The Descendants

of

Hugh Thomson

by Donald C. Thomson

with major contributions by

Jack Light
Jeanette Anderson
Fred Swenson
Elsie E. Foster
George Wiley Beveridge
James McCleery Beveridge, M. D.
John R. Beveridge
Hazel Yule
Dorothy Joyce
Phil Graham

ISHI PRESS INTERNATIONAL

The Descendants of Hugh Thomson

by Donald C. Thomson

Compiled by

Donald C. Thomson
203 Drovers Way
Stevensville MD 21666-3929

with major contributions by

Jack Light, Jeanette Anderson, Fred Swenson, Elsie E.
Foster, George Wiley Beveridge, James McCleery
Beveridge, M. D., John R. Beveridge, Hazel Yule, Dorothy
Joyce, Phil Graham

First Published in 2001
Copyright © 2001 by Donald C. Thomson

This Printing in July, 2013
by Ishi Press in New York and Tokyo

ISBN 0-923891-61-7
978-0-923891-61-9

Ishi Press International
1664 Davidson Avenue, Suite 1B
Bronx NY 10453-7877
USA
1-917-507-7226
samhsloan@gmail.com

Printed in the United States of America

Introduction by Sam Sloan

The Descendants of Hugh Thomson

by Donald C. Thomson

Introduction by Sam Sloan

With the rapid advances in DNA testing and technology, it is becoming possible to know exactly how we are all related to each other, since it has been established that we are all relatives, if we go back far enough, which is often not far.

I did not even know that I was a member of the Thomson Family until this book became available. My name is on pages 173 and 344 of this book. I am number 1165511. With this number, one can calculate my relationship to every other person listed in this book using the method described on page x. The author, Donald C. Thomson, is number 1151213, so we are 4th cousins.

What impelled me to reprint this book is I have joined a DNA Genealogical Testing group: 23andme.com This group does Autosomal DNA testing. This is in contrast to the other main company that does DNA testing for genealogy purposes, Family Tree DNA. Family Tree DNA does primarily two kinds of DNA Testing: Y-DNA Testing and mtDNA Testing. Y-DNA Testing provides information about your father's father's father's father, etc. This is because the Y-Chromosome is passed from father to son. Women do not have a Y-chromosome and thus cannot be tested for it. mtDNA is carried by both men and women but women pass it on to their daughters. mtDNA testing will help determine who your mother's mother's mother was.

The problem with this is that although Y-DNA testing and mtDNA testing produces accurate results at what it does, it does not provide information about other branches of your family tree, such as who your mother's father's mother's father was.

Autosomal DNA testing tests other sections of DNA. Since every person inherits some DNA from their mother and some from their father, Autosomal DNA testing holds the unfulfilled promise of being able to determine who all your ancestors were. Accordingly, I sent off to have my Autosomal DNA tested.

The result was surprising. It said that I have no first or second cousins that have been tested, but that I have 191 third or fourth cousins and 798 more distant cousins, none of whom I know.

My correspondence thus far with those few "Third and Fourth Cousins" who have responded shows that they know even less about their genealogy than I do. Most do not know anything beyond their grandparents and many do not even know that much. I have decided to send a copy of this book to all of my genetic cousins I can find through mtDNA testing, so they can go through it and see if they can find any of their ancestors in this book. Anybody whose mtDNA matches mine and is a 3rd or 4th cousin is likely a descendant or a relative of Elizabeth McRobert who is pictured on page 27 of this book or of Ann Milwain who is pictured on page 10.

According to 23andme, my Y-DNA type is R1b1b2a1a2f* and my mtDNA type is T2f1

Family Tree DNA gives slightly different designations.
Y-DNA = R1b1a2 = Shorthand R-M269
mtDNA = T. Family Tree DNA has me in Little Scottish Cluster - Y-DNA SNP

All of these types are typical of Scot-Irish.

My direct maternal ancestry is not Scot-Irish but rather Scottish. This is because my mother's mother's mother came directly from Scotland without stopping in Ireland. She was Elizabeth Grace Thomson, born 25 May 1851 in Dhuloch, Kirkcolm Parish, Wigtownshire, Scotland and died 12 June 1932 in Afton Iowa. Her mother was Elizabeth McRobert, born 1 August 1812, Kirkcolm, Stranraer, Wigtownshire, Scotland, died 19 February 1879, Madison County, Iowa. My mother, a medical doctor, was a notoriously tight-fisted person, reluctant to spend money on anything. She even made her own soap. When anybody would complain about this, she would say, "That is because of the Scotch in me".

My mtDNA type of T2f1 comes from Elizabeth McRobert (1812-1879). Her branch is the subject of this book, "The Descendants of Hugh Thomson" by Donald C. Thomson. Her picture is on page 27 of this book. Her story is on pages 26-30. As recounted in this book, the entire family came to America the ship **"Andrew Foster"** which departed from Liverpool on 23 September 1856. There were 530 passengers on this voyage. Unfortunately, their new born baby Samuel became sick on the ship, died, and had to be buried at sea. They arrived in New York on 22 October 1856 and took a train to Illinois where they met relatives who had preceded them to America.

This book is part original research and part compiled from other sources. Among the other sources is the book, **David Graham of Chester County, South Carolina and His Descendants 1772-1989**, which I have reprinted as **ISBN 0923891072**. I am thankful to co-author Philip Graham for giving me permission to reprint that book and for even giving me the original page proofs.

Sam Sloan
Bronx, New York
USA
July 19, 2013

INTRODUCTION

In the course of compiling the history of this Thomson family, the compiler discovered the existence of several unpublished manuscripts, and a few published books, that contain genealogies on several branches of the Thomson family. This demonstrates that there has been a widespread interest in our Thomson ancestry for many years. These documents have proven to be very helpful for piecing together a comprehensive story of the family.

Probably the earliest bit of information on our ancestry is contained in a hand-written note by Jeanette "Nettie" Thomson, daughter of John Thomson, a Scottish immigrant. She recalled an interview she had with her father seventeen days before his death in 1904. Jeanette's brothers, Rev. John J. Thomson, and his younger brother, Samuel, wrote more extensively about the origins of the Thomson family. John's granddaughter, Margaret Corson, provided the compiler with a copy of these documents.

A document titled "Brown-Mekemson Ancestry," dated 1902, was prepared by A.L. Brown of Eustis, Fla., and was revised in 1923 to include Thomson ancestry. An extensive family history was compiled in 1923 by James McCleery Beveridge, a medical doctor. This very valuable document provided a lot of information not contained in the other manuscripts. It followed all the lines down from our progenitor, in various degrees of detail.

Lawrence Thomson became interested in his roots and documented the results of his research in a manuscript prepared about 1953. It was not very broad in scope and, unfortunately, very few references were given for his information. He used some material published earlier by others.

A book on the history of the Brokaw family,[1] which included descendants of Anne (Thomson) Weir, was compiled about 1960 by Elsie E. Foster of Junction City, Ore.

In 1962, George Wiley Beveridge, then a newspaper editor, prepared a booklet on the family of James McCleery and his wife, Margaret Graham, and their descendants. This document has proven to be very helpful in providing information on a branch of the family that would have required considerable research by the compiler.

A genealogy of the Robinson family was prepared in 1964 which includes the descendants of Thomas Henderson Robinson who married Elizabeth McCleery, and Nellie May Robinson who married William Russell McCleery, all of whom are descended from Jean Thomson, another Scottish immigrant. A copy of this valuable document, whose compiler is unknown, was provided by John B. Robinson of Mountain Lake, New Jersey.

The family tree of Jeanette and William Brown Mekemson was contained in a small document that was prepared about 1965.

James H. Beveridge II compiled a 110-page manuscript *Church of the Pioneers* in 1971.[2] It is an excellent source of information on the history of Somonauk United Presbyterian Church of DeKalb Co., Ill., and its elders, some of whom were Thomson descendants. Included are lists of members throughout the history of the church.

More recently, another effort to establish the family tree of Samuel Melvin Thomson was accomplished by Hazel Thomson Yule.[3] After her death, the effort was finished in 1978 by her husband, Robert Yule. This booklet mainly contains family statistics (family group sheets), but it also includes copies of precious letters and memoirs written by descendants of Samuel Thomson that describes life in Scotland around 1850, life in Madison County, Iowa, and the unfortunate consequences of moving to the Sandhills of Nebraska.

John R. (Ron) Beveridge put together a supplement to the *Somonauk Book*[42] that has biographical information on many families of DeKalb Co., Ill., including the Beveridge and McCleery families. Ron's supplement, dated about 1973, follows the children of John C. Beveridge and his wife, the former Mary Ann McCleery. Ron's sister, Dorothy Beveridge Joyce, provided excerpts from a book she was instrumental in compiling in 1979 that traces her mother's side of her family.[4] Dorothy has been very active in genealogy as a member of the DAR. She was especially interested in proving the story that claims a connection between her ancestors and John Paul Jones, a story that is prevalent in diverse segments of the Thomson family.

In 1983, Jack Light compiled an eloquently written history of the McCorkle family who are descendants of Samuel Thomson. Later, he updated the material for inclusion in this book.

Wyman Graham provided excerpts from a large book which compiled the history of one Graham family, another branch of the Samuel Thomson family.[5] A co-author, Phil Graham, gave permission to use his material. We are indebted to him for his generosity.

.A large section from a book, *Savilles Then and Now*, prepared recently by Jeanette Anderson, has been utilized in this compilation. Her book included information on yet another branch of the family of Samuel Thomson, and was used with her permission.

A considerable amount of updated information on the Weir family was provided by Barbara (Milligan) Baylor in 1998 based on information she acquired from family members. The compiler is very grateful for her hard work in support of this effort.

Fred Swenson prepared "Genealogy Chart For Edna Ethel Mekemson" in Apr 1998. The document is filled with interesting stories, and related accounts from other sources.

By far, most of the information on the Thomsons of younger generations has been acquired through correspondence and telephone conversations with relatives. A lot of information has been exchanged with other Thomson family genealogy researchers, mainly, Tom Fulton, Wendell Chestnut, Jack Light, Linda Clark, Barbara Baylor, Jeanette Anderson, and Fred Swenson.

The document that did the most to inspire the compiler to prepare a family history of all the known Thomson descendants was a copy of a three-page letter written in 1933 by Samuel Alexander Thomson, son of John Thomson the Scottish immigrant. In the letter, Samuel had written brief sketches about his own family and cousins. In 1996, the compiler, unaware of most of the family history manuscripts, began to follow up on the information in the letter. Eventually, data on all branches of the family began to materialize.

Several relatives have submitted photographs of their ancestors to the compiler which are used in this book, including Iola Lovely, Mary Haxby, Ruth Sorensen, Roland Thomson, Helen Evans, Thomas Reston, Eleanor Thomson, John Bishop and Donald Huber.

The greatest effort was made to ensure the accuracy of the data presented in this book. In several cases different sources gave conflicting dates, especially of births. Where possible, birth dates listed in Social Security records were used because the birth date was provided by the applicant.

Errors that appear in other publications might unfortunately have been repeated in this compilation. Without a doubt, some errors crept into the records because of typos that occurred when transcribing vital statistics; this compiler is probably as guilty as any others. The compiler regrets any mistakes that may occur in some biographies; I can only say I did my best.

BITS and PIECES

I write this at the conclusion of the task, to reflect on the effort undertaken.

During the several years the compiler researched the Thomson family, nothing new has surfaced regarding our oldest known ancestor, Hugh Thomson I. His existence can only be supported by family tradition since he is not mentioned in any "official" documents. Because he rented land, and was not a landowner, he was not listed in land records, and with few assets, he probably had no reason to write a will. He separated from the Church of Scotland, so the birth of his children and his death were not mentioned in the parish registers.

We believe we did succeed in finding a death record of the William Thomson who left Scotland and lived in Australia. We also located some 'new' Scottish cousins, but we did not succeed in tracing down to present time the family of William Thomson, son of James Thomson of Lochwinnoch, Scotland. And after extensive research, we still haven't been able to learn anything more about a Samuel Thomson, mentioned as being a weaver who lived in Paisley, Scotland. Likewise, we gained no ground in locating the brothers William and Robert Thomson and their sister who left Ireland about 1776 and settled near Fort Pitt, Pa.

It can be seen that the Thomson name is actually not prominent in this book; if the Thomson line only was followed down male lines, this would have resulted in a small publication. Obviously, the reason for this is the prevalence of female children. For example, Samuel Melvin Thomson had six children, five of whom were females. The Thomsons alive today that are descended from Samuel and carry the Thomson name are few, yet a large segment of this book is devoted to Samuel's descendants with a multiplicity of surnames.

In a few instances it was difficult to obtain biographical information from some of my cousins alive today. More often than not, correspondence was not returned, a problem reported by most genealogists today. Oftentimes, telephone calls were placed when correspondence was not forthcoming. The compiler was usually well received, although one never knew what response to expect. In a few instances, cousins made it known that they were not at all interested in providing genealogical information, or wouldn't accept the fact that they were related to the compiler. In these rare cases, biographical data obtained from their close cousins was substituted.

THE NUMBERING SYSTEM

More than likely, a reader will quickly find their name in the index and will then turn to their biography. When they see the number in front of their name it will be an enigma to all but genealogists. However, the prefix is actually a code and each digit has a special meaning. This numbering procedure is certainly not new, and it seems much less cumbersome than systems used in other genealogy publications. Many published genealogies have unusual numbering systems where their compilers have strove to invent unique systems when actually no new system is required; the compiler truly hopes that the system used herein is easily grasped by his many, many cousins.

The oldest relative we have documented proof of is Hugh Thomson II (the second), from his marriage record. It is accepted as fact that his father was Hugh Thomson I (the first) who is given the designation "1 Hugh Thomson I." The siblings of Hugh Thomson I are designated as 2, 3 and 4.

The children of Hugh Thomson I are designated by two digits which indicates that they were of the second generation. They are numbered in regard to birth order, i.e., Hugh Thomson II (the second) is given the designation "11 Hugh Thomson II."

In the third generation we have "111 James Thomson" who was the oldest son of the oldest son. Next in order of birth was "112 Elizabeth Thomson." This routine continues through seven generations.

Some families were large and contained ten or more children. In this event the tenth child was designated in parenthesis, i.e., 1138(10) Fannie E. McCleery was the tenth child of 1138 William Doig McCleery.

The compiler desired to make this book more than a boring compilation of names and dates by including interesting information about the lives of each person, but regrets that he did not always succeed. In this regard, it is apparent, and perhaps odd, that generally more was written on the oldest generations than on living relatives. This might be explained because of modesty or desires for privacy.

The book almost exclusively follows bloodlines--kin of spouses of the Thomsons are infrequently mentioned.

There is an easy way to determine how you may be related to any other blood relative in this book.   It utilizes the numbering system just mentioned.

For example, Cassandra Robinson (with prefix 1137415) may wish to know her relationship to Roland Marts (with prefix 1162952).   The best way to make the determination is to arrange the prefixes vertically, as shown below, then compare digits in each row.   By following the example, it is shown that they are fourth cousins. The relationships of their forefathers is also listed.

$$1 \text{ ----- same person ------ } 1$$

$$1 \text{ ----- same person ------ } 1$$

$$6 \text{ -------siblings -------- } 3$$

$$2 \text{ ----- 1st cousins ------ } 7$$

$$9 \text{ ----- 2}^{nd}\text{ cousins ------ } 4$$

$$5 \text{ ----- 3}^{rd}\text{ cousins ------ } 1$$

$$2 \text{ ----- 4}^{th}\text{ cousins ------ } 5$$

In cases where there is a differnce in generations, then the relationship between two people would use the term "once removed" or "twice removed", etc.

THE EARLY YEARS

Scottish people were members of clans until the early 1600s, and it wasn't until the end of the tribal system that people took up surnames. Unless a connection to royalty is made, there is little hope of tracing a family before the 1600s.

Presbyterianism was the established religion of Scotland, but in 1733 there was a secession which took place as a result of congregational dissatisfaction with the method of selecting ministers. These Seceeders were not attending the Church of Scotland, therefore significant events such as births, marriages, and deaths were not recorded in the parish registers.

Several stories handed down through the generations tell that the Thomsons suffered religious persecution in Scotland. One such story was told by 115 John Thomson, shortly before he died, to Jeanette, his daughter, and passed on to Margaret (Thomson) Corson. The story relates how the Thomsons were persecuted, their property in Ayrshire (Ayr County) was confiscated, and most of the family killed. During one raid, sometime before 1628, soldiers came onto the farm and began rounding up members of the family. Two uncles and a little boy hid in a haystack until dark, then under cover of darkness, found a boat and fled across the North Channel of the Irish Sea to the coast of County Down, Ireland, a distance of about 20 miles.

During this time of religious persecution, several of our Thomson ancestors suffered martyrdom. Two Thomson ancestors were tied to stakes at low tide and left to drown on the flood tide. That these atrocities occurred was recorded in *Copy Extract Minute of Kirk Session of Kirkinner according the Sufferings of the Wigtown Martyrs*, dated 15 April 1711, LDS film 0102348. There is no mention, however, of Thomson martyrs. One was burned at the stake, according to a story written by Bessie (Thomson) Kench in *The Yule Booklet*,[3] and repeated in the Beveridge manuscript.

SCOTTISH CUSTOM OF NAMING CHILDREN

The custom in Scotland was to name children after their forebears.[6]
The tradition was to name them as follows:
    The eldest son after the paternal grandfather
    The second son after the maternal grandfather
    The third son after the father
    The eldest daughter after the maternal grandmother
    The second daughter after the paternal grandmother
    The third daughter after the mother

An examination of the names in the early generations seems to bear
out this tradition. There were other variations in the naming of
children, probably the most usual was reversing maternal and
paternal priority, but usually a child's name was chosen to honor
close family relatives. This provides us with important clues as
to the names of our oldest ancestors.

Hugh Thomson II named his first daughter Elizabeth, which could be
the name of Elizabeth's grandmother Thomson, a wife of Hugh Thomson
I.

FOUR-GENERATION DESCENDANCY CHART

The first four generations of the family tree, as we know it, are
as follows:

First Generation
1 Hugh Thomson I (ca. 1740-ca. 1800), twice married, one wife
    possibly Elizabeth
2 Unknown Thomson (female), married, lived near Fort Pitt ca.
    1776 ?
3 Robert Thomson, lived near Fort Pitt, ca. 1776 ?
4 William Thomson, lived near Fort Pitt ca. 1776 ?

Second Generation
11 Hugh Thomson II (ca. 1775-1840), m. Ann Milwain
12 Mary Thomson (ca. 1791-ca. 1841), m. Samuel Abernethy
13 Samuel Thomson, lived in Paisley, Scotland ?

Third Generation
111 James Thomson (1804-1807)
112 Elizabeth Thomson (1805-1894), m. 1st Thomas Fulton,
      2nd James Cole
113 Jean Thomson (1808-1858), m. James McCleery
114 Hugh Thomson III (ca. 1810-1895), m. Jane Lyle
115 John Thomson (1813-1904), m. 1st Elizabeth Maley, 2nd
      Margaret Catherine McClelland, 3rd Mary Ann Parks
116 Samuel Melvin Thomson (1815-1903), m. Elizabeth McRobert
117 Anne Melvin Thomson (1818-1914), m. Alexander Weir
118 William Thomson (1821-alive in 1901), of Australia
121 Nancy Abernethy (1822-1827)
122 John Abernethy (1824- ?), alive in 1841
123 William Abernethy (1826-ca. 1830)
124 Margaret Abernethy (1828-1866)
125 James Abernethy (1830-1866)
126 William Abernethy (1832- ?), alive in 1881

Fourth Generation
1121 Anna Fulton (1835-1890), m. William John Knowles
1122 Hugh Fulton, died young
1123 John Fulton, died young
1124 Thomas W. Fulton (1842-1869), unmarried
1125 James Fulton (1846-1925), m. Jane E. Gray
1126 Isabelle Cole (1848- 1932), m. John Armstrong
1127 Robert J. Cole (1851-1935), m. Margaret E. Beveridge
1131 John McCleery (1834-1917), m. Ann McCall
1132 James W. McCleery (1835-1903), m. Margaret Graham
1133 Hugh McCleery (1837-1837)
1134 Robert McCleery (1839-1842)

1135 Mary Ann McCleery (1841-1907), m. John C. Beveridge
1136 Margaret McCleery (1843-1916), m. Alexander Howison
1137 Elizabeth McCleery (1845-1922), m. Thomas Henderson
        Robinson
1138 William Doig McCleery (1848-1903), m. 1st Mary
        Jeanette Randles, 2nd Jennie Elizabeth Maxwell
1139 Jane Catherine McCleery (1851-1855)
1141 Margaret Thomson (ca. 1836- ?)
1142 James Thomson (1838-1916), m. Martha Farquhar
1151 William Maley Thomson (1846-1920), m. Catharine Strauser
1152 Anne Melvin Thomson (1846-1863)
1153 Mary Jean Thomson (1857-1906), m. John Spence
1154 John J. Thomson (1860-1917), m. 1st Belle Stuart, 2nd
        Sarah I. Dickson
1155 Elizabeth Thomson (1861-1939), m. David Taylor Spence
1156 Margaret McAllister Thomson (1863-1916), unmarried
1157 Abraham Lincoln Thomson (1865-1926), m. Gertrude L. Nees
1158 Janette Mekemson Thomson (1868-1940), unmarried
1159 Nancy Moreland Thomson (1868-1941), unmarried
115(10) Frances Clokey Thomson (1870-1895), m. Samuel Spence
115(11) David Paul Thomson (1875-1939), m. Rosabel Mearns
115(12) Samuel Alexander Thomson (1875-1946), m. Clara Alida
        Hunter
1161 Mary Buchanan Thomson (1842-1920), m. James Gawn Beck
1162 Jeanette M. Thomson (1844-1925), m. William B. Mekemson
1163 Hugh Thomson IV (1847-1923), m. Cynthia Ann Bard
1164 Annie Melvin Thomson (1849-1934), m. Andrew Applegate
1165 Elizabeth Grace Thomson (1851-1932), m. Samuel Allison
        Graham
1166 Samuel Thomson (1856-1856)
1167 Jane Eleanor Thomson (1858-1946), m. Edward L. McCorkle
1171 William Thomson Weir (1853-1927), m. Annie C. Knustrom
1172 John Weir (1858-1937), m. Jennie McMillan

REFERENCES

1. Foster, Elsie E., *Our Brokaw-Bragaw Heritage*, ca. 1960
2. James H. Beveridge II, *Church of The Pioneers*, a manuscript prepared in 1971.
3. Yule, Robert, A manuscript of notes on the Thomson family, LDS film 1321298 item 15, 1978.
4. Conley, Avlyn Dodd, compiler, *The Darnall, Darnell Family*, Gateway Press, Inc., Baltimore, 1979.
5. *David Graham of Chester County, South Carolina and His Descendants*, by Katharine Tolle Kell and Phillip James Graham, 1990, Birmingham, Ala.
6. Hamilton-Edwards, Gerald, *In Search of Scottish Ancestry*, Genealogical Pub. Co., Balt., Md., 1972, p. 71
7. Harpster, John W., editor, *Pen Pictures of Early Western Pennsylvania*, 1938, p. 100
8. *The National Cyclopdia of American Biography*, bio of John Paul Jones
9. Lorenz, Lincoln, *John Paul Jones, Fighter for Freedom and Glory*, 1943
10. Morison, Samuel Eliot, *John Paul Jones, A Sailor's Biography*, An Atlantic Monthly Press Book
11. *The Encyclopedia Britannica*, 14th Edition, Vol 13, p. 140, bio of John Paul Jones
12. De Koven, *The Life and Letters of John Paul Jones*, Vol 2, Charles Scribner & Sons, New York, 1930
13. *The Dumfries and Galloway Standard*, 24 Aug 1953, Paul Jones's Family
14. Durning, William and Mary, *The Scotch-Irish*, Published by the Irish Family Names Society, 1991, LeMesa, CA.
15. Gilmour, David, *Paisley Weavers of Other Days, The Pen Folk*, 1876, LDS film 0873658.
16. *Past and Present of De Kalb County* (Ill.), Vol. 2, 1907, p. 561, bio of (11252) William J. Fulton
17. *Portrait and Biographical Album, De Kalb County, Illinois, 1885*, bio of (1125) James Fulton, pp. 548, 553, and (1132) James McCleery, pp. 591-592
18. Tweedsmuir, *History of North Walsingham* (Norfolk County, Ontario), ca. 1966, pp. 41, 28 and 190, re: Knowles family
19. *The Hartford City* (Ind.) *News*, 3 Dec 1930, obit of (11251) George T. Fulton
20. *The Quebec Gazette*, Montreal, Canada, 6 Jun 1832, arrival of Brig *Fisher of Mary Port* from Stranraer, Scotland

21. Wakefield, George Mighell, *De Kalb County Illinois Families*, 1938 (Utilizes some material from *Waterman Yearbook* by George E. Congdon)
22. *Aledo* (Ill.) *Democrat*, 23 Feb 1904, obit of (115) John Thomson
23. *Index to Marriage Records, Warren County* (Ill.), p. 365, (115) John Thornson (sic) and Elizabeth Maley
24. *The Times Record*, Aledo, Ill., 23 Apr 1903, 90th birthday celebration for (115) John Thomson
25. *The New York Times*, 22 Oct 1856, "Marine Intelligence", p. 8, arrival of ship Andrew Foster
26. Ship Passenger Lists, National Archives, 20 Oct-17 Nov 1856, Film Roll 237/168
27. *The Times*, London, England, 4 May 1857, p. 9, re; sinking of *Andrew Foster*
28. Map of Jackson Township, Madison County, Ia., 1875, shows farms of Thomson relatives
29. *The History of Madison County, Iowa*, 1879
30. Cemetery Records Online, Stringtown Cemetery, Douglas Township, Madison County, Iowa: List includes Applegate, Chase, McCorkle, and Thomson families
31. Map of Douglas Township, Madison Co., Ia., 1912, shows cemetery locations
32. *Madisonian*, Winterset, Ia., 23 Jul 1919, item on village of Stringtown
33. *The Daily Review*, Monmouth, Ill., 9 Jan 1914, obit of (117) Anna (Thomson) Weir
34. *Stronghurst* (Ill.) *Graphic,* 18 Nov 1897, obit of (117) Alexander Weir
35. *Dunolly and Bet Bet* (Australia) *Shire Express,* 19 May 1905, obit of (118) William Thomson
36. Talbot District (Simcoe, Ontario) Marriage Register, 1837-1857, marriage of (1121) William John Knowles and Anne Fulton on 3 May 1853
37. *Carholme-Knowles Cemetery, Concession 9, Lot 18, Walsingham Township, Norfolk County*, transcribed Jul 1994 by Judith Buchanan, William Terry, and Grace Morris
38. *Roster of Wisconsin Volunteers, War of The Rebellion, 1861-1865*, Vol. 1, p. 257, 1886 (Copy at Janesville Public Library, Janesville, Wisc.)
39. *The Coeur d'Alene* (Ida.) *Press.* 8 Jan 1925, obit of (1125) James Fulton
40. *Birthday Book*, of Anne Fulton, transcribed and annotated by James Thompson Fulton, Sep 1999
41. *The Sandwich* (Ill.) *Free Press*, 22 Dec 1921, obit of (1126) John A. Armstrong
42. Patten, Jennie M., *History of the Somonauk United Presbyterian Church, near Sandwich, De Kalb County, Illinois*, 1928.

43. *The Sandwich* (Ill.) *Free Press*, 22 Jan 1925, obit of (1125) James Fulton
44. *The Newark* (N.J.) *Evening News*, 22 Jul 1932, obit of (1126) Mrs. Isabelle Armstrong
45. *Hebron, A Century In Review*, p. 216, 1987, Published by the Hebron Preservation Society, Glen Falls, N.Y., re: marriage of Margaret Beveridge to married Robert Cole
46. *The Coeur d'Alene* (Ida.) *Press,* 24 Apr 1925, obit of (1125) Mrs. Jane Gray Fulton
47. *The Spokane-Review,* Spokane, Wash., 18 Aug 1935, obit of (1127) Robert J. Cole
48. *The Coeur d'Alene* (Ida.) *Press,* 16 Aug 1920, obit of (1127) Mrs. Margaret E. Cole
49. *Grundy Herald*, Grundy Center, Ia., 6 Aug 1907, obit of (1135) Mrs. Mary A. (McCleery) Beveridge
50. *The Biographical Record of De Kalb County, Illinois*, 1898, bios of Alexander Howison and Margaret McCleery.
51. *History of Cedar County* (Ia.), pp. 141-142, bio of (1151) William M. Thomson and pp. 456-457, bio of (11512) William F. Thomson
52. *The Stanwood* (Ia.) *Herald*, ca. 3 Apr 1920, obit of (1151) William Maley Thomson
53. *Ibid.,* 26 May 1921, obit of (1151) Mrs. William M. Thomson
54. *Oklahoma Life*, Oklahoma City, Okla., 2 May 1908, cartoon featuring (1154) John J. Thomson
55. *Madisonian*, 25 Apr 1939, obit of (1155) Mrs. Elizabeth (Thomson) Spence
56. Ibid., 1923, obit of (1155) David T. Spence
57. Winterset Cemetery Files, page 125, burial locations of the Spence family
58. *From the Ashes, The Story of the Hinckley Fire of 1894*, by Grace Stageberg Swenson, North Star Press of St. Cloud, Inc., 1979.
59. *Times-Record,* Aledo, Ill., 18 Sep 1894, (1157) Abraham Lincoln Thomson's experience with a forest fire
60. *Madisonian,* Winterset, Ia., early Jan 1924, obit of (1163) Hugh Thompson (sic)
61. Ibid., early Feb 1934, obit of (1164) Annie (Thomson) Applegate
62. Ibid., Sep 1917, obit of (1164) Andrew Applegate
63. *Reporter*, Winterset, Ia., 30 Jun 1915, attendance at Thomson family reunion at home of (1163) Hugh Thomson
64. *Madison County* (Ia.) *Marriages, 1849-1880*
65. *Kansas City Star,* 25 Oct 1946, obit of (1167) Mrs. Jane Eleanor McCorkle
66. *Stronghurst* (Ill.) *Graphic*, 25 Aug 1927, obit of (1171) William T. Weir
67. Ibid., 12 Aug 1937, obit of (1172) John Weir

68. *The Hartford City* (Ind.) *News*, 19 June 1899, wedding of (11251) George T. Fulton to Nettie Leonard
69. *From Oxen to Jets*, A History of De Kalb County, Ill,, 1835-1963, edited by Harriet (Wilson) Davy, 1963, p. 216, mention of (11252) William J. Fulton
70. *The True Republican*, Sycamore, Ill., 28 Mar 1961, obit of (11252) Justice William J. Fulton
71. Letter from Anne Fulton to her brother, William Fulton, dated 1915, transcribed by James Thompson Fulton, 1999
72. *The Coeur d'Alene* (Ida.) *Press.*, 6 Jun 1932, obit of (11253) Ann(e) E. Fulton
73. *Who Was Who In American History*, p. 190, bio of (11255) Walter Scott Fulton
74. *Army Register*, Retired List, 1943, p. 1166, (11255) Walter S. Fulton
75. Ancell, R. Manning with Christine M. Miller, *The Biographical Dictionary of World War II, Generals and Flag Officers, The U.S. Armed Forces*, item re: (11255) Walter Scott Fulton
76. *Columbus* (Ga.) *Enquirer*, 25 Jun 1950, obit of (11255) General Walter Scott Fulton
77. *The Coeur d'Alene* (Ida.) *Press*, 18 Jun 1934, obit of (11256) James Thompson Fulton
78. Ibid., 20 Oct 1964, obit of (11256) Mrs. James Thompson (Olive Wood) Fulton
79. Sandusky, Ohio, 5 Aug 1967, obit of (11257) Frederick Fulton
80. *The Bloomington Herald-Telephone*, 17 Mar 1966, obit of (11258) Ella Carter
81. *Columbus* (Ga.) *Ledger,* 5 Dec 1952, p. 27:2, obit of (11258) Henry H. Carter
82. *Daily Herald-Telephone*, Bloomington, Ind., 3 Dec 1952, obit of (11258) Henry H. Carter
83. *The Morning Tribune*, Minneapolis, Minn., 17 Jun 1965, obit of (11259) Frank O. Koehler
84. *Asbury Park* (N.J.)*Press,* 6 Jan 1949, obit of (11261) James D. Stirling
85. *The Chicago Tribune*, 21 Aug 1980, obit of (11263) Ruth Armstrong Shannon
86. *The Cleveland* (Ohio) *Plain Dealer*, 18 Sep 1927, obit of (11263) William Kennedy Armstrong
87. *The Spokesman-Review,* Spokane, Wash, 10 Dec 1966, obit of (11271) Andrew James Cole
88. *The Somonauk* (Ill.) *Reveille*, 5 Apr 1951, obit of (11312) John A(lexander) McCleery
89. Ibid., 17 May 1956, obit of (11318) Bessie (McCleery) Gilbert
90. Ibid., 28 Nov 1968, obit of (11319) Mary Eliza (Hastings) McCleery

91. *Ibid.*, 6 Nov 1936, obit (11321) Sara Jane (McCleery) Graham
92. *Ibid.*, 2 Feb 1955, obit of (11329) Raymond McCleery
93. *Daily Tribune*, Ames, Ia., 3 Apr 1956, obit of (11351) Mrs. Mary M. Beveridge
94. *Waterloo* (Ill.) *Courier*, 11 Jan 1950, obit of (11328) William R. McCleery
95. *News-Gazette*, Champaign, Ill., 29 Dec 1956, obit of (11352) Mrs. Mary H. Beveridge
96. *The Ladysmith* (Wisc.) *News*, 19 Sep 1930, obit of (11355) Rea L. Beveridge
97. Ibid., 28 Jun 1962, obit of (11355) Bertha (McGoech) Beveridge
98. *Washington Evening Journal* (?), Washington, Ia., Dec 1952, obit of (11356) Miss Mae Beveridge
99. *American Women, The Standard Biographical Dictionary of Notable Women*, Vol. 111, 1939-40, items on (11358) Mrs. Alice Hess Beveridge and (113514) Elizabeth Beveridge
100. *Daily Press*, Eau Claire, Wisc., 2 Feb 1921, obit of (11358) Archibald G. Beveridge
101. *The Somonauk* (Ill.) *Reveille.*, 22 Oct 1952, obit of (11361) George A. Howison
102. Ibid., 10 Dec 1943, obit of (11362) Miss Margaret Jean Howison
103. *The Cleveland* (Ohio) *Plain Dealer*, 30 Oct 1967, obit of (11389) Dr. John M. McCleery
104. *The Press*, Renfrew, Scotland, 27 Jun 1947, obit of (14111) Hugh Thomson
105. *The Cedar Rapids* (Ia.) *Gazette*, 4 Oct 1956, obit of (11512) William F. Thomson
106. Ibid., 12 Jul 1972, obit of (11512) Mrs. Sarah Thomson
107. Ibid., ca. 21 Oct 1955, obit of (11514) Mrs. Frank Thomson
108. Ibid., 26 Oct 1967, (11514) obit of Frank Marion Thomson
109. *Daily Herald*, Oskaloosa, Ia., 21 Jan 1961, obit of (11515) John E. Thomson
110. *Monticello* (Minn.) *Times*, 15 Aug 1961, obit of (11541) Mary Isabelle (Thomson) Barron
111. *The Times*, St. Cloud, Minn., 7 Jan 1978, obit of (11541) Alexander M. Barron
112. *Madisonian*, Winterset, Ia., 20 Feb 1957, obit of (11552) William J. Spence
113. Ibid., 22 Sep 1923, marriage announcement of (11554) Vasha Spence and Christian Sorensen
114. *The Washington Post*, 1953, obit of (11554) Christian Sorensen
115. *History of Madison County* (Iowa), 1915, pp. 100-101, bio of (11615) Jeannette E. Beck
116. *Orient* (Ia.) *History Book*, 1982, obits of (11657) Walter N, Graham, (11657) Olive Mae Stream, and (116571) Ruth Josephine (Graham) Butler
117. Monmouth, Ill. (?), 12 Oct 1972, obit of (11578) Alice (Thomson) *Burkett*

118. *Stronghurst* (Ill.) *Graphic*, 7 Dec 1967, obit of (11724) Roy W. Weir
119. *History of Madison County, Iowa*, 1984, pp. 316-7, an account of the Spence Family
120. *Muskingum College Bulletin*, Apr 1959, pp. 7-8, item re: retirement of (11389) Dr. John McCleery
121. *The* Simcoe (Ontario) *Reformer*, 22 Feb 1967, obit of (112161) Mrs. William (Annie Knowles) McInally
122. *The Muncie Evening Press*, 6 Mar 1981, obit of (112513) Charles H. Goddard
123. *Celebrity Register,* p. 617, biography of (112524) James Reston
124. *The Washington Post*, 7 Dec 1995, obit of (112524) James "Scotty" Reston
125. *The Atlanta Journal*, 30 Jul 1987, obit of (112551) Rev. Stephen W. Ackerman Sr.,
126. *The Coeur d'Alene* (Ida.) *Press*,, 29 Nov 1978, obit of (112561) Elsie H. Fulton
127. Ibid., 25 Apr 1978, obit (112561) Robert G. Fulton
128. Atlanta, Ga., 27 Nov 1990, obit of (112551) Mrs. Helen (Fulton) Ackerman
129. *The Coeur d'Alene* (Ida.) *Press.*, 2 Feb 1954, obit of (112562) Richard W. Fulton
130. *Sarasota* (Fla.) *Herald-Tribune*, 17 Mar 1977, obit of (112522) William J. Fulton
131. *The Eugene Register-Guard,* Eugene, Ore., 1 Jun 1981, obit of (112576) Virginia Fulton Place
132. Ibid., 2 Jul 1988, obit of (112576) Stewart Dalmon Place
133. *Countyline Magazine*, Lincoln, Neb., Feb 1989, re: (112577) Janet Gauger
134. *The Coeur d'Alene* (Ida.) *Press.*, 22 Jun 1971, obit of (112711) Bruce Cole
135. *The Spokesman-Review*, Spokane, Wash., 25 Apr 1978, obit of (112561) Robert G. Fulton
136. *The New York Times*, 8 Apr 1977, obit of (112581) Jane Elizabeth Kenworthy
137. *The Washington Post,* 26 Jan 1993, obit of (112581) E. W. Kenworthy
138. *Who's Who in America*, 1998 52nd Edition, Vol. 2, (112583) Dudley Bradstreet Tenney
139. *Minneapolis Star-Tribune*, 14 Dec 1988, obit of (112592) Fulton Koehler
140. *Austin* (Tex.) *American-Statesman*, 18 May 1988, obit of (112632) Vivian Armstrong Rose
141. Ibid., 30 Nov 1995, obit of (112632) Howard N. Rose
142. *The Seattle Post-Intelligencer*, 22 Jan 1969, obit of (112731) Col. Robert W. Brumwell

143. *The Seattle Times,* 21 Aug 1994, obit of (112733) Dr. George "Keith" Brumwell

144. *The Washington Post,* 8 Apr 1977, obit of (112581) Jane Elizabeth Kenworthy

145. *Aurora* (Ill.) *Beacon,* 11 Nov 1953, obit of (113121) Wayne E. McCleery

146. *The Somonauk* (Ill.) *Reveille,* 9 Nov 1945, obit of (11313) James A(ndrew) McCleery

147. *Illinois State Journal,* Springfield, Ill., 8 Nov 1961, obit of (113265) J. Ray Graham

148. *The Spokesman-Review,* Spokane, Wash., 25 Apr 1971, obit of (113282) Helen A(delaide McCleery) Postle

149. *Monmouth College Scots Newse,* Vol. 3, Spring 1988, item re: dedication of Hewes Library, (113273) Don Beveridge

150. *The Virginia* (Ill.) *Gazette-Times,* 2 May 1974, obit of (113264) Thomas Roy Graham

151. *The State Journal-Register,* 30 Oct 1979, obit of (113265) Bessie L. Graham

152. *Memphis Democrat,* Memphis, Mo., 16 Jun 1988, obit of (113274) Reid Graham Beveridge

153. *The Pantagraph,* Bloomington, Ill., 7 Mar 1991, obit of (113275) Glen W. Beveridge

154. *St. Joseph News-Press,* 4 Mar 1975, obit of (113292) Creighton Francis (113583) Frank M. Joyce

155. *Daily Tribune,* Ames, Ia., 20 Dec 1963, obit of (113511) Bruce L. Beveridge

156. Ibid., 17 Feb 1978, obit of (113514) Miss Elizabeth Beveridge

157. *The Ladysmith* (Wisc.) *News,* 13 Mar 1958, obit of (113555) Wallace Beveridge

158. Ibid., 24 Feb 1994, obit of (113551) Miss Evalyn M. Beveridge

159. *The Pittsburgh Post-Gazette,* 29 Jan 1969, obit of (113512) George M. Beveridge

160. *The Progress-Index,* Petersburg-Colonial Heights, Va., 13 Mar 1960, p. 23, item re: AFrogman@

161. *Rolla* (Mo.) *Daily News,* 27 Aug 1978, editorial and obit of (113723) Thomas R. Beveridge

162. *Peoria* (Ill.) *Journal Star,* 14 Sep 1988, obit of (113762) Glen L. Borden

163. *The Times,* London, England, 30 Jun 1992, obit of (113823) Ruth (McCleery) Stephens

164. *Conservative-Advertiser,* Tipton, Ia., 24 Jun 1971, obit of (115128) Evelyn (Thomson) Blayney

165. *The Cedar Rapids* (Ia.) *Gazette,* Apr 1995, obit of (115151) Alice Mae (Thomson) Barron Groenendyk

166. *The San Diego Union,* 17 Jul 1984, obit of (115175) Donald K. Harper

167. *The Times-Union*, Jacksonville, Fla., 25 Feb 1996, murder of (115512) Margaret Oppen

168. *Times-Citizen*, Iowa Falls, Ia., 28 Feb 1996, murder of (115512) Margaret Oppen

169. Ibid., 28 Dec 1991, obit of (115512) Allan M. Oppen

170. *Dallas County* (Ia.) *News, 17 Dec 1992,* obit of (115532) Carl Burgett

171. *The Topeka* (Kan.) *Capital Journal*, 3 Jul 1988, obit of (116112) Mrs. Isla M. (Dooley) Taylor

172. *The Milwaukee Journal*, 22 Nov 1988, obit of (116122) Matthew P. Zenzian .

173. *New York Times*, 13 Jun 1974, obit of (116161) James Eldredge Miller

174. *El Dorado* (Kan.) *Times*, 4 Jun 1975, obit of (116243) James Doty

175. *The Indianapolis News,* 19 Dec 1962, obit of (116252) Alvin T. Jones

176. *The Milwaukee Journal*, 10 Feb 1972, obit of (116562) Strande A. Bishop

177. *The Des Moines* (Ia.) *Register*, 3 Feb 1998, obit of (116564) Elizabeth (Bishop) Morris

178. *Kansas City Times*, 10 May 1989, p. B-6, obit of (116755) Clyde C. Parker

179. *Roswell* (N.M.) *Daily Record*, 30 Jan 1992, obit of (117121) Jean Marie (Bowersox) Baker

180. *The Hawkeye*, Burlington, Ia., 13 Jan 1999, obit of (117232) John W. Brokaw

181. *Current*, Oquawka, Ill., 24 May 2000, obit of (117233) Evelyn Ruth (Brokaw) Service

182. Shadduck, Louise, *At The Edge of The Ice--Where Lake Coeur d'Alene And It's People Meet*, 1996, ISBN 1-886609-08-X

183. Ross, Virginia and Jane Evans, *Henderson County, Illinois, Cemeteries,* Vol. I, p. 51, South Henderson Cemetery, (inscriptions of the Weir family)

184. *The Augusta* (Ga.) *Chronicle*, 20 Sep 1978, obit of (113582) John R. Beveridge

185. Reston, James Barrett, *Deadline, A Memoir*, Random House, New York, 1991

186. *Stanwood* (Ia.) *Centennial, 1869-1969*, Cedar Co., Ia., Genealogical Society, Tipton, Ia.

187. Porter, H. Leonard III, *Destiny of the Scotch-Irish*, 1990

188. Anderson, Jeanette, Editor and Publisher, *Savilles Then and Now*, 1993, copies at DAR, Washington, D.C.; LDS, Salt Lake City; Genealogical Society, Portland, Oregon

189. Eagle Grove (Ia.) *Eagle*, 22 Oct 1953, obit of 11383 Albert McCleery

190. Marquis *Who's Who in America,* 56th Edition
191. McKerlie, P.H., *History of the Lands and Their Owners in Galloway* (Scotland), 1906

FIRST GENERATION

1 Hugh Thomson (I)

Just before his death, 115 John Thomson told his daughter, Jeanette, a little of the Thomson history. He recalled stories about how the Thomsons who lived in Ayrshire, Scotland, were persecuted and most of the family killed. Three men in the family escaped and fled to Ireland sometime before 1628. The Thomsons then lived in Ireland for several generations. In another version handed down, it is mentioned that Hugh Thomson (I), our oldest known ancestor, had three uncles, unnamed, who suffered martyrdom in one of the persecutions in Scotland. Hugh (I) lived in County Down, Ireland, until after the birth of his son, Hugh Thomson II, in 1775. Dr. Beveridge stated that they relocated to Scotland when Hugh II was a small boy, age not given. Hugh (I) rented some moorland west of Stranraer in Wigtownshire (or Wigtown County) located in the southwest portion of Scotland.

The Thomson home may have been a small structure with a fireplace. There may not have been a chimney, just an opening in the roof for the smoke to escape. The house may have been constructed of stone, or just as likely, of more primitive materials, including a roof of branches and straw. Living conditions were undoubtedly crude by today's standards.

Because of distrust of officials of the church and government, the Scottish became known for being tight-lipped and secretive, while being hard-working and thrifty.

Hugh Thomson (I) is said to have been married twice, but the names of his wives are not recorded; one may have been Elizabeth, since Hugh's first granddaughter had that name. Several manuscripts mention that he had a daughter, Mary, by his first wife. As will be discussed later, Mary was born about 1791 in Ireland. After 1791, Hugh (I) could have married a second time, either in Ireland or Scotland. There are no known children by his second wife.

The Beveridge manuscript mentions that Hugh Thomson (I) had two sons, William and Robert, who emigrated "in an early day" to America and settled near Fort Pitt, now Pittsburgh. Dr. Beveridge mentioned that descendants lived there as well as being scattered all over the U.S., but he failed to name any of the relatives. This is similar to a story contained in the manuscript by Samuel Thomson, who, without giving references, mentioned that Hugh Thomson (I) had two or three brothers, not sons, who "came to America about the time Hugh went to Scotland." Hugh Thomson (I) most likely died in Wigtownshire, but no record of his death has

his death has been found in the local parish registers or
elsewhere. Family records mention that Hugh Thomson I died of
cancer.

Counties of Scotland

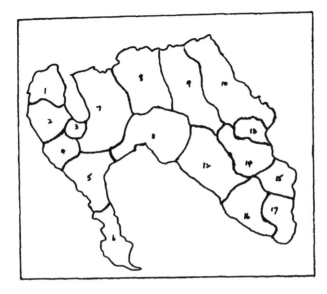

1.	Kirkcolm
2.	Leswalt
3.	Stranraer
4.	Port Patrick
5.	Stoneykirk
6.	Kirkmaiden
7.	Inch
8.	New Luce
9.	Kirkcowan
10.	Penninghame
11.	Old Luce
12.	Mochrum
13.	Wigtown
14.	Kirkinner
15.	Sorbie
16.	Glasserton
17.	Whithorn

Parishes of Wigtown County (Wigtownshire)

The Church of Jesus Christ of Latter-day Saints (LDS) has filmed an enormous number of official records all over the world. One such film, number 0231258, contains probate records of Wigtownshire, Scotland. Mentioned is a Hugh Thomson, a taylor (tailor), who died intestate about 1803, but the parish in Wigtownshire was not mentioned. Samuel Thomson, his brother, was considered to be his nearest of kin. A Hugh McClelland was mentioned as having found some money in Hugh's pocket after his death. This might be the Hugh McClelland who married Sarah Thomson on 1 Dec 1798 in Kirkinner, which is located in the eastern part of Wigtownshire. In the churchyard at Kirkinner is a gravestone with inscriptions that reveal that Hugh McClelland died in 1807 at the age of 42, and that Sarah Thomson died 2 Dec 1846 at the age of 66, placing her birth about 1780. It can be assumed that Sarah Thomson was the daughter of this Hugh Thomson.

Considering the poor means of travel in 1803, it seems that Kirkinner would be a long distance from the western part of Wigtownshire where our Thomsons are known to have lived, which would lessen the possibility of these being relatives of "our" Hugh Thomson. (This information has been included herein for the benefit of future researchers).

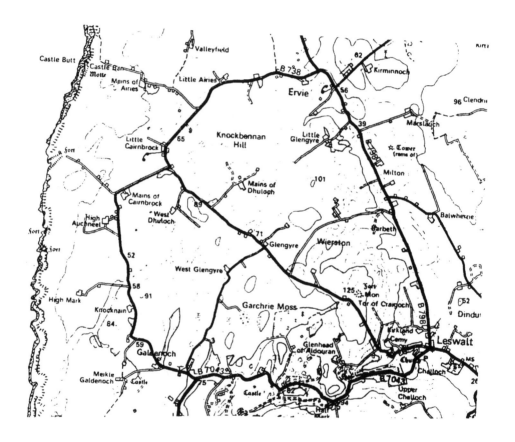

Detail Map of Area West of Stranraer (Thomson home
located at West Dhuloch was northwest of Stranraer)

2 Unknown Thomson

Hugh Thomson (I) and an unnamed sister "were among the first to accept the doctrines of the Secession Church or Associate Presbyterian, when preached in Ireland." A secession from the Church of Scotland occurred in 1733 resulting from a dispute over the appointment of clergy.[187] If they were young adults when they made their acceptance, it would seem to place their birth dates in the early 1700s. The sister was "married in Ireland and with her husband settled near Fort Pitt near the breaking out of the Revolutionary War," according to the manuscript prepared by Samuel Thomson. However, it was more usual for emigrants to be young adults, therefore their birth in the mid-1700s would be more believable.

3 Robert Thomson
4 William Thomson

On the order of thousands of hours of research has been spent tracing a Robert and a William Thomson in the area of Fort Pitt, now Pittsburgh, Pa. Their given names were used in the fourth generation which to some degree supports their existence, given the previously mentioned practice of using names of forebears, the Scottish practice.

The manuscript of Lawrence Thomson included a story about an attack by the Indians upon the home of this family located near Fort Pitt. The attack occurred while the husband was away to the mill, leaving his wife and children at home. Warned of the approach of the Indians, the wife and children fled on foot toward the fort as the Indians set fire to the cabin. Fortunately, some soldiers came along and drove away the Indians. The soldiers then helped her to the fort where she found her husband, nearly crazed with grief. It is not known how Lawrence Thomson learned of this event. This is similar to another account of early Fort Pitt.[7]

Searches have been launched in Allegheny, Westmoreland, and other neighboring counties. This has proven to be a difficult task, primarily because the surname is misspelled in available records, and Thompson is a much more common spelling. (From "PhoneDisc USA 1994" it is learned that the number of people with the surname Thompson is 20 times greater than Thomson). The correct spelling is sometimes determined by examining their true signature on legal documents, especially land records and wills. Attempts to find the correct family primarily have involved a process of elimination: Each possibility is explored until it is proven to be a wrong lead. Research to learn details about the Thomsons of Fort Pitt will likely continue after this book is published.

The basic premise has been that our Robert or William Thomson remained in the Fort Pitt area and did not migrate west at a young age, otherwise their names would not be recorded in official records, and tracing where they went would be next to impossible. Dr. Beveridge claimed in his manuscript that some descendants of Robert or William were in the Pittsburgh area in 1923 while other members had migrated widely throughout the U.S. But it's unfortunate that he didn't name these relatives.

Of interest has been *Record of Indentures of Individuals Bound Out as Apprentices, Servants, Etc. and of German and Other Redemptioners in the Office of the Mayor of the City of Philadelphia.* This covers the period October 3, 1771, to October 5, 1773. It was published by the Genealogical Publishing Co., Baltimore, Md., 1973. On 15 Jun 1772, a William Thomson was indentured to William Carson and his assigns, of Philadelphia, to serve for two years, nine months, and for a fee of fifteen pounds. On June 23, 1772, a Robert Thomson, apparently from an Irish port, was indentured to James Caldwell of Philadelphia for two years, ten months, 23 days as an apprentice, "to be taught the art and mystery of a mariner and navigation and found meat and drink only." It is possible that they later migrated to the area near Fort Pitt.

SECOND GENERATION

11 Hugh Thomson II

If the Scottish tradition of naming children was followed, as mentioned earlier, it would appear that Hugh Thomson II was the third son of Hugh Thomson I, and very unlikely his first son. He was born about 1775 in Ireland. As will be seen, his wife was born in 1778, so it is reasonable to assume that Hugh II was born a few years earlier.

Scottish parish records, which were photographed by members of the Church of Latter-day Saints (LDS), list the marriage of Hugh Thompson (sic) and Ann Melwain (sic) as occurring 2 July 1803 in the parish of Portpatrick, Wigtownshire, Scotland. Ann Milwain was born 20 Apr 1778, and was christened 26 Apr 1778 in Stoneykirk. Hugh was mentioned as being from the parish of Kirkcolm, which lies to the north. Portpatrick and Kirkcolm lie on the western coast of Scotland.

In 1900, 11354 Dr. George Beveridge visited the old farm called "Dhuloch" located west of Stranraer, Scotland. Dhuloch is derived from a Gaelic word meaning black loch.[191] Dr. Beveridge interviewed two people who remembered Hugh's wife, Ann, even though she had left the area around 1850. No traces of the old home exist today.

Ann Milwain was the daughter of James Milwain and Jean Saul as recorded in the old Leswalt Parish registers. A James Milwain, probably Ann's father, was christened 2 Dec 1755 in Stoneykirk, the son of Andrew Milwain and Sarah Fee. James Milwain and Jean Saul were married 27 Sep 1775 at Stoneykirk as shown in records for Wigtown, Scotland. James died 1 Jun 1829 at the age of 78 at Dhuloch. Jean Saul was stated to have died at the age of 90 on 17 Aug 1835 at Dhuloch, placing her birth about 1745. In addition to Ann, they had other children: Janet, christened 3 Sep 1776; John, christened 31 Jul 1780; Jean, christened 23 Apr 1786; and James, christened 16 Sep 1788.

According to a tradition widely held in our Thomson family, Jean Saul was the brother of John Paul Jones, the Revolutionary War hero. Jean's daughter, Ann Milwain Thomson, widow of Hugh Thomson II, should have known of John Paul Jones, who would have been Ann's uncle. Surely she would have known of an uncle who was the notorious naval hero in the eyes of the Scottish. Ann emigrated to America with her daughter and son-in-law, Alexander Weir, in 1856.

Later, Ann was known to be living with her grandson, John Weir, in Henderson Co., Ill. A direct descendant of 1172 John Weir is 1172111 Marilyn Fowler of Gladstone, Ill. She has an oblong mirror that has been passed down from Ann.

John Paul was born 6 Jul 1747, the son of John Paul Sr. and Jean McDuff or MacDuff, as written in OPR (Old Parish Register) baptism records. John's father was a gardener in the old county of Kirkcudbright located east of Wigtown County. John Paul Sr. died 24 Oct 1767 in Scotland. The literature consistently claims that the first child of John Paul Sr. and Jean MacDuff was William, who emigrated to Fredericksburg, Va., was a merchant, and died there without children in 1774. Next came Elizabeth who died unmarried. The third child was Jannet recorded in Kirkcudbright Parish registers of births and baptisms as the "lawful daughter of John Paul and Jean Duff of Mehnhull," who was baptized 22 Apr 1739. Jannet became the wife of William Taylor, a watchmaker in Dumfries, Scotland. Fourth was Mary Ann, who was born 2 Mar 1741 and was baptized 8 Mar 1741. Mary Ann married twice, first to a Mr. Young, then to a Mr. Lowden or Louden. John Paul (Jones) is widely considered to be the fifth surviving child. Lastly came Jean, who was born 25 Apr 1749 and was baptized 28 Apr 1749; she was probably one of two children younger than John Paul who died in infancy. Never in these parish registers is the name written as Saul.

Papers of John Paul Jones were reviewed at the Nimitz Library at the U.S. Naval Academy in Annapolis in 1996. The compiler could find no evidence to prove that John Paul Jones was a Thomson relative. (Of course, it is often said that one can't prove a negative, or in this case, that an event never occurred). Another relative, 113583 Dorothy Beveridge Joyce of Clemson, S.C., has spent many years researching John Paul Jones and also has been unable to prove her relationship to the famous naval hero. She has generously provided the results of her efforts to the compiler.[8-12]

The notion of a relationship to John Paul Jones can be dismissed for two important reasons. None of the records reviewed by the compiler use Saul as the spelling for the family of John Paul Jones. Secondly, the sister of John Paul, Jean Paul, was born in 1749 and supposedly died as an infant. Jean Saul, wife of James Milwain, was born ca. 1745 based on the fact that she died at the age of 90 in 1835. If Jean Paul and Jean Saul were one and the same, it is hard to believe that John Paul Jones would have ignored this sister in the several letters he wrote to other siblings, considering his expressions of love of his siblings and his strong desire for unity in the family.

While visiting in Scotland in 1999, the compiler had a chance meeting with David Williamson, a John Paul Jones descendant, of Dumfries, Scotland. He very generously mailed copies of newspaper items from the *Dumfries and Galloway Standard*, written 15 Aug 1953 and 24 Aug 1953 by his aunt, Agnes J. Spalding, of Surrey.[13] Again, there is no indication of a relationship to our Thomson family.

Hugh Thomson II and Ann Milwain had eight children. First came James who was born in 1804 and died in 1807. Elizabeth was born in 1805, Jean in 1808, Hugh III in 1810, John in 1813, Samuel Melvin in 1815, Anne, mentioned above, in 1818, and William in 1821. Shortly after 1851, Ann took her daughter, Anne, and son, William, to Glasgow where they remained until 1856. All of this family emigrated from Scotland except Hugh III.

We learn from several of the manuscripts that Hugh II had a cancerous leg amputated. His daughter, Anne, later stated that he sat on the side of the bed and, without any restraint, anesthesia, or opiate of any kind, let the surgeons remove the leg. He had said that if he died he wanted to "go before his maker with an unclouded mind." (It's hard to believe such a painful and bloody operation would have taken place as stated; perhaps the surgery was of a less serious nature). Unfortunately, the cancer recurred and Hugh Thomson II died in 1840. He is probably buried near Stranraer, however, his grave site has never been located.

In the census reported for the year 1851, contained in LDS film 0103775, for the parish of Stranraer, there was a listing for Ann Milven, head of a household on Glenwell Street, widow, age given as 72, who was born in "StoneKirk" (sic). It was customary for widows to use maiden names. Also in the household was Ann(e) Thomson, daughter, age 27, dress maker, unmarried, born in Kirkcolm. If the ages were correctly reported, the mother would have given birth at the age of 45. It is possible Anne the spinster shaved a few years off her age so as to appear younger. Family records list the birth of Anne Thomson as having occurred in 1818 in Scotland, so her correct age would have been close to 33.

Ann (Melvin or Milwain) Thomson came to America with her daughter and son-in-law in 1856. She lived with the Weirs in Biggsville, Ill., until her death 17 Feb 1875, just a few years shy of her 100th birthday. Her burial was in South Henderson Cemetery in the Weir family burial plot. Her grave is marked with a beautiful stone.

Ann was a religious person whose faith was expressed in a poem she penned a few days before she met her Savior:

O strengthen faith, encourage hope
And warm my love for Thee.
For Thou of life art the sure prop,
And long hast stood by me.

Oh let my soul be safe with Thee,
That it may not be lost.
For it was bought on Calvary,
And Jesus paid the cost.

Long did I o'er life's ocean sail,
And many a storm have stood.
Help me to weather the last gale,
And find my anchorage good.

The Pilot knows the rocky coast,
The Captain is the King.
The cargo, purchased at His cost,
He safely home will bring

O may He claim what He has bought
When all is brought on shore.
May I obtain what I have sought,
A calm safe passage o'er.

Ann Milwain Thomson

12 Mary Thomson

Mary married Samuel Abernethy and settled in the parish of
Kirkcolm, Wigtownshire. Parish records copied by LDS reveal that
Samuel Abernethy and Mary Thomson of Kirkcolm had Nancy, John,
William, James, Margaret, and another William. Abernethy was a
common name in County Down, Ireland, but uncommon in Wigtownshire.[4]
From the christening dates of the children, it can be estimated
that Mary Thomson and Samuel Abernethy were married about 1820. The
earliest census record available, taken in 1841, for the parish of
Kirkcolm, lists Samuel Abernethy, age 43, joiner, born in Ireland.
Mary's age was given as 50, which in accordance with accepted
practice of the census enumerators, could have been rounded down to
the next lowest increment of five years, from as high as 54 years.
Therefore, her birth year could have been between 1787 and 1791.
Her birthplace was Ireland. John was 16, Margaret was 14; James
was 10, and William was 8.

If Mary Thomson was born in Ireland between 1787 and 1791, then her
father, Hugh Thomson I, of course would have left Ireland after her
birth. When Hugh's first wife died, Hugh remarried, either in
County Down, Ireland, or in Wigtownshire, Scotland. This somewhat
agrees with a comment in Lawrence Thomson's paper in which he
claims that Hugh II was taken with his father's family "when young"
to Scotland (he would have been in his 'teen' years).

Mary (Thomson) Abernethy must have died before 1851, since she is
not listed in the census of that year with Samuel Abernethy of
Kirkcolm. Their home was named Cairnbrock, an area located within
short walking distance of the McRoberts, the Fultons, and the
Thomsons. Samuel, a widower, 52, was a farmer of 9 acres, and was
born in Ireland. Margaret was his daughter, age 24, born in
Kirkcolm. James, his son, was 20, and William was 18, which agrees
with the 1841 census data.

Some early Abernethys, of the Protestant faith, were originally
from Fife County in Scotland and migrated to County Down, Ireland.[14]
They lived in a parish called Drumbo which is located in the north-
central part of the county. Research by Jeanette Anderson during a
visit to the Family History Library of LDS in Salt Lake City
resulted in her locating a map of County Down which was accompanied
by a list of original inhabitants by surname of the many parishes,
no dates given. The Thomson family was listed in several parishes,
most of which were in the lower half of County Down, including the
parishes of Inch, Kilcoo, Kilmegan, Newry and Seapatrick. This
tends to indicate that the Abernethy and Thomson families did not
intermingle in Ireland, but met in Wigtown County, Scotland, and
married there.

The 1861 census data shows that Samuel Abernethy was living in an area called South Lenicarr in the parish of Kirkcolm. He was 62, then a farmer of 18 acres of land. His house had 2 rooms with one or more windows, an odd category by today's standards. Still at home were Margaret, "farmer's daughter," 28; James, "farmer's son," 26; and William, 24. (It is evident that the ages do not agree with ages of the previous censuses when adjusted for the census year, a common observation). Samuel died 10 Feb 1866 in Cairnbrock, Kirkcolm Parish. His death record mentions that his father was John Abernethy who worked as a joiner. Samuel's mother was Mary Morrow. Since Samuel was born in Ireland, it is fairly safe to assume that his parents were born there as well.

The 1871 census listed William Abernethy, age 36, unmarried, farmer of 26 acres, living in Croft Cairnbrock. He had a male servant living with him. He was listed in 1881 as being a retired farmer, unmarried, 40, (perhaps misread as 40 instead of 46), born in Kirkcolm. His residence had changed to Spoutwell in the parish of Inch.

13   Samuel Thomson

Hugh II is stated to have had one brother, Samuel Thomson, a weaver by trade, who spent most of his life in Paisley in Renfrew County, Scotland. This is supported by the observation that Samuel was a given name used frequently in the Thomson family in several generations.

Upon reviewing the 1841 census records taken in Paisley, Renfrewshire, LDS film 1042728, a listing was found for a Samuel Thomson, 45, whose occupation was "cloth lapper." But it indicated that he was born in Renfrewshire which would rule him out as being "our" man, but on the other hand, his birthplace may not have been correctly listed. In the household were Jean, age 25, John 15, Esther 9, Andrew 7, Jean 3, and Alexander 1, all born in Renfrewshire. Jean, age 25, may have been his second wife. Perhaps a review of the 1851 census to locate the data for this Samuel Thomson would be beneficial.

A professional researcher in Edinburgh was unable to find a death record for a Samuel Thomson who may have been a weaver or who worked in the textile industry,[15] although there were nine with that name who died between 1855 and 1900 in Renfrewshire. Four more were located who died in Wigtonshire during the same period, but again they didn't match. A search of monument inscriptions in several Paisley cemeteries did not include a Samuel Thomson in any of the eleven cemeteries examined. The researcher also could not

find birth records for the above children of Samuel, but this is
not too surprising since many Presbyterian Seceders did not
register births in their parish prior to 1855. The report from the
researcher seems to indicate that this Samuel Thomson and his
family emigrated from Scotland.

THIRD GENERATION

111 James Thomson

James was the first child of Hugh Thomson II, born in 1804, and he died in 1807 according to old family records. He may have been named for his maternal grandfather, James Milwain.

112 Elizabeth Thomson

Elizabeth Thomson was born 9 Dec 1805 in Wigtownshire, Scotland. She was probably named after her paternal grandmother named Elizabeth, but we have no documented proof of such a person, who would have been one of the wives of Hugh Thomson (I).

Elizabeth Thomson Fulton Cole

The original records of Kirkcolm Parish list a marriage of
Elizabeth Thomson to Thomas Fulton of Barony Parish in Glasgow on
25 May 1834.   The old records of Kirkcolm Parish indicate that
Thomas Fulton was living in Barony Parish in Glasgow.   They may
have lived in Glasgow after their marriage.

Some background information was obtained of the Fulton family, as
follows: A review of the 1841 census returns of Kirkcolm Parish in
Wigtownshire indicated listings for several Fulton families.   The
name of Thomas' second son was John who probably was named after
his paternal grandfather. There was a John Fulton, an agricultural
laborer (farm hand), age 55, born in Ireland, who resided at
Goldenoch, an area about a mile south of where the Thomsons lived.
His wife was Flora Wright, age 60, also born in Ireland.   There is
no record of their marriage in Wigtownshire.   They had a son,
Thomas, who was born 14 Jul 1809 in Leswalt Parish, Wigtownshire,
as listed in records filmed by LDS.   They had other children,
including Anne, christened 16 Apr 1811; James, christened 30 Jan
1814; and Samuel, christened 5 Sep 1815, and Agnes.   If this is the
correct family, Thomas would have been 25 when he married Elizabeth
Thomson who was then 28.

Flora (Wright) Fulton died at the age of 80 on 11 Jan 1860 at
Goldenoch, Leswalt Parish.   She was the daughter of Thomas Wright
and Jane Macbrain.   She was buried in the Reformed Presbyterian
Churchyard in Stranraer, although no monument was found by the
compiler during a visit in 1999.   John Fulton died at the age of 93
on 26 Mar 1879 at Greenvale Street in Stranraer due to "old age and
general frailty."   The informant on his death certificate was his
daughter, Agnes Fulton.   The certificate listed his father as John
Fulton, a quarryman; his mother was Ann Semple.   An Agnes Fulton,
formerly of Stranraer, died in Glasgow as mentioned in the Wigtown
Free Press published on 29 Jul 1880.

John Fulton and Ann Semple also had a son, Samuel, a laborer who
was married, and died at the age of 75 at Dhuloch in Kirkcolm
Parish on 16 Apr 1858.   The cause of his death was listed as old
age, and he was buried in the "new churchyard at Kirkcolm."   Again,
no tombstone was found.   The informant on his death certificate was
James Fulton, his son.

Elizabeth and Thomas Fulton had children who were born in Scotland,
and later in Canada to which they emigrated in 1842.[16]   Their
children were Anna, John, Hugh, Thomas, and James.   A history of
DeKalb County, Ill., states that there were six children, but only
five are known.[17]

Map of Ontario with old Counties Indicated

The Beveridge manuscript mentions that Thomas Fulton died in Nanticoke, which is in the former county of Haldimand in Ontario. Thomas died in 1846, a few months before the birth of his youngest son. A search for his gravesite has been unsuccessful.

Elizabeth was soon married a second time to James Cole who was born in Northern Ireland. They had two children, Isabella, born in 1848, and Robert J., born in 1851, apparently after James Cole died. The Haldimand Genealogical Society has records showing that James Cole was buried in the Cheapside-McGaw Cemetery in Cheapside, Walpole Township, Haldimand County, Ontario, located near the northern shore of Lake Erie. He died 12 Aug 1850 in his 50th year; this could be our James Cole. A visit was made to the graveyard in 1998 but no stone was found for James Cole.

The same records suggest that James Cole was previously married. James was witness to the marriage of Margaret Cole to William Nunn on 20 Mar 1844, and to the marriage of Jane Cole to Titus Hoover on 5 Mar 1845, both in Haldimand County. Both of these women were

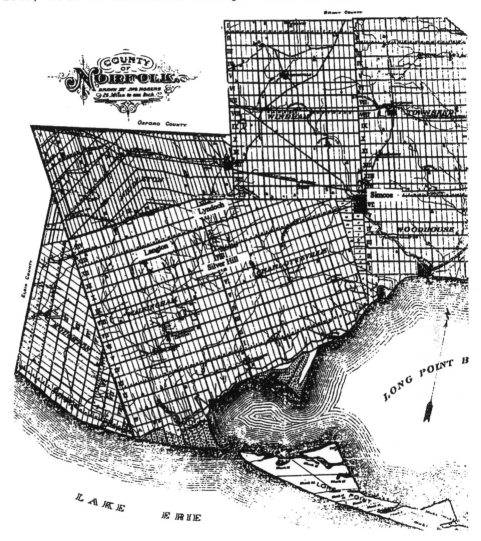

Old Norfolk County, Ontario

possibly his daughters from a previous marriage. Buried in the same cemetery with James Cole is William Nunn (1818-1908) and his wife Margaret Cole (1824-1868), plus their children, Joseph, Robert, Henry, and two infants.

The 1851 census returns listed Elizabeth Cole as a widow and she had relocated to Norfolk County, Ontario. An account of the Gray family written in 1896 by an unknown author mentions that as of 1853 Mrs. Cole operated a small store in Silver Hill, located a few miles below Lynedoch. The census record showed that she had a post office in the store, perhaps part of the 1-1/2 story plank house they lived in. On her next birthday she would be 43 years old. It appears that she deducted a few years off her age; she was really closer to 46. Her religion was indicated as "Free Church;" of which the United Presbyterian Church was a part. The following children were at home: Ann Fulton, 17; Thomas Fulton, 8; James Fulton, 6; Isabella Cole, 4; and Robert J. Cole, age 1. All of the Fulton children were listed as having been born in Scotland, which was a mistake; James had to have been born in Canada. The Cole children's birthplace was listed as Canada. The history of DeKalb County, Ill. indicates that the boys attended school away from home.[17]

In 1861, Elizabeth was still residing in Charlotteville Township in Norfolk County, Ontario. The census data had Elizabeth, 51, in charge of a post office, probably in Silver Hill. The Fulton children were, Thomas, age 17, born in Scotland, and James, age 14, born in Canada, both incorrectly identified as Cole children. Also listed were Isabella Cole, age 12, and R. J. Cole, age 9. As commonly occurred with census records, ages did not always change by ten years from one census to the next.

A review of the 1871 census determined that Elizabeth Cole was the only person by that name in Charlotteville Township. She was still "postmistress" in Silver Hill, District No. 11. She was living with Henry and Hannah Gifford, storekeepers. None of her children were listed as living in the household.

The Tweedsmuir History of North Walsingham[18], page 41, mentions that Elizabeth Cole was the first postmaster of Silver Hill, from 6 Oct 1851 to 29 Apr 1871. Our relative, Evans Knowles, who lives near Langton believes that the old post office building burned down not too many years ago. Silver Hill today is a small town.

The De Kalb County, Ill., history[17] published in 1885 claims that Elizabeth Cole was still in Ontario. However, a search of the 1881 census did not reveal her name. The obituary of her grandson, George T. Fulton, which appeared in *The Hartford City (Indiana)*

News in 1930, mentioned that his parents moved to Waterman, Ill., in 1880.[19] The manuscript of the Gray family stated that they arrived in Sandwich, Ill., in July 1880. Elizabeth Cole may have arrived with them, since she was then 74 years of age. This arrival date would make them too late to have been recorded in the 1880 census of Illinois which was taken on 1 June 1880. Elizabeth died 22 May 1894 at the home of her son, Robert Cole, and was buried in Oak Mound Cemetery located five miles north of Somonauk, Ill., and close to the Presbyterian Church. Her grave is marked with an impressive granite stone.

113   Jean Thomson

Jean was born near Stranraer, Scotland, 5 Mar 1808. Keeping with the method of naming her two older siblings, Jean may have been named for her maternal grandmother, Jean Saul. Lawrence Thomson reports that she and her brother, John, set sail for America on the old sailing brig, Fisher of Mary Port, 16 Apr 1832. The vessel was not in good condition and they were fearful it would break up in the stormy seas during their six-week voyage. They landed in Montreal, Quebec in June 1832, just when a cholera outbreak occurred; their vessel was held in quarantine in the river of Quebec for a week before they could go ashore.[20]

Jean and John Thomson spent one or two years in and near Galt, Ontario, which today is in the heart of Cambridge in old Waterloo County, Ontario. In Galt in 1833, Jean married James McCleery who was born 5 June 1803. Here, the following children were born: John, James, Hugh, Robert, and Mary Ann.[21] The Beveridge manuscript reported that the town of Galt was built on some of the McCleery farms.

Some background information on the McCleery family may be of interest to many family members, as follows: Dr. Beveridge read a paper he had written on the history of the McCleery and Thompson (sic) families in honor of the golden wedding anniversary of James' younger brother, John McCleery, on 10 Sep 1912. (Here is further evidence that the Thomson name was misspelled.) The McCleary family was living in Glasgow, Scotland, in 1771, but the name was spelled differently then, i.e., McCleary. John McCleary was born in Glasgow in 1771, and served as an apprentice at a trade in England, although his father appears to have been a wealthy man.

One night, about 1795, while standing near a fountain in London, John was attacked by the Press Gang. John was a powerful man and knocked down several of the party, but he was overpowered and put on board a man-o-war. John refused to enlist, but was compelled to serve. On a passage to Quebec a young officer struck him with his sword and John promptly knocked down the officer. For this he was sentenced to be shot but was pardoned by the Captain with whom he is said to have found favor.

At Quebec, he obtained leave to go ashore and started off through the woods. With no weapons but a club, he traveled at least 350 miles through a mountainous country, and came upon the home of Thomas Cook in Cambridge, Washington County, N.Y., in a state of almost complete exhaustion. John was taken into the Cook home and kindly cared for. He remained in the community of Cambridge and went to work. It was at this time he changed the spelling of his name to obscure his original identity.

He married Margaret Cook in 1797, the daughter of the family that received him. To them were born ten children: Robert, who lived about three months, James (who married Jean Thomson), Mary Ann, Jane, who lived to 18, Thomas, Edward Cook, John, Margaret, Elizabeth, and Catherine.

John and Margaret lived in various places in Washington County, N.Y., the last being Putnam near Tyconderoga. In 1827 they moved to Canada near Niagara, going first to Stamford and soon after to Dumfries, where they lived until 1841. (The paper describes problems they had with the Presbyterian Church, which culminated in a visit in 1838 to Philadelphia by James McCleery).

Reference has been made to the McCleery Farms located where Galt now exists, in the heart of the city of Cambridge, North Dumfries Township, Waterloo County, Ontario. The compiler visited the land registry Office in Kitchener, Ontario, in 1998, and the city archives in Galt. It was learned that the farm was located on Lots 6 and 7 in Concession 11, and totaled 100 acres. The Concessions in North Dumfries Township are long strips of land numbered from one at the south end to twelve at the north end, while the lots are numbered in sequence from east to west.

The so-called McCleery Farms today are mainly a residential area in the eastern portion of Galt. The old farm property, rectangular in shape, is bounded by Highway 97 to the south, Chalmers Street to the west, Gore Street to the north, and Flora Street to the east. Highway 8 runs diagonally across this area, and was described as a macadam road on a very early map developed by McDonald in 1826. Although family tradition has it that the McCleerys didn't arrive there until 1827, land owned by John and his brother, Edward McCleery, is clearly indicated on this map. James McCleery purchased a total of 100 acres being part of lot 4 in the 8th

Concession and lot 2 in the 9th Concession. Edward McCleery owned land in lot 1 of the 11th Concession.

The records at the archives indicate that the McCleerys sold their land in Sep 1841 to Henry Husson. Although the archives had copies of the old land transactions, they could not be found in the records of the Land Registry Office, and apparently were never officially recorded in the county. An Indenture (deed) identified as no. 3422 in book 9, dated 22 Nov 1876, still referred to Edward McCleery's property as McCleary's (sic), however. The land once owned by James McCleery's was described in Indenture no. 8429 of book 20 of the township of Dumfries, recorded 5 Sep 1912. This deed did not refer to the McCleery name. Time did not allow for a more thorough search of the records, unfortunately.

In 1842, John McCleery moved his entire family, including the family of his son, James, to Dalton, Wayne Co., Ohio. They came by wagon, but at one point James' wife, Jean (Thomson) McCleery, was walking and carrying Mary Ann when Jean fell and dislocated or broke her hip. This was never properly treated, causing chronic lameness and probably later became tubercular, causing her death. Here, several more children were added to the family: Margaret, Elizabeth, William, and Catherine. James' father, John McCleery, died near Dalton, Ohio, on 14 Dec 1849. They remained in this location until 1851 when most of the McCleery family migrated to Somonauk Twp., De Kalb Co., Ill. James McCleery purchased 300 acres of land at a cost of $1.25 per acre.

Jean's brother, Samuel Thomson, and his family stayed with them a short while upon immigrating from Scotland in 1856. In Victor Township, at the home of her son, Robert Cole, Jean died 25 May 1858. Jean was buried in Oak Mound Cemetery in a plot with her husband and his second wife, Eliza Elliott. James McCleery died in Washington County, Iowa, 22 Feb 1892. Their graves are marked with a large granite monument.

114 Hugh Thomson III

Hugh was the only one of his family that remained in Scotland; he was born about 1810 near the parish of Leswalt, on the family farm called Dhuloch Farm, in Wigtownshire, Scotland. He also appears to have been named according to tradition.[6] He married Jean (or Jane) Lyle on 9 Feb 1834 in Riccarton, Ayrshire. They had a daughter, Margaret, and a son, James, as indicated in the notes from the collection of Lawrence Thomson.   In the 1851 census, Jean was listed as head of the household, living on Glasgow Street in Ardrossan, a seaport located on the west coast of Scotland. Hugh evidently was at sea. Also in the family was Margaret, age 15, "seamstress," and James, age 13, "scholar." In 1861, they were in Glasgow with Hugh as the head of the family, age 50, "steam boat fireman." Jane was 52, "wife."

In a letter written in 1922 by his nephew, Hugh Thomson IV, Hugh III was remembered as working on a tugboat that operated on the Firth of Clyde. He thought it was possible that Hugh III was in Paisley, but thought it more likely that he lived in Glasgow. The Beveridge manuscript mentions that Hugh was Assistant Engineer on the Cunard steamers for years.

The 1881 census listed Hugh Thomson, age 70, head of a household in Lochwinnoch, Renfrewshire, which is located nine miles southwest of Paisley. His birthplace was reported as Kirkcolm Parish in Wigtonshire. His occupation was that of a general laborer. His wife was Jean, age 75, born in Monkton, Ayrshire. Living with them were two grandchildren, James, age 7, and Mary, age 5, both born in Lochwinnoch. On the same page of the census record there was a listing for a James Thomson, age 42, whose occupation was "joiner," and he was born in Dreghorn, Ayrshire, which is located within a few miles of the city of Ayr. He was the father of Mary and James, as well as Hugh and William who were living with their father, ages 11 and 9. For the 1891 census, Hugh was living alone in Boghead, Lochwinnoch, and was described as "poultry keeper," age 80.

The above suggests that Hugh Thomson III left Wigtonshire as a young man, met and married Jean in Ayrshire where their children were born. They lived in Glasgow in 1855 according to his direct descendant, Agnes McArthur. She has a diary Hugh kept while serving as a stoker on S.S. Sinla in 1854-1855. The ship was taking cavalry, horses and soldiers to the Crimea.

Agnes McArthur remembers a letter she once possessed that was written about 1860 by Ann (Milwain) Thomson to her son, Hugh III. She exhorted Hugh to read his Bible and stay off the drink! The letter was full of family news but, unfortunately, the letter seems to have been lost.

Hugh lived to old age and was visited by Alexander Howison about 1890. His death has been determined to have occurred on 22 May 1895 at 119 High Street in Renfrew, a suburb of Paisley, in Renfrewshire. The death record listed [incorrectly ?] his age as 83 and he was classified as a labourer. The record shows that his father was Hugh Thomson, farmer, and mother Ann Milncain (sic), both deceased. His wife, Jane or Jean (Lyle) Thomson, daughter of George Lyle and Margaret Latta, died 10 Dec 1888 at Boghead, Lochwinnoch, Renfrewshire. It is not known where they are buried.

115   John Thomson

John was born in Wigtownshire, Scotland, 17 Apr 1813.[22] There was no one that we know of in the Thomson family named John before him, so it's not clear who he was named after.

He joined his sister, Jean, on a voyage to America just a day before his 19th birthday, and they landed in Montreal, Canada in June 1832. A microfilm copy of a Montreal newspaper, *The Quebec Gazette,* was recently reviewed. The edition of Wednesday, 6 Jun 1832, mentioned that the brig *Fisher* had indeed left Stranraer, Scotland, on 16 Apr 1832 under the command of Captain Skay; the boat was owned by H. Gowan and Co. The brig transported ballast as well as 69 "settlers."   The brig departed Montreal on 7 Jul 1832, headed for Wales.

After spending a year or two in Galt, Ontario, John went to Massilon, Ohio, where he spent a year working as a carpenter. His next residence was in Mariette, Ohio, then he road a steamboat down the Ohio River, then up the Mississippi River before debarking at Oquawka, Ill. He resumed his trade as a carpenter in partnership with a Mr. Hibbard.

In Little York, Ill., he married[23] 15 Nov 1844 Elizabeth Maley who was born 24 Feb 1816, from Bible records contained in Lawrence Thomson's genealogical collection, now held by Linda Clark.

John Thomson

They had twins, William Maley Thomson and Ann Melvin Thomson, born 9 Nov 1846. Elizabeth died 1 Aug 1849 and was buried near Little York, Ill., in a plot with her parents and possibly her daughter, Ann. The 1850 census listed John Thompson (sic) in Oquawka, Ill., working as a carpenter.

John married again, this time to Margaret Catherine McClelland, 11 Sep 1855. She died without children 28 Apr 1856. Thirdly, John married Mary Ann Parks 5 Nov 1856. She bore him ten children after they moved to Aledo, Ill.: Mary Jean, John J., Elizabeth, Margaret M., Abraham L., Janet M., Nancy M., Frances C., David Paul, and Samuel Alexander. The Thomson home was located at the corner of 3rd St. SE and Rose St.

John built many of the first houses in Aledo as well as in Oquawka and Little York. He had a creative mind, and always strove to improve modes of work. He obtained several patents, one of which was for a door weather strip, patent number 121,912. Another patent of great importance was for *check-row planters*, patent number 129,624, shown in part in the next figure. Patents can be viewed and purchased on-line at Getthepatent.com. John is said to have sold patent rights to Haworth Brothers of Decatur, Ill. They marketed the check-row planter and made a fortune from its sale.

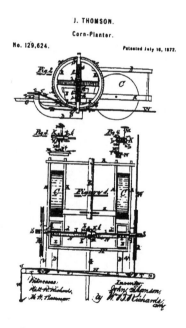

One of John Thomson's Patents

John volunteered for the Civil War but was rejected three times because he was in his forties and not in good health (an odd comment since he survived to the age of 90.) At home John helped the families of those who had lost husbands and fathers at the front.

John Thomson and Family, ca. 1883

Front, L-R: Abraham, John, twins Samuel and David (standing), Mary, John J.

Rear: twins Nancy and Jeanette, Elizabeth, Margaret (?), Mary (?), Francis

In an undated letter, John gave George Beveridge instructions on how to find where the old Thomson home in Scotland once stood:

> When you are at Stranraer, go west past Leswalt Church. That is three miles about half way to where I was raised. Inquire for a farm called "Mains of Douloch." When there inquire for the Dogstone Hill. That is where I used to sit and watch the cows. There you will have the best view of any place I ever saw in my life. You see the Merrick Hills (2,764 ft elev) 30 miles NE, the Craig Ailsa, 20 miles north, which is at the mouth of the Firth of Clyde, you see the Isle of Arran, the Mull of Kintyre, the Rathlin Isles, the Fair Head of Ireland and the Galin Haugh Bluff, where King William's men drove the Papists over into the sea.

> You will see the mountains of Mourne and on a clear day, you can see the Isle of Man. I have counted if I remember right on the West side of Dogstone Hill. Near its base, was the little house where I was born, but I am told that it is gone and all landmarks-- the little farms grouped into large ones. Perhaps some of the old ones can tell you where Hugh Thomson's home used to stand. When you come back, I want to see or hear from you.

John was a religious man, a strong supporter of the Presbyterian Church. He inherited a love for poetry from his mother and he was a great admirer of the Scottish poets, Scott and Burns. On his 90th birthday, all of his children and his sister, Anne (Thomson) Weir, gathered at his home in Aledo for a celebration.[24] He read a poem he had composed which is contained in the Appendix, page 384. In it he mentions that his parents and sister (two actually) have died, but no mention of his brothers, including James, who died in infancy. John died not long afterward, 19 Feb 1904. In his obituary,[22] Anne Weir is described as the last surviving member of his family, which was most likely true. John was buried in Aledo Cemetery where a large monument marked 'Thomson/Spence' was erected. Mary died 11 Jun 1903. Later, other family members were buried in the family plot.

116 Samuel Melvin Thomson

[Most of the following is from a manuscript specially prepared for this book by Jack Scott Light in 1998]. Samuel was born 15 Jul 1815 in Duloch, Kirkcolm Parish, Wigtownshire, Scotland. He was given the name of his uncle. Samuel grew to manhood near Stranraer, Scotland. He excelled in education and when he was a young adult he became a school teacher in or near Stranraer. After marriage to Elizabeth McRobert in Aug 1840, he became an engineer

Samuel and Elizabeth Thomson

on ferry boats operating on the Cylde River out of Greenock in Renfrew County.

After four years at Greenock, and with two young children, Samuel took his family back to Dhuloch farms. Samuel's brother, John, and sister, Jean, had migrated to America several years earlier, and Samuel yearned to go there also but Elizabeth would not leave her aging mother behind, so they stayed in Scotland. The children born to Samuel and Elizabeth were Mary Buchanan, Jeannette McRobert, Hugh Thomas, Annie Melvin, Elizabeth Grace, Samuel, and Jane Ellen.

Samuel did not relish farm life, so he returned to the sea for his livelihood. He signed on as engineer on an ocean-going vessel. In Nov 1851 Samuel said fond farewell to his family and steamed across the North Atlantic, not to be seen by his family for three and a half years. For part of his voyage he served as second engineer on a mail vessel that sailed from Valparaiso, Chile, to Panama. He sent half of his earnings home to Elizabeth. While he was away his family lived with his mother-in-law, Mary Buchanan McRobert at Ervie and they made a meager living raising vegetables, fowl, and a few head of livestock on the small farm they rented.

After Samuel returned he found that Elizabeth had saved about all the money he had sent home. The 1851 census records of the parish of Kirkcolm, LDS film 0103774, show that Samuel, age 35, laborer, was living with his mother-in-law, Mary McRobert, age 77. His wife, Elizabeth, was reported to be 38. Also listed were Samuel and Elizabeth's children, Mary, Janet, Hugh, and Ann, plus Helen McRobert, Elizabeth's sister, age 35. Elizabeth's mother soon died and Elizabeth was then willing to migrate to America. However, she was pregnant and the trip was delayed until the baby, named Samuel, arrived.

In 1856, Samuel's mother, Ann Melvin Thomson, age 78, his married sister, Annie Thomson Weir and her family, initially thirteen people in all, made their way to Liverpool, England, where they boarded the ship *Andrew Foster,* and departed on 23 Sep 1856.[25]

Henry Wakeman Swift was the captain of this ship that displaced 1,286 tons and carried a total of 530 passengers on this voyage. The ship's passenger list had Sam'l Thompson, engineer, age 41, of Scotland. Baby Samuel was four months old.[26] The Weirs were listed as Thompsons by mistake; Alex was listed as a blacksmith, age 26, and Anne was 28. Their son William was age 2, and they had a daughter, Jane, age 10 months. Ann Thomson was listed as being 55 years of age. (The ages recorded of the married women were considerably less than their actual ages.) They encountered rough weather during the ocean crossing which caused much sea sickness for the family, including Elizabeth; she became dehydrated and had no milk for baby Samuel. The baby became sickly and died on 14 Oct 1856, as indicated on the passenger list, and had to be buried at sea, greatly adding to the distress of the trip. (The ship *Andrew Foster* later collided with *Tuscarora* in the Irish Sea on 28 Apr 1857 and was sunk.)[27]

They arrived in New York City on 22 Oct 1856 and made their way by train to the home of Samuel's sister, Jean (Thomson) McCleery in Somonauk, Ill. They soon departed for Little York, Ill., to visit John Thomson, then settled in Oquawka, Ill. The 1860 census of Henderson Co., Ill., described Samuel Thomson, age 50, laborer, with a personal estate worth $300, born in Scotland. In the family were his wife, Elizabeth, and children Mary B., Jeannette, Hugh, Anna, Elizabeth, and Jane. Jane was the only one born in Ill.

Samuel was reluctant to become naturalized because of his loyalty to Queen Victoria. When his son, Hugh, turned twenty-one and applied for citizenship, Samuel followed suit. Samuel was quoted as saying "England was to him as a mother and America as a wife; loving his mother did not make him love his wife less." On 17 Oct 1866, Samuel swore on oath to renounce Queen Victoria of Great Britain in Circuit Court in Henderson County, Ill.

Samuel farmed near Biggsville, in Henderson County, Ill., for several years. Oddly enough, there was a Samuel F. Thompson who lived nearby and had just received a large inheritance.

In Sep 1867, the families of Samuel Melvin Thomson and William B. Mekemson, married to Samuel's daughter, Jeannette, traveled by wagon with some livestock in tow, and had to cross the Mississippi River by ferry at Burlington, Ia. When the ferry arrived at the west shore, two of the cows swam the river back to Ill., and had to be rescued. The closest railhead to their new farm was Des Moines; their heavier farm equipment and household goods were shipped there and hauled by wagon the remainder of the way. Oddly enough, Samuel F. Thompson, their neighbor, also moved to Madison County, and bought land in Jackson Twp., which, understandably, caused some confusion in tracing the land records.

After Samuel and his family arrived in Jackson Twp., Madison Co., Ia., Samuel bought his first land in America on 9 Sep 1867. The purchase was for eighty acres of land located in the west half of the northwest quarter of section 24 in Jackson Twp.[28] Log houses were immediately constructed and prairie hay cut for winter feed. With courage, the family confronted the challenge of rugged pioneer life for a few years until the new farm became productive. The following year, 1868, his son-in-law, James Beck and his daughter, Elizabeth, also left Henderson Co., Ill. and joined the Thomsons as neighbors in Madison Co. Samuel farmed his land the remainder of his life and all his younger children were raised to adulthood there.

The Thomson farm was located about two miles east of the new village of Pitzer where the Thomsons, Becks, and Mekemsons were charter members of the Union United Presbyterian Church. Their Scottish Christian heritage as Presbyters was not neglected; once a month they attended preaching services conducted by Dr. McCaugham in a little rural schoolhouse. On other Sabbaths, when the weather was nice, they drove ten miles to Winterset. When winter weather closed in, Samuel organized prayer meetings at his home for the local farmers for the intervening Sabbaths. Using the Bible and the Catechism, a Sunday school was started. This local union became the nucleus for the new church at the crossroads of Pitzer. The original membership of the new church was 35 members.[29]

Nearby is located Stringtown Cemetery[30-32] where Samuel Thomson is buried; he died in Redding, Ringgold Co., Ia., 6 Jun 1903 at the home of his daughter, Jeannette Mekemson. His grave is marked with a tall obelisk stone. No death certificate was to be found for Samuel by the Iowa Health Department, as recording of vital records not yet compulsory. Elizabeth (McRobert) Thomson was born 1 Aug 1812 (Lawrence Thomson's notes have her born in 1814) on Dhuloch farm, in the parish of Kirkcolm, Wigtownshire, Scotland. She was an exceptionally pious Christian and very affectionate to her family and friends. She died 19 Feb 1879. At the age of 68, Samuel married Mary Orr who was born Feb 1845 in Ireland, according to the 1900 census records. Samuel sold the farm to his daughter, Jane and her husband, Edward McCorkle, on 22 Feb 1888. In 1900 Samuel and Mary were living in Penn Twp., Madison Co., Ia.

117 Anne Melvin Thomson

"Annie" was born in Scotland 6 Apr 1818 and was named after her mother.[33] The 1841 census had her listed in Dhuloch, parish of Kirkcolm, Wigtownshire. Anne Thomson, whose birthplace was listed as Stoneykirk, was 63; Samuel was 25; and Anne was 20, both born in Kirkcolm. As previously mentioned, the 1851 census had Ann Thomson unmarried, living with her widowed mother, in Stranraer. Sometime later, her mother took her daughter, Annie, and her son, William, to Glasgow. Annie married Alexander Weir in 1852 and they lived in Glasgow where their son, William Thomson Weir, was born.

Alexander's obituary[34] states that he was born in Oct 1830 in Scotland and at an early age was apprenticed to a firm of shipbuilders. The census of 1851 listed an Alexander Weir, age 18, living in the parish of Stoneykirk, village of Sandhead. This Alexander Weir was born in the parish of Inch in Wigtownshire and was an apprentice to James W. McNillie, blacksmith. Old documents held by Jane Weir, who lives in Biggsville, Ill., mention that Alexander Weir was employed as an iron worker at Clyde Bank Iron Shipyard for three years preceding 1856. The Beveridge papers mention that he was a shipbuilder and a wonderfully fine mechanic. Dr. Beveridge was frequently at their home near Gladstone when he was attending Monmouth College.

Along with a number of other family members, the Weirs emigrated to America in 1856. They spent their first year in Little York, Ill. Their daughter, Janie, survived the ocean crossing but died at the age of two and was buried in Little York, Ill.

The 1860 census of Henderson Co., Ill. recorded Alex's occupation as "blacksmith." They made their home in Coloma, near Biggsville, where they also farmed. Here, their son John was born. Records obtained at the National Archives in Washington, D.C., indicate that Alex was naturalized in Circuit Court in Henderson County 30 Aug 1867. Annie's obituary mentioned that on 23 Oct 1857 she and her husband were received by letter from Scotland into South Henderson Presbyterian Church.[33]

Dr. Beveridge visited her when she was about ninety. She was home alone that day and had gotten out a lot of carpet rags and washed and dyed them herself. She said that she had to do them as they would not let her do it when they were home. Her mind was very clear. After a long life, at the age of 95, Annie died 6 Jan 1914. She was buried in South Henderson Cemetery in the same plot as her mother and husband, Alexander, who died 12 Nov 1897.

118   William Thomson

William, who may have been named for a great-uncle, was born in 1821, and was in Glasgow sometime after his father died, then he departed for Australia. When a young man, as the story goes, he was disappointed in love and went to Australia, saying he would not return until he had acquired $250,000. He wrote to relatives on his 80th birthday, but the letter has not survived.

A lot of effort and expense has gone into obtaining a copy of his death certificate: Inquiries were made in all the states in Australia. A death certificate that could be his was obtained from the State of Victoria. A William Thomson who had been a miner and an old age pensioner from the State of Victoria died 16 May 1905 at the age of 85. His death occurred in Moliagul, County of Gladstone, District of Dunolly, and was recorded as death number 5108. The cause of death was listed as "old age and debility, and died whilst being conveyed to Dunolly Hospital." An inquest into the cause of his death was ruled unnecessary. The names of his parents were unknown, but he was said to have been born in Edinburgh, Scotland, and had been in Victoria, Australia, for 53 years. The record shows that he was not married.

His obituary mentioned that he had been engaged in mining and "fossicking" and was well known and highly respected throughout the district.[35] No survivors were mentioned. He had been a resident of Moliagul for 40 years. The facts closely fit what we know about him. He may have worked the gold fields, and may have come close to acquiring his monetary goal, but then lost it, as one story handed down relates. If he had been in Australia for 53 years, he would have left Scotland about 1852, a date which fits well.

121   Nancy Abernethy

Original records reveal that Nancy was born at Dhulach Farms and was christened 22 Sep 1822 in Kirkcolm Parish, Wigtownshire, Scotland. She is probably the Agnes Abernethy who died at the age of four on 30 Mar 1827 at Doulach as recorded in the Leswalt Parish register.

122   John Abernethy

John was born at Dhulach Farms and was christened 29 Aug 1824. *The Free Press* listed the birth of a son (James) on 17 Aug 1864 to the wife (Agnes Watson) of John Abernethy, umbrella maker, of Friar's Vannel in Dumfries, possibly our relatives.

123   William Abernethy

William was christened 16 Oct 1826. There were two children christened with this name, indicating that this William died in infancy.

124 Margaret Abernethy

Margaret was born in 1828 in Wigtownshire and died unmarried 25 Nov 1866 at Cairnbrock, Wigtonshire, as appeared in *The Free Press* which described her as the only daughter of the late Samuel. Her death record at the New Register House in Edinburgh listed her mother as Mary Thomson. Her brother, William, was the informant.

125   James Abernethy

James was born 10 Sep 1830 in Cairnbrock and was christened 13 Sep 1830. The census records show that he attained manhood. James was not married. At Cairnbrock, parish of Kirkcolm, James died 13 Mar 1866, the same year his father and sister died.

126   William Abernethy

The second William was christened 5 Dec 1832 and is believed to have remained unmarried his entire life. He had been a farmer and was alive for the 1881 census, living in the parish of Inch.

FOURTH GENERATION

1121   Anna Fulton

Anna was listed in the Ontario census records from which her birth
year of 1835 is derived. Born in Scotland, she may have been named
after her paternal grandmother, Anne Melvin Thomson. Annie married
William John Knowles in the town of Simcoe, Norfolk Co., Ontario on
3 May 1853.[36] The marriage was listed in Talbot District Marriage
Register of 1837-1857, per records filmed by LDS. William was born
in 1828 (per his obit) in County Antrim, Ireland, and died 24 Sep
1903 at Carholme. Their children were Robert, Thomas Fulton,
Elizabeth A., Bessie A., Margareta, William John Jr., and James
Fulton. Tuberculosis about wiped out the family. Anna died 4 Jan
1890, "in her 55th year," and was buried in Carholme-Knowles
Cemetery in Walsingham Twp., Norfolk Co., Ontario.[37] Descendants
of Anna live in Langton, Ontario.

Anna Fulton

The above photograph of Anna was obtained from Agnes McArthur of
Renfrew, Scotland.

William purchased the main portion of his farm in 1861 which was
added to the part purchased by his father, Robert Knowles, in 1849.
In 1878 he erected a large cheese factory on his farm which he
operated; in 1905 it was sold to George Gray of Lynedoch. "Century
Farm" has remained in the hands of the Knowles family who increased
its size to 334 acres by 1966. Tobacco, corn, beef cattle, and a
few hogs are the enterprises now operated on the farm.[18]

By an indenture dated 3 Apr 1889, William and Annie Knowles sold, for $1.00, a tract of three and one-half acres of land to the trustees of Carholme Presbyterian Church, for the purposes of establishing a cemetery.

1122 Hugh Fulton

Hugh was not listed in census records, which would indicate he died in infancy.

1123 John Fulton

The dates of birth of John and Hugh are unknown. Since they were not listed in the 1851 census, they were thought to have died young, as the Beveridge manuscript mentioned. Hugh would have been named for his paternal grandfather, Hugh Thomson. John's maternal grandfather may have been John Fulton. Both must have been born in Scotland before 1841 but no record of their birth has been found.

1124 Thomas W. Fulton

Information recently obtained from Fulton descendant Mary Gray (Koehler) Haxby included photographs of Anne Melvin (photo identifies her as Grandmother Thompson (sic)), Elizabeth (Thomson) (Fulton) Cole, and three pictures of Thomas Fulton. Inscriptions on the photos indicate that Thomas served in the Civil War with the

Thomas W. Fulton

First Wisconsin Heavy Artillery from 1863 to 1865.[38] A notation on two photos gives his birth date as 20 Oct 1842 and his death date as Dec 1869. He was given his father's name in accordance with tradition for naming a third-born son.

A review of his service records at the National Archives reveals that he was born in Glasgow, Scotland, and was a resident of Fulton Township, Rock County, Wisconsin, when he enlisted 6 Nov 1863 in Milwaukee to serve a term of three years. Fulton Township is located west of Edgerton, on the Rock County, Dane County line. He listed his occupation as farmer and gave his age as 19, which doesn't agree with the age marked on his photographs.

His service records indicate he was 5' 11" tall, had brown eyes and hair, and had a fair complexion. A muster roll dated 18 Aug 1865 reveals that Thomas had deserted from Battery Rodgers, and the U.S. was due 1 screwdriver, 1 wiper, 1 tampion, 1 spring vise, and half of a double bed-sack. Thomas may have become ill during the war which could have led to his early death, in Michigan, according to Dr. Beveridge. He had no pension file, and was probably unmarried.

VOLUNTEER ENLISTMENT.

STATE OF *Wisconsin*   TOWN OF *Fulton Rock County*

I, *Thomas W. Fulton* born in *Glasgow* in *Scotland* aged *Nineteen* years, and by occupation a *Farmer* Do HEREBY ACKNOWLEDGE to have volunteered this *Sixth* day of *November* 186*3*, to serve as a **Soldier** in the Army of the United States of America, for the period of *THREE YEARS*, unless sooner discharged by proper authority: Do also agree to accept such bounty, pay, rations, and clothing, as are, or may be, established by law for volunteers. And I, *Thomas W. Fulton* do solemnly swear, that I will bear true faith and allegiance to the **United States of America**, and that I will serve them honestly and faithfully against all their enemies or opposers whomsoever; and that I will observe and obey the orders of the President of the United States, and the orders of the officers appointed over me, according to the Rules and Articles of War.

Sworn and subscribed to, at *Milwaukee Wis* this *Sixth* day of *November* 186*3*   *Thomas W Fulton*

BEFORE

Capt I CERTIFY, ON HONOR, That I have carefully examined the above named Volunteer, agreeably to the General Regulations of the Army, and that in my opinion he is free from all bodily defects and mental infirmity, which would, in any way, disqualify him from performing the duties of a soldier.

Thomas Fulton's Enlistment Record

1125 James Fulton

James Fulton was the subject of a biographical sketch published in an 1885 history of DeKalb Co., Ill.[17] He was described as being the youngest in his family and was born in Dunnville, Haldimand County, Ontario on 12 May 1846. According to his granddaughter, Dorothy Fulton Cope, James was born a month after the family arrived from Scotland. She thought that her grandfather's middle name was Thomson, the same as her father's middle name. The obituary of George T. Fulton, his grandson,[19] confirms James' birthplace as Dunnville, Haldimand Co. James attended grade school in Silver Hill (where his mother lived), high school in Seneca, and advanced grammar school in Toronto. He was listed in his mother's household for the 1861 census.

A copy of the certificate of marriage between James Fulton and Jane C. "Jennie" Gray on 14 Nov 1871 has been obtained. Jane was born 19 May 1845 in Portage, N.Y., and was a resident of Walsingham at the time of her marriage. James' birthplace was recorded as Dunnville. The marriage was performed in Walsingham Twp., Norfolk Co. by George Chrystal, a minister. The witnesses to the ceremony were Abraham Gray, and Isabella Cole, his half-sister. Their wedding trip was to Somonauk, Ill., where James had friends. At the time, James taught school and was a bookkeeper in Lynedoch.

James Fulton and Family

Sitting in Front: Thomas
Middle Row, L-R: Nell, James, Fred, Jane Gray, Mary
Back Row, L-R: Walter, William, Anne, George, Robert

In 1872, James opened a store in Langton, located a few miles west of Silver Hill in Norfolk County, Ontario. He was assisted by his father-in-law, George Gray, Jr. After being open for about a year, James decided to erect a brick building that was large enough for his store and dwelling space for his family. Initially, he sold a large quantity of goods and was prospering. However, the store cost two thousand dollars to build, which took much of the capital from his business. The business ended disastrously as a result of bad debts and other losses. James was obliged to close the store at a significant loss not only to himself, but to Mr. Gray, and to Mr. John Charlton who had backed his business.

James resumed his teaching profession in the autumn of 1874 which he continued until 1880. He was also a bookkeeper during this time. He was an excellent teacher, and the parents of his students were sorry to see him leave. In July 1880, he moved the family to Waterman, Ill., where he once again engaged in general mercantile business. He was in a partnership with J. A. Armstrong (who married Isabella Cole, his half-sister) until 1884 when he purchased his partner's interest. Then, in 1893, he moved to Hartford City, Ind., where he opened a grocery store. In 1898 he had a hardware store which failed in the depression. They remained in Hartford City until 1908, after which they relocated to Coeur d'Alene, Ida., in 1910. They had nine children: George T., William J., Anne E., Robert B., Walter S., James T., Frederick G., Ella C., and Mary. The last three were born in Ill. The Fultons maintained their religious faith with the Presbyterian Church as had their forefathers. James died 6 Jan 1925 in Coeur d'Alene, after seeing all of his children during the last few weeks of his life.[39,43] Jane died 22 Apr 1925.[46] Both are buried in Forest Cemetery in Coeur d'Alene.

1126 Isabella Cole

Isabella or "Beth", was born[40] in Lynedoch, Norfolk Co., Ontario, Canada 4 Jul 1849. She married John Alexander Armstrong, a native of Washington, New York. John, who was born 17 Jul 1847, was the son of William Armstrong and Phebe McClellan. He died 20 Dec 1921, supposedly in Chicago, however, his obituary was not found in *The Chicago Tribune* or *Daily News*.[41] John was buried in Oak Mound Cemetery. John at one time was a business partner with James Fulton in Waterman, Ill. They had five children according to the 1910 census, and three were living. Isabella indicated to the census enumerator that she had been married 34 years, placing her marriage about 1876. The *Somonauk Book*[42] appendix listed their children as Jean Elizabeth, Margaret M., William K., Charles S., and Grace L. Isabella had the distinction of being listed twice in the 1920

census. She was listed with her half-brother, James Fulton, in
Coeur d'Alene, Ida., and with James Stirling, her son-in-law, in
Chicago. In both cases, her age was listed as 71, and birthplace
Canada. She was listed in the 1923 City Directory as "widow of
John." Isabella had been a member of Women's Missionary Society of
United Presbyterian Church in Chicago. She died 22 Jul 1932 in East
Orange, N.J.[44] Burial was in Mt. Hebron Cemetery in Montclair, N.J.

1127 Robert James Cole

Robert was born 24 Mar 1851 near Simcoe in Norfolk Co., Ontario. He
entered the United States and declared his intention to become
naturalized 21 Jun 1880 according to Circuit Court records of
DeKalb Co., Ill. A certificate of naturalization was granted 23
Oct 1882 with James McCleery and Andrew Graham standing as
witnesses as recorded in Naturalization Docket, book 16, page 2.

Naturalization Record of Robert J. Cole

On 27 Mar 1879, he married Margaret Elizabeth Beveridge. Margaret
was born 24 Sep 1854 (per death certificate) in New York state, the
daughter of Andrew L. Beveridge and Jennett Hutton. The 1860
census returns listed them as residents of West Hebron, Washington
County, N.Y. Ancestors of Andrew L. Beveridge (1820-1898) have

been traced back to Alexander Beveridge (1793-1874), to Andrew
Beveridge (1752-1835, a Scottish immigrant), and to George
Beveridge of Strathmiglo, Scotland. The information on the
Beveridge family is contained in *Hebron, A Century In Review, 1987*,
which was published by the Hebron (New York) Preservation Society.[45]
Robert Cole and his wife, Margaret Beveridge, had ten children:
Andrew James, Elizabeth, Mary Jeanette, William J., Sarah,
Margaret, Annabelle, Robert H., Ernest, and Ruth Agnes. Two others
died young.

In 1906 the family removed to Yellow Grass, Saskatchewan, Canada,
where they homesteaded. In 1920 they were living in Coeur d'Alene,
Kootenai County, Ida. The census data confirms that he spent some
time in Canada and returned to the U.S. in 1919. In the household
were his wife, Margaret E., age 64, and two grandchildren, Robert
B., age 8 years-seven months, and Isabel, age 6 years-3 months,
both born in Canada. The ages were relative to the date of the
census which was 1 Jan 1920. Margaret died 14 Aug 1920 in Coeur
d'Alene and was buried in Forest Cemetery.[48] Isabelle Scriven
remembers that every meal was served with elegance. Her
grandfather always served dinner, and on warmed plates. She also
recalls that he was an excellent checker player.

Robert James Cole died 17 Aug 1935[47] in Spokane and was buried
alongside his wife in Forest Cemetery in Coeur d'Alene. Buried
with them are his unmarried daughters, Sarah Cole and Elizabeth
Cole.

Robert James Cole and Family

L-R: Andrew, Elizabeth, William, Robert, Ernest, Ruth, Sarah,
Margaret Beveridge, Janet, Bert, Margaret

1131 John McCleery

John was born 23 Jan 1834 in Ontario, Canada, and died 24 Jan 1917 in Victor Twp., De Kalb Co., Ill., based on the dates on his tombstone in Oak Mound Cemetery. He married 22 Sep 1862 Ann McCall who was born 31 Dec 1840 and died 14 Jan 1920. John and Ann lived to celebrate their golden wedding anniversary. They had nine children: Robert Francis, John A., James Andrew, Margaret, Annie, Lula May, William Carlisle, Elizabeth Rose, and Benjamin Henderson. Robert Francis and James Andrew are buried in their parents' plot.

1132 James W. McCleery

James was born near Galt, Waterloo County, Ontario, Canada, 18 Jun 1835.[17] His parents took the family to Dalton, Ohio, in 1842, then to De Kalb Co., Ill., in 1851. On 1 Feb 1858 he married Margaret Graham, who was born 15 Jun 1837 and died 16 Aug 1926 in Waterman, Ill. Their children were Sara Jane, John Andrew (two in succession), Margaret, Mary, Fannie Elizabeth, Adeline Isabelle, William Russell, Raymond, and Jeannette (Nettie). Their dates of birth, and some deaths, appeared in *De Kalb County Illinois Families* by George Wakefield, 1938.[21] G. Wiley Beveridge published a genealogy of this family in 1962.

James was appointed supervisor of Clinton Twp. in 1883. The family was aligned with the Presbyterian Church. He died 23 May 1903 on his farm in Clinton Twp., De Kalb Co. James and Margaret were buried in Oak Mound Cemetery, along with four of their children: John, Andrew, Margaret and Jeanette. A large granite stone marks their plot.

1133 Hugh McCleery

Hugh, named after his paternal grandfather, was born 10 Mar 1837 in Canada and died three days later.

1134 Robert McCleery

Robert was born 15 Nov 1839 near Galt, Ontario, Canada. He died in Dalton, Ohio 22 Mar 1842.[17]

1135 Mary Ann McCleery

Mary Ann was born 22 Jan 1841 in Galt, Ontario, Canada.[17] On 10 Jan 1865 she married John C. Beveridge, the son of Alexander Beveridge (1793-1874) and Sarah "Sally" McClellan (1794-1888). During their first years of marriage, they lived in a log cabin. Then, in 1871, John put his carpentry skills to use and built a house and several

farm buildings. John was a successful hog raiser and farmer, but
also contributed to his community by holding positions such as
assessor, supervisor, and school treasurer. John was born 3 Feb
1826 in Washington County, N.Y., lived in Illinois for 44 years,
all on his farm, and died 3 Jan 1906. Their picture was included
in a photograph of a large group in the *Somonauk Book.*[42]

Mary Ann (McCleery) Beveridge and Family

Front Row, L-R: James, John C., Archibald, Mary Ann, Alexander,
Mae, Margaret. Back Row, George, Albert, Jennie C. Reed, Rae

In Mar 1907, Mary moved to Reinbeck, Ia., to live with her son, Dr.
George Beveridge. She died in Reinbeck 31 Jul 1907.[49] She was
buried alongside her husband in Oak Mound Cemetery. The children
of John C. and Mary Ann Beveridge were Alexander William, James
McCleery, Albert Elmer, George, Rea L., Mae, Margaret, and
Archibald. All but Archibald, who was born later, were listed in
the census returns of Victor Twp., DeKalb Co, Ill., in 1880.

1136 Margaret McCleery

Margaret was born in Dalton, Ohio 22 Feb 1843 and died 23 Aug 1916
in Squaw Grove Twp., De Kalb Co., Ill. She married Alexander
Howison who was the subject of a biographical sketch in *The
Biographical Record of De Kalb County, Illinois, 1898.*[50] From this
source we learn that Alexander was born on 22 Nov 1826 in
Roxburyshire, Scotland, the son of George

Howison and Margaret Brown. Alexander arrived in Illinois in 1847.
He ventured to California in 1852 and there he spent several years
prospecting for gold, and also was a gardener. Alexander and his
brother, James, safely returned home by way of the Isthmus of
Panama after surviving shipwreck and yellow fever. Margaret and
Alexander were married 18 Nov 1862 and they took up farming in
Squaw Grove Twp. They had seven children: George Andrew, Margaret
Jean, Mary Jeannette, Archie H., Ralph James, Isabella Catherine,
and Elizabeth Ann. Alexander died 24 Aug 1907; he and Margaret are
buried in Oak Mound Cem.

1137 Elizabeth McCleery

The Robinson genealogy lists the birth date of Elizabeth as 28 Mar
1845 in Somonauk, Ill.   Other sources give her birthplace as
Dalton, Ohio.[17] Elizabeth died 3 Sep 1922 in Somonauk Twp., De Kalb
Co., Ill.   She married 10 Sep 1873 Thomas Henderson Robinson who
was born 12 Jul 1849 at Sheakleyville, Pa., and died 6 or 7 Jan
1937. Both are buried in Oak Mound Cem. Their seven children were
James McCleery, Isabelle Beveridge, Benjamin, John Beveridge, Lee,
Margaret, and Jean Elizabeth.

1138 William Doig McCleery

William was born 10 Jan 1848 near Dalton, Ohio.[17] He married twice:
First to Mary Jeanette Randles 25 Dec 1870 (Somonauk Book). Their
children were Andrew J., Howard, Albert, Clarence T., and Ralph.
Mary was born 14 August 1850 and died of tuberculosis 6 Feb 1881.
William married a second time, Jeanette (Jennie) Elizabeth Maxwell,
21 Feb 1882.   By Jennie he had five more children: Ruth, Harry,
Archie, John Maxwell, and Fannie E. Jennie was born 24 Nov 1858,
and died 22 May 1943. Her grave marker reads "Jennie E., 1858-
1943." William died at his home in Victor Twp. 29 Apr 1903 and was
buried in Oak Mound Cem.

1139 Jane Catherine McCleery

Catherine was born in Dalton, Ohio, 22 May 1851 and died of scarlet
fever in Victor Twp., De Kalb Co., Ill., 25 Mar 1855. She was
buried in Oak Mound Cem., in the same plot with her parents.

1141 Margaret Thomson

Margaret was born about 1836 in Monkton, Ayrshire. In 1851 she
was living in Glasgow and working as a seamstress.

1142 James Thomson

James was born about 1838 in Dreghorn, Ayrshire. His first wife died without issue. For the 1861 census, he was a widower, age 23 "blockmaker", living with his parents in Glasgow. Secondly, he married Martha Farquhar on 16 Apr 1867 in Blythswood, Glasgow, Lanarkshire. Martha was born ca. 1844. Their children, as listed in the 1881 census, were Hugh, William, James, and Mary. Their birthplaces suggest the family lived initially in Glasgow and later in Lochwinnoch, Renfrewshire. Martha died in Lochwinnoch in 1879, so the children were brought up by their Thomson grandparents. When his mother died in 1888, James lived at 28 Hairst Street in Renfrew.

James lodged in Renfrew where he worked as a journeyman joiner in Simons or Lobnitz Shipyards. He walked home to Lochwinnoch on Saturday afternoons and back to Renfrew on Sunday afternoon, a one-way distance of about eleven miles, quite a feat in itself. Considering the bad winter weather that often occurs in Scotland, his walks in that time of year would have been quite remarkable. James died at the age of 78 on 28 Feb 1916 in Renfrew, Scotland, of osteo-arthritis.

1151 William Maley Thomson

William was a twin, born in Little York, Ill., 9 Nov 1846.[51] At the age of two, his mother died and he and his twin sister went to live with their Maley relatives. The 1850 census of Warren Co., Ill., had William Thompson (sic), (and his twin sister, Ann M.), age 4, in the household of William Mealey (sic) farmer, age 72, born in Pa., in addition to several other family members. He spent his youth in Warren County, Ill., then, on 17 Feb 1865, William enlisted in Company 'B', 83rd Illinois Volunteer Infantry. He served with his unit in the south for seven months, then was transferred to Company 'E', 61st Illinois Infantry. His pension file mentions repeatedly that he was honorably discharged at Nashville, Tenn., on 8 Sep 1865. His papers described him as having a dark complexion, brown eyes, black hair, weighing 145 pounds at a height of 5' 6".

William M. and Catherine Thomson

In Jan 1867 he moved from Little York, Ill., to Cedar Co., Ia., where he lived with Mr. and Mrs. A. W. Maley, his aunt and uncle. There he remained except for the years 1875 and 1876 spent in Taylor Co., Ia. William Thomson and Catharine Strauser were married 24 Feb 1876 by Rev. Forsyth, near Mechanicsville, Ia. Catharine was born 2 Aug 1855 in Jonesborough, Green County, Ind.

They established a household in Corning, Iowa, where they lived for three years, then they moved to Stanwood. Cedar County land records indicate that Catharine Thomson and W. M. Thomson purchased 160 acres of land in Section 13 of Township 82 for the consideration of $7,700 on 22 Feb 1895. This farm was later sold in Mar 1907 for $14,400. They then purchased for $17,200 a new farm of 160 acres located in Section 4 of Township 81. They had nine children: Margaret Elizabeth, William Forsythe, Arthur Elias, Francis Marion, John Edwin, Clara Ann, Agnes Belle, Ella Ruth, and Chester Lawrence.

William inherited a gift for poetry, as evident from the following poem penned 11 Mar 1881:

My Wants

I want a calm secluded place
In the kind thoughts of all my race
I want that men should speak of me
In gentle tones of charity

And even more
I want to feel deep in my heart
I've acted well my humble part
And when my earthly course is run
I want the Master's kind "well done"
All this I want and nothing more

William M. Thomson
Stanwood, Iowa

William first applied for, and received, as an "invalid", a pension of $6.00 per month, commencing in Oct 1890. He had injured his left eye when filing a steel plow in 1875 and his left wrist in a fall from a haywagon, and suffered from shortness of breath and rheumatism. His pension was increased several times through the years, and was up to $22.50 in Nov 1921, certainly not much by today's standards. William was a tenant farmer as of 1891 and claimed that all his possessions were worth not more than $500. He was asking for an increase in his pension to support his wife and six children. William and Catharine retired and moved to a home in Stanwood in 1909. He was civic-minded as reflected by his service as an assessor and membership on the school board.   Politics played a part in his life and, as a Republican, he was a delegate to various conventions.   He and Catharine were members of the United Presbyterian Church where he served as clerk of the official board. After being bed-ridden for two and a half years, William died 1 Apr 1920.[52]   Catharine died of blood poisoning 22 May 1921;[53] both are buried in Stanwood Cem.

1152 Ann Melvin Thomson

A twin, Ann was born 9 Nov 1846. She was raised by Maley relatives after the death of her mother in 1849. Ann died of disease about 10 Jan 1863. She may be buried next to her mother in Sugartree Grove Cemetery in Hale Twp., midway between Monmouth and Little York, Ill., although there is no headstone to mark her grave.

1153 Mary Jean Thomson

Mary was born of her father's third wife, Mary Ann Parks, 22 Nov 1857. She was educated in schools in Aledo, Ill., then married John Spence on 13 March 1883. John was born 17 Mar 1832 in Wigtownshire, Scotland, and emigrated to Canada in 1856, and to Ill., in 1858. John was a veteran of the Civil War, having served with Company K, 84th Regiment, Illinois Volunteer Infantry.[29] John arrived in Madison Co., Ia., in 1869 and took up farming. Both Mary and John were members of the United Presbyterian Church in Pitzer. Mary died without issue on 7 Feb 1906; John died 14 Jan 1916; both were buried in Eppard-Pitzer Cemetery located northwest of Winterset, Ia.

1154 John J. Thomson

John was born 14 Apr 1860 in Aledo, Ill. There was no middle name, just the letter 'J', but he signed his name with a period after the middle 'J'.

John was educated in the schools in Aledo, then taught school for a few years. He worked his way through Monmouth College and the Xenia Seminary where John studied to become a Presbyterian minister, and was ordained as pastor at Clayton, Ill., 18 Jun 1891. From 1894 to 1898 he was principal of the academy at Stuttgart, Ark. He answered the call to serve in the War with Spain: He enlisted with the 2nd Arkansas Infantry on 2 May 1898. John served in Company 'I' as a 1st Sergeant, then was promoted to a 2nd Lt. In Company 'F' he was a 1st Lt. His service was spent in Florida until his discharge at Camp Shipp in Ammiston, Alabama, on 25 Feb 1899. The members of his company presented him with his sword, a prized possession.

During his period of military service, John contracted malaria from which he never fully recovered. His pension records mention that he suffered an injury to the lower end of his spinal column.   The medical reports described him as having a ruddy complexion, gray eyes, black hair, and he stood 5' 10" tall.   In Feb 1902 he was awarded a pension for his injuries.

John married Isabelle Stuart on 21 Aug 1890 at Aurora, Ill.   She died childless at Clayton, Ill., on 17 Oct 1891.   He married secondly, Sarah Isabelle Dickson on 1 Jan 1900 at the home of the bride's mother in Tarkio, Atchison Co., Mo. Sarah was one of Tarkio's best known and most popular young ladies and was the daughter of Alexander Reid Dickson and Alice Louisa Mitchell. At this time, John was pastor of the Park Avenue United Presbyterian Church in Omaha, Neb., where they made their home.   The children from his second marriage were Mary Isabelle, John Alexander, and David Reid.   In 1902 he removed from Monroe, Ia., and settled in Findlay, Ohio.

Cartoon Featuring John J. Thomson

In 1908, John was involved in regulating the quality of intoxicants sold in Okla. He was featured in a "friendly" cartoon[54] in 1908. John died 28 Feb 1917 in Monmouth, Ill. While in Muncie, Ind., about 1912, he had an accident while riding a bicycle during a thunderstorm. He collided with a team of horses and suffered head injuries from which he never fully recovered. His widow, Sarah, received a pension. John was remembered as having been a fine student who helped his fellow students with higher mathematics that came easily to John. In 1920 Sarah lived in Sterling, Kan., and in 1935 she was in Guthrie, Okla. Sarah, who was born 19 Feb 1870 in Monroe, Ia., may have died 5 Dec 1939 in Oklahoma City, Okla.; John and Sarah are buried in the Thomson/Spence plot in Aledo Cemetery in marked graves.

1155 Elizabeth Thomson

Known as "Lizzie", she was born in Aledo, Ill., 12 Dec 1861. As a young girl, she joined the United Presbyterian Church in Aledo. Lizzie and David Taylor Spence were married 23 Sep 1884 in the Thomson home in Aledo, Ill. After moving to Douglas Twp., Madison Co., Ia., Lizzie transferred her membership to the Union United Presbyterian Church in the village that was formerly known as Pitzer. Lizzie lived on the farm until two months before her death when she moved to north of Earlham. She died 19 Apr 1939[55] and was buried in Winterset Cem.[57]

David was born in Kirkcolm Parish, Wigtownshire, Scotland in Sep 1841, one of 15 children of John Spence and Mary Ritchie. The census taken in Kirkcolm Parish in 1851 listed David, age 9; three siblings, Margaret, Andrew, and William; his aunt, Elizabeth Ritchie; and his parents. He came to America in 1866 and was naturalized in 1872. He was one of five brothers who settled in Madison County, with David arriving in 1877. When he was married, he was a cheese maker and lived with his brother, John, in Jackson Twp. After his marriage he lived in Douglas Twp. for the rest of his life. He was a successful farmer, and at his death owned 115 acres of land in Section 18 of Douglas Twp. When David died 11 July 1923, his obituary mentioned that he was one of the early settlers of the area called Stringtown, and he had a wide circle of friends.[56,57]

Lizzie and David were the parents of six children: Margaret Mary, William John, Elizabeth Melvin, Vasha Isabelle, David Taylor, and Janet Frances, all of whom survived their parents.

1156 Margaret McAllister Thomson

Margaret McAllister Thomson was born in Aledo, Ill., 20 Apr 1863.

She attended schools in Aledo and was a member of United Presbyterian Church. Margaret never married and died at the old home on 9 Feb 1916. She was buried in the family burial plot in Aledo Cem.

1157 Abraham Lincoln Thomson

"Link" was born in Aledo, Ill., 29 Jun 1865. He married Lena Gertrude Nees 2 May 1889. Their children were Mary Elizabeth, Nina Hazel, George William, Edgar Lincoln, David Leroy, Effie Lillian, John Howard, and Alice May. Starting in 1883 he worked as a telegraph operator at railroad stations in Little York, Ill.; and in Mont., S.D., Minn., and Colo. In a letter written in 1933 by his brother, Samuel, Link was said to have injured his health in a forest fire. Details of the incident are described in *From The Ashes*.[58] Link wrote his own account[59] of the fire in *The Aledo Time Record*.

On 1 Sep 1894, brush was being burned five miles south of Hinckley, Minn. Fires had been burning all summer, so initially the fire was not of much concern. The summer had been unusually hot and very dry, creating a tinderbox. Eventually, the fires got out of hand and began sweeping in a northeasterly direction, gaining in strength. Link, employed by St. Paul and Duluth Railroad, was working as a telegraph operator at Miller station located north of Hinckley. Link, his wife, and two children lived at the depot. The sky darkened and there was an eery silence. It was so dark from the huge cloud of smoke that they had to light all the lamps in the house. The fire gained momentum, and developed into a firestorm.

The fire lasted only two hours, but consumed six towns and covered 400 square miles. Link was able to alert passenger trains already in the vicinity, and many hundreds of residents ran for their lives to catch the train. Hundreds of lives were lost, however. Link and his family lost everything except the clothes on their back. For gallant and faithful discharge of duty while manning his station at great risk to himself, Link was awarded a gold watch, which was presented by the St. Paul and Duluth R.R. Co.

Link applied for relief after the fire, and lived in Centerville for a while. In later years, Link lived in Biggsville, Ill., across the street from their train depot. The old house no longer stands. Link suffered a stroke and was barely able to get around for several years. He couldn't speak, but he understood what was spoken to him. Link died 26 Sep 1926 and was buried in Biggsville (Ill.) Cemetery. Lena died 31 Dec 1928.

1158 Jennett Mekemson Thomson

A twin, "Nettie" was born in Aledo, Ill., 20 Jun 1868. She lived her life at the old homestead and was never married. The twins fell into reduced circumstances in their later years. She died 12 Mar 1940 and was buried in the family plot in Aledo Cem.

1159 Nancy Moreland Thomson

"Nannie" lived her whole life with her twin sister in Aledo. She never married and died 16 Jan 1941. Burial was in the family plot.

115(10) Francis Clokey Thomson

"Fannie" was born 26 Jan 1870 in Aledo, Ill. She attended public schools in Aledo and professed her faith in the Presbyterian Church. On 30 Jan 1890 she and Samuel Spence were married and farmed in Douglas Twp., Madison Co. They became members of the Presbyterian Church at Pitzer on 11 Jan 1896. They had a son, John, evidently named for his grandfather, John Spence. "Fannie" died at an early age 28 Dec 1895. She was buried in Aledo Cemetery in the Thomson family plot marked with an impressive monument marked "Thomson/Spence." Samuel, born a member of the large Spence family from Scotland, had several brothers that lived in Madison Co. and married into the family. Samuel is believed to have died about 1940; his burial location is uncertain.

115(11) David Paul Thomson

John Thomson fathered three sets of twins, including David and Samuel, born 11 May 1875. David was educated in the Aledo schools, then settled in Seattle in 1903. There, he and Rosabel "Rose" Mearns were married 21 Jun 1905. They had five children: Helen Virginia, Rose Elizabeth, Howard Mearns, Marjorie Lois, and Paul Lincoln. Rose was born in Guide Rock, Neb., 17 Feb 1882 and died 2 Oct 1936 in Seattle. David passed away 19 Jul 1939. Burial was in Wachelli Cemetery in Seattle.

115(12) Samuel Alexander Thomson

A twin, born 11 May 1875 in Aledo, Ill., Samuel attended school in Aledo, then worked as a house carpenter for five years, a skill passed down naturally from his father. In 1899, he went to business college in Quincy, Ill., graduated, and assumed a position in Omaha, Neb. Three years later he arrived in Moline, Ill., where he was employed by implement manufacturers, and at the Montgomery Elevator Co.

Thomson   Family   Reunion, 1915

Thomson Family Reunion Photograph of 1915

Identified by number counting from the left:
<u>Front Row:</u> 6- Stewart Beck, 7- Floyd Beck, 8- Kenneth Amick (?),
<u>10-</u> Dale E. Jessup (?), 12- Mildred Beck Kuyk, 17- Elizabeth Bishop
Morris

<u>Second Row:</u> 1- baby in lap, 2- Howard Amick, 5- Laura Beck, 7-
Marguerite Beck Zendzian, 8- Alberta Amick (?), 10- Dale E. Jessup
(?), 12- Charlotte Bishop Augustine

<u>Middle Row:</u> 3- William Gooding McCorkle, 5- Samuel Allison Graham,
6- James Beck, 7- Mary Thomson Beck, 8- Jeanette Thomson Mekemson,
9- Hugh Thomson IV, 10- Annie Thomson Applegate, 11- Lizzie Thomson
Graham, 12- Jane Thomson McCorkle, 13- David T. Spence, 14- Andrew
Applegate

<u>Fourth Row:</u> 1- Jeanette McCorkle (in white dress in front of tree),
2- Anna Applegate Chase (partially hidden), 3- Mabel Stewart
Graham, 4- Hazel Chase (hair parted in middle), 5- Verle Andrew
Chase (young boy), 6- Ed Chase, 7- Etta Beck, 10- Jeanette Beck,
11- Floss Beck, 12- Jeannette Mekemson Amick, 14- Harriet Mekemson
Jessup (?), 16- Jennie Graham Bishop, 19- Mabel McCorkle (?), 20-
Margaret Thomson (?), 21- Elizabeth Thomson Spence

<u>Back Row:</u> 2- Mabel Chase Black, 3- Robert C. Graham, 4- Samuel
Beck, 5- John Beck (?), 8- Margaret Spence Bates, 9- Ray Sherman
Bates, 10- William McRobert Thomson (?), 11- Pearl Rash Thomson,
12- John Spence, 14- Gertrude Addy Spence, 16- Isla Mary Dooley
Taylor (?), 18- Janet Spence Gibson, 20- Bessie Agnew Thomson
Kench, 21- Vasha Spence Sorensen, 22- David T. Spence Jr., 26-
William Spence, 27- Edward McCorkle

(The compiler is indebted to those who identified their ancestors
in the above photograph. Unfortunately, the identity of many has
not been determined.)

Samuel and Clara Alida Hunter were married 2 Jul 1908 and had Lawrence Hunter, Margaret Parks, and Marybelle McKee. Samuel died 7 Jul 1946; Clara, who was born 30 Jul 1878 in Cadiz, Ohio, died 24 Jan 1970. They are buried in Riverside Cemetery in Moline, Ill.

His letter written to his nephew, Frank Thomson, of Mechanicsville, Ia., in 1933, has provided considerable insight regarding the genealogy of Samuel's siblings.   This, coupled with Samuel's discussion of some of his aunts, uncles, and cousins was of such great interest to the present compiler that it provided the spark leading to research of the entire Thomson family.

1161 Mary Buchanan Thomson

[From a manuscript written by Jack Scott Light].   Mary was born near Stranraer, Scotland, 8 May 1842.   She vividly remembered the arduous trip across the Atlantic to America in 1856.   When she was eighteen, then living on a farm in Henderson Co., Ill., she met a young Irish immigrant named James Gawn Beck. James, known as "Pa", was born 1 Mar 1839 in County Antrim, Ireland, and arrived in America in 1857. When the Civil War started he enlisted in Company E, 7th Iowa infantry.   During a furlough he returned to visit her and proposed marriage, and Mary accepted.   They were married 4 Feb 1864 in Henderson Co., Ill.   During the four years of war, James was captured, was imprisoned at Andersonville, and later released. He fought in several major battles, but to the delight of Mary, he returned home unscathed.   She gave birth to her first child in Henderson Co. in 1867 and, in 1868, they migrated to Iowa and settled on an 80-acre farm located near the village of Pitzer in Jefferson Twp., Madison Co.   Their children were Elizabeth Thomson, John Craig, Samuel Melvin, Jeanette Eleanor, Mary Ethel, and Clarence Blaine. Mary and James were charter members of the Pitzer United Presbyterian Church where James was a Deacon.   In 1909 they left the farm and retired to Winterset, and transferred to the Winterset congregation.   They lived to celebrate their golden wedding anniversary.   Mary died in Winterset 28 Sep 1920; James died 25 Sep 1925; both are buried in Winterset Cemetery where there is a stone to mark their graves.

1162 Jeanette McRobert Thomson

Jeanette was born near Stranraer, Scotland, 1 Jan 1844 and may have been named after her great-grandmother, Jean Saul.   During the voyage to America in 1856, all of the family members were sick except her father and herself. They had to care for the sick and carry food to the big kitchen to be prepared by the cook, which was more difficult than the present mode of serving steamer passengers. The cook and sailors took great interest in little Jeanette as she had to press through crowds and go on the dangerous deck alone. One sailor held her out overboard to frighten her so she would not again take such great risks.

In Henderson Co., Ill., she married William Brown Mekemson 28 Dec 1865. They farmed in Henderson Co. for a few years, then moved to Madison Co., Ia., in 1867. They had a large family: Elizabeth Eleanor, Ralph, Harriet M., Anna Belle, Jessie Lodena, Jeanette, Maggie Lois, Andrew Thomson, Zelza Grace, Archie Raymond, and Edna Ethel. The parents and all but the younger children were listed in the 1880 census in Iowa; but only their initials were used. They were members of the Presbyterian Church at Pitzer.

William was born 28 Aug 1842 near Biggsville, Henderson Co., Ill., the eldest child of Andrew Mekemson and Eleanor McQuown. William's grandfather was Andrew Mekemson who, in 1818, obtained a federal land grant in western Illinois. William enlisted with Company G of the 84th Regiment of Illinois Volunteers on 28 Jul 1862 in Biggsville, Ill. He was honorably discharged at Clinton, Ia., 13 Jul 1865. His pension file indicates that he contracted rheumatism while on guard duty. He had been exposed to wet and cold conditions on a march from Louisville, Ky., to Nashville, Tenn., which was attested to by John Spence who served in the same unit. He received a pension for his disability which caused him considerable pain and allowed him to do about half the work he could before the war. This pension file had his wife's name spelled "Jannette", but her signature was not on any of the records.

The last thirty years they spent in the vicinity of Redding, Ia. Jeanette died in Diagonal, Ia., 17 Jun 1925, followed closely by William's death 5 Nov 1926. Both are buried in Redding Cemetery.

1163 Hugh Thomson IV

Much has been learned of the life of Hugh IV from accounts in *The Yule Booklet* of 1978.[3] He was born 28 Feb 1847 "in Greenock on the brown banks (of) Clyde", as he described it in his letter of 1922. Shortly after he was born, his father was hired on a ship that sailed around South America, so his mother took her family back to the old home at Dhuloch (black lake farm), located about six miles west of Stranraer. A story handed down involves an incident in which Hugh, a young boy at the time, was lost one day, and was found near dusk, wandering, crying and stumbling along the River Clyde. There may have been a big event that day involving a visit from Queen Victoria.

When his father returned after three and a half years at sea, his mother had saved enough money to pay for the family's passage to America. In 1856, Hugh and a large party of Thomsons left their ancient homeland and sailed toward a new and strange land. They debarked in New York City which Hugh vividly remembered. Their first stop was at the home of Hugh's aunt, Jean (Thomson) McCleery in Somonauk, Ill. After a short stay, they went to Little York, Ill., to see Uncle John Thomson. Then they made their way to Oquawka, Ill., where his father, Samuel, found work for a short while, then farmed near Biggsville.

In 1867, his parents moved to Madison County, Ia. Hugh IV courted Cynthia Ann Bard who lived in Stringtown, located about two miles east of the Thomson home. After a few years of becoming acquainted, they were married in the Bard home 14 Sep 1871. Hugh must have been quite slim as he was 5'9" tall and weighed just 118 lb. However, he was probably in excellent physical condition since he built a log house and barn plus dug a well with little outside help. Their home was half a mile from his father's farm. The 1880 census shows that Hugh lived next door to his father, in Jackson Twp. of Madison Co.

Hugh and Cynthia had six children: Hugh Caldwell, William McRobert, Leonard Samuel, Bessie Agnew, Nan Bard, and Ray Sherman. The first two boys were born in the log cabin that was cold. Before the next baby arrived, Hugh had built another small house that had two rooms and a cellar for use as a kitchen. Hugh was a successful farmer and was able to buy yet another house that they attached to the rear of their present house, giving them much more living space, and allowed moving the kitchen to the first floor.

These were prosperous times, with Hugh raising a herd of fine Hereford cattle. Cynthia was even able to afford a hired girl, Cousin Minnie Wilcox. Just when they achieved the peak of their prosperity, Hugh decided it was time to "go west." At the Presbyterian church he attended, Hugh heard great things about land in Neb. Hugh wanted to give his sons a better start than he had, so he decided to sell his place in Madison Co. in the fall of 1887. They spent the winter in the home of his father, Samuel Thomson.

In Neb., west of Gordon, they again lived in a sod house. There were no farm buildings nor was there a well initially, and water had to be hauled in a barrel from a neighbor. Hugh had been given some bad advice to leave Iowa and move to the sand hills of Nebraska. The first year he produced a good crop of corn. After that, the crops failed because the sandy soil did provide the nutrients required year after year as did Iowa soil. In addition, they suffered through drought conditions for seven years. Fed up with life in Nebraska, Hugh took his family to Minnesota in 1895 and farmed in the vicinity of Lake Wilson. Finally, in 1906, Hugh returned to Madison Co. when he bought a farm located about a mile west of the Stringtown Cemetery. Hugh hosted a family reunion in 1915 that was very well attended.[63]

Cynthia was born 3 Apr 1847 and died 10 Mar 1914, followed by Hugh 30 Dec 1923.[60] Both are buried in Stringtown Cemetery where there is a large upright stone that marks their graves.

1164 Annie Melvin Thomson

Annie was born in Greenock, Scotland, 21 Jul 1849 and was given the name of her ancestor. Her family emigrated to America in 1856 and lived for a while in Henderson Co., Ill. Annie married Andrew "Andy" Applegate in Madison Co., Ia., 7 Oct 1869 and they took up farming for a living. In 1897 they were living in Earlham, Ia; and in 1899 in Dexter. Their children were Anna Rachel, Robert Thomson, and Ralph Earl. Two other children died in infancy.

Andy was born 10 Feb 1844 in Youngstown, Ohio, and came to Ia. with his parents when he was about 15 years old. Andy served three years with Company I of the 4th Iowa Cavalry during the Civil War. He died 1 Sep 1917[62] at the home of his daughter, then Anna Chase, near Winterset. Annie died 30 Jan 1934[61] and was buried alongside her husband in Stringtown Cemetery. Their funerals were held in the Presbyterian Church in Pitzer. Their graves are marked with a monument.

1165 Elizabeth Grace Thomson

"Lizzie" was born 25 May 1851 on the old farm in Dhuloch, Kirkcolm Parish, Wigtownshire, Scotland. Her family departed Scotland in 1856 and settled in Henderson Co., Ill. Later, they lived on a farm northwest of Winterset in Madison Co., Ia. She married Samuel Allison Graham 3 Jun 1869[64] at the Macksburg United Presbyterian Church. Samuel was born 18 Mar 1848 in Biggsville, Ill., the son of William M. Graham and Jane Popham. Samuel was a farmer in Jackson Twp., Madison Co. as indicated by the 1880 census returns. Later he lived in Adair Co. With farming not being a successful endeavor, he moved to Orient, Ia., where he became part owner and operator of a grain storage elevator. He was an affable person and was a better salesman than farmer. This was demonstrated by his ability to buy cattle and hogs for meat packers.

Their children were William Allison, Thomas Edward, Robert Culbertson, Lillie Maude, Elizabeth Mary, Jane Grace, Walter Nelson, and Samuel Roscoe. Samuel died in Adair Co., Ia., on 1 Oct

1931, followed closely by the death of Lizzie on 12 Jun 1932. Both are buried in Orient Cemetery, Orient, Ia.

1166 Samuel Thomson

Samuel was born 21 May 1856 in Kirkcolm Parish, Wigtownshire, Scotland per LDS records. He was just four months old when his family set out for the New World.[26] They encountered very stormy weather on their voyage, which caused widespread sickness amongst the family, including his mother. With his mother unable to provide the baby with adequate nourishment, he died at sea on 14 Oct 1856, just eight days before they were to reach America. One can imagine the misery and suffering they must have endured, coupled with the tragic loss of the child.

1167 Jane Eleanor Thomson

Jane was born in Oquawka, Ill., 27 Jan 1858. As a young child, she moved with her family to Madison Co., Ia. There, she later married Edward Lindsay McCorkle 28 Oct 1880. Edward was born 21 May 1854 in Carpentersville, Putnam Co., Ind. His parents had moved to Jackson Twp., Madison Co., in 1878. Their children were Norma Minta, George Elmer, Nina Elizabeth, Mabel Eleanor, Winnie Bell, Edna Mae, Harold Edward, and Jeannette Esther. While they lived in Madison County, they attended the West Star Methodist Church. In 1909 they moved to an 80-acre farm located near Ridgeway, Mo., and later the farm was sold for $10,000. In 1919 they moved to Smith Center, Kan. Their children organized a gala 50th wedding anniversary party for their parents. Mr. McCorkle passed away 20 Oct 1935 in Hastings, Neb., while visiting at the home of his daughter, Jeannette.

Jane then went to live with her children and died at the home of her daughter, Winnie Light, 24 Oct 1946 in Kansas City, Mo., and was buried with her husband in Stringtown Cemetery.[30,65] [Jack Light is to be credited with providing information on the McCorkle family, in this and ensuing generations].

1171 William Thomson Weir Sr.

William was born in Glasgow, Scotland in Apr 1853, and was brought to America in 1856. He spent the remainder of his life in Henderson Co., Ill. where in 1884 he started the Oak Grove Fruit Farm. He married Annie C. Knustrom of Gladstone, Ill., about 1896 and they had Anna Hazel, Bess L., and William Jr. The 1910 census listed his occupation as fruit farmer. He developed a large apple orchard and processing plant that is still very productive today.

Annie was born in Jun 1869 in Iowa and died of tuberculosis 16 Apr 1924. William died of a lingering illness 19 Aug 1927 in Long Beach, Calif. Both are buried in Biggsville Cemetery.[66]

Samuel Thomson and His Children, Circa 1890

Front Row, L-R: Mary, Samuel, Jeanette
Back Row, L-R: Jane, Elizabeth, Hugh IV, Annie

1172 John Weir

From his obituary[67] it is learned that John was born in Coloma, Henderson Co., Ill., 18 Jan 1858. John and Jennie Florence McMillan were married 11 Jan 1883 in Henderson Co. They had four children: Jessie Mae, Grace Lillian, Annie Susan, and Roy William. The 1910 census indicated that Annie Weir, John's mother, was living with them at age 92. Her year of immigration was listed as 1856. She stated that she had given birth to four children, and two were living. John had his own blacksmith shop in Gladstone Twp. Jennie was born 21 Jul 1860 and died 8 Mar 1934; John died 6 Aug 1937. Both are buried in Biggsville Cem.

FIFTH GENERATION

11211 Robert Knowles

Robert was born about 1853 and was a teacher when he died 12 Mar 1889, "in his 36th year", as inscribed on his marker[37]. Robert, his wife, Mary F. Tisdale, who died 21 Nov 1892 in her 34th year, and a son, William E., who died 30 Nov 1894 in his 18th year, are buried in Carholme-Knowles Cemetery. They all died of tuberculosis.

11212 Thomas Fulton Knowles

Thomas was born in 1855 and died 22 Mar 1884,[37] probably unmarried. He was buried in the Carholme-Knowles Cemetery in North Walsingham Twp., Norfolk Co., Ontario.

11213 Elizabeth A. Knowles

Elizabeth lived for two years and died 9 Apr 1859. She was buried in Carholme-Knowles Cem.

11214 Bessie A. Knowles

Bessie was born in 1859. She was a school teacher and was unmarried. She died 10 Mar 1886 and was buried in Carholme-Knowles Cem.

11215 Margareta Knowles

Margareta died in her third year, 27 Mar 1864. She was buried in Carholme-Knowles Cem.

11216 William John Knowles Jr.

William was born 1864 and died 4 May 1914 in North Walsingham Twp., Norfolk Co., Ontario. He firstly married Osceola Gordon and they had a daughter, Annie. Osceola died 27 Mar 1899 in her 27th year. Secondly, on 26 Dec 1901 in Lynedoch, William married Edith Maude Halliday who was born 12 Jul 1871 and died in 1952. They lived near Lynedoch in Norfolk County and had William David and John Evans. William and Maude are buried in Carholme-Knowles Cem.[37]

11217 James Fulton Knowles

James was born in 1866 and died in 1918. His wife was Victoria Morgan who was born in 1870 and died in 1946. When his father died

in 1903, James was located in Moosejaw, Saskatchewan.   Their
children were William Morley, Anna Victoria, Leslie Kingston,
Bessie, and Ella Morgan.   James and Victoria are buried in
Carholme-Knowles Cem.

11251 George Thomas Fulton

George was born in Lynedoch, Norfolk Co., Ontario 7 Aug 1872. In
1880, his family moved from Langton, Ontario, to Waterman, Ill.,
where his father engaged in the mercantile business.   The 1920
census records indicate that he was naturalized in 1883. At the
age of nineteen he entered the University of Illinois where he
majored in civil engineering. While there, he played third base on
the baseball team.

In 1893, he moved with his parents to Hartford City, Ind., where he
spent a year working for his father, then put his engineering
skills to use. He was city engineer of Hartford City until 1900.
He then worked for the Johnson Glass Factory, eventually serving as
general manager.   Shortly before his death, George organized the
Fulton Glass Company.

George and Mary Nettie Leonard were married in her parents' home 18
Jun 1899.[68] The family worshiped at the Presbyterian Church where
George served as trustee and was the teacher of a boys' class. They
had three children, George Leonard ("Junior"), James P. A., and
Susanna. George developed leukemia and died 1 Dec 1930 in Hartford
City.[19] He had many friends and was highly respected. Nettie was
born 4 Feb 1875 in Montpelier, Ind., and died 28 Dec 1970. Both are
buried in I.O.O.F. Cem., Hartford City.

11252 William John Fulton

Will was born in Lynedoch, Norfolk Co., Ontario on 14 Jan 1874 or
1875.   In 1880 his parents moved to De Kalb Co., Ill., where he
attended the public schools and the University of Illinois; he
graduated with the class of 1898. On the university baseball team,
he was a standout at second base. The athletic director named him
to his all-time university team, and he was considered capable of
playing in the major leagues. At the university he was a member of
Phi Beta Kappa, an honorary scholastic fraternity.   In his senior
year he was chosen class president.   William continued in post-
graduate work studying law for two years, and was admitted to the
bar while employed in the office of Carnes, Dunton and Faissler.

He established his own practice in 1904, then was appointed City
Attorney of Sycamore, Ill.   William's illustrious career
accelerated with his appointment as judge of the circuit and the

appellate court, then he was elected to the Illinois Supreme Court
in 1942. He was Chief Justice in 1945 and administered the oath of
office to Adlai Stevenson when he was elected governor in 1949.
Because of his wife's poor health, he retired from the Supreme
Court on 1 Nov 1954.[69]

William married his college sweetheart, Laura Busey, 26 Nov 1902.
Their children were Frederick Henry, William John Jr., Robert B.
and Sarah Jane. For the 1910 census, it was recorded that Laura
had been married 8 years and had given birth to three children, two
of which were living. In the 1920 census records, William was
shown to have immigrated in 1880 and was naturalized in 1888. A
search for his naturalization records at the courthouse in Sycamore
was unsuccessful.

Judge Fulton died 24 Mar 1961 in Sycamore, Ill.[70] His wife, Laura,
born 1 Feb 1877, died 17 Jan 1961. Both are buried in Section 'G'
of Elmwood Cemetery in Sycamore, Ill. As a tribute to his stature
as a great judge and humanitarian, his portrait hangs in the lobby
of the DeKalb County courthouse in Sycamore.

11253 Anne Elizabeth Fulton

Anne was born in Lynedoch, Norfolk Co., Ontario on 19 Oct 1875. In
1880 she was taken with her family to Waterman, Ill. She attended
public schools in Hartford City, Ind., then went on to Oberlin
College from which she graduated in 1904 and became a Latin teacher
in Coeur d'Alene High School. She changed careers to sell
insurance for New York Life Insurance Company, an occupation at
which she excelled. She became one of the top salespersons in the
country, and her picture was used in promotional materials. Anne
felt that she needed extra income to help in the support of her
aging parents after they moved to Coeur d'Alene. [We appreciate
the efforts of Mary (Koehler) Haxby of St. Paul, Minn. for
furnishing most of the above material on Anne Fulton.]

When her father died in 1925, Anne wrote a long letter to her
brother, Will, elaborating on the events surrounding her father's
death.[71] (The letter has been preserved and is in the possession of
Will's grandson, Thomas Reston, of Washington, D.C.) Anne remained
at the home in Coeur d'Alene until her death 5 Jun 1932 in
Spokane.[72] Her body was cremated and her remains were buried
between her parents in Forest Cemetery in Coeur d'Alene.

Anne kept a book of birth dates of her relatives.[40] This very
valuable source of genealogical information has been passed down to
Tom Fulton of Boise, Ida., and into the hands of the compiler. The
information forms an important part of this compilation.

11254 Robert Bruce Fulton

Bruce was born 13 May 1877 in Lynedoch, Ontario. At a young age his family moved to Waterman, Ill., then to Hartford City, Ind. He graduated from the University of Illinois in 1901 with a degree in civil engineering. During his college years he played second base on the varsity baseball team. As a civil engineer, his work took him all around the country building water pipe lines. Once his work took him from Maine to Alaska. In Seattle he met Alpha Weltzin who was teaching school there. Bruce was a captain in World War I, but being forty years old he was not sent overseas. Immediately after the war Bruce and Alpha were married in her hometown of Mayville, N.D., 21 Dec 1918.

Bruce worked one summer in West Virginia and that is where he applied for his social security card. They also lived in Hendersonville, N.C., in Vermont, and East Orange, N.J. In East Orange, Bruce was an elder in the Presbyterian Church, and Alpha taught Sunday school. Their daughter, Elizabeth Marie, sang in the choir. He suffered from asthma, so in 1937 he moved the family to Calif. Bruce was very ill for several years, but managed to work in a defense plant during World War II. Then he sold real estate for a while. Bruce died 8 Nov 1962 in Menlo Park, Calif. Alpha then moved to Pullman, Wash., where she lived with her daughter and son-in-law. Alpha was born 2 Oct 1887 and died 11 Aug 1985 in Pullman. Both are buried in Alta Mesa Cemetery in Palo Alto, Calif.

11255 Walter Scott Fulton

Walter, known as Scotty to family members, was born 23 Mar 1879 in Lynedoch, Ontario.[73] He came to Illinois with his family in 1880, and later lived in Ind. He was interested in attending the U.S. Military Academy, and one day he took off on his bicycle and road for about 50 miles to seek an interview with his senator. The senator was so impressed with Scotty's feat that he won an appointment and became a cadet on 19 Jun 1900. He received the Bachelor of Science degree and was commissioned a Second Lt. of infantry 15 Jun 1904. His ranking in his class was 118. He was accepted for promotion to First Lt. 11 Mar 1911; to Captain 1 Jul 1916, to Major 1 Jul 1920, to Lt. Colonel 27 Oct 1928, to Colonel 1 Aug 1935, and to Brigadier General in 1942.[74,75]

He served in the Philippines during the 1906 campaign, and at Vera Cruz, Mexico, during the American occupation in 1914. He served in France during World War I with the 88th Division. He was professor of military science and tactics at the University of Ohio in the

late '30s. He was a graduate of the Command and General Staff
school at Fort Leavenworth, Kan., and of the Army War College.
General Fulton served as Executive Officer then as Post Commander
of Fort Benning. After his retirement in Jan 1944, he was active
in community civic affairs, including the Red Cross in which he was
chapter chairman.

Foremost in promoting many of the civic improvements in the
Columbus-Fort Benning area, he participated in a successful drive
against vice conditions early in 1942, and did much to foster
harmonious relations between the military and civilian leaders of
the community.

In Denver, Colo., Walter married 27 Feb 1911 Helen Rose Bennet who
was born 2 Feb 1890. Their children were Helen Bennet and Walter
Scott Jr. General Fulton died 24 Jun 1950 in Columbus, Ga.[76] He
was buried at Fort Benning Cemetery. Helen died 6 Jan 1974 in
Atlanta, Ga.

11256 James Thompson Fulton

James (Tom) was born 26 Sep 1880 in Waterman, Ill.[40] It appears
that he was named for his Thomson ancestors, but the spelling was
changed. He was the only one in his family that did not graduate
from college. In Hartford City on 25 Nov 1902 he married Olive Wood
who was born there 26 Jun 1883. They moved to Coeur d'Alene, Ida.,
in 1913 where Tom started the Fulton Grain and Feed Store.[182] He was
a champion at tennis and golf in Coeur d'Alene. In addition, he
enjoyed playing chess. He was active in civic affairs, was a
member of the Presbyterian Church and the Elks lodge. Their
children were Robert Gray, Richard Wood, and Dorothy Louise.
Included in the household in 1920 was Jane Wood, his mother-in-law,
age 74, born in Ohio. He started a brokerage business and was just
getting the business going, following the Great Depression, when he
died from cancer 16 Jun 1934.[77] Olive died 19 Oct 1964; she and Tom
are buried in Forest Cemetery in Coeur d'Alene.[78]

11257 Frederick Gray Fulton

Frederick was born 30 Sep 1882 in Waterman, Ill. On 14 Jan 1909,
in Mercer, Pa., Fred married Helen Graham Thorne who was a 1905
graduate of Oberlin College; their license no. was 10326. Helen
was born 9 Jan 1884 and died 29 Dec 1958. They lived in Spokane,
Wash., and in Moscow, Ida. They had seven children: Anna Thorne,
Mary Belle, Helen Graham, Ruth Eleanor, Frederick Gray, Virginia,
and Janet Margaret. Fred was a 1907 graduate of Oberlin College
and was a salesman for N.Y. Life Insurance Co. in Spokane, and
later lived in Berlin Heights, Ohio. After Helen's death, Fred

married Alice Judson Jones on 16 Apr 1959 in Sandusky, Ohio. Alice had been previously married to Emlin Jones. The Fultons were members of the First Congregational Church of Berlin Heights. Fred died 4 Aug 1967 in Sandusky Memorial Hospital in Sandusky, Ohio, and his body was cremated.[79]

11258 Ella Charlton Fulton

Nell was born 25 Aug 1884 in Waterman, Ill. In Spokane, Wash., she married Henry Holland Carter 10 Aug 1910. Nell was a graduate of Oberlin College in 1908 with a A.B. degree in education. She was a member of the Trinity Episcopal Church, the 19th Century Club, and P.E.O. When she died, she was a resident in the Indiana University Memorial Union Building. She had been on the staff of the University Bureau of Public Discussion. They had four daughters: Jane Elizabeth, Mary Snow, Margaret Gray, and Bertha Ann. Nell died 16 Mar 1966 in Bloomington, Ind., and was buried next to her husband in City Cemetery, Richfield, Ohio.[80]

Henry Carter was born 16 Aug 1884 and grew up in Brecksville, Ohio. He was granted the A.B. degree from Oberlin College in 1907, an A.M. degree from Yale, then his Ph.D. from Yale in 1914. He taught at Miami Univ., and at Carleton College in Northfield, Minn. He was hired by The University of Indiana and was chairman of the English Department from 1923 to 1941 when he resigned so as to devote full time to teaching and research. He was author or co-author of several textbooks, and was recognized as one of IU's outstanding teachers and scholars. Professor Carter died in Bloomington 3 Dec 1952 and was buried near where he grew up.[81,82]

11259 Mary Belle Fulton

Mamie was born 25 May 1886 in Waterman, Ill. She graduated from Hartford City High School and, like her sisters before her, she graduated from Oberlin College (1909) and became a teacher. She married Frank Oliver "Stoney" Koehler 10 Aug 1910 in Spokane, Wash., in a double wedding with her sister, Ella. They had Jean Elizabeth, Fulton, Mary Ann and Mary Gray. Frank was a 1908 graduate of Oberlin College. He joined the YMCA staff in 1912 as a boys' work secretary. He became general secretary in 1925, a post he held until 1948. He then left Minneapolis to become general secretary of the World Youth Fund of the International Committee of YMCAs. Frank retired in 1949 and returned to Minneapolis. Mary died on 16 Jun 1944 in Minneapolis. Frank was born 28 May 1884 in Lenox, Ia., and died 15 Jun 1965[83] in Minneapolis. Both were buried in Lakewood Cemetery in Minneapolis.

11261 Jane Elizabeth Armstrong

Jane, or Jeannie, was born 18 Dec 1876 in Ill. On 16 Dec 1903 she married James Duncan Stirling who was born 24 Sep 1876. Their child was Agnes Isabelle. In 1910 James was office manager of a railroad station in Chicago where they rented a home at East 62nd St. Isabelle was their only child. James became vice president of an oil company and resided in East Orange, N.J., in the 1930s. In 1937 James and his daughter moved to Sea Girt, N.J., where he was general traffic manager of the Socony-Vacuum Oil Co. James wrote his will on 14 Nov 1941 and made no mention of a wife, which indicates that Jane was deceased, sometime between 1932 and 1941. James died 5 Jan 1949 in Sea Girt,[84] but Jane did not die there.

11262 Margaret McClellan Armstrong

Maggie was born 22 Aug 1878 in Somonauk, Ill. She married Joseph Edward "Ed" Curran on 11 Jun 1908 in Kansas City, Mo. Ed was born 19 May 1877 in Howard, Kan., and died 8 Mar 1967 in Miltipas, Santa Clara County, Calif. He served in the U.S. Army and took part in the Spanish-American War in the Phillipines. They were residents of Chicago where Ed was employed as a baker. They had William Edward, Elizabeth Elizabeth, and Robert John. Margaret moved to Calif., where she died on 28 Aug 1959 in San Francisco.

11263 William Kennedy Armstrong

William was born 13 Oct 1880. About 1913 he married Ruth Kavanaugh who was the daughter of Stephen H. Kavanaugh and Mary McElroy. They had two daughters, Grace Vivian and Mary Belle. William died 15 Sep 1927 in Cleveland, Ohio, and was buried in Lakewood Park Cemetery.[86] From the 1943-44 Cleveland City Directory, Ruth was listed at 1241 West 112th St., Apartment 6. Her daughter, Mary Belle, was a member of the Womens' Army Auxiliary Corps (WAC) and resided with her. Ruth secondly married Jack Shannon.

Ruth lived in Cleveland until 1960, then lived in a nursing home in Chicago, Ill., where she died about 20 Aug 1980.[85] Ruth's obituary mentioned that a mass was at St. Bernadett Church in Chicago with interment at St. Mary.

11264 Charles S. Armstrong

Charles was born 22 Sep 1882. He died 21 Aug 1887.

11265 Grace L. Armstrong

Grace was born 25 Sep 1884 and died 26 Dec 1885.

11271 Andrew James Cole

Andrew was born 22 Jun 1880 in Ill. He was a graduate of Moody
Bible Institute in Chicago.   He interred as a Presbyterian
missionary but his voice gave out, as recalled by his daughter,
Lois. He married Olga Jacobson 11 Sep 1910 and they farmed near
Central Butte, Saskatchewan, until about 1916. Olga may have lived
in Chicago and been a graduate of Northwestern Univ. Andrew and
Olga had Robert Bruce, Margaret Isabelle, Ralph William, and
Donald, who was born in Mar 1919 and died the next month.   Olga
died in Apr 1919 of peritonitis in Moose Jaw, Saskatchewan, where
the baby, Donald, and mother were buried. Andrew was living in
the area of Spokane, Wash., in 1925 when he helped care for James
Fulton of Coeur d'Alene, Ida., shortly before James' death.

Secondly, Andrew married Florrie Anne Faulkner on 23 Jul 1927 in
Pasadena, Calif. Their child was Eloise Lois. Andrew left Florrie
about 1934, but neither remarried.   Andrew obtained his social
security card in Oregon, and died 8 Dec 1966 in Spokane, Wash.[87] His
birth date was based on his Social Security record. Burial was in
Fairmount Memorial Park.   His obituary mentioned that he was a
self-employed carpenter and had been in the area for 46 years. Upon
his death, he had 10 grandchildren and 3 great-grandchildren.
Florrie was born 23 Jul 1891 in St. James, Mo., obtained her social
security card in Montana, and died 4 Jan 1976 in Pasadena, Calif.
Florrie was buried in Northview Cemetery in nearby Ontario, Calif.

11272 Elizabeth Cole

Lizzie was born 5 Feb 1882 in Ill. She never married, and died 7
Jan 1982 in Spokane. She was short in stature, about 5'3" tall.
Lizzie was a nurse and owned a nurse's registry in Spokane. She
spent her last years living at Rockwood Manor, a retirement home,
in Spokane. She was buried in the family plot in Forest Cemetery
in Coeur d'Alene.

11273 Mary Jeannette Cole

Janet was born 7 Aug 1883 in De Kalb Co., Ill. On 11 Aug 1911, she
married George Brumwell in Moose Jaw, Saskatchewan. George was
born in 1883 in Canada. They lived in Whitefish, Mont. They had
three children; Robert William, Helen Jeannette, and George Keith.
After the death of her husband in 1953, Mary lived at Rockwood
Manor, a retirement home, in Spokane, Wash., and died 8 Dec 1977.
Burial was in Whitefish, Mont.

11274 William John Cole

Willie was born 1 Oct 1884 in Sandwich, Ill. He served during
World War I as a private (no. 148678) in the 78th Battalion of the
Expeditionary Forces of Canada. His Attestation Papers (military
records) describe him as standing 5' 10" tall with blue eyes and
brown hair. He was a farmer. He died of wounds in a hospital in
France 29 Apr 1917 and was buried in Flanders Field.

Death Record of William John Cole

11275 Annabelle Cole

Annabelle was born 5 Sep 1887 and died 9 Oct 1889.

11276 Sarah Cole

Sadie was born 29 Sep 1889 in Ill. She was an executive secretary
at one of the large banks in Spokane. She was never married, lived
at Rockwood Manor in Spokane. She died 13 Feb 1974 in Spokane, and

was buried in Forest Cemetery in Coeur d'Alene, Ida.

11277 Margaret Cole

Margaret was born 30 Sep 1892 in Ill. She married Colin B. Hughes in 1919. Colin was born in 1885 and died in Jun 1932. Their children were Margaret Joyce and James William. Margaret is remembered by her daughter, now Margaret Joyce Norris, as being an excellent homemaker as well as hostess. She carried on the family tradition of serving every meal with elegance. She made the children's clothes as well as her own. She enjoyed bridge parties, traveled frequently, and attended church. Margaret died 31 Mar 1975 and was buried in Moose Jaw, Saskatchewan.

11278 Robert Hutton Cole

Bert was born 3 Oct 1894 in Somonauk, Ill. *The Somonauk Book* states, in part, that he served with the Canadian Expeditionary Forces during World War I, and was a lance-corporal (no. 427587) in the 16th Battalion. His military records (Attestation Papers) stated he was 5' 8" tall, had blue eyes and brown hair. He was a law student with an affiliation with the Presbyterian Church. Isabelle Scriven has his death date as 6 Sep 1916, whereas his death certificate prepared by the Canadian Expeditionary Force states that he was killed in action between 4 and 7 Sep 1916. He was buried in Flanders Field.

11279 Ernest Cole

Ernest was born 23 May 1896 in Ill., and served with the Canadian Army during World War I. He was wounded but recovered and returned to Canada. In 1935, he was living in Saskatchewan. Ernie worked as a lumberjack in several areas and was a bit of a roamer. In Aug 1974 he married Jennie who was born 7 Jan 1896. Jennie is claimed to have lived to the age of 102. Ernest died in 1981 in Victoria, British Columbia, Canada, and was buried there.

1127(10) Ruth Agnes Cole

Ruth was born 13 Mar 1899 in Ill. She married Howard Mitchell Betters 22 Jun 1922 and lived in Canada. They had Margaret Grace, Dorothy Jean, Patricia Louise, and Robert Julian. Ruth died 13 Dec 1983 in Victoria, British Columbia, Canada.

1127(11) Robert Bruce Cole

Robert was born 10 Mar 1903 and died 14 Mar 1906.

13111 Robert Francis McCleery

Robert was born 1 Feb 1864 in Victor Twp., De Kalb Co., Ill. He died 19 Oct 1918 in De Kalb Co. and was buried in Oak Mound Cem. Robert was never married.

11312 John Alexander McCleery

John was born 10 Dec 1865 in Victor Twp. and was a farmer there for most of his life. He married Elma Agnes Weddell (Fraser) who was born in Nov 1866 and died in 1944. They had a son, Wayne Edward. John lived on part of the old family farm, but spent the last three years of his life in Florence Rest Home in Marengo, Ill., and died there 28 Mar 1951.[88] John and Elma are buried in Oak Mound Cem.

11313 James Andrew McCleery

James was born 3 Dec 1868 on the McCleery homestead in Victor Twp., De Kalb Co., Ill. He attended Monmouth College and a business college in Chicago. James dropped out of college and returned home to help his father with the farm work. He was a faithful member of United Presbyterian Church, and was made an elder 15 May 1907. He was never married, and was considered a substantial citizen of his community. He died 5 Nov 1945 after having been in poor health for sixteen years.[146] Burial was in Oak Mound Cem.

11314 Margaret J. McCleery

Margaret was born 7 Dec 1870 in De Kalb Co. She was a teacher of considerable ability and may never have married. She died 20 Dec 1906 and was buried in Oak Mound Cem.

11315 Annie M. McCleery

Annie was born 18 Oct 1872 and was unmarried. She lived with her sister, Lula May. Annie, who was in poor health in 1923, died 8 Jan 1937 and was buried in Oak Mound Cem.

11316 Lula May McCleery

Lula May was born 10 Aug 1875, and died 14 Jun 1930 in Sandwich, Ill. She was unmarried and kept house for her brother, James. Burial was in Oak Mound Cem.

11317 William Carlisle McCleery

Carlisle was born 17 Sep 1880 in Somonauk, Ill., and married Bessie Bull 5 Jun 1913 in Xenia, Ohio. He was ordained a United

Presbyterian minister. They had three children: William Carlisle Jr., Margaret Ann, and Ralph. His first appointment was to North Henderson, Ill. In 1923 he was a preacher in Idaville, Ind. Bessie died 31 May 1952. Carlisle died 13 May 1958 in Newark, Ohio, where he had resided with his daughter, Margaret, since 1952. They were buried in New Concord, Ohio.

11318 Elizabeth Rose McCleery

Bessie was born 2 Aug 1883 in Victor Twp., De Kalb Co., Ill. Bessie was a graduate of Earlville High School and De Kalb Normal State Teachers College. She taught at Rollo, Troy Grove, and Hinckley. She married Hoyt Ezra Gilbert at Victor on 30 Jun 1910, and they lived in Hinckley, Ill. For the last six years of her life, she lived in Somonauk and was a lifelong member of the United Presbyterian Church. For many years she taught the adult Sunday School class. They had three children: Wallace Dale, Donald L., and Elizabeth I. Hoyt was born about 1877 in Pa., and died 28 Jan 1926, possibly in Hinckley, Ill. Bessie died 10 May 1956 in Victor Twp. and was buried in Oak Mound Cem.[89]

11319 Benjamin Henderson McCleery

Benjamin was born in Feb 1887 and died 21 Jan 1949 in Victor Twp. Benjamin was married on 3 Sep 1924 to Mary Eliza Hastings and they lived on the home farm. They have one son, Hugh Hastings McCleery. Mary was born 6 Oct 1887 in Chillicothe, Ill., and died 19 Nov 1968 in Sandwich, Ill.[90] Benjamin and Mary were buried in Oak Mound Cem.

11321 Sarah Jane McCleery

Jane was born 28 Oct 1858 in Clinton Twp., De Kalb Co., Ill. Jane and Nathan Orcutt Graham were married 14 Dec 1877. Nathan was born 4 Jan 1851 in Schuyerville, Saratoga Co., N.Y. Their "love letters" have been saved by family members. To this union were born seven children: Richard Mallory, Susan E., Nora T., Grace G., Ruth F., Helen Daisy, and Margaret. Nathan died of typhoid fever 17 Jun 1895 in Viola, Kan. In 1920, Jane was living in Waterman, Ill., along with two nieces, Margaret McCleery and Ruth McCleery, both born in Iowa, the children of 11328 William Russell and Nellie McCleery. Jane died in Waterman 3 Nov 1936 and was buried in Oak Mound Cem.[91]

11322 John Andrew McCleery

John was born 27 Sep 1860 in Clinton Twp. He died 4 Oct 1860 and was buried in Oak Mound Cem.

11323 John Andrew McCleery

When a baby died it was common practice to give the next baby of the same sex the deceased baby's name. John Andrew was born 17 Dec 1861 in Clinton Twp. He died 23 Jan 1865 and was buried in Oak Mound Cem. The first child was referred to as simply John and the second as Andrew in Wakefield's document.[21]

11324 Margaret McCleery

Margaret was born 24 Feb 1864 in Clinton Twp. and died 31 Jan 1865. She joined her brothers in Oak Mound Cem.

11325 Mary McCleery

Mary was born 10 Apr 1866 in Clinton Twp. Mary and Alexander Maxwell were married 17 Dec 1884; they had a son, Andrew. Mary died 4 Jan 1922 and was buried with her husband in Oak Mound Cem.

11326 Fannie Elizabeth McCleery

Fannie was born 9 Nov 1868 in Clinton Twp., DeKalb Co., Ill. She married Wilson David Graham 30 Dec 1890. They may have been in Kansas in 1894. Their children were Margaret, Eva Lucile, Howard Scott, twins Thomas Roy and James Ray, and Maude Greeley. Fannie died 23 Oct 1938. Wilson was born 25 Aug 1860, and died 15 Apr 1948 in Los Angeles, Calif.

11327 Adaline Isabelle McCleery

Adaline was born 2 Jul 1870 and died 17 May 1927. She was married 25 Dec 1895 to Taylor Reid Beveridge who was born 5 May 1869 in New York state and died 1 Sep 1935 in Monmouth, Ill. They lived near Goldfield, Iowa, in 1920. They had eight children: George Wiley, Luella, Hugh Raymond, Reid Graham, Glen Walker, Ralph, Paul Hutton, and Jeannette McCleery. Adaline and Taylor are buried in Glenwood Cem., Goldfield.

11328 William Russell McCleery

William was born 12 Jul 1873 in Waterman, Ill. He married Nellie May Robinson 2 Jan 1895 and they had: James Austin, Helen Adelaide, Kathryn, Lee R., Mary Elizabeth, Margaret, and Ruth Jeannette. William died 10 Jan 1950 in Waterloo, Ia. Nellie was born 29 Apr 1873 in Kan., and died 25 Feb 1919 in Waterloo. Both were buried in Oak Mound Cem.[94]

11329 Raymond McCleery

Raymond was born 5 Apr 1876 in Clinton Twp. on a farm located three and a half miles south of Waterman. He attended school in Clinton Twp., and also studied at Monmouth College. For many years he was a restaurant employee. He married Louise Victoria Jenkins on 19 Oct 1915. Their children were Raymond Oswald and Margaret L. She divorced Raymond and married Clarence W. Tombaugh who adopted Louise's children. They lived in the Kansas City, Mo. area. Raymond died 28 Jan 1955 in a Dundee nursing home after retiring to Aurora in his later years.[92] Raymond was buried in Oak Mound Cem. Louise was born in Ill., 21 Feb 1898 and died in Breckenridge, Mo., in Aug 1977; smoking in bed led to her death. She was married to a Mr. Hunt when she died.

1132(10) Jeanette McCleery

"Nettie" was born 2 Aug 1878 in Clinton Twp. She married 7 Jun 1928 Taylor Reid Beveridge apparently after the death of her sister, Adaline. Nettie died 24 Apr 1960 in Ill., and was buried in Oak Mound Cem. There were no children. Taylor died 1 Sep 1935.

11351 Alexander William Beveridge

Alexander was born in Victor Twp., De Kalb Co., Ill., on 2 Feb 1866. He was married first to "Jennie" Jane Charlton Reid 25 Dec 1888. She bore him a son, Bruce. Jennie was born 11 Sep 1867 in Lynedoch, Ontario, Canada, and died near Waterman 27 Feb 1897.[93] She was buried in Oak Mound Cem. Secondly, Alexander married Mary B. Maxwell 27 Dec 1899 at Logans Porte, Ind. They had George Maxwell, Wilson McNitt, and Mary Elizabeth. Alexander was a graduate of Chicago Veterinary College in 1900 and practiced in Ohio, Ill., and Colo. Alexander died 17 Dec 1940 in Olathe, Colo. Mary was born 10 Feb 1864 in Salem, N.Y., lived thirty years in Olathe, and had lived in Washington, D.C., before moving to Ames in 1953. She died at the home of her daughter in Ames 3 Apr 1956. Alexander and Mary are buried in Olathe.

11352 James McCleery Beveridge

James was born 23 Nov 1867 in Victor Twp. He finished Monmouth College in 1893 and University of Illinois Medical School in 1898. Dr. Beveridge spent one year in Chicago at Baptist Hospital. He then practiced seven years at Buckingham, Ill., and after 1906 at Oregon, Ill. On 28 Dec 1899 he married Mary Ellen Hayes who was born in Lynedoch, Norfolk Co., Ontario, on 7 Jul 1873. She died

28 Dec 1956 in Urbana, Ill.[95] They had two children, Ralph Hayes and Helen Mae. James died 21 Nov 1935 in Oregon, Ill. James and Mary are buried in Oak Mound Cem.   On 10 Sep 1912, Dr. Beveridge read a paper he had written on the occasion of the golden wedding anniversary of John and Ann (McCall) McCleery. It was unfortunate that he misspelled Thomson.

11353 Albert Elmer Beveridge

Albert was born 3 Jul 1871 in Somonauk, Ill., and was never married. He attended Monmouth College and then ran a farm. He died 30 Apr 1904 in Chicago, Ill., and was buried in Oak Mound Cem.

11354 George Beveridge

George was born 19 Aug 1874 near Somonauk, Ill. George finished Monmouth College in 1899 and University of Illinois Medical School in 1904. He was considered to have exceptional ability. In 1900, he visited Stranraer, Scotland. He was unmarried, died 3 Oct 1907 in Reinbeck, Ia., and was buried in Oak Mound Cem.

11355 Rea L. Beveridge

Rea was born 30 Oct 1876 near Somonauk, Ill., in Victor Twp. There he attended local schools and, for a time, Monmouth College. He married 30 Aug 1900 Bertha McGeoch of Cambridge, N. Y., and they had five children: Mary Evelyn, Willard, Max, John, and Wallace. He engaged in farming in Ill., and Ia. For several years he was in business in Cambridge, N.Y., and Chicago. In 1907 they were in Cambridge, N.Y. Since 1913 their home was near Sheldon, Wisc. Rea was kicked in the abdomen by a horse and died from peritonitis 13 Sep 1930 in Ladysmith, Wisc.[96] Bertha was born 24 Oct 1877 and died 26 Jun 1962 in Ladysmith, Wisc.[97] Burial was in Woodlawn Cem. near Sheldon in a plot used by the entire family.

11356 Mae Beveridge

Mae was born 30 Oct 1876 near Somonauk, Ill. She attended rural schools in De Kalb Co., then attended Monmouth College for two years and Moody Bible Institute for two additional years. In 1907 she was living with her brother, Dr. George Beveridge, in Reinbeck, Ia. She was not married, and died 20 Dec 1952 in Washington, Ia.[98] Mae was on the staff at Knoxville College in Knoxville, Tenn., and at Frenchburg, Ky. Burial was in Oak Mound Cem.

11357 Margaret Beveridge

Margaret was born 18 Dec 1878, lived in Reinbeck, Ia. for some time, and later was living in Frenchburg, Ky. She and her sister, Mae, were associated with Knoxville College in Knoxville, Tenn. She died 13 Sep 1964 at the United Presbyterian home in Monmouth, Ill., and was buried in Oak Mound Cem.

11358 Archibald G. Beveridge

Archibald was born 29 Jan 1885 in Somonauk, Ill. His mother's obituary, which appeared in the Grundy (Iowa) *Herald* 6 Aug 1907, stated that he was in Regina, Saskatchewan. He married Alice Magdalene Hess on 12 Aug 1908 in Somonauk. Alice was born 4 Aug 1885 in Somonauk and died 1 Apr 1956 in Demorest, Ga., where she had taught music at Piedmont College. She was an author and composer, and had published music to a number of poems, scores for rhythm bands, pageantry and poetry. Her name was included in *American Women*, Vol. III, 1939-1940.[99] They lived for a time in Saskatchewan where their three children were born: Albert Henry John Ronald, and Dorothy Margaret. Archibald died 1 Feb 1921 in Chippewa Falls, Wisc.[100] Burial was in Oak Mound Cem. in De Kalb Co., Ill. After his death, the wife and three children lived in Somonauk. In 1926 they relocated to Demorest, Ga.

11361 George Andrew Howison

George was born 23 Nov 1864 in Squaw Grove Twp., De Kalb Co., Ill. He remained on the original homestead in Squaw Grove. In 1920 his sisters, Jean M. and Mary J., were living with him. He spent his entire life in the Frank Community. He was a member of Somonauk United Presbyterian Church. He died 16 Oct 1952 and was buried in Oak Mound Cem.[101]

11362 Margaret Jane (Jean) Howison

Margaret was born 22 Sep 1867. She lived on the farm with her brother, George. Margaret died 6 Dec 1943 in Sandwich, Ill.[102] She received her elementary education in the local district school, and attended high school in Sandwich. She obtained her collegiate training in Monmouth College and at Ferry Hall in Lake Forest, Ill. She was buried in Oak Mound Cem. in the family plot.

11363 Ann Elizabeth Howison

Ann was born in Mar 1870, and died while a student at Monmouth College 3 Jun 1888. She was buried in Oak Mound Cem.

11364 Archie H. Howison

Archie was born 4 Jan 1873 in DeKalb Co., Ill. He married Martha

A. Randles 8 Feb 1899. Martha's mother was Annette Gray who was a first cousin to Mary Ann Reid and Mary Ellen Hayes. Archie died 24 Jun 1901 and was buried in Oak Mound Cem. They had no children.

11365 Mary Jeannette Howison

Mary was born 17 Dec 1875 and died in Jul 1948. She had lived with George and Jean on the old farm. She was a graduate of Monmouth College. Burial was in Oak Mound Cem.

11366 Ralph James Howison

Ralph was born 9 Feb 1880 in De Kalb Co., Ill. On 13 Jun 1906, he and Margaret Helen Beveridge were married in De Kalb Co. Margaret was the daughter of William G. Beveridge and was born 19 Nov 1881 and died 22 Jul 1939. They had Donald, then adopted Robert Wendell and Evelyn Mae. Ralph died in Mar 1963; both were buried in Oak Mound Cem.

11367 Isabella Catherine Howison

Isabella was born 12 Jan 1883 in De Kalb Co., Ill. She died 30 Jul 1886 and was buried in Oak Mound Cem.

11368 Elizabeth Ann Howison

Elizabeth was born 24 Feb 1885 in De Kalb Co. She died 3 Jun 1888 and was buried in Oak Mound Cem.

11371 James McCleery Robinson

James was born 20 or 21 Sep 1874 and died 24 or 26 Aug 1879 in De Kalb Co. He was buried in Oak Mound Cem.

11372 Isabelle Beveridge Robinson

Isabelle was born 22 Jun 1877 in De Kalb Co., Ill. She married on 10 Sep 1904 Merritt Hoy Beveridge, son of James Hoy Beveridge and Elizabeth A. Disbrow. Merritt was born 17 Jun 1869 and died 8 Dec 1944 at Somonauk, Ill. Their children were James Hoy, Thomas Robinson and Margaret Jean. Isabelle died 3 Apr 1923 in De Kalb Co. and she and her husband are buried in Oak Mound Cem.

11373 Benjamin Robinson

Benjamin was born 29 Aug 1879 in De Kalb Co. When he descended from a tree, he was bitten by a rattlesnake and died 20 Jul 1892 in De Kalb Co. Burial was in Oak Mound Cem.

11374 John Beveridge Robinson

John was born 19 Dec 1881 in De Kalb Co. and died 17 Sep 1952 at Winterset, Iowa. He married on 29 Jun 1910 at Indianola, Ia., Margaret Ethel McCoy and they had three children: Thomas Clyde McCoy, James Keith, and John Beveridge Jr. Margaret was born 4 Oct 1882 in Iowa and died 7 Apr 1942 in Monmouth, Ill. The family was living in De Kalb Co. in 1920. They farmed 200 acres south of Waterman, Ill. Both were buried in Oak Mound Cem.

11375 Lee Robinson

Lee was born 4 Jul 1884 at Somonauk, Ill., and died 21 Jan 1885. He was buried in Oak Mound Cem.

11376 Margaret Robinson

Margaret was born 5 or 15 Mar 1886 in De Kalb Co., Ill. She married Wallace J. Black on 20 Jun 1907 at Sandwich, Ill. Wallace was born 12 Jan 1884 at Washburn, Ill., and died 24 Jan 1962 in Peoria, Ill. where he was a successful lawyer. They had two children, Kenneth Wallace and Constance Isabel. Margaret died 20 Aug 1959 in Peoria, and both she and her husband are buried in Mt. Vernon Cemetery in Washburn, Ill.

11377 Jean Elizabeth Robinson

Jean was born 13 Oct 1888 near Somonauk, Ill. Jean received an advanced education at Monmouth College, Monmouth, Ill. She taught English and speech in Blackfoot High School, Blackfoot, Idaho and in rural Illinois. On 5 Aug 1915 at Waterman, Ill., she married Wendell Abel Potter, born 22 Dec 1890 at South Granville, N.Y. He was a graduate of Monmouth College and the Univ. of Chicago where he was magna cum laude. He then studied for his medical degree in Rush Medical School, Chicago. He practiced medicine in northern Illinois. They had two daughters, Jean Elizabeth and Jo Ann Temple. Jean died 3 Mar 1948 at Geneseo, Ill., and was buried in Oak Mound Cem. Dr. Potter died 8 Oct 1964 in Springfield, Mo.

11381 Andrew J. McCleery

Andrew was born 9 Oct 1871. He died 12 Sep 1872 and was buried in Oak Mound Cem.

11382 Howard J. McCleery

Howard was born 1 Apr 1873, and died 1 Apr 1940 in Vegreville,

Alberta, Canada.   He married 2 Apr 1902, in Illinois, Ethel Carouthers and they had issue: Marion, Evelyn, Ruth, and Marjorie. In 1927 he was farming in Vegreville, Alberta, Canada. Ethel died in 1923.

11383 Albert McCleery

Albert was born 4 May 1875 in De Kalb Co., Ill., and died 9 Oct 1953 in Eagle Grove, Ia. On 20 Feb 1902, he married Mary Ellen Henry who was of Goldfield, Ia. Albert lived in Wright Co., Ia., since his marriage, except for about thirteen years spent in Alberta, Canada, and Siloam Springs, Ark. They owned a farm near Eagle Grove. Albert first became a member on 21 Mar 1902, and upon his death was a senior member of the Session of the United Presbyterian Church. Their children were Mary Jeanette, Irene Ellen, Lois Isabel, and Sarabelle. Mary was born 17 Oct 1875 died in 1927.[189] They were buried in Goldfield, Ia.

11384 Clarence Thomson McCleery

Clarence was born 28 Jan 1877, died 2 Apr 1877, and was buried in Oak Mound Cem.

11385 Ralph McCleery

Ralph was born 15 Aug 1878, died 15 Jan 1880, and was buried in Oak Mound Cem.

11386 Ruth McCleery

Ruth was born 14 Jan 1883, died 19 Jun 1884, and was buried in Oak Mound Cem.

11387 Harry Robinson McCleery

Harry was born 3 Dec 1884 in Somonauk, Ill. He married 25 Dec 1906 Ethel L'Hommedieu who used the name Graham up until her marriage. In 1927 they were farming near Butler, Ind. Their adopted children were Howard Dean, and Beatrice Belle. Ethel was born about 1883 and died in 1963. Harry died 19 Aug 1955. Both are buried in Fremont, Ind.

11388 Arch McCleery

Arch was born 24 Sep 1888, probably in Somonauk, Ill., and died in Nov 1964, in Ypsilanti, Mich. He was a veteran of WW I. He married 5 Feb 1913 Alice A. Ashenhurst who was born 28 Apr 1891 and died in Dec 1984 in Ypsilanti. They are buried in Fremont,

Ind., where they once lived. They had Jane E., Mary Alice and William Ashenhurst. He was a grocer, and later was in the office supply business.

11389 John Maxwell McCleery

John was born 14 Aug 1890. John was reared on a farm near Waterman, Ill., and was a graduate of Muskingham College in 1916 and of Western Reserve Medical School in 1917. John served in the U. S. Army for a year and a half during World War I. He married 7 Sep 1920 Pearl M. Roe and they had two children, Grace Eileen and Dorothy Ruth. John spent a few years as a medical missionary to the Sudan in Africa, and returned because of ill health in 1923. Later, he was the college physician and professor of biology at Muskingham College in New Concord, Ohio.[120] John, who was a modest man with a keen sense of humor and a quick repartee, retired in 1959. He died 26 Oct 1967 in Cleveland, Ohio.[103] Pearl died 29 Sep 1964 in Cleveland; both are buried in New Concord, Ohio.

1138(10) Fannie E. McCleery

Fannie was born 13 Jun 1892 in Vegreville, Alberta, Canada, and died there on 16 May 1960. She married in 1921 Kenneth Thomas Ferguson in Alberta, Canada, and had four children: Ralph McCleery, Helen Daisy, Lila Jennette, and Leonard Keyes. Kenneth was born 10 Feb 1889 in Manitoba, and farmed in Alberta, Canada. He died 23 Jul 1984.

11421 Hugh Thomson

Hugh was born 24 Sep 1869 in Anderston, Glasgow, Lanarkshire, Scotland, from records held by LDS. He left school at age twelve, and at fourteen began working in the shipyard. In 1890 he became a member of the Associated Iron Moulders of Scotland. On 23 Feb 1894 he married Agnes Keith at Rosebank Hall, Renfrew, Renfrewshire. Witnesses to the wedding were William McLintock and Susan Thomson Risk, relationships, if any, unknown. Agnes was born about 1867, the daughter of Duncan Keith, boilermaker, and Agnes McMurray. Their child was Agnes McMurray. Hugh was a well-known horticulturist in Renfrew. Under the name "Meadowside", he wrote a weekly series on gardening in *The Renfrew Press*. Starting in 1939, he gave tips on the growing of plants, flowers and vegetables. He had a small garden behind his house where he developed quite a reputation for growing chrysanthemums. He was also manager of a co-operative poultry farm in Broadloan, and was once president, then treasurer, of Renfrew Horticultural Society. Hugh was found dead in bed on 18 Jun 1947 at 49 Ferry Road, Renfrew.[104] He was 77. He had suffered acute rheumatism 56 years prior, but died of heart disease. The informant was Alex J. McNeil, his son-in-law. Agnes died on 1 Jan 1940 at the same address at age 72. Agnes had heart disease and died of pneumonia.

11422 William Thomson

William (Willie) was born 3 Aug 1871 in Lochwinnoch, Renfrewshire, Scotland, according to records held by LDS. He was living in Lochwinnoch working as a servant when the 1891 census was recorded. (By way of interest, there were over 2,300 William Thomsons listed in all of Scotland for the 1891 census.) Soon thereafter, on 10 June 1892 in Cleland, West District of Shotts, Lanarkshire, he married Jessie Rodger in the Free Church. Jessie was 22 years of age, the daughter of John Rodger and Agnes Ferguson of Cleland. Jessie had also been working as a farm servant when she married William.

Originally, William was believed to have married in Renfrewshire, but the results of considerable research did not find a William that matched what we knew about him. Later, another approach was taken wherein it was assumed that the first-born son was James, named after his grandfather in the Scottish custom. This in fact proved to be the case, and a birth record for a James Thomson born in 1892 in Lochwinnoch disclosed that he was the son of William Thomson and Jessie Rodger.

The family grew in size; John was the second-born child, named after his maternal grandfather most likely. They also had a daughter named Agnes who was named for one of her grandmothers. By the time of the outbreak of WW I, there were five children in the family. Agnes McArthur provided a photo that shows three boys, a girl and another young child. They then emigrated to Ontario where William is thought to have spent the remainder of his life. He is known to have been alive in 1943. A search for a death record for him in Ontario has not been successful for the period of 1943 through 1962. A story passed down in the family relates how the sons of William worked with combine harvesters in the wheat fields in the west. Perhaps later in his life, William joined one of his sons in another province of Canada, or the U.S., and died there.

11423 James Thomson

James (Jimmy) was born 27 Jun 1873 in Lochwinnoch, Renfrewshire. He never married. After his father died, and his sister Mary married, he lived on his own. Georgina and Agnes remember that he had dinner with them every day. "He was always teasing us and making

us laugh", remembers Georgina. He was a joiner in the shipyards.
He died 21 Jun 1945 at 51 Ferry Road in Renfrew.

11424 Mary Thomson

Mary was born about 1875 in Lochwinnoch. She married John Leiper;
no children. She lived in Renfrew and died 8 Mar 1942.

11511 Margaret Elizabeth Thomson

Elizabeth was born near Lenox, Adams Co., Ia. 18 Feb 1877, and was
baptized in Adams United Presbyterian Church in 1878. She married
Samuel Sedam Strieby 11 Oct 1906 in Stanwood. Samuel had a career
as a plumber.   They were members of the Presbyterian Church.
Elizabeth died 27 Mar 1971 in Clinton, Henry Co., Mo., and was
buried there in Englewood Cem. Samuel was born in 1881 and died in
Feb 1953; burial was in Mankato, Kan. Their children were twins,
LaRue Thomson and Frances LeRoy.

11512 William Forsythe Thomson

William's biography appeared in a 1910 History of Cedar Co., Ia.[51]
A family Bible lists his birthplace as being near Lenox, Ia., on 13
Dec 1878. He was baptized in Adams United Presbyterian Church in
1879. He was two years old when his parents moved to Cedar Co. He
attended grade school and high school in Stanwood and became a
member of the United Presbyterian Church 6 Feb 1896.   On 4 Apr
1904, in Tipton, he married Sarah Ann Wertz. "Sadie", the daughter
of Isaac Wertz and Martha Fraseur, was born in Red Oak Twp., Cedar
Co., on 5 May 1884, and died 12 Jul 1972.[106] Of German descent, her
ancestry has been traced to a Wertz family in Bedford Co., Pa.
William rented a farm soon after they were married. It wasn't
until 7 Mar 1927 that William purchased, at a cost of $42,000, a

William F. Thomson

farm of 240 acres in Section 26 of Fremont Township 82, located two miles south of Stanwood. He continued growing crops and raising hogs and cattle until his retirement to Stanwood in 1938. He served as County Supervisor from 1940 to 1953. The family worshiped with the United Presbyterian Church of Stanwood. Their nine children were Paul Estel, Richard Elwood, Everett Strauser, Charles William, George Marion, Eloise Ruth, Edwin Isaac, Evelyn Mae, and Emma Lou. Sadie worked hard raising nine children and attending to all the domestic duties, without the modern conveniences of today.

His daughter, Emma Lou, remembered her father as being very intelligent, and a strong man. The compiler didn't know his grandfather well, but remembers his advice, "don't follow the crowd." He died in Stanwood, Ia., on 3 Oct 1956.[105] His death was caused by a lingering battle with cancer which began with a lesion on his lower lip, although he was never a smoker. William was the first in his family to die, and he was survived by four brothers and four sisters. William and Sarah are buried in Stanwood Cem.

11513 Arthur Elias Thomson

Arthur was born 12 Dec 1880 near Stanwood, Ia. On 12 Sep 1906 he and Edna Mae Bannister were married in Clinton, Ia. Initially they farmed near Stanwood, then homesteaded near Hamill in Tripp Co., S. D. In their later years, they lived near their daughter, Ruth, in Idaho, then in Gardena, Calif., to be near their son, Bill. Arthur died 26 Jan 1962. Edna was born 20 Sep 1880 and died 7 Nov 1952 in Gardena, Calif., where both are buried. Their children were Olive Mae, Edna Ruth, and William Martin.

11514 Francis Marion Thomson

Frank was born 1 Jan 1884 near Stanwood, Ia., and was baptized 21 Jun 1884 in Stanwood United Presbyterian Church. On 15 Aug 1906 he and Nellie Edna Robinson were married in Clarence, Ia. Their children were Thelma Lucile, Ethyl Charlene, Donald Paul, Dale Marion, Jean, Murl Howard, Francis Glen, and Doris Lorraine. Frank farmed his entire life in Cedar County, most recently near Mechanicsville. He was a member of the First Presbyterian Church, the Masons, Lions Club, and Cedar Rapids Consistory. Nellie was born 21 Aug 1885, and died in Chicago 17 Oct 1955 as the result of a collision between the car her husband was driving and a delivery truck.[107] Frank died in Mount Vernon, Ia., 18 Oct 1967.[108] Frank and Nellie were buried in Stanwood Cem.

11515 John Edwin Thomson

Ed was born 19 May 1886 near Stanwood, and was baptized 21 Nov 1886 in Stanwood United Presbyterian Church. Ed and Faira Mae Abbott were married 25 Feb 1914, and were farmers. They lived near Fremont until 1923, then near Hedrick until 1931. They were members of the Presbyterian Church. Their children were Alice Mae, Eddyth Marie, Carol Illa, and Eathol Arlene. Ed was living in Oskaloosa, Ia., when he died 21 Jan 1961.[109] Burial was in Memorial Lawns in Ottumwa. Faira was born 15 Aug 1889 and died 20 Oct 1971.

11516 Clara Ann Thomson

Clara was born near Stanwood, Ia., 15 Dec 1889. She married Frank James Tenley 2 Mar 1908. Their children were Beryl Thomson, Kathryn Elizabeth, Joseph Myron, Mary Louise, Chester Robert, and William Kenneth. Mr. Tenley was born 18 Aug 1886 and died 21 Oct 1962. Clara died 1 Dec 1966 in Rochester, Minn.

11517 Agnes Belle Thomson

Agnes was born 11 Oct 1891 near Stanwood, Ia. She married Edgar Harrison Harper 27 Jan 1915. Agnes died 13 May 1958 in Lebanon, Linn Co., Ore; Edgar was born 15 Jun 1887 and died in Dec 1968 in Ore. Their children were Hazel Ola, Howard Thomson, Cecil Ralph, John William, Donald Kenneth, and Marvin Earl.

Children of William M. Thomson and Catherine Strauser

L-R: Elizabeth, William F., Arthur, Francis, John, Agnes, Clara, Ruth, Lawrence, 1922

11518 Ella Ruth Thomson

Ruth was born 22 Jan 1894 near Stanwood, Ia., and died 6 Jul 1971 in Durham, N.H.   She graduated from The University of Iowa where she earned a master's degree in genetics, a special accomplishment in that time. She married 18 Jun 1925 Clarence Henry McQuade who was born 18 Jun 1889 in Alpena, Mich., and died 5 Sep 1931.   They had a daughter, Elizabeth Ann.   Old notes in Lawrence Thomson's papers indicate that Ruth went on a tour to a foreign country in 1966. Ruth is buried alongside her parents in Stanwood Cem.

11519 Chester Lawrence Thomson

Lawrence was born 25 Apr 1897 in Stanwood, Ia. He was a graduate of The University of Iowa. Most of his career was spent at Indiana State Teachers College in Pa., where he taught English and literature.   While in Pa., he became aquainted with the actor, Jimmy Stewart, and his parents. Later, he returned to Bettendorf, Ia., to be nearer to home and family. He headed a Scott Co., Ia., relief office for several years. He was of immaculate dress, and was well spoken. He never married. Lawrence spent his later years researching his roots and wrote a manuscript on his Thomson ancestry that is widely held in the family and has been a source of enlightenment regarding the Thomson genealogy for many years. Lawrence died in Phoenix, Ariz., 19 Jun 1971.

11541 Mary Isabelle Thomson

Isabelle was born 26 Oct 1900 in Monroe, Ia.   In her youth she moved with her parents to Ia., Okla., Ohio, Fla., Ga., Ill. and Kan.   Isabelle was a graduate of Sterling College in Kan., then taught school in Kentucky and Kan.   She married Alexander Montgomery Barron Sr. in Sterling, Kan., 2 Aug 1926. Alexander was born 21 Dec 1890 in Kirkwood, Del., and was a veteran of WW I having served in the U.S. Army in France in the ambulance corps. While in the service he was awarded the French Croix de Guerre. After the war, he was a livestock feeder for Swift and Co. for more than 30 years. Alexander worked in Omaha, St. Paul, and Watertown, S.D. When Isabelle drove her husband to work one day, she somehow lost her hand bag which contained her diamond engagement ring and her wedding ring, as well as some money. Their two children were John Reid and Alexander Montgomery Jr. Isabelle was an active member of the Presbyterian Church. She died[110] 15 Aug 1961 in Buffalo, Minn., and is buried in Ft. Snelling National Cemetery, St. Paul, Minn., alongside her husband who died on 6 Jan 1978.[111]

11542 John Alexander Thomson

John was born 7 Mar 1902 in Monroe, Ia.   He enlisted for service in

WW I on 24 Oct 1918 and was discharged 8 Jun 1919. He married Carrie Isabelle Hubenett 1 Sep 1927 and they had Carol Christine and John Dennis. John died in Wichita, Kan., 4 Mar 1972. Carrie was born 23 Nov 1900 in Little River, Kan., and died 8 Jul 1976 in Hutchison, Kan.; burial was in Wichita.

11543 David Reid Thomson

Reid was born 17 Nov 1903 in Findley, Ohio. From a copy of a letter he wrote on 16 Dec 1980, we learn that Reid attended Sterling College in Sterling, Kan., a United Presbyterian school, where he met his first wife. He married Vivian Moffett who was born 25 Oct 1902 and died 15 Oct 1969 in Fort Dodge, Ia. Reid was employed by Curtis Publishing Co., and during his 32 years with them, they moved several times. His last assignment took them to Detroit. Their son was David Reid Jr. David secondly married Lorraine McAlpin in the fall of 1970. Lorraine was born 13 Oct 1909 and died in Aug 1996. After living in Detroit a year, Reid decided to retire and moved to Ft. Dodge, Ia., where Lorraine was raised. David died in Fort Dodge, Ia., in Feb 1987.

11551 Margaret Mary Spence

Maggie was born 3 Jul 1885 and died in Nov 1963, probably in Iowa Falls, Ia. She was a medical doctor and was married to Rev. Forest E. Bates who was born 1 Jul 1897 and died in Jun 1964 in Iowa Falls. In 1957 they were living in Telluride, Colo. They also lived in Marengo, Ia., and were owners of a farm. Their children were Edwin and Margaret Grace.

11552 William John Spence

William was born 12 Oct 1888 in Douglas Twp., Madison Co., Ia. He was a 1908 graduate of Earlham High School. Later he farmed on the "home place" until 1939. William farmed in Dallas County until 1943 when he moved to Waterloo to live with his sister, Janet. He had been a member of the Pitzer Church. Never married, he died[112] 10 Feb 1957 in Waterloo and was buried in Winterset Cem.[57]

11553 Elizabeth Melvin Spence

"Bessie" was born 23 May 1891 and died in 1957. She married Forrest Huff on 18 Dec 1911. They had Forrest Jr. (Harry), and raised Mary Pearl Ludwig. Forrest was born 24 May 1888 and died in Dec 1977 in Dawson, Ia. "Frosty" and "Bessie" were buried in Pleasant Hill Cemetery located west of Dawson, Ia.

11554 Vasha Isabelle Spence
Vasha was born 22 Nov 1892 near Winterset, Ia., and attended grade

school in Winterset, Ia. She was a graduate of Earlham Academy (high school) in Earlham. She attended Iowa State College where she studied home economics. She then taught at a country school for a short time. She met Christen Sorensen whom she married 20 Sep 1923.[113] They had Donald, Ruth, and Betty. Vasha was a member of Clarendon Presbyterian Church in Arlington and was active in Women's Circles. Vasha died 1 Oct 1969. Christen was born 11 Apr 1892 in Denmark and emigrated to the U.S. when he was 17 years old. He was a graduate of Iowa State College with a degree in civil engineering. Vasha and Christen moved to Arlington about 1927 where he worked for the Veteran's Administration as a landscape architect, and prepared designs for facilities in many places in the U.S. Christen was killed in an automobile accident 4 Jan 1953 in Greene Co., Va.[114] Vasha and Christen were buried in Arlington National Cem.

11555 David Taylor Spence Jr.

David was born 2 Aug 1895 near Winterset, Ia. He married Mabel Lorene Black 2 Mar 1921, and they farmed west of Winterset and near Hawkeye, Ia. Their childen were Esther Ruth, Margaret Helen, Robert Eugene, and Mildred Lucille. Mabel died 4 Jan 1970. Secondly, David married in Mar 1971 Golda Van Cleave who died in 1980. David died 27 May 1972.

11556 Janet Frances Spence

Janet was born 30 Jun 1898. She married Alexander Gibson in 1943. Janet had no children and died in May 1964. Alexander was born 30 Jul 1893 and died in Apr 1977 in Waterloo, Ia.

11571 Mary Elizabeth Thomson

Mary was born 25 Jul 1890. She was a schoolteacher, and in 1915 she married Fred Walter Johnson. Fred was a druggist in New Richland, Minn. They had Fred Holton, and a son that was stillborn. Fred Sr. died in 1931 was buried in New Richland; Mary died in 1963 and her body was cremated.

11572 Nina Hazel Thomson

Hazel was born 24 Jan 1893. She was married briefly to Ole Jensen in 1955 and worked for the Minneapolis-St. Louis Railroad. There were no children. She died in 1964; Ole died 3 Jan 1958.

11573 George William Thomson

George was born 16 Oct 1894 in Monmouth, Ill., and died 22 Sep 1920 in the hospital in Aurora, Ill; his latest residence had been

Plano where he worked as a telegraph operator. Burial was in Berean Cemetery in Westfield Twp., Bureau Co. Ill. George married in 1915 Ruby Plym who was born about 1894 and died in 1949.

11574 Edgar Lincoln Thomson

Edgar was born 1 Aug 1897 in Alpha, Ill., died 26 Sep 1930 in Cook Co., Ill. He was last married to Zella Oconner (sic ?); no issue. He was a stenographer in Minneapolis and died of Hodgkin's disease. Burial was in Minneapolis. His wife survived him.

11575 David Leroy Thomson

David was born 10 Oct 1902. He married in 1920 Lola Maude Mercer and they had Betty Gene. David was an agent and operator for Burlington Railroad in numerous towns. David died 7 Mar 1959 and was buried in Township Cemetery, Plano, Ill. Lola was born 2 Jun 1903, and died 17 Jul 1973 in Bristol, Ill.

11576 Effie Lillian Thomson

Effie was born 9 Mar 1905 in Minnesota and died in Oct 1977. She married 25 Jul 1928 Delbert Dale Gillette who was born 7 Oct 1906 and died 13 Mar 1982 in Minneapolis. Both were cremated. Delbert was a house painter and liked to write. Both were active in their church. They had a daughter, Laverna Darlene.

11577 John Howard Thomson

John was born 8 (or 9) Sep 1909. He married in 1934 Lucille Ethel Wilson who was born 28 Jul 1908 in Dover, Ill. In 1933 they were living in the small town of Zearing, Ill. Their children were John Kay and Shirley Anne. John died 11 Sep 1989; Lucille died 12 Feb 1999; both are buried in Elm Lawn Cem., Princeton.

11578 Alice May Thomson

Alice was born 5 Jul 1911 at Biggsville, Ill. Alice married 7 Apr 1935 Arthur Vaughn Burkett at Monmouth, Ill., where they lived out their lives. They had Arthur Vaughn Jr. ("Sonny") and Lenna Gail. Vaughn was born 10 Jan 1901 and died 12 Sep 1976. Alice died 12 Oct 1972 in the Monmouth Community Hospital; both are buried in Monmouth Memorial Park Cem.[117]

11579 Gladys Lucille Thomson

Gladys was born 21 Feb 1908 and died 8 Dec 1908.

115(10)1 John Spence

John was born 15 Mar 1891 in Douglas Twp., Madison Co., Ia., an only child whose mother died in 1895. On 24 Dec 1914 he married Gertrude Mae Addy, who was born 24 Dec 1891 in Madison Co., Ia., and died 2 Apr 1991. Their children were Mary Josephine, Lyda Frances, and John Wallace. Mr. Spence, who was a rural mail carrier, died 12 Apr 1951 in Winterset, Ia., after 30 years of service.[119]

115(11)1 Helen Virginia Thomson

Helen was born a twin 17 Apr 1906. In 1925 she started working for the Extension Service. By 1933, she was employed as a stenographer at University of Washington in Seattle. Helen never married and died in Seattle on 9 Sep 1999.

115(11)2 Rose Elizabeth Thomson

Rose was born a twin 17 Apr 1906. She began working for the Dean of the College of Mines in 1925. On 13 Jul 1934 she married Kenneth Guy Skinner who worked for the Bureau of Mines, which took him to York, Pa., and to the University of Washington. They had a daughter, Chelsea, who died at eighteen months. Ken died about 1970 and Rose died 30 Jul 1989.

115(11)3 Howard Mearns Thomson

Howard was born 13 Jul 1908 in Seattle. From the letter written in 1933 by his uncle, Samuel Alexander Thomson, we learn that Howard was a 1930 graduate of Washington State University with a degree in electrical engineering. He then was employed by Bell Telephone Co. of New York. He drove a Model 'T' Ford from Seattle to New York, taking in the sights via San Francisco, Yosemite Valley, Salt Lake City, Yellowstone Park, Omaha, Des Moines, and other mid-western cities, which totaled about 6,000 miles.

From correspondence with Howard, we learn that he married Alvina Cora Breithaupt 7 Jan 1936 in San Diego, Calif., at the home of Frank Heilman, a cousin of Alvina's father. Alvina was born 25 Nov 1908 in Mondovi, Wash., and was educated in schools in Idaho and eastern Washington. She graduated from Willamette University in Salem, Ore., in 1930. She graduated from Mercy Hospital School of Nursing in San Diego in 1935. She tied for first place out of 250 nurses in the Calif. State examination for nurses in March 1935 and became a surgical nurse in Mercy Hospital. She didn't have her RN long before she gave up her nursing career to become a mother. Howard remained with Bell Telephone until his retirement in 1969.

Alvina died 2 Mar 1999 at Wingate Nursing Home in Andover, Mass. She had suffered a stroke in 1995. She was cremated and her ashes placed in her flower garden. They had Kenneth and Marian who live near Howard in North Andover, Mass.

115(11)4 Marjory Lois Thomson

Marjory was born 9 Sep 1912. She once had a job in Seattle, but was out of work in 1933 due to the Great Depression. She married William Arthur "Bill" Goold on 27 Oct 1940 at Pacific Palisades, near Santa Monica, Calif. They had four children: Chelsea Louise, Karen Judith, William Paul, and Peggy Ann. Bill was born 11 Jan 1911 and died suddenly of polio 13 Sep 1949. Marjory was living in Seattle in 2001.

115(11)5 Paul Lincoln Thomson

Paul was born 8 Jul 1915 in Seattle, Wash. He married Mary Pearson 19 Jul 1941, in Everett, and they had four children: Ruth, twins Jean Rose and Joan Helen, and Donald Paul. Paul was a letter carrier in Seattle for 31 years. Interestingly enough, Mary had been a secretary at none other than **Thomson** Junior High School in Seattle. Paul died 24 Jun 1999.

115(12)1 Lawrence Hunter Thomson

Lawrence was born 11 Jul 1909, died 13 Dec 1965. He graduated from high school in 1927, and spent two years at Monmouth College. In the summer of 1930 he worked for the Government in the Teton National Park. He then resumed his education while attending Augustana College in Rock Island, Ill. Lawrence married Helen Jane Park on 25 Jun 1949. They adopted Robert Lawrence.

115(12)2 Margaret Parks Thomson

Margaret was born 27 Oct 1911 in Moline, Ill. She attended Iowa State Teacher's College to become a kindergarten teacher. On 19 Aug 1939 in Moline, Margaret married Chester Elliot Corson who was born 19 Jun 1913 in Toledo, Ia. They had a son, William, who was stillborn, Craig Edwin, Donald Lawrence, and Margaret Jean. Margaret provided considerable assistance to this compilation. She was a an active member of Baraboo United Methodist Church. Margaret died 4 Mar 2001 and was buried in Walnut Hill Cemetery.

115(12)3 Marybelle McKee Thomson

Marybelle was born 25 Feb 1913. In 1931 she graduated from high school in Moline, Ill. She married C. Norman Jones; no issue. Marybelle died 7 Dec 1983.

11611 Elizabeth Thomson Beck

Lizzie was born 12 May 1867 in Biggsville, Henderson Co., Ill.
Lizzie married Andrew Jackson Dooley 12 Mar 1891 in Winterset, Ia.
Andrew was born 13 May 1859 in St. Paul, Minn.   Before she was
married she served as president of the Pitzer Presbyterian Church
women's group. They spent most of their married life in Topeka,
Kan.   Their children were Max Beck, Isla Mary, Lucile America, Webb
W., and Jeanette Fern.   Lizzie died in Topeka 13 Dec 1936. Burial
was in Memorial Park in Topeka.

11612 John Craig Beck

John was born 15 Apr 1869 in Madison Co., Ia.   He married 2 Feb
1904 Flora (Floss) K. Stewart who was born 21 Jul 1879 in
Macksburg, Ia. They had three children: Lora Isla, Mary Marguerita,
and James Stewart.   The 1920 census listed them as living in
Madison Co.   John died 29 Jun 1963; Flora died in Jul 1963, and
both were buried in Winterset, Ia.

11613 Samuel Melvin Beck

Samuel was born 13 Dec 1870.   In Stuart, Ia., he married 26 Feb
1902 Etta Brown who was born 31 Nov 1871 and died in 1938.   In 1920
they were residents of Adair Co., Ia.   They had Ruth Helene, Floyd,
and Mildred.   Samuel died in 1932.   Both Samuel and Etta are buried
in Orient Cemetery in Orient, Ia.

11614 James Agnew Beck

James was born 8 Mar 1875 and died 3 Sep 1875.   He was buried in
Pitzer-Eppard Cemetery in Madison Co., Ia.

11615 Jeanette Eleanor Beck

Jeannette was born 11 Oct 1881 in Jackson Twp., Madison Co., Ia.
She was raised on a farm and completed her basic education in the
public schools.   She had a leg amputated at the age of 19 years,
but she was able to get around quite well with the use of her
artificial leg. She never married.   A 1915 history[115] of Madison
County, Iowa, featured Jeannette; in 1912 she was elected to the
office of Madison County Recorder. Her excellent performance was
awarded by her reelection and she stayed in her position until
1918.   She died 14 Jan 1976 in Glendale, Calif., and was buried in
Winterset Cem.

11616 Mary Ethel Beck

Ethel was born 20 Apr 1883 and married Walter O. Miller 2 Mar 1904.

Walter was born 2 Feb 1883 in Bloomington, Ill. They remained in Iowa until 1906 when they moved to North Dakota, then to Kansas in 1909. They had two sons, Joseph Keith and James Eldredge. The 1915 history of Madison County mentions that they were living in Winfield, which is in Cowley County, Kan. On 15 Jan 1916, Walter was killed when an ice-making plant exploded. Ethel then returned to Iowa and was employed as "house mom" at Grinnell College, and later as "house director" at the Law School in Iowa City. Ethel died in Glendale, Calif., 18 May 1963 and was buried in Winterset Cem.

11617 Clarence Blaine Beck

Clarence was born 19 Sep 1886 and died 17 Jan 1887. Burial was in Pitzer-Eppard Cemetery in Madison Co., Ia.

11621 Elizabeth Eleanor Mekemson

Nellie was born 19 Jan 1867 in Henderson Co., Ill. She married 20 Jun 1917 Alex T. Hagan in Redding, Ia. Alex had children from a previous marriage: Belle, Frank, and John. They lived near Abilene, Kan. and later, Manhattan, Kan. Nellie died 17 Oct 1955 and was buried in Redding Cemetery, Redding, Ia.

11622 Ralph Mekemson

Ralph was born 27 Oct 1868 and died in Jan 1869.

11623 Harriet M. Mekemson

Hattie was born 21 Feb 1870 in Madison Co., Ia. In Creston, she married 2 Mar 1896 Dr. Arthur E. Jessup. Arthur was a graduate of the Medical Department of The University of Iowa in 1895. He began his practice of medicine in Caledonia, Ia., where they remained until 1899. They briefly relocated to Airlie, Ore., and by Nov 1899 were in Sharpsburg, Ia. In Jun 1909 they had moved to Diagonal, Ia., where Dr. Jessup continued his medical practice and operated a drug store. They had a child who died in infancy 29 Apr 1897, also Vera Leta, Ruth Jannette, Byron Marin, twins Dale Ernest and Dorothy Mae. A baby born 9 Nov 1909 died after two weeks. Dr. Jessup was born 15 Nov 1869 and died in Jan 1944. Hattie died at the age of 100.

11624 Anna Belle Mekemson

Belle was born 8 Mar 1872 in Madison Co., Ia. and died in 1965. She married 17 Oct 1890 Jacob R. Doty in Macksburg. Jacob was born 6 Nov 1865 and died in 1957. Their children were Jessie Maude, Waldo Emerson, and James Lowell. They lived on a farm near Creston, Ia.,

and later at Benton, Kan. Both were faithful members of the
Christian Church in Benton, Kan., where Belle taught Sunday school
for over 40 years. The family had a letter that circulated around
for probably 70 years by which they kept in touch.

11625 Jessie Lodena Mekemson

Jessie was born 15 Jul 1874 near Winterset, Ia. She married 27 Oct
1897 in Redding, Ia., Birt Amick born 8 Apr 1869 near Redding, Ia.
They had Howard Charles, Muriel Alberta, and Kenneth Dean. They
Also raised Elder William from Birt's former marriage. Birt was
initially engaged in real estate in Redding, then, for a short
time, took up faming near Loup City, Neb. They lived in Des Moines
starting in 1906. Birt died 7 Apr 1928 and Jessie died 2 Jun 1959,
both in Des Moines, Ia. They are buried in Redding.

11626 Janett Mekemson

Nettie was born 8 Nov 1876 in Madison Co., Ia. She married 4 Apr
1900 George F. Saville, who was born 3 Apr 1877. They lived on a
farm near Redding, Ia. They had Emma Jeanette, Chester Vernon,
Nellie Bernice, Archie Leland, Lloyd George, Wendall Keith , Henry
Henderson, Annabelle Lee, and Ethel Etta. Nettie died 27 Aug 1960
in Audubon, Ia. George Sr. died 21 Apr 1949.

11627 Margaret Jane Lois Mekemson

Maggie was born 21 Mar 1879 in Ia., and may have died young.

11628 Andrew Thomson Mekemson

Andrew was born 15 Sep 1882 in Biggsville, Ill. He married 2 Sep
1903 Effie Belle Lytle in Redding, Ia. The first year of their
married life was spent on a farm near Bassett, Neb. They returned
to Ia., then went west and lived in Prosser, Wash., then Klamath
Falls, Ore. In 1910 they once again returned to Ia. and located on
the old Mekemson farm near Redding. Their children were Herbert
Monroe, Esther Eveline, Eleanor Lucille, Andrew Voight, Harold
Lytle, and Frances. Andrew died 20 Mar 1958. Effie was born 24
Sep 1884 in Sterling, Ill., and died 1 Aug 1960. They were buried
in Ashland, Ore.

11629 Zelza Grace Mekemson

Zelza was born 14 Nov 1883 in Biggsville, Ill., and died there in
Sep 1952. She married 25 Nov 1903 Arthur Wilburn Marts, who was a
bank cashier. For nearly two years they were located in Colorado
City, Colo., then moved to Comstock, Neb. where they remained until

1909 when they moved to Diagonal, Ia. After a year in Ia., they
again moved to a farm near Bassett, Neb. Here Mr. Marts decided to
dedicate his life to missionary work. He was ordained a minister of
the Gospel in the Baptist Church.   Their children were Mildred
Beryl, Marie Jannette, Ila Wilburna, Roland Thomas, Nancy Jo, and
Wilma.   Wilburn was born 20 Dec 1880 and died in Aug 1972 in
Colorado Springs, Colo. Both are buried in Long Pine, Neb.

1162(10) Archie Raymond Mekemson

Archie was born 23 Oct 1887 near Winterset, Ia. He married Mina
Mae Williamson, who was born 9 Sep 1894 in Jasper, N.Y., and died
5 Feb 1985.   They had Edna Pauline, Stuart Evert, and William
Brown. Archie was in the lumber business in Pawnee, and they lived
in Kinsley and in St. John, Kan.   Archie died 10 Jul 1966 in
Creston, Ia.

1162(11) Edna Ethel Mekemson

Edna was born 27 Mar 1890 in Pitzer, near Winterset, Ia. At the
age of 18, she began teaching at a country school, and by 1910 she
was teaching in Manhattan, Kan. She attended Drake Univ. in Des
Moines for a year and a half while she stayed with her sister,
Jessie. In 1921 she was teaching school in the primary grades in
Powell, Wy. There, she met Harold Emil Swenson who was born 22 May
1888 in New York City. They married 22 Aug 1924 in Powell. Edna
and Harold went to Seattle to look for work and they remained there
only a few months before leaving for San Francisco by boat. Their
children were all born in San Francisco: William Herman, Frederick
Harold, and twins, Herbert Jack and Hilma Janet. On Friday, 13 May
1938, the family drove their 1931 Ford sedan, pulling a utility
trailer, to the home of Harold's parents in Dunellen, N.J. Harold
died 3 Jul 1971 in Shippensburg, Pa.   Edna died 14 Jun 1984 in
Maryville, Tenn. Both are buried in Lake Nelson Cemetery in
Piscataway, N.J.

11631 Hugh Caldwell Thomson

Hugh was born 10 Jul 1872 in a log cabin in Madison Co., Ia. When
he was about 15, his father decided to relocate to a farm near
Gordon, Neb. There they lived in a sod house, and there were no
out buildings; living conditions were worse than what they had left
behind in Ia. Hugh even attended school in a sod building before
wooden buildings were erected. Hugh must have left the Sandhills
of Neb., and headed for S.D. There he met Sena Marie White at the
Lee and Prentice Ranch near Vermillion, S.D. They were married 19
May 1897 in Dell Rapids, Minnehaha Co., S.D.   They had three
children: Ethel Ruby, Hazel White, and Ruth May who were all born
in Minn.

Hugh was killed in a train accident while a mail clerk; he died 31 May 1909 in Oeabody, Marion Co., Kan. He was buried in Dell Rapids Cemetery. After Hugh's death, Sena married Henry Andrew Olson in Sioux Falls on 28 Sep 1914. Sena was born 9 Jun 1875 and died 26 May 1966 in Sioux Falls, S.D. Her burial was in Dell Rapids.

11632 William McRobert Thomson

Will was born 4 Mar 1874 in a log cabin in Madison Co., Ia. He made the journey to a ranch west of Gordon, Sheridan Co., Neb. in 1888, and was upset after he realized what a bad move his father had made. He attended school in a sod building with his siblings. Later, a drafty wood school house was constructed. The Thomson children became friends of the Rash family that lived within walking distance. At the age of 36, Will married Pearl Mildred Rash on 8 Jun 1910 in Gordon, Neb. But this was long after the family had left Neb. for Minn. and Ia. Pearl was born 23 Oct 1884 in Wessington, S.D. They had six children, all born in Madison County, Ia., except their second child, who was born near Gordon, Neb., in 1913. The children were Donald Glenn, Kenneth Earl, Dorothy Esther, Hugh Clair, Marjorie Clara, and an unnamed daughter who died at birth on 22 Jan 1927. Will died 25 Apr 1930 in Des Moines, Ia. He was buried in Stringtown Cemetery. Pearl died 13 Jun 1971 in Winterset and was buried with her husband.

11633 Leonard Samuel Thomson

Leonard was born in Madison Co. 28 Sep 1876. He spent his youth in Ia. and in Neb. He served during the Spanish-American War. At the age of 38, he married Lydia Irene Kendall 20 Jan 1915 in Tingley, Ringgold Co., Ia. They did not have any children. Lydia was born 1 Nov 1876 and died 6 Aug 1938 in Shannon, Ia; Leonard died 18 Jan 1952. Both are buried in Tingley Cemetery.

11634 Bessie Agnew Thomson

Bessie was born 25 Nov 1878 in Madison Co., Ia. She moved with her family to west of Gordon, Neb. in 1888 and attended school in a drafty board shanty before a better school house was built. In the winter, she and her siblings did a lot of ice skating and sliding on a toboggan. The 1910 census returns of Sheridan County, Neb., listed a Bessie Thomson living in the household of Alva Rash, very near the time Bessie's brother, William, was married to Pearl Rash. Bessie and Ralph Kench were married 16 Oct 1917 in Storm Lake, Ia. They were childless. Bessie died 6 Apr 1964 in Washington, Ia; Ralph, born 12 Aug 1881, died 13 Jan 1925 in Woodstock, Minn. Bessie was buried in Stringtown Cemetery.

11635 Nan Bard Thomson

Nan was born 10 Jul 1885 in Ia. As a young girl, she was taken by her family to Neb., where they lived in a sod house. Later, the family moved to Minn., then back to Ia. In Winterset, Nan married Andrew John Surratt on 3 Sep 1912. They had four children: Kathryn Cynthia, Margaret Nan, Andrea Jean, and Robert Andrew. The first child was born in Minn., the next two in N.D., and the last one in Ill. He was a crop statistician and gained national recognition. Andrew died in an auto accident in Rolla, Mo., on 18 Nov 1948. Nan died 26 Oct 1962 in Springfield, Ill., and was buried there alongside her husband.

11636 Ray Sherman Thomson

Ray was born 26 Jan 1891 in Sheridan Co., Neb., probably in a sod house. As a young boy, he was taken to Minn., then to Ia. He was educated in schools in Madison Co., Ia. Ray was a veteran of World War One. He married Eunice Caroline Bissell on 27 Jun 1927, making him another of his family to marry late. Eunice was born 5 Dec 1895 in Des Moines and died 11 Oct 1967 in Sandstone, Minn. Ray and Eunice had three children: Lois Ruth, Paul Bissell, and Elmer Hugh. Ray died in Sandstone on 7 Jul 1972 and was buried in Danforth Cemetery, as was his wife.

11641 Anna Rachel Applegate

Anna was born 15 Aug 1872 near Winterset, Ia. On 13 Oct 1892 she married Wilson Edmund Chase. Wilson was born in Madison Co. on 14 May 1867 and died 11 Nov 1938. Their children were Mabel Roberta, Lilla Hazel, and Verl Andrew. Anna died 2 Jul 1944 in Dexter, Ia. Burial was in Chase-McDonald Cemetery located west of Winterset.

11642 Robert Thomson Applegate

Robert, a twin, was born 18 Dec 1874. His twin died at childbirth. He and Mable Iris Fairholms were married 19 Feb 1896 at Fontanelle, Ia. He died in Douglas Twp., Madison Co., seven weeks later on 9 Apr 1896 at the age of 21 years, 3 months, 22 days, and was buried in Stringtown Cemetery. Cause of death was "lung fever and pleurisy." Mable was born 19 Sep 1876.

11643 Ralph Earl Applegate

Ralph was born 5 Apr 1882 in Madison Co. He died when 16 years old, 17 Nov 1898 at Earlham, Ia. Burial was in Stringtown Cem.

11651 William Allison Graham

William was born near Pitzer in Madison Co., Ia., 30 Dec 1870. He married Ora Alma Bonham 30 Dec 1896. Ora was born 17 Mar 1876 in Madison Co., died in Spokane, Wash., 7 Jul 1974. Their residences included Macksburg, Ia.; Fort Shaw, Mont.; and Spokane, Wash. They were members of Metzger Methodist Church. Their children were Mary Edna, Leslie Bonham, George Allison, Clarence Samuel, Merton, Ruby Ellen, and Chester William. William died in Spokane on 16 Dec 1959; both were buried in Pines Cemetery in Spokane, Wash.

11652 Thomas Edward Graham

Ed was born 3 Mar 1872 near Pitzer in Madison Co. He married Charlotte Mabel "Lottie" Johnson in Jun 1908 in Creston, Ia. Charlotte was born 4 Jun 1883 in Creston, Ia. and died in Long Beach, Calif., 27 Dec 1968. They had residences in Great Falls and Fort Shaw, Mont., and Long Beach. Tom was a plant operator for Lomita Gasoline Co. Their children were Philip Edward, Gordon Albert, and Robert Johnson. Tom died in Long Beach 9 Feb 1943.

11653 Robert Culbertson Graham

Robert was born 18 Aug 1873 and died in Creston 28 Oct 1948. He married Mabel Ethel Stewart 9 Mar 1897 in Macksburg, Ia. Mabel was born 26 Jul 1877 and died in Winterset 29 Aug 1943. Robert was a farmer. Their children were Arlie Harold, Earl Stewart, Dorothy, Lorene Mabel, Robert Russell, and Wyman Lee.

11654 Lillian Maude Graham

Lillie was born near Pitzer in Madison Co. 30 Jun 1877. She married Samuel Howell Wimmer 2 Jul 1895 in Orient, Ia. At first Sam continued working on his father's farm, then rented another nearby farm. In 1898 they set off with their possessions in a horse-drawn wagon for Yuma Co., Colo. This venture was unsuccessful, and in 1901 they moved to Turner Co., S.D., where they rented a farm. Lillie barely survived a ruptured appendix and they were forced to return to Ia. in 1904.

They moved several more times, including a period in Fort Shaw, Mont., where Sam opened a general store. The enterprise was successful, however, his store was blown up by town rowdies. Again, they were forced to move, and by 1917 they had arrived in Spokane, Wash. Sam worked in lumberyards, and later became a residence building contractor. Still later they lived in Calif. Lillie was an active church member wherever she lived, and was a member of The Order of the Eastern Star.

Lillie died 2 Dec 1945 in Modesto, Calif.   She was buried in
Fairmont Memorial Park in Spokane.   Sam died 14 Mar 1965 in Spokane
and was buried next to his wife.   Their children were Max Rolland,
Gladys, and Lyle Graham.

11655 Elizabeth Mary Graham

Mary was born 13 Jun 1879 in Madison Co., Ia.   She married Peter
Wesley Jacobson 2 Jun 1909 in Spaulding, Ia. Peter was born 16 Apr
1877 and died in Creston, Ia. 30 Aug 1963.   Their residences were
Spaulding, Ia.; Towner, Colo.; and near Afton, Ia. They had Helen
Marjorie, Victor Graham, Wesley Cassel, Jeanette Eleanor, Alden
Dale, and Newell Edward.   Mary died in Creston on 23 Sep 1956;
burial was near Spaulding.

11656 Jane Grace Graham

Jennie was born 9 Feb 1883 in Spaulding, Ia.   She married Claude O.
Bishop   22 Jun 1904 in Spaulding.   Claude, born 6 Oct 1881 in
Stanton, Ia., was the son of Tracy Straud Bishop and Sara Nicotte
Rogers Moore.   Claude was a telegraph operator and depot agent in
Orient, Ia.   Their children were Myrle Graham, Straud Allison,
Charlotte Mae, and Elizabeth Mary. Jennie died in Indianola, Ia.,
on 11 Mar 1959.   Claude died 2 Nov 1958.

11657 Walter Nelson Graham

Walter was born near Macksburg in Madison Co. 13 Oct 1885. He
finished high school at Cutler Academy in Colorado Springs, Col.,
then attended Colorado College where he was a member of Kappa Sigma
Fraternity. He was quite the athlete, and pitched left-handed for
the college team.   He was also very interested in golf, and he
helped to develop two golf courses.   He started as a farmer near
Orient, Ia., then was a banker in Ia. from 1921 to 1939, and in Oil
City, La. until 1963.   Walter married, first, Olive Mae Stream on
22 Feb 1911.   They had a daughter, Ruth Josephine.   Olive died 20
May 1962.   In Mar 1963 Walter married Adele Smith.   Walter died at
Vivian, La., 6 May 1979.[116] He and Olive are buried in Prairie Lawn
Cemetery in Spaulding.

11658 Samuel Roscoe Graham

Rock, or Roscoe, was born 19 Jul 1888 in Madison Co.   In Chariton,
Ia., on 16 Jun 1908, he married Addie Reed.   He worked for the *Des
Moines Register and Tribune* for over fifty years.   He was a life
member of the Crusade Masonic Lodge in Greenfield, Ia. Roscoe and
Addie retired to Long Beach, Calif., where he died 2 Feb 1968.
Addie, born 31 Oct 1887, died 3 Sep 1972.   They came from large
families but they had no children.

11671 Norma Minta McCorkle

Norma was born 5 Dec 1881 in Madison Co., Ia.   There she married Frank Lawrence Eyerly 28 Oct 1902. Frank was born 1 Oct 1874 in Madison Co., and died 11 Jul 1956 in Los Angeles Co., Calif. Frank and Norma moved to Ridgeway, Mo., and farmed on the north side of town. About 1920 they moved to Brighton, Colo., where they had a grocery store.   In 1940 they went to Calif.   They had four children: Raymond McCorkle, Irma Lorraine, Glenn Lawrence, and Jeannette Alice.[119] Norma died in Pasadena, Calif., 21 Aug 1970; she and Frank are buried in Mountain View Cem.

11672 George Elmer McCorkle

George was born 21 Oct 1883 in Madison Co., Ia., and died 16 Dec 1975 in Earlham, Ia. He married Edith Isabell Benjamin 22 Feb 1906 in Madison Co. Edith was born 31 Oct 1884 in Iowa and died in Jun 1966.   Both are buried in Earlham Cem. Their children were Gladys Delight, Lois Isabel, Walter Edward, and Mary Jeanette.

11673 Nina Elizabeth McCorkle

Nina was born 6 Jan 1886 in Madison Co. She married, first, Guy Lloyd Wright on 11 Aug 1908 in Madison Co., and they had Byrne McCorkle, Wilma Jeanetta, and Elizabeth Ellen. Guy was born in 1887 in Adair Co., Ia., and died 20 Aug 1924 in Pueblo Co., Colo. He had been a railroad worker. Secondly, Nina married Leo Crumby. She died in Pueblo on 9 Oct 1977. Guy and Nina are buried in Mountain View Cemetery in Pueblo.

11674 Mabel Eleanor McCorkle

Mabel was born 12 Feb 1887 in Winterset, Ia., and died 19 Apr 1977 in Lewistown, Mont. Mabel went to Mont., where her sweetheart, Harry Perkins Morse, was working. He had previously mailed her a diamond engagement ring. They were married on 12 Feb 1916 in Lewiston.   Harry was born 27 Dec 1883 and died 10 Jan 1968; Both were buried in Sunset Gardens Cem. Their children were Margaret Jennie, George Nicholas, Edward Lindsay, Ruth Alice, Harry Perkins Jr., and Mabel Eleanor.

11675 Winnie Belle McCorkle

Winnie was born 1 Nov 1888 on the Thomson farm in Jackson Twp., Madison Co., Ia. Winnie was born on the Thomson farm located two miles east of the village of Pitzer. She obtained her elementary education in a little country schoolhouse located near her home. Winnie took note of Claude Light who had moved to near the West

Star Church which they regularly attended. Claude was 5 ft, 7 in. tall, had a light build, and was wiry and agile.

Claude was raised in the farming communities of Douglas Co., Ill., and Whiting and Winterset, Iowa. Winnie and Claude became fond of each other and by the time they were sixteen they had thoughts of marriage. But the parents of both would not hear of a marriage at that early age. The situation became so serious that Winnie was sent to live with her Aunt Jeannette near Redding, Ia., some forty miles away. However, absence made the heart grow fonder and Claude went to Redding where he found Winnie and eloped to Omaha, Neb., and were married 10 Oct 1905. Claude was born 2 Nov 1888 in Coles Co., Ill., and died 20 Mar 1964 in Kansas City, Mo. They farmed in Madison Co., Ia. In 1914, Claude, his father, and their families migrated to Winfield, Kan., where Claude worked at the city ice plant. In 1917 they moved to Wichita, Kan. where Claude worked as a refrigeration specialist in an ice cream plant. In 1922 they were on the move again, this time to Kansas City.

Throughout the depression years of the 1930s, Claude was mostly unemployed. He worked in the laundry of his son-in-law, Clyde Parker, from 1938 to 1947; thereafter he pursued the vocation as a stationary engineer until he reached 65. He and Winnie lived apart during the latter portion of their lives, but maintained a cordial relationship. They had Edson McCorkle, Claude Ivan, George Edward, Helen Onabelle, and Ruth Marie. Winnie died 3 Aug 1966 in St. Luke's Hospital in Kansas City, Mo. Burial was in Floral Hills Memorial Gardens in Kansas City, Mo.

11676 Edna Mae McCorkle

Edna was born 11 Mar 1891 in Madison Co., Ia. She met Elden Landes Sr. who was a widower who farmed about two miles from Ridgeway. He had two children by his marriage to Lillian Maude Jincks: Loren Delane and Lila Delores. Edna and Elden were married 28 Feb 1917 in Bethany, Mo. Six children reached adulthood: Gerald Harlen, Wilbur Lee, Bobby Dean, Elden Jr., Glen D., and Margaret Jean. Edna lived to almost 90 before she died in Ridgeway, Mo., 29 Mar 1980. Elden Sr. was born 9 Nov 1889 in Trail Creek Twp., Harrison Co., Mo., and he died 27 Feb 1966 in Bethany. They are buried in Ridgeway Cem.

11677 Harold Edward McCorkle

Harold was born 28 Jun 1895 in Madison Co., Ia. Harold obtained most of his elementary education at the little country schoolhouse near the family farm. After the family moved to Ridgeway, Mo., he completed his education and graduated from Ridgeway High School in 1916. As a young man, he helped out with the chores on the farm.

Not long after World War One broke out, and Harold enlisted in the U.S. Navy. He spent his entire enlistment stationed in Florida. Afterwards he rented a farm near Athol, Kan. He soon met Mable Hazel Scott of Athol and they were married in Sep 1920. They had several children: Howard Earl, Dolly Walen, Mae Earnestine, Donald Edward, Scott, Margaret Jane, Robert Alden Sr., and Myron George. Mabel was born 27 Jun 1899 and died 28 Apr 1955 at Cedar, Kan. After Mable died, Harold married Ada Hillyard in Henderson Co., Mo. Harold died 21 Sep 1961 in Athol, Kan. Harold and Mabel were buried in Pleasant View Cemetery in Athol.

11678 Jannette Esther McCorkle

Jannette was born 20 Nov 1899 in Jackson Township, Madison County, Ia. Jannette was still living at home with her parents in 1920 when they decided to sell the farm near Ridgeway, Mo., and retire near Jannette's brother, Harold, at Smith Center, Kan. Jannette lived at home during the winter of 1920-1921 and worked at the courthouse for the county assessor, and later worked at an insurance office. She was courted by Ellis Halsie Lary of Hastings, Neb., during that time. She would take the train to Fairbury, Neb., where they would meet on dates. They were married in Fairbury on 25 Jun 1921, and lived in Hastings where Ellis was employed at the lumberyard.

They had three children, Charles Marion, Edward Halsie, and Alice Ann. In 1941 the family moved to Portland, Ore., where Ellis worked for two years. Then they moved to Kelso, Wash., where Ellis worked for the Copeland Lumber Co. until he retired. Ellis was born 21 Jan 1897 in Gentry Co., Mo., and died 25 Sep 1963 in Longview, Wash. He was buried in Cowlitz View, Kelso, Wash. Jannette was a member of the First Presbyterian Church of Kelso and was active in the YMCA in Kelso. Over the years Jannette kept a keen interest in her family, friends, family history, her church and the Bible. Her 97 years of fruitful life is a testament to the strong genetic heritage passed down by the McCorkle and Thomson family lines. She died 6 Dec 1996 in Kelso, Wash., and was buried with her husband in Cowlitz View, Kelso, Wash.

11711 Anna Hazel Weir

Hazel was born 28 Jun 1896 in Henderson Co., Ill. She married 5 Aug 1927, at Idaho Springs, Colo., Albert Marion "Dutch" Salsman. Their child was Robert. Her death came 11 Mar 1985 in Golden, Colo. Albert was born 26 Jul 1894 and died in Mar 1968 in Golden, Colo.

11712 Bessie Lucille Weir

Bessie was born 25(?) Feb 1900 based in part on the 1900 census results. She moved to New Mexico to treat her tuberculosis in the 1920s, and taught school in Raton, N.M. She married Marvin Wayne Bowersox, who was an inventor by trade. Their children were Jean Marie and Lou Anne. Bessie was very active in the First Methodist Church in Roswell, N.M. After her divorce in the 1950s, she went to live near her daughter, Jean. She suffered a series of strokes and died about 19 Nov 1965; she was buried in South Park Cemetery in Roswell, N.M., on 22 Nov 1965. Marvin is not buried there.

11713 William Thomson Weir Jr.

William was born near Biggsville in Henderson Co., Ill., 10 Aug 1905. He married, at Kahoka, Mo., Pauline Dorothy Smith 12 Dec 1926. They had William Ray, Shirley Ann, Milton Smith, Jane Kay, and Carol Marie. William was very successful with the Weir Fruit Farm. William died 11 Jun 1979 in Burlington and was buried in Biggsville Cemetery. Pauline was born 13 Nov 1907 and died 27 Nov 1997 after living her last years in a nursing home.

11721 Jessie Mae Weir

Jessie was born 17 Aug 1883 in Henderson Co., Ill. She married 27 Feb 1907 William John Gibb who was born 15 Mar 1879 in Biggsville and died 30 Mar 1945 of cancer. They had Paul Douglas, John Dale, and Gail. Jessie died ca. 1967 and she and her husband were buried in Biggsville Cem.

11722 Grace Lillian Weir

Grace was born 5 Jun 1886 at Colona in Henderson Co., Ill., and married in Burlington, Ia., on 4 May 1903, Francis Shaw Gibb who was born 21 Nov 1882 and died 31 May 1969. Francis was a farmer, and both were members of the United Presbyterian Church. They had Lloyd, Ellen, Jean, Winifred, Eva, Frances Elizabeth, and Louise. Grace died 1 Apr 1967 in Burlington. Grace and Francis were buried in Biggsville Cem.

11723 Anna Susan Weir

Anna was born 28 Jul 1889 in Colona in Henderson Co., Ill., and died 6 Feb 1974 at Mercer County Hospital, Aledo, Ill. She married Abraham Leonard Brokaw 5 Oct 1909. They owned and operated a farm near Aledo and Viola, Ill. Abraham was born 1 Oct 1888 and was raised on a farm near Raritan, Ill.; he died 9 Aug 1963 in Mercer County Hospital. Burial was in Aledo Cem. Their children were Allan Vandevere, John Weir, Evelyn Ruth, Leonard Harold, Robert Edwin, and Richard Dean.

<u>11724 Roy William Weir</u>

Known as "Ted", he was born 1 Mar 1894 at Stronghurst, Henderson Co., Ill. He married Louise Wittman 26 Aug 1946 in LaSalle, Ill. They initially operated a general store in Biggsville. Later, he followed the carpenter and building trade in the Biggsville community where he spent his entire lifetime. He was a member of the United Presbyterian Church, the American Legion, and the Lions Club. During WW I he served in the U.S. Navy. Louise was born 18 Apr 1900 and was a schoolteacher and storekeeper. Louise died 10 Jan 1973 in Burlington Hospital. There were no children. Ted died 1 Dec 1967 in the hospital in Monmouth, Ill.; he and his wife are buried in Biggsville Cem.[118]

Samuel and "Lizzie" Graham

SIXTH GENERATION

112111 William E. Knowles

William died 30 Nov 1894 in his 18th year. Burial was in Carholm-Knowles (C-K) Cem.

112161 Annie Knowles

Annie was born 27 Jan 1899 at Carholme in North Walsingham Township, Norfolk County, Ontario, and died 21 Feb 1967. She married William McInally and they had a daughter, Mary Lou. William died in 1954. They were members of St. James United Church in Simcoe where Annie was active in her church. They were buried in Oakwood Cemetery in Simcoe.

112162 William David Knowles

William was born 16 Feb 1908 and married Vera Mildred Masterson who was born in 1914. William was elected to Parliament from 1968 through 1979. He taught school before World War II, and for a year afterwards. William then returned to the farm and helped his brother, Evans, with the farm operations. Their children were William Robert and James Kirby. William died 23 Nov 2000.

112163 John Evans Knowles

Evans was born 30 Nov 1914. He married 23 Aug 1957 Shirley J. White, who was born 14 Nov 1926 in Scotia Junction, Ontario. Shirley graduated from New Liskeard Secondary School in 1944, and from North Bay Teacher's College in 1945. She then taught school for 36 years while being very active in her community. They did not have any children. About 1940, Evans assumed management of what was his father's farm, and was joined by his brother, William, in 1947. The farm has grown in size to several hundred acres and was known as "Knowles Brothers Farm", then changed to "Big Creek Farms" when it was sold. Evans was active politically and was elected to Parliament in 1957 and served until 1962. Shirley died of cancer 11 Jul 1999; her body was donated to science and cremated later. Burial was in C-K Cemetery.

112171 William Morley Knowles

Morley was born in 1890 and died in 1976; burial was in C-K Cem. He served in WW I and was wounded. He was married to Evelyn Beacall. Morley was principal of a public school in Thunder Bay, Ontario. Their children are Hugh, Barbara, and Shirley.

112172 Anna Victoria Knowles

Anna was born 13 Mar 1892. She married J. Guy McChesney who was born 24 May 1890 and died 4 Feb 1962. Anna was a school teacher. Their children are Margaret Elizabeth, Laurel, James, and Robert. Anna died 17 Jun 1984 and was buried in C-K Cem.

112173 Leslie Kingston Knowles

Leslie was born in 1895. He served with the Canadian Army in France during WW I and was wounded. He married Grace P. Cline, and they had James and Jeanne. His entire working career was spent with the Ontario Compensation Board in Toronto. Leslie died in 1959; Grace was born in 1898 and died 2 Nov 1975; both are buried in C-K Cem.

Knowles Family, ca. 1942

Front Row, L-R: Leslie Knowles, Evans Knowles, Bob McChesney, Middle Row: Mary Lou McInally, Annie McInally. Back Row: William David Knowles, Vera Knowles, Grace Knowles, Maude Knowles, Morley Knowles, Anna McChesney, Victoria Knowles, Bessie Knowles, William McInally.

112174 Bessie Knowles

Bessie was born 17 Jun 1897. She married James Earl Whitelock, who was born 10 Aug 1895, died 29 Jul 1963. They had no children. Bessie died 30 May 1990 and was buried in Milton, Ontario.

112175 Ella Morgan Knowles

Ella was born 5 Aug 1902. She married Frank Knight and they had William John. Secondly, Ella married William Harris. She went to Calif. where she worked for Paramount Studios as a receptionist and may have had some minor roles in films. Ella died 13 Feb 1994 and was buried in C-K Cem.

112511 George Leonard Fulton

George was born 17 Oct 1900 in Hartford City, Ind. He married Wilma Searcy Wadsworth 12 Jun 1928 in Muncie, Ind. They had a stillborn on 16 Aug 1930, George Leonard II, Anne Wadsworth and Susanna Gray. Wilma was born 13 Jan 1902 and died 29 Sep 1981. Mr. Fulton died 31 Oct 1953; both are buried in Hartford City Cem.

112512 James Peter Agustus Fulton

James was born in the family home in Hartford City, Ind., on 11 Feb 1903. As a young man Jim worked in the Johnston Glass Factory. After high school he chose to attend the University of Illinois. Also attending was Loyce Barnett, born 31 Oct 1903, who was enrolled in the School of Music. Jim and Loyce were married 18 Apr 1923 in Urbana, Ill. They had Molly Jane and James P. A., Jr.

In 1929, around the time of the stock market crashes, Jim, his brother, George, and his father founded the Fulton Glass Co. They produced glass doors, glass shelving, and table tops. Jim was a veteran of World War II, having served with the Army Air Corps in the Galapagos Islands. He was a member of the Board of Directors of Indiana Manufacturers. A Republican, he served as district chairman for nineteen years. Loyce was an associate member of Kappa Kappa Kappa Sorority.

During their later years, they enjoyed travel to South America, Mexico, and Canada. They especially enjoyed river cruising in the U.S. Both were active members of the Presbyterian Church. [From a history of Hartford City.] Jim died 13 Mar 1991 in Ft. Wayne, Ind. Loyce died 28 Apr 1991. Burial was in Hartford City Cem.

112513 Susanna Jane Fulton

Susanna was born 8 Jul 1905 in Hartford City, Ind. There, she was educated in the local schools. She married Charles Huston Goddard Sr. in Jun 1931. Charles was born 23 Nov 1901 in Muncie and was a graduate of Muncie High School and Wabash College. He was president of Joseph A. Goddard Co., a wholesale grocery firm, for many years. He was a member and former Deacon of the First United Presbyterian Church, and a member of the Masonic Lodge and the

Kiwanis Club. They had a son, Charles H. Jr. Mr. Goddard died 6 Mar 1981 in Muncie and his body was cremated.[122] Susanna died 6 May 1997 in Muncie and was placed to rest in the Goddard Mausoleum; her husband's remains were interred in her vault.

112521 Frederick Henry Fulton

Frederick was born 6 Jan 1905. Death occurred 27 Mar 1906. He is buried alongside his parents in Elmwood Cemetery, Sycamore, Ill.

112522 William John Fulton, Jr.

William was born 12 Feb 1907 in Sycamore, Ill. He was a 1929 graduate of the University of Illinois where he was a member of Phi Delta Theta fraternity. He served in the U.S. Army during World War II as a meteorologist. Immediately after the war he became chief of the *Chicago Tribune* London Bureau. In 1949 he moved to Greenwich, Conn., where the family remained until his retirement to Fla., in 1972. He was a reporter for the *Chicago Tribune* for 35 years and served as its U.N. correspondent in New York for many years. William was a member of the Chicago Press Veterans Club.

His first marriage was to Alberdine Hatcher on 19 Jun 1935. Shortly after the wedding, Alberdine became seriously ill and she returned to live with her parents. Secondly, William married Joan Eileen Twelftree in London, England, in 1948. Joan, born 4 Jun 1917 in London, England, was a reporter with the *United Press* in London where she met Bill. Their children were Jill Mary, Sally Ann, Elizabeth, and William Scott. William died 16 Mar 1977 in Sarasota, Fla., largely the result of polio he contracted in 1953.[130] As of 1999, Joan was working as a literary agent and residing in New York City.

112523 Robert Busey Fulton

Robert was born 15 May 1909 in Sycamore, Ill. He attended the University of Illinois and had taken most of the courses required for a degree, but he did not graduate. He went to work for Anaconda Wire and Cable as a mill worker, then worked his way up the ladder to become vice president of the parent company--Anaconda Copper Co. He married Ruth Pogue in the "Little Church Around the Corner" in New York City on 21 Dec 1934. Ruth had worked for Anaconda in a clerical position. They had two children, Pamela and William John, and in 1977 they were living in Sarasota, Fla. Robert died there on 2 Apr 1988. Ruth, who was born 2 Sep 1910 in South Kortright, N.Y., died 4 Sep 1990 in Sarasota. Both were cremated and their ashes spread over the Gulf of Mexico.

112524 Sarah Jane Fulton

Sally was born 5 Sep 1912 in Sycamore, Ill. She was a graduate of the University of Illinois where, in 1930, she met her future husband, James Barrett Reston. They were married 24 Dec 1935 in the Larchmont Avenue Church, Larchmont, N.Y. James was born 3 Nov 1909 in Clydebank, Scotland, which earned him the nickname "Scotty." He came to America with his parents in 1920. James attended school in Dayton, Ohio, and entered college in 1928. After graduation with a A.B. in 1932 from the University of Illinois, James accepted a position with the *Daily News* of Springfield, Ohio, where he was a sports writer.

Jane and James both were newspaper correspondents in London at the outbreak of World War II. James had joined the *New York Times* in London on 1 Sep 1939. In 1942 he was the author of a book *Prelude To Victory*. Later, James was a Washington correspondent and bureau chief for *The New York Times*.[123] Jane and James made their home in Washington, D.C., where James retired on his 80th birthday. During his career Scotty had twice won the Pulitzer Prize, journalism's highest honor. Their children were Richard Fulton, James Barrett Jr., and Thomas Busey. James was author of the book, *Deadline*, *A Memoir*[185], published in 1991. James died 6 Dec 1995.[124] Sally and her son, Tom, both of whom are very interested in their family roots, have been of considerable assistance to the compiler.

112541 Elizabeth Marie Fulton

Betty was born 19 Dec 1919 in Hendersonville, N.C., and grew up in East Orange, N.J. She moved with her parents to Calif. in 1937. While they were living in Palo Alto, Betty commuted daily to San Jose State College. At school she met her future husband, George Frykman. Betty had to quit school because of her father's hospitalization, then she did secretarial work. On 14 Jun 1942 she and George were married. George soon thereafter left for the service in World War II. Betty was able to join her husband when he was sent to different posts. They ended up in Washington, D.C. where George headed up the photography laboratory of the Overseas Technical Unit, Air Transport Command. They have three daughters, Alice Elizabeth, Jean Fulton, and Mary Ellen.

After the war, George returned to school and earned a Ph.D. in history from Stanford University. In 1950 they moved to Pullman, Wash., where George was a professor of history at Washington State Univ. for 37 years. He wrote the history of the university when it celebrated its centennial anniversary, *Creating the People's University: A History of Washington State University*.

Betty and George have done a lot of traveling and have made several trips to Sweden to visit his cousins.

112551 Helen Bennet Fulton

Helen was born 8 Apr 1912. Her first marriage was to Roger Barton Derby. They had a daughter, Angela Fulton. Secondly, she married Rev. Stephen Wilson Ackerman on 5 Sep 1940 in Fort Benning, Ga. They had a son, Scott Fulton Ackerman. Rev. Ackerman also had a son by a previous marriage, Stephen W. Ackerman Jr. Helen attended the Visitation Convent School at Georgetown University in Washington, D.C. She shared classes with her husband at Suwanee Episcopal Seminary at the Univ. of the South, one of the first women to do so. She was director of the Jr. Daughters of the King for the Diocese of Atlanta. She died 25 Nov 1990 in Atlanta, Ga.[128] Burial was in Fort Benning Military Reservation, Columbus, Ga.

Rev. Ackerman was born 3 Jan 1902 and died 29 Jul 1987 of heart failure at the Veterans Administration Medical Center in Atlanta, Ga. Rev. Ackerman was a priest of the Episcopal Diocese of Atlanta and retired from the U.S. Army as a Colonel. He is buried next to his wife.[125]

112552 Walter Scott Fulton, Jr.

Walter was born 4 or 5 Sep 1926. He was a graduate of Emery University of Atlanta with a B.A. degree; his major was English. He had attempted to enlist in the R.A.F. when he was sixteen, but he would have had to relinquish his U.S. citizenship which he didn't want to do. Walter then served with the Merchant Marines, then enlisted in the U.S. Navy during WW II. Later, he was involved with the Georgia Vocational Rehabilitation Program, and spent five years as a state employee at the Atlanta Federal Penitentiary. He also worked with the American Red Cross, and was involved as an interior decorator. His third marriage was to Elizabeth Middleton; no issue. Elizabeth died about 1986. Walter was living in a care center in Cleveland, Ga., in 1998.

112561 Robert Gray Fulton

Robert (Bob) was born 14 Oct 1903 in Hartford City, Ind. Bob had polio when he was three years old, which left him with a bad leg, but he was never heard to complain. He was able to play tennis and he was a good swimmer. He never attended college but did graduate from business school. He was remembered by Dorothy Fulton Cope as one who wasn't interested in studying, but was well liked by everyone. He was never able to live down the time he slept through most of the opera Madame Butterfly. In 1927 he married Elsie Louise

Fulton Family

L-R: Margaret Fulton, Jean Fulton, Robert Fulton, Elsie Fulton

Hopkins who was born 23 Jun 1903 and died 26 Nov 1978.[126] They had
Margaret Louise and Jean Roberta. Bob and Elsie worked for a motor
parts store in Spokane for about thirty years; he was the credit
and office manager, and she was a stenographer and bookkeeper. Bob
was a member of Otis Orchards Community Church, a Mason, a charter
member of the Toastmaster's Club, and past president of the
Wholesale Credit Managers Association. Bob died 23 Apr 1978 in
Spokane, Wash. His body was cremated.[127,135] Their remains are buried
in Forest Cemetery in Coeur d'Alene, Ida.

112562 Richard Wood Fulton

Richard ("Dick") was born 1 Aug 1906 in Hartford City, Ind. Dick
enjoyed tennis, badminton, basketball, and golf. As a teenager he
injured his back from lifting heavy sacks of feed in his father's
store. Later in life this resulted in his having the lower
vertebrae fused. Dick attended schools in Coeur d'Alene, Ida., and
had three years of college, two at the University of Minnesota and
one at the University of Idaho. He worked at the City Beach as a
life guard and in a lumber camp to help pay for his college
expenses. He ended up a banker and was vice-president of First
Federal S & L Assoc.[182] In Superior, Mont., on 1 Aug 1943, he
married Iva Lee Mildred Huffman who was born 22 Jun 1920 in Kossuth
Co., Ia.   They had James Thompson, Richard Wood Jr., Michael
Robert, and David Gray. Richard was a resident of Coeur d'Alene
when he died 1 Feb 1954.[129] He had been active in civic affairs,
was a member of the Rotary Club, the Masonic Lodge, Scottish Rite

and Shrine Club, and the Elks Lodge. He was very well thought of by everyone. Burial was in Forest Cemetery. Iva Lee later married William Howard Potts of Coeur d'Alene.

112563 Dorothy Louise Fulton

Dorothy was born 22 Apr 1917 in Coeur d'Alene, Ida. She attended Oberlin College in 1935. On 20 Jan 1942, in Coeur d'Alene, she married Robert William Cope who was born 13 Aug 1912. Bob eventually took over the family appliance store after the war and sold the business in the 1970s. They retired in Waianae, Hawaii, where Bob gave tennis lessons and Dorothy arranged social events for a condo complex. They had two children, Thomas William and William (Bill) Fulton. In 1983, Dorothy wrote "Remembrances of the Tom and Olive Fulton Family," which was for the benefit of her close family members. She told of the family moving to Saskatchewan about 1912 to farm. Dorothy's mother disliked life on the prairie where the hot winds blew in the summer, followed by blizzards in the winter. Her father, on the other hand, loved the two years they spent there before returning to Coeur d'Alene.

Dorothy's aunt, Anne Fulton, taught English and Latin in Coeur d'Alene and helped Dorothy with her studies. Dorothy considered her aunt a great person who was loved by the entire family. Dorothy recalled that her father had a crystal (radio) set with all its squeaks and squawks, and how thrilling it was to receive a station from Calif. After Dorothy graduated from high school in May 1934, and shortly after her father's death, she applied for secretary to the high school principal. She thinks she was given the job out of sympathy for her family. Dorothy got along splendidly with her brothers whom she dearly loved. Her mother told her that it was seldom that her grandparents had a meal for less than fifteen people, what with visitors, relatives and friends of the children. Grandfather Fulton had a saying for a person of means: "And they could have pie for breakfast!"

Robert Cope died in Hawaii on 27 Nov 1998; interment was in St. Thomas Catholic Cemetery in Coeur d'Alene. Dorothy returned to the mainland to be near her sons and was residing in Tacoma, Wash., in 2001.

112571 Anna Thorne Fulton

Anna was born 19 Nov 1909 in Wash. As the eldest of seven siblings, she was relied on by her entire family. Anna remained single, and operated a bookstore that helped the family survive the Great Depression. Anna died in a car crash on 28 Dec 1936. Their car skidded on ice and collided with a bus.

112572 Marybelle Fulton

Marybelle was born 23 Mar 1914 in Spokane, Wash. In college she majored in fine arts. She married 27 Sep 1939 Karl Zeise and they lived in Needham, Mass. She was editor of a Boston newspaper. Karl was born 12 Mar 1901 and died 24 Nov 1992. He had been a musician for the Boston Symphony. They had Frederick Fulton, Eric Karl, and Karl III. She contributed to a pouch of letters that were circulated amongst the Fulton family. Marybelle died 20 Aug 1969; later, Karl married Janet Weeks Roberts.

112573 Helen Graham Fulton

Helen was born 1 Jan 1916 in Wash., and died 6 Apr 1921 due to an ear infection.

112574 Ruth Eleanor Fulton

Ruth was born 17 Aug 1917 in Spokane, Wash. She married 5 Jun 1943 Dexter Newell Richards, Jr., and they lived in Berkley, Calif. Ruth was a stock trader, a business she conducted from her family home. The family often joked about how Ruth sometimes earned more than her husband the surgeon. Joy Brown remembers her as being "vibrant and vivacious, always there for us as we grew up." Dexter, born 22 Feb 1918, graduated magna cum laude from Harvard Medical School in 1942. He was a flight surgeon with the rank of captain in the U.S. Air Force before he returned to private practice in Berkeley, Calif. They had Ruth Louise, Dexter Newell III and Chesley Fulton. Ruth Eleanor died 25 Nov 1983 in Trinidad, Calif.; she was cremated. Dr. Richards was living in Danville, Calif., in 2001.

112575 Frederick Gray Fulton, Jr.

Fred was born 28 Mar 1919 in Wash. He was a graduate of the University of Idaho with a degree in business administration. He was a 2nd Lt. in the U.S. Army, 10th Infantry Regiment, 5th Infantry Div., when he earned a Purple Heart, and died near Metz, France, 21 Sep 1944 during World War II. He was buried in Luxembourg American Cem.

112576 Virginia Fulton

Virginia was born 27 May 1922 in Spokane, Wash. Virginia received a BA in primary education from Oberlin College in Ohio in 1948. Following graduation she moved to Hood River, Ore. There, she taught in public schools. In Hood River, on 10 Jun 1951, she married Stewart Dalmon Place who was born 2 Aug 1922 in Raliegh, N.D. Stewart was a minister as well as the son of a minister. The elder Rev. Place performed the marriage ceremony. A year after the marriage they moved to Eugene, Ore., so Stewart could continue his education. There, she taught at Condon Elementary School until she they started a family. She was very involved in organizing a Goodwill chapter and as a result received the National Goodwill Volunteer of the Year award in 1961. She served as secretary of the Oregon State Employees Assoc., and was active in her church where she taught Sunday school. Following the death of her mother, Virginia organized Multi-Denominational Church Women's Groups, and set up weekly visitors to every nursing home in Eugene and Springfield, Ore. Their children were Anna Joy, Stewart Douglas, David Fulton, and Melanie Fulton. Virginia died on Memorial Day, 25 May 1981, in Eugene, Ore.[131] Stewart died 30 Jun 1988 in Monmouth, Ore.[132] Burial was in Lane Memorial Gardens in Eugene.

112577 Janet Margaret Fulton

Jan was born 30 Oct 1928. She earned a BA from the University of Idaho. On 22 Nov 1954 she married Wendell Gauger who was born 7 Nov 1927. They had Carl Christian, Christine Anne, Kathryn Helen, and Sarah Fulton. They also supported Doug Place, Jan's nephew. Wendell obtained a Ph.D. in biology and taught at the University of Nebraska. In 1991, Jan and Wendell were divorced. In Nov 1971, Jan had the distinction of being the first woman to be elected to serve on the Lancaster Co., Neb., board of supervisors. She retired from that position after having been presented with many awards and commendations during a sixteen-year career.

112581 Jane Elizabeth Carter

Elizabeth (Betts) was born 21 Jun 1913. She was a 1934 graduate of Oberlin College, where she earned a degree in English. She then taught English at Indiana University and at the University of Illinois before moving to Washington, D.C. in 1943. She was married to Edwin Wentworth (Ned) Kenworthy. They also lived in Baltimore, London, and New York. Betts had worked since 1957 as a writer and editor with Health and Education Resources, Inc. of Bethesda, Md. Betts died 7 Apr 1977 of cancer at Johns Hopkins University in Baltimore, Md.[136,144] Ned was born 23 Sep 1909 in Attleboro, Mass. He graduated from Oberlin College with a master's degree in English. After college, he was an English teacher at Oberlin and Western Reserve Academy in Ohio, Classical High School in Providence, R.I., and at Indiana University. Ned changed careers to become a journalist late in his life: About 1982 he became a reporter for *New York Times* and joined the Washington bureau headed by James B. Reston. Ned died of cancer on 25 Jan 1993 in Washington, D.C.[137] They had John, Thomas and Jane.

112582 Mary Snow Carter

Mary was born 10 May 1915 in Northfield, Minn. She graduated from
Oberlin College in 1936. She married Jacob Wernli Schaefer who was
an engineer on the research staff of Bell Telephone where he helped
design guided missiles. They had William Scott and Joanna Snow.
Mary and Jacob were living in N.J., in 2001.

112583 Margaret Gray Carter

Margaret was born 6 Nov 1918 in Northfield, Minn. In 1940, she
graduated with honors from Oberlin College where she majored in
English. In Cambridge, Mass., she was married on 13 Jun 1941 to
Dudley Bradstreet Tenney who was a graduate of Oberlin College,
then Harvard Law School. He was a partner of a Wall Street firm in
1958.[138] He was a major in the U.S. Army during WW II and served in
China, and elsewhere. Their children are Anne and Janet. Margaret
and Dudley are divorced. Margaret had an apartment adjoining Janet
in 1999.

112584 Bertha Anne Carter

Bertha was born 31 Jan 1926, and was in St. Coletta School in
Jefferson, Wisc., in 1958. She was never married, and was living
in Madison, Ind., in 1977. She died in Oct 1984 in New York City.

112591 Jean Elizabeth Koehler

Jean was born 3 Sep 1913. She married Ben Rogers Gossick 22 Aug
1941. Ben was born 6 May 1914 and died 12 Nov 1977. Children born
to them were Elizabeth Ann, Mary Fulton, Katherine Rogers, and
Victoria Jean. Ben was a member of the physics faculty at Purdue
Univ. He is the author of *Waves in Periodic Structures*, published
by Dover. Jean died 21 Aug 1998 in Lexington, Ky.

112592 Fulton Koehler

Fulton was born 22 Feb 1915. He grew up in Minneapolis and was
president of his senior class at West High School. He attended
Oberlin College in Oberlin, Ohio, and the Univ. of Minnesota, where
he was a member of Phi Beta Kappa. In 1939 he earned his doctoral
degree. His first employment was in the actuarial department at
Northwest National Life Insurance Co. in Minneapolis. After that
he joined the faculty of the Univ. of Minn. in 1942. He became a
professor of mathematics at the university, where he taught from
1942 to 1972. During his career he published many research papers
and was a consultant to several local companies. Fulton left the

university and was co-founder of a company that served as a resource for energy exploration firms. His last experience was with a consulting firm in Houston, Tex., where he was senior vice-president.

Fulton married Mary Jane Confer. Their children are George, Ruth, James, and Thomas. Mary was born 8 Sep 1914. Fulton and Mary were divorced. They were members of the Westminster Presbyterian Church. Fulton died 11 Dec 1988, as the result of a heart attack, at Fairview Southdale Hospital in Minneapolis.[139]

112593 Mary Anne Koehler

Mary was born 16 Nov 1922 and died 8 Jul 1923.

112594 Mary Gray Koehler

Mimi was born 29 Mar 1925 in Minneapolis, Minn. She graduated from the University of Minnesota in 1947 and worked as a teacher for ten years, and as a book seller for ten years, in addition to raising a family. She married Bernard Van Loan Haxby 5 Dec 1944 in Minneapolis. Their children are Robert Gray, William Fulton, James Van Loan, and Mary Alice. In 2001, Mimi was living in St. Paul, Minn. Bernard, known as Jim, was born 30 Nov 1921 and died 28 Dec 1997. His body was cremated and the remains buried in Lakewood Cem. in Minneapolis.

112611 Agnes Isabelle Stirling

Isabelle was born 27 Jan 1906. She was listed in the 1920 census of Chicago as being 13 years old. She lived with her parents in East Orange, N.J., up to 1937, then in Sea Girt, N.J. She inherited her father's estate when he died in 1949. She was never married and may have died in East Orange, N.J.

112621 William Edward Curran

William was born 21 Mar 1911 in Liberty, Mo. He graduated from Purdue University in 1938 with a BS degree and became an industrial engineer. On 5 Sep 1941 in Chicago, he married Alice Marie Hajek who was born there on 30 Sep 1913. Their children were Barbara Alice, Donald Robert, James Edward and Janet Elizabeth.

112622 Margaret Elizabeth Curran

Elizabeth was born 21 Oct 1912 in Chicago and died there 29 Jan 1990. She married Sylvester Joseph "Bud" Tuohey on 18 Mar 1939 in Chicago. Bud was born 3 Dec 1915 in Brooklyn, N.Y., and died 2 Oct 1980 in Chicago. Bud was once vice president of the J.M. Sweeney Co., and worked 31 years for the Iron Fireman Co., manufacturers of stokers. They had Kathleen Mary and Robert Joseph. Elizabeth and Bud are buried in Queen of Heaven Cem.

112623 Robert John Curran

Robert was born 5 Dec 1918 in Chicago. He served in the U.S. Army during WW II and spent time in China, Burma and India. After returning home from the war, he was a machine parts inspector for Lockheed Aircraft. He married Dorothy Dolbert, a widow, on 20 Jul 1987 in Reno, Nev. Dorothy was born 16 Nov 1906 in East St. Louis, Ill., and died 8 Aug 1997 in Los Altos, Calif.

112631 Mary Belle Armstrong

Mary was born 27 Nov 1914 in Cleveland, Ohio. She was a 1932 graduate of West High School in Cleveland. In 1936 she graduated from Lake Erie College at Painsville, Ohio. In 1938 she was working as a clerk and lived with her mother at 10612 Joan Ave. In 1943-44, she was listed as a member of the Women's Army Auxiliary Corps, and was living at 1241 West 112th St, Apt. 6. Mary Belle graduated to become a captain in the U.S. Army.

On 14 Apr 1945 in Hattiesburg, Miss., Mary Belle married John Leonard Maier, who was born 6 Jul 1915. John graduated Cum Laude at Loyola and became a physician. During WW II, he served in the U. S. Army at Shelby, Miss., and later was in practice near Chicago, Ill. They had Mary, John, and Stephen. Mary and John later lived in Saint Petersburg, Fla.

112632 Grace Vivian Armstrong

Vivian was born 24 Oct 1917 in Cleveland, Ohio, and died following surgery for cancer 16 May 1988 in Austin, Tex.[140] Vivian attended Lake Erie College and Western Reserve University. She married 8 Aug 1941 Howard N. Rose in Cleveland. Their children were William S. and Laurence D. Vivian was a member of D.A.R. and AMORC, Martinest. Howard was born 29 May 1913 in Cleveland, and graduated from Glenville High School in 1931. He served with the U.S. Army and the U.S. Army Air Corps during World War II. He was a highly successful manager of the May Department Stores, and after 37 years he retired in 1971. Howard and Vivian then moved first to Austin, Tex., then to Lakeway, where Howard worked as a real estate salesman. He was active in Lakeway civic organizations. Howard was considered to be a genuinely happy and optimistic person. He died 28 Nov 1995 after fighting a lingering illness.[141]

112711 Robert Bruce Cole

Bruce was born 21 Jun 1911 in Moose Jaw, Saskatchewan, and came to the states about 1936. He married Freda Brooke, and they later were divorced. He lived in Coeur d'Alene where he worked as a fireman for Northwest Timber Co. When he died in the Kootenai Medical Center on 19 Jun 1971, he had a step-son, Calvin Lingo, and a step-daughter, Charlotte Morse.[134] He was buried near his grandparents in Forest Cemetery in Coeur d'Alene.

112712 Margaret Isabelle Cole

Isabelle was born 26 Sep 1913 in Saskatchewan. She lost her mother at the age of six and went to live with her grandparents for a short while. When her grandmother died in 1920, she and her brother were placed in foster homes, and saw their father infrequently. When her father remarried, she lived with them from 1927 until the Great Depression. Isabelle then moved to Coeur d'Alene where she found work to support herself. Isabelle studied to become a R. N. from Walla Walla College of Nursing. She married Wayne Albert Scriven 22 May 1944, and they produced three sons, Charles Wayne, Donald Cord, and Richard Ralph. Wayne, a minister, was born 25 May 1914, and received his M.A. from Andrew's Univ. in Berrien Springs, Mich. They make their home in Coeur d'Alene.

112713 Ralph William Cole

Ralph was born 5 Aug 1915 in Central Butte, Saskatchewan, Canada. He was raised by Mrs. Margaret Kerr, of no relation. He married 2 Oct 1939 Jeanette Evelyn Juhnke at Tugaske, Saskatchewan. Jeanette was born 12 Jan 1922 in Tugaske, the daughter of Paul and Hilda Juhnke. Their children were Ronald Ralph, Isabelle Jeannette, and Patricia Faye. Initially, Ralph farmed near Central Butte, and later worked primarily as a storekeeper in Central Butte, Broadview, and Maple Creek. He was active in the Masons and was a member of Central Butte Senior's Club. Jeannette worked as a homemaker and was an active member of the United Church and the Eastern Star. Ralph contracted Guillan-Barre Syndrome, a nerve disorder. He died 28 Jan 1993 in Regina, Sk. Burial was in Moose Jaw Cemetery alongside his mother.

112714 Donald Cole

Donald was born in Mar 1919 in Saskatchewan. His mother died of a child-birth infection shortly after his birth. The doctors couldn't find anything to agree with the baby, and he also perished, in Apr 1919. Donald was buried in the same lot as his mother in Moose Jaw.

112715 Lois Eloise Cole

Eloise was born 25 Jan 1929 in Pasadena, Calif. On 29 Sep 1950 she
married Harold J. Rupp in Pasadena. Harold was born 14 Jun 1913 in
Phoenix, Ariz., and died 5 Jan 1979 in Duarte, Calif; his body was
cremated. Harold worked in Pasadena as an electronics technician in
research and development, and had a hand in developing a camera for
use in the stratosphere. Eloise was a technician in the school
system and helped juniors and seniors in occupational programs.
Their children were Kerry Elizabeth, James Michael, Wayne Riley,
Hugh Jay, and Donna Jean.

112731 Robert William Brumwell

Robert was born 10 May 1910. He married Joan Kirby in London,
England. He was a Colonel in the U.S. Army Reserves and died 13
Jan 1969 in Seattle, Wash., where he had a military funeral and was
laid to rest in Washelli Veterans Cemetery, Seattle. He had been
a member of University Lodge No. 141 F & AM, Scottish Rite Body,
Nile Temple, and the Seattle Reserve Officers Association. Joan
survived him; no issue.[142]

112732 Helen Jeannette Brumwell

Helen was born 15 May 1915 in Moose Jaw, Saskatchewan. She
graduated from the University of Montana, then taught in a high
school for two years before she married William Richard Evans 24
Aug 1941 in Whitefish, Mont. William was born in 1916 and died in
1995. William was a superintendent of schools. Helen has been
active in civic affairs evident by her serving on the school board,
and acting as chairman of the hospital board, her church board, and
the library board. Their children are William Richard Jr., Janet,
and David. Helen makes her home in Red Lodge, Mont.

Wedding Day, 24 Aug 1941

L-R, Front row: Helen Brumwell Evans, Bill Evans, Annie Evans Wood,
Bob Brumwell. Back row: George Brumwell, Janet Brumwell, William
Evans, Eva Evans

112733 George Keith Brumwell

Keith was born 13 Apr 1919 in Morse, Saskatchewan.   He was a
graduate of the University of Oregon, then enlisted in the U.S.
Navy as a dental officer. He was proud of his service in Southeast
Asia during WW II.   Later, he had a dental practice and was a
professor at the University of Washington. He was considered to be
an extraordinary dentist who was well respected locally as well as
internationally. He married, first, Kathy Kernaghan, and secondly,
Susan Johnson in Great Falls, Mont.   He died 17 Aug 1994 in
Seattle, Wash.[143] The funeral was conducted by Bleitz Funeral Home
of Bellevue, Wash., and burial was in Seattle. He was the father
of Pamela Diane, Keith George, and Craig Lloyd.

112771 Margaret Joyce Hughes

Joyce was born 7 Aug 1929. She married Warren J. Norris on 6 Oct
1962. They had a son, Geoffrey. Warren was born 21 Jan 1925 and
died 26 Sep 1981. Warren was an aero engine technician having
retired from the air force in 1975. He enjoyed working at the
Western Development Museum in Moose Jaw until his untimely death.
Joyce graduated as a RN in 1952, worked in Moose Jaw, Vancouver,
B.C., and in Saskatoon, Sk. From 1956 to 1962 she was charge nurse
of the phychiatric department at the Union Hospital in Moose Jaw.
While there she studied and received her certificate of nursing
administration.   Later, she also studied at the University of
Toronto School of Nursing. Her hobbies include needlework, sewing,
gardening, reading, and caring for her dog.

112772 James William Hughes

William was born 10 April 1932. He married Yvonne Richardson 23
Jun 1954. Yvonne was born 14 Sep 1935. They had Beverly Anne,
Arthur William, and Donna Elaine. James joined the Bank of Nova
Scotia in 1952 and was appointed to branches in Manitoba,
Saskatchewan, and Alberta, and worked until 1977. He then purchased
a general Insurance Agency and finally retired from that in 1994.
His hobbies have included playing golf, fishing, camping,
gardening, wood working, and lately, carving birds. They are
residents of Shellbrook, Saskatchewan.

1127(10)1 Margaret Grace Betters

Peggy was born 11 Aug 1923 in Briercrest, Saskatchewan.   She
married Thomas E. Patterson 22 May 1953 in Toronto, Ontario. Thomas
was born 23 May 1919. Secondly, she married Robert James Cameron 17
May 1992 in Victoria, British Columbia. There were no children.

1127(10)2 Dorothy Jean Betters

Dorothy was born 2 Mar 1925 in Moose Jaw, Saskatchewan. She married William Robinson 28 Apr 1947 in Winnipeg, Manitoba. Their four children are Robert Richard, Michael William, Lauri Jean, and James Edward.

1127(10)3 Patricia Louise Betters

Pat was born 6 Nov 1926 in Briercrest, Saskatchewan. She married Joseph Spencer Pearn 1 Sep 1951 in Toronto, Ontario. Their two children are Susan Ruth and Jane Elizabeth.

1127(10)4 Robert Julian Betters

Bobby was born 29 Feb 1928 in Briercrest, Saskatchewn. He married Theresa Abril in Honolulu, Hawaii. Bobby died 16 May 1977 in Honolulu. They had five children: Michelle Tolani, Collette Roberta, Palakiko Frank, John Polimoro, Brenda Joy Schott, and they adopted Joanie Betters.

113121 Wayne Edward McCleery

Wayne was born 22 Jun 1906 (his obit said 22 Jan 1906) in Victor Twp., DeKalb Co., Ill., and died 11 Nov 1953 in Aurora, Ill. He graduated from Waterman Community High School in 1924, then completed a two-year course at the Northern Illinois State Teacher's College in 1926. Wayne continued his education and graduated from the University of Illinois with a bachelor of science degree in education in 1930. He earned a master of science degree in Aug 1935 by attending summer sessions at the University of Illinois. Wayne also took additional summer courses at Northwestern University and at the University of Chicago. He taught in Aurora, and was superintendent at Mokena, Leland, Marengo, and Crystal Lake, Ill. Wayne was a member of several clubs and associations which earned him mention in *Who's Who in American Education*. Upon his untimely death, he was superintendent of West Aurora schools.

Wayne had seen his family doctor about a cold and a sore throat. He was given a penicillin shot, and Wayne collapsed and died soon after leaving the doctor's office due to anaphylactic shock, an allergic reaction to the penicillin.[145]

He was married to Ethel J. Johnson who was born 7 Feb 1907 in DeKalb Co., Ill. They had Nancy Ann and Margaret Beth. After Wayne's death, she married Theodore H. McKee. Ethel died 4 Jun 1985 in Aurora, Ill.

McCleery Accelerated Elementary School in Aurora, built in 1957, is named for Wayne. In the front hall hangs a portrait of Superintendent McCleery.

113171 William Carlisle McCleery Jr.

William was born 23 Nov 1917 in Lisbon, Ohio. He was an ambitious person and was selling magazine subscriptions at the age of fourteen. During World War II he was serving in the U.S. Coast Guard. He was a state trooper, and held a position with the Masons. He married Evalyn Fisher who was born 20 Jun 1916 and died 22 Apr 1998. They had two daughters, Patti Mae and Sandra Sue. Evalyn was a WAC during World War II and later worked as a travel agent. William died 16 Aug 1989 in Hendersonville, N.C.

113172 Margaret Ann McCleery

Margaret was born 12 Nov 1919 in Lisbon, Ohio. She married 24 Dec 1947 Warner Stasel Wolverton who was born 2 Nov 1920 in Alberta, Canada. Both were school teachers. Their children are Elizabeth Ann, Katherine Cristina, John Warner, Mary Margaret, and Martha Susan. The Wolvertons were living in Newark, Ohio, in 1999.

113173 Ralph Addison McCleery

Ralph was born 2 Mar 1922 in Idaville, Ind. He graduated from New Concord High School in 1940, then went on to Muskingum College for three years. He served in the U.S. Army in Africa and Italy during World War II. He returned home and finished his advanced education with a BA in economics. He was an insurance adjuster for a short time with Travelers Insurance Co., a job he didn't like. He then became a salesman for American Sterilization Co., a firm that specialized in hospital sterilization equipment. He married Betty Eaton on 28 Mar 1946 in Smethport, Pa. Betty was born 28 Sep 1922. They lived in Erie, Pa., for 43 years, then moved to be closer to a daughter in Wooster, Ohio. They had two daughters, Deborah Mae and Phyllis Jean.

113181 Wallace Gilbert

Wallace was born 22 Apr 1912 in Hinkley, Ill., and died 10 Dec 1934 of Marfan Syndrome, a hereditary disease that has affected many family members.

113182 Donald L. Gilbert

Donald was born 19 Mar 1916 in Hinkley. He died 15 Feb 1963 in Somonauk. Burial was in Oak Mound Cemetery; a marker was erected. He never married.

113183 Elizabeth Gilbert

Betty was born 10 Jul 1920 in Hinkley. She was married to Horace Eugene Curts 14 Feb 1947 in Victor, De Kalb Co., Ill. Horace was born 9 May 1917 and died 24 Dec 1994 in Quincy, Ill. Betty died 13 Sep 1991. Both are buried in Oak Mound Cem. Their children were James Craig and Denise Lynn.

113191 Hugh Hastings McCleery

Hugh was born in 1925 in De Kalb Co., Ill. He married Joyce in 1955 and they were residing in Leland, Ill. in 1997. Dr. Joyce McCleery was installed as the moderator of the Black Hawk Presbytery of the Presbyterian Church U.S.A., on 9 Jan 2001.

113211 Richard Mallory Graham

Richard was born 13 Oct 1878 near Eden, Kan. He married Mary Alice Dewey 26 Apr 1910 in Ware, Tex. Mary was born 19 Nov 1887 and died in Jun 1976 in Sandwich, Ill. Their children were Hugh D., Charles Anson, Richard Worth, Ruth Alice, Milton Orcutt, Daniel Dean, and Helen Jane. Richard died in Sandwich, Ill., 5 Oct 1960. Richard and Mary are buried in Oak Mound Cem.

113212 Susan E. Graham

Susan was born 26 Mar 1881 in Eden, Kan. She married Harry Souder 29 Dec 1904 in De Kalb Co., Ill. Their children were Grace, Mary, Ralph, Ruth, Richard, Adelbert, and Donald. Harry died 10 Apr 1950; Susan died 15 Oct 1945 in De Kalb Co. Burial was in Oak Mound Cem.

113213 Nora T. Graham

Nora was born 25 Apr 1883 in Sumner Co., Kan. She married 29 Dec 1916 Arthur N. Gordon who was born 2 Nov 1877 and died 12 Aug 1962 in Waterman, Ill. They had Sarah Jane, Jeannette M., and George Graham. Nora died 7 Feb 1934 in Clinton, Ill., and was buried in Oak Mound Cem.

113214 Grace G. Graham

Grace was born 18 May 1885 in Sumner Co., Kan. She married Adam John Boyle 21 Jul 1911 in Waterman, Ill. Adam was born 12 Sep 1875 in Sparta, Ill., and died 25 Jun 1965. Their children were Reid Graham, and Jean M. Grace died 6 Dec 1963 in De Kalb Co., Ill. Burial was in Oak Mound Cem.

113215 Ruth F. Graham
Ruth was born 26 Aug 1889 in Viola, Kan. She and Harold "Roxie"

Nowers were married in Clinton, Ill. 16 Jun 1921. They raised a foster child, Joyce Ann. Roxie died 24 May 1953 in Bushnell, Ill. Ruth died 6 Dec 1972 in Macomb, McDonough Co., Ill. She was buried in Oak Hill Cemetery, Geneseo, Ill.

113216 Helen Daisy Graham

Helen was born 10 Aug 1891 in Viola, Kan. She died in Sandwich, Ill., on 27 Apr 1985 and was buried in Oak Mound Cem.

113217 Margaret Graham

Margaret was born 16 Jun 1894 in Viola, Kan. She died in Waterman, Ill., on 24 Jul 1918 and was buried in Oak Mound Cem.

113251 Andrew Maxwell

Andrew was born 25 Apr 1893 and died 31 Jul 1910.

113261 Margaret Graham

Margaret was born prematurely and died in 1891.

113262 Eva Lucille Graham

Social Security Death Benefit Records give Eva's birth date as 7 Oct 1893. Her birthplace was in Kan. She worked as a registered nurse at Huntington Memorial Hospital in Pasadena, Calif. She was married to James Lyle Marshall 18 Feb 1922. They had James Graham, Robert Howard, and William D. Eva died of heart disease 18 Oct 1988 in Pasadena, and her body was cremated.

113263 Howard Scott Graham

Howard was born 29 Sep 1895. He fought during World War I and was killed in action in France 19 Jul 1918.

113264 Thomas Roy Graham

Thomas was born a twin 3 Apr 1898. His obituary mentioned that he was born in Iowa. The 1920 census listed him as a hired man living with his uncle, Raymond McCleery, in DeKalb Co., Ill. He was never married and farmed near Chandlerville, Ill. He was a member of the Fairdale, N.D., Presbyterian Church and was a veteran of WW I. He died at St. John's Hospital in Springfield, Ill., on 25 Apr 1974.[150] Burial was in Fairview Cemetery north of Chandlerville.

113265 James Ray Graham

James, a twin, was born 3 Apr 1898 in Waterman, Ill., and died 7 Nov 1961 in Springfield, Ill., where he had lived for 24 years.[147] He married Sophia Livermore 2 Feb 1920. They had James Wilson and James Ray Jr. Sophia died 6 Jul 1927. James married, secondly, Bessie L. Quick of Springfield on 7 Mar 1936. He received a B.A. degree from Monmouth College and a M.S. degree from the Univ. of Illinois. He was a former principal and superintendent of schools at Aledo, Easton, and Mason City. He was the author of various publications related to his field of education and has also served as a special lecturer in the field of exceptional children. He was at one time the president of the International Council of Exceptional Children, a past president of the Springfield Rotary Club and past district governor of Rotary International. A small building at North Illinois University is named in his honor.

Bessie was born 11 Sep 1906 in Mason City, Ill., the daughter of John Quick and Minnie Hienefeldt. She was a member of the King's Daughters. She died in Springfield on 29 Oct 1979 and was buried in Oak Ridge Cem.[151]

113266 Maude Greely Graham

Maude was born 27 Mar 1903 and died of cancer on 28 Jan 1957 in Los Angeles, Calif. She attended Monmouth College in the 1920s but may not have graduated with her class of 1927. She never married and once lived in Temple, Calif., where she gave music lessons at home.

113271 George Wiley Beveridge

"G. Wiley" was born in Ill., 7 Dec 1896. In 1920, he, his parents and siblings were living in Goldfield, Ia. He married 18 Aug 1928 Margaret E. Gracey and they had a son, Reid Kyle. G. Wiley was a newspaper man in Williamsburg, Ia., and compiled a family history of his forefather, James McCleery, in 1962. Wiley died 22 Dec 1976. Margaret died 22 Jan 1995; burial was in Williamsburg, Ia.

113272 Luella Beveridge

Luella was born 17 Aug 1898 and died of spinal meningitis 27 Jan 1920 while attending Monmouth College. Burial was in Glenwood Cem. in Goldfield, Ia.

113273 Hugh Raymond Beveridge

Hugh was born 21 Dec 1899 in De Kalb Co., Ill., and attended school in Goldfield, Ia. In 1918, Hugh came to Monmouth College in

Illinois to do military duty under the Student Army Training Corps, the World War I equivalent of ROTC. Hugh was a 1923 graduate of Monmouth College. He earned his Ph.D. from the University of Illinois in 1929 and assumed the position of head of the math department. He married 6 Aug 1932 Dorothy Mertz who was born 2 Aug 1898 in Gladstone, Mich. She attended Lawrence College and Michigan Normal School in Marquette, Mich. After World War I she lived in Chicago and taught school in Chicago suburbs. Their children were Robert Hugh, Donald Reid, and Dorothy Jean. Hugh served Monmouth from 1929 until 1961 as a professor of mathematics and dean of the College. Dorothy served the College for 46 years as a hostess, sorority advisor, and friend. In 1988 the Hewes Library had been renovated and several rooms on the second floor were named in their honor. Their son, Don Beveridge, spoke eloquently of his parents at the dedication ceremony.[149] Hugh died of cancer 31 Dec 1961. Dorothy died suddenly of a heart attack 15 Mar 1978 in Monmouth. Both are buried in Warren Memorial in Monmouth.

113274 Reid Graham Beveridge

Reid was born 20 Oct 1901 near Goldfield, Ia., and died 5 Jun 1988 in Memphis, Mo.[152] He was never married and was a member of First Presbyterian Church. He attended schools in Goldfield and was a graduate of Monmouth College in 1925. He worked several years in Chicago, then purchased a small farm near Arbela, Mo. Later, he retired to Memphis, Mo. Burial was in Glenwood Cemetery, Goldfield, Ia.

113275 Glen Walker Beveridge

Glen was born 21 Aug 1903 near Goldfield, Ia., and died[153] 5 Mar 1991 in Clinton, Ill. He was a 1924 graduate of Monmouth College. A newspaper publisher, he had purchased Heyworth Star in 1934 and was publisher and editor until 1972. He was a member of the Presbyterian Church where he was an elder and sang in the choir. He was a member of the McLean County Farm Bureau, and Illinois Press Association, and was at one time the president of Heyworth Lions Club. In Sparta he married Elizabeth V. McLaughlin 22 Aug 1928; they had a son, James Martin. Elizabeth was born 22 Jun 1903 and died in Apr 1972. Both were buried in Heyworth Cem.

113276 Ralph Beveridge

Ralph was born 12 Mar 1905 and died 27 Mar 1905.

113277 Paul Hutton Beveridge

Paul was born 3 Jun 1909. He was a Monmouth graduate with the class of 1934. He and his wife of 51 years, Elizabeth Helen Henry, lived in Palo Alto, Calif. They were married 5 Oct 1946 and had a daughter, Diane Winslow. Paul died in Sep 1998.

113278 Jeanette McCleery Beveridge

Jeanette was born 17 Jan 1913. She was a graduate of Monmouth College in 1935. She married 3 May 1941 Owen Kramer of Chandlerville, Ill. Jeanette died 6 May 1968; Omar died 4 Mar 1998. They had Linda Margaret and Kent William.

113281 James Austin McCleery

James was born 4 Oct 1895 in Waterman, Ill., and died 6 Oct 1958 in Hampton, Ia. He married 4 Oct 1916 Eva Muryl Shannon at Sioux Falls, S.D. They had Eileen Lucille and James Austin Jr. Eva was born 28 Jul 1896 in Clarksville, Ia., and died 8 Oct 1979 in Hampton, Ia.

113282 Helen Adelaide McCleery

Helen was born 10 Aug 1898 at Waterman, Ill. Her first marriage was to Guy E. Walker 15 Nov 1915. Guy was born 9 Jul 1897 at Decorah, Ia. They had Richard Lee Sr., Bobby, DeWayne Edwin, and Charles LaVerne. Secondly, she married Orland Postle of Medical Lake, Wash., who had four daughters from a previous marriage. Orland was born 6 Feb 1890 at Danville, Ill., and died 12 Jan 1971 in Airway Heights, Wash. Helen died 24 Apr 1971 in Lancaster, Calif.[148] She had been a resident of Airway Heights for 23 years.

113283 Kathryn McCleery

Kathryn was born 4 May 1900 and died 10 Sep 1903.

113284 Lee R. McCleery

Lee was born 11 Jan 1902 and died of measles in Feb 1920.

113285 Mary Elizabeth McCleery

Mary was stillborn 7 May 1905.

113286 Margaret McCleery

Margaret, with no middle name, was born 2 Sep 1906 at Waterloo, Ia. On 10 Dec 1927 she married Rev. Mervin H. Wright who was born 29 Jun 1905 at Lancaster, Ill., and died in May 1969 in Ind. They had Dorothy Jeannette, Mervin McCleery, William George, Robert Lawrence, Margaret Ann, Grace Eileen, James Merrill, and John

David. Margaret died 28 Aug 2000 in Lakewood, Calif.

113287 Ruth Jeannette McCleery

Ruth was born 14 Jun 1908 at Waterloo, Ia. She married 3 Feb 1940
Kenneth Charles Wielert, who was born 19 Aug 1908 at Waterman, Ill.
They had a daughter, Karen Elizabeth. Ruth was employed as a
nurses aide in the Hammond-Henry Hospital in Geneseo. Kenneth was
an employee of Skinner's Meat Market and the De Kalb Locker
Service. All three were killed instantly in an automobile accident
on the night of 23 Jul 1966 on Hwy 81 west of Geneseo, Ill. They
were buried in Lutheran Church Cemetery located west of Hinkley,
Ill.

113291 Raymond Oswald McCleery

Raymond was born 16 Sep 1916 and died in 1932 in Kansas City, Mo.

113292 Margaret L. McCleery

Margaret was born 15 Jun 1919 in Ill. She was adopted by her step-
father, Clarence W. Tombaugh, and attended school in Kansas City,
Mo. Her first marriage was to Rollan LeRoy Hearn 12 Jun 1937; he
was killed in a gory motorcycle accident 26 Nov 1944 in Kilgore,
Tex. Interment was in Floral Hills Cem. in Kansas City, Mo. They
had James, Ruth, and Twila. Margaret was most definitely not the
typical upstanding McCleery. Margaret later married Creighton Roy
Francis[154] then James Nelson Wasson. Margaret was murdered in a
western state about 1962.

113511 Bruce L. Beveridge

Bruce was born 15 Nov 1889 in Lenox, Ia. He married Rachel
Campbell, and they had a son, Reid Garfield. Rachel died in 1941;
Bruce died 19 Dec 1963 in Iowa Methodist Hospital in Des Moines.
He came to Ames, Ia., in 1953 where he managed Ames Stationers up
until his death.[155] Burial was in Oak Mound Cem.

113512 George Maxwell Beveridge

George was born 8 Feb 1901 in Kenton, Harding Co., Ohio. He married
Elizabeth Loy Welker 15 Sep 1934. Elizabeth was born 27 May 1899
in Pittsburgh and died 20 Oct 1971 in the same city. George
graduated from the University of Colorado with a degree in civil
engineering, then worked at Republic Steel Corporation. Their
children were Elizabeth Welker and Mary Ann. George lived in Mt.
Lebanon, a Pittsburgh suburb, and was an elder of the Southminster
Presbyterian Church. George died 28 Jan 1969 in Mercy Hospital in
Pittsburgh and was buried in Homewood Cem.[159]

113513 Wilson McNitt Beveridge

Wilson was born 18 Apr 1903 in Somonauk, Ill. He graduated from Iowa State College in forestry, and worked for the U.S. Forest Service in N.M. and in Ariz. In Phoenix, he married Retha Bolding; no known children. Wilson died 2 Jun 1964 in Sun City, Ariz.

113514 Mary Elizabeth Beveridge

Known as Elizabeth, she was born 22 Jul 1905 in Somonauk, Ill. She obtained her social security card in New York state. Elizabeth was a graduate of Colorado State in 1928 and received a master's degree in 1934 from Iowa State College. She returned to Ames in 1953 as professor and head of household equipment in the department of home economics. From 1963 to 1966, she participated in the Ford Foundation's Baroda project at Baroda University in India. Elizabeth was author of the book, *Choosing and Using Home Equipment*. She died at Mary Greeley Hospital in Ames 14 Feb 1978 after having suffered several years with arthritis.[156] Her body was left to the University of Iowa for research.

113521 Ralph Hayes Beveridge

Ralph was born 11 Jan 1904 in Buckingham, Ill. He graduated from Ripon College, Wisc., in 1925, and worked for Kable Printing Co. On 22 Feb 1936 in Oregon, Ill., he married Harriet Lillian Thomas. Harriet was born 19 Dec 1910 in Oregon, and died there 24 Mar 1988. She was a graduate of Northern illinois Univ., and had a teaching career. Their child was John Thomas. Ralph died in Mar 1987 in Oregon, Ill.

113522 Helen Mae Beveridge

Helen was born 10 Jan 1907 in Oregon, Ill. She graduated from Monmouth College, and received a master's degree from the University of Mich. She was assistant professor of English for foreign students at U. Ill. She married John W. Brennan 12 Jun 1952 in the Panama Canal Zone. They had no children. John was born in 1894 and died 4 Feb 1955; he was a veteran of WW II. Helen died 22 Mar 1964 in Urbana, Ill. Both are buried in Oak Mound Cem.

113551 Evalyn Mary Beveridge

Evalyn was born 8 Jul 1902 in Humboldt Co., Ia. She was unmarried and died 18 Feb 1994 at Rusk County Memorial Nursing Home in Ladysmith, Wisc.[158] Burial was in Woodlawn Cem. near Sheldon.

113552 Willard Albert Beveridge
Willard was born 2 Nov 1903 in Humboldt Co., Ia. He died 7 Sep

1966 in Chippewa Falls, Wisc., and was buried in Woodlawn Cem.

113553 Rea Maxwell Beveridge

"Max" was born 29 Dec 1907 (or 1908?) in Cambridge, N.Y., and   He was not married, and died in Sep 1980 with burial in Woodlawn Cem.

113554 John Beveridge

John was born 2 Oct 1911 in Evanston, Ill. He died 20 Nov 1920 in Chippewa Falls, Wisc. He was not married. Burial in Woodlawn Cem.

113555 Wallace Beveridge

Wallace was born 2 Sep 1917 in Sheldon, Wisc. He died on the family farm 5 Mar 1958.[157] Unmarried, he was described as having a cheerful, loving disposition. Burial was in Woodlawn Cem.

113581 Albert Henry Beveridge

Albert was born 10 May 1910 in Moose Jaw, Saskatchewan, Canada. He attended Piedmont College in Demorest, Ga., and worked for International Harvester Co. in Indianapolis, Ind. He enlisted in the military during World War II. He was captured during the Battle of the Bulge and was held in Stalag 10B. When a Russian prisoner was shot the bullet ricocheted and hit Albert who was not in the best of health to begin with; he died 5 Mar 1945 and was buried in the U.S. Military Cemetery, Neuville-en-Codrez, Belgium. He was not married.

113582 John Ronald Beveridge

John was born 21 Nov 1911 in Moose Jaw, Saskatchewan. He graduated from Piedmont College in Demorest, Ga., in 1933. John served in the U.S. Army during World War II and retired as a reserve Lt. Col. He later was employed at a textile firm, then became Personnel Officer of the Youth Development Center in Augusta, Ga. John was a military historian and a member of the Sons of the American Revolution. He wrote a supplement to the *Somonauk Book*. He married Edith E. Schmiedeskamp in Atlanta, Ga. on 23 Apr 1955. Edith was born 1 Feb 1921 in Radersburg, Mont. She received training as a nurse at Peabody College, Nashville, Tenn., and was employed by the Richmond County Health Dept. in Augusta. Their children were Alice Anne and Albert Henry II. John died[184] 18 Sep 1978 at Fort Gordon, Ga., with burial was in Yonah Memorial Gardens in Demorest, Ga. Edith was living in Augusta in 1999.

113583 Dorothy Margaret Beveridge

Dorothy was born 20 Feb 1913 in Yellow Grass, Saskatchewan, Canada.
She was a student at Piedmont College, then was employed as a civil
service employee in the USDA. She also worked as a clerk in a
textile firm in Cornelia, Ga. About 1940 she became interested in
genealogy which led to her becoming an active member of the DAR.
She married Frank Michael Joyce on 20 Mar 1954 in Atlanta, Ga.
Frank was born in Cleveland, Ohio, 14 Jul 1907 and died 7 Jun 1991.
He attended Toledo College, Toledo, Ohio. During WW II he served
with the Underwater Demolition Team in the Navy Seabees in the
South Pacific with the rating of Chief Petty Officer. He was a
construction engineer for large corporations. His last assignment
was on the staff at Clemson University, Clemson, S.C., as a
resident engineer.[160]

113661 Donald D. Howison

Donald was born 31 May 1910. He died 4 Aug 1916 after falling off
a wagon which then ran over him. He was buried in Oak Mound Cem.

113662 Evelyn Mae Howison

Evelyn was born 10 May 1920 in Kansas City, Mo. She graduated from
Waterman High School and Monmouth College. She received a master's
degree from Northern Illinois University in DeKalb, and taught
English in high school for 17 years before she retired. She was
very active in the Somonauk Presbyterian Church. During WW II, she
was in the U.S. Navy as a WAVE, stationed in Hawaii. She married
Raymond J. "Pat" Lafferty 20 Apr 1946 in Somonauk. Pat was born 17
Jul 1912 and died 15 Jul 1995 in Somonauk, Ill. Their children
were Richard James, Michael Ralph, and Patrick Kevin. Evelyn died
of cancer in Somonauk on 25 Mar 1999 and was buried in Oak Mound
Cem.

113663 Robert Wendell Howison

Robert was born 25 Nov 1915. He married Margaret "Florence"
Sylogye who was born 16 May 1921. Florence was of Aurora, Ill.,
and was a nurse. They had a daughter, Margaret Helen. Robert died
31 Mar 2001 after being a resident of a De Kalb County nursing home
for a few years. Florence died 8 Mar 1981 in the Sandwich
hospital; both are buried in St. Michael's Cem. in Aurora, Ill.

113721 James Hoy Beveridge II

James was born 6 May 1907 in Somonauk, Ill. He married Ruth Vera
Goynes 15 Oct 1927. Their children were Jacqueline Isabelle and
James Hoy. James was a farmer and died 4 Mar 1972 in Aurora, Ill.

Burial was in Oak Mound Cem. He wrote *Church of the Pioneers* about 1971, a history of the United Presbyterian Church located near Somonauk, Ill. Ruth was born 30 Nov 1907 at McVeytown, Pa., was living in Aurora, Ill., in 1964, and died in Madison, Wisc., on 12 Jan 1989.

113722 Margaret Jean Beveridge

Jean was born 16 Oct 1914 at Somonauk, Ill. She served as a secretary for the United States Relief and Rehabilitation administration during WW II. Later, she worked for the Franklin D. Roosevelt Foundation and assisted Grace Tully in editing and publishing Tully's book, *F.D.R., My Boss*. Also, she was Advertsing and Nielsen Marketing Research Coordinator for Lever Bros., New York City. She married 14 Oct 1964 Franklin Newhall who was born 13 Jan 1914 in Chicago. In 1932, he graduated from high school in Muskegon, Mich. He then received a BS from the University of Chicago in 1939 and was a chemist with US Steel Corp. until 1942. He served as a meteorologist and weather forecaster in the Army Air Corps from 1943-1946, and retired a major. He received a master's degree in 1947 from the University of Iowa. He then worked for the US Department of Commerce. They were living in a retirement community in Bowie, Md., when Margaret died 15 May 1999.

113723 Thomas Robinson Beveridge

Tom was born 30 Jun 1918 near Sandwich, Ill. He graduated from Monmouth High School, and at Monmouth College he earned a BS degree in geology. Next, he received a BS in mining engineering from Missouri School of Mines in 1942. He then enlisted in the U.S. Army Air Corps and served as a navigator in heavy bombardment based in Italy. He completed almost fifty missions over Europe including strikes on oil refineries in Romania. On one mission, Tom's plane was shot at and damaged after a bombing mission over Ploesti and was forced to ditch in the Adriatic Sea. The bombing seriously crippled the Luffwaffe. In 1944 he returned home and received the Purple Heart and the Distinguished Air Medal. After his military career, he continued his education by earning a Ph.D. at the University of Iowa in 1949. He was professor of geology at the University of Missouri-Rolla and became chairman of the department. Tom died 25 Aug 1978 in Rolla, Mo.[161] His lengthy obituary and eulogy by the editor of the Rolla newspaper attested to his fine character. He was highly intelligent, well-liked, and always willing to serve his fellow man. Burial was in Oak Mound Cemetery near Somonauk, Ill. He was married to Nancy Mary Lytle 12 Jun 1946 at Monmouth, Ill. Nancy was born 11 Apr 1921 at Youngstown, Ohio. They had Nancy Lourie and Mary Isabelle.

113741 Thomas Clyde McCoy Robinson

Thomas was born 17 Aug 1912 at Grassy Lake, Alberta, Canada. He
was a graduate of Monmouth College. He married 1 Jan 1942 Doris
Ethel Loehr who was born 13 Nov 1919 at Mystic, Ia. Thomas was
with the State Dept. until 1951, then became director of Program
Operations Division, World Food Program in Rome, Italy. Their
children were John Clement, Margaret Jill, Samantha Jane, Kathleen
Jean, and Cassandra. Thomas died 6 Dec 1984 in Harlingen or
Cameron, Tex., and was buried in Oak Mound Cem.

113742 James Keith Robinson

James was born 24 Jul 1916 on the Robinson farm which was located
five and a half miles south of Waterman, Ill. James was in the
U.S. Navy during WW II, with the rank of LCDR. He earned a BA at
the University of Tenn., then a MA and Ph.D. at Harvard. He taught
for ten years at Northwestern University, then he became Professor
of English at the University of Cincinatti. On 11 Jul 1945 he
married Pamela Ruth Lyne at Plymouth, England. Pamela was born 16
Jul 1924 at Dartmouth, England. She taught speech and theatre at
UC. Their children were Christopher Lyne and Nicholas Keith. James
died 4 Jan 1993 in Cincinnatti and was buried there in Spring Grove
Cem. Pamela was living in Albany, Calif., in 2001.

113743 John Beveridge Robinson Jr.

John was born 5 Oct 1917 at Waterman, Ill. He was a graduate of
the University of Tennessee with a bachelor of science degree in
commerce. He then became a certified public accountant and a
partner in the firm of Arthur Andersen and Co. He married 26 Jun
1948, at Chicago, Elizabeth Jane Brown who was born 16 Aug 1924 at
Chicago. Their children were Jean Kathleen and Kay Louise. John
was contacted and generously provided the compiler with a copy of
the Robinson Genealogy.

113761 Kenneth Wallace Black

Kenneth was born 10 Dec 1912 at Peoria, Ill. He was an accomplished
tennis player and served as captain of the Peoria High School and
Bradley University tennis teams. He won the greater Peoria singles
championship ten times, and doubles championship 14 times. He
graduated from Bradley University in 1934, then the University of
Chicago Law School in 1937. He had a law office in Peoria and in
Washington, Ill., and was senior partner in the law firm Black,
Black and Brown. He served on the board of directors at First
National Bank for over 25 years, and was an active citizen of his
community. He married 10 Aug 1938, at Peoria, Edith Adele Lowry
who was born 15 Mar 1914 in Peoria, and died 15 Sep 1977. Their

children were Barbara Kay, Kenneth Lowry, and Bruce Wallace. Kenneth later married Dorothy Powell. He died 11 Jul 2000 in Washington, Ill., and was buried alongside Edith in Glendale Cemetery in Washington.

113762 Constance Isabel Black

Constance was born 29 Sep 1916 at Proctor Hospital, Peoria, Ill. In Peoria, she was married 21 Jun 1941 to Glen Lafon Borden who was born 8 Jan 1911 at Edison, Neb. Glen was a resident of Wyoming, Ill., when he died 13 Sep 1988 at Methodist Medical Center in Peoria.[162] Glen graduated from Kearney State Teachers College in 1935. He then attended Stanford University and the University of Iowa where he received a master's degree in history in 1940. After a brief teaching career, he attended the University of Illinois Law School and was admitted to the Illinois Bar in 1942. He received his juris doctor degree from the University of Illinois in 1953. During World War II, he was a lieutenant in the U.S. Army and received the Purple Heart. He practiced law in Peoria and Wyoming. Glen was buried in Linn-Mount Vernon Cemetery in Washburn, Ill. Their children were Scott Wallace and Stuart Paul. Constance was living in Wyoming, Ill., in 2001.

113771 Jean Elizabeth Potter

Jean was born 7 Feb 1918 at Chicago, Ill. Jean is a graduate of Iowa State College where she studied to become a dietician. In Sandwich, Ill., she married 21 Oct 1939 Albert Ernest Ehrke who was born 29 Aug 1914 at Randolph, S.D. They had Thomas Wendell and Jean Elizabeth. Albert was also a graduate of Iowa State with a B.S. degree in mechanical engineering; he then worked as a manufacturer's representative. In 1964 they were living in Cleveland, Ohio, and in 1998 they were in Boynton Beach, Fla.

113772 Jo Ann Temple Potter

Jo Ann was born 9 Oct 1925 at Eureka, Ill. She studied at Iowa State College (now Iowa State University), at the University of Minnesota and at Kent State University. Jo taught school in suburban Cleveland. On 14 Jun 1947 she married Albert Henry Taube who was born 11 May 1925 at Geneseo, Ill. Albert received his advanced education at Coe College in Cedar Rapids, and at Iowa State College, and became a forester with the Bureau of Land Management. He died 3 Jun 1960 at Eugene, Ore., and was buried at Geneseo, Ill. Their children were Eric Paul, David John, Kathryn Ann, and Jean Marie. Jo Ann was living in Solon, Ohio, in 1998.

113821 Marian McCleery
Marian was born 12 Aug 1904 and died 8 Apr 1982. She was

handicapped and never married.   She lived in Vegreville, Alberta, Canada.

113822 Evelyn McCleery

Evelyn was born 29 Aug 1908 and died 21 Feb 1976 in Vermilion, Alberta.   She married 27 Jun 1933 in Vegreville, Alberta, Clifford Edwin Cunningham.   Edwin died in 1956.   They had Bruce Wesley, Allan Howard, Clifford Edwin, and Rex Burton.

113823 Ruth McCleery

Ruth was born 15 Jul 1909, and died 24 Jun 1992, in London, England.   She married Digby Lloyd Stephens 2 Aug 1939 in London. Their children were Digby Lloyd, Hedley, and Gareth.   Ruth's death notice appeared in the *London Times* on 30 Jun 1992.[163]   It mentioned that her husband had predeceased her, and that she had the above named sons as well as five grandchildren.   Digby died 16 Feb 1971 near London.   She was described as "a treasured Aunty and steadfast friend to many in this and other countries around the world."   Her body was cremated.

113824 Marjorie McCleery

Marjorie was born 7 Jan 1911 in Vegreville, Alberta.   She married 14 Sep 1937 Howard M. Wilson in Ohio.   They had no children. Marjorie died 20 Mar 1995 in Butler, Pa.   Howard was born 18 May 1903 and died in Dec 1974.

113831 Mary Jeanette McCleery

Mary was born 11 Aug 1904 in Ia., and died 22 Jun 1995 in Menlo Park, Calif.   She married Dr. John R. Christensen 17 Jan 1970. John was born 29 Sep 1886 in Ia., and died 24 Dec 1975 in Calif.

113832 Irene Ellen McCleery

Irene was born 22 Oct 1908.   She married 1 Jan 1931 G. Hugh Foster.   Their baby was born 10 Jan 1933 and died 19 Jan 1933. Irene died during childbirth on 10 Jan 1933.

113833 Lois Isabel McCleery

Lois was born 6 Dec 1912, and died 26 Jan 1913.

113834 Sarabelle McCleery

Sarabelle was born 6 Mar 1914 in Edmonton, Alberta, Canada.   She was a graduate of Monmouth College in 1936, and was director of child services in Ore. and Calif. She was living in El Cerrito, Calif., in 2001. She never married.

113871 Howard Dean McCleery

Dean was born 23 May 1918 in Chicago. He married 16 Aug 1941 Mary Ann Vejupek in Cleveland, Ohio. Howard was a graduate of Butler High School in Indiana. He then attended Tri-State University where he graduated as an electrical engineer in 1939. He worked for Fairbanks-Morse, then as a self-employed manufacturer's rep for twenty six years. They had David Dean and Richard Frederick. They make their home in East Aurora, N.Y.

113872 Beatrice Belle McCleery

Beatrice (known as Bea) was born 3 Jul 1922 in Chicago, Ill. She was a 1940 graduate of Butler, Ind., High School. She and Warren Emory Snyder eloped and were married 4 Oct 1940 in Elkhart, Ind. Their six children are Jerry Lee, Roger Allen, Keith Eugene, Linda Ann, Lance Robinson, and Michael Warren. Warren was born 31 Aug 1916 and died in Aug 1982. Beatrice died 30 Mar 2000; Warren and Beatrice are buried in Butler Cem.

113881 Jane E. McCleery

Jane was born about 1915 and died soon after birth.

113882 Mary Alice McCleery

Mary Alice was born 28 Sep 1920 in Chicago, Ill., and died 26 May 1996 in Fort Walton Beach, Fla. In Berea, Ohio, she married Henry Rockwell on 4 Oct 1940. Henry died 30 Nov 1997; both were cremated. Their children were David William and Robert Henry.

113883 William Ashenhurst McCleery

William was born 13 Mar 1925 in Chicago, Ill. He was a graduate of Baldwin-Wallace College in Berea, Ohio, in 1949, then spent a year at Michigan State before he earned a master's degree at Kent State in 1962. He was a high school and college educator. He married 7 Sep 1946 Iris Olsen. Iris holds a BS degree in home economics from Michigan State. She worked at St. Lukes in Cleveland and after marriage she was dietician at Baldwin-Wallace. She later received a teaching certificate and taught from 1963 to 1980. William died 10 Nov 2000 and was cremated. They had Carol Anne and Nancy Louise. Iris was living in Berea, Ohio, in 2001.

113891 Grace Eileen McCleery
Eileen was born 20 Oct 1922 in Doleib Hill, Sudan. She married

Paul Hawthorne Johnson on 2 Sep 1950.   Their children were Eric
Roe, Mark Hawthorne, and Marcia Jean.   Eileen had a master's degree
and was a pediatric nurse.   Paul earned a BS in engineering from
Pitt and a MS from Stanford, and was a sales engineer for Air
Control Products of Cleveland.   Paul also served in the U.S. Army
during WW II.   Paul was born 3 Jun 1919 in Crafton, Pa., and died
11 May 1984 in Waverly, Ohio, followed four days later by Eileen's
death; both are buried in New Concord, Ohio.

113892 Dorothy Ruth McCleery

Dorothy was born 14 May 1927 in Cleveland, Ohio.   She attended
Muskingum College in New Concord, Ohio, and earned a BA in home
economics and English in 1948.   In 1951 she received an MRE at
seminary in Pittsburgh.   She occasionally taught school at several
locations.   She married 16 Jun 1951 David Asbury Redding in New
Concord, Ohio.   David was born 24 Nov 1923 in Marietta, Ohio.   Their
children are Marion Telford, John Maxwell, David Mitchell, and Mark
McCleery.   Dorothy and David were living near Delaware, Ohio, in
2001.

1138(10)1 Ralph McCleery Ferguson

Ralph was born 31 Mar 1922 in Vegreville, Alberta.   He was raised
on a farm in Alberta, Canada, and later was a civil engineer
employed mainly by steel fabricators. He married Ruth Irene Myers
on 30 Jun 1951.   Ruth was born 28 Oct 1920 in Saskatoon,
Saskatchewan, and was a bookkeeper before her marriage.   They had
Joyce Charlotte, Brian Arthur, Douglas Keith, and Neil Edwin.   Ruth
died 26 Jun 1999 in Mississauga, Ontario.   In 2001 Ralph was living
in Mississauga.   His generous contributions to this compilation are
appreciated.

1138(10)2 Helen Daisy Ferguson

Helen was born 13 Feb 1924 and became a registered nurse.   She
married 14 Jun 1947, in Vegreville, Peter Noster who was born 7 Apr
1913.   They were farmers. Their children were Linda Mary, Kenneth
John, Eileen Bernadette, and Christopher Peter Joseph. Helen died
2 Feb 1987 in Vermilion, Alberta.

1138(10)3 Lila Jennette Ferguson

Lila was born 27 Mar 1926 in Vegreville, Alberta.   On 26 Jul 1958
she married Donald Lee Davidson who was born 26 Jul 1925.   They
were farmers. Their children were Jennifer Jean, Frances Elizabeth,
Margaret Rose, Ralph William, and Helen Daisy.   They now live in
Alliance, Alberta.

1138(10)4 Leonard Keyes Ferguson

Leonard was born 27 Mar 1926 in Vegreville, Alberta. He was a farmer and for several years he was director of Federated Co-Ops. He married 24 Oct 1949, in Alliance, Alberta, Mary Margaret Davidson who was born in Mar 1922 and died in Aug 1992. She had been a dietician. They had Leslie Dale and Valerie Margaret. Leonard lives in Vegreville.

114211 Agnes McMurray Thomson

Agnes was born 5 Apr 1906 in Renfrew, Scotland. Her daughters recalled that she was very artistic and attended art classes in high school. She played a piano that was bought for her by her grandfather, James Thomson. During the Clydebank Blitz of WW II, the female side of the family was packed off to Millport on the Isle of Cumbrae for nine months. On 21 Sep 1934 she married Alexander John McNeil at North Manse, Renfrew. Alexander was born 28 Apr 1902 in Renfrew, the son of Alexander McNeil and Georgina Stewart. Alexander was an "engineer turner" living at 2 Thomson Street in Renfrew when he married Agnes. Agnes was working as a drapery saleswoman. Their children were Agnes Keith and Georgina Stewart. Mother Agnes died at the age of ninety on 7 Nov 1996 at Royal Alexandra Hospital in Paisley. Her latest residence had been Stewart House Residential Home, Glendee Road, Renfrew. The informant on her death record was Agnes McArthur, her daughter, of 2 Arran Road, Renfrew.

Children of William Thomson

L-R: Agness, James, baby, John, unknown son

114221 James Thomson

James was born 24 Aug 1892 in Lochwinnoch, Renfrewshire, Scotland. He emigrated to Canada with his family when a teenager.

114222 John Thomson

John was born in Lochwinnoch on 2 Jul 1894, and came to Ontario just prior to WW I. He and his brother may have worked the wheat fields in the western provinces of Canada.

114223 Agness Thomson

Agnes(s) was born in Scotland, shortly after 1900, and emigrated with her family to Ontario sometime before WW I. She is believed to have married Frank Osbeck, but no records of them have been located.

115111 LaRue Thomson Strieby

LaRue was born a twin on 22 Jan 1911. He married Hazel Christensen who was born in 1913. Hazel had previously been married to Lane Fredrickson on 4 Nov 1933. They had a daughter, Marjean, born 15 Jan 1936. When Lane abandoned Hazel, she sued for divorce. LaRue and Hazel lived in College Park, Md. for about thirty years where LaRue was a manager of civil service employee retirements. Their child was Serena Beth. Later they retired in Cleveland, Ohio, to be near their daughter. LaRue died 3 Oct 1989 and was buried in Western Reserve Cemetery in Cleveland. Hazel was living in Cleveland in 1998.

115112 Frances LeRoy Strieby

LeRoy was born a twin on 22 Jan 1911. He married Cindonia Dana Maynor 9 Jun 1935 in Parkville, Mo. LeRoy was a mail carrier. Their adopted child is Dana Frances. Cindonia was born in 1909 and died 28 May 1971. LeRoy died 11 Apr 2001.

115121 Paul Estel Thomson

Known his entire life as Estel, he was born 26 Jun 1904 on a farm near Stanwood, Ia. Being the oldest son, some of the hard work on the farm fell on his shoulders. In the middle of summer when the corn was up, Estel would rise before sunup, hitch a team to a cultivator, and they would wait at the end of the field until there was enough daylight to see the rows. They would continue cultivating until nightfall. Estel was a member of the Boy Scouts of America and in 1919, the troop was pictured in the Stanwood centennial booklet.[186]   Estel may be the one shown in the back row, next to last on the right, not in uniform. The same booklet lists Estel as a member of the Mason organization.

Estel was educated in the local schools and graduated from Stanwood High School on 25 May 1923. During high school, he played baseball with his brothers. Charles remarked to the compiler not too many years ago that "Estel could really hit a baseball." Estel played basketball and won awards (ribbons) during his participation in track.

He entered Iowa State Teacher's College in Cedar Falls on 12 Sep 1923 as indicated on a transcript of his records. His major was manual arts; his minor was agriculture. Scholastically, he received excellent marks in mechanical drawing and woodworking. Estel attended summer school in 1924 and 1925 and received a diploma in manual arts education in 1925. During the summer of 1928, Estel took courses in crops and animal husbandry at Coe College.

His first teaching assignment was in Springville, Ia., followed by Dysart, Armstrong, Springville again, Morning Sun, Oakville, and finally, Kanawha, where he taught the longest. Even though he had coached a championship baseball team, drastic budget cuts cost Estel his teaching job at Armstrong in 1932 during the depths of the Great Depression. Throughout his career he primarily taught industrial arts, and was a baseball and basketball coach.

His teams often did well in tournaments, and he coached numerous baseball teams that made it to the final game in state tournaments. While at Armstrong his team reached the final round in the District tournament in the spring of 1931, losing to Ledyard by a score of 11-8. The following spring his team defeated North Des Moines by a score of 21-11 to win the state crown, certainly a case of David defeating Goliath; all schools, large and small, were enjoined in the same tournament. Most of his championship teams were from Kanawha where the display case was filled with trophies.

Estel married 8 Jun 1929 Leota Mae Knight in Vinton, Ia. Leota was born in Anamosa, Ia., 6 Feb 1909. She attended school in Viola where her parents, Lester and Clara (Staley) Knight farmed. Estel and Leota spent the first year of their marriage in Springville where they rented an apartment. Their children were Lowell Estel, David Lee, Donald Claire, Lyle Ivan, and three children who died at birth: a son in 1946, Robert Louis, who died in 1948, and Linda Mae, who died in 1953, all of whom went full term, but died because of an improper blood transfusion Leota had years ago. During the years of World War II, they lived in Oakville, and Estel gave up

teaching temporarily to work in an army ordnance plant near
Burlington, Ia. He was foreman of a crew that crated bombs, a
rather dangerous occupation. The family lived in Burlington the
last year of the war.

In the fall of 1945, Estel resumed his teaching career by accepting
a position at Kanawha. He continued teaching there until he
resigned in late 1954 to take a full-time position as an insurance
adjustor. In 1966 they left Kanawha and moved to Clear Lake where
they resided for several years, then they moved to West Liberty,
Ia. On 12 Mar 1971 in Cedar Rapids, Estel was inducted into the
Hall of Fame of Iowa High School Baseball Coaches Association for
his outstanding success as a coach.

In his last few years, Estel spent time playing golf, caring for
his lawn, planting a garden, and working on projects in his garage.
He re-established the tradition of holding annual family reunions,
which have been held on the second Sunday of June in Stanwood.
Estel was a quiet man with a special sense of humor, and he enjoyed
exchanging banter with his friends downtown at the coffee shop. He
developed cancer and died suddenly 21 Dec 1976 in the hospital in
Iowa City, Ia. He was buried 23 Dec in Stanwood Cemetery where his
parents, grandparents and numerous relatives are buried.

Estel had a cane that has been passed down from oldest son to
oldest son. The tradition may have started with John Thomson. The
cane is now in the hands of Estel's great-grandson, Bryce Thomson,
of Texas.

Thomson Brothers, ca. 1939

L-R: Everett, George, Charles, Edwin, Richard and Estel

115122 Richard Elwood Thomson

Richard, known to his family and friends as Dick, was born 5 Dec 1905 on a farm located near Stanwood in Cedar Co., Ia.   In his youth, he helped in the operation of the farm, which involved growing crops, raising hogs and cattle, and managing the land. Dick attended elementary and high school at Stanwood. With his brothers, he was active in the athletic programs of the school.   Most notably, he was the catcher on the baseball team that won the state championship in 1925.[186]   The brothers often reminisced about baseball during family reunions.   Dick graduated from Stanwood High School in 1925.

Dick married Anne Viola Williams 12 Jan 1927 at the Methodist Church parsonage in Iowa City, Ia.   Anne was born 1 Feb 1910, the daughter of George Washington Williams and Fanny Ruby Smith.   Dick and Anne spent many years of their married life engaged in farming in Cedar Co.   Together, they worked long tedious hours to make farming a successful operation.   Dick was also a salesman of animal feed supplements, and seed corn.   He was a kind and generous man, widely known among farmers as a friend.

They had four children: Roland Dean, Leland Arnold, Shirley Lee, and Gary Alan.   Dick died at Mercy Hospital in Iowa City 31 May 1989.   Anne preceded him in death at the Cedar Manor Nursing Home in Tipton 29 Nov 1986.   Both were interred in the rural Red Oak Grove Presbyterian Church Cemetery located between Stanwood and Tipton.

115123 Everett Strauser Thomson

Everett was born 17 Apr 1907 in Stanwood, Ia.   Everett attended schools in Stanwood.   In 1925, his junior year, he was the pitcher on the Stanwood High School baseball team that won the state championship.   His brother, Dick, was the catcher, and Chick played second base.   In Everett's senior year, the team lost in the final game of the district tournament.[186]   He was also a player on the football team.   Everett was president of his small senior class. He married Marie Lillian Gibbs in 1933 in Webster City, Ia.   Marie was born 17 Jul 1905 and died in Davenport, Ia., 13 Mar 1996.   Marie was a graduate of Iowa State Teacher's College with a degree in elementary education.

Everett attended the University of Iowa with intentions of becoming a medical doctor.   After a year, he changed his mind, and spent the next two years at Iowa State Teacher's College where he obtained a teaching certificate.   He played on the college baseball team.   He taught in Preston, Ia., for a few years, then opened up

a restaurant. Next, Everett went into the insurance business and
had offices in Muscatine and Davenport. Marie taught school in
Preston, Ia., for ten years before joining her husband in business.
They enjoyed traveling in their retirement years. Everett died 14
Nov 1989. They are buried in Davenport Memorial Park.

115124 Charles William Thomson

Charles was born 21 Aug 1908 and was better known as "Chick". He
attended schools in Stanwood and was an outstanding baseball and
football player.[186] He was a 1927 graduate of Stanwood High School.
Chick married Eleanor Evelyn Hass in Stanwood 26 Mar 1938 and took
up residence on the Thomson farm. They acquired his father's farm
located near Stanwood and remained there until they retired to
town. Chick often drove to Chicago to attend major-league baseball
games. He and Eleanor traveled extensively in their retirement
years. Chick died 13 Oct 1993 and was buried in Stanwood Cemetery.
Eleanor was born 7 Mar 1917 and resides in Stanwood. She
generously arranges for the annual Thomson family reunion held the
second Sunday of June in Stanwood Park.

115125 George Marion Thomson

George, known as "Joe", was born 26 Feb 1910. He attended schools
in Stanwood and graduated from high school in 1929. In 1926 Joe
played second base on an excellent team that was narrowly defeated
in the final game of their district tournament held in Ames. Joe
then attended Iowa State Teacher's College and received a teaching
certificate in 1931 after two years of study. He continued his
education by attending summer school and eventually earned a BA
degree. Joe taught in Stanwood for a few years, then accepted
employment with the Farm Credit Administration in Tipton. In May
1942, he was drafted into military service, and was inducted into
the U.S. Army in Des Moines. He was immediately sent to Douglas,
Wyoming, where there was a German prisoner of war camp. The war
ended the day he was scheduled to embark for overseas duty. He
eventually was discharged in 1946.

Joe then resumed his teaching career, with all but one year spent
at Roosevelt High School in Cedar Rapids. There, he taught
industrial arts, and was a coach of their baseball, basketball and
football teams. In 1955, he was awarded a master's degree from the
University of Iowa. In 1971, Joe and his brother, Estel, were
inaugurated into the Iowa High School Baseball Coaches Association
Hall of Fame, perhaps the only brothers to claim such an honor. He
is in the Iowa High School Coaches Association 500th Win Club. He
retired in 1975 after teaching for 34 years. Joe has been active
in many organizations and won the Tait Cummins award from the South

Side Civic Club for his contribution to youth activities and athletics.

Joe and Edna Caroline Engelking were married 2 Jun 1937 in Davenport, Ia. After two years at Iowa State Teacher's College, Edna received a certificate in Home Economics, and was a teacher. Their children were Mary Ann, Ruth Ellen, and Max William. Joe and Edna observed their golden wedding anniversary in 1987. Edna died 2 Jan 1995 in Cedar Rapids. Joe played golf almost daily in his retirement years until health problems intervened. Joe died 16 Jan 2001 and he was buried beside Edna in Stanwood Cem.

115126 Eloise Ruth Thomson

Eloise was born 18 Dec 1911. She attended schools in Stanwood, then married Harold Negus on 10 Nov 1930 in Aledo, Ill. Their son was Edwin Earl. Harold, who operated a service station in Muscatine, was born 29 Sep 1907 and died in Apr 1970 in Muscatine. Eloise married, secondly, Harold Sinkler on 28 Jan 1971, and they lived in Florida for a while, then returned to Muscatine. Mr. Sinkler was born 10 Dec 1910, probably in Michigan, and died in Apr 1981 in Muscatine. Eloise died in Davenport, Ia., 11 Apr 1992 and was buried in Muscatine Memorial Park.

115127 Edwin Isaac Thomson

Edwin was born 15 Jun 1913. His brother, George, remembers that he was the best looking of the bunch. Then as a young boy in the third grade, he had the misfortune of being thrown off a horse-drawn wagon and hitting his face on the hub of a steel wheel. The injury to his face was serious, but he would have been better cared for with today's medical practices. He had to have many stitches to close the wound. His life was changed as a result of that accident. "Bub" spent his years working on the farm of his brother, Charles, and had an 80-acre farm of his own. He was always delighted to have close family members visit him on the farm, and he was always present for the annual family reunions. In his later years, he suffered from hearing loss which, unfortunately, made it difficult to visit with him. In later years he lived in the Cedar County Care Facility for 17 years. His death came 30 Sep 1997 at Elmview Nursing Home in Burlington. Burial was in Stanwood Cem.

115128 Evelyn Thomson

Evelyn was born 28 Dec 1915. She attended schools in Stanwood, and graduated from high school in 1933. The same year, she and Darrell Price Blayney were married. Darrell, it turns out, was a distant cousin of Leota (Knight) Thomson. Their children were Keith Dale, Karen Kay, and Kathy Sue. Evelyn had a fabric business in a store

in Tipton until her premature death from cancer 18 Jun 1971.[164]
Darrell was born 3 Oct 1912 and died 16 Feb 1978. He had a dry
goods store in Anamosa, then, about 1954, became a butcher for a
chain store and lived in Tipton. Burial was in Green Cemetery near
Morley, Ia.

A Thomson reunion

L-R: Eloise, Emma Lou, Edwin, Sarah, William, Evelyn, Estel,
Charles, George (Children not identified)

115129 Emma Lou Thomson

Emma Lou was born 4 Sep 1917 in Stanwood. She graduated from
Stanwood High School in 1935, then attended a junior college in
Clinton, Ia., where she studied business. Her first job was with
Aetna Casualty and Surety Co. in San Diego. On 13 Sep 1943, in
Seattle, Emma Lou married Carrol James Smith who was born in 1919.
With Carrol being in the U.S. Navy, they had residences in Norfolk,
Va., and several cities on the west coast--San Diego, San
Francisco, Seattle, and Portland. After he retired with twenty
years of service, Carrol managed a paint store in San Diego. They
had Bruce Emerson and Mary Ann. Carrol died 29 Mar 2001 and
received a military funeral; he was buried in Rosecrans Military
Cemetery, Point Loma, near San Diego.

115131 Olive Mae Thomson

Olive was born in 1907 and died in 1911 as inscribed on her
tombstone in Stanwood Cem.

115132 Edna Ruth Thomson

Ruth was born 26 May 1919 in Hamill, S.D. She graduated from
Gregory, S.D., High School in 1937. On 11 Aug 1940 at Whitten,
S.D., she married Emfred Albin Anderson who was born 15 Aug 1905 in
Spencer, Neb. While living at Blackfoot, Ida., Emfred worked for
the Fish and Wildlife Service until 1975 when he retired. He

developed macular degeneration of his eyes and was in a care center
for his last two years of life. He died in Blackfoot, Ida., 5 Jan
1998, and was buried in Riverside-Thomas Cemetery in Blackfoot.
Edna was enjoying good health in Blackfoot in 1999, and was often
traveling to visit friends and relatives.   Their children are
Philip Fred, Gary Carl, and Laura Ruth.

115133 William Martin Thomson

William (Bill) was born 17 Feb 1921 in Hamill, S.D., and died 15
Nov 1997. Bill was an instrument specialist on U.S. Navy airplanes.
Later he was manager of airplane instruments for Genani Aircraft
near where he lived in Hemet, Calif.   On 8 May 1944, while
stationed at Pensacola, Fla., he married Dorothy Mae Sigler who was
born 20 Oct 1919 and died 5 Sep 1997 in Hemet.   Their children are
Dorothy Carol and Donna Jean.

115141 Thelma Lucile Thomson

Thelma was born 6 Mar 1908 near Stanwood, Ia., and was a member of
the 1926 class of Stanwood High School. She was married to Merlyn
Sperbeck whom she later divorced. Thelma died of tuberculosis 6
Jul 1932 and was buried in Stanwood Cem. There were no children.
Merlyn was born 30 Aug 1910 and died 30 Aug 1991, location unknown.

115142 Ethel Charlene Thomson

Charlene was born 15 Mar 1910 near Stanwood, Ia.   She married 14
Jun 1941 George D. Reid who was born 30 Nov 1901 and died 4 Jun
1974.   They lived in Cove, Ark., for a short while, then in Hot
Springs for about 25 years. Secondly, she married David Sholeen 30
May 1980. Charlene died 8 Oct 1988. David died 4 May 1989; both
were buried in Alexander, Ark. They had no children.

115143 Donald Paul Thomson

Donald was born 30 Nov 1911 in the Red Oak area near Stanwood.   He
was married 29 Nov 1934 to Bonnie Beveda Bittner who was born 4 Apr
1911 near Wheatland, Ia.   Donald was a tool and die maker at
Douglas Aircraft in Calif., and later farmed near Mechanicsville,
Ia.   They had David Winslow, Paula Jane, and Douglas Alan.   Bonnie
died 4 Jan 1985; Donald died 13 Sep 1989, both in Mount Vernon,
Ia.; they are buried in Lisbon Cem.

115144 Dale Marion Thomson

Dale was born 15 May 1914 near Tipton, Ia. He married 30 Nov 1937
Lillian Josephine Aaron who was born in 1918. Their son was Larry

Francis.   Dale died 10 Mar 1975 and was buried in Stanwood
Cemetery. Lillian was in a nursing home in 2001.

115145 Jean Thomson

Jean was born 6 Sep 1917 near Tipton, Ia. She was married 26 Jan
1941 to John Duncan whom she later divorced; no children. Secondly,
Jean married 31 Dec 1964 Bernice W. (Bud) Griffith; he died 23 Feb
1997.   Bud had two children from a previous marriage: Diane Jean
and Richard Verl.   Jean was living in Rogers, Ark., in 1998.

115146 Murl Howard Thomson

Murl was born 16 Mar 1921 near Tipton, Ia. He attended school in
Mechanicsville, and was a 1939 high school graduate.   He then
enlisted in the Coast Guard in 1940, and took his basic training at
Curtis Bay, Md. His service included patrol duty off Greenland and
convoy escort. Murl was discharged from the Coast Guard in 1943,
then he worked for military intelligence (G-2) in Washington, D.C.
where he helped crack the Japanese code. He was married on 19 Sep
1942 to Marie Josephine (Jo) Tiedemann in Des Moines, Ia. Jo was
born 7 Apr 1924, the daughter of Henry J. Tiedemann and Marie G.
Boyle.   Murl and Jo owned and managed a steak house in Branson,
Mo.,   then sold the business in 1980.   They now reside in
Springfield, Mo. Their children are John Vincent, Jo Ann, Gary
Lynn, and Robert Alan.

115147 Francis Glen Thomson

Francis was born 14 Mar 1924 near Tipton, Ia. He married 5 Jan
1949 Marie Alice Kamberling in Iowa City. Marie was born 6 Oct
1928. They had six children: James Allen, Danny Lynn, Linda Kay,
Catharine Marie, Ricky Francis, and Tina Ann. Francis and Marie
have been farming in the Mechanicsville area since their marriage.

115148   Doris Lorraine Thomson

Lorraine was born 15 Nov 1927 near Mechanicsville, Ia. She married
30 Apr 1949 Gene Leroy Nielsen who was born 27 Aug 1922.   They
lived and taught school in Iowa where Marcia Jean was born. They
then moved to Mich. and continued teaching. Gene died in Mich. on
19 Sep 1955. Secondly, Lorraine married 4 Sep 1964 Wayne William
Webber, born 9 Apr 1934, and they had Carol Lynn and Kristin Ann.
They live in St. Joseph, Mich.

115151 Alice Mae Thomson

Alice Mae was born 30 Dec 1914 and died 18 Apr 1995.[165] Firstly,
she married Corby Arthur Barron who was born 7 Nov 1902 and died 29

Apr 1975 in an Iowa City hospital. Corby was a farmer, and an elder in the Presbyterian Church. Their children were Evelyn Eileen, Edwin Eugene, Jon Laverne, Faira Louise, and Carolyn Kay. Secondly, she married, in 1980, Dennis Groenendyk. Corby Barron and Alice were buried in Memorial Lawn Cemetery, Ottumwa, Ia.

115152 Eddyth Marie Thomson

Eddyth was born 8 Feb 1918 at Martell, Ia. She attended grade school near Fremont, and high school in Hedrick, where she graduated in 1935. She married 8 Feb 1940 Glenys Cummins Rice who was born 5 Nov 1913 and died 18 Jul 1994 in Sigourney, Ia. He was buried in Mt. Zion Cemetery near Martinsburg, Ia. They had Lois Ann, Lynn Glenys, Clarence Allen, and Glenda Paulette.

115153 Carol Illa Thomson

Carol was born 12 Sep 1924 and married Leonard Allen Messer in 1945. Leonard was born 6 Apr 1921 and died 26 Mar 1996 in New Sharon, Ia. Burial was in Friends Cemetery, New Sharon. He had been a teacher, and served in the U.S. Army from 1942 to 1945. Their four children were Kathleen Mae, Lawrence Allen, Mark Thomson, and Lorraine Ann.

115154 Eathol Arlene Thomson

Eathol was born 2 Jun 1930 in Fremont, Ia. She attended the community college in Oregon City, Ore., for two years and worked as an electronics assembler. On 30 Jun 1951 in Hedrick, Ia., she married Wallace James De Young who was born in 1932 and died 19 Oct 1999 from complications with diabetes. They had Jerold Lynn who was born 23 Mar 1953 in Rapid City, S.D.; James Edwin who was born 1 Feb 1955 in Rapid City;, and John Thomson who was born 4 Sep 1962 in Phoenix, Ariz. After her divorce, Eathol married, on 21 Sep 1968 in Bellevue, Wash., Victor Duane Marska who was born in 1924. Duane was once a manager of Superior Fast Freight and later worked at a storage facility in Peoria, Ariz.

115161 Beryl Thomson Tenley

Beryl (Ben) was born 1 Mar 1908 in Stanwood, Ia., and died 10 Aug 1978 in Rochester, Minn. Ben was a horse trainer and also worked as a custodian at the Mayo Clinic. On 25 Dec 1942, in El Reno, Ok., he married Dorthy Marie Chappell who was born 10 Nov 1916 in El Reno. Dorothy was living in Rochester.

115162 Kathryn Elizabeth Tenley

Kathryn was born 24 Jul 1909 in Stanwood, Ia., and died 22 Nov 1995 in Rochester, Minn. On 4 Sep 1934 she married Orville Berry Cooper who was born 3 Jul 1905 and died 24 Sep 1972. Orville had a TV and radio repair business in Rochester. They had Robert Bruce, Carol Louise, and Dale Thomas.

115163 Joseph Myron Tenley

Joseph was born 2 Nov 1911 in Stanwood, Ia., and died 6 Mar 1974 in Rochester, Minn. He was a railroad engineer and lived in Rochester. He married Flora Marie Anderson on 17 Oct 1931 in Rochester. Flora was born 15 Nov 1908 in Westbrook, Minn. Their children were Richard Arthur, Beverly Ann, and Beatrice Evon.

115164 Mary Louise Tenley

Mary was born 14 Sep 1913 in Stanwood, Ia., and died 6 Dec 1993 in Rochester, Minn. On 5 Sep 1935 she married Lewis Henry "Hank" Partner who was born 26 Jul 1908 in Spokane, Wash., and died 18 Dec 1975 in Rochester. Hank was a plumber in Rochester, Minn. They had no children.

115165 Chester Robert Tenley

Chester was born 1 Oct 1916 in Stanwood, Ia., and died 19 Apr 1994 in Rochester, Minn. He married Viola Mae White 2 Jan 1942 in Rochester. Viola was born 15 Jan 1918 in Wadina Co. Chester was a carpenter in Rochester. They had three children: Mary Kathryn, Cary Robert, and Joel Lynn.

115166 William Kenneth Tenley

Kenneth was born 8 Aug 1920 in Pratt, Minn., and died 25 Oct 1980 in Rochester, Minn. He married 19 May 1941 Myra Ellen McConnell who was born 22 Feb 1920 in Muncie, Ind. Ken held several jobs which included being a trucker in Rochester. They had a son, James McConnell.

115171 Hazel Ola Harper

Hazel was born 23 Sep 1915 near Stanwood, Ia. On 23 Sep 1936 in Kelso, Wash., she married William Earl Boag who was born 11 May 1907 in Portland, Ore., and died in 1968. They had a son, Wayne Edward. Secondly, Hazel married on 26 May 1947 in Kelso, Wash., Clarence Huntley who was born 12 Apr 1904 and died 6 Nov 1976 in Corvallis, Ore; burial was in Gilland Cemetery in Sweet Home, Ore. They had Cecil Clarence. Thirdly, Hazel married Leslie Eugene Chaney who was born 13 May 1915 and died 21 Jan 1991. They had no children.

115172 Howard Thomson Harper

Howard was born 25 May 1917 near Winner, Tripp Co., S.D. In 1936
he graduated from high school in Aumsville, Ore. He served with
the U.S. Army Air Corps during WW II, and was an aerial engineer on
8 Dec 1941 when he was wounded during an attack in the Phillipine
Islands. He was one of a few who were fortunate to avoid capture
by the Japanese and made it to Sydney, Australia, on an inter-
island hemp boat. Howard spent 23 years in the military before
changing to a civilian career with the IRS. He worked in San
Bernardino Co., Calif., for 22 years. He married 6 Aug 1941 Clara
Alice Pinson, in Ironton, Ohio. Clara was born 17 Nov 1913 in
Sidney, Ky., and died 28 Nov 2000. They met in Ky., when Howard
was in miliary school. Later they lived in Riverside Co., Calif.
Their two children are Karen Lorraine and Shirley Ann.

115173 Cecil Ralph Harper

Cecil was born 3 Dec 1918 near Winner, S.D. On 22 Nov 1942 in
Turner, Ore., he married Pearl Olive Nelson. He served in the U.S.
Army during WW II, and later was an electrical engineer for
Bonneville Power Administration. They had Martha Belle and Carolyn
Rae. Cecil and Pearl divorced, and he secondly married Helene
Agnes Reus. Cecil died 18 Aug 1994 in Milwaukie, Ore. His body
was cremated.

115174 John William Harper

John was born 26 Dec 1926 in Winner, S.D. On 27 Aug 1945 in
Vancouver, Wash., he first married Ruby Reva Scott who was born 27
Dec 1926 in Albany, Ore. They had three children: Mark William,
Roy Allen, and Jerry Dean. John's second wife was Hazel Lucy
Johnson who was born 19 Oct 1920, probably in Ala., and died 12 Jan
1994 in Kissimmee, Fla. There were no children from his second
marriage. John, who lives in Milwaukee, Ore., has a stiffness
regarding his genealogy.

115175 Donald Kenneth Harper

Donald was born 14 Feb 1928 near Winner, S.D., and later moved to
Oregon with his parents. He was a veteran of the U.S. Air Force
and at one time a member of the Oregon State police. Donald was a
letter carrier in San Diego, Calif., when an illness forced his
retirement. He first married 18 Oct 1953 Carol Jenne Jaynes who
was born in 1927; they divorced. Secondly, he married Barbara
Clark who was born in 1930 and they were divorced. Thirdly, he
married Buryl Ann Bicknell who was born 28 Aug 1929 and died 8 Sep
1986 in San Diego Co., Calif. Donald adopted Buryl's children from
a previous marriage, Pamela and Gayle. He was very active in his

church.   Donald died in San Diego 14 Jul 1984;[166] his body was cremated and his ashes were scattered at sea.

115176 Marvin Earl Harper

Marvin was born 26 Dec 1929 in Winner, S.D. He married Marvel Katherine Chrisman on 26 Jul 1952 in Vancouver, Wash. She was born 29 Aug 1934 and died of cancer in Nov 1977 in Beaver Creek, Ore. They had Marvin Earl and Marvel Elaine. Marvin's second wife was Nancy Lee Belnap, and they divorced in 1998, without children. Marvin was living in Beaver Creek, Ore., in 1999.

115181 Elizabeth Ann McQuade

Elizabeth was born 16 Nov 1928 in Alpena, Mich.   She was a 1946 graduate of Iowa Falls High School. Her advanced education was obtained at The University of Iowa where she graduated with a BA in 1950.   She participated in a Danforth Graduate fellowship program from 1950-1951. Elizabeth obtained a MA from the University of Chicago in 1955. After serving as Assistant Dean of Women at Oberlin College in Ohio, Elizabeth arrived at the University of New Hampshire in 1960 and eventually became Associate Dean of Women. Elizabeth was never married and died in Durham, N.H., 3 Dec 1976; she left a will dated 1970 wherein she bequeathed her personal effects to Everett and Marie Thomson. The proceeds from the sale of her remaining estate were to go toward the purchase of an organ at the Durham Community Church where she had been involved in the music program. She was also a member of the American Association of University Women. Her body was cremated and the remains were interred in Durham Cemetery.

115411 Alexander Montgomery Barron, Jr.

Montgomery was born 17 Dec 1927 in South St. Paul, Minn. "Monte" enlisted in the United Staes Marine Corps 8 Dec 1949, was promoted to Sgt. 13 Apr 1951, and was discharged as a Staff Sgt. 28 Oct 1952.   He served in Korea from 11 Dec 1950 to 4 Nov 1951.   He married 22 Mar 1958 Shirley Ann Banks Harkins in New Bern, N.C.   He died there of pneumonia on 19 Jun 1959 and had full military services; interment was in National Cemetery in Cherry Point, N.C.

115412 John Reid Barron

John was born 25 Jan 1929 in South St. Paul, Minn. After junior high school his family moved to Watertown, S.D., where his father operated a feed lot for Swift & Co. He graduated from high school in 1947 and entered Macalester College in St. Paul where he studied for two years. John was an accomplished swimmer on his college team and won several medals in backstroke competition. At this time John enlisted in the Naval Reserve. He continued his education by attending St. Cloud State College, then he re-enlisted in the U.S. Navy and took pilot training at Pensacola, Fla. He accumulated 230 hours of flight time before being discharged in 1952. John loved to sing as evident by his participation in the college choir and with the Naval Avaiation Choir.

John returned to St. Cloud, resumed his studies, and graduated in 1954 with a BA in Industrial Arts. He was then primarily employed as a mechanical design draftsman, eventually working exclusively with computer drafting software. John retired in 1994. On 18 Dec 1954 he married Lois May in Clearwater, Minn., where Lois was born 21 May 1932. Their children were Laura May, Linda Ray, Paul Reid, and Mary Elizabeth. In their retirement years, John and Lois have traveled to both coasts and to Europe. They keep busy with volunteer work at their church and are members of a bike riding club which tours the state.

115421 Carol Christine Thomson

Christine was born 13 Oct 1929 in Wichita, Kan. She earned a BS degree from Wichita State University in business and accounting. She and Donald LaVerne Huber were married 23 Nov 1951 in Wichita. Don was born 4 Nov 1926 in Wichita and obtained a BA degree in geology from Wichita State University in 1951. Christine died as the result of breast cancer 24 Jan 1987 in Liberal, Kan., where she was buried. Their children were Julie Lynn and Clay Randall. Don was living in McPherson, Kan., in 2001.

115422 John Dennis Thomson

Dennis was born 11 Oct 1935 in Wichita, Kan. He graduated with a BS in fire protection and safety engineering from IIT, Chicago. Dennis spent 1958 to 1978 in the U.S. Air Force. He married Virginia Baumgartner 5 Oct 1957, and later they divorced. Their children were Janice Lynn, Lory Christine, and Cheryl Lee. John has a large collection of documents passed down from his grandfather, John J. Thomson, and has generously shared them with the compiler.

115431 David Reid Thomson, Jr.

David was born about 30 Aug 1942. He married Donna (?) Niedemus and they lived in Columbus, Ohio. They may have adopted Scott Reid and Shannon. David worked as an accountant and was in some degree of trouble when he took his own life in Jul 1985.

115511 Edwin Bates
Edwin had a leg injury as a youth and it is believed to have

developed into bone cancer. He is buried in a plot with his parents and sister.

115512 Margaret Grace Bates

Margaret was born 29 Nov 1929 in Des Moines, Ia. She attended grade school in Marengo and graduated from Iowa State Teachers College. She taught English in area high schools, and coached speech and drama. She received a master's degree in child development and psychology from the University of Northern Iowa in 1971. She was of the Lutheran faith, and enjoyed travel, theater, and community activities. She married Allan Milo Oppen in 1955 and they divorced in 1986. Their children were Eric Bates and John David. Margaret was murdered in Jacksonville, Fla., in Feb 1996 while she was staying in her condominium during the winter.[167,168] The case was still under investigation as of 1998. Her remains were cremated and buried in her parent's plot. Allan died at the age of 69 on 26 Dec 1991 and was buried in Slayton, Minn.[169]

115531 Forrest (Harry) Huff

Harry was born 20 Aug 1927. He served in the U.S. Air Force from 1950 to 1952. He married Mary Kennedy 2 Jul 1952 in Wichita Falls, Tex. On their farm they fed cattle, and grew crops of corn and soy beans. In 1998 they were residing in Mineola, Tex. They had no children.

115532 Mary Pearl Ludwig

Pearl was born 16 Aug 1913 and was cared for and raised by the Huff family; she was not adopted. On 18 Dec 1935 she married Carl Burgett who was born 21 Mar 1911 near Fort Pierre, S.D., and died 12 Dec 1992.[170] He had been a member of DeSoto United Methodist Church, the Madison County Coon Hunters Association, Dallas County Farm Bureau, McCreary Community Center at Perry, and Heartland Co-op at Dallas Center. He had farmed for fifty years near Adel, Ia. They had a son, Rex, and daughters, Eunice and Alice. Pearl died 24 Aug 1994. Burial was in Ellis Cemetery near DeSoto.

115541 Donald Spence Sorensen

Donald was born 11 May 1926 in Minneapolis, Minn. He graduated from Washington-Lee High School in Arlington, Va., in Feb 1948 after serving in the U.S. Army. He was briefly married to Marilyn Fast. He secondly was briefly married to Leona Elizabeth. There were no children from either marriage. Donald died in Mar 1993 and was buried in National Memorial Park in Falls Church, Va.

115542 Ruth Elaine Sorensen

Ruth born 23 Apr 1930 in Washington, D.C. She graduated from Washington-Lee High School in Arlington, Va., in 1948, then obtained her B.S. in education at Madison College in Harrisonburg, Va., in 1952. She taught school briefly, then worked at the C.I.A. from which she retired. Ruth has provided assistance for this compilation, including rare photographs of ancestors.

115543 Elizabeth Christine Sorensen

Betty was born 17 Sep 1931 in Washington, D.C. She attended Washington-Lee High School in Arlington where she graduated in 1949. She then went on to Madison College where she earned a B.S. degree in education in 1953. She taught school in Berryville, Va. She married Donald O. Levi and they had Mark Spence, Keith Winterton, and Susan Virginia. Donald died 10 Apr 1999 and was buried in Green Hill Cemetery in Berryville, Va. Elizabeth was living near Charles Town, W. Va., in 1999.

115551 Esther Ruth Spence

Esther was born 2 Jun 1922 in Earlham, Madison Co., Ia. She died 21 Jun 1922 and was buried in Winterset Cemetery, Winterset, Ia.

115552 Margaret Helen Spence

Margaret was born 25 Jul 1923 in Earlham, Ia. She was a 1940 graduate of Hawkeye High School. After graduation she went to Waterloo where she worked. She married 20 Apr 1943, at Elkader, Ia., Eugene Peter Klein. Eugene was born 20 Dec 1916 in Waterloo, Ia., and died of cancer 3 Oct 1998; burial was in St. Mary's Cemetery in Gilbertville. He was the son of John Klein and Anna Funfsinn Schmitz Klein. Eugene graduated from High school in Waterloo, then became a member of the Coast Auxiliary, and served in the South Pacific in World War II. He started the Washburn Knife Company and worked there until his retirement in 1988. Eugene was very civic minded as evidenced by his participation in many organizations. Their children are Patrick Eugene, Rita Ann, Elaine Marie, Keith Joseph, David John, Doris Margaret, Larry James, Annette Lorene, and Angela Mary. They were members of Immaculate Conception Catholic Church in Gilbertville. Margaret was the source of the photograph taken in 1915 at the Thomson family reunion held near Winterset; her generosity for sharing the photograph is greatly appreciated.

115553 Robert Eugene Spence

Robert was born 7 Mar 1926 in Winterset, Ia. He graduated from

Hawkeye High School in 1943, then went into the U.S. Army. He
married first, Anna Kathryn Willey 1 Oct 1946. Secondly, he
married Lea Austin 1 Aug 1961. Thirdly, he married Wanda Jordan in
Oct 1966. No issue from any of his wives. Robert died 20 Sep 1973
in San Antonio, Tex., and was buried there in Military Cem.

115554 Mildred Lucille Spence

Lucille was born 28 Aug 1929 in Winterset, Ia. She boarded in West
Union, Ia., and graduated from Olewein High School in 1947. She
married 17 Mar 1950 William Russell. Lucille inherited an antique
walnut table, spoons made from cow horn, and a model of a sailboat
passed down from her grandfather, David Taylor Spence Sr. Their
children were Elizabeth Catherine and John David, both adopted.
Lucille and her husband, Bill, are kept busy working as travel
agents in Austin, Tex.

115711 Fred Holton Johnson

Fred was born 16 Aug 1923 in Minneapolis, Minn. He graduated from
Central High School in Minneapolis in 1941, and was soon drafted
into the U.S. Army. He served in the European Theatre from 1943 to
1945. He attended the University of Minnesota where he majored in
industrial education and earned a MA degree in 1948. He worked for
Rohr Corporation 46 years before retiring in 1998. He married Ruth
Virginia Kottke about 1948 in Minneapolis. Virginia was born 22 Aug
1920 in S.D. and died 20 Jan 1998; her body was cremated and her
ashes were cast over the Pacific Ocean. Fred was living in El
Cajon, Calif., in 1999. They had Ronald L. and Terri Lynn.

115731 Leroy George Thomson

Leroy was born about Aug 1919 in Ill., and died 29 May 1920 in
Plano, Ill.

115732 Ruby Hazel Thomson

Ruby was born 11 Nov 1920, perhaps in Ladd, Ill. Ruby never
married and died in Kankakee State Hospital on 7 Nov 1962. She may
have been buried in Berean Cem. in Westfield Twp., Bureau Co., Ill.

115751 Betty Gene Thomson

Betty was born 14 Dec 1923 in Gillett, Wyoming. She attended school
in Somonauk, Ill., and graduated with the class of 1941. Betty
married 11 Jan 1944 Glenn DuWayne Young at the Plano Baptist Church
in Plano, Ill. Betty was a stenographer for Burlington Railroad.
DuWayne was a B-24 pilot during WW II and later worked as an
operator and agent for Burlington Railroad. Their children are

Richard Arlan, Patricia Louise, and Jonathan Russell. Betty and DuWayne were residing in Bristol, Ill., in 1998.

115761 Laverna Darlene Gillette

Darlene was born 27 Aug 1929 in Zearing, Ill. She graduated from Central High School in Minneapolis in 1947. She then attended the University of Minnesota where she majored in Spanish and earned a BS in education in 1951. Darlene then taught in high school in Staples and Wayzata, Minn., for four years, then was a tutor for ten years. She married Gayle LeRoy Basford on 21 Mar 1952 in Edina, Minn. They both are active in their church. Darlene is now a self-employed Christian Science practitioner while Gayle retired in 1999 as a financial aid director at Dunwoody Institute in Minneapolis. They had no children.

115771 John Kay Thomson

John was born 30 Jun 1944 in Princeton, Ill. He enlisted in the U.S. Navy at the age of 18 and served four years. His first marriage was to Carol A. Walsh in May 1966, and ended in divorce in 1984. Secondly, he married Sandra Hoover 11 Sep 1987. John and Carol had Paula Ann, James Patrick, and Michael Shawn. John has worked in Princeton 31 years as a boiler operator for a chemical plant, Geon Co., that produces PVC resin. He has provided the compiler with information about his grandfather, Abraham Lincoln "Link" Thomson, who was involved in a forest fire in Minn.

115772 Shirley Anne Thomson

Shirley was born 4 May 1937 in Aurora, Ill. On 14 Aug 1954 she married Gerald Olin in Palmyra, Mo. Gerald was born 14 Dec 1931. Shirley worked at Jostens Jewelry Co. for 21 years as a plater. Gerald did carpentry work until his retirement. They have two children, Linda Jean and Victoria Renee. They live in Princeton, Ill.

115781 Arthur Vaughn Burkett Jr.

Vaughn was born 2 Apr 1937 in Monmouth, Ill., and attended school there. Before completing his senior year, he enlisted in the U.S. Air Force on 21 Jan 1955. He was in the service for 23 years and attained the rating of Master Sargent. In 1984 he earned a BS degree in business at Upper Iowa University in Fayette, Ia. He then went to Central Michigan University and obtained a MBA in 1987. Vaughn was a staff management engineer at several hospitals and clinics, and is currently employed as an industrial engineer working with the Navy. On 20 Dec 1958, in Mount Clemens, Mich., he married Gloria Swirko who was born 24 May 1938 in Wallington, N.J. They reside in Orange Park, Fla. Their children are Kori Elaine and Kristyn Anne.

115782 Lenna Gail Burkett

Lenna was born 12 Sep 1944 in Monmouth, Ill. She attended the University of Iowa for a year, then worked 8 years as a school-age care provider, then she became a department store manager. In Mount Clemens, Mich., on 21 May 1966 she married Gerald Joseph Platkowski. They have a daughter, Karen Sue.

115(10)11 Mary Josephine Spence

Josephine was born 14 Apr 1918 in Douglas Twp., Madison Co., Ia. She worked most of her life with Iowa Farm Bureau Insurance Co. in Winterset and in Des Moines. She was never married, and died on 8 Aug 1998; burial was in Winterset Cem.

115(10)12 Lyda Frances Spence

Known as Frances, she was named after her grandparents, Frances Thomson and Lyda Addie Spence, and was born 16 Nov 1919 in Douglas Twp., Madison Co., Ia. She married, first, John Walter Duff, and they had Kenneth John and Harriett Jo. They divorced about 1945. John was born 21 Nov 1915, and died 27 Jun 1995 at Grenola, Kan. Secondly, she married 13 Jun 1948 Elwood Beem who adopted the two children. Frances died of cancer on 22 Aug 1956 in Neb., and was buried in Winterset Cem.

115(10)13 John Wallace Spence

Known as Wally, he was born 7 Nov 1922 in Douglas Twp., Madison Co., Ia. He married, first, Bernice Smith 21 Jun 1942.   Their children were Michael Andre, Marilyn Louise, and Anne Marie. Bernice was born 8 Aug 1924 and died of cancer on 28 Nov 1984; burial was in Winterset Cemetery. Secondly, John married Ruth (Hackett) Irwin 16 Aug 1969.   Ruth was born 20 Jun 1920 in Estherville, Ia., and had been previously married. Wally worked for Northwestern Bell Telephone Co., starting as a lineman, and progressed to personnel staff supervisor in Des Moines. He retired after thirty years of service 2 Mar 1978. Wally and Ruth now reside in Ft. Myers, Fla.

115(11)31 Kenneth Edmund Thomson

Kenneth was born 9 Oct 1936. He married Beth Joann Hubley 23 Aug 1963. Beth was born 14 Apr 1932. They had Neal Joshua and

Jennifer Rachel. Ken teaches German, French, math, and chemistry at Wakefield High School. His avocation involves the repair of bicycles; he also enjoys bike riding long distances. Beth is a school nurse in North Reading, Mass., where they make their home.

115(11)32 Marian Thomson

Marian married Peter Carter Cain. They adopted Joel at the age of about five. Marian is a free-lance editor and formerly worked in Boston for D.C. Heath. Peter is a therapist at Tewksbury, a state mental institution.

115(11)41 Chelsea Louise Goold

Chelsea was born 25 Mar 1942. In Nov 1993, she married Gary Walker who was born 19 Jan 1947. They did not have any children.

115(11)42 Karen Judith Goold

Karen was born 19 Jan 1944. On 17 May 1965 she was married first to John Lapham, and they had three children: Lorene Kay, John Joseph, and Kathy Lynn. Karen divorced John, then married Harold "Bud" Stott on 22 Jun 1996. Bud was born 15 May 1937. In 2001 they were living in Tucson, Az.

115(11)43 William Paul Goold

Bill was born 26 Jan 1948. He married Pamela Butler on 16 Aug 1968. Pamela was born 13 Dec 1948. They had Rebecca Aileen, Leah Rae, William Michael, Joshua David, and Rachel Joy. They lived in Everett, Wash., in 2001.

115(11)44 Peggy Ann Goold

Peggy was born 1 Aug 1949. Peggy was married to Eugene Young and they had Ian Eugene. Peggy and Eugene were divorced and she married Tim Mann on 15 Sep 1990. Tim was born 10 Apr 1948. They were living in Edmonds, Wash., in 2001.

115(11)51 Ruth Elizabeth Thomson

Ruth was born 31 Jul 1945 in Seattle. There she attended Lincoln High School and graduated in 1963. At Seattle Pacific University she majored in physical education and graduated in 1967. Ruth married Wayne Brown. Ruth and Wayne worked for Washington State University. Their children are Nathaniel and Lyndsey. They were living in Vancouver, Wash., in 2001.

115(11)52 Jean Rose Thomson

Jean was born a twin 21 Sep 1946. She married Phil Peterson and they reside in Olympia, Wash. Jean works for Washington State Hist. Soc. Their children are Callie Jean and Jennifer Lee.

115(11)53 Joan Helen Thomson

Joan was born 21 Sep 1946. She married Peter Hanson of Renton, Wash. They did not have any children. Joan is retired after working for Human Resources of the State of Washington. Pete operates a charter fishing business.

115(11)54 Donald Paul Thomson

Don was born 21 Feb 1949. He graduated from Lincoln High School in 1967, and spent two years at Seattle Pacific and Shoreline County Colleges. Don works for Cummins Rocky Mountain of Billings, Mont. He married Debbie Stickler who was born 20 Oct 1953, and is employed by the Comptroller Industrial Communications and Electronics. Their children are Shawn and Kara.

115(12)11 Robert Lawrence Thomson

Robert was born 18 May 1948 in Rock Island, Ill. He received his education in Rock Island schools and attended Black Hawk College in East Moline. On 2 Aug 1980 he married Linda Gartner who was born 3 Jan 1947. Robert is an optician while Linda works at Wal-Mart. They adopted Nicholas Robert. Linda has a daughter, Edina Lee, by a previous marriage. Robert and Linda were living in Rock Island in 1998.

115(12)21 Craig Edwin Corson

Craig was born 18 Sep 1941. He graduated from Moline High School in 1959 and from Illinois Western University in 1963. He married 13 Jun 1964 Helen Diane Stith and they live in Ames, Ia., where Craig is a city bus driver. Their children are Schuyler Eugene and Andrew Craig.

115(12)22 Donald Lawrence Corson

Donald was born 11 Jun 1944. Don graduated from Moline High School in 1962 and from Coe College in 1966. He also attended Kansas State University for a year, then served a year in the U.S. Air Force in Vietnam from 1969-1970. He holds a master's degree from the University of Louisville and works for Jefferson County School System in Louisville, Ky. He married, first, Charlotte E. Lynch and later they divorced. Secondly, he married Joyce Deddin Martin 13 Dec 1979. His third wife is Kathy Rose whom he married on 7 Jun 1997. They live in Sellersberg, Ind.

115(12)23 Margaret Jean Corson

Jean was born 6 Mar 1946. She attended Moline High School and graduated in 1964. Then she graduated from Coe College in 1968. She married 7 Sep 1968 Howard William Wolvington who was born in 1945. Howard is employed by Boeing Aircraft in Seattle, Wash. They have two children, Sandra Leigh and Matthew Allan.

116111 Max Beck Dooley

Max was born 5 Jul 1892 in Madison Co., Ia. He married 2 Feb 1918 Isabel Wilson who was born 20 May 1895 in Galveston, Tex., and died in Feb 1948. Their children were Betty Jane and James Beck. Max died 1 Jan 1948 in Topeka, Kan., and was buried in Memorial Park Cemetery, Topeka.

116112 Isla Mary Dooley

Isla was born 11 May 1894 in Dexter, Dallas Co., Ia. She was a graduate of Washburn College in Topeka, Kan., in 1917. She taught Sunday school and held Bible classes while a member of First Presbyterian Church in Topeka. She worked at Panama Air Depot, and as a clerk at the Kansas State Board of Barber Examiners before she retired in 1964. She married 27 Aug 1926 Loren Ayre Taylor. Loren died 3 Aug 1953 and was buried in Memorial Park Cemetery, Topeka, Kan. Isla died 2 Jul 1988[171] and was buried alongside her husband. Their child was Dot Elizabeth.

116113 Lucile America Dooley

Lucille was born 4 Aug 1896 in Dexter, Ia. She attended Kansas State Normal College. In Nov 1916 she married Joseph G. Rosacker who was born 13 Jun 1895 in Stafford Co., Kan., and died in Feb 1980. Lucile died in Sep 1994, possibly in Washington, D.C. Their children were J. Warren, Joseph Jackson, Mary Elizabeth, and William Keith.

116114 Wilbur Graham Dooley

Webb was born 16 Dec 1899 in Dexter, Ia., and died 16 May 1972 in Topeka, Kan. He had been a student of Chicago Art Institute. He married 24 Jun 1930 Margaret Anne Peterson who was born 24 Dec 1901 and died in Jun 1975 in Topeka. Burial was in Memorial Park Cemetery in Topeka. Their children were Jay Allen, Margaret Anne, and Stephen Peterson.

116115 Jeannette Fern Dooley

Jeannette was born 16 Mar 1902 in Topeka, Kan., and was a student at Washburn College in Topeka. She married 5 Nov 1925 Cecil Perry McDonald who was born 16 Apr 1902 and died 9 Feb 1966 in Alexandria, Va. Jeannette died 27 Nov 1995 in Alexandria, Va. Their children were Thomas Andrew, Keith Dooley, and James.

116121 Lora Isla Beck

Lora was born 27 Dec 1904 in Madison Co., Ia. She married Orville Wilcox and lived on a farm near Winterset, Ia. Orville also was a county supervisor. They were childless. Lora died in Iowa about 1991 and was buried in Winterset Cem. Orville remarried after Lora died.

116122 Mary Marguerite Beck

Marguerite was born 24 Dec 1905 in Madison Co., Ia. She married Matthew (Matt) Zendzian who was born 28 Dec 1905 in Providence, R.I. He attended Brown University and became involved in insuranceand a travel agency. They had a daughter, Karen. Marguerite and Matt were later divorced. Marguerite was living in Milwaukee Catholic Home, an assisted living facility in 2001. Matt died 20 Nov 1988 in Milwaukee and was buried there in Memorial Park Cem.[172]

116123 James Stewart Beck

Stewart was born 17 Aug 1910 in Madison Co., Ia. He married Lucille Foster, who was of Manhattan, Kan., and they had two daughters, Lynn and Barbara. Stewart died at about the age of 59 of cancer and was buried in Miami, Fla. Social security death records list a James Beck who was born 3 Aug 1910 and died in Jan 1969 in Pensacola, Fla.

116131 Ruth Helene Beck

Ruth was born 19 Mar 1904 in Madison Co., Ia. She married Leland Wilhelm who was born 31 Mar 1906 and died 12 May 1992. Ruth died 14 Sep 1989 in Lee's Summit, Mo., and both are buried in Branson, Mo. Their were no children.

116132 Floyd Brown Beck

Floyd was born 21 Sep 1905 in Madison Co., Ia., and died 30 May 1991 in McAllen, Tex., where he was buried. Floyd was a graduate of Grinnell College about 1930. He married Mary Louise Musmaker

who was born in Sep 1915. Their children were Larry Allen, Jane
Frances, Thomas James, and Daniel Joseph (?).

116133 Mildred Jeannett Beck

Mildred was born 7 Dec 1909 in Adair Co., Ia. She married in 1953
Ben Kuyk who was born 12 May 1888 and died in Sep 1979. They had
no children. Mildred, who was living in Pella, Ia., in 1999, and
still driving, was a big help in identifying the people in the 1915
Thomson reunion photograph.

116161 James Eldredge Miller

Eldredge was born 4 Jul 1905 in Madison Co., Ia. He was married to
Lois when he died in New York City on 12 Jun 1974.[173] There were no
children.   He was at one time the Advertising Manager of
Architectural Building Products Div. of the Johns-Manville Corp.

116162 Joseph Keith Miller

Known as Keith, he was born 11 Nov 1909 in Topeka, Kan. He was a
salesman for Hemphill Shoe Co., and had worked for them 28 years
when he died of a heart attack on 12 Sep 1980 in Huntington Beach,
Orange Co., Calif. His body was cremated. He married Virginia
Ellen Rhea who was born 7 Jan 1912 in Kan., and died 13 Feb 1990 in
Huntington Beach.   They are probably the parents of Ethel Adelle
who was born 27 Mar 1943 in Los Angeles Co., Calif.

116231 Vera Leota Jessup

Vera was born 8 Oct 1899 in Airlie, Ore. She married in Creston,
Ia., on 16 May 1919, Paul A. Beymer who was born 24 Apr 1899 in
Diagonal, Ia. Their children were Ruth Pauline, Beth Maxine, and
Ronald Arthur. Paul died in Sep 1982 in Cedarville, Mich.

116232 Ruth Jannette Jessup

Ruth was born 5 Mar 1901 in Sharpsburg, Ia. She married 1 May 1920
Eugene Joseph Greene who was born 12 Jun 1896 in Hatfield, Mo.
Their children were Robert Byron, Shirley Louise, Phyllis Marie,
and Alberta Jeannette. Secondly, she married in 1963 Ora Virgil
Payne. Ruth died 25 Jul 1996 in Simi Valley, Calif.

116233 Byron Marin Jessup

Byron was born 19 Nov 1904 in Sharpsburg, Ia. He died in Jun 1919
as the result of an accidental explosion in a drugstore where he
was employed.

116234 Dale Ernest Jessup

Dale was born 9 Oct 1909 in Diagonal, Ia. He married Florence Leota Wiley in Des Moines on 6 Oct 1933. She was born 5 Sep 1912. Dale graduated from Diagonal High School. He then attended Northwestern College of Minnesota, received a BA degree from the University of Minnesota, and a MA from the University of Denver. He became a Baptist minister. Florence graduated from Diagonal High School and received a AA degree from Citrus Community College in Calif. Their two sons are Byron Dale and Dwight Wiley. Dale and Florence were residents of a nursing home in Ind., in 1999.

116235 Dorothy Jessup

Dorothy was born 9 Oct 1909, a twin to Dale. She never married and died in University Hospital in Iowa City 27 Sep 1951. She was buried in Diagonal, Ia.

116241 Jessie Maude Doty

Maude was born 30 Jun 1892 in Macksburg, Ia. She was in California when she developed typhoid fever and died 12 Jan 1911 in Des Moines, Ia.

116242 Waldo Emerson Doty

Waldo was born 6 Jan 1898 in Redding, Ia. He was in the U.S. Army during WW I. He died 21 Sep 1936 in San Francisco, Calif., and was buried in Calif., exact location unknown. He was never married.

116243 James Lowell Doty

James was born 31 Mar 1903 near Creston, Ia. In Wichita, Kan., James married 3 Oct 1925 Mary Elnor Dickerson who was born 15 Nov 1906. James and Elnor were graduates of Wichita University. They had a daughter, Mary Belle. James was a school teacher for 44 years including the fifteen years he served as principal of Towanda Grade School. He was also on the faculty of Oil Hill School. He recently lived in El Dorado and was also an associate realtor with J. C. Hoyt and Co. He died suddenly of a heart attack 3 Jun 1975 and was buried in Benton Cemetery, Benton, Kan.[174] Elnor was living in El Dorado, Kan., in 2001.

116251 Howard Charles Amick

Howard was born 5 Jul 1903 in Loup City, Neb. He was a graduate of North High School and the University of Chicago. He was a department head for Northwest Bell Telephone Company for over forty years. On 15 Jul 1930 in Pine City he married Blanche Miller who was born 8 Dec 1906 in Sioux City, Ia. Their children were Richard Charles, Marjorie Ellen, and Martha Ann. Howard died of a liver ailment 10 Jul 1980 in Des Moines, Ia., where he had lived most of his life.   Shortly before his death he had been a doorkeeper at the Iowa Senate for two sessions. He was an elder and trustee of Westminster United Presbyterian Church. He was a past president of Polk County Historical Society and the Rotary Club. He was buried in Jordon Cemetery in West Des Moines. Blanche died 14 Mar 2001 in Des Moines, Ia.

116252 Muriel Alberta Amick

Alberta was born 19 Dec 1905 in Redding, Ia., and died in 1967 in Des Moines. She graduated from Roosevelt High School in Des Moines in 1924, then graduated from Drake University about 1928. She married 14 Jun 1930, in Des Moines, Alvin Turner Jones who was born 13 Jul 1902 and died 18 Dec 1962 in Indianapolis, Ind.   Alvin graduated from Coe College in Cedar Rapids about 1926, then worked for Northwestern Bell Telephone Co. as a directory planning supervisor in Des Moines and in Omaha, Neb. They had Verlee Faye, Susan Marie, Nancy Ann, and Thomas Alvin. Alvin died of injuries suffered in a two-car accident on U.S. Hwy 31 in Hamilton Co., Ohio., which also claimed the life of his mother, Hannah (Turner) Jones. Alvin was buried in Des Moines.[175]

116253 Kenneth Dean Amick

Kenneth was born 1 Oct 1912 in Des Moines, Ia. He graduated from high school in Des Moines, and then graduated from Georgetown University in 1937 with a law degree. Kenneth served an officer in the U.S. Army from Dec 1941 through Oct 1946, and spent his entire tour of duty in several countries in Europe and Africa. Later, he practiced law, initially in Washington, D.C., then in New York City, followed by Duluth, Minn., where he worked for Etna Insurance. He married 17 May 1947, in Washburn, Wisc., Ruth Barbara Hill who was born 31 Aug 1919 in Minneapolis, Minn. Barbara graduated from Washburn (Minn.) High School in 1937. They had Laurie Jayne, Birt Clyde, and Jabez Hill. Kenneth died 17 Feb 1987 in Tucson, Az. Barbara was living in International Falls, Minn., in 2001.

116261 Bernice Saville

"Nellie" was born 18 Mar 1901 in Ringgold Co., Ia. She married 25 Dec 1923 Theodore Larsen at Elk Horn, Ia. Their children were Jeannette, Theodore Jr., and Nellie Faye. Nellie died 8 Oct 1991 in Atlantic, Ia., and was buried in Elk Horn Lutheran Cem.

116262 Archie Leland Saville

Leland was born 8 Jan 1903 near Redding, Ia. He married 25 Nov 1925 Zanita Margaret Fullerton. Their children were George Lewis, Eva, and Pearl. Archie died 31 Oct 1983 in Mount Ayr, Ia.; burial was in Rose Hill Cemetery, Mount Ayr, Ia.

116263 Lloyd George Saville

Lloyd was born 26 Oct 1904. He married Mildred Worthington 1 Jun 1935 in Clearfield, Ia. Their children were Jacob, Paula, Anna Mary, Ellen, and James. Lloyd died 19 Jan 1987 in Mount Ayr, Ia. and was buried in Rose Hill Cem.

116264 Emma Jeanette Saville

Emma was born 24 Nov 1906 near Redding, Ia., and died there of dyptheria 14 Aug 1911.

116265 Wendell Keith Saville

Keith was born 16 Nov 1908 near Redding, Ia. He married, first, in St. Joseph, Mo., Marjorie Rifie 6 Dec 1932; they divorced in 1960. Their children were Thomas and Roger. Secondly, he married Betty Stephens. Keith died 8 Feb 1997 in Green Valley, Ariz.

116266 Henry Henderson Saville

Henry was born 13 Feb 1912 near Redding, Ia. He married 22 Oct 1938 Hazel Mary Dimiz in Atlantic, Ia. Their children were Shirley, Larry, Lloyd, and Kenneth. Henry died 17 May 1975 in Atlantic, Ia. and was buried there in Catholic Cem.

116267 Chester Vernon Saville

Chester was born 27 Jan 1915 near Redding, Ia. He died of a stomach tumor 12 Mar 1916 and was buried beside his sister, Emma Jannett, in Middleford Cem.

116268 Annabelle Saville

Annabelle was born 28 Sep 1917 near Redding, Ia. She married Robert Bristol 10 Jan 1942 in Des Moines, Ia., and they had Alan and John. Later they divorced. She was in Stuart, Ia., in 1998.

116269 Ethel Saville

Ethel was born 16 Aug 1919 near Redding, Ia. She married Warren Martin 18 Jun 1945 in Watsonville, Calif., and were divorced in

1969.   Their children were Susan, Marilyn, Rebecca, and David.
Ethel was living in New Providence, Ia., in 1998.

116281 Herbert Monroe Mekemson

Herbert was born 30 May 1904 in Bassett, Neb. He married Marjorie
Marshall and they had Curtis. He adopted the children his wife had
by a previous marriage: Marshall Cox and Nancy Cox. He died 10 Jan
1992 in Sacramento, Calif.

116282 Eleanor Lucille Mekemson

Eleanor was born 29 Nov 1907 in Prosser, Wash., and died 7 Aug 1986
in Sacramento Co., Calif. On 17 Feb 1937, she married Keith
Johnstone who was born 7 Apr 1893 in Grinell, Ia., and died 4 Dec
1970 in Sacramento Co. They both are buried in Sacramento. They
had Robert, James, and Elaine.

116283 Harold Lytle Mekemson

Harold was born 19 Sep 1910 and died 4 Mar 1963 in Seattle. He was
married 11 Sep 1929 to Vera Xoreta Bryan who was born 5 Jan 1911
and died 23 Dec 1973. Their daughter was Roberta Joyce. After
Harold's death, Vera married Kenneth Bolton.

116284 Esther Eveline Mekemson

Esther was born 7 Dec 1915 and married Bruce Schilling who died 30
Oct 1966 in Grants Pass, Ore., and was buried there. They had
Carol, Patricia, Doris, Andy, and Bruce. Secondly, Esther married
Beecher Lucky who was born 17 Dec 1902 and died in Apr 1982 in Coos
Bay, Ore. Esther suffered a stroke and died on 13 Jun 1999 in
Salem, Ore. She was buried in Grants Pass, Ore.

116285 Andrew Voight Mekemson

Andrew was born 17 Aug 1923 in Redding, Ia. He served in the U.S.
Navy during WW II. He was a refrigeration repairman for Bumblebee
Seafoods and became plant engineer. In his possession is a Bible
that has been in his family for many generations; it contains vital
statistics. His first marriage was to Geraldine Harris; they later
divorced. Their children were Laura and Jeannette. Secondly, he
married Mabel Nelson 30 Sep 1953 in Toledo, Ore. Their children
are Douglas Voight and Howard Allan. Andrew died 18 Mar 2001; his
body was cremated.

116286 Frances Mae Mekemson

Frances was born 10 Jul 1927 in Redding, Ia. She married Robert

Grisham on 7 Jul 1946 in Ashland, Ore. They had Susan, Deborah, Craig and Jonathan. Robert died in an automobile accident 12 Aug 1972 in Las Vegas, Nev. Frances secondly married Richard Timmerhoff 3 Apr 1978 in Coeur d'Alene, Ida.; they live in Greenacres, Wash.

116291 Mildred Beryl Marts

Mildred was born 14 Dec 1904 in Colorado City, Colo. She had a master's degree. She married Raymond Hulshizer and they had Berneta Ray and Dorris Ann. They were of Brush, Colo., where Raymond was a farmer, machinery salesman, and preacher. Gardening was his main hobby. Mildred died 2 Nov 1987; Raymond was born 1 Sep 1919 and died in Jul 1962. Both are buried in Ogallala, Neb.

116292 Marie Jannette Marts

Marie was born 24 May 1907 in Comstock, Neb., and died 16 Jan 1995. She was buried at Shrine of Rest in Colorado Springs, Colo. She married Marridy "George" Hubby and they had Bonnie Delores and Bruce. George was born 8 Sep 1902 and died 3 Mar 1988. His body was cremated and his ashes were scattered over Cripple Creek, Colo.

116293 Wilma Marts

Wilma was born 24 Mar 1913 and later lived in Crista Senior Community in Seattle, Wash. She married Paul Berg who died 28 Dec 1948 in Tacoma, Wash., and was buried in Boone, Ia. Paul was a minister with the Christian Missionary Alliance. They had Paul Wilburn, David John, and Daniel Joe.

116294 Ila Wilburna Marts

Ila was born 20 Jun 1914 in Bassett, Neb. She married Ellis (Ike) Wiley and their children were Roger Ellis, Max Allan, Mark, and Ann Jeanette. Ila died 14 Sep 1994 in Albuquerque, N.M. Ellis was born 16 Mar 1915 and died 7 Oct 1997 in Portland, Ore.

116295 Roland Thomas Marts

Roland was born 20 May 1919 in Hay Springs, Neb. He graduated from Diagonal High School in 1937 and had two years of college before becoming a superintendent in commercial construction. He married Ardyce and they had Theodore and Thomas. They lived in Colorado Springs, Colo.

116296 Nancy Jo Marts

Nancy was born 28 Aug 1923 and died 10 Jan 1978 in Wallace, Neb. She married Ralph Mord and later divorced. She obtained her social security card in Washington state, indicating her residence there at a young age. Ralph was born 25 Feb 1923 and died 1 May 1992 in Tex. They had Shirley Rae, Betty, Rahe Sterling, and Judy Kay. Nancy secondly married Clarence Williams.

1162(10)1 Edna Pauline Mekemson

Pauline was born 9 Sep 1917 in Kinsley, Kan., and died 19 Apr 1991 in Crete, Neb.   She married John Brenneman and they lived near Hastings, Neb. John died 16 Dec 1987 and was buried in Riverside Cemetery in Crete, Neb. They had Elizabeth, Robert, and Kenneth.

1162(10)2 Stuart Everett Mekemson

Stuart was born 12 Jan 1921 in St. John, Kan., and died 4 Aug 1991. He married Jane Graham and they had John Robert, David Graham, Ann Sheldon, Wendy Jane and Leslie Elizabeth.   Stuart and Jane both graduated from Monmouth College. He was a personnel director.

1162(10)3 William Brown Mekemson

William was born 18 Jan 1925 in St. Johns, Kan. He was a graduate of the Univ. of Minnesota, and obtained a master of arts degree from the Univ. of Iowa. William was in the Navy R.O.T.C. program at the Univ. of Minn., and was in the U.S. Navy from 1943 to 1946. He then taught Spanish, music, social studies, and, occasionally, mathematics. He married 23 Dec 1951, in Emmettsburg, Ia.,   Dorothy Mae Brown.   Their children are Mary Janine, William Brown, Paul Randall, and Joseph Gilbert.   The Mekemsons were living in Humboldt, Ia., in 2001.

1162(11)1 William Herman Swenson

Bill was born 5 Jul 1925 in San Francisco, Calif. Bill graduated from Dunellen (N.J.) High School in Jun 1943, and in Oct 1943 he was drafted into the U.S. Army.   His   extensive and detailed account of his wartime experiences as a radio operator in Italy are contained in a manuscript *A Genealogy Chart for Edna Ethel Mekemson,* compiled by his brother, Fred. Bill attended Maryville College, the McCormick Theological Seminary in Chicago, and earned a BAE in 1956 and a MAE in 1960.   He went to the School of Art Institute in Chicago, and taught art at Maryville College before he retired in 1990. He married Esther Cornelius and they had William and Esther. After a divorce, William married Peggy Tippins 7 Aug 1973 in Maryville, Tenn. See "Late Additions," p.381.

1162(11)2 Frederick Harold Swenson

Fred was born 6 Aug 1927 in San Francisco. He graduated from

Dunellen (N.J.) High School in 1945. Fred then spent two years in the U.S. Navy. Later he attended night school at The State University of Rutgers in Brunswick, N.J., for almost four years but did not receive a degree; he was majoring in math. Fred decided to go into the trucking business which he started in N.J., and continued in Calif. He married 31 Jul 1965 Rita Giso who was born 17 May 1936; no issue. Rita is a graduate of Boston University and became a school teacher in Boston and in San Francisco. Rita retired in 1998.

1162(11)3 Herbert Jack Swenson

Jack, a twin, was born 20 Sep 1930 in San Francisco, Calif. During the Korean War, he was in the Medical Corps and was stationed on USS Haven, a hospital ship. In 1954 the ship was deployed to Vietnam to aid the French servicemen who were defeated in northern Vietnam. The ship took the French soldiers to their homeland, then sailed across the Atlantic, through the Panama Canal and to San Francisco where Jack completed his enlistment in the U.S. Navy. In Dunellen, N.J., he married Lois Jean Stransky who was born 6 Jul 1932 in Plainfield, N.J. They had Carol Jean, Todd Jack, Stephen Jack, and Ted. Jack and Jean are divorced.

1162(11)4 Hilma Janet Swenson

Janet was born 20 Sep 1930 in San Francisco, Calif. After graduating from Dunellen (N.J.) High School, she attended Taylor University in Upland, Ind., for two years. She then studied at Colombia Presbyterian Medical Center in New York City, and received her R.N. and a B.S. degree in 1953. From 1954 to 1956 she was at Biblical Seminary in NYC and earned a master's degree in religious education. She went to Pakistan as a missionary nurse in 1958, and returned to the U.S. in 1962. She later lived in Shippensburg, Pa., where she worked as a nurse. In 1995 she retired from nursing. She was married to Richard White, and they have since divorced. They had Elizabeth Florence (Beth).

116311 Ethel Ruby Thomson

Ethel was born 17 Feb 1898 in Lake Wilson, Minn. On 15 Aug 1917 she married Harry Clarence Crisp who was born 17 May 1893 in Chester Lake, S.D., and died 23 Jan 1966 in Dell Rapids, S.D. Their children were Lucile Mildred, Ralph Glenn, Betty Ann, Robert Hugh, Reginald Keith, Max Thomson, and Harriet Ruth. Ethel died in May 1984.

116312 Hazel White Thomson

Hazel was born 22 Oct 1899 in Lake Wilson, Minn. In Harrison,

S.D., she married 28 Jun 1926 Robert Burns Yule, who was born 10 Jun 1898 in Tipton, Ia. Their children were James Oliver, Roger Thomson, and Roberta Ruth. Hazel compiled a history of the Thomson family which remained for her husband to complete when she died 18 Jan 1978 in Mesa, Az. Robert did complete the task, and the document was widely circulated. The material contained in it has formed an important component of this compilation. Robert died in 1987; both are buried in Red Oak Cem. in Cedar Co.

116313 Ruth May Thomson

Ruth was born 1 Jun 1902 in Lake Wilson, Minn. She married 24 Aug 1931 Howard Wirth Lackey who was born 27 Sep 1902 in Sioux Falls, S.D. Ruth died 25 Nov 1943 in Dell Rapids; Harold died 7 Jul 1988 and both are buried in Woodland Cem., Sioux Falls.

116321 Donald Glenn Thomson

Donald was born 31 May 1911 in Madison Co., Ia., and died in Apr 1983 in Kila, Mont. He married Edith Brown Black 15 May 1939 in Kallspell, Mont. Edith was born 13 Apr 1917 in Glendive, Mont. Their children are David Hugh and Pamela Adele. Edith was living in Joliet, Mont., in 2001.

116322 Kenneth Earl Thomson

Kenneth was born 19 Jan 1913 in Gordon, Sheridan Co., Neb. He had a ninth-grade education. During W W II he was classified 4-F, so he didn't have to serve. In Estherville, he married on 29 Dec 1938 Charlotte Melvina Zerfuss who was born 23 Mar 1915 near Superior, Ia. She graduated from high school in 1932. They had Janet Jean, Dorothy Marlene, Ruth Marie, and Mary Kay. Kenneth died 9 Dec 1988 in Superior, Ia.

116323 Dorothy Esther Thomson

Dorothy was born 16 Sep 1916 in Madison Co., Ia. She married 13 Aug 1936 Alvin Walter Roby, who was born 16 Feb 1908 in Truro, Ia., and died 5 Jul 1976 in Cedar Rapids, Ia. Dorothy died 22 Dec 1998. Their children were Clark Walter and Carol Ann. Alvin and Dorothy are buried in Young Cemetery, Truro.

116324 Hugh Clair Thomson

Hugh was born 29 Nov 1917 in Madison Co., Ia. He married 12 Jul 1943 in San Luis, Calif., Doretha Laverne Beasley who was born 17 Jan 1922 in Davis City, Ia. Their children were Jackie Gwenn and Christine Sue.

116325 Marjorie Clara Thomson

Marjorie was born 29 Nov 1917 in Winterset, Ia. On 31 Dec 1937 she married Donald R. Wilson who was born 28 Sep 1913 in Winterset and died 9 Oct 1969 in Branson, Mo. Burial was in Ozark Memorial Cemetery in Branson. Their children were Sharon Lee and Donald Dennis.

116351 Kathryn Cynthia Surratt

Kathryn (Kay) was born 12 Sep 1913 in Fergus Falls, Minn. Kay is a graduate of Monmouth College class of 1935. Kay taught Spanish at the University of Wisconsin as well as in outlying areas. She was also a professional photographer. She married 21 Jun 1942, in Madison, Wisc., Richard Woodrow Reierson who was born 25 Nov 1913 in Madison, Wisc., and died in May 1983 in Madison, Wisc. Kay died 22 Aug 1996. Their children were Richard Andrew, Michael Eric, and Patricia Jean.

116352 Margaret Nan Surratt

Margaret was born 18 Jul 1916 in Grand Forks, N.D. In 1938 she graduated from Monmouth College, and taught a year at Princeton, Ill. She married 28 Aug 1939, in Springfield, Ill., Arthur Elliot Morgan who was born 6 Oct 1916 in Denver, Colo. Arthur was an executive with Swift and Company before he died 3 May 1976 in Batesville, Ark., of a heart attack while on a trip. Their children were Robert Elliot, James Shorter, William Arthur, and Thomas Bard. Margaret was living near Kissee Mills, Mo., in 2001.

116353 Andrea Jean Surratt

Andrea was born 13 Jan 1919 in Grand Forks, N.D. In 1940 she graduated from Monmouth College. She married Carroll Steward Hinman 26 Jun 1943 in Springfield, Ill. Carroll, who was born 16 May 1913, worked for the federal government in the State Department. Their children were John Carroll, Andrea Jean, Donald Lee, Keith Russell, and Nancy Caroline. Carroll died 26 Sep 1986 and was buried in Arlington National Cemetery in Va.

116354 Robert Andrew Surratt

Robert was born 15 Nov 1923 in Springfield, Ill. He attended Monmouth College for about a year before he enlisted in the U.S. Army Air Force. Later, he graduated from the University of Illinois with a degree in geology. This occupation took him to Turkey where he was involved in developing air bases. He married Carol Cook in 1961. They were divorced in 1962 without children.

Robert then worked for a filming company in Kansas City, and finally as a postal employee. Robert died at the age of 58 on 6 Aug 1982 in Kansas City where he had lived most of his life.

116361 Lois Ruth Thomson

Lois was born 22 Dec 1928 in Sandstone, Minn. She married Alvan Harold Holmes 22 Dec 1948. Their children were Sheila Ruth, Loren Errol, Alice Carolyn, Michael Ray, Glen Howard, David Brian, Susan Lori, Sharon Elizabeth, and Tamara Iris. Lois and Alvan make their home in Viola, Ark.

116362 Paul Bissell Thomson

Paul was born 19 Nov 1930 in Askov, Minn. He had a BS degree in animal husbandry and a master's in food technology from The University of Md. He married in Clinton, Ia., on 1 Aug 1959, Bette Manning who was born 15 Jan 1940 in Alpena, Mich. Their children were Robin Lynn, Randy Ray, Holly Lynn, and Jennifer Ruth.

116363 Elmer Hugh Thomson

Elmer was born 23 May 1934 in Sandstone, Minn., and died 7 Nov 1996. He was buried in Danforth Cemetery in Sandstone. He had been a corrections officer at the federal prison at Sandstone, and farmed extensively. He married 12 Oct 1963 Irene Louise Eaton who was born 6 Apr 1945 in Sandstone. Their children were Jacelyn Kay, Hugh Ryan, and Gary Eugene.

116411 Lillie Hazel Chase

Hazel was born 30 Jun 1893 in Madison Co., Ia. Late in her life she was married, for a short time, to Frank Athey, then they divorced. Hazel died 26 Jun 1981 at Winterset, Ia.

116412 Mabel Roberta Chase

Mabel was born 23 Aug 1897 in Madison Co., Ia. She was married there 26 Dec 1917 to Charles Earl Black who was born 28 Apr 1896 in Arcola, Ill. Charles enlisted in the U.S. Army 8 Aug 1918 at St. Louis, Mo. He was sent to Camp McArthur in Waco, Tex., where he was posted until 16 Sep. He eventually landed in France 7 Oct 1918 and was put into the Army of Occupation, Co. E, 16th Regiment Infantry, and served one year. He was subjected to shellfire one week before the Armistice was signed. He was discharged 19 Aug 1919 at Camp Upton on Long Island. Mabel lived with her parents during her husband's absence. Mabel died 2 Oct 1936 in Madison Co. and was buried in Winterset Cemetery. Charles died 2 Jan 1980

in Greenfield, Ia. and was buried there.   Their children were
Roberta Mae, Iola Maxine, Earl Chase, and Eva Rachel.

116413 Verl Andrew Chase

Verl was born 3 Dec 1904 in Madison Co., Ia.   He married Dorothy
Chapman and later they divorced.   Their child was Charles Edmund
Chase, who lived just six months. Secondly, Verl married Eunice
Wright 26 Sep 1934 at Broken Bow, Neb.   Eunice was born 7 Aug 1905
and died 25 Dec 1983.   They had Verl Andrew Jr., John Edmund, and
Marilyn Ann. Verl was a farmer as well as a school bus driver. Verl
died 8 Mar 1962 in Madison Co.; Verl and Eunice are buried in
Chase-McDonald Cemetery located a few miles west of Winterset, Ia.

116511 Mary Edna Graham

Mary was born 3 (or 8) Nov 1897 in Macksburg, Ia. She graduated
from Whitworth College, became a high school teacher, and taught in
Hartline, Wash., and Wallace, Ida.   She was married on 14 Jun 1933
to Edward Edwards who was born 1 Aug 1895 and died at the age of 98
on 24 Mar 1994 in Wilbur. He had been a farmer in Hartline, Wash.
Their child was Richard Lewis. Mary died 8 Mar 1976 in Spokane,
Wash., and was buried alongside her husband, in Hartline, Wash.

116512 Leslie Bonham Graham

Leslie was born 10 Jun 1900 in Macksburg, Ia. He married, first,
Marguerite Miller 15 Oct 1928. Marguerite was born 14 May 1903 in
Walla Walla, Wash. Secondly, on 5 Jun 1978, Leslie married Mouck
Teria who has celebrated her 100th birthday.   Leslie died 23 Feb
1985.

116513 George Allison Graham

George was born 20 Nov 1903 in Macksburg, Ia., and died 25 Mar 1993
in Spokane, Wash. He married, first, Edith Aebrisher 20 Oct 1928
in Chicago, Ill.   They had Fred Allison and Frances Mildred.
Secondly, he married 12 Dec 1945 Bernice Lucile Kirk.   Bernice was
born 2 Aug 1908, possibly in Minn., and probably died of cancer in
Spokane, Wash., 29 May 1987, where she had lived since 1942.
Bernice was buried in Fairmont Memorial Park.

116514 Clarence Samuel Graham

Clarence was born 3 Aug 1906 in Macksburg, Ia.   He married 17 Aug
1929 Wynona Gretorex in Seattle.   His second marriage was to
Bernice Adelaide Blake (?) 24 Jun 1961. His children were Diane

and Jacqueline.   There is a social security death record for a
Bernice Graham who was born 18 Oct 1905 and died in Jun 1983.
Clarence was living in Yuma, Ariz., in 1999.

116515 Merton Graham

Merton was born 26 Jul 1911 in Macksburg, Ia. He died 25 Jan 1914
in Fort Shaw, Mont.

116516 Ruby Ellen Graham

Ruby was born 3 Aug 1915 in Fort Shaw, Mont. She graduated from
North Central High School in Spokane in 1933. She then attended
Whitworth College for a semester. In Seattle she was married on 28
Sep 1935 to Roy Phillipy who was born 25 Nov 1906 in Velpen, Ind.,
and died 4 Mar 1995 after suffering from a stroke. Roy was buried
in Spokane Memorial Gardens Cemetery. Roy had previously been
married to Inez Rider and they had a son, Mark. Roy and Inez later
divorced. Roy had a fifth-grade education, and at the age of
fifteen he became an apprentice painter for the Great Northern
Railway. He learned to do the mahogany interiors of railroad
executive cars that he painted in gold trim. Later, his work mainly
consisted of painting the "Billy Goat" decals on freight cars; he
worked for the railroad for almost fifty years. He was a member of
the Masons and other organizations. In retirement he enjoyed
travelling, and painting landscapes in oils. Ruby worked as a
saleslady at a locally-owned Crescent Department Store.   Their
children were Lawrence Eugene, David Allen, and Keith Leroy. Ruby
was living in Spokane, Wash., in 1999, and was especially helpful
and generous with information on her family for which the compiler
is thankful.

116517 Chester William Graham

Chester was born 26 May 1920 in Spokane, Wash. He spent time in
the U.S. Air Force. He married 14 May 1944 Frances Elizabeth
Maberry in Deming, N.M. Frances was born 23 Apr 1920 in McCaulley,
Tex. They had William Leonard and Janice Fern, and lived in Wash.,
and Tex.

116521 Philip Edward Graham

Phil was born 18 Dec 1911 in Cascade, Mont. He died 26 Jun 1990 in
Long Beach, Calif. In 1933, he graduated with a BS degree from the
University of Calif. He married, first, in 1935, Wauneta Vickers
who was born 21 Apr 1910 in Mitchell, S.D., and died 7 Jul 1937.
They had Philip Edward Jr. Secondly, he married Bernice Margaret
Hammett 4 Aug 1940 in Riverside, Calif. They had Mary Margaret,

and cared for Patricia Louise Dobyns. Bernice died 26 Apr 2001 in Long Beach, Calif., and is buried with her husband and infant son in Forest Lawn Memorial Park in Long Beach.

116522 Gordon Samuel Albert Graham

Gordon was born 8 Jul 1916 in Great Falls, Mont. He graduated from the University of California-Berkeley in 1938 with a BA degree in political science and economics. Gordon managed Longs drug stores and later was a partner in developing the Teton Village ski resort. He was owner of a real estate company in Jackson, Wyo. He married in Glendale, Calif., 7 Jul 1938, Betty June Richesin who was born 16 Jun 1916 in Long Beach, Calif., and died in Jackson, Wyo., 28 Aug 1994. Their children were Judith Lynne, Darleen Joan, and Thais June. Gordon was living in Jackson, Wyo., in 2001.

116523 Robert Johnson Graham

Robert (Bob) was born 5 Oct 1921 in Great Falls, Mont. In Corona, Calif., on 29 Jan 1949, he married Gladys Mildred Korsgarden who was born 27 Jun 1921 in Twin Valley, Minn. Bob was in the U.S. Marine Corps from 1943 to 1970 and spent time as a test pilot. He held a master's degree in electrical engineering. Their children are Thomas Edward, Christine Diane, and Robert David. Bob enjoys playing golf and is a car restorer at home in Tustin, Calif.

116531 Arlie Harold Graham

Arlie was born 3 Apr 1898 in Macksburg, Ia. He married 4 Dec 1917 Ruth Mary Ritter who was born 14 Aug 1897 in Afton, Ia., and died in Jan 1971 in Ia. Their child was Robert Layman. Arlie died 5 May 1934 in Des Moines, Ia.

116532 Earl Stewart Graham

Earl was born 19 Aug 1900 in Macksburg, Ia., and died about 25 Feb 1986 in Creston, Ia. He married, first, Helen Black 26 May 1926. Helen was born 22 Apr 1902 in Cumberland, Ia., and died 7 Mar 1969 in Omaha, Neb. Their child was Margaret Karen. Secondly, he married Bernice Oshel Farquhar 8 Jul 1970. Bernice was born 20 Jan 1899 in Orient, Ia., and died 2 Apr 1982 in Creston, Ia.

116533 Dorothy Graham

Dorothy was born 17 Nov 1902 in Macksburg, Ia. She married, first, Arnold Light 22 Oct 1923 in Leavenworth, Kan. They had a son, Raymond Earl Light. Secondly, she married 24 Oct 1942 Joseph Robert Vogt who was born 23 Nov 1903 in Omaha, Neb.

116534 Lorene Mabel Graham

Lorene was born 19 Jan 1906 in Macksburg, Ia. She married 29 Dec 1934 John Wesley Ross at Dunlap, Ia. Their children were Carol Lee, Donald Frank, and John Edward. John was born 17 Jan 1905 at Macksburg, Ia. Lorene died 22 Feb 1960 in Winterset, Ia.

116535 Robert Russell Graham

Robert was born 9 Mar 1908 in Macksburg, Ia. and died 12 Aug 1974 in Long Beach, Calif. He married Lucile Jeannette Conway who was born 15 Jul 1908 in Orange, Calif. Their children were Margaret Jean, Betty Mae, and Harold Edward.

116536 Wyman Lee Graham

Wyman was born 1 Jan 1921 in Macksburg, Ia. He married in Pasadena, Calif., 12 Jul 1947, Shirley Louise Hayman who was born 20 Apr 1924 in Glendale, Calif. Their children are Kenneth Lee, William Robert, and Mary Louise.

116541 Max Rolland Wimmer

Max was born prematurely 7 Apr 1896 in Adair Co., Ia. He died of pneumonia and measles 13 Apr 1896 and was buried in Liberty Baptist Church Yard, next to the monument of his grandmother.

116542 Gladys Wimmer

Gladys was born 5 May 1899 in Wray, Yuma Co., Colo., and died 10 Jan 1990 in Spokane, Wash. She married Raymond Otis Haworth on 8 Jun 1921 at Spokane, Wash. Raymond was born 1 Mar 1896 in Belvedere, Neb., and died 16 Mar 1973 in Eugene, Ore. He was buried in Fairmont Cemetery. Their children were Robert Lyle, Donald Raymond, and Gerald Samuel.

116543 Lyle Graham Wimmer

Lyle was born near Parker, S.D. on 23 Jun 1902. He moved to Spokane, Wash., in 1915 where he graduated from high school. In Spokane he married Mildred Bernice Roberts on 17 Sep 1924. She was born in Spokane 22 Mar 1902, the daughter of Samuel Louden Roberts and Bertha Jane Hevener. Mildred was a graduate of Washington teacher's college, later known as the Univ. of Eastern Washington. She taught school before she was married and remained active in church work. Their children are Ruth Evelyn and Gordon Lyle. Lyle spent his youth exploring the wilderness near Fort Shaw, Mont. At the age of eighteen he started working for Fairbanks Morse and Co. while also attending college. He graduated with a degree in electrical engineering in 1927 from the University of Washington. He continued his studies and was elected to Tau Beta Pi, an honorary engineering society. The Graham Genealogy continues with details of his outstanding career. In 1932 he left Fairbanks-Morse and took on a new career with Hartford Steam Boiler Inspection and Insurance Co. in Berkeley, Calif. In 1940 he was transferred to Connecticut, and in 1944 he switched to The Travelers Indemnity Co. He traveled extensively, which included several trips to Scotland. He published many articles on boiler and machinery insurance. Lyle entered into semi-retirement in 1967 while still serving as a litigation consultant and special witness. Lyle was active in church work wherever he lived, including the Presbyterian Church in Berkeley, Calif. Lyle died in Boca Raton, Fla., on 26 May 1995. Mildred died there 20 Apr 1997, and was buried in Spokane.

116551 Helen Marjorie Jacobson

Helen was born 17 Mar 1910 in Spaulding, Ia. Helen received a AS degree from Cottey College in 1930, a BS degree from the University of Iowa, and her medical degree from UI in 1936. She was a child psychiatrist in Virginia until 1984 when she retired. She married LeRoy Bayfield Sloan. LeRoy was born 2 May 1910 in Chicago, Ill. He had a JD degree from the University of Iowa and became an income tax attorney with the IRS. LeRoy died 19 Jan 1986 and was buried in Spring Hill Cemetery in Lynchburg, Va. They had Samuel Howard and Creighton Wesley. Helen was divorced from LeRoy, and was living in Aiken, S.C., in 1999.

116552 Graham Victor Jacobson

Victor was born 16 Jun 1911 in Spaulding, Ia., and was employed as a steam fitter for contractors most of his working career. He married 3 May 1943, in Iowa City, Ella Margaret Peters who was born 6 Feb 1912 and was living in Los Alamos in 1999. Graham died 31 May 1977 in Cedar Falls, Ia., and was buried at the Illyria Community Church near Wadena. Their child was Edward Graham.

116553 Wesley Cassel Jacobson

Wesley was born 21 May 1913 in Towner, Colo. He married, first, in Washington, D.C., Marion Margaret Mahoney who was born 20 May 1919 and died 13 May 1976 near Silver Spring, Md. Their children were Carol Elizabeth and Karen Jeanette. Secondly, he married Tessie Dordal. They were living in Rockville, Md., in 1998.

116554 Jeannette Eleanor Jacobson

Jeanette was born 24 Oct 1914 in Afton, Ia., and died 19 Jan 1989 in Long Beach, Calif. Burial was in Prairie Lawn Cemetery, near Spaulding, Ia. She was unmarried.

116555 Alden Dale Jacobson

Alden was born 4 Jun 1916 in Afton, Ia. He graduated from high school there in 1933, then attended college for four years. Alden then became an air force cadet and obtained a pilot's rating. He was in the U.S. Army Air Corps for 24 years and retired as a Lt. Col. He was a basic instructor, then was a B-29 pilot and flew 31 missions in combat during World War II. He married, first, Elizabeth Berger and they had Robert Dale, Richard Wesley, William Allison, and Philip Alden. Secondly, he married Lillian Lorraine Suttle Dula 24 Mar 1968. Lillian was born 28 May 1921 at Black Mountain, N.C. They were living in Fla. in 1999.

116556 Newell Edward Jacobson

Newell was born near Grafton, Union Co., Ia., on 7 Jun 1918. He married 22 Jun 1946 Dorothy Mae Myers in Creston, Ia. Dorothy was born 3 Dec 1919. Newell is a retired major in the U.S. Army and had lived in Homestead, Fla. They had no children. Newell died 25 Apr 1989, and was buried near Trinity, N.C.

116561 Myrle Graham Bishop

Myrle was born 19 Jun 1905 in Orient, Ia., and died in Chicago 10 Nov 1964. His first marriage was to Jeannette Ritter on 11 May 1929 in Chicago, Ill. They had Joanna Myrtle and Barbara Jean. Secondly, Myrle married on 16 Dec 1961 Inger Olson who was born 27 Jun 1907 and died 26 Feb 1990 in Beloit, Wisc.

116562 Straude Allison Bishop

Known as Al, he was born 30 Nov 1906 in Orient, Ia. He served two years in the U.S. Navy, then worked for the railroad as a traffic manager. He was married to Betty Edith Calkins on 9 Jun 1933; she was born 7 Jul 1914. They had John Allison, Mary Jane, Thomas Wayne, and Kenneth Claude. Al died[176] 9 Feb 1972 in Milwaukee, Wisc., and was buried there in Holy Cross Cem. Betty was living in Milwaukee in 2001.

116563 Charlotte Mae Bishop

Charlotte was born 19 Jul 1909 in Orient, Ia., and died in Sep 1974 in Indianola, Ia. She married 26 May 1935 Floyd "Pete" Franklin Augustine who was born 22 Aug 1907 and died in Apr 1975 in Indianola. Their children were Claudette Jane, Jim O., and Jack G.

116564 Elizabeth Mary Bishop

Elizabeth, who went by Elizabeth B. because she didn't like the name of Mary, was born 17 Feb 1912 in Orient, Ia. She married 1 Oct 1934, in Chicago, Ill., Mathew Elmer Morris, known as Mat. Mat served in the U.S. Navy during WW II. Their children were Richard Alan and Peter Jon. Elizabeth was a homemaker in Indianola, Ia., and died of cancer in Des Moines on 3 Feb 1998.[177] Mat was born 21 May 1908 and died 4 Oct 1992; both are buried in Orient, Ia.

116571 Ruth Josephine Graham

Josephine was born 5 Oct 1916 in Creston, Ia. In 1934 she graduated from Orient High School. She married, in Oil City, La., on 25 May 1942, Jerry Keithley Butler Jr. who was born 27 Dec 1915 in Mansfield, La. Josephine graduated from Grinnell College in 1938 and taught English in the high schools of Oto and Osceola, Ia. Jerry was in the U.S. Marine Corps in which he enlisted on 10 Mar 1935 and from which he retired on 1 Jun 1958. He then went into the oil business with his brother and father. Their children were Jerry Keithley III, Robert Graham, Ellen Ruth, and Lawrence Walter. They lived in Calif., N.C., Hawaii, and Oil City, La.

116711 Raymond McCorkle Eyerly

Raymond was born 30 May 1903 in Madison County, Iowa. His first marriage was to Floy Lillian Lyon who was born 5 Feb 1905 in Kan., and died of a stroke on 30 Dec 1943 in Los Angeles Co., Calif. They lived in Brighton, Colo., then in Calif. Secondly, Raymond married Doris Naanes who was born 18 Jan 1921 and died 31 Dec 1969 in Los Angeles Co. Doris previously had a daughter, Virginia Lee Petitt, who was born 4 Jan 1943. They had a son, Frank Raymond. Thirdly, Raymond married Bernice. Raymond died 9 Sep 1995 in Edmonds, Wash.; he and Doris are interred at Mountain View Mortuary in Altadena, Calif.

116712 Irma Lorraine Eyerly

Irma was born 25 Jul 1904 in Madison Co., Ia., and died 30 Nov 1981 at Hawthorne, Calif. She married Victor E. Billiter in Colorado about 1949. Their daughter was Joan Lorraine. Victor was born 25 Apr 1908 and died 24 Sep 1974 in Hawthorne, Calif; he and Irma are buried in Inglewood Cemetery in Los Angeles.

116713 Glenn Lawrence Eyerly

Glenn was born 28 Nov 1906 in Madison Co., Ia., and died 9 May 2000 in Calabasas, Calif. His social security card was issued when he was living in Colo. He worked in a grocery store with his parents. Glenn served in the U.S. Marine corps during WW II as part of the "Home Guard" on the west coast. He suffered from asthma and was classified 4-F, but wanted to serve his country during the war. At a late age, he married Virginia G. Grondahl who was born 9 Sep 1919 in Washington state and died 9 Apr 1995 in Arcadia, Calif. They were buried in Pasadena, Calif. They did not have any children.

116714 Jeannette Alice Eyerly

Jeannette was born 21 Nov 1922 in Brighton, Colo. She married Howard Lincoln Mills 22 Aug 1947 in Pasadena, Calif. She attended Colorado University in Boulder, and graduated from Whittier College in Jun 1945. She was a first grade teacher for twenty-five years. Howard was born 12 Feb 1914 in Oklahoma City, and died 7 Nov 1987 in Redlands, Colo. He was laid to rest in Mountain View Mortuary in Pasadena, Calif. Howard had a degree in business from the University of Oklahoma, and was a realtor and a building contractor in Pasadena. Jeannette was enjoying living in a retirement community in Santa Barbara as of 2001. Their children are Millicent Jean and Patricia Ann.

116721 Gladys Delight McCorkle

Gladys was born 6 Jun 1907 in Madison Co., Ia., and died 5 Jan 1993 in San Antonio, Tex. She was buried in Van Meter, Ia. On 6 May 1931 she married Johnnie Delmar Sandusky who was born 2 Mar 1903 in Labette County, Kan., and died 28 Jan 1951 in Dallas Co., Ia. Their children were Ruth Ilene, Evelyn Lenora, and Mary Isabelle. Secondly, she married John Loschen 8 Aug 1953 at Hopkinton, Ia. John died 16 Apr 1974 at Van Meter, Ia., and was buried there.

116722 Lois Isabel McCorkle

Lois was born 20 Jul 1910 in Madison Co., Ia., and died 29 Apr 1972 in Omaha, Neb. She married 6 Aug 1940 John P. Gieber in Omaha, Neb. They had Lenamae, Connie Jo, and John Edward. Mr. Gieber was born 18 Sep 1911 and died 21 Jan 1979 in Omaha; burial was in Hillcrest Cemetery.

116723 Walter Edward McCorkle

Walter was born 29 Nov 1912 in Winterset, Ia. He married 1 Aug 1940, in Cedar Rapids, Myrtle Ratcliff who was born 15 Dec 1917 in Coggan, Ia. Walter farmed near Independence, Ia., until he retired in 1976 and moved to town. Myrtle was a nurse and worked in the Monticello, Ia., hospital. Later, she was director of a nursing home. They had Nancy Mae and Virginia Anne. Walter died 1 Apr 1999.

116724 Mary Jeanette McCorkle

Jeanette was born 8 Dec 1923 in Madison County, Ia. She graduated from Earlham High School in 1941, then became a medical records technician. Her first marriage on 14 Dec 1941 in Omaha, Neb., was to Ivan Rold who was born 29 Jul 1916 in Neb., and died 24 Jan 1974 in Omaha; burial was in Forest Lawn in Omaha. Their children were Patricia Jean and Terri Joanne. Secondly, she married, then divorced, Homer Doyle. Jeanette was living in Omaha in 2001.

116731 Byrne McCorkle Wright

Byrne was born 8 Feb 1909 in Madison County, Ia. and died 14 Aug 1976 in Wheatridge Colo.; he had lived in Arvada, Colo. He was married to Eva Malvina Kirk on 11 Feb 1946, perhaps in Portland, Ore. Eve was born 27 May 1919 and died 29 Sep 1995 in Edgewater, Colo. Byrne served in the U.S. Navy during WW II and later worked for the Beatrice/Meadowgold Co. before he retired. Both were buried in Crown Hill Cem. in Wheatridge. They had Joanne Elizabeth.

116732 Wilma Jeanetta Wright

Wilma was born 23 Nov 1910 in Douglas Township, Madison Co., Ia., and died 28 Aug 1992 in Pueblo, Colo. She married, first, Wilson Duff on 6 Oct 1951, and they adopted Warren L. and Carole L. Secondly, she married Bruce Earnest Watkins Jr. who was born 21 Apr 1908 and was living in 1999. Bruce was the father, and Wilma the step-mother, of Nancy A.

116733 Elizabeth Ellen Wright

Elizabeth was born 8 Jul 1912 in Madison County, Ia., and died 12 Feb 1946. She married Everett C. (Red) Barnes about 1930 and they had a daughter, Shirley. Red may have been born 7 Dec 1914 and died in Mar 1965 in Denver, Colo.

116741 Margaret Jennie Morse

Margaret was born 25 Dec 1918 in Denton, Mont., and was living in Colfax, Wash., in 2001. She married Vernon Iowa Clow on 22 Nov 1969. There were no children. Vernon was born 6 Dec 1898 in Whitman, Wash., and died there 29 May 1977.

116742 George Nicholas Morse

George was born 11 Mar 1920 in Denton, Mont. He married Dora Lenora Janson on 20 May 1960. Dora was born 4 Dec 1929. They had Carol Lenora, Paul Nicholas and Julie Ann. They live near Lewistown, Mont.

116743 Edward Lindsay Morse

Edward was born 9 May 1921 in Denton, Mont. He married, in Great
Falls, Mont., on 24 July 1952, Eva Louise Frederickson who was born
27 Sep 1928 in McCone Co., Mont., and died 8 Aug 1997 in Denton
where she was buried in Hillcrest Cemetery. They had the following
children: Gregg Edward, Karen Ione, Eric Lindsay, Mark Harry, Dale
Frederick, and Carla Jean.

116744 Ruth Alice Morse

Ruth was born 17 Oct 1922 in Denton, Mont. She married 20 Aug 1954
Gerald Kenneth Randall. They had no children. Gerald was born 2
Jun 1926 and died 8 May 1982 near San Jose, Calif.

116745 Harry Perkins Morse Jr.

Harry was born 29 Mar 1927 in Denton, Mont. He married, first,
Marcella Elaine Harrington 7 Apr 1951. They had six children before
they divorced: Michael Patrick, Rebecca Marie, Patricia Ann, Thomas
John, Juanita Elaine and Joan Ellen. Harry was living in Reno,
Nev., in 2001, when not on a journey in his motor home.

116746 Mabel Eleanor Morse

Mabel was born 5 Aug 1928 in Denton, Mont. She graduated from
Montana State College in 1951 as a nurse. She worked in several
western states, and was living in Cheyenne, Wyo., in 2001.

116751 Edson McCorkle Light

[The following biography was compiled by Jack Scott Light in 1998].
Edson was born 9 Aug 1906 in Winterset, Ia., and died 13 Jun 1976
in Kansas City, Mo. His body was cremated and the ashes were
spread over the graves of his mother and father at Floral Hills
Cemetery in Kansas City, Mo. He was a smoker which eventually
caused throat cancer and his death. Edson's first wife, Bernice
White of Wichita, Kan., was about four years older than Edson; they
married in 1924 in Wichita when he was eighteen. He attended
barber's school and practiced in Milwaukee, Wisc., in his wife's
uncle's shop. The marriage lasted only a year and they were
divorced. Edson's second marriage was to Beatrice Kirby in 1929;
his third marriage on 29 Jan 1930 was to Bernice Amelia Scott who
was born 7 Dec 1907 in Stippville, Kan. In 1998 she was living
alone in Columbus, Kan. Their children were Shirley Lee and Jack
Scott. Fourthly, he married Buelah Scheilz in 1934; and lastly to
Georgia Frances Kaiser 29 Mar 1937. Georgia was born 22 Feb 1908 in
Woolridge, Mo., and died 10 May 1997 in Kansas City, Mo. They had
Edson Leonard and Paul Albert.

116752 Claude Ivan Light

[Compiled by Jack Scott Light]. Claude was born 10 May 1910 in Madison Co., Ia., and died 17 Oct 1971 in the hospital in La Marque, Tex. He spent most of his life in Independence, Mo., where he worked as a purchasing agent for Panhandle Eastern Pipeline. He spent some time in Canada, then moved to La Marque, Tex., where he worked as a civil engineer. He was a Mason and a member of the Christian Church. He married Virginia Blackburn 28 Dec 1935 in Kansas City, Mo. Virginia was born 16 Jul 1904 and died in Dec 1990 in Independence, Mo. She was a school teacher until they moved to Tex. They did not have any children. Both are buried in Blue Springs Cem., Blue Springs, Mo.

116753 George Edward Light

[Compiled by Jack Scott Light]. George was born 17 Feb 1912 in Winterset, Ia., and died of lung cancer on 3 Sep 1989 in Kansas City, Mo. Burial was in Memorial Gardens Cemetery, K.C., Mo. He loved sports and excelled in football and basketball in high school. Later, in the military, he played basketball for his unit. George was stationed at the Army Air Base at Eagle Pass, Tex. George was transferred to Wright Patterson Air Base before leaving the military at the end of World War II. After the war, George took a position with the U.S. Postal Service and moved up to postmaster at Ridgeway, Mo. He was married on 18 Jul 1936, in Excelsior Springs, Mo., to Margaret (Pat) Lucille Rooney. Margaret was born 18 Feb 1916 in Osceola, Mo., and died in Reno, Nev., about 1995. They had Georga Anne.

116754 Helen Onabelle Light

[Compiled by Jack Scott Light]. Helen Onabelle was born 18 Oct 1913 in Jackson Twp., Madison Co., Ia. and died 1 Nov 1991 in Kansas City, Mo. When she was a baby the family moved to Winfield, Kan., then returned to Winterset in 1919 and lived with her grandparents, Will and Linnie Light. At the age of ten, the family moved to Kansas City, Mo., where Helen attended Ashland Elementary School, and later, East High School, and graduated in 1933. She married, first, 29 Apr 1934, Earl E. Redd who worked for a White Castle Cafe. Later, Earl ran Earl's Hamburger Restaurant with Helen's assistance. After Earl died 12 Nov 1960, Helen married Howard Phillips on 4 May 1963 in Kansas City, Mo. They operated the restaurant until they retired in 1984. Earl was buried in Mount Mariah Cem., Kansas City, Mo. They had William Claude.

116755 Ruth Marie Light

Ruth was born 10 Mar 1920 in Wichita, Kan. She married 11 Oct 1937

Clyde Carson Parker in Kansas City, Mo. Clyde was born 11 Oct 1920 in Kansas City, Mo.[178], and died of kidney failure 8 May 1989 at Research Medical Center in Kansas City, Mo. Clyde was a veteran of World War II having served in the U.S. Navy. Before 1950 he was a manager for Purity Textiles in Kansas City. From 1950 to 1965 he owned Clyde's Hamburgers located at 78th Street and Wornall Road. Next he was assistant manager for Skaggs Drug Stores until he retired in 1975 and moved to Bella Vista, Ark. Later, he and Ruth returned to Kansas City. Clyde was a member of Grandview Masonic Lodge, the Scottish Rite bodies and Ararat Shrine. He was a life member of the Hughes-Marvin post of the Veterans of Foreign Wars. He was buried in Mount Moriah Cemetery. Ruth died on 21 Nov 1996 in Vacaville, Calif. Their children were Connie Ruth and Earl C.

116761 Gerald Harlen Landes

Edd was born 12 Mar 1918 in Harrison County, Mo., and died there on 24 Feb 1972; burial was in Bethany, Mo. In 1946 in Troy, Kan., he married Ermadean Updegraff who was born 27 Aug 1919.

116762 Wilbur Lee Landes

Wilbur, known as Brown, was born 2 Feb 1920 in Harrison Co., Mo. On 25 Oct 1947 in Bethany, Mo., he married Barbara June Bartlett who was born 7 Jun 1925 in Harrison Co., Mo. They had Ricky Lee and Deborah June. Brown died 8 Aug 2000.

116763 Bobby Dean Landes

Bobby was born 17 Jul 1925 in Harrison Co., Mo., and married Leta Lenoir Blessing on 31 Oct 1946 in Troy, Kan. Leta was born 27 Oct 1928 in McFall, Mo. They had Brenda Rea, Alan Lynn, and Tony Ray.

116764 Elden Landes Jr.

Junior was born 14 Jun 1928 near Ridgeway, Mo., and married Evelyn Jean Taylor on 6 Nov 1955 in the Blue Ridge Christian Union Church, Blue Ridge, Mo. Evelyn was born 25 Dec 1932 in rural Harrison Co. Junior assumed the management of the farm that had been his father's, and worked it most of his life. Junior and Evelyn had David Eugene and Gloria June. They were making their home in Ridgeway, Mo., in 1998. At age 65, Junior moved to the town of Ridgeway where they were enjoying retirement in 1999.

116765 Edward Lindsey Landes

Edward was born 26 Aug 1929 in Ridgeway, Mo., and died that day. He was buried in Ridgeway Cem.

116766 Glen D. Landes

Glen was born 29 Jan 1935 in Harrison Co., Mo. He was never married and moved into the Harrison County Group Home in 1981.

116767 Margaret Jean Landes

Margaret was born 13 Oct 1937 in Harrison Co., Mo. She married Eugene Frankie Schratter on 17 Sep 1961 and they were divorced on 19 Apr 1977. Secondly, she married Luther Lee Reynolds on 12 Nov 1981 in Ark.; they divorced 16 Feb 1983. There were no children from either marriage. Margaret now uses her maiden name.

116771 Howard Earl McCorkle

Howard was born 18 Jul 1921 in Athol, Kan. He married Dollieann Marie Whalen on 12 Jul 1946 in Seattle, Wash. Dolly was born 25 Nov 1927 in Butte, Mont., and died 10 Dec 1997 in Seattle. She was buried near Bothell, Wash. They had Toni Ann and Terry Lee.

116772 Mae Earnestine McCorkle

Mae was born 21 Mar 1923 in Athol, Kan. She married Carroll John McDonald in Smith Co., Kan., on 3 Oct 1943. Carroll was born 7 Jul 1922 in Smith Co., and died in Smith Center, Kan., on 5 Jul 1985. He is buried in Fairview Cemetery in Smith Center. Mae was living in Smith Center, Kan., in 1998. They had Nancy Carol, Kenneth Ray, Jean Loree, Larry Allen, Cathy Arlene, and Gary Steven.

116773 Donald Edward McCorkle

Donald was born 13 Jul 1924 in Athol, Kan. He married Tressie Elizabeth Casteel on 28 Jul 1946 in Phillipsburg, Kan. Tressie was born 29 Nov 1926 in Sterling, Colo. They had Donna Beth and Ronald Allen. Donald moved his family to Puyallup, Wash. He and Tressie were living in Yelm, Wash., in 1998.

116774 Scott McCorkle

Scott was born 28 Oct 1925 in Athol, Kan. His wife was Roma Jean Norton whom he married 4 Dec 1949 in Denton, Mont. Roma was born 9 Feb 1931 in Bellaire, Kan. Their children were Sharon Kay, Dennis Scott, Carl Eugene, Darrell Lynn, Jeffery Harold, and Norma Jean. In 1998 he was living in Sabetha, Kan.

116775 Margaret Jane McCorkle

Margaret was born 12 May 1927 in Athol, Kan. She married Richard Dale Trent 19 Jul 1952 in Osborne, Kan. Richard was born 28 Mar

1927 in Omaha, Neb.   They had Janet Marie, Richard Dean, Marcia Jane, and Sheri Lou.   They lived in Phillipsburg, Kan., in 1998.

116776 Robert Alden McCorkle Sr.

Robert was born 30 May 1933 in Athol, Kan.   Right after graduating from high school, he enlisted in the U.S. Navy and served from 1951 to 1954, mainly aboard USS Breckenridge, APD 176, a troop transport.   On 14 Jun 1959 in Denver, Colo., he married Margaret Ellen Walker who was born 4 Oct 1937 in Hallidayboro, Ill.   They had Robert Alden Jr., and Elizabeth Ellen.   Robert Sr. worked for Martin-Marietta for 32 years before retiring. They were living in Salida, Colo., in 2000.

116777 Myron George McCorkle

Myron was born 9 May 1940 in Athol, Kan.   George married Rosita Katarina Csizmar in Oct 1965 in Denver, Colo.   She was born 14 Nov 1948 in Amberg, Germany.   They had Peggy Sue.   George secondly married Verda Martha Morton on 27 Apr 1969 in Estes Park, Colo. They were making their home in Aurora, Colo., in 2000.

116781 Charles Marion Lary

Charles was born 2 Nov 1922 in Hastings, Neb., and died 9 Jul 1994 in Eugene, Ore.   He was buried in Willamette National Cemetery, Portland, Ore. On 1 Feb 1950 in Kelso, Wash., he married Charlene Utley and they had Linda Jane, Charles Halsey, Randall Edward, Susan Ann, and Robert McLain. Charlene was born 12 Aug 1929 and was living in Kelso in 1997.

116782 Edward Halsie Lary

Edward was born 21 May 1925 in Hastings, Neb., and died there 4 Apr 1927.   He was buried in Hastings Cem.

116783 Alice Ann Lary

Alice was born 17 Feb 1930 in Hastings, Neb., and died 15 Jul 1981 in Hood River, Ore.   She married 27 Mar 1954 Herman Albert Peters in Kelso, Wash.   Their children were Mathew Lary, Danise Lea, Timothy Henry, and Julann Carol.   Herman was born 12 Apr 1930 in Grass Valley, Ore.; in 1999 he was in Hood River, Ore.   He owned a carpet cleaning/installing business.

117111 Robert Salsman

Robert was born 3 Feb 1929 in Rapid City, S.D.   He was married 23 Dec 1952, in Tracy, Calif., to Juana Clark. They had Thomas M.,

Larry E., Kathline, Teresa G., and James R. Robert enlisted in the U.S. Navy for three years, but the Korean War caused his enlistment to be extended to four years. Robert was a graduate of the University of Denver in 1957 with a degree in public administration. He began a career working for the U.S. Soil Conservation Service in Colo. They retired in Golden, Colo.

117121 Jean Marie Bowersox

Jean was born 29 May 1929 in Albuquerque, N.M. She married 15 Aug 1948 James Roscoe Baker in Arkansas City, Kan. Their children were Steve, Jim, Allen, and Doris. James died 7 May 1991. Jean had been a resident of Roswell for 40 years. When she retired in 1991 she had been office manager for Colin McMillan, consulting geophysics. She had been named Pecos Valley outstanding secretary in 1984 by the Roswell Chapter of Professional Secretaries International. She was a member of Trinity United Methodist Church. Jean died of gastro-intestinal cancer on 27 Jan 1992 in Roswell, N.M., and was buried in South Park Cemetery in Roswell.[179]

117122 Lou Anne Bowersox

Lou Anne was born 14 Dec 1932. She became a nurse in Lubbock, Tex., where she worked for several years. She was unmarried and died of lung cancer. She was buried in South Park Cemetery on 29 Aug 1978.

117131 William Ray Weir

William was born 30 Oct 1927 in Burlington, Ia., and died 8 Jul 1992 in Biggsville, Ill.[183] He was buried in Biggsville Cem. He married 30 Dec 1948, in The Little Brown Church in Nashua, Ia., Mabel Jane Bigger who was born 25 Apr 1929 in Biggsville. They continued the operation of the Weir Fruit Farm, which mainly involved the growing and processing of many varieties of apples. Their children were Peggy Ann, William Ray Jr., and John Milton.

117132 Shirley Ann Weir

Shirley was born in May 1929 and died 25 Jun 1938. She was asphixiated while riding in the back seat of a new Packard that for some reason had a defective exhaust pipe.

117133 Milton Smith Weir

Milton was born in 1931 and suffered the same fate as his sister.

117134 Jane Kay Weir

Jane was born 6 Jun 1935 and married Laurence A. Anderson. Jane was a school teacher for 24 years. They had three children: Mark Lawrence, Susan Marie, and Laura Kay.

117135 Carol Marie Weir

Carol was born 28 Jul 1939 in Henderson Co., Ill., and died 29 Jul 1939; burial was in Biggsville Cem.

117211 Paul Douglas Gibb

Paul was born 18 Nov 1907 in Henderson Co., Ill., and died in Nov 1991. Paul was a ham radio operator for over fifty years. He married 28 Jul 1928 Eloise Marcia Jamison who was born 23 May 1908 in Henderson Co., Ill., and died 29 Aug 2000 in Galesburg, Ill. Their children were Marilyn Jeanne and Dennis Lee.

117212 John Dale Gibb

Dale was born 26 Jul 1910 at Biggsville, Ill.   In Palmyra, Mo., he married Irene Blake on 7 May 1938. Irene was born 7 Oct 1920 and died 1 Dec 2000. Their children were Linda Lee and Dana Lynn. Dale farmed in the Fall Creek area. Dale died of a heart attack 10 Jan 1977 in Biggsville; he and Irene are buried in Oquawka Cem.

117221 Eva Pauline Gibb

Eva was born 30 Oct 1903 in Biggsville, Ill. She was a graduate of Biggsville High School and attended Knox College in Galesburg, Ill., and Western Illinois University, Macomb, Ill., where she earned a master's degree in education.   She then taught in elementary and high schools in Illinois and Iowa for 27 years.   In St. Charles, Mo., she married 11 Apr 1925 Leon A. Price who was born 6 Apr 1902 in Denver, Ill.

Leon attended school in Loraine, Ill., and then attended Western Illinois University, and finally received his master's degree from the University of Iowa. He was a school teacher and superintendent during his 26-year career.   They were members of the United Presbyterian Church.   After his initial retirement, he taught classes at Burlington Junior College. Their children were Donn F., Robert Leon, and Ellen Jane. Eva died 29 Mar 1994 at Henderson County Retirement Center in Stronghurst; Leon died 16 Oct 1994 in Stronghurst and both were buried in Biggsville Cem.

117222 Lloyd Weir Gibb

Lloyd was born 28 Aug 1906 in Biggsville, Ill., and died of lung problems 17 May 1986 in Burlington, Ia. Lloyd attended school in Biggsville and at Knox College. Initially, he was foreman on Weir's fruit farm, then became a farmer until he retired. In Monmouth, he married 26 Jan 1932 Doris C. Reynold who was born 25 Oct 1911 and died 4 Jun 1986; burial was in Biggsville Cem. They were members of the United Presbyterian Church. Doris attended beauty school and was an accomplished musician. They did not have any children.

117223 Ellen Gibb

Ellen, who had no middle name, was born 13 Mar 1909 near Biggsville and married in Jacksonville, Ill., on 11 Sep 1931, Stephen Wendell Graham. They were members of Biggsville United Presbyterian Church. They had Stephen Wendell Jr., Mary Ellen, Jon Kendall, and Owen Gibb. Ellen was a secretary as well as a housewife, while Stephen farmed. Mr. Graham was born 6 Nov 1907 in Biggsville and died 16 Aug 1975 in Burlington, Ia.; he was buried in Biggsville Cem. Ellen is in a nursing home in Oquawka, Ill.

117224 Jennie Louise Gibb

Known as Bunny, she was born 26 Feb 1912 near Biggsville and died from complications with lupus 30 Jan 1991 in Mount Pleasant, Ia. She married, in Oquawka, 26 Apr 1930, William Earl Milligan who was born 18 Nov 1909 in Gladstone, Ill. Earl farmed most of his life in the Biggsville area. For a while, they ran a dry goods store in Biggsville. He was also a good carpenter, and he and Bunny refinished furniture, including two pieces that had been in the family for several generations. Earl died of lung cancer 1 Sep 1987 at Mount Pleasant Hospital. They were buried in Biggsville Cem. Their children were Barbara Jean, Jimmy Lee, and Gerald Earl.

117225 Frances Elizabeth Gibb

Frances, whose nickname was Billie, was born 11 Dec 1917 in Biggsville, Ill., and died 30 Jul 1941 in Galesburg, Ill., of surgical malpractice. In Davenport, Ia., she married 16 Jun 1933 Charles K. Stotts who was born 23 Jun 1914. Their children were Doris Joan, Ronald Keith, Myrna Bernita, and Evelyn Jean. Frances was buried in Biggsville Cemetery alongside her parents.

117226 Jean Shaw Gibb

Jean was born 13 Oct 1919 in Biggsville. She married 8 Sep 1939, in Burlington, Ernest Edward Leinbach who was born 3 Oct 1917. Their sons were Terry Edward and Guy Lynn. Jean has worked as a bookkeeper at the Ford Garage since 1955.   Ernest was in the plumbing business and was postmaster for 25 years before retiring in 1984.   In 1998, Jean and Ernest were residing in Stronghurst, Ill.

117227 Winifred Lucille Gibb

Winifred was born 31 Dec 1922 in Biggsville, Ill. She was married at the home of her parents in Biggsville 3 Mar 1942 to Donald Willard Tinkham who was born 9 Nov 1922 in Galesburg, Ill. Winifred was employed as a secretary. Their children were Charles Francis and Michael Bradley. Winifred was living in Maxwell, Ia., in 1998.

117231 Allan Vandevere Brokaw

Allen was born 26 Feb 1912 on a farm near Gladstone, Ill. He married Mildred Letitia Speer on 9 Dec 1944 in Hanover, Ill. Mildred was born 21 Mar 1910 and died 7 Oct 1992 at a nursing home in Elizabeth, Ill. Burial was in Log Church Cemetery in Hanover, Ill. Mildred had taught high school in Viola, Sterling, and Galena. Allan served in the U.S. Navy during World War II with most of his service spent on New Caledonia. After the war he returned to farming near Hanover, Ill. Their children were Leonard Edwin and Louise Anne.

117232 John Weir Brokaw

John was born 9 Nov 1914 on a farm near Stronghurst, Ill. He was a lifetime grain and livestock farmer in Mercer Co., until his retirement in 1988. Being a farmer, John was exempt from the service during World War II. He was a member of Mercer County Farm Bureau, and an elder of the former United Presbyterian Church in Aledo where he taught Sunday school. He recently was a member of Trinity Presbyterian Church. He was active in the 4-H Club where he was a leader for many years. He was an avid sports fan and enjoyed golfing and bowling. On 11 Apr 1941 he married Pearl Marie Parkinson in Viola, Ill. Pearl was born 4 Dec 1919 in Mercer Twp., Mercer Co. Their children were Karen Sue, James Kurtis, Philip Weir, Dennis Craig, and Michael Jon. Pearl died 14 Apr 1989 in Mercer County Hospital in Aledo. She was buried in Aledo Cem. On 16 Mar 1991 John married Dona Baker in Chandler, Ariz. Dona, born 14 Nov 1921, had children from a previous marriage: Jerry Baker, born 28 Nov 1940; and Mark Baker, born 10 Jun 1960. John died 8 Jan 1999 at Mesa General Hospital in Mesa, Ariz.[180]

117233 Evelyn Ruth Brokaw

Ruth was born 19 Nov 1918 near Stronghurst, Ill. She married John Wilber Service on 7 Jun 1940 at the United Presbyterian Church in

Viola, Ill. John was born 15 May 1911 and was a sales manager for the John Deere Spreader Works, an occupation that required frequent trips to all parts of the country. His last four years were spent at Deere Administrative Center in Moline where he was division manager in salary administration. John retired in 1973. They lived in Moline, Ill. John was a trustee at Monmouth College. Their children were Shirley Marie, John Dean, and Robert Kent. They celebrated their 50th wedding anniversary on 10 Jun 1990. Evelyn died 24 May 2000 and was buried in Viola, Ill.[181]

117234 Leonard Harold Brokaw

Harold was born 16 Feb 1921 near Stronghurst, Ill. He married 17 Jun 1948 Barbara Jena Moss in Aledo, Ill. Barbara was born 12 Aug 1927 in Indianapolis and died 21 Jan 1996 at Franklin, N.C. Burial was in Bradenton, Fla. She was once a personal banker at First Union National Bank. She was a member and elder at Kirkwood Presbyterian Church. Harold was a Corporal in the U.S. Army in France and Germany during WW II, was wounded, and received a Purple Heart. He was employed with the Maas Bros.' store in Sarasota, Fla., and lived in Holmes Beach, Fla. They had Paul Scott and Elizabeth Ann.

117235 Robert Edwin Brokaw

Robert was born 6 Mar 1923 near Stronghurst, Ill. He was exempt from service during World War II because he was classified 4-F. On 9 Dec 1950, in Aledo, Ill., he married Helen Lee Peterson who was born 16 Jan 1930 at Green Twp., Viola, Ill. They operate a farm near Aledo, Ill. Their children are Sharon Ruth, Debra Dee, and Robert Mark, Bradley Kyle, and Christina Marie.

117236 Richard Dean Brokaw

Richard was born 16 Sep 1925 near Stronghurst, Ill. He served with the U.S. Army during the Korean Conflict, was wounded, and received a Purple Heart. Prior to his going to Korea, he married, in Rock Island, Ill., on 14 Apr 1951, Lois Laurine Long who was born 23 Oct 1930. They have a son, John Andrew. Richard retired from International Harvester Co. in Aledo, Ill.

MODERN-DAY GENERATIONS

1121611 Mary Lou McInally

Reverend Mary was born in 1930 in Ontario, and died 24 Jun 1979. She attended Simcoe, Ontario, High School, then teachers college in Toronto where she studied and became a minister. She held BA and a BD degrees. She lived in Mount Elgin, Oxford County, Ontario. She performed the marriage of her aunt and uncle, J. Evans Knowles and Shirley White, in 1957. In 1967 she was living in Claxton Bay, Trinidad. She was not married and died of a heart attack. At the time of her death she was United Church minister of the Mount Elgin pastoral charge. Her body was cremated and her ashes were buried in the family plot in Oakwood Cemetery in Simcoe, Ontario, in a marked grave.

1121621 William Robert Knowles

William was born in 1945. He married Sydney Leyland and they had three children: William Edward, Kimberly Jane, and Kristine. William was a building contractor, an occupation that took him to foreign countries. They lived in Langton, Ontario.

William is not married. Kimberly married 26 Aug 2000 Stanley Baer. Kristine married 27 Jun 1998 Christopher Coulthard.

1121622 James Kirby Knowles

James was born 14 Jun 1951 in Simcoe, Ontario. He attended the University of Western Ontario and in 1974 received a BS degree in geology, with honours. In 1977 he earned a master's degree in business administration at UWO. He became a chartered accountant (CPA) in 1979. James began his working career with Energy, Mines and Resources of the Government of Canada. Today, he is vice president of finance for Blackburn Group Inc., in London, Ontario, where he lives. On 30 Sep 1978 he married Maria Antoinett Durante and they had Sarah Angela born 4 Nov 1983 and Stephanie Marie born 24 Nov 1986.

1121711 Robert Hugh Knowles

Hugh was born 15 Feb 1920 in Fort William, Ontario, Canada. He graduated from Drew School, then attended Fort William Collegiate and earned a BS degree in agriculture at the University of Toronto. He obtained a high school teaching certificate at the University of Toronto, and held a master of science degree in plant physiology from the University of Alberta. Hugh continued his higher education by attending Michigan State University where he earned a BS degree in landscape architecture. Hugh married Jessie McGregor Wishart on 3 Aug 1945 at the First Presbyterian Church in Fort William. Hugh was a teacher at Ontario High School and was a professor at the University of Alberta for 35 years. Hugh's hobbies include writing and outdoor recreation; they live in Edmonton, Alberta. Jessie was born 8 Nov 1919 and has worked as an office administrator in addition to being a mother and a housewife. Their children are Kathryn Jane who was born 14 Nov 1946 in Brantford, Ontario; Ann Elizabeth who was born 14 Dec 1949 in Edmonton, Alberta; and Donna Lesley who was born 14 Jun 1954 in Edmonton.

Kathryn was educated in Edmonton public schools and graduated from the University of Alberta School of Nursing with a BS degree. In the First Presbyterian Church of Edmonton, Kathryn married Clifford John Revell who was born 2 Jan 1944. Cliff is a periodontist. Their children are Nancy Eileen who was born 1 Sep 1974 in Edmonton, Alberta, and Lesley Ann who was born 25 Oct 1976 in Edmonton. Nancy Eileen was educated in Edmonton public schools and graduated from Augustana University with a BA degree in physical education. She married Daniel David Osness on 8 May 1999. Nancy is a personal trainer while Daniel, who was born 5 Oct 1969, is a forester.

Ann married Gregg Pierce of Olympia, Wash., in 1974 in Edmonton; they divorced in 1997. They had Alison Ann who was born 17 Jun 1977 in Portland, Ore., and Kelsey Knowles who was born 29 May 1985 in Olympia. Ann secondly married Frank R. Willson of Everett, Wash., on 23 Aug 1998 in Olympia. Ann attended schools in Edmonton, and graduated from the University of Alberta with a BS degree in education. She later received a master of education degree at the University of Washington. Ann is teaching in public schools. Frank is an attorney at law.

Donna Lesley was educated in public schools in Edmonton, then attended the University of Alberta where she earned a BS degree in household economics. She is a dietician at Calgary General Hospital. On 3 Jul 1982 she married Michael John Patterson at St. Paul's United Church in Edmonton. Michael was born 10 Sep 1955 and is an electrical engineer for an oil industry and is a businessman. Their children are Lauren Elizabeth who was born 4 Apr 1984, Claire Jessie who was born 7 Feb 1987, and Hugh John who was born 24 Nov 1988.

1121712 Barbara Knowles

Barbara was born 4 Jul 1922 in Thunder Bay, Ontario, and died 21 Apr 1969 in Vancouver, B.C. She married John Norman Olsen on 15

Jul 1949 in Vancouver and they had Karen, Janet Evelyn, Christopher, Mark, and Eric.

Karen married Tom Truesdale on 24 Dec 1976 and they had Claire. Janet married Darrel Arthur Mansbridge and they had Blake and another child. Christopher married Ruth and they had Brian and Jennifer.

1121713 Shirley Knowles

Shirley was born in 1927 and married, first, James Thompson. They had Ian and David. Ian was born in 1953 and married Wendy Roberts. They have a son, Owen Morgan, born 23 Jun 1992. David married Donna. Shirley secondly married Don Wilson and they live in Dryden, Ontario.

1121721 Margaret Elizabeth McChesney

Margaret ("Betty") was born 6 Aug 1923. She served in the Canadian Armed Forces during WW II during which she spent time abroad. After the war, she became a nurse, and has been a world traveler. Betty was living in Folsom, Calif., in 2001.

1121722 Laurel McChesney

Laurel was born 25 Nov 1924 and married Cedric Harrop who was born 11 Aug 1923. Their four children are Victoria Leigh, Verle Margaret, Dorothy Carol, and Cedric Malcolm.

Victoria was born 15 Aug 1948 and married, first, Gregory Cottrell and they had Todd Ian who was born 1 Jun 1970. (Todd's last name has been changed to Harrop). Secondly, Victoria married John Farrell and they had Laurel Anna who was born 19 Dec 1974, and Lincoln who was born 14 Mar 1977. Verle was born 21 Aug 1952 and married John Fredric Archibald. They had Ian Edwin, born 25 May 1978, Hilary Margaret, born 28 Aug 1980, and Elizabeth, born 9 Apr 1983. Verle secondly married Ken Scott.

1121723 James McChesney

James was born 19 Aug 1928 and married Joan M. Dutt who was born 24 Apr 1930. Their children were David James and Jeffrey Scott.

David James McChesney was born 22 Jul 1959 and married Mari Lee Haselhuhn. They had Cori Jane, born 28 Apr 1984, and Ian James, born 10 Apr 1987. David secondly married Burma _____ . They had Clayton born 29 Jan 1999. Jeffrey Scott McChesney was born 21 Mar 1961 and married Celeste Ann Lewallen. Their son is Riley Lewallen.

1121724 Robert McChesney

Robert was born 21 May 1932 and married Cecelia Perrault. He is a mining engineer. They had Robert who was born 10 Apr 1960. Robert married Pamela and they had Jessica Marie in 1992.

1121731 James Knowles

James was born in 1916 and is deceased. Burial was in C-K Cem. He married Dorothy Sullivan who was born in 1922 and is deceased. Their children were Diane Jeanne, born 14 Mar 1951; Janice, born 28 Mar 1953; Debbie, born 18 Feb 1954; William, born 2 Jun 1958; and John, born 9 Sep 1962.

Diane married Stephen Leslie Hammond who was born 24 May 1951; they live in Whitby, Ontario.

John married Suzanne Wallace who was born 3 Aug 1962.

1121732 Jeanne Knowles

Jeanne was born 6 Mar 1917 in Walsingham, Ontario. She attended Vaughan Road Collegiate and Toronto Western Hospital Nursing College. She was a nurse at Western Hospital for about 16 years, then worked as a social worker for 15 years. Her first marriage was to George Oliphant who was killed during WW II. About 1978 she married Ian Armour in Toronto; Ian is now deceased. There were no children. In 2001, she was living with her niece, Diane Hammond.

1121751 William John Knight

William married Marcia Greenleaf and they had Karen, Patricia, James, and Kathleen. William died 24 Nov 1970. Karen married Harry Martin Saunders and they had Robyn and Ryan Martin who were born in 1977. Patricia was born 8 Mar 1946 and married Ralph Scaramella who was born 20 Jun 1942. Patricia and Ralph had Laurie born 1 Dec 1965, Ralph born 29 Jun 1967, Peter born 29 Jun 1977, and Lisa born 3 Dec 1981. James Knight married Patsy and they had Valerie, William, Roberta, and Mercy. Kathleen Knight was born in 1948 and married Richard Williams. They had Kimberlie born 19 Jan 1969, Tamyra born 14 Jan 1971, and James Trauis born 3 Feb 1980.

1125111 George Leonard Fulton II

George was born 26 Oct 1931. He is a graduate of Hartford City High School and of Hanover College of Hanover, Ind., in 1953. He served in the military then worked as a civilian at the Pentagon in Wash., D.C. In 1967 he married Diana Buffington; they are now divorced. There were no children. He lives in Dayton, Ohio.

1125112 Anne Wadsworth Fulton

Anne was born 21 Mar 1937. She married Phillip Harden Smith who was born 13 Feb 1936. They had three children: Louis Porter, born 19 Sep 1957; Phillip Brett, born 24 Feb 1962; and Lisa Fulton, born 10 May 1965. Anne and Phillip were divorced in Sep 1978. Secondly, Anne married 27 Mar 1982 Walter Francis Jones who was born 17 Jun 1925. They were living in Golden Valley, Minn., in 1999.

Louis Porter Smith married 16 Jun 1990 Nadia Flores Najarro who was born 4 Apr 1959. They had two children: Eva Najarro, born 28 May 1992, and Daniel Najarro, born 10 Mar 1995. They live in Minneapolis, Minn.

Phillip Brett Smith married 6 Jul 1985 Kelly Lynn Spaulding who was born 27 Apr 1962, and died 26 Nov 1989. Secondly Phillip married 17 Jul 1992 Jody McCormick who was born 26 Mar 1953. Their address is White Bear Lake, Minn.

Lisa Fulton Smith married 26 Jun 1993 Kraig Shonle Bruer who was born 13 Jun 1956. They had Parker Phillip, born 30 Oct 1994, and Rheo Fulton, born 17 Jan 1997. Their home is in Big Torch Key, Fla.

1125113 Susanna Gray Fulton

Susanna was born 19 Sep 1939 in Hartford City, Ind. She and Donald Merrill Landis were married on 6 Sep 1958. Donald was born 22 May 1940 in Hartford City. They had Jeffrey Allen, born 24 Mar 1959, and Robert Fulton, born 13 Oct 1961. They live in Hayward, Calif.

Jeffrey married 17 Oct 1981 Donna Joy Camping. They had Benjamin Jeffrey, born 25 Aug 1986, and Joel Edward, born 29 Aug 1989. Rev. Jeffrey Landis lives in San Jose, Calif.

Robert married 30 May 1981 Cathlene Joy Gray and they had Donald Gray, born 6 Jul 1982, and Melissa Joy, born 14 Jan 1985. They live in Castro Valley, Calif.

1125121 Molly Jane Fulton

Molly was born 26 Aug 1924 in Champaign, Ill. She graduated from Hartford City High School in 1942, then spent a year attending Western College and three years at Bell State where she graduated with a BA in education. She taught a year at Eaton High School before she married James Dolan on 28 Sep 1947 in Hartford City, Ind.

James was born 26 Dec 1923 in Hartford City. He graduated from high school in 1942. From 1943 to 1945 Jim served with the U.S. Army Air Corps and flew A-20 attack bombers on many missions in New Guinea. Jim attended Indiana University for 2-1/2 years where he majored in business. He then went into the family glass business in Hartford City, and also spent ten years in Okla. He moved back to Hartford City in 1964 where he remained until his retirement in 1989. Since then he has served on the city council for four years, been active in the Democrat party, and now serves as Door Keeper at the State House. Molly died on 18 Aug 1998 in Hartford City and is buried there. Their children are Cynthia, Nancy, and Jane Fulton.

Cynthia (no middle name) was born 3 Jan 1950 in Hartford City. She married Ron McMillin and they had Mary Kathleen, born about 1982, and David, born about 1984.

Nancy was born 7 Feb 1953 in Hartford City. She married Tom Rea and they live in Bethel, Wash.

Jane was born 9 Jan 1957 in Okmulgee, Okla. She married John Westermeier and they had James Robert, born about 1988, and John Patrick, born about 1989. They live in Carmel, Ind.

1125122 James P. A. Fulton, Jr.

Jim was born 23 Apr 1930 in Hartford City, Ind. He earned a journalism degree at Indiana University followed by service in the U.S. Army from 1952 to 1954. His career as a reporter and editor for newspapers in Indiana and California spanned 40 years, most of which was with *The Progress Bulletin* in Pomona, Calif. He was married and has a daughter, Elizabeth. Jim is now divorced and living in Upland, Calif.

Elizabeth was born 24 Nov 1967 in Pomona, Calif. She married Corey Schmidt on 27 Nov 1993 in Pomona, Calif. Corey was born 5 Mar 1963 in Omaha, Neb. Both are graduates of the University of Southern California Film School in Los Angeles. Elizabeth began a career in film editing in 1989, which was interrupted when she entered into motherhood. Corey is a production manager for a graphics design company. Their son, Evan, was born 5 Dec 1996. The family lives in Glendale.

1125131 Charles Huston Goddard Jr.

Charles was born 9 Mar 1935 in Muncie, Ind. He has a BA degree in history and psychology from Wabash College, which he was granted in 1957. His first marriage was on 11 Sep 1960 in Muncie, Ind., to Corlis Sue Stanley who was born 31 Jan 1940. Their children are Amelia, Angela, Charles Huston III, and Amanda. Charley married

Carol Guilkey on 21 Mar 1998. Charley presently works for an automobile dealership in Muncie.

Amelia was born 18 Mar 1961 in Muncie. She is a graduate of Indiana University with a BA in 1983. She is a schoolteacher. She married William A. Galloway on 2 May 1987 at Brown County State Park, Nashville, Ind. They had William Angelo, born 21 Nov 1994.

Angela was born 23 Mar 1963 in Muncie. She graduated from Ball State University with a BA in 1985 and a MA in 1986; her major was Speech Communications. She is now self-employed as a meeting facilitator consultant in Los Angeles, Calif. Angela is not married.

Charles III was born 8 Jul 1967 in Defiance, Ohio. He briefly attended St. Vincent University. On 8 Jul 1995 he married Traci Helms who is from Centerville, Ind., the place they were married. Traci had Cody on 17 Sep 1988 from a previous marriage. Charles and Traci had Ceara Tylan on 15 May 1996 and Sunni Ki on 5 Aug 1997. Charles is an artist while Traci is a computer operator. They live in Phoenix, Ariz.

Amanda was born 27 Oct 1970. She is not married and manages a jewelry store.

1125221 Jill Mary Fulton

Jill was born 13 Mar 1947 in London, England. She graduated from the University of Colorado in 1969, and is currently working on her Ph.D. at the University of Texas. Jill is fluent in Spanish, knowledgeable on Amazon flora and fauna, and a student of Latin American cultures. She writes songs (music for guitar and lyrics) for youngsters. She made tapes concerning ecology which are widely used in schools in Florida. In Florida she was involved with an environmental group at Pine Jog in West Palm Beach. She was married to Mr. Jarboe and later they divorced. Jill was of Austin, Tex.

1125222 Sally Ann Fulton

Sally was born in London on 3 Oct 1948. Sally attended high school at the Washington School of the Ballet in Washington, D.C. She was engaged in ballet teaching and some modeling after her senior year before marrying Tom Clay in New York in 1965. She was living in Daytona Beach, Fla. in 1977. Later she and Tom were divorced. Sally retired and was planning to move to northern Calif. in 1999. A daughter, Willow Spring, was born in Jersey City in 1970. Willow is a flight attendant with a charter airline.

1125223 Elizabeth Fulton

Elizabeth was born in New York City on 31 May 1950. Liz attended Greenwich Academy, then Skidmore College, and graduated from New York State University in Purchase, N.Y., in 1973. She took a year off to travel Europe, the Middle East and Asia before getting married to Clyde Lawrence (Larry) Caldwell in Calif., in 1983. Their daughter, Margaret (Maggie), was born 1 Feb 1984 in New York City. While rearing her daughter, Liz remained home in Manhattan and in Redding, Conn., where she wrote two novels. Liz is currently a producer with NBC for the TODAY show. She has several years experience on and off the air with the three major networks. Maggie attends Ridgefield High School in Conn.

1125224 William Scott Fulton

Scott was born in Greenwich, Conn., 20 Sep 1954. He attended Greenwich High School and the University of Colorado in Boulder in 1974 and 1975. He is interested in music and formed a band and traveled around the country before settling in Idyllwild, Calif. He plays drums and writes soft rock music and lyrics. He is also interested in landscaping. Scott is unmarried.

1125231 Pamela Fulton

Pam was born 14 Apr 1939 in Yonkers, N.Y. She grew up in Dobbs Ferry, N.Y., and then Pleasantville, N.Y. She attended Skidmore College for two years, then married Albert A. Hopeman III on 12 Sep 1959. They lived in Rochester, N.Y., and had five children: Anna Messer, born 14 Jun 1960; Susan Elizabeth, born 21 Aug 1963; Albert Arendt IV, born 20 Apr 1964; Leslie Sharon, born 19 Apr 1966; and Robert Fulton, born 19 Mar 1968, all born in Rochester.

Pam returned to college at the University of Rochester and received a BS in 1967 and a master's degree in public policy analysis in 1978. Pam was divorced in 1983. She received a master's in divinity in 1986 from Colgate Rochester Divinity School in Rochester, N.Y. Pam became the executive director of Advent House Ministries in Lansing, Mich., and there married Edward M. Havitz in 1989. In 1990, they adopted two children: Jimmy Morgan who was born in 1978 and Faith Ann who was born in 1981. The family moved to Manistique, Mich., in 1994 where Pam is now pastor of Church of the Redeemer-Presbyterian and Gould City Community Church.

Anna, married to Robert Dees, is a pediatric otolaryngologist at Stanford University Medical School in Palo Alto, Calif. They have two children.

Susan, who married Mark Davidson, is president of Gordon's Jewelers and they are living in Coppell, Tex. They have two children.

Albert married Cindy Starks and is a senior software engineer with Oracle in Boston. They have two children.

Leslie is an occupational therapist in Longmont, Colo. She has a child.

Robert is a data analyst for an environmental testing firm in Oakland, Calif. Robert is not married.

1125232 William John Fulton

Bill was born 21 Jul 1943 in Yonkers, N.Y., and lived until the age of ten in Dobbs Ferry, N.Y., a small town near Hastings. The next two years he lived in Pleasantville, N.Y., then moved with his family to Mexico City, Mexico, for another two years. Next he lived in Orange County, Calif. Bill graduated from high school at the Army and Navy Academy in Carlsbad, Calif., in 1961. He completed two years of study at the University of Arizona in Tucson where he met Helen Kay Harper. In 1963 he joined the U.S. Army and served with the Army Security Agency in Germany until 1967. Bill married Kay on 19 Feb 1965.

Upon completing his military service he finished a BA in Russian studies at the University of Arizona in 1969. He and Kay moved to Washington, D.C. where Bill was employed by the FDA until 1981. Bill obtained a masters degree in social work in 1983 and went to work for Bethesda Naval Hospital as an addictions counselor. Next, Bill moved to Salt Lake City, Utah, where he worked at a LDS hospital. In 1988 Bill began private practice in psychotherapy which continued as of this writing. They had two children; Russell Erik who was born 4 Sep 1974 and Mindy Fulton who was born 11 Jul 1978. Bill and Kay were divorced in 1986; he secondly married Carol Jesslen Bird on 9 Jun 1990. They reside in Salt Lake City, Utah.

1125241 Richard Fulton Reston

Richard was born 14 Jul 1937 in London, England. He married Mary Jody O'Brien on 16 Oct 1965 in Washington, D.C. Richard was a 1955 graduate of St. Albans School and a 1960 graduate of the Univ. of Wisc. with a liberal arts degree. In his junior year he studied at the Univ. of Edinburgh in Scotland.

"Dick" became a newspaperman, and in his early years he was a correspondent for several publishers, including *Madison Times, San Francisco Chronicle,* and *Los Angeles Times.* In 1972 he became editor of *Vinyard Gazette*, published in Martha's Vinyard, Mass. The paper is the oldest weekly in the U.S. in constant circulation. In recent years it has received prestigious awards for journalism. Dick is now editor and publisher, and since 1972, has been assisted by his wife, Mary Jo, who serves as general manager.

Mary Jo was born in Delavan, Wisc., and is a graduate of the Univ. of Wisconsin where she majored in speech. She worked for Blue Cross/Blue Shield, worked for the Republican National Committee for a while, and lived in Moscow when Dick was a correspondent for the *Los Angeles Times*. They do not have any children.

1125242 James Barrett Reston Jr.

James was born 8 Mar 1941 in New York City. On 12 Jun 1971, in Hume, Va., he married Denise Brender Leary who was born in The Bronx, N.Y. Jim grew up in Washington, D.C., where he attended St. Albans School. He attended the University of North Carolina on a "Morrehead Scholarship," and graduated in 1963. He studied at Oxford University in England during his Junior year.

Jim is a writer of numerous novels and popular histories. Some of his publications include *The Last Apocalypse, Gallaleo* (a biography), *Lone Star* (a biography of Gov. John Connelly of Texas), and *Our Father Who Art In Hell*. His talents have been used in the production of documentaries for PBS and "Frontline."

Denise is a graduate of Boston University and Duke Law School; she was admitted to the bar about 1974. She has been involved in employment discrimination cases, and is now Deputy Council for National Public Radio in Wash., D.C. Jim and Denise have three children: Maeve, born about Jan 1977, who was to begin her senior year at Cornell in 1998; Devin Fitzgerald, born in Jan 1980; and Hillary Rory McTier, born about Dec 1984.

1125243 Thomas Busey Reston

Tom was born 4 July 1946 in New York City. He attended schools in Washington, D.C., and graduated from St. Albans School in 1964. Tom achieved his higher education at Harvard College where in 1968 he earned his A.B. in social studies and graduated cum laude. Tom then worked about two years for a newspaper as a foreign correspondent. He was involved in Virginia state politics and in Democrat campaigns, and was secretary in the Democrat party of Virginia from 1972 to 1977. In 1974 Tom graduated from the University of Virginia School of Law with a J.D. degree. He practiced law from 1974 to 1976, then worked for the State Department as deputy assistant secretary of state for public affairs. He was deputy spokesman at the State Department from 1977 to 1980, and often appeared at televised briefings. Since 1980 he has been practicing international law in Washington, D.C. Tom and Mary Victoria Kiechel were married 5 May 1990 in Hume, Va. Their children are Laura Kiechel, born 20 Nov 1992, and James Kiechel, born 27 Oct 1995, both born in Washington, D.C.

1125411 Alice Elizabeth Frykman

Alice was born 19 Aug 1946 in Palo Alto, Calif. She graduated from Washington State Univ., Pullman, Wash., in 1967. Alice married in Sep 1973 Alphusain J. Marong who was a student at WSU from The Gambia, West Africa. Their child is Serign M., born 29 Jan 1979 in Las Cruces, N.M. He was an honor student at WSU with a football scholarship. Alice is employed at WSU in Pullman.

1125412 Jean Fulton Frykman

Jeanie was born 6 May 1949 in Palo Alto, Calif. She is a graduate of WSU, Pullman, Wash. On 16 Dec 1972 she married Gerald Wayne Morse. Jerry is now principal of the high school in Colton, Wash., a town sixteen miles south of Pullman. They live in Pullman where Jeanie works at WSU. They have a daughter, Lisa Marie, born 4 Feb 1979 in Pullman. Lisa was now an honor student at WSU. She loves to ride and has her own horse. Lisa competed in English-type riding trials in the western states.

1125413 Mary Ellen Frykman

Mary was born 10 Feb 1954 at Pullman, Wash. She later graduated from Washington State Univ. On 27 Dec 1980 she and Phillip Andrew Braun were married. He was a grad student at WSU when they married, and died 9 Oct 1988. They had no children. Mary is living in Albion, Wash., while working at WSU.

1125511 Angela Fulton Derby

Angela was born 4 Nov 1934 in New Orleans, La. She graduated from high school in 1952 in Columbus, Ga. Angela has a BA degree from University of Chattanooga, Tenn., and a MSW from Syracuse in New York. She worked as a clinical social worker in the medical field. Before her recent retirement, she served as a hospice social worker for about six years. She married Vernon DeLon Hagen on 9 Jun 1956 in Toccoa, Ga. They had Audrey Angela who was born 8 Jul 1957 in Columbia, S.C.; and David Vernon, born 23 Oct 1959 in Laredo, Tex. Vernon received a BS from Omaha University and a MBA from Georgetown University. In 1980, he retired as a colonel from the U.S. Air Force.

Audrey married John Allen Hummel and they had Priscilla Lynn who was born in Des Moines, Ia.; Jeremy who was born in Syracuse, N.Y.; and Heather Leigh, born 3 Jul 1991 in Syracuse, N.Y.

David married Gale Irvin on 14 Aug 1983 in Williamsport, Pa; she died in Jul 1996. They had two children, David Jr., born 14 May 1991, and Douglas, born 24 Apr 1995. Secondly, David married Suzanne on 16 May 1998 in Vienna, Va.

1125512 Scott Fulton Ackerman

Scott was born 10 Apr 1944 in New Orleans. He was a graduate of Westminster High School in Atlanta in 1962. He was then a Moorehouse Scholar at North Carolina University. He studied at Eastern Theology Seminary in Cambridge, Mass. After being ordained, he served in Brooklyn and in Atlanta. He married Susanne Kittles, then they were divorced in 1994 without issue. Rev. Fulton died 5 Sep 1996. Recently, Susanne was living in Dallas, Tex.

1125611 Margaret Louise Fulton

Margaret (Peggy) was born 26 Jun 1930 in Spokane, Wash. Her fond childhood memories are of festive family gatherings in Coeur d'Alene, Ida., on holidays and birthdays. Margaret attended Whitworth College (Presbyterian) in Spokane for a year. Later she enlisted in the U.S. Navy where she trained as a Meteorological Technician, and during her four-year hitch she attained a rating of Petty Officer, Second Class. After she left the military, she worked at various jobs, but enjoyed the weather work so much that she applied to the U.S. Weather Service where she worked for six years in San Francisco and seven years in Anchorage, Alaska. Her last ten years of employment were with the Forest Service near Coeur d'Alene, where she currently lives. Margaret now volunteers at her church as a receptionist and record keeper. The compiler is indebted to Margaret for providing several photos of her family, as well as considerable family data.

1125612 Jean Roberta Fulton

Jean was born 19 Mar 1936 in Spokane, Wash. On 28 Nov 1959 in Spokane, Wash., she married LeRoy Harold Pierce. Their children were Linda Lee and Karen Marie. Jean was living in a nursing home in 1998; LeRoy lived in Newman Lake, Wash.

Linda was born 10 Feb 1964 in Spokane and first married Edwin Criswell. Her second marriage on 29 Apr 1995 was to Carl Leon Hansen who was born 11 Oct 1963. Linda and Ed Criswell had three daughters: Sharon Grace, born 6 Nov 1984; Amber Lynn, born 12 Sep 1986; and Hillary Jean, born 27 Dec 1991.   Jean and Carl had Michelle Lindsey who was born 20 Aug 1995.

Karen was born 28 Feb 1967 and married Cory Wall on 10 Sep 1988 in Spokane. No children.

1125621 James Thompson Fulton

James (Tom) was born 6 Feb 1944 in Coeur d'Alene, Ida. He graduated from high school in 1962, then attended the University of Idaho where he earned a BS degree in business administration.   He was drafted into the U.S. Army in 1968, and served with a field artillery unit at Giessen, Germany, until his discharge in Mar 1970. In Boise, he married Carol Ann (Ferguson) Carroll on 18 Feb 1989.   Carol was born 23 Nov 1946 in Anaconda, Mont.   Tom has a step-son, Michael Joseph Carroll, born 1 Apr 1972 in Hagerstown, Md.   Tom followed in his father's footsteps to become a bank manager in Boise.   Tom's hobbies include photography and bird watching.

Tom shares a special interest in genealogy. He has transcribed and annotated the information in a birth date book, once maintained by Anne Fulton of Coeur d'Alene.   The compiler is grateful for sharing the results of his enormous efforts which contained dates on a wide segment of the Fulton family.   We have discussed with Tom the fact that his middle name is spelled wrong!   Carol received a master's degree in education from Boise State University in 1991. Carol was awarded the Presidential award for Excellence in Teaching Science and Mathematics for Idaho in 1997 which she received in Washington, D.C.   She was awarded a Fullbright Memorial Program Teacher Scholarship in 1999.   In Oct 1999 she traveled to Japan to observe Japanese education.

1125622 Richard Wood Fulton Jr.

Dick was born 5 May 1945 in Coeur d'Alene.   He is a graduate of Coeur d'Alene High School, class of 1964, and graduated from Eastern Washington University in 1969.   Dick served in the U.S. Army from 1969 to 1971.   He has been a banker in Coeur d'Alene since 1972.   His first marriage was to Nancy Rhodes; no issue. Secondly, in LaClede, Ida., he was married on 11 Mar 1978 to Laura Dawn Glazier who was born 15 Mar 1958 in Spokane.   She is a realtor in Coeur d'Alene.   They have two sons: Trevor Gene who was born 5 Sep 1983, and Richard Wood III who was born 7 May 1985, both born in Spokane.   They make their home in Rathdrum, Ida.

1125623 Michael Robert Fulton

Mike was born 27 Feb 1946 in Coeur d'Alene, and was married there on 9 Jul 1966 to Dianne DeWitt who was born 29 Jan 1946. Their children are Joseph Robert, Heather Marie, and Sarah DeWitt. Mike is a 1970 graduate of Eastern Washington University with a degree in biology. He spent four years in the service of his country in the U.S. Air Force. Mike has been employed by the U.S. Postal Service for many years; Dianne works as a nurse.

Joseph (Joe) was born 22 Oct 1967 at the Fairchild AFB in Spokane County, Wash. He graduated from Cheney High School in Spokane County and served in the U.S. Air Force from 1994 to 1998. On 20 Apr 1996 he married Gretchen Sean Tyler in Cahokia, Ill. Gretchen was born 8 Feb 1973. They have a daughter, McKenzie Suzanne, born 16 May 1997 in Belleville, Ill.

Heather was born 1 Apr 1973 in Spokane. She is a 1991 graduate of Cheney High School. On 26 Apr 1992 she married Timothy Michael Lieseke in Cheney. Tim was born 29 Apr 1970 in Coupeville, Wash., and served in the military from 1991 to 1998, and now works for Burlington Northern Railroad. They have a son, Ren Michael, born 5 Sep 1992 in Honolulu, Hawaii, and a daughter, Haydn Gray, born 10 Jun 1996 in Spokane.

Sarah was born 2 Aug 1974 in Spokane and is not married.

1125624 David Gray Fulton

Dave was born 2 Aug 1947 in Coeur d'Alene, Ida. He attended Eastern Washington University for three years, and served in the U.S. Air Force from 1968-1972. In Spokane he was married on 9 Aug 1975 to Gayle Eileen Garner who was born 9 Jul 1954. They have two adopted children: Tara Nicole who was born 6 Sep 1979 and Derek James who was born 27 May 1983. Dave has worked for a distributor of NAPA auto parts for many years. Gayle works as a receptionist in a doctor's office.

1125631 Thomas William Cope

Tom was born 19 May 1947 in Coeur d'Alene, Ida. He earned degrees from Spokane Community College in 1976 and 1986. Tom is a vascular technologist for Cascade Vascular Medical Clinic. He enjoys music and has played in several bands for many years. He also likes to travel and scuba dive. Tom lives in Tacoma, Wash.

1125632 William Fulton Cope

William (Bill) was born 16 Nov 1955 in Washington and was adopted as a baby. He married Cecelia Scott on 13 Aug 1990 in Tacoma, Wash. Cecelia was born 7 Aug 1942. Bill attended culinary school in San Francisco about 1978. He currently is a chef in Tacoma and is married.

1125721 Frederick Fulton Zeise

Fred was born 27 Jul 1943 in Boston, Mass. He did like several other cousins and moved from his home in Boston to Calif., to be near his cousins. Fred is a skilled computer programer in the Silicon Valley. He married 15 Sep 1984 Ann Alden Peterson who was born 3 Nov 1947. They live in Milpitas, Calif. They had Scott Eric, born 19 Feb 1985.

1125722 Eric Karl Zeise

Eric was born 28 May 1950 in Boston, Mass. He obtained a Ph.D. in electronic imaging. He married Ellen Henry 27 Oct 1984. Ellen was born 28 Oct 1953 and has a Ph.D. in toxicology. Their son, Evan, was born 25 Oct 1992, and their daughter, Karen, was born in Sep 1995. They were living in Pittsford, N.Y.

1125723 Karl Zeise III

Karl was born 26 Dec 1957 in Boston, Mass. He, too, left Boston to be near his cousins, the Richards, in Calif. He had a daughter, Amber Leigh, born 5 Aug 1995, by Juli Gaeth. Karl is a skilled carpenter and woodworker: He designs furniture and is a building contractor and remodeling specialist in Calif.

1125741 Ruth Louise Richards

Ruth was born 3 Apr 1944 in Lincoln, Neb. She received a BS with honors from Stanford University in 1965. Her MA was earned at University of California, Berkeley, in 1969, followed by a Ph.D. in 1971. In 1980, she graduated from Harvard Medical School. She was Diplomate American Board of Psychiatry and Neurology, and was a licensed physchologist in Mass. She was associate attending physchiatrist at McLean Hospital, Belmont, Mass. By 1994, she was professor of psychology at Saybrook Graduate School, San Francisco. She sat as chair on Counciousness and Spirituality from 1999–2000. Ruth has contributed numerous scientific articles to professional journals and chapters to books.[190] She has ongoing research and clinical affiliations with Harvard, and UCSF. Her avocations include visual art, creative writing, photography and physics. Ruth married Jim Holtz in 1967 and they divorced in 1974. Secondly, she married Sandy Ruby in 1984, and they divorced in 1992. Ruth and Sandy adopted Lauren Jo who was born 1 Jan 1990. Ruth has her home in San Francisco.

1125742 Dexter Newell Richards III

Dexter was born 24 Jun 1946 in Boston, Mass. At the University of California, Berkeley, he earned a BA degree in economics in 1974. His career mainly involved working on integrated circuit development, and then he became director of research and development for Integrated Wave Technologies, Inc., in Santa Clara, Calif. He is also a photographer, has psychic abilities, and founded an invention company--Brevity, Inc. Dexter is not married. His sister and her husband were unable to have a child, whereupon Dexter became a sperm donor who, along with Donna _____, made it possible for Lauren Jo to come into this world and be adopted by his sister's family (see above).

1125743 Chesley Fulton Richards

Chesley (Chet) was born 18 Sep 1951 in Alameda Co., Calif. He earned a BA in physics at the University of California, Berleley, in 1974. He married Carine Wustefeld in Belgium in 1988 and they divorced in 1992. Secondly, he married Sandra (Choi) Hoey in 1996. In 2001, they were living in Danville, Calif., where Chet works in the field of computers and computer storage.

1125761 Anna Joy Place

Joy was born 7 Jul 1952 in Eugene, Ore. On 17 Mar 1973 she married Roland Harold Brown who was born 8 Oct 1947 in Detroit, Mich. In 1999, they lived in Monmouth, Ore., where they originally met as undergraduates. Joy and Roland obtained their master's degrees from the University of Oregon. Joy is in special education and counseling psychology, while Roland is in labor and industrial relations. Joy has served as State President for the Arc of Oregon, and is on numerous boards and advocacy organizations. Their son is Nathaniel Harold Ernest Brown, born 3 Oct 1980 in Seaside, Ore.

1125762 Stewart Douglas Place

Stewart was named after his father but went by his middle name, Doug. He was born 24 Aug 1953 in Eugene, Ore. Doug was a conscientious objector during the Vietnam War. He played the viola and guitar. He moved to Lincoln, Neb., and lived initially with Janet Gauger and her family until he settled. He married Martha on 4 Jul 1984; they had no children. Doug worked as a construction and equipment operator contractor for the railroad in Neb. and the surrounding states. On 20 Jun 1988, he was driving a heavily loaded truck down a mountain when a tire blew. He swerved to avoid a car but the truck crashed and burned; Doug was incinerated. Martha was living in Tuscon, Ariz., in 1999.

1125763 David Fulton Place

David was born 22 Nov 1954 in Eugene, Ore. He married Deborah Lynn Beckett on 17 Nov 1978 in Eugene. Debi's sons, Jerome and Todd, were adopted by David. David spent two years attending Western Oregon State College, then became an accomplished landscaper. He at one time owned and operated K&D's Hamburger Restaurant in Glenwood, Ore., just outside Eugene. His hobbies included square dancing, chess, and coaching and playing tennis. He also played the violin. He died of a stroke, related to his seizure disorder, on 23 Apr 1994 in Eugene. Burial was in Lane Memorial Gardens in Eugene.

1125764 Melanie Fulton Place

Melanie lives in Corvallis, Ore., with her life partner, C. Bummet. Melanie earned a BS degree in library science, and now works for the state of Oregon in the employment division.   She is an accomplished flutist, and coordinates a musical performance group that plays Celtic music.

1125771 Carl Christian Gauger

Carl was born 24 Mar 1954 In Lafayette, Ind.   In 1981 he married Rochelle (Shelly) who was born in Jun 1958.   Their children are Briana Justine, born 17 Mar 1982; Jerome Owen, born 13 Jun 1984; Carl Christian III, born 25 Jun 1988; and Mariel Grace, born 26 Jun 1997.   Carl has a associate degree in drafting and is employed as a design engineer in Kansas City, Kan. Shelly attended college and has home-schooled her children.

1125772 Christine Anne Gauger

Christine was born 6 Jan 1956 in Lafayette, Ind.   She married Lee Leighton in Jun 1989. Lee has a B.A. degree from Whittier College in Calif., and a master's degree in regional planning from the University of Nebraska in Lincoln. He worked five years as a city planner in Tualitan, Ore., and later for a private consulting firm. Christine has a B.A. from Evergreen College in Olympia, Wash., and a masters in dance from Ohio State University.   Chris owns two women's consignment stores in Portland, called "Here We Go Again," that have been successful.

1125773 Kathryn Helen Gauger

Kate was born 19 Jan 1958 in Lincoln, Neb. She is a graduate of Southeast Community College in Lincoln with a degree in computer science. She married Scott Colborn in Jun 1986. He attended the University of Neb. at Lincoln but did not graduate. He was involved in real estate for several years, but now he and Kathryn own and operate a music and book store in Lincoln called "The Way Home Music and Books." They had Melissa Ann, born 19 Jul 1994, and Asher Robert, born 8 Apr 1997.

1125774 Sarah Fulton Gauger

Sarah was born 8 Nov 1959 in Lincoln, Neb. She graduated with a B.A. degree from the University of Neb., in Lincoln. She married Charles Duerschner in Jan 1989. Charles is a graduate of the same university, with a degree in civil engineering. He subsequently obtained his professional engineers' license. He is with the Department of Environmental Control for the state of Neb. They have twins, Christopher Arthur and Jonathan Wendell, born 13 May 1997. The family lives in Lincoln, Neb.

1125811 John Kenworthy

John was born 10 Oct 1940 in Hammond, Ind. He graduated from Western High School in Washington, D.C., about 1958, then attended Oberlin College and the American University where he graduated with a degree in economics about 1966. He has worked in the computer field for several major corporations. John married Ann Caldwell on 19 Jun 1965 in Oberlin, Ohio. Their children are Jennifer and Catherine. John and Ann lived in Washington, D.C., for 34 years, then moved to Lothian, Md.

Jennifer graduated from veterinary school in Blacksburg, Va., and is in practice in Denver, Colo. Catherine completed medical school in San Francisco and was in her second year of residency. She is married to David Allan.

1125812 Jane Elizabeth Kenworthy

Jane was born 3 Oct 1945 in Washington, D.C. She graduated from Woodrow Wilson High School in 1963, then attended Oberlin College where she majored in English literature and earned a BA degree in 1968. Next, Jane enrolled at the Manhattan School of Music in New York City which she attended for over a year, then worked there in an arts management position. She was working in Boston when she married Richard A. Arenberg in May 1973 in Washington, D.C. They had Joshua Abraham on 13 Nov 1976 in Washington, D.C.; Meg Elizabeth on 14 Oct 1979 in Alexandria, Va.; and Ned Aaron on 11 Dec 1982 in Alexandria, Va. Secondly, Jane married Paul Schorsch. They were divorced, and Jane has re-acquired her maiden name. Jane was involved with the Baltimore Symphony Orchestra, the Annapolis Symphony Orchestra, and then became executive director of the Twin Cities Youth Symphonies, an organization that oversees eight

College in 2000 with a dual degree in music and political science. Meg is a member of Oberlin College class of 2001. Ned will attend Guilford College in 2001.

1125813 Thomas Kenworthy

Tom was born 4 Feb 1948 in Washington, D.C. After graduating from Woodrow Wilson High School in 1966, he attended Cornell University and earned a BA degree in history in 1970. He married Nancy Wood on 24 Jun 1972 at Clifton Springs, N.Y. Nancy earned a BS degree from Cornell in 1971 and a MS degree in education from Tufts University in 1972. Nancy is a self-employed management training consultant. Their children are Nora Jane born 14 Sep 1982 in Baltimore, Md., and Max Andrew born 12 Nov 1984 in Baltimore. Both children were attending Golden High School and were expected to graduate in 2000 and 2002, respectively. Tom is a newspaper reporter who has spent time in Amherst, N.H., and recently became a correspondent for *USA Today* in Denver, Colo.

1125821 Joanna Snow Schaefer

Joanna was born 3 Aug 1943 in Philadelphia, Pa. In 1965 she graduated from the University of Rochester with a BA degree in economics and mathematics. Joanna works for City Corps Investment Management Group, a division of INVESTCO, and heads up a Computer Systems Department in New York City. She married Clem Fiori on 12 Feb 1966 in Watchung, N.J. Clem was born 29 Mar 1943 and is a 1965 graduate of The State University of Rutgers where he majored in English. He currently is a publisher of books on photography of fine art and landscapes. He also is engaged in environmental activities. Their children are Nicholas Snow born 7 Sep 1974 and Daniel Scott born 13 Mar 1979, both born in Princeton, N.J. Joanna and Clem are living in Blawenburg, N.J.

Nicholas is a graduate of Brown University where he majored in mathematics and music. Currently, he is teaching math at St. Ann's School (K-12) in Brooklyn, N.Y. In 1999, Daniel was in his junior year at Brown University where he was majoring in music and art.

1125822 William Scott Schaefer

W. Scott was born 9 Jan 1949 in Summit, N.J. He graduated from Watchung Hills Regional High School in 1967. He then simultaneously earned a BS and MS in mechanical engineering at Ohio State University in 1972. Next, he earned a MBA at the State University of New York-Binghamton in 1976. He married Ardeen Lea Wills on 19 Jun 1982 in Zoar, Ohio. Ardeen was born 1 Jul 1942 in Cleveland, Ohio. Ardeen holds a BS degree in education in 1964 from Ohio State University. She taught second grade for awhile, served a year on an educational research council, and for the last nine years has been teaching at the pre-school level. From a previous marriage, Ardeen had Randall Thomas Gerber on 30 Mar 1968, Todd Michael Gerber on 28 Feb 1970 and Bradford Wills Gerber on 14 May 1972, all born in Parma, Ohio. Scott and Ardeen had Sharon Lorelle on 3 Jun 1984 in Buffalo, N.Y. They were living in East Aurora, N.Y., in 2001.

1125831 Ann Fulton Tenney

Ann was born 16 Feb 1946 in Washington, D.C.   After attending school in her early years in Roslyn, N.Y., she graduated from Paul D. Schreiber High School in Port Washington, N.Y., in 1965.   Then she attended Radcliffe (Harvard) College and Harvard University where she majored in social relations and earned a AB degree in 1969. She was awarded a MS degree in 1995 from Springfield College and is presently pursuing a doctoral degree in clinical psychology. Ann also attended New Hampshire Technical College in Concord where she earned an associate-in-nursing degree in 1979. She has spent twenty years as a nurse and the last twelve years as a family therapist. Ann married Thomas John Bindas on 6 Nov 1971 in Boston, Mass. Tom, who was born 3 Nov 1945, holds a degree in physics from Harvard in 1967, and is now construction manager for Appalachian Mountain Club.   They had Jan Bindas-Tenney on 7 Jun 1980 in Lewiston, Maine. Jan graduated from Gorham High School in 1998 and is a student at Vassar College, class of 2002. The family resides in Gorham, N.H., where they are members of the Gorham Congregational Church.

1125832 Janet Tenney

Janet was born 4 Jan 1948 in New York City and attended early grades at Roslyn, N.Y. In 1965, she graduated high school in Port Washington.   She began college as a physics major but left to become active in civil rights and anti-war movements. Later she attended Boston College where she graduated in 1979 with a BS degree in nursing; she is now a registered nurse. She married Anthony Hurst in Kalamazoo, Mich., in 1970. They had Ann Marie who was born 11 Feb 1972, at home, in Chicago, Ill., and Corey who was born 25 Sep 1974 in Boston, Mass. Secondly, Janet married Clayton Greene on 11 May 1985 in Boston. Clayton was born 17 Feb 1941 in Trinidad. Clayton served in the U.S. Army during the Vietnam War. He is a musician and plays the drums. He is a self-employed courier.

Ann Marie attended the University of Massachusetts and is now manager of Healthworks, a health club in Salem, Mass. Ann married Brian Baga.

Corey graduated from Tulane about 1996 with a degree in psychology. Presently she manages Nine-West, a shoe store in Nashua, N.H., while living in Salem. She is not married.

1125911 Elizabeth Ann Gossick

Elizabeth was born 22 Jun 1943. She married James Lauer who was born 17 Oct 1942; later they were divorced. Their children were Karen, born 2 Apr 1971, and Tanya, born 30 Jun 1972.

1125912 Mary Fulton Gossick

Mary was born 17 Mar 1945. She married, then divorced, Harold Symms who was born 16 Dec 1943. They had John Clifton, born 10 Nov 1965, and Laura Jean, born 23 Nov 1968. Laura married 27 Apr 1996 Raymond Albert Wallace who was born 11 Nov 1969.

1125913 Katherine Rogers Gossick

Katherine was born 27 Jul 1948. She married 4 Jan 1972 Kenneth Doyle Petrey who was born 16 Jan 1948. Their two children are Samuel Harlan, born 19 May 1985, and Rachel Katherine, born 8 Feb 1989.

1125914 Victoria Jean Gossick

Victoria was born 5 Feb 1955. She was alive as of 2001.

1125921 George Fulton Koehler

George was born 9 Nov 1941. He married 29 Jul 1972 Carolyn Kenney who was born 11 Jan 1943. They had Michael James, born 19 Mar 1976, and Daniel Fulton, born 17 Sep 1978. They lived in North Andover, Mass., in 2000.

1125922 Ruth Koehler

Ruth was born 16 Apr 1944. She married 28 Dec 1967 John Frederick Bergerson who was born 17 Jul 1943. They had John Palmer, born 27 Jan 1970; Eric Andrew, born 15 Oct 1972; and William Frederick, born 4 Mar 1977. As of 2000, Ruth and John lived in St. Paul, Minn.

In Snowbird, Utah, John was married on 29 May 1994 to Amy Aldous who was born 10 Apr 1966. Their child is John Charles who was born 14 Dec 1997.

1125923 James Fulton Charles Koehler

James was born 22 May 1950. In Minneapolis, Minn., he was married on 18 Aug 1973 to Susan Bailey who was born 9 Jun 1950. They had Lucas Charles, born 3 Dec 1982, and Allison Ruth, born 16 Aug 1985. They were living in Richardson, Tex., in 2000.

1125924 Thomas Edward Koehler

Thomas was born 25 Aug 1952. On 1 Aug 1980 in St. Paul, Minn., he married Stephanie Nielsen who was born 28 Mar 1949. Their two children are Erin Nielsen, born 7 Aug 1982, and Kathleen Nielsen, born 1 May 1985. Their home was in Duluth in 2000.

1125941 Robert Gray Haxby

Robert was born 4 Jan 1948 in Minneapolis, Minn. He graduated from the University of Minnesota Medical School, and was a emergency room physician. On 8 Aug 1970 he married Elisabeth Grams who was born 28 Jul 1949. They had Mikael Caley Grams who was born 26 Apr 1979, and Sara Elisabeth Grams who was born 29 Jun 1982.

1125942 William Fulton Haxby

William was born 3 Oct 1949 in Minneapolis. He was married on 24 Dec 1970 to Nan Hawkins who was born 28 Jul 1947; later they divorced. They had Jane Fulton who was born 11 Dec 1976 in Ithaca, N.Y., and graduated from Yale in Jun 1999. Bill earned a BS degree from the University of Minnesota, and his Ph.D. from Cornell University in N.Y.   He is a geophysicist with Lamont Earth Observatory at Columbia University in N.Y.

1125943 James Van Loan Haxby

James was born 20 May 1951 in Minneapolis. On 9 Sep 1973 he married Barbara Garey who was born 30 Sep 1951. They had Andrew Warren, born 24 Oct 1981 and Matthew Fulton, born 9 Jul 1984. James graduated from Carlton University with a BS degree, then achieved his Ph.D. at the University of Minnesota. He is a neuro-scientist at the National Institute of Health in Bethesda, Md.

1125944 Mary Alice Haxby

Mary was born 8 Jul 1954 in Minneapolis. In Rhode Island, she was married on 10 Sep 1983 to Dennis Gibbons who was born 23 Aug 1953. They had two children, Katherine Haxby, born 11 May 1986, and Samantha Lauren, born 19 Oct 1987. Mary graduated from the University of Minnesota as a registered nurse and is in that practice part time.

1126211 Barbara Alice Curran

Barbara was born in Chicago on 30 Apr 1942.

1126212 Donald Robert Curran

Donald was born in Chicago 14 Sep 1943 and died in Santa Clara, Calif., on 28 Mar 1990.

1126213 James Edward Curran

James was born 14 Sep 1946 in Philadelphia, Pa. He was in the U.S. Air Force and served in Vietnam.

1126214 Janet Elizabeth Curran

Janet was born 24 Nov 1952 in Concord, Calif.

1126221 Kathleen Mary Tuohey

Kathleen was born 3 Oct 1945 in Chicago, Ill., and was living in 2001. She is not married.

11266222 Robert Joseph Tuohey

"Bob" was born 29 Dec 1947 in Chicago. He was in the U.S. Marine Corps and served in the Vietnam War. He was married to Marilyn, and they had a daughter, Jennifer Catherine, born 21 Oct 1971, and a son, Christopher Michael, born 19 Nov 1974, both born in Chicago. Bob is presently single, living in the Chicago area.

1126311 Mary Frances Maier

Mary was born 14 Jan 1958 in Chicago. She graduated from Evergreen Park High School in 1976, then attended Marquette University where she earned a BS in nursing. Mary works as a public health nurse.

She married Mr. Hildebrand who has a dairy heard of 500 cows in Wisc.   Their children are Jo-Allen, and twins Ryan Allen and Bradley Jo.

1126312 John Leonard Maier Jr.

John was born 8 Jul 1949.   He is a lawyer in Wisc., and in Ill. On 18 Dec 1999 he married Trisa.   He was previously married and has a son, Michael.

1126313 Stephen Peter Maier

Stephen was born 1 Jul 1952.

1126321 William Stuart Rose

Bill was born 23 Nov 1942 in Cleveland.   He married Paula Elizabeth Robertson on 22 Sep 1974 in Austin, Tex.   Bill is a 1964 graduate of Williams College of Williamstown, Mass., with a BA degree in English.   He then studied at the University of Texas Law School in Austin and earned a LLB in 1968.   Paula earned a Ph.D. in English from the University of Texas, and has been a professor at Austin Community College for the past 23 years.   Their children are Austin Lindsay who was born 30 Nov 1975 in Austin and Lincoln John Howard who was born 9 Mar 1981 in Austin.

Austin has been awarded a BA degree from the University of Virginia, and he is now pursuing a master's degree in architecture from the University of Texas.   Lincoln will graduate from high school in 1999 and plans to attend Washington and Lee College in Lexington, Va.

1126322 Laurence David Rose

Larry was born 25 Aug 1945 in Cleveland, Ohio.   He received a BA and a MBA from California Coast University, and was a financial advisor before working for John Hancock Insurance.   On 9 Jan 1971 he married Danielle Grace Martin who has a BA from Erie College in Painesville, Ohio. Their children are Tiffany Ellen who was born 20 Dec 1980 and Brittany Shannon who was born 8 Oct 1982, both born in Phoenix, Ariz.

1127121 Charles Wayne Scriven

Chuck was born 7 Jul 1945 in Prineville, Ore.   While teaching he also studied at Berkeley where he earned a Ph.D.   He is now president of Columbia Union College in Takoma Park, Md.   He married Marianne Sjoren in Jun 1970.   Marianne was born 1 Feb 1947. Their children are Charles Jonathan, born 14 Jun 1971, now a teacher;

Christina Annemarie, born 27 Mar 1975, working as a student nurse; and Jeremy Cord Edward, born 27 Oct 1983.

1127122 Donald Cord Scriven

Donald was born 24 May 1948 in Grants Pass, Ore. He married in Apr 1990 Nelda Cowles. He spent two years in the military before graduating from Tulane Law School in 1974. He and two partners have a law firm in Columbus, Ohio. Donald and Nelda were living in Upper Arlington, Ohio, in 1999 and they are the parents of Peter Alexander, born in Jul 1991, and Emily Elizabeth, born in Sep 1993.

1127123 Richard Ralph Scriven

Richard was born 17 Mar 1954 in Spokane, Wash. He graduated from Loma Linda University Medical School in 1978. Dr. Scriven is a urologist at Rockwood Clinic in Spokane, Wash. He married Suzie Johnson in Jun 1975. Suzanne was born 16 May 1952. They had Stacy Errin, born 13 Nov 1978, and Sabrina Allison, born 2 May 1982.

1127131 Ronald Ralph Cole

Ronald was born 7 Sep 1941 at Central Butte, Saskatchewan. He received his education in Central Butte and in Moose Jaw. On 23 Oct 1965 he married Wilma Margaret Wilhelmson in the United Methodist Church in Central Butte. Wilma was born 30 Apr 1944 in Yarmouth, Nova Scotia, the daughter of Truman and Mary Wilhelmson. Ronald worked in his father's store and did construction work in Central Butte. He was a volunteer ambulance driver and paramedic. From 1966-1967 he was a police officer, then he moved to Swift Current where he is working as a claims adjuster with Saskatchewan Government Insurance.

They have three children: Teresa Annette, born 26 Aug 1966 in Central Butte; Leanne, born and died 25 Feb 1970 in Swift Current; and Kevin Ronald Andrew, born 8 Jul 1974 in Swift Current. Teresa and Kevin are not married.

1127132 Isabelle Jeannette Cole

Isabelle was born 14 Mar 1944. She married 19 Apr 1963 Bill Newton, and they have four children: Rhonda Michelle, born 20 Oct 1963; Denise Lynn, born 22 Oct 1966; Craig Dean, born 2 Jun 1973; and Corey M., born 27 Oct 1969, all born in Central Butte. Isabelle and Bill Newton were divorced 13 Dec 1982. Isabelle was living in Regina, Sk., in 1998.

Rhonda married Phil Hanison in Regina in Dec 1989. They have two children, Kyle Matthew, born 8 Jul 1992, and Nathan Andrew, born 12 Jan 1995, both in Regina.

Denise married Gary Fedreau 5 Oct 1985 in Central Butte. They currently live in Camrose, Alberta.   They have three children: Jennifer Dawn, born 12 Dec 1986 in Central Butte; Dylan Sean, born 27 May 1989 in Central Butte; and Courtney Breanne, born 1 Jul 1996 in Cambrose, Alberta. Craig, a resident of Atwater, Sk., and Corey, a resident of Central Butte, Sk., were not married as of 1998.

1127133 Patricia Faye Cole

Patricia was born 9 Dec 1956 in Central Butte, Sk. On 2 Aug 1975 she married, in Regina, Wayne Styles; they were divorced in Dec 1990.   Their children were Mark Kenneth, born 20 Nov 1976 in Regina; Kirk Robert, born 9 Jan 1978 in Regina; Kent Andrew, born 14 Jan 1980 in Regina; and Jordan Patrick, born 28 Mar 1991 in North Battleford, Sk. As of 1998, Mark was not married and living in Saskatoon; Kirk was unmarried living in Kingston, Ontario, and has a child, Justin, born 16 Sep 1997 in Kingston; Kent was not married, living in Regina; and Jordan, whose father is not revealed, resides in Lloydminster, Alberta, with his mother.

1127151 Kerry Elizabeth Rupp

Kerry was born 3 Mar 1951 in Pasadena, Calif. She has a daughter, Jesse Elizabeth Stuart, born 17 Sep 1980 in Pocatello, Ida. Kerry is a graduate of the University of Idaho with three bachelor degrees. She is a health inspector for the county of Klamath in Ore. Jesse was attending the University of Oregon in 2001, pursuing a business degree.

1127152 James Michael Rupp

James was born 15 Aug 1952 in Pasadena.   He was married, then divorced in 1990. He is in the printing business in the L.A. area. He is a graduate of Pasadena Community College, and has taken courses at other colleges.

1127153 Wayne Riley Rupp

Wayne was born 26 Oct 1954 in Pasadena. He married Christine Anthony in 1979 and they divorced in 1983. They have a son, Riley Jay, born 5 Mar 1980 in McMinnville, Ore. He attended junior college in McMinnville and at the University of Oregon. Wayne is a long-distance truck driver, and lives in Woodland, Wash.

1127154 Hugh Jay Rupp

Hugh was born 12 Jan 1957 in Duarte, Calif. He married Christine Andres in Jun 1984 and divorced in 1989. They have a daughter, Stephanie Andres, born 12 Nov 1983 in Arcadia, Calif. Hugh died 14 Jun 1999 due to complications with a back injury. His body was cremated. Stephanie was a freshman at the University of Mich. in 2001.

1127155 Donna Jean Rupp

Donna was born 26 Mar 1959 in Duarte, Calif. She obtained a business degree at the University of Idaho and now lives in Beaverton, Ore. She married Sam McKeehan 23 Dec 1980 in Moscow, Ida., then divorced in 1985. They had Adrienne Anne, born 28 May 1981 in Moscow, Ida., and Allison Alycia, born 18 Apr 1983 in Moscow. Adrienne attended college in Molalla, Ore., while Allison is a member of her high school graduating class of 2001.

1127321 William Richard Evans Jr.

William was born 18 Dec 1942. He graduated from the University of Montana and from the University of Washington College of Dentistry. He served in the Vietnam War, and retired as a Lt. Commander. He has a dental practice in Eagle River, Alaska. William also teaches and trains dogs for agility trials. He married Diane Arthur and they had Erika and Karen.

Erika graduated from Pacific Lutheran Univ. in Tacoma, Wash. She is working for 'CellularOne.' She married Brian Flattum and they have a son, Jared. Karen graduated from Eastern Washington Univ., and is teaching school in Wenatchee, Wash.

1127322 Janet Helen Evans

Janet was born 30 Mar 1945. She was an exchange student in Switzerland for a year before she graduated from the University of Montana. Janet has traveled to Europe, Africa, New Zealand and Australia. She teaches in the high school in Bozeman, Mont. She married Terry Anderson who is a economics professor at Montana State University. They had Sarah Elizabeth and Peter Novak. Sarah was a senior at M.I.T. in 1999. Peter is on a trip around the world after graduating from high school.

1127323 David George Evans

David was born 16 Jan 1952. He graduated from Montana State Univ. and from the Univ. of Minnesota Dental College. He has a dental practice in Red Lodge, Mont. He has a son, Jeffrey Ryan, who in 2000 graduated from Red Lodge High School, then entered MSU.

1127331 Pamela Diane Brumwell

Pam was born 5 Aug 1949 in Seattle. She is a graduate of the University of Washington where she earned a degree in English literature and creative writing in 1972. She then attended an interior design school and has worked in fashion merchandising and interior design. She married John Othart who was born 11 Jun 1949 in Bakersfield, Calif., and holds a degree in Ag Business and Accounting from Fresno State University. They were living in Irvine, Calif., in 1999.

1127332 George Keith Brumwell Jr.

Keith was born 15 May 1952 in Seattle and attended several colleges. He achieved a two-year degree in landscape maintenance and design. He is now a landscape designer, unmarried, living in Seattle.

1127333 Craig Lloyd Brumwell

Craig was born 18 May 1957 in Seattle and is married to Mary; they have a daughter, and live near Boston, Mass.

1127711 Geoffrey Norris

Geoffrey was born 20 Jul 1966. He received a BS degree in pharmacy at the University of Saskatchewn, and graduated with great distinction, in May 1991. He received the Campbell prize as the 2nd-most distinguished graduate in pharmacy. He works as a pharmacist in the hospital in Red Deer, Alberta. He married Janis Hataley on 4 Jul 1992. Janis was born 4 Nov 1973. Their children are Simon, born 19 Sep 1994, and Sean, born 29 Oct 1997.

1127721 Beverley Anne Hughes

Beverley was born 10 Nov 1954. She is a graduate of Saskatchewan Business College. She married Thomas McLeod 9 Apr 1977. They have three sons; David Ari, born 6 May 1980; Kenneth William, born 6 Jun 1984; and Matthew Thomas, born 13 Mar 1987. Beverley works for Saskatchewan Telephone in the business office.

1127722 Arthur William Hughes

Arthur was born 28 Dec 1957. He is a graduate of the University of Saskatchewan with a bachelor of arts and science degree. He is employed as a sales rep for a food wholesale co. His first marriage was to Natalie Kachur on 29 Jul 1978. They had Patricia Nicole, born 2 Oct 1979. Secondly, he married Shelley Fauser on 12 Dec 1986. Their children are Nicholas Arthur, born 9 Apr 1990, and Katherine Ruth, born 10 Dec 1992.

1127723 Donna Elaine Hughes

Donna was born 24 May 1961. She married Terrance Campbell on 18 Nov 1978. Donna has worked for an insurance company for nine years, as a part-time employee at a funeral home, and as a teacher's aide. Their children are Terrance Tyral, born 16 May 1979, and Amy Nichole, born 31 Aug 1982. Secondly, Donna married Lorne Warren Valuck on 15 Jan 1988. They had Bethany Alexandria, born 31 Mar 1989, and Joshua Andrew, born 5 Sep 1990. Donna and Lorne live on an acreage and enjoy all their animals, plus the work of a market garden.

1127(10)21 Robert Richard Robinson

Bobby was born 18 Jun 1948 in Portland, Ore. He married Margaret Lynn (Peggy) Bramble 21 Dec 1969 in Honolulu, Hawaii. Peggy was born 7 Jan 1946. Their children are Jessica Ean (sic?), born 23 Nov 1970 or 1971, and Robert Nathaniel, born 12 Jan 1975. Both children were born in Doylestown, Pa.

1127(10)22 Michael William Robinson

Michael was born 12 Oct 1950 in Seattle, Wash. He is not married.

1127(10)23 Laurie Jean Robinson

Laurie was born 16 Dec 1953 in Seattle, Wash. She first married Alan Cartor (Bo) Tabagogon 27 May 1975 in Honolulu. They had Daniel Kahana born 20 Nov 1976 in Honolulu, and David Ka'aina born 3 Jun 1981 in Portland, Ore. Laurie secondly married Duane Pratt 17 Mar 1990.

1127(10)24 James Edward Robinson

James was born 22 Apr 1958 in Hawaii. He married Beth Aleson Hall 15 May 1989. They had Mitchell Julian Aukai born 15 Mar 1991 in Vancouver, Wash.

1127(10)31 Susan Ruth Pearn

Susan was born in Toronto, Ontario, 1 Oct 1957. She married Michael Anthony on 23 Dec 1978. They have no children.

1127(10)32 Jane Elizabeth Pearn

Jane was born 8 Sept 1959 in Toronto, Ontario. She married Graham Scott on 1 Feb 1979.

1127(10)41 Michelle Iolani Betters

Michelle (Shelly) was born in Honolulu 22 Oct 1961. She lives in Honolulu, Hawaii, with her daughter, Lauren Nicole Hi'ilani Betters-Dung who was born 1 May 1992 in Honolulu. Michelle attended various elementary schools on Oahu and in Guam. She graduated from St. Francis High School in 1979, then from the University of Hawaii, Manoa, in 1997 with a BBA in Human Resource Management. Currently, Michelle is employed at Theo. H. Davies and Co. as a benefits administrator. Her hobbies include traveling, cooking and gardening, and she enjoys her time with Nicole. Nicole is attending Ma'ema'e Elementary School in Nuuanu, Hawaii. Nicole plays soccer and dances hula.

1127(10)42 Collette N. Betters

Collette (Coco) was born 10 Nov 1962 in Hawaii. She has no children.

1127(10)43 Frank Robert Lemieux

Frank was born 25 Nov 1963 in Honolulu, Hawaii, and has two children, Nuri Andrian Lemieux, born 1 Dec 1994, and Nalani Aline Lemieux, born 26 Apr 1996.

1127(10)44 John Palimoo Betters

John was born 17 May 1958 in Hawaii.

1127(10)45 Brenda Joy Schott

Brenda was born 15 Mar 1959 in Hawaii; she has two children.

1131211 Nancy Ann McCleery

Nancy was born ca. 1937 in Leland, Ill. She appeared on College Quiz Bowl radio program in 1955 while a freshman at U. Ill. Allen Luden was quiz master. Her team lost. She married Simon Mein. Their son is Andrew.

1131212 Margaret Beth McCleery

Margaret married Gordon Cota. Their children are Matthew and Elizabeth Ellen. Neither she nor her sister were interested in providing more information.

1131711 Patti Mae McCleery

Patti was born 25 Sep 1950 in Columbus, Ohio. She graduated from Jefferson Union High School in Richmond, Ohio in 1968. In 1972 she graduated from Ohio State University with a degree in physical education. She is not married.

1131712 Sandra Sue McCleery

Sandra was born 28 Mar 1954. She married John P. Reilly Jr., and they have two sons, Matthew born 3 Jan 1988 and Peter born 25 May 1993. Their home is in Wilmette, Ill.

1131721 Elizabeth Ann Wolverton

Elizabeth was born 5 Jun 1950. On 29 Jul 1989 she married Vincent A. Kleinknecht. There are no children.

1131722 Katherine Christina Wolverton

Katherine was born 28 Jul 1951; married 14 Jul 1973 to John A. Jordan. They have three children: Karen A. born 3 Feb 1979, Timothy Russell born 2 Apr 1981 and John Frederick born 8 Sep 1983.

1131723 John Warner Wolverton

John was born 30 May 1953. He married Nancy Clare Rachal on 6 May 1978. John is an M.D. Their children are Brian Peter born 31 Mar 1979 and Michael Joseph born 5 Dec 1983.

1131724 Mary Margaret Wolverton

Mary was born 7 Jun 1955. She married John R. Bartos 17 Jun 1978. They had Frank Warner born 30 Apr 1987. Secondly, Mary married Gregory Van Atta on 19 Apr 1997.

1131725 Martha Susan Wolverton

Martha was born 17 Jan 1958. She married Jeffrey B. Hargis, an M.D., on 29 Sep 1984. Their children are Libia Kathryn born 29 May 1989, Natalie Christine born 10 Jun 1991 and Meredith Anne born 24 Jan 1995.

1131731 Deborah Mae McCleery

Deborah was born 24 Dec 1953 in Erie, Pa. She married Foster Hinkle, and later they divorced. They had no children. Deborah lives in Wooster, Ohio.

1131732 Phyllis Jean McCleery

Phyllis was born 18 Jan 1957 in Erie, Pa. She is married to James Franks, Jr. They had two daughters, Jennifer, born 1 Jul 1983 and Emily born 10 Sep 1985. They live in Pittsburgh, Pa.

1131831 James Craig Curts

James was born 19 Feb 1948 in Sandwich, Ill. He was a 1966 graduate of Somonauk High School and later he attended college. He worked as a computer programmer. He married Kathleen Burkardt on 1 Jun 1973 at Somonauk Baptist Temple. James died 15 Oct 1973 in Chicago, Ill. He had no children. Kathleen remarried.

1131832 Scott Allen Curts

Scott was born 15 May 1952 in Sandwich, Ill. In 1970 he graduated from Somonauk High School, then he attended college but did not graduate. He is now a television engineer for WGN in Chicago. Scott is a member of the Naval Reserves, and lives in Glendale Heights, Ill. He is not married.

1131833 Denise Lynn Curts

Denise was born 24 Sep 1953 in Sandwich, Ill. She is a 1971 graduate of Somonauk High School. She earned a BS degree in business administration in 1976 followed by a MS degree in 1980 from Aurora University. She is employed by Farmers Insurance Group in Aurora. She married Charles Edward Lueth on 9 Jun 1979 at Somonauk United Presbyterian Church. Charles was born 4 Mar 1940, has a degree in mechanical engineering and is a graduate of the United States Naval Academy. He earned a master's degree from Roosevelt University in Chicago and works primarily as a contract engineer. He also is a professor at Waubonsee Community College in Sugar Grove, Ill.

1132111 Hugh Duane Graham

Hugh was born 5 Jan 1912 in Ware, Tex., and died 3 Aug 1966 in Bentonville, Ark. He married Christine Kirby 26 Dec 1935. Christine was born 6 Jul 1908. Their adopted child is Marilyn Sue, born 15 Sep 1946 in Rogers, Ark. Marilyn Sue married Charles Turner in 1963, and they have two daughters, Christine and Kim, both married and divorced with children.

1132112 Charles Anson Graham

Charles was born 3 Sep 1915 in Clay Co., Kan. He married 24 May 1941 Harriet Jane Grubb who was born 26 Dec 1915 in Hayward, Calif. They had Glory Anne, born 13 Feb 1943 in Indio, Calif., and Charlene Ruth, born 14 Oct 1946 in Berkeley, Calif. Glory Anne married 8 Jun 1963 John Laffey; Glory died 18 Apr 1999 in San Jose, Calif. They had John Charles, born 10 May 1966, died 2 May 1996, and Richard Clark, born 6 Dec 1967. Charlene Ruth married Gary Detlefs 19 Aug 1967 and they had Robert Graham, born 27 Oct 1970, and John Peter, born 11 Sep 1973. Charlene divorced Gary and married Philip Duval; no children.

1132113 Richard Worth Graham

Richard was born 25 Oct 1917 in Clay Co., Kan., and died in Jun 1967. He married 7 Apr 1940 Kathleen Fuller who was born 29 Aug 1919 in Galva, Ill. They adopted Richard Gary who was born 12 Oct 1946 in Aurora, Ill. Richard Gary married Melody Rogers 22 Oct 1966 and later divorced. They had Tammy Kay, born 7 Jun 1967 in Aurora. Tammy Kay gave birth to Richard Worth Graham. Secondly, Richard Gary married Katherine Olivia Medina 18 Sep 1971, and they had Kevin, born in 1979, and Clayton Marseiles, born 16 Apr 1987 in Wausau, Wisc.

1132114 Ruth Alice Graham

Ruth was born 31 Mar 1920 in Viola, Kan. On 13 Jul 1940 she married Everett Newton Teal who was born 11 May 1911 in Ottawa, Ill. Their children were Juanita Merle, born 24 May 1941; Mary Caroline, born 19 Jul 1944; Linda Louise, born 11 Aug 1947; Delores Rae, born 12 Sep 1950; and Alice Wendy, born 17 May 1955, all born in Sandwich, Ill. Everett died 10 May 1999 and was buried in Oak Mound Cem.

Juanita Merle married Gerald D. Guiterrez 27 Jun 1970 and later were divorced. Their children were Christopher Graham, born 27 Jul 1972 in Fremont, Calif., and Caroline Boston, born 30 Jul 1975 in Calif. Secondly, Juanita married Don Furtado in May 1991 and they divorced in 1996.

Mary Caroline married John O'Benar 18 Jun 1971 in Berkeley, Calif. John was born 11 Apr 1943 and died 15 Mar 1997 in San Antonio, Tex. No children.

Linda Louise married 11 Sep 1971 William Renc in Somonauk, Ill. William was born 17 Feb 1949 in Ill. They had Christine Alice, born 16 Apr 1975 in Clearwater, Fla.

Dolores Rae married William Moseley 30 Mar 1972 and later they divorced. She adopted William's children from a prior marriage: William Scott, born 30 Sep 1968 in Kan.; and Mark Aaron, born 7 Dec 1969. Together, they had Amy Kaye, born 28 May 1975 in Lawrence, Kan.

Alice Wendy married James Moseley 2 Apr 1976 in Kansas City, Kan. They had Tara Marie, born 30 Nov 1982 in Kansas City, Kan.

1132115 Milton Orcutt Graham

Milton was born 30 Apr 1922 in Viola, Kan., and died 3 May 1992 in R.I. He married 23 Jun 1942 Doris Elizabeth Wilson who was born 16 Jul 1923 in South Kingston, R.I. They had Marsha Elizabeth, born 10 Aug 1946 in South Kingston; Richard Winfield, born 20 Jul 1948 in Sandwich, Ill.; and Cheryl Kathleen, born 17 Mar 1953 in South Kingston.

Marsha married and divorced without children; she died in Sep 1991. Richard Winfield married Jaqualine Ann Arnet and later divorced. They had Heather Marijah who was born 13 Jun 1976 in Tacoma, Wash. Secondly, Richard married Orpha Mae Cockburn. Cheryl Kathleen married Steve Resentes 31 May 1974 and they had a daughter, Roxanne Kanani, born 26 Feb 1983 in R.I. Later they divorced.

1132116 Daniel Dean Graham

Daniel was born 3 Feb 1930 and died 17 Jun 1939.

1132117 Helen Jane Graham

Helen was born 30 Aug 1931 and died 31 Jan 1941.

1132121 Grace Souder

Grace was born 29 Oct 1905 in Victor Twp., DeKalb Co., Ill., and died 4 Jun 1994 in Kewanee, Ill. She married 21 Feb 1931 James Creighton "Heck" Elliott who was born 26 Jul 1899 in Stark Co., Ill., and died 6 Oct 1984 in Ill. She was buried in Elmira Cemetery in Stark Co., Ill. They had Lois Ann, John Curtis, Eunice Belle, and Alice Marilyn. From Wendell Chestnut's notes we learn that Grace was interested in many things. She was accomplished at quilting, and enjoyed crocheting and making hand-braided rugs. She was a poet and had some of her writings published in a book *County Roads*. Grace was a member of Elmira United Presbyterian Church where she held various positions. She taught Sunday school and served as an officer in the Women's Association. Grace was a graduate of Northern Illinois State Teacher's College of DeKalb, Ill., and she taught school in Lake County before her marriage.

Lois Ann was born 4 Jan 1933 and married Robert M. Segar 25 Sep 1956 in Rogers City, Mich. They had Ellen Jean, born 11 Feb 1961 in Port Huron, Mich., Janet Elizabeth, born 21 Jul 1963 in Rogers City, and Nancy Lou, born 6 Apr 1968 in Clinton, Ia.   Janet Elizabeth married Steve Para.

John Curtis was born 3 Jun 1934 in Kewanee, Ill., and married Donna Kay Parrish 18 Feb 1962 in Toulon, Ill. They had James Clifton, born 2 Dec 1963, and Beth Ann, born 13 Jan 1966, both born in Kewanee, Ill. James Clifton married Deborah Davis.

Eunice Belle was born 4 Jul 1936 in Kewanee. On 10 Nov 1957 in Elmira, Ill., she married Donald L. Daniels who was born 17 Apr 1937 in Kewanee.   They had Gary Lee, born 3 Jul 1958 in Jacksonville, Fla.; Duane Lawrence, born 16 May 1959 in Kewanee; and Thomas Eldon, born 20 Jul 1962 in Kewanee. Gary Lee married Diane White and later were divorced. They had a daughter, Leanne, born 25 Sep 1979 in Kewanee. Duane Lawrence married Joy Osborne 13 Sep 1987. They had Stephen Elliott, born 5 Aug 1989 in Moline, Ill. Thomas Eldon married Mary Melendez in Apr 1982. Their two children are Matthew Thomas, born 5 Nov 1982, and Samantha Christine, born 4 Dec 1989.

Alice Marilyn was born 6 Feb 1938 in Kewanee, and married Robert E. Griswold 7 Aug 1960. Their children were David Earl, born 14 Jul 1961; Joanne Kay, born 7 Feb 1963; Stephen Robert, born 29 Jul 1965; and Cheryl Ann, born 25 Apr 1971. Joanne Kay married Henry Thurston.

1132122 Mary Souder

Mary was born 29 Apr 1907 in DeKalb Co., Ill. She married 16 Feb 1929 Dale M. Bend who died 26 Mar 1960 in DeKalb Co.   Their children were Richard M., born 18 Apr 1930; Jean Patricia, born 24 Mar 1933; Phyllis Grace, born 6 Nov 1939; and Mary Carole, born 16 Sep 1945.

Richard married Marilyn Boegner 8 Aug 1954. Their children were Linda Sue, born 8 Jan 1956 in Germany; Ronald Richard, born 29 Jul 1960; Jon Merritt, born 2 Feb 1963; Beth Kaye, born 10 Aug 1966; and Richard Harvey, born 19 Oct 1971. Beth Kaye married a Mr. White. Jean married Richard Barr 29 Jun 1954.   They had six children: Patricia Marie, born 13 Mar 1955; Theresa Kaye, born in Oct 1956; Barbara Jean, born 11 Feb 1959; Margaret Mary, born 2 Aug

1960; Edward Thomas, born 14 Sep 1961; and Kellie Michelle, born 12 Nov 1968. Patricia Marie married Dana Philip Austin and they had Honna Lee, born about 1980; Holly Cristal, born About 1982; Danae, born about 1985; Joel Jacob, born about 1987; Philip David, born about 1988; Garrett, born about 1990; and Trevor, born about Mar 1993. Thersea Kaye married Michael Konan and they had Ellie, Carlye, James, and Nicholas. Barbara Jean married Ronald Schoo and they had Molly, Benjamin, and Andrew. Margaret Mary has a son, Jacob Thomas.

Phyllis Grace married Daniel Christianson 8 Sep 1960. Their two children are Cathryn Carole, born 11 Jul 1961, and Heather Ann, born 31 Dec 1964. Cathryn Carole had a son, Kyle, by Mr. Abraham. Mary Carole married 10 Sep 1966 LaVerne Jordal and they had Sean Dale, born 8 Jun 1968, and Jason Kenneth, born 20 Mar 1971.

1132123 Ralph Souder

Ralph was born 17 Sep 1909, and was of Libertyville, Ill. He recently celebrated his 89th birthday and has lived in the Fairhaven Christian Home in Rockford, Ill., for many years.

1132124 Ruth Souder

Ruth was born a twin 21 May 1911 and married Warren Reimensnider 28 Sep 1935. Ruth was in a nursing home in Aurora, Ill., in 1998. Warren was born in 1906 and died in 1989. Their son was David Warren, born 24 Aug 1939. David married Doris Trout 14 Mar 1964 and they had Christine Rhea, born 15 Jun 1965; Lauralynn, born 13 Apr 1968; Deann Kay, born 13 Mar 1970; and Robert David, born 1 Mar 1972. Christine Rhea married Mark Olson.

1132125 Richard Souder

Richard was born 21 May 1911, a twin, but died two days later.

1132126 Adelbert Souder

Adelbert was born 14 Mar 1914 in DeKalb Co., Ill., and died there 2 May 1969. He married Edna E. Strong 1 Feb 1936 in DeKalb Co., Ill., Edna was born 14 Oct 1914. They had Sandra Sue, born 10 Aug 1938 and Mary Sheryl, born 1 Apr 1946.

Sandra Sue married Ronald Zerkle 9 Sep 1961 at Holy Name Catholic Church in Chicago, Ill., and they had (1) Mary Lisa, born 9 Sep 1962, who married Richard Pliskin on 16 Jun 1990 in N.Y. and they had a child, Emma Barrie, born 10 Jul 1993 in Convent Station, N.J.; (2) David Karl born 31 Dec 1963, married Carolyn Beer 7 Oct

1991 in Cincinnati, Ohio, and they had Sandra Ann, born 29 Oct 1991. (3) Andrew Joseph, born in 1966, married Lisa Marie Pappas 7 Jul 1990 in Cincinnati.

Mary married Christopher E. Dries 23 Sep 1967 and they had twins born 28 Nov 1969, Mary Jennifer and Joanne Marie.

1132127 Donald Souder

Donald was born 16 Apr 1916 in DeKalb Co., Ill. He married Mary Ruth Nelson 24 Dec 1938 in Somonauk, Ill. Mary Ruth was born 23 Sep 1915 in Somonauk and died 4 Jul 1990 in Canandaigua, Ontario Co., N.Y. They had Charlotte Marie, born 6 Oct 1937; Karon Ruth, born 29 Jun 1945; and Susann Louise, born 2 Feb 1953. Charlotte married John Wood and they had Van John born 17 May 1972, and Cheryl Marie. Karon married Nyal Ernest Laird and they had James Nyal, born 1 Sep 1963, and Ronald Ernest, born 3 Feb 1966. Susann married Kenneth Wurster on 30 Jun 1973 and their children were Dennis Allen, born 29 Feb 1976; Donald Edward, born 23 Feb 1980; and Michelle Suzanne, born 4 Sep 1986.

1132131 Sara Jane Gordon

Sara was born 31 Oct 1917 and married Forrest Frederick Thurow on 4 Apr 1942 in Somonauk, Ill. Forrest was born 11 Mar 1915. Their children were Gene F., born 2 Sep 1944 in Hinckley; Dwane Gordon, born 26 May 1947 in Aurora; Donald F., born 2 Apr 1949 in Aurora; and Merrill L., born 23 Nov 1953 in Aurora. In 1999 they were living in Sandwich, Ill.

Gene married Patricia Loring 31 Dec 1965 in Hinckley and they had Scott Loring, born 26 Aug 1966 in Aurora, Ill. Secondly Gene married Denise Sprinkle who was born 5 Jul 1943. Gene and Denise had Melissa Jean born 3 May 1970 in Aurora.

Scott married 1 Jul 1995 in Shamburg, Ill., Joanne Santiago, born 11 Dec 1964. Melissa Jean married Timothy Schomer, and later were divorced. They had Ashley Jeane who was born 26 Jan 1993 in Aurora. Secondly Melissa married on 1 Jun 1997 Rodney Jandt who was born 8 Mar 1970. They had Lucas Ronald who was born 19 Jan 1998 in Aurora.

Dwane married 9 Sep 1967 Mary Bromeland who was born 29 Dec 1946. Their children were John Douglas, born 25 Sep 1970, and Allison Jane, born 14 Dec 1979, both in Aurora, Ill. Donald married 3 Apr 1982 Cheryl Covell who was born 17 Jun 1953. They had Tiffany Ann, born 19 Feb 1983 in Aurora. Cheryl had two children by a previous marriage, Michele and Kristy Pereklita.

Merrill married Diana Rohman who was born 27 Dec 1952 in Aurora. They had Lisa Ann born 13 Sep 1977, and Michael E. born 27 Feb 1980.

1132132 Jeannette M. Gordon

Jeannette was born 31 Oct 1917 in Waterman, Ill. She was a 1941 graduate of Copley School of Nursing, and was a registered nurse for over 35 years at Dreyer Medical Ceneter before she retired. Jeannette was a member of Somonauk United Presbyterian Church where she was very active in all church activities and in the choir. She was active in the Sandwich Opera House, Meals on Wheels, Food Pantry and many community affairs. Never married, she died at Copley Memorial Hospital in Aurora on 11 Feb 1993.

1132133 George Graham Gordon

George was born 1 or 21 Feb 1921 in Waterman, Ill. In Sandwich, Ill., he married 2 Sep 1944 June M. Greenwood who was born 26 May 1924 in Chicago, Ill., and died 5 Jun 1983; burial was in Oak Mound Cemetery. Their children were David L., born 9 Jul 1946; Roger L., born 16 Mar 1951; and Carol Ruth, born 13 Feb 1953. George secondly married 5 Dec 1990 Betty Phillips who was born 24 Aug 1929 in Plano, Ill. George died 14 Apr 1998 in his home in Sandwich, Ill.

David married Beverly Sheetz who was born 25 Nov 1945 in Calif. They had Jeff, born 3 Feb 1980, and Jodi, born 23 Feb 1982, both in Calif.

Roger married in Plainfield, Ill. on 15 Apr 1978 Carol Lynn Francis who was born 16 Mar 1951 in Sandwich, Ill. Their children are Timothy, born 24 Mar 1980, and Ellen Ruth, born 17 Apr 1983.

Carol married 20 Mar 1993 Thomas Gowdy at the Somonauk Presbyterian Church in DeKalb Co., Ill. Thomas was born 1 Nov 1946.

1132141 Reid Graham Boyle

Reid was born 20 Jul 1912 in Clay Center, Clay Co., Kan., and died 9 May 1966. In 1962 he was residing in Edwardsville, Ill. He married Helen Jensen on 25 Mar 1937, and they had James Martin, born 20 Jun 1942, and Martha Ann, born 12 Jan 1948. Helen died 5 Dec 2000 at Edwardsville, Ill.

James married Jean Echternach and they had Heather and Adam James; Martha married James Borgstede, a dental surgeon, and their children were Kimberley and Laura.

1132142 Jean M. Boyle

Jean was born 23 Feb 1926 in DeKalb Co., Ill. On 25 Jun 1948 she married Clair L. Boyd at Somonauk United Presbyterian Church in DeKalb Co., Ill. Clair was born 10 Jan 1928 and died 9 Feb 1997 near Sioux City, Ia. They lived at Creston, Ia., in 1962. They had Constance Louise, born 31 Aug 1949; Barbara Jean, born 24 Jul 1951; and Ronda Claire, born 16 Oct 1953.

Constance married Peter Marcellus and they had Theron, Jennifer, and Amanda. Barbara was married three times and had issue; she is deceased. Ronda was married and is now divorced.

1132151 Joyce Ann Nowers

Joyce was born 22 Jun 1925 (or 30 Oct 1925) and was a foster child. She married Victor Carl Nagel on 25 Dec 1945. Their three children were Lynn Nowers, born 1 Sep 1947; Vicki Carol, born 22 Nov 1948; and Bruce Alan, born 12 Jul 1955. They made their home in Creston, Ia., in 1962. Joyce may have died in Oct 1978 in Woodbury, Ia.

1132621 James Graham Marshall

James was born 11 Dec 1922 and married Janet Miller 21 Jan 1961. They once lived in Pasadena, Calif. No known children. James died in Jul 1995 in Garden Grove, Calif.

1132622 Robert Howard Marshall

Robert was born 5 Nov 1924 in Waterloo, Ia. He married Katherine Colton 7 Aug 1948 in Somonauk, Ill.   Katherine was born in 1926 in San Luis Obispo, Calif. They had two sons, Stephen Alan, born 31 Jan 1950 in San Luis Obispo, and Jeffrey Kent, born 6 May 1952 in St. Charles, Ill. They once lived in Pasadena, Calif., and in 1988 they were in Covina, Calif.

1132623 William D. Marshall

William was born 10 Mar 1926 in Waterloo, Ia. He married Donna Jean Hoag 29 Jul 1948. They had Michael D., born 3 Jul 1949; Sharon E., born 19 Sep 1950; Rosemary L., born 10 Feb 1953; and Wayne L., born 9 May 1954. William and Donna later divorced. William died 27 Nov 1995 at Pico Rivera, Calif.

1132651 Ralph Wilson Graham

Ralph was born 20 Dec 1920 and died 12 Jun 1936.

1132652 James Ray Graham Jr.

James Jr. was born 20 Aug 1923 and married Eileen Frank 9 Aug 1945. They had Sondra Lee, born 13 Apr 1952, and Cynthia Christine, born 14 Oct 1953. In 1962 they lived in Los Angeles. An Eileen Frank was born 1 Oct 1921 and died in Jan 1995 in Vancouver, Wash.

1132711 Reid Kyle Beveridge

Reid was born 20 Oct 1942 in Sumner, Ia. In 1964 he graduated from Monmouth College with a BA degree in English. In 1965 he earned a MS degree in journalism from Columbia University. He then began his journalism career with the *Houston Chronicle* in Houston, Tex., and after seven years moved on to Williamsburg, Ia., to assume operations of the newspaper started by his father. In 1975 he went to Madison, Wisc., where he worked as a legislative and political reporter for the *Wisconsin State Journal*. From 1981 to 1996 he was editor of the National Guard magazine in Washington, D.C.

Reid enlisted in the National Guard as a private in 1965 and worked his way up to become a second lieutenant in 1968; by 1995 he had earned the rank of brigadier general. He was still active in the Guard as of 1999. Reid married Eileen Davies on 23 May 1998 in Milford, Del., where they were living in 1999.

1132731 Robert Hugh Beveridge

Robert was born and died 19 Jun 1934.

1132732 Donald Reid Beveridge

Donald, a twin, was born 3 Mar 1937 in Monmouth, Ill. There he attended Monmouth College and graduated with a degree in math and physics in 1959. Don spent some time in the Army Reserves. He worked as a computer systems analyst for Time, Inc., in Chicago, and now does consulting work. He married Carol Anderson 16 Oct 1965. Their children are Donna, born 11 Apr 1971, and Paula, born 11 Feb 1973, both unmarried. The Donald Beveridge family was living in Kalamazoo, Mich., in 1998.

1132733 Dorothy Jean Beveridge

Jean, a twin, was born 3 Mar 1937. She married Michael Meyers and they live in Montclair, N.J. They have a daughter, Lynn, who is married to Elliott West of the Boston area.

1132751 James Martin Beveridge

James was born 10 Jul 1929. He married 30 Jun 1956 Nancy Mortland

and they had a daughter, Sonia, born 28 Feb 1959.   They live in Heyworth, Ill., where Jim has a printing business.

1132771 Diane Winslow Beveridge

Diane was born 3 Apr 1957. She was previously married to Mohammud Nikfor and lived in Santa Clara, Calif. They have two sons, Isaac, and Amin.

1132781 Linda Margaret Kramer

Linda was born 7 Dec 1947 in Springfield, Ill.   She is a 1966 graduate of Balyki High School in Bath, Ohio.   She received a BS degree in home economics education at Illinois State University in 1970 and a MS at Purdue University in 1976.   She finished her advanced education by earning a Ph.D. in consumer economics at Purdue in 1979. She taught at Oak Park Elementary School. She married John Zimmermann on 24 Jun 1973 in Bath, Ill., and they live in Greenfield, Ind. John is a veterinarian patholgist who earned his degree at the University of Illinois.

1132782 Kent William Kramer

Kent was born 18 Nov 1952. He had Down's Syndrome and died of kidney failure in 1967.

1132811 Eileen McCleery

Eileen, known as "Bunny", was born 27 Jul 1920 in Mitchell, S.D. She was married in Waterloo, Ia., on 9 Dec 1939, to Glenn Leroy Hendricks who was born 7 Dec 1918 in Lohrville, Ia.   They had Kathie Joan. Eileen married, secondly, Wilbur H. Yeutter on 12 Jul 1951 in Milford, Ia. Eileen died 13 Jun 1996 in Geneva, Ill., and was buried in Hampton, Ia.   Wilbur was born 27 Jun 1919 at Emmetsburg, Ia.

Kathie, born 12 Aug 1940 in Waterloo, is a graduate of Iowa State University.   She married Edmond J. Walsh 26 Jun 1965 in Hampton, Ia.   Their children are Anne Shannon who was born 27 Nov 1968 at Arlington Heights, Ill., and they adopted Magan who was born 23 Jan 1974.   Edmond was born 13 Sep 1943 in Norristown, Pa., and died 24 May 1991 at Maywood, Ill.; burial was in Garfield Cemetery in Kane Co., Ill.   Kathie, who was living in Geneva, Ill., in 1999, is interested in genealogy, and has assisted with this compilation.

Anne married Matthew Cesarone on 30 Sep 1995 in Geneva, Ill. They had Patrick who was born 29 Jun 1999 in Geneva.

1132812 James Austin McCleery Jr.

James was born 6 Aug 1929. He graduated from East Waterloo High School in 1947. On 1 Jul 1950 he and Luanna Wood were married. Luanna was born in Omaha, Neb. They had Michael James, born 20 Nov 1951, and Patrick W., born 7 Oct 1956. James is a 1951 graduate of Iowa State Teacher's College (now UNI). They lived in Omaha for a while, then in Knoxville, Ia., where he operated a funeral home.

1132821 Richard Lee Walker Sr.

Richard was born 30 May 1917 in Waterloo, Ia., and married 7 May 1937 Mary Angela Elder who was born in Waterloo. They had Richard Lee Jr., born 9 Mar 1938; Danny Gene, born 15 Feb 1940; Mary Sue, born 18 Jul 1946; and Michael Paul, born 7 Jun 1958. Richard Sr. died in Waterloo, 11 Apr 1989.

Richard Jr. married Ruth Dawn Bishop 12 Jun 1960 at Cedar Falls, Ia.

1132822 Bobby Walker

Bobby was born 15 Sep 1921 in Waterloo, Ia., and died 25 Jun 1923. He was buried in Waterloo.

1132823 DeWayne Edwin Walker

DeWayne was born 6 Dec 1925 in Eldora, Ia., and married Marlys Jean Yarrington 8 Nov 1947. Marlys was born 14 Nov 1931. They had Kathy Jo, born 26 May 1954; Paula Ann, born 21 Mar 1957; and Theresa Marie, born 26 Jul 1961. DeWayne died in May 1974.

1132824 Charles LaVerne Walker

Charles was born 10 Jun 1927 in Waterloo, Ia. He married Dorothy Mae Morgon 22 Jul 1944. Dorothy was born 4 Nov 1927. They had three children: Gary Lee, born 4 Sep 1944; Carol Kay, born 6 Jul 1949; and Karen Lynne, born 7 Dec 1960. Charles died in Nov 1971 in Waverly, Ia.

1132861 Dorothy Jeannette Wright

Dorothy was born 22 Jul 1928 in Waterman, Ill., and died 12 May 1961 in Gary, Ind. She was buried at Schererville, Ind. Dorothy married 25 Jul 1948 Rev. Fred J. Green who was born 1 Mar 1928 in Gary, Ind. Their children were Margaret Anne, born 3 Jul 1950 at Washington, Mo.; Fred Joseph, born 29 Nov 1951 at Washington, Mo.; Dorothy Elizabeth, born 19 Dec 1953 at Knox, Ind.; Joy Eileen, born

4 Dec 1955 at Knox, Ind.; and Julia Alice, born 20 Jan 1959 at Marion, Ind.

1132862 Mervin McCleery Wright

Mervin, known as Mac, was born 10 Oct 1929 in Lancaster, Ill. On 3 Jun 1951 he married Anna Lou Armes. They had Mark Stephen, born 1 Feb 1953; Joretta Sue, born 17 Oct 1955; and David Paul, born 11 Mar 1963. Rev. Wright and his family arrived in Calif. in 1958 and lived in Palmdale in 1964.

1132863 William George Wright

William was born 25 May 1931 in Leland, Ill., and married Helen Frances Webber 24 Aug 1952 in Escondido, Calif. Helen was born 16 May 1935 in Gary, Ind. Their children were William George Jr., born 19 Nov 1953 at Washington, Ind.; Deborah Ilene, born 4 Aug 1955 at Inglewood, Calif.; and James Mark, born 20 Dec 1958. They were living in Escondido, Calif. in 1964.

1132864 Robert Lawrence Wright

Robert (Bob) was born 22 Jun 1933 in Lancaster, Ill. On 22 Oct 1954 in Flora, Ill., he married Myrna Gannon who was born in Lava Hot Springs, Ida. Both are graduates of Cincinnati Bible Seminary, Myrna in 1952 and Bob in 1957. Bob was a minister in the First Christian Church until he retired in 1977. In 1978 he went into the insurance business and established his own agency in 1988, and they are still active in the daily operation. They had John Bradford, born 10 Oct 1956; Janna Beth, born 29 Dec 1957; and Jeffrey Brent, born 6 May 1960, all in Cincinnati; and Jerald Blaine born 2 Mar 1963 and Joel Bryan born 28 Aug 1966 in Calif. They once lived in Cynthiana, Ky., and arrived in Calif. in 1961. They were in Pomona, Calif., in 1999.

1132865 Margaret Ann Wright

Margaret was born 8 May 1936 in Ill. She graduated from high school in 1954 and from Cincinnati Bible College in 1959. She married Jack Porter Harney on 18 Dec 1959. Jack was born 23 Nov 1938 in Lexington, Ky. He graduated from high school in 1957 and from Cincinnati Bible College in 1962. They had Dorothy Sue born 28 May 1962 in Cincinnati and J. Michael born 12 Jun 1964 in Rushville, Ind. They were living in Rushville, Ind. in 1964 and presently reside in Georgetown, Ky.

Dorothy Sue (Dotty) graduated from high school in 1980 and from Ozark Christian College in 1987. She was living in Columbia, Mo., in 1999.

J. Michael graduated from high school in 1982 and from Ozark Christian College in 1987. He married Julia Ellen Rowoth on 8 Dec 1985. Their children are Daniel Bryan born 8 Feb 1989, Joel Porter born 28 Aug 1991, Caleb Michael born 2 May 1995 and Ellen Corrine born 2 Jan 1999. They lived in New Berlin, Ill., in 1999.

1132866 Grace Eileen Wright

Grace was born 22 Apr 1938 at Elnora, Ind. She graduated from Young America High School in Metcalf, Ill., in 1956, and from Cincinnatti Bible Seminary in 1961. She married Howard Joseph Kelsey, Jr. on 26 Mar 1988. Joe was born 16 Nov 1938. They live in Lakewood, Calif.

1132867 James Merrill Wright

James was born 10 Aug 1941 at Villa Grove, Ill. He went to California after graduating from high school in 1959. He attended Pacific Christian College and Long Beach State and graduated in 1965. He married Diane Marie Parker on 17 Dec 1966. Their children are Susan Elizabeth and Dana Marie. James is an insurance broker, and lives in Anaheim Hills, Calif.

Susan was born 12 Apr 1971 and married Paul Alan Grady on 15 Jul 1995. They had Erin Elizabeth who was born 24 Mar 1999. They live in Placentia, Calif.

Dana was born 8 Jan 1974. She had Lauren Nicole who was born 17 Oct 1993. Dana then married married John Carter. John had a son he brought into the family. Dana and John cross-adopted Lauren and Cody. They live in Anaheim Hills, Calif.

1132868 John David Wright

John was born 3 Mar 1943 at Villa Grove, Ill. He moved to Long Beach, Calif., in 1961. John and Diane Lynn Woodard were married there on 23 Feb 1968. They have two children, David John born 11 Feb 1970 and Christa Lynn born 26 Jul 1971. Secondly, John married Linda Rhea Light on 21 Dec 1990. John and Linda have an insurance agency in Cerritos, Calif. They were living in Huntington Beach, Calif., as of 2001.

1132871 Karen Elizabeth Wielert

Karen was born 26 Apr 1947 in Elgin, Ill. She graduated from Cambridge High School in 1965 and had attended Western Illinois University the following year. She and her parents were killed in an automobile accident 23 Jul 1966 that occurred west of Geneseo, Ill. on Illinois Hwy 81. She was buried in Immanuel Lutheran

Church Cemetery west of Hinckley.

1132921 James Hearn

James was born 8 Nov 1938 in Kansas City, Mo. He was raised by
John W. and Lulu Hearn, his grandparents. He married Esther Eskam
5 Jul 1960, was in serious trouble with the law and may have fled
to Canada.

1132922 Ruth Marie Hearn

Ruth was born 29 Aug 1941 in Kansas City, Mo. She was legally
adopted by her aunt and uncle, Olin and Ruth (Hearn) Ruth. She
attended school in the KC, Mo., area. Young Ruth married David
Brewer and they had Kathy.   After a divorce, Ruth married a
wrestler named Marshall, and they divorced. Ruth may be of Calif.

1132923 Twila Hearn

Twila was born 9 Oct 1942 in Kansas City, Mo. She was adopted
after her mother left the family. She married David James, a
salesman. He died of a heart attack. They had several girls, the
oldest being Janice, then Mary, Carolyn, two more girls and a boy.
Secondly, Twila was briefly married to David's brother, who also
had several children. Twila may be in Calif.

1135111 Reid Garfield Beveridge

Reid was born 23 Aug 1917 in Yellow Grass, Saskatchewan, Canada. He
enlisted in the U.S. Navy at the beginning of World War II and
studied to achieve the rating of Aviation Chief Mechanic, the
highest enlisted rating. During his 4-1/2 years in the service he
spent 13 months aboard aircraft carrier USS Yorktown in the South
Pacific. On 11 Jul 1942 in Chicago, Ill., he married Jean
Richardson who was born 1 Sep 1924 in Boone, Ia. After the war,
Reid was the manager of a hardware store, then worked as a manager
for a subsidiary of IBM Corp. Jean was a switchboard operator
before she became a bookkeeper for Heineken Beer Distributors in
Chicago. They had two sons, Karl Edward, born 23 Mar 1945, and
Allan Dale, born 28 Jun 1951. Reid died of heart trouble 29 Feb
1992 in Chicago. Jean was living in Burbank, Ill., in 2000.

Karl first married Jane Hein and they had Bruce, born 1 Nov 1958 in
Chicago, Ill. Bruce married Lisa in 1997. Secondly, Karl married
Marilyn Custardo about 1990; no children.

Allan married Shirley Janusch about 1971 and they have three
children: Theresa Ann, born about 1976, Reid Carl, born in 1982,
and Rachel, born about 1975. Theresa lives in Maywood, Ill., with

her daughter, Mariah Ann Easley.

1135121 Elizabeth Welker Beveridge

Elizabeth (Betty) was born 10 Oct 1935 in Pittsburgh, Pa. She graduated from Mount Lebanon High School in 1953, then attended Penn State University where she majored in home economics and education. She received a BS degree in 1957. Her first career opportunity was with Mount Lebabon School District when she taught home economics. Next, she worked for Scotch Plains Fanwood High School in New Jersey. Since 1977 she has been in the real estate business. Betty married Ned Harpster Finkbeiner on 12 Jul 1958 in Mount Lebanon. Ned is retired from Alcoa where he worked in sales, and now has his own business. Their children are Kathy Ann, twins David Allen and Donald George, and Karen Lee. Betty and Ned lived in Birmingham, Mich., in 1999.

Kathy Ann was born 5 Aug 1960 in Plainfield, N.J. She married James Wayne Douglas on 21 Jul 1984. Their children are Lea who was born 19 May 1988; Chase Wayne who was born 22 Oct 1990; and Hunter who was born 24 Nov 1995.

David Allen was born 29 Dec 1962 in Plainfield, N.J. He married Tressia Bailey on 22 Oct 1988. David works for Kraft Foods and is now living in Grand Rapids, Mich. They have Samantha who was born 30 Jun 1990; Tyler who was born 21 Sep 1991; and Payton who was born 28 Apr 1998.

Donald George was born 29 Dec 1962 in Plainfield, N.J. He is not married.

Karen Lee was born 6 Apr 1967 in Mount Lebanon. Pa. She married Bryan Best on 28 Dec 1991. Their children are Brandon who was born 2 Sep 1995 and Blake who was born 25 Nov 1997.

1135122 Mary Ann Beveridge

Mary Ann was born 1 Aug 1937 in Pittsburgh and died of cancer at the age of 37 in 1974. She was a graduate of Penn State with a major in home economics, and after graduation she had a business in that field. On 20 Oct 1963 in Pittsburgh she married George Joseph Rudolph; George now lives in Kettering, Ohio. He received a degree in business administration from Ohio Wesleyan University, and a master's degree from Cornell University. In 1973 he was the manager of an engineering consultation firm in Dayton, Ohio. They had George Beveridge on 7 Sep 1966 at Akron, Ohio, and Sherrin Ann on 11 Aug 1967 at Coshocton, Ohio. George married Michelle and they live in Cascade, Mich. Sherrin married Bryce Kristo and they live in Chicago, Ill.

1135211 John Thomas Beveridge

John was born 14 Aug 1947 in Oregon, Ill. He is a graduate of Oregon High School, class of 1965. John continued his education by attending several colleges, and eventually took up the occupation of fireman. He first married Sally Patzer 27 Jun 1969 at Oregon, Ill. Sally was born 29 Feb 1948 in Geneva, Ill. They had Scott Thomas, born 29 Jan 1970 in Sterling, Ill., and James Michael, born 12 May 1974 in Dixon. Secondly, on 10 Jul 1982 in Oregon, Ill., John married Diane Mina Levan who was born 4 May 1951 in Dixon. Today they operate a nursery in Dixon.

Scott married Michele Smith on 16 Apr 1994 in St. Simon's Island, Ga. They had twins, Graham Thomas and Nathan Hayes, born 19 May 1999 in Athens, Ga.

1135821 Alice Anne Beveridge

Alice was born 1 Apr 1956 in Gainsville, Ga. She graduated from Butler High School in Augusta, Ga., about 1973. She became a registered dietician. She married Douglas Conte in 1984, and they presently make their home in Ocean Side, Calif. They have no children.

1135822 Albert Henry Beveridge II

Albert was born 27 Jan 1959 in Gainsville, Ga. On 28 Oct 1989 he married Laura Leigh Hooker in Augusta, Ga. Their children are Connor Ronald, born 29 May 1991 in Augusta, and twins Grayson Arthur and Tanner Herbert, born 17 Dec 1994 in Augusta. Albert is a manager for Club Car, a manufacturer of golf cars. He is a Civil War buff.

1136621 Richard James Lafferty

Richard was born 27 Apr 1948 in Sandwich, Ill. He is a graduate of Purdue University. His children are Jennifer Leigh, born 21 Feb 1970; Gregory Daniel, born 29 Jul 1971 and Kathleen Sinead, born 24 Nov 1975. Kathleen has a daughter, Rachel Kathleen Seely who was born 10 Sep 1998. They were of Ft. Wayne, Ind., in 1999.

1136622 Michael Ralph Lafferty

Michael was born 1 Dec 1949 in Sandwich, Ill. He graduated from Waterman High School in 1967, then graduated in general studies from Kishwaukee College in Malta, Ill. He served in the U.S. Army, and afterwards worked for Caterpillar. He married Elizabeth Eure and they later divorced. Their children are Susan Evelyn and

Christian Allen. Michael was living in Somonauk, Ill., in 2001.
Susan had Christopher and Nicholas.

1136623 Patrick Kevin Lafferty

"Pat" was born 12 May 1953 in Sandwich, Ill. In 1971 he graduated
from Waterman High School and then attended Kewanee Community
College. He earned a degree in agra-business in 1972, and took up
farming for a while. He is currently working for Vermeer Midwest
in sales and service of machinery. Pat married Carla Sue Oksa and
they had Katrina Susanne on 15 Nov 1976, Kevin Ralph on 22 Mar 1979
and Kelli Rae on 20 Mar 1986. Secondly, Pat married Michelle Lynn
Harrinestine who was previously married. They were living in
Somonauk, Ill., in 2001.

1136631 Margaret Helen Howison

Known as Peggy, she was born 7 Aug 1946. She graduated from
Waterman (Ill.) High School. She attended Southern Illinois
University before she transferred to Northern Illinois University
where she graduated with a BS in nutrition and food science. On 30
Nov 1968, at St. John the Baptist Catholic Church in Somonauk, she
was married to Lyle Merton Tuestad Jr., who was a graduate of
Waterman High School in 1962. Their child was Timothy Robert who
was born 23 Mar 1969 in DeKalb, Ill. Tim graduated from Loyola
University in Chicago, and was living in Chicago in 2001. Secondly,
on 5 May 1980, Peggy married Marvin O. Trepton, M.D., and they
have a daughter, Kellie, who was born 4 Dec 1981 and was a freshman
at the University of Wisconsin, Madison, in 2001. The family was
living in DeKalb, Ill., in 2001.

1137211 Jacqueline Isabelle Beveridge

Jacqueline was born 6 Apr 1934 in Waterman, Ill. She married 31
Dec 1960 Roger Lee Ross who was born 5 Jul 1932 in Ill., and died
in 1995; he was a salesman. They had Lynn Patricia, James Ralph and
John David. Jacqueline and Roger divorced in 1982. She spent a
combined two years at Knox College and at Northern University of
Illinois. She has worked as a medical secretary, and was residing
in Middletown, Wisc., in 2001.

Lynn was born 27 Nov 1961 in Elmhurst, Ill. She is not married and
lives in Madison, Wisc.

James was born 13 Dec 1964 and is unmarried.

John was born 15 Jul 1966. He married Heidi Dvorak and their
children are Jacob Paul who was born 10 Nov 1997 and Carley
Elizabeth who was born 2 Sep 1999, both born in Madison, Wisc. They

live in Middletown.

1137212 James Hoy Beveridge, III

James was born 22 Sep 1936 in Sandwich, Illinois. He graduated from Waterman High School in 1954 and then volunteered for duty in the U.S. Army in 1955, and was assigned to 86th Infantry Regiment for two years. He worked for DeKalb Hybred Seed Co., and later worked for General Motors in Arizona where he was involved with car testing on the proving grounds. Presently, he is the leader of the emmisions testing lab. He married Edith Ann Hunter 29 Jun 1968 at the Christian Church in Jewell, Kan. Edith was born 23 Dec 1937 on the family farm in Jewell Co., Kan. She graduated from Jewell Rural High School in 1955, and received a BS in education in 1959 and a MS in library science in 1964, both from Emporia State University in Kan. She moved to Ariz., and worked in the Scottsdale Public Library. She also gives piano lessons at home. They had Jamie Leigh and Jonna Ann.

Jamie was born 12 Oct 1971 in Scottsdale, Ariz. She graduated from Mountain View High School in 1989 and worked as an accountant before before starting a family. She married 4 May 1991 Darcy Swaim who was born 22 Sep 1967 in Jacksonville, Fla. Darcy holds degrees from the Community College of the Air Force, from Mesa Community College, and Scottsdale CC. He presently is a RN administrator. Their children are Payton Leigh, born 21 Feb 1995; Aubrey Lynn, born 29 Jul 1997; and Riley Darcy, born 25 Aug 2000. They live in Mesa, Ariz.

Jonna was born 14 Nov 1975 and graduated from Mountain View High School in 1994. She went on to Mundus Institute where she graduated in 1995. She was employed as a travel agent for a few years before attending college full time. In 2001, she was attending Arizona State University.

1137231 Nancy Lourie Beveridge

Nancy was born 13 Jul 1947 in Monmouth, Ill. She graduated from Rolla High School in 1965, and began her advanced eduacation by first attending Wellesley College in Mass., where she graduated with a BA in Russian history in 1969. She earned a MA and Ph.D. at the University of Michigan in 1979 where she majored in Russian. After completing her studies, she joined "The Voice of America" where she is a broadcaster. She married 24 Apr 1982 in Rockville, Md., Frank C. Beardsley, and they live in Springfield, Va. Frank is retired from The Voice of America. He attended Southern Methodist University, and was in the U.S. Marine Corps for nine years where he served as a combat correspondent. They had Thomas Franklin who was born 1 Dec 1983 in Washington, D.C.

1137232 Mary Isabelle Beveridge

Mary was born 23 Nov 1953 in Rolla, Mo. Mary graduated from Worcester College in Ohio with a degree in history. She then earned a master's degree in library science at the University of Illinois. She also earned a master's in history at Drake University in Des Moines, Ia. Mary is a librarian at Kansas City, Mo., Public Library. She is not married.

1137411 John Clement Robinson

John was born 13 Nov 1942 in Washington, D.C. He attended Swarthmore College, and graduated from The University of Wisconsin after serving four years in the Army Security Agency as a Chinese translator. He lived in Taiwan and Thailand during the Vietnam War. He presently lives in Madison, Wisc., where he works for a hotel that serves as a cancer hospital. John is not married.

1137412 Margaret Jill Robinson

Margaret was born 3 Oct 1944 in Olney, Md. She graduated from Swarthmore College, then earned a master's degree at the University of Wisconsin. She is currently an English teacher at Mt. Gilead, Ohio. She married Thomas Christmas Grubb on 24 Aug 1968. Thomas has a Ph.D. from UW and is a professor of zoology at Ohio State University in Columbus. Their children are Joshua Thomas, Elizabeth Ruth and Benjamin Robinson. Margaret and her husband live on 56 acres near Columbus. In the summer they enjoy traveling in their truck camper.

Joshua was born 17 Sep 1972 in Hunterdon Co., N.J. He was a National Merit Scholar and valedictorian of his high school. He graduated with a BA from Oberlin College, and earned an MFA at Yale School of Drama. He is currently an actor in New York and works for the Open Society Institute. In 1998 he married Colene Flynn and they took Robinson as their surname.

Elizabeth was born 20 Oct 1974 in Mt. Vernon, Ohio. She was salutatorian at her high school, then received a BA from Oberlin and a master's in education from Ohio State. She is a middle school language arts and social studies teacher in Gahanna, Ohio. She was engaged to be married to Scott Debney.

Benjamin was born 23 Sep 1977. He was a Merit Scholar and valedictorian, and graduated from Oberlin College and is a member of Phi Beta Kappa. He was planning to move to San Francisco where he will resume working for Habitat for Humanity.

1137413 Samantha Jane Robinson

Samantha was born 24 Jun 1947 in Washington, D.C. After graduating from Overseas High School in Italy in 1965, she studied at Marietta College in Ohio and earned a BA degree in English drama. She has worked for 25 years as a show room manager at a Susan Bristol store in Atlanta. She married Robert Lynn Whetsell on 28 Dec 1969 in Marietta, Ohio. Robert was born 22 Apr 1947 in Parkerburg, W.V. He earned a business degree at Marietta College, and works in sales. Their children are Amanda Robin and Cassandra Blythe.

Amanda was born 27 Jul 1972 in Kansas City, Mo. She graduated from Rollins College, then married Ratford Wayne Smith. Their child is Mia Devi who was born 13 Oct 2000.

Cassandra was born 29 May 1974 in Hinsdale, Ill. She is a graduate of Rhodes College of Memphis, Tenn. She married Jonathan Theodore Runnels, and they had Jackson Theodore on 13 Nov 2000.

1137414 Kathleen Jean Robinson

Kathleen (Jingle) was born 21 Dec 1950 in Sydney, New South Wales, Australia. With her father being in the State Dept., her family also lived in Pakistan, Italy, and finally, Iowa. Jingle graduated from Overseas School of Rome (Italy) High School in 1968, then attended Earlham College, a Quaker college, in Richmond, Ind., where she earned a BA in elementary education in 1972. She married Marvin G. Pretorius on 12 Dec 1970, and they had April Elsie and Noel Christian. Secondly, she married George Samuel Robinson on 8 Nov 1986. They reside in Washington, N.C.

April was born 26 May 1974 in Charleston, S.C. She graduated with honors from The University of Georgia with a BA in Latin in 1996. She is a member of Phi Beta Kappa honor society. Currently, she is an insurance underwriter.

Noel was born 18 May 1977 in Springfield, Ohio, and is a graduate of Woolford College with a BS in business and Spanish. He works for Milken Mills in Greenville, S.C.

1137415 Cassandra Robinson

Cassandra was born 5 Jun 1957 in Washington, D.C. She graduated from Overseas School of Rome (Italy) High School in 1975. Raised in a Quaker home, Cassandra then spent two years studying at William Penn College in Oskaloosa, Ia. She was baptized 18 Dec 1977 and chose Marie as her middle name. She married Bryan Mydosh on 6 Aug 1977 at St. Stanislaus R.C. Church in Pine Island, N.Y. Bryan was born 21 Mar 1955 at Fort Bragg, N.C. Bryan graduated valedictorian from William Penn College in 1977, then received a master's degree at Illinois State University in 1978, and completed 40 hours toward a Ph.D., then accepted an engineering position in Oskaloosa. Their children are Heather Dawn, born 23 May 1985, Joseph McCoy, born 1 feb 1988, Alyssa Roseann, born 12 apr 1991 and Anna Marie, born 11 Sep 1995. All were born in Hillsdale, Mich. The family was residing in Munith, Mich., in 2001.

1137421 Christopher Lyne Robinson

Christopher was born 17 May 1949 in Evanston, Ill. Known as "Kit", he graduated from Yale about 1972 with a BA degree. He is a published poet, and is involved with a computer software company in public relations. He married Andrea Barker who was born 22 Aug 1944. They had no children, although Kit has a step-child, Ericka. They live in Berkeley, Calif.

1137422 Nicholas Keith Robinson

Nicholas (Nick) was born 24 Dec 1953 in Evanston, Ill. He is a graduate of the University of Calif., Santa Cruz, with a BA in theater. He first married Ileene Corder who was born 2 Jan 1953. They had Columbine Corder who was born 9 Jul 1984 in Albany, Calif. Secondly, Nick married Laura Moriarty who was born 8 Apr 1952. He is a librarian in public health at the University of Calif., and is also a musician in a Balinese orchestra. They live in Albany.

1137431 Jean Kathleen Robinson

Jean was born 7 Sep 1952 in Chicago, Ill. She attended high school at Westtown, Pa., Friends School and graduated in 1970. She then went to Earlham College in Richmond, Ind., and earned a degree in education in 1975. On 30 Aug 1975 she married Wayne Perry in Covington, Ky. Wayne works for Lear Corp. Their child is Nicole Elizabeth who was born 16 Jan 1989.

1137432 Kay Louise Robinson

Kay was born 10 Nov 1958 in Palatine, Ill. She graduated in 1976 from King Alfred School in London. She then spent two years at a community college in Morris, Ill., and two years at Drew University in N.J. where she earned a degree in political science. At Rutgers University she earned a MS in library studies in 1992, and works part time at a private school.

1137611 Barbara Kay Black

Barbara was born 10 Jan 1940 in Peoria, Ill. She graduated from

Washington, Ill., Community High School in 1958. She received a BS degree from Bradley University in 1975, and a MS degree in liberal studies in 1991. She is director of major and planned gifts at Bradley. She was married 3 Jan 1960 at Washington, Ill., to Robert Walker Brown who was born 9 Jul 1940 in Peoria. Robert holds a MBA from Bradley, and is CEO at Bank Plus in Morton, Ill. Their children are Robert Walker Jr., born 6 Sep 1960 in LaFayette, Ind.; Martin Thomas, born 24 Nov 1961 in Peoria, Ill., David Anthony, born 1 Feb 1964 in Peoria; and Katherine Anne, born 29 Oct 1965 in Peoria. They live in Morton, Ill.

Robert Walker Jr. is a 1978 graduate of Morton High School. He then attended Bradley University where he graduated in 1982 with a BS degree. He received a juris doctorate degree from Southern Illinois University in 1985, and is an attorney with Black, Black and Brown in Washington, Ill. He married Sarah Jean Ferko and they had Steffan Walker on 15 Jan 1989 and Mitchell Robert on 21 Nov 1991.

Martin Thomas is a 1979 graduate of Morton High School, and Bradley University with a BS degree in 1983. He is an agent for Farmer's Insurance in Boise, Id. He married Julie Daughhetee who is owner of Pinnacle actuarial firm in Boise, Ida. Their sons are Walker Thomas born 10 Aug 1992 and Andrew David born 17 Feb 1996.

David Anthony graduated from Morton High School in 1982, from Bradley in 1986, Indiana University in 1990 with a MS degree, and attained his JD degree from Indiana University in 1990. He is an attorney with Black, Black and Brown. He married Suzanne Witcher, MSN, OSF St. Francis, Peoria, Ill. They have twin sons born 30 Jul 1990, Anthony David and Hunter Thomas.

Katherine graduated from Morton High School in 1983 and from Bradley University in 1987 with a BS degree. She earned a MBA from Pepperdine University in 1988 and is regional sales manager for Match Logic in Chicago, Ill.

1137612 Kenneth Lowry Black

Kenneth was born 5 Dec 1942 in Peoria, Ill. In 1961 he graduated from Washington Community High School, then went on to Bradley University where he earned a BS degree in 1966. He was awarded a juris doctorate from the University of Louisville in 1974 and is an attorney with Black, Black and Brown in Washington, Ill. He married Paula Prutsman, then Carolyn Coulter on 27 Nov 1998. Their son, Travis Paul, born 2 Jul 1977, earned a BS degree from Tulane University in 1999, and now works for a brokerage firm in New Orleans.

1137613 Bruce Wallace Black

Bruce was born 16 May 1944 in Peoria, Ill.   He graduated from Washington Community High School in 1962 and went on to Bradley University where he earned a BA in 1966.   In 1971 he earned a juris doctorate at the University of Illinois.   He married Janice Landwehr and they had Colin Landwehr who was born 10 Apr 1974. Secondly he married Patricia Bass on 11 Oct 1997.

Colin received a BA in 1996 and a JD in 1998, both from Tulane University. He is an attorney in Washington, D.C.

1137621 Scott Wallace Borden

Scott was born 12 Mar 1948 at Methodist Hospital in Peoria, Ill. He graduated from Wyoming High School in 1966 and from Bradley University in 1970 with a BA in history. He then went to Drake University where he graduated a JD in 1973. He is a practicing attorney in Wyoming, Ill. Scott is not married.

1137622 Stuart Paul Borden

Stuart was born 23 Nov 1951 at Methodist Hospital in Peoria. He graduated from Wyoming High School in 1969, from Bradley University in 1973, and then attended Southern Illinois University where he received a juris doctorate degree in 1977. He is a circuit court judge. He married Pamela A. Butke 17 Sep 1977. Their children are Caroline E., born 12 Mar 1979 in Peoria, and Jonathan S., born 16 Dec 1981, both born in Peoria, Ill.

Caroline graduated from Stark Co. High School in 1997 and was in her fourth yaer at Bradley University in 2001.

Jonathan graduated from high school in 2000 and then entered Bradley University.

1137711 Thomas Wendell Ehrke

Thomas was born 16 Jul 1942 in Marshalltown, Ia. He married 25 Jul 1981 in Pepper Pike, Ohio, Lynn Vinzant who was born 12 Jan 1949. Tom attended Ohio Wesleyan University in Delaware, Ohio, and Case Western Reserve in Cleveland, Ohio. He is an attorney. Lynn attended Virginia Polytechnical Institue in Blacksburg, Va., and the University of Pittsburgh. Lynn is an environmental engineer. Their child is Christopher Thomas, born 10 Dec 1983. The family is living in Aiken, S.C.

1137712 Jean Elizabeth Ehrke

Jean Beth was born 28 Nov 1945 in Marshalltown, Ia. She married

Michael Farrar who was born 3 Feb 1941 in Cleveland, Ohio. They later divorced. Jean attended Iowa State University in Ames, Ia., and is a dietitian. She is living in Houston, Tex. Jean and Michael had three children: (1)Jeanne Elizabeth, born 12 Jun 1970 in Detroit, Mich., married Joseph Kaliszewski and they live in Portland, Ore. Jeanne graduated from Rice University and Joseph from MIT in electrical engineering; (2)Katherine Marie, born 6 Mar 1973 in Detroit, married in Jan 1997 Joseph Ernst. Katherine was educated at the University of Texas, Irving, Tex., and Joe at Texas A&M; (3) Michael William, born in Cleveland, Ohio, 6 Dec 1974, an engineering student at the University of Texas in Austin.

1137721 Eric Paul Taube

Eric was born 15 Jan 1950 in Ames, Ia. He died 8 Mar 1972.

1137722 David John Taube

David was born 26 Nov 1952 in Davenport, Ia. He died 5 Aug 1971. He and his brother, Eric, were buried in Solon, Ohio.

1137723 Kathryn Ann Taube

Kathryn was born 27 Apr 1955 in Davenport, Ia. She married 18 Sep 1976 Kenneth William Lazo in Pepper Pike, Ohio. Kenneth graduated from the University of Houston, and now is the director of personnel at Premix Corporation in East Kingsville, Ohio. They are residents of Geneva, Ohio. Kathryn attended Heidelberg College in Tiffin, Ohio, and the University of Houston, Houston, Tex. Their children are Kenneth William, born 27 Jun 1979; Kathryn Elizabeth, born 14 Nov 1981; and Ann Marie, born 6 May 1985, all born in Houston, Tex.

1137724 Jean Marie Taube

Jean was born 5 Sep 1957 in Milwaukee, Wisc. She attended Kent State University in Kent, Ohio. She married 8 Sep 1979 in Pepper Pike, Ohio, Robert Edward Vargo who was born 20 Apr 1957 in Cleveland, Ohio. They currently live in Solon, Ohio. Jean is employed by the Orange City Schools in Moreland Hills, Ohio. Robert is a manager with Clay Matthews Pontiac in Cleveland. Their children are Lindsay Marie, born 16 Aug 1982; Alison Christine, who was born 4 May 1985; and Nathan Robert, born 21 Mar 1987, all born in Cleveland, Ohio.

1138221 Bruce Wesley Cunningham

Bruce was born 26 Dec 1934, and died 25 Dec 1967 in Edmonton, Alberta.

1138222 Allan Howard Cunningham

Allan was born 3 Dec 1936 in Vegreville, Alberta. He married 25 Jun 1977 Ann Christine Ullman. They had Laura Mary, born 25 Jul 1978, and Ruth Danielle, born 23 Nov 1979. They were living in Sherwood Park, Alberta, in 1998.

1138223 Clifford Edwin Cunningham

Clifford was born 3 Jul 1940 in Vegreville, Alberta. He married Rose Marie Dalgliesh on 1 Aug 1964. Their children are Cameron Lee, born 24 Mar 1969 in Zambia, and Stuart Martin, born 14 Apr 1971. Cameron was married to Ilka and lived in Vancouver, B.C., before his death there on 7 Feb 1996.

1138224 Rex Burton Cunningham

Rex was born 4 Nov 1945 in Vegreville, Alberta. He married 6 Jul 1968 in Camrose, Alberta, Joyce Victoria Olsen. Their children are Scott Wesley, born 19 Feb 1971 in Mannville, Alberta; Murray John, born 5 Nov 1973 in Mannville; Jayne Evelyn, born 1 Nov 1976; and David Rex, born 21 Dec 1980. They currently live in Manville.

Scott married 31 Jan 1998 Heike Britta Mathiesen. Murray married 12 Jul 1997 Nadine Lee Traptow.

1138231 Digby Lloyd Stephens Jr.

Digby was born 11 Dec 1940.

1138232 Hedley Stephens

Hedley was born 23 Oct 1944. Hedley declined to provide family data in preference for privacy.

1138233 Gareth Stephens

Gareth was born 23 Oct 1944.

1138711 David Dean McCleery

David was born 24 Apr 1943 in Rochester, N.Y. He attended Canisius College in Buffalo, N.Y. He is an accountant in Richmond, Va. He married Joan Russell Traver who was born 1 Jul 1943. Joan is a graduate of Buffalo College at Buffalo, N.Y. She holds a master's degree in teaching and has taught in Virginia. They adopted Rebecca Susan who was born 15 Sep 1970 in Bristol, Va.; adopted Michael David, who was born 15 Sep 1971, and they had Heather Leslie, who was born 15 May 1978 in Tenn., and was a senior at

Salem College in 1999.

Rebecca married James Wood. Michael, an expert mechanic, married Jenny, a special-ed teacher.

1138712 Richard Frederick McCleery

Richard was born 26 Nov 1944 in Rochester, N.Y. In 1967, Richard received a BA in political science at the School of International Service of the American University in Wash., D.C. At Duke University he received a masters of divinity at the Divinity School in 1971. In 1974, he earned a master's of theology in pastory psychology at Duke. In 1981, he obtained a MBA in transportation management from the School of Business of Syracuse University. In 1987 he became a licensed customs broker. He is now employed as a global logistics analyst for ITT Industries, and lives in Palm Coast, Fla. Richard married Carole Aldrich who was born 26 Oct 1944. Carole holds a Ph.D. in mathematical economics from Carnegie Mellon University in Pittsburgh. She is teaching economics at Stetson University in DeLand, Fla. They had Mary Elizabeth who was born 11 May 1975 in Durham, N.C.

Mary earned a BS degree at Allegheny College and is working to complete a MS from American University in political science. She married Vi Min Choong who was born 5 Aug 1975. Vi Min holds a MS degree in computer science from the College of William and Mary, and is a computer programmer for the Federal Reserve Bank. They reside in Silver Spring, Md.

1138721 Jerry Lee Snyder

Jerry was born 7 Sep 1942 in Auburn, Ind. He was a volunteer fireman in Cedar Canyon, Ind., and died of a heart attack on 17 Jun 1997. Burial was in Leo, Ind. He married Sharon Rose Timmerman 28 May 1962. They had Brent Allen who was born 9 Jan 1963 and Susan Irene who was born 25 May 1965. See "Late Additions" on page 381.

1138722 Roger Allen Snyder

Roger was born 30 Aug 1944. He died 5 Feb 1945; burial was in Butler, Ind.

1138723 Keith Eugene Snyder

Keith was born 22 Aug 1945 in Auburn, Ind. He was a truck driver when he collapsed in his cab and died of a heart attack on 28 Feb 1996 in Ohio. He was in the U.S. Army and spent four years in Germany. Keith was married on 26 Jul 1976 to Janis (Myers) Treesh who was born 26 Jul 1948. See page 381, "Late Additions."

1138724 Linda Ann Snyder

Linda was born 25 Feb 1950 in Auburn, Ind. On 25 May 1968, in
Butler, Ind., she married Robert Edward Evanoff who was born 2 Apr
1949. Their children are April Renee who was born 1 Jun 1971 and
Troy Edward who was born 11 Jul 1973, both born in Auburn. They
live in Butler, ind., where Bob has his own cleaning business.
Until recently, Linda was employed in accounting. April had Chaz
Lee Davis on 4 Oct 1995 and Dylan Edward Davis on 13 Aug 2000, both
born in Auburn. Their father is Perry Lee Davis.

1138725 Lance Robinson Snyder

Lance was born 21 Dec 1958 in Auburn, Ind. His first marriage was
to Jacqilyn and they had Joshua Clinton on 17 Jul 1980 and Jillean
Janelle on 1 Jun 1982. They adopted Ashley Shanee who was born 30
Dec 1989. His second marriage was to Kimberly Kay Mynhier on 23
Oct 1998. Lance is a machine operator and programmer.

1138726 Michael Warren Snyder

Michael was born 26 Nov 1960 in Hicksville, Ohio. He married Cheryl
on 20 Apr 1992. They had Gaylon Michael Emery on 31 Jul 1991 and
Halie Michelle on 12 Jul 1993, both in Auburn, Ind. Michael works
at Dura Automotive and Cheryl works at the school in Garrett, Ind.

1138821 David William Rockwell

David was born 13 Apr 1943 in Calif. He married Cathy, and they
are living in Sierra Vista, Ariz.

1138822 Robert Henry Rockwell

Robert was born 6 Mar 1951 in Berea, Ohio. He graduated from
Ypsilanti, Mich., High School in 1969, and briefly attended East
Michigan State. He has been involved in selling musical
instruments primarily. He married Sherry Patrice Leonard on 24 Mar
1973 in Fort Walton Beach, Fla. Their children are Robert H. Jr.
born 7 Sep 1983 in Fort Walton Beach, and Andrew James born 23 Apr
1986 in Pensacola, Fla.

1138831 Carol Anne McCleery

Carol was born 2 Jul 1950 in Manistee, Mich. Is a 1968 graduate of
Berea, Ohio, High School. She then attended Albian College where
she earned a BS degree in German in 1972. She taught German in
Ohio schools for twenty years before the program was dropped. She
is not married and is living in Berea, Ohio.

1138832 Nancy Louise McCleery

Nancy was born 17 Oct 1952 in Mt. Clemens, Mich., and graduated from Berea High School. She is a graduate of Ohio University in 1975 with a degree in elementary education. She has been a teacher since her graduation. She married Peter Buehler on 13 Jun 1981 in Berea where they currently live. Peter is co-owner of a computer business. Daughter Megan Anne was born 8 Sep 1985 in Berea.

1138911 Eric Roe Johnson

Eric was born 3 Feb 1952. He is married to Gayle. Their children are Ben, Rachel, and Asher. Their home is in Mt. Juliet, Tenn.

1138912 Mark Hawthorne Johnson

Mark, a twin, was born 9 Feb 1955. His wife is Carol. They have Emily, Trevor, Lee, and David. They live in Bay Village, Ohio.

1138913 Marcia Jean Johnson

Marcia, a twin, was born 20 Jan 1957. She is married to Duane Binkley and are living in Chiang Mai, Thailand. Their children are Sean, Shanon, and Erin.

1138914 David McCleery Johnson

David, a twin to Marcia, died 23 Jan 1957.

1138921 Marion Telford Redding

Marion was born 25 Sep 1953 in Marysville, Ohio. She married Charles Lizanich and they later were divorced. Their children were twins, Katrina Pearl and Alexei Maxwell, who were born 25 Feb 1984 in Rutland, Vt.

1138922 John Maxwell Redding

John was born 3 May 1955 in Marysville, Ohio. He was married first to Jean Parsons. He married Shari Dean 7 Jun 2001.

1138923 David Mitchell Redding

David was born 4 Oct 1957 in Springdale, Ohio. He married Bobbie LeMaster. Their children are Alicia Mae, born 14 Apr 1987, Ian Maxwell, born in 1995 and Cameron Andrew, born in 1997.

1138924 Mark McCleery Redding

Mark was born 8 Nov 1960 in Springdale, Ohio. He married Sarah

Alward.   Their children are Hannah McLeod who was born in Nov 1992,
Kate McCleery who was born in May 1994, and David Wallace who was
born 28 Feb 1999.

1138(10)11 Joyce Charlotte Ferguson

Joyce was born 27 Apr 1952 in Calgary, Alberta.   She married George
M. Fingland 13 May 1972.   Both are graduates in textile technology.
Joyce was dye technician and is now a school librarian.   George is
a technical representative for knitting yarns.   They have three
sons: Edward George, born 16 Jun 1977; Ian Thomas, born 5 May 1979;
and Jonathan Hugh, born 4 Sep 1980.

1138(10)12 Brian Arthur Ferguson

Brian was born 23 Jul 1954 in Calgary, Alberta, and is an
electrical engineering graduate. He is a supervisor of
communication system designers.   He married Ximena Elizabeth
Antezena who worked for the Bolivia Military Attache in Washington,
D.C.   They have a daughter, Sabrina, born 13 Jul 1988.

1138(10)13 Douglas Keith Ferguson

Douglas was born 17 Jan 1962 in Winnipeg, Manitoba, and is now a
computer programmer.

1138(10)14 Neil Edwin Ferguson

Neil was born 11 Aug 1965 in Hamilton, Ontario, and is a civil
engineer.   He is a technical representative regarding computer
aided design of roof trusses.   His company produces steel connector
plates for wooden trusses.

1138(10)21 Linda Mary Noster

Linda was born 16 Aug 1949 in Vermilion, Alberta.   She married
Michael Joseph Frederick Jacejko who was born 6 Feb 1945.   Their
children were Christa Marie, born 14 Mar 1972, married 16 Jul 1994
David Gary Caruthers, born 21 Oct 1969; Aaron Michael, born 23 Nov
1973;   Monica Helen, born 19 Mar 1976; Rebecca Magdelena, born 26
Oct 1977; and Mary Bernadette, born 1 Jun 1982.

1138(10)22 Kenneth John Noster

Kenneth was born 29 Jan 1952 in Vermilion, Alberta.   In Vermilion,
he married Marlane Marie Madge Herklotz who was born 16 Mar 1954.
Their children were Toby Lourna, born 3 Jun 1981; Simon Peter, born
14 Feb 1985; Kyra Marlene, born 15 Nov 1987; Naomi Arielle, born 11

Aug 1989; Ezra Joseph, born 8 Mar 1992; and Saul Fergus, born 29 Jun 1994. This family resides in Derwent, Alberta.

1138(10)23 Eileen Bernadette Noster

Eileen was born 19 Mar 1954 in Vermilion, Alberta. She married 28 Dec 1974 Russell Mike Yarmuch who was born 23 Mar 1954. They had John Joseph, born 30 Nov 1974; Alena Katheleen, born 3 Apr 1977 in Vermilion, Alberta; and Matthew Allen Russell, born 17 Dec 1980. Katheleen married 22 Aug 1998 Larry Walter Thompson in Bonnyville, Alberta. The Yarmuchs live in Bonnyville.

1138(10)24 Christopher Peter Joseph Noster

Christopher was born 12 Jul 1956 in Vermilion, Alberta. He married Linda Joy Marie Stamp who was born 20 Oct 1957. They had four children: Jennifer Irene Magdalena, born 29 Nov 1981; Heather Marie Grace, born 2 Mar 1983; Tiffany Nicole Beth, born 1 May 1987; and Graham Christofer John, born 19 Feb 1991.

1138(10)31 Jennifer Jean Davidson

Jennifer was born 20 Jun 1959. She is a RN. She married 25 Jul 1981 Ralph Boone who was born 24 Dec 1956. They have Jennette Joanna, born 20 Sep 1984, and Clifford Lee, born 4 Mar 1991.

1138(10)32 Frances Elizabeth Davidson

Frances was born 26 Jul 1960 and married 30 Jul 1983 Craig LuVerne Holte who was born 3 May 1958. He is a farmer. They have Heather Danielle, born 4 Nov 1988; Michelle Lynn, born 12 May 1990; Cassandra Fay, born 11 Feb 1992; and Jeffrey Adam, born 9 Mar 1994.

1138(10)33 Margaret Rose Davidson

Margaret was born 9 Feb 1962. She works as an "information analysis coordinator."

1138(10)34 Ralph William Davidson

Ralph was born 27 Jun 1963; he is a farmer.

1138(10)35 Helen Daisy Davidson

Helen was born 17 Jan 1965. On 28 Jun 1988 in Alliance, Alberta she married Steven Madge, born 7 Oct 1960. They operate a farm. They have two children, Brianna Rae, born 8 Apr 1994, and Tyler Jeffery, born 11 Mar 1997.

1138(10)41 Leslie Dale Ferguson

Leslie was born 11 Jun 1954 in Edmonton, Alberta. He married 2 Oct 1982, in Vegreville, Alberta, Darlene Ann Hewko. Their children are Ashley Dawn, born 9 Jan 1988, and Carlie Rae, born 22 Jul 1991.

1138(10)42 Varlerie Margaret Ferguson

Varlerie was born 26 Apr 1956 in Edmonton, Alberta. She married 28 Jan 1984 John Stewart Gray in Wellington, New Zealand. Their children are Nicholas James Theodore, born 13 Sep 1987; Andrew John, born 28 Aug 1991; and twins Catriona Mary Stewart and Moira Joslin Mackay, born 14 Jan 1994.

1142111 Agnes Keith McNeil

Agnes was born 13 Jun 1935 in Renfrewshire, Scotland. She began her primary education at the Blythswood School, then at the age of twelve entered Renfrew High School, followed by the John Halston Institution in Paisley. At the age of sixteen she began work in Scottish Cables Ltd. and attended night school at the West of Scotland Commercial College, Glasgow where she studied shorthand and typing. She met William (Bill) Whyte McArthur in Scottish Gables and they were married 12 Sep 1957. Bill was born 21 May 1932 in Paisley. They have two children, Elaine Anne and Alan. Their home in 1999 was in Renfrew, Scotland.

Elaine was born 18 Jul 1959 in Westlands Nursing Home, Paisley, Scotland. On 5 May 1983 she married Colin Houston Whiteford who was born 6 Jan 1959. They had Craig Alexander born 12 Nov 1983 in Paisley and Andrew born 10 Mar 1986 in Paisley. In 1999 they were living in Paisley.

Alan was born 13 Jul 1961 in Renfrew, Scotland. On 31 May 1985 he married Ann Hackett in Holy Cross Church, Croy, Dunbartonshire. Ann was born 28 Jun 1961. They have Ross born 12 Jan 1987 in Glasgow, Scott born 28 Nov 1988 in Glasgow, and Christopher born 7 Sep 1990 in Glasgow. In 1999 he was living in Ballock Estate, Cumbernauld, Dunbartonshire.

1142112 Georgina Stewart McNeil

Gina was born in 1937 in Renfrew, Scotland. On 21 Jun 1974 she married Gordon Hamilton in Renfrew. Gordon was born 28 Jun 1937 in Glasgow, and died in Jan 2001. She was chief cataloguer in Jordonhill College Library until she retired in 1995.

1151111 Serena Beth Strieby
Serena was born 10 Aug 1950. A terrible tragedy struck when Serena

went white-water rafting on 13 May 1978. With the river unusually rough, Serena was tossed overboard and drowned.

1151121 Dana Frances Strieby

Dana, who was adopted, was born in 1944. She married Robert B. Moore and they had a son, James LeRoy, born in 1974. Later, Dana and Robert divorced.

1151211 Lowell Estel Thomson

Lowell was born 2 Mar 1931 on his grandfather Knight's farm near Viola, Ia., and spent his first year in Armstrong, Ia. He attended grade school in several towns where his father was teaching, junior high school in Burlington, Ia., and graduated from Kanawha High School in 1948. While in high school, Lowell played basketball and baseball on teams coached by his father. Lowell played short stop on the team that made it to the state tournament his senior year.

Lowell played baseball at Iowa State Teacher's College (now UNI) where he graduated in 1952. His first teaching position was with the high school at Ledyard, Ia. He also taught physical education at Plymouth, Ia., before relocating to Mason City. In Mason City he was also baseball coach. Lowell obtained a master's degree in secondary education in 1961 while attending summer school at Greeley, Colo., and a master's in physical education in 1967.

Lowell and Maryen Johnson were married 22 Dec 1951 in Waterloo, Ia. Maryen was born 18 Dec 1932 in Kanawha, Ia., and died of leukemia 9 Apr 1974 in Mason City, and was buried there in Memorial Park Cem. They had four children: Leslie Jean, Robert Lowell, LuAnn Sue, and William Paul.

Lowell was named Iowa Baseball Coach of the Year in 1980. On 6 Feb 1999 Lowell was admitted into the Iowa Baseball Hall of Fame for his outstanding career as a player and as a baseball coach. His teams won 354 games and lost 201 during his coaching career of twenty years. Lowell enjoys playing golf, fishing in Canada, and attending athletic events. Lowell married Meryleen in Sep 2000. During the winter months they reside near Brownsville, Tex.

Leslie was born 26 Sep 1952 in Buffalo Center, Ia. She graduated from Mason City High School in 1971, then attended Iowa State University where she graduated in 1975 with a BA degree in interior design. While in college she met and later married Gordon Lee Meyer 13 Sep 1975. Their children are Kristopher Lee, born 9 Dec 1980, and Sarah Elizabeth, born 7 Apr 1984, both in Knoxville, Tenn. Chris became an Eagle Scout and graduated from high school in 1999. In 1994 Leslie earned the title of registered interior designer. Leslie and Gordon divorced, and then Leslie married William Hoover 22 Apr 1995. Leslie and Bill live in Louden, Tenn., and have a son, James Ellis Boyd, born 21 Jul 1996 in Knoxville.

Robert was born 30 Jun 1954 in Buffalo Center, Ia. In 1973 he graduated from high school in Mason City, and in 1977 he graduated from Iowa State University with a degree in chemistry and biology. He married Sandra Martinson 28 Feb 1976 in Mason City. Sandy was born 11 Jan 1955 in Des Moines. They had Bryce Lowell, born 11 Mar 1979 in Nevada, Ia., and Ryan Isiah, born 16 Dec 1980 in Houston, Tex. They make their home in Houston, Tex., where Bob is a kitchen designer.

LuAnn was born 25 Aug 1955 in Mason City and graduated from high school in 1974. She attended the University of Iowa for three years. She married 19 May 1984 Mark Worden in Iowa City. They have no children. Lately, LuAnn works at the University of Iowa Hospital.

William (Bill) was born 1 Apr 1958 in Mason City, Ia. In 1976 he graduated from Mason City High School where he played baseball on his father's team. Bill is now a truck driver and is unmarried. He lives in Mason City.

1151212 David Lee Thomson

Dave was born 28 Jan 1934 in Springville, Ia. He attended grade school in Oakville and Burlington, and high school in Kanawha where he graduated in 1951. During high school he played basketball and baseball. In his youth in Kanawha, Dave worked at the local movie theater, and later was a carpenter in the summer months. He then spent about three years at Iowa State College in Ames studying engineering and industrial economics. On 25 Oct 1953 in Rockwell City, Ia., he married Rita R. Morris, born 1 Aug 1937 in Kanawha, Ia., the daughter of Hershel Morris and Alma Josephine Holm. Dave and Rita lived in Mason City, West Des Moines, and Omaha before settling in Overland Park, Kan. Dave had a long career as agent for State Farm Insurance Co., and retired in Dec 1999. They are the parents of Steven James, Kimberly Jean, and Scott David. Dave and Rita have traveled extensively world-wide and they enjoy playing bridge, golf, and attending baseball and football games in Kansas City. Rita is active in church work.

Steven was born 23 Mar 1954 in Belmond, Ia. While growing up, he was active in the Boy Scouts of America and earned the Eagle Scout award in 1969. In 1972 he graduated from Shawnee Mission West High School in Overland Park, Kan. He then attended the University of Kansas and graduated with honors in 1976 with a BA degree in microbiology. From there he attended Creighton University, School of Dental Science, in Omaha, where he earned his Doctor of Dental Surgery (DDS) degree in 1981. Following graduation he accepted a commission as an officer in the U.S. Air Force and was stationed in Okinawa, Japan, as a general dental officer.

In 1984, he returned to the states and was assigned to Offutt Air Force Base in Omaha, Neb., where he was Chief, Family Dentistry and Special Projects Assistant to the Straegic Air Command Dental Surgeon. He then attended a 2-year post-graduate residency in General Dentistry at Keesler AFB, Biloxi, Miss. Following residency graduation, he was assigned to McConnell AFB, near Wichita, Kan., as Chief, Dental Professional Services and Clinical Dentistry Flight Commander. In 1996, he was assigned to Izmir Air Station, Turkey, as Director, Base Dental Services. In 1998, he was selected to be a squadron commander and was reassigned to Aviano Air Base, Italy, as Commander, 31st Dental Squadron. During his assignment to Aviano, he was responsible for providing comprehensive dental support to all combat forces assigned to Operation ALLIED FORCE, who successfully repelled the Serbian aggression in Kosovo. Steve was promoted to the rank of Colonel in July 1999. Steve died of cancer 3 Apr 2001 and received a military funeral in San Antonio with burial in Fort Sam Houston National Cem. Steve married Jamee Sue Newby of Charleston, Ill., on 6 Jun 1981. They adopted Travis James who was born 19 Jun 1990, and Trevor Alan, born 17 Feb 1992.

Kimberly was born 15 Mar 1958 in Belmond, Ia. Kim graduated from high school in 1976 and went on to Kansas State University where she graduated with a BA in 1980. On 14 Apr 1984 she and Everett Roy (J.R.) Bretches were married at Hillcrest Covenant Church in Prairie Village, Kan. J.R. was born 14 Mar 1951 in Kansas City, Mo., and he has a son from his first marriage, Evan Ross, born 7 Jul 1979. J.R. and Kim had Chase Austin, born 27 Jun 1991, and Taylor David, born 9 May 1993.

Scott was born 8 Apr 1961. He attended Shawnee Mission West High School and graduated in 1979. On 27 Jul 1983 he married Kathleen Marie Donovan who was born 19 Jul 1961 in Kansas City, Mo. Their children are Monica Marie, born 8 Jan 1988, Bailey Elizabeth, born 24 Jan 1999 and Erika Lee, born 4 Apr 2000. The family was living in Overland Park, Kan., in 2001.

1151213 Donald Claire Thomson

Don was born 30 Dec 1936 in Morning Sun, Ia., where his father taught school for a year. He started first grade in Oakville, attended second grade in Burlington, then finished his elementary education in Kanawha, Ia. Don was active in the Boy Scouts of America organization and earned the Eagle Scout award in Oct 1953.

At Iowa State Univ., he graduated with a BS degree in mechanical engineering in Feb 1960. He accepted a position with a naval research facility in Annapolis, Md., where he worked until his retirement in Jan 1992. Most of his career was involved with the reduction of sound levels of naval craft, especially patrol boats. Genealogy later became his hobby as evidenced by this publication. He recently spent several hundred hours of his retirement in a volunteer effort preparing indexes of the 1870 and 1880 census returns of Anne Arundel County, Md., which results are available to the public on-line. Don enjoys taking his yellow lab for long walks in view of the Chesapeake Bay.

Don married Kathryn (Kay) Anne Small 27 Jan 1962 in Calvary United Methodist Church, formerly located on State Circle in Annapolis. Kay was born 26 Sep 1942 in Annapolis, Md., the daughter of Kathryn Sarah Powers and James Francis Small, Sr. Kay graduated from Annapolis High School in 1960 after attending lower grades in Glen Burnie schools. Don and Kay lived in Annapolis until 1977, then moved to Kent Island where their home is located about eight miles south of the village of Stevensville. Kay has worked as a self-employed decorator, then as a retail sales clerk. They had four children: Mark Alan, born 18 Apr 1963; Barry Estel, born 2 Feb 1965; Laura May, born 1 Apr 1966; and Daniel Eric, born 26 Jul 1967, all in Anne Arundel General Hospital in Annapolis. They were baptized at Trinity United Methodist Church.

Mark attended elementary schools in Annapolis and graduated from Queen Anne's County High School in Centreville in 1981. He then attended the University of Maryland where he graduated with a BS degree in electrical engineering. He subsequently accepted a position with BGE at the Calvert Cliffs Nuclear Power Plant. Mark was in the Maryland Army National Guard and went through basic training. He married 16 Jan 1988 Kathrine Elizabeth Horn in Trinity United Methodist Church in Annapolis. Kathrine was born 11 Oct 1965 in Wilmington, Del., the daughter of Calvin Horn III and Margaret (Peg) Evers. They had Jessica Lynn, who was born 4 Apr 1994, and Matthew Alan, who was born 29 Jul 1998, both in Annapolis. The Mark Thomson family is living in Dunkirk, Md.

Barry graduated from Queen Anne's County High School in 1983. He is an accomplished tradesman and achieves a high degree of excellence in whatever task he undertakes. More recently, Barry has entered the field of financial management. He has a daughter, Stephanie Nicole Thomson, born 9 Apr 1990 in South Baltimore Hospital. Stephanie lives with her mother and step-father, Julie and Bryant Myers, in Glen Burnie, Md.

Laura is a 1984 graduate of Queen Anne's County High School. She attended Anne Arundel Community College for two years and earned an

associate's degree in accounting, and worked in that field for
several years. Later, she graduated from nursing school in New
York state and is an RN in a New York state hospital.   Laura
married   Thomas Anthony Ranalli 3 Jun 1989 at the new Calvary
United Methodist Church in Annapolis. Thomas was born 13 Jul 1962
in Rhineland Pfalz, West Germany. He is a 1980-graduate of Orchard
Park High School near Buffalo, and attended the State University of
N.Y. at Buffalo. They make their home in Batavia, N.Y., and have
a daughter, Cara Mia, born 23 Jun 1997 in Amherst, N.Y.

Dan graduated from high school in 1985, then attended Anne Arundel
Community College. Until recently, he was employed as a machinist
and programmer for computer-assisted machining operations. Dan
has resumed his advanced education at Chesapeake Community College
in pursuit of a degree in computer networking. Dan enjoys scuba
diving, weight lifting, and skiing. He and Daphne Elise Ewing were
planning to be married in Sep 2001.

1151214 Lyle Ivan Thomson

Lyle was born 23 Dec 1938 in Oakville, Ia. He graduated from
Kanawha High School in 1957. In high school Lyle was a star on the
baseball and basketball teams. He threw right handed as a pitcher
but batted left handed just like his brother Lowell. Lyle was a
great hitter, and holds a record for hitting the ball to the top of
the high school building. This helped earn him a position on the
baseball team at UNI in Cedar Falls. Lyle graduated from State
College of Iowa (now UNI) with a BA degree in 1962, then enlisted
in the U.S. Army which took him to Germany for most of his
enlistment period. Returning home in 1965, Lyle accepted a
teaching position at Lake Mills High School where he primarily has
taught industrial technology. He also served as baseball coach
from 1988 to 1992, and as boys golf coach from 1983 to the present.
Lyle was on-call as an ambulance attendant for several years. Lyle
earned a master's degree from the University of Wisconsin in 1972.
Lyle retired in 2000, although he occasionally fills in as a
substitute teacher. Otherwise, he spends time with hobbies, which
include gardening and playing golf.

In Lake Mills, Lyle married 26 Jun 1966 Orloue Mae Halvorson who
was born 5 Jan 1941 in Mason City, the daughter of Henry Halvorson
and Elvina Groe. Orloue graduated from Lake Mills High School,
then received a BA degree from UNI in 1963. She taught math in
area schools and later served as a substitute teacher. She is
active in her church and in community affairs. Their two sons are
Paul Curtis, born 11 Jul 1969, and Neal Aaron, born 24 Sep 1972,
both in Albert Lea, Minn.

Paul graduated from Lake Mills High School in 1987 where he

continued the Thomson tradition of playing baseball. He attended
Iowa State University and earned a BS degree in 1992 and a MS
degree in 1995, both in meteorology. Paul is employed in Overland
Park, Kan., with Black and Veatch, Inc. Paul holds a pilot license
and has flown since 1984. Paul married Shawn Stelter 29 Feb 2000.

Neal graduated from high school in 1991 and played on the baseball
team, as well as other sports. He graduated from ISU with a BS
degree in 1996 and with a MS degree in mechanical engineering in
1998. Neal is employed by the Delavan Company in Des Moines, Ia.

1151221 Roland Dean Thomson

Rollie was born 28 Jul 1927 in Stanwood, Ia.   He attended
elementary schools in Clarence, Tipton, and in Stanwood where he
graduated from high school in 1945. He then attended Cornell, Iowa
State Teachers College and Coe College where he received a B.S.
degree in psychology and physical sciences in 1958. Next, he earned
a master's degree in educational school administration at the
University of Iowa in 1963. Rollie worked toward a doctor's degree
but never completed the task. He taught at elementary, junior and
senior high school levels at several towns in Iowa over a period of
37 years.

On 22 May 1955 in Tipton, Ia., he married Shirley Ann Kimberling
who was born in 1936. They had Wendy Sue who was born 31 Mar 1956
and died 25 Nov 1960, and Diane Kay, who was born 7 Nov 1958.

Diane first married Rick Jay Stull. Secondly, Diane married Robert
Joseph Rummelhart and they had a son, Benjamin Robert, born 9 Jun
1990. Diane is a registered nurse and works at Iowa Methodist
Hospital in Des Moines. Diane is currently married to Greg Landry
who is an attorney.

1151222 Leland Arnold Thomson

Lee writes that he was born 16 Aug 1929 on a farm three miles
southwest of Stanwood, Ia. Lee graduated from high school in
Stanwood in 1947, then he enrolled at Iowa State Teachers College
in Cedar Falls. Before completing his undergraduate studies, he
was hired to teach in the Brooklyn Junior High School and to coach
junior high athletic sports. His teaching career was interrupted
by the Korean War when Lee was drafted into the U.S. Army on 21 Jan
1952. He served with the Counter Intelligence Corps and was
released from duty two years later. Lee resumed teaching at Royal,
Ia., then finshed his studies at ISTC where he earned his
bachelor's and master's degrees. Lee's next teaching assignment
was with the Montezuma Community Schools where he was a coach,
principal and superintendent from 1956 to 1966. He then accepted

a position at the University of Denver, in the Bureau of Educational Research. During his time there, he was able to complete his requirements for the Doctor of Education degree in Aug 1968.

Next, Lee became Director of Planning of Northern Iowa in Cedar Falls, a position he held for the next 23 years. Lee took early retirement on 28 Jun 1992. Now he lives on a small farm near LaPorte City, Ia., and also manages a grain farm near Spencer. Lee is active in the Lion's Club, El Kahir Shrine, UNI Alumni Board and Firstar Bank Board. Lee has faithfully attended the annual Thomson family reunions in Stanwood.

On 9 Jun 1957, in Des Moines, Lee married Virginia Ann Jordan who was born 1 Feb 1936 and died 7 May 1977 in Rochester, Minn., as the result of an aneurism. Their daughter is Margaret Ann who was born 21 Aug 1960. Margaret graduated with a BA from Iowa State University in 1982, and from Drake University with a JP degree in 1985. Margaret is a lawyer and works for the Iowa Legislature in Des Moines.

1151223 Shirley Lee Thomson

Shirley was born 7 Mar 1931. She graduated from Stanwood High School in 1949. Her first marriage on 14 May 1950 was to Cecil Eugene Slach who was born in 1928. Their children were Cecil Richard, born 28 Oct 1951; Patti Dee, born 26 Jan 1955; and Lori Lee, born 10 Mar 1958. Secondly, Shirley married Stanley Gourd and they later were divorced. Thirdly, in 1972, Shirley married Robert Frederick Walter Ehlers who was born in 1927.

Cecil married 3 Jul 1976 Mary Ann Wright who was born in 1954. They had Courtney Marie, born in 1984. Patti Dee on 14 Sep 1974 married Thomas Michael Pelzer; no issue. Secondly, Patti Dee married James Joseph Fonteyne on 17 Sep 1977. They had Matthew James, born in 1978, and Lindsey Leigh, born in 1983. Lori Lee married John James Foley who was born in 1958. They had Kelly Jo, born in 1981, and Katie Lee, born in 1983.

1151224 Gary Alan Thomson

Gary was born 24 Apr 1940. He was a 1958 graduate of Tipton High School. Gary received a BA from Coe College and a MS from Penn State. He has taught school and farmed. He has been a supervisor with Fontanelle Seed Co., and executive secretary of the Missouri Sheep Association. He married on 1 Nov 1959 Joanne Lucille Seitz who was born 24 Apr 1940. They had Tamara May who was born in 1960, Kandace Rae who was born 20 Nov 1962, and Terre Jo born 13 Nov 1965.

Tamara married William Terry Campbell who was born in 1958. They had Justin William, born in 1985, and Kylee Jo, born in 1990. Kandace married Alan Douglas Schminke who was born in 1962. They had Cody Alan born in 1988, and Chelsea Rae, born in 1991. Terre Jo married Jeffrey James McVay who was born in 1965. They had Tyler James, born in 1986.

1151251 Mary Ann Thomson

Mary was born 22 Oct 1942 in Cedar Rapids, Ia. On 28 May 1963 she married Gary Douglas McMurry at The Little Brown Church in Nashua, Ia. The family operates a custom plastic injection molding plant in Cocoa, Fla. They had five children: Adam Todd, born 4 Oct 1964; Eric Ryan, born 31 Dec 1966; Dawn Marie, born 4 Jun 1969; Lance Blake, born 21 Jul 1971; and Dana Ann, born 18 Apr 1974. Home is Melbourne, Fla.

On 14 Feb 1987 in Indiana, Adam married Laura LeAnn Waninger who was born 22 Dec 1965. They live in St. Charles, Mo.

Eric works with the family in the plastics plant in Cocoa, Fla.

Dawn married Robert Thomas Meeks III, a captain in the USAF, on 15 Oct 1996 in Orlando. As of 2000 they were stationed in Alabama where Trey is a helicopter flight instructor. They had Robert Thomas Meeks IV who was born 28 Jan 1999 in Santa Maria, Calif.

Lance recently moved to San Francisco where he works for Charles Schwab. He married Young Mi Yun on 15 May 1999 in Orlando, Fla.

Dana lives in Cincinnatti and is employed as a flight attendant with Comair. She married Christopher Dale in Nov 2000.

1151252 Ruth Ellen Thomson

Ruth was born 25 Jan 1947 in Cedar Rapids. Ruth received a BA and MA in history from the University of Iowa in 1969 and 1970, respectively. On 1 Jul 1972 in Iowa City, she married Scott Roy Nelson who was born 5 Oct 1947. Their daughter, Amy Caroline, was born 23 Aug 1978 in Royal Oak, Mich. Ruth was named assistant vice president for The Chubb Group, an insurance company, in Chicago. Scott is an insurance salesman for The Hartford. Amy graduated from St. Olaf College in 2000 and in 2001 was spending a year of service with the Lutheran Volunteer Corps in Baltimore, Md.

1151253 Max William Thomson

Max was born 20 Nov 1950 in Cedar Rapids. On 25 Aug 1973 he married Candana Jean Marsh who was born in 1951. Max was a newspaper publisher in Mexico, Mo., before assuming that role in New Castle, Pa. They have two daughters, Brooke Laura, born 30 May 1979, and Joanna Elaine, born 10 Jun 1982. Candi teaches English at Hampton Township High School in a suburb of northern Pittsburgh. Brooke is a chemical engineering student at Penn State. Brooke has worked in an engineering cooperative studies program for Union Carbide's Technical Research Center in Charleston, W.Va. Joanne graduated from Neshannock High School and competed for nine years as a gymnast until she was injured. Later, she attended Penn State where she majored in biology.

1151261 Edwin Earl Negus

Ed was born 15 Jun 1931 and died in Davenport, Ia., on 15 May 1991 of cancer. He was buried in The Arsenal, a military cemetery located near Moline, Ill. On 14 Mar 1953, Ed married Delores Ament who was born 21 Jan 1937 in Wapello, Ia. They had Kathleen Marie, born 17 Jul 1953 in Pensacola, Fla.; Kenneth Earl, born 2 Feb 1955 in Muscatine, Ia.; Connie Sue, born 20 Sep 1957 in Muscatine; Christine Ann, born 18 Jan 1961 in Davenport, Ia.; and Karen Lynn, born 3 Nov 1963 in Davenport. Ed adopted Kevin Jay, son of Dolores, born 29 Nov 1968. Secondly, Ed married Lois Jackson. Ed and Lois had Terri Lynn who was born 18 Feb 1968 in Davenport.

Kathleen (Kathy) was married to Larry Ashby. They had Shawn Earl who was born 8 Dec 1970 in Davenport, and Heather Marie who was born 5 Jul 1974 in Davenport. Shawn has a child, Lucas M. Ashby, who was born 22 Dec 1995 in Burlington, Ia. Heather married Steve Gaarder on 14 Nov 1996 in Las Vegas. Steve was born 8 Dec 1973 in Iowa City. Their children are Shelby Marie who was born 12 Mar 1992, Brook Ashley who was born 6 Sep 1996, and Haley Aliane who was born 2 Mar 1998, all in Davenport. Secondly, Kathy married Dennis Jorgenson on 16 May 1974 in Davenport, Ia.. Dennis was born 4 Aug 1953 in Davenport. They had Nathan Tyson who was born 30 Mar 1970 in Davenport and Aaron Michael who was born 21 Apr 1983 in Davenport. Thirdly, Kathy married Ralph Miller and they had Sara Amanda who was born 25 Apr 1991 in Davenport.

Kenneth married Tanya Kay Goold on 16 Feb 1989 in Rock Island, Ill. Tanya was born 30 Apr 1956 in Rock Island, Ill. They had Jason Earl, who was born 10 Jun 1981 in Davenport, and Rebecca Renea, who was born 1 Jul 1983 in Davenport. Ken's step-children are Jeremy Michael Goold who was born 30 Jan 1974 in Rock Island; Fred Gustav Goold who was born 18 Jun 1981 in Rock Island; and Annie Goold who was born 19 Aug 1982 in Rock Island.

Connie had Jerome David Eickstaedt, born 11 Nov 1985 in Davenport, and Jamie Rae Eickstaedt, born 20 Jun 1988 in Davenport. On 16 Apr 1994 Connie married Randy Provick in Rock Island, Ill.

On 17 Jun 1979 in Des Moines, Christine married Raul Arnold DeAnda who was born 21 Aug 1951 in Davenport.   Christine had Angela Christine Sanchez who was born 26 Dec 1978, and Candice Petra Sanchez who was born 27 Sep 1981, both born in Davenport.

Karen married Scott Donald Briegel on 1 Apr 1994.   Scott was born 7 May 1969. They had Rachel Elizabeth who was born 20 May 1985 in Kinston, S.C.

1151281 Keith Dale Blayney

Keith was born 8 Feb 1937 in Anamosa, Ia. After graduation from Monticello High School in 1955, where he lettered in football all four years, he attended the University of Iowa.   He earned a bachelor's degree in 1959 and a master's degree in 1961, then spent three years in the U.S. Air Force.   In 1964 he returned to UI and within two years he received a doctor's degree in hospital and health administration.   He arrived in Birmingham, Ala., in 1966 where he became director of the University Hospital and Clinics in the University of Alabama, in Birmingham.   In 1971 he was founding dean of the School of Health Related Professions.   Keith gained a national and international reputation where he is respected as the authority when it comes to addressing health care issues.   In 1991 Keith accepted the position of Chancellor of the Osteopathic Medical University in Des Moines, Ia.   He now resides in Birmingham.

On 14 Sep 1958, Keith married Joyce Ann Bryan who was born in 1937. They had two sons, Michael Bryan, born 9 Jan 1961, and Steven Price, born 27 Feb 1963. Keith is now divorced.

Michael received his Ph.D. at the University of Maryland and is employed as head of Environment Health at Dartmouth.   He married Lillian Burke, an M.D. They had two children, Edward Michael, born in 1985, and Elizabeth Marie, born in 1988. Michael and Lillian later were divorced. Michael remarried in Mar 1999.

Steven graduated from the University of Washington where he received a master's degree in Asian Studies. He also studied in the Stanford program in Taipei.   He finished law school at Washington University in St. Louis.   In 1998 he was living in Hong Kong where he is a lawyer with a large international law firm.

1151282 Karen Kay Blayney

Karen was born 27 Nov 1945 in Monticello, Iowa.   After she graduated in 1964 from Tipton High School, she attended St. Luke's School of Nursing in Cedar Rapids for two years, then quit when she got married. In 1978 she became a RN at Clinton Community College.

On 31 Dec 1966 she married Larry Lee Lang who was born in 1945. Their children are Vanessa Sue, born 14 Aug 1967, and Bethany Ann, born 25 May 1970.

Vanessa earned an associate degree in computer sciences from Kirkwood Community College in 1998. Vanessa married, and later divorced, Scott Russell Miller who was born in 1966. They had a son, Jesse James Miller, who was born in 1990. Vanessa secondly married Jeff Tumulty in Nov 1995 and they had Wyatt Jeffery Tumulty who was born in Oct 1996.

Bethany has a son, Daniel Lee Lang, born in 1988. She married Tad Seiler and they had Dallas who was born 1 Jun 1997.

1151283 Kathy Sue Blayney

Kathy was born 29 Jul 1950 in Monticello, Iowa. She is a 1968 graduate of Tipton High School. In Tipton, she was married on 23 Aug 1968 to Richard William Lahmon who was born 15 Jun 1949 in Cedar Rapids. Their children are Jennifer Mae, born 12 Mar 1972, Melony Marie, born 20 Aug 1974, and William Richard, born 15 Sep 1978 in Iowa City.

Jennifer married Chad Strathman on 6 Aug 1997. Chad was born 18 Nov 1970. Chad graduated from law school in 1996 at the University of Iowa. He is now in practice in Minneapolis. They had Annabelle Rose on 23 Dec 1999 in Minneapolis, Minn.

Melony married Shawn Mittelstadt who was born 6 Sep 1973. Their children are Brooke Levi, born 22 Feb 1995 and Breyden, born 10 Jul 1998. Shawn earned a degree in business at the University of Iowa in 1997.

1151291 Bruce Emerson Smith

Bruce was born 8 Apr 1947. He graduated from Hoover High School in Jun 1965, then he joined the U.S. Air Force where he served for four years. He spent one year in South Vietnam. Upon discharge, he attended A. E. School in Phoenix, Ariz. Bruce then worked for Pacific Southwest Airlines in San Diego, where, on 11 Jan 1969, he married Jaline Kay McGill who was born in 1950. Bruce is now working in Charlotte, N.C. Their children are Brian Emerson, born 6 Oct 1975 in Westlake, Calif., and Daniel James, born 28 Sep 1977 in Westlake. Bruce and Jaline are divorced.

1151292 Mary Ann Smith

Mary was born 3 Jun 1958 in San Diego. Mary graduated from Buena High School in Ventura, Calif., and then went to work for a oil company where she worked in the drafting department, now performed using computers. On 11 Nov 1980 she married Timothy George Cook who was born in 1954. Their children are William George who was born 8 Jul 1987 and Lauren Michelle who was born 12 Nov 1991 in Ventura, Calif.

1151321 Philip Fred Anderson

Philip was born 26 Apr 1942 in Blackfoot, Ida. He graduated from Snake River High School, then from the College of Idaho with a BA degree. On 10 Nov 1965 in Blackfoot he married Denise Browning. Denise is an LPN in surgery at the hospital. Philip is with the advertising department of the *Post-Register*. They had Roger Alan, born 22 May 1968, Carol Denise, born 9 Jun 1970, and Julie Ann, born 18 Jan 1973, all born in Idaho Falls.

Roger earned a degree in animal science from Montana State in Billings. Carol received a master's degree in occupational therapy at St. Paul, Minn.

1151322 Gary Carl Anderson

Gary was born 16 Feb 1947 and died 31 Dec 1982 in Blackfoot, Ida. His delivery was mishandled and he received brain damage. His parents cared for him his entire life. His death occured as a result of complications with the flu.

1151323 Laura Ruth Anderson

Laura was born 18 Aug 1953 in Pocatello, Ida. On 1 Aug 1975 in Blackfoot, she married Thomas William LaFrenz who was born 31 Aug 1947. Tom operated Tom's Auto Clinic and is the pastor at Forks, Wash. Their two children are David Thomas, born 17 May 1978, and Robin Jeanette, born 9 Sep 1979, both in Blackfoot. Laura and Tom are residents of North Bend, Wash. David is a graduate of Nazarene College and is a pastor. He married August Olsen 26 May 2001. Robin has a degree in Elementary Education, and married on 10 Jul 1999 in Sequoia, Wash., Jason Person, a pastor with Social Ministries.

1151331 Dorothy Carol Thomson

Carol was born 18 Sep 1944 in Los Angeles Co., Calif. She lived in Azusa, Calif., and married Tom Charles Ford who was born in 1944. They had Debbie Christine, born in 1969, and Janice Coleen, born in 1973. Debbie married Robert Keith LaFountain who was born in 1964. Janice married Todd Joseph Ball who was born in 1972.

1151332 Donna Jean Thomson

Donna was born 23 Apr 1949 in L.A. Co., Calif. She attended South
Hills HS in West Covina, Mt. San Antonio College in Walnut, Calif.,
and Orange Coast College in Costa Mesa. She is a licensed interior
designer and taught art. (For more, see "Late Additions" p. 381).

1151431 David Winslow Thomson

David was born 17 Nov 1937 in Cedar Rapids, Ia. He began his
elementary school education in California, then entered the fifth
grade in Iowa when his parents moved. He graduated from Mount
Vernon High School in 1955, then received a BA degree in general
science at the University of Iowa in 1959, and a BS in chemistry
there in 1960. He then served in the U.S. Air Force from 1961
through 1989, during which time he primarily was involved with
flying fighters and trainers. Dave retired as a colonel, and is
now working part time teaching aviation safety and risk management,
both in the U.S. and overseas. During his military career he
earned a master's degree in chemistry from Ohio State University in
1964. On 17 Dec 1963 he married Millicent Ann Becket who was born
4 Aug 1938 in Brookings, S.D. Their children are David Andrew,
born 18 Dec 1963 at Wright Patterson Air Force Base, Ohio, and Amy
Elizabeth, born 10 Jan 1968 at Reese Air Force Base, Lubbock, Tex.
 David and Millicent were making their home in Canon City, Colo.,
in 1999.

David Andrew married Lisa Jane Coleman in Jun 1987. They had
Ashley Elizabeth who was born 23 Jan 1980 at Ellsworth AFB, S.D.;
and Sarah Ann who was born 24 Sep 1993 at Ellsworth AFB. Amy
married Ted Cason and they had Zachary David who was born 25 Jul
1993 at Eglin AFB, Fla., and Courtney Ann who was born 27 Apr 1999
at Fort Walton Beach, Fla.

1151432 Paula Jane Thomson

Paula was born 17 Sep 1945 in Pasadena, Calif. She graduated from
Mount Vernon, Iowa, High School in 1963, then attended the
University of Iowa where she earned a BA degree in English and a
secondary teaching certificate in 1967. She continued her
education by earning a MA degree in library science from the
University of Iowa in 1971, then a MS degree in creative studies at
State University College in Buffalo, N.Y., in 1980. She taught
school for 28 years before becoming a professional photographer for
portraits and social functions in the Des Moines area where she
lives. On 14 Aug 1966 in Mount Vernon, Ia., she married Robert J.
Colon, and changed her name back to Thomson after they divorced.
They have a daughter, Cara Dance, who was born 13 Aug 1979 in
Buffalo, N.Y., and graduated from Purdue University in 2001.

1151433 Douglas Alan Thomson

Douglas was born 1 Aug 1953 in Cedar Rapids, Ia. He married Pam Sheets, they divorced, and he remarried. They had Aaron Douglas who was living in Portland, Ore., in 1999.

1151441 Larry Francis Thomson

Larry was born in Jan 1943 in Jones Co., Ia. He was not married. He died in New York City 1 Sep 1991 and was buried in Stanwood Cemetery.

1151461 John Vincent Thomson

John was born 30 Oct 1947. He married 21 Jun 1968 Mary Lou Jensen, and they were later divorced. Their children were Heather Victoria, born 27 Jun 1968 in Cedar Rapids, Ia., and Seth Gabriel, born 29 Aug 1974 in Greene, Ia. Heather is the mother of Drew Brendon Thomson, born 15 Dec 1988, and Jaedon, born in 1993.

1151462 Jo Ann Thomson

Jo Ann was born 18 Jul 1952 in Cedar Rapids, Ia. She received a BS degree in education at Iowa State University in 1974, then taught for a year. She was then married in Mount Vernon on 24 Apr 1971 to David Virgil Stoner who was born 3 Apr 1948 in Cedar Rapids. Their children are Bradley David, born 23 Jul 1975 in Cedar Rapids, and Kyle Joseph, born 3 Jan 1979 in Cedar Rapids. Jo Ann has hosted annual reunions of her grandfather's branch. David assists in farming 5500 acres near Mount Vernon. Jo Ann returned to teaching two years ago.

Brad is a 1998 graduate of ISU with a degree in industrial technology. Kyle attends ISU, class of 2001, in pursuit of the same degree as his brother.

1151463 Gary Lynn Thomson

Gary was born 20 Mar 1954 in Cedar Rapids. He graduated from Mount Vernon High School, then earned a BS degree in industrial technology at Oklahoma State, and is now pursuing a master's degree. Gary has had a kidney transplant. He is a licensed real estate broker and was previously married.

1151464 Robert Alan Thomson

Robert was born 8 Jun 1957 in Cedar Rapids. On 2 May 1981 he

married Sheryle Kay Clark who was born 23 Oct 1957. They have
Nathan Alan, born 14 Sep 1981 in Branson, Mo., Natasha Marie, born
19 Dec 1986 in Minden, La., and Nicholas Howard, born 15 Feb 1989
in Minden.

1151471 James Allen Thomson

James was born 7 Jul 1951 in Cedar Rapids, Ia. He had a child,
Shawn Michael Knepp, born 30 Apr 1976. He married 25 Feb 1978
Kristi Renee Wenndt in Stanwood, Ia. Their children are James
Jeffrey, born 14 Mar 1979 in Cedar Rapids, and Brandon Joe, born 8
Jan 1981 in Cedar Rapids. Shawn married Jenna Clowers 2 Dec 1994.
Their children are Shawn Michael Jr., born 4 Oct 1994, and Samantha
Breanne, born 15 Nov 1996.

1151472 Daniel Lynn Thomson

Danny was born 20 Aug 1953 in Cedar Rapids. He married Deborah J.
Reynolds 21 Apr 1973 and later divorced. They had a child,
Christine M., born 8 Oct 1973 in Iowa City, Ia. Christine married
11 Sep 1993 Jerry Grey in Wichita, Kan. They had Jennifer Elaine,
born 4 Jun 1993, and Jerry Christopher, born 9 Sep 1995. Danny
married 15 Jul 1983 Julie Ketchum in Tipton, Ia. Their children
are Ryan D., born 26 Sep 1983; Nicholas T., born 2 Nov 1984; and
Mitchell G., born 26 Feb 1994, all born in Iowa City.

1151473 Linda Kay Thomson

Linda was born 20 Sep 1955 in Cedar Rapids, Ia. She married 12 Aug
1972 Edwin Ray Clark who was born 15 Feb 1952. Their children are
Michelle Lynn, born 17 Dec 1970; Mandi Kay, born 22 Sep 1977; and
Brandon Edwin, born 28 Mar 1981, all born in Cedar Rapids.

1151474 Catharine Marie Thomson

Catharine was born 26 Jul 1958 in Cedar Rapids. She married 3 Jul
1992 Joel Farrell Kruse.   Catharine has a child, Megan Renee
Thomson, born 21 Dec 1978 in Iowa City.

1151475 Ricky Francis Thomson

Ricky was born 26 Jun 1963 in Cedar Rapids. He married 22 May 1992
Jolene Kay Thomsen Walter, born in 1961. Two step-children are
Brandon Allen, born 13 Apr 1982, and Levi Curtis, born 21 Jun 1984.

1151476 Tina Ann Thomson
Tina was born 27 Jun 1967 in Cedar Rapids. She married 26 Sep 1987
Clifford Paul Krutsinger. They had Katie Renee, born 20 Feb 1994
in Iowa City.

1151481 Marcia Jean Nielsen

Marcia was born 24 Dec 1949 in Cedar Rapids. She graduated from St. Joseph, Michigan, High School in 1968, and graduated from Michigan State with a undergraduate degree in 1972, and with a master's degree in education in 1975. She married 10 Jun 1972 Ross Richard Reck, born 27 Apr 1945. Their children are Phillip Ross, born 10 Oct 1976; Katherine Elizabeth, born 17 Oct 1980; and Nancy Kim, born 30 Nov 1986. Ross holds a Ph.D. from Michigan State in 1977. He is a management consultant and an author, including *Win-Win Negotiator*.

1151482 Carol Lynn Webber

Carol was born 12 May 1965 in Benton Harbor, Mich. She graduated from Arizona State and Indiana University with a master's degree. She is employed in the human resources department at Whirlpool Corp. She married 27 Jun 1987 Douglas Summersgill who was born 24 Apr 1962. Douglas is an electrical engineer and works in the computer field. Their children are twins Andrew Douglas and Christopher Edward, born 8 Aug 1995, and Sarah Katherine, born 22 Jun 1998.

1151483 Kristin Ann Webber

Kristin was born 11 Nov 1966. She is a graduate of Western Michigan University in Kallamazoo. She is employed in sales in Stevensville, Mich. Kristin is not married.

1151511 Evelyn Eileen Barron

Evelyn was born 3 Mar 1938 in Hedrick, Ia. On 16 Aug 1957, in Hedrick, she married Richard Murray Criner who was born 15 Dec 1934 in Burlington, Ia. They met at Parsons College, Fairfield, Ia. Evelyn attended college for two years, then taught kindergarten for three years at Batavia, Ia. After staying home when her children were young, she became a reading associate in Boone, Ia., at the second grade level for 23 years. Dick received a BS from Parsons College and a MA while attending Northwest Missouri, Iowa State, and Drake. Dick taught high school math at Cardinal Community of Eldon, Ia., and at Boone High School. He retired after 32 years of service, and now keeps busy with home repairs, churchwork, and enjoys hunting and fishing. Evelyn is active in her church and enjoys spending time with their grandchildren. Their children are Terri Linn, Linda Dee, and Timothy Lee.

Terri Linn was born 6 Sep 1958 in Fairfield, Ia. On 1 Oct 1988 she married, in Clive, Ia., Dale Edward Bunting who was born 10 Sep 1952. Terri is a Life Flight nurse at Iowa Methodist Medical

Center in Des Moines.   She is working towards becoming a nurse practitioner.   Dale is a firefighter for the city of Des Moines. They had twins on 13 Aug 1989, Daniel Edward and Emily Anne, and Alec Joseph on 12 Mar 1993.

Linda Dee was born 29 Oct 1961 in Fairfield, Ia.   She earned a BS and a MS in social work and is a psychotherapist.   Linda married Hal F. Ream on 8 Jul 1995 in Des Moines.   Hal was born 26 Dec 1957, and is an engineer for the Union Pacific RR.   Linda was previously married and has a daughter, Lydia Marie Givens, born 29 Aug 1989. Lydia takes dancing lessons and plays soccer.   Linda and Hal enjoy boating and bike riding.

Timothy was born 10 Jan 1966 in Boone, Ia.   He holds a MA in business administration and is a CPA.   He is Chief of Child Support Fiscal Bureau of the Iowa Dept. of Human Services.   Tim married Kristine Kay Rademaker on 11 Sep 1993 in West Union, Ia.   Kristine was born 18 Nov 1964.   Kris has a BA in business and also is a CPA. She works for the State Auditor for State of Iowa.   They have Nicole Kristine, born 3 Oct 1994, Katelyn Lea, born 25 Jul 1996 and Tyler Richard, born 9 Jun 1999.   Tim enjoys outdoor activities like running, fishing and golfing.

1151512 Edwin Eugene Barron

Edwin was born 30 Aug 1942 in Hedrick, Ia.   His first wife was Joann Morgan whom he married in Dec 1960 in Oskaloosa, Ia. Secondly, he married Rita Kay Sheddy on 14 Feb 1987 in Williamsburg, Ia.   (Both were previously married).   Rita was born 4 Mar 1936.   Both are high school graduates.   Ed is a farmer and also has an auto body shop.   His children are Rhonda Sue, and Lee Allen.

Rhonda was born 8 Feb 1963.   She married Michael Grimm on 20 Sep 1986.   They live in Billings, Mont.; no children.

Lee was born 21 Dec 1960.   He has a son, Corby Jonathan, born in Oct 1998.   Lee lives in Euless, Tex.

1151513 Jon LaVerne Barron

Jon was born 21 Jun 1944 in Ottumwa, Ia.   His first marriage was to Roxie Mae Fortner.   He secondly married Linda Hughes on 18 Sep 1993 in Cedar Rapids, Ia.   By his first marriage Jon had Tamera (Tammy) Kay who was born 8 Dec 1964, and Susan Lynette who was born 4 Mar 1974.

In Wyoming, Tammy married Steven Vaughn who was born 7 Jul 1961. They have a daughter, Ashley Mae who was born 5 Dec 1989.

1151514 Faira Louise Barron

Faira was born 24 Mar 1947 in Ottumwa. She married Gary DenHartog.
Secondly, on 19 Sep 1982, she married Donald Homer King who was
born 7 Jul 1951, and was previously married.   Faira had three
children from her first marriage: Brenda Louise, Belinda Mae, and
Brian Dean, all with last name of DenHartog.

Brenda was born 7 May 1970.   She married Alfonso Lopez on 3 Jun
1995. He was born 3 Oct 1961. They have Courtney Cheynne, born 23
Sep 1994, Lierra Nykole, born 20 Jan 1996 and Colby Rae, born 23
Mar 1999.

Belinda was born 12 Jul 1975, and married Sean Jeffrey Wursta on 27
Jul 1996. Sean was born 25 Mar 1970. They have Chance Jeffrey,
born 13 Nov 1995, and twins, Bret Charles and Bryce Corby, born 7
Mar 1997.

Brian was born 21 Mar 1973.

1151515 Carolyn Kay Barron

Carolyn was born 7 Jun 1953 in Ottumwa.   On 21 Apr 1972, in
Oskaloosa, Ia., she married Eugene Keith Ryken who was born 15
Nov 1952. Their children are James Arthur, Anthony Eugene, and
Geoffrey Ryan. They were living in Ark. in 1999.

James was born 28 Oct 1973 and married Jennifer Elaine Wakefield on
30 Jun 1997. Jennifer was born 23 Dec 1972. Anthony was born 19
Jun 1975 and on 14 Mar 1998 he married Renee Denise McHaha, born 22
Aug 1975.   Geoffrey was born 10 Jan 1980.

1151521 Lois Ann Rice

Lois Ann was born 2 Jan 1943 in Ottumwa, Ia. She graduated from
Farson High School in 1961 and briefly attended the University of
Northern Iowa.   On 27 Dec 1961 in Hedrick she married William
(Bill) Allen Martin who was born 6 Nov 1941. Bill died 18 Dec
2000. Bill sold and installed water conditioning systems.   They had
Susan Michelle, born 16 Jul 1962; Timothy Allen, born 21 Oct 1963;
and Callan Aaron, born 13 Jun 1985.

Susan married Albert Robert Ashby Jr. on 19 Jun 1993 in Accomack
Co., Va. Albert was born 9 May 1960 in Exmore, Va. Susan is a
doctor of chiropractic and has her own practice--Eastern Shore
Chiropractic. Albert graduated from William and Mary College and
is a CPA. In 1999, he was a special investigator with the Virginia
State Police.

1151522 Lynn Glenys Rice

Lynn was born 19 Nov 1945 in Ottumwa, Ia., and died 6 Feb 1971. He was buried in Mt. Zion Cemetery near Martinsburg, Ia.

1151523 Clarence Allen Rice

Clarence, who goes by Allen, was born 14 Apr 1948 in Ottumwa, Ia. On 23 Nov 1971 he married Christine Ruth Webber who was born 13 Jul 1951 in Evanston, Ill. Their children are Kristin Alanna, born 28 Dec 1980; Allison Christine, born 15 Jan 1984; Alexandra Christine, born 22 Jun 1986; and Clinton Allen, born 9 Mar 1989. Allen owns an equipment leasing business.

1151524 Glenda Paulette Rice

Glenda was born 29 Nov 1955 in Ottumwa. She married on 21 May 1977 Russell James Sieren who was born 1 Mar 1957 in Ottumwa, Ia. They had Jeremy Lynn, born 17 Aug 1979; Clinton James, born 9 Feb 1981; Josiah Rice, born 22 Feb 1985; Hanna Jo, born 31 Mar 1988; and Rachel Renee, born 3 Sep 1991 and died 5 Sep 1991. Clinton James died in a motorcycle accident 26 Mar 2000.

1151531 Kathleen Mae Messer

Kathleen was born 19 Jun 1948 in Ottumwa, Ia. She married Arthur Lee Lillie on 1 Mar 1969. Their children are Tonya Lorraine, born 27 Nov 1969 in Ames, Ia., and Daniel Patrick, born 6 Apr 1974 in Hampton, Ia. Secondly, she married John McLaughlin in Dec 1995 in Lake Tahoe. Kathleen has a BA from Iowa State University in graphic arts. Presently, she is a real estate broker.

Tonya married Mark Alan Cisek on 28 Aug 1999 in Chicago. Mark is an attorney. Tonya has an MA from Illinois State University. Her work involves locating programming flaws. Daniel has a degree in art from Northern Illinois University at DeKalb. He has worked at design window displays.

1151532 Lawrence Allen Messer

Lawrence was born 24 Aug 1952 in Mount Pleasant, Ia. He married Becky Lu Tumilty 28 Jun 1974 in Shellsburg, Ia. Their children are Benjamin Allen who was born 15 Nov 1978, Thomas James, born 2 Oct 1981; and Katy McKensie, born 27 Apr 1985, all born in Winterset, Ia. Lawrence has a BA from William Penn in Oskaloosa, Ia., and earned a teaching certificate at the University of Northern Iowa (UNI). He is a social studies teacher in Winterset Middle School. He also coaches cross country and volleyball. Becky is a coordinator of events planning at a hospital.

Benjamin attended Ellsworth CC, then transferred to Southwest CC in Creston, Ia. He enlisted in the U.S. Marines in Sep 1999. Tom is a student of aviation at Indian Hills CC in Ottumwa, Ia.

1151533 Mark Thomson Messer

Mark was born 10 Jun 1956 in Oskaloosa, Ia. He married Jeanette Alese Bishop on 22 Mar 1986 at Belmond, Ia. Jeanette was born 10 Jan 1961. Mark has a BA from Central College in Pella, Ia. and a MA from UNI. He teaches English at Northern Iowa Area Community College in Mason City. Their children are Alese Christine, born 3 Jun 1987; Jennifer Marie, born 28 Sep 1990 in Mason City, Ia.; and Christopher Lyle, born 25 Jun 1993 in Mason City. Jeanette holds a MA from UNI as a speech therapist.

1151534 Lorraine Ann Messer

Lorraine was born 2 Jul 1962 in Clinton, Ia. She married Steve Versteegh in 1982 in Lake Tahoe, Nev.. Their child is Jeffrey Allen who was born 29 Jan 1981 in Grinnell, Ia. Secondly, Lorraine married Afton Richards on 21 May 1991 in New Sharon, Ia. Lorraine is a LPN nurse.

1151535 Brent Leonard Messer

Brent was born 3 Jan 1965 in Cedar Rapids, Ia., and died 27 Oct 1985 in Oskaloosa, Ia. He served three years in the U.S. Navy and traveled below the equator. Family records mention that he was shot. Burial was in Friends Cemetery, New Sharon, Ia.

1151541 Jerold Lynn De Young

Jerold was born 23 Mar 1953 in Rapid City, S.D. In Oct 1971, in Minneapolis, Minn., he married Bonnie Rae Irwin who was born 31 Mar 1954. They had Pauline Rae who born 31 Mar 1972 in Minneapolis, Minn. After Jerold and Bonnie divorced, Jerold married Susan Kay Gramm on 25 Mar 1978; Susan was born in 1956.

Pauline married Brian Baughman and were in the midst of a divorce in 1999. Pauline and Douglas Holden had Ashley Rae who was born 7 Apr 1993 in Tacoma, Wash.

1151542 James Edwin De Young

James was born 1 Feb 1955 in Rapid City, S.D. He married Christa Lynn Taylor on 21 Apr 1984 in McKinney, Tex. Christa was born 19 Mar 1959. They had Wil Jamison, born 15 Oct 1992 in Plano, Tex.

1151543 John Thomson De Young

John was born 4 Sep 1962 in Phoenix, Ariz. On 1 Sep 1984, in
Zweibruchn, Germany, he married Lydia Esther Zayas who was born in
1959. They had Matthew John, born 14 Oct 1986 in Germany. John
adopted Lydia's daughter, Melissa Ann Cavender, who was born 19 Nov
1980 in Phoenix, Ariz. John spent two years in the U.S. Air Force
and is now working towards a bachelor's degree.

1151621 Robert Bruce Cooper

Robert was born 4 Feb 1935 in Rochester, Minn. In Long Beach,
Calif., he married in Aug 1957 Carmella Satter who was born in 1937
in Long Beach. Their child was Erin Dawn, born 2 Dec 1958 in
Rochester, Minn. Secondly, Robert married Billie Jo Ford who was
born in 1929.

1151622 Carol Louise Cooper

Carol was born 3 Jan 1936 in Rochester, Minn. She married Heye
"Junior" Renken in Rochester. Junior was born 4 May 1932 and died
2 Jul 1986. Carol died 1 Jun 1969 in Rochester. They had a
daughter, Deanna, who was born 24 Jan 1958 in Rochester. They
adopted Randal who was born 28 Nov 1965.

Deana married Jeffrey McEachern on 17 May 1980 in Rochester. Deana
and Jeffrey had Joshua who was born 8 Dec 1980 in Minneapolis.

Randal married Amy Dubbles who was born 30 Sep 1966 in Rochester,
Minn. Their children are Jake Heye who was born 11 May 1990; Holly
Lucinda who was born 26 Dec 1991; and Jon Randal who was born 30
Jan 1995.

1151623 Dale Thomas Cooper

Dale was born 1 Dec 1945 in Rochester, Minn. He married Lavonne
Claire Schultz on 26 Dec 1966 in Rochester. Lavonne was born 4 Feb
1947 in Rochester. They had four children: Debra, born 7 Jun 1969
in Germany; Tonya, born 29 Jun 1971 in Rochester; Jason, born 10
Mar 1974 in Rochester; and Chad, born 13 Jul 1976 in Rochester.

Tonya married 5 Sep 1992 John Pearson in St. Cloud, Minn. They do
not have any children.

1151631 Richard Arthur Tenley

Richard was born 25 May 1932 in Rochester, Minn. He enlisted in
the U.S. Navy and served from 1951 to 1955. He attended the
University of Minnesota and earned a BS degree in electrical

engineering. He worked for Hughes, Litton and IBM before retiring
in 1990. He married 8 Aug 1964 Katherine Gail Hess in Towson, Md.
Katherine was born 21 Jul 1941 in Bethlehem, Pa.   Their children
are Susan Darlene, born 31 May 1968 in Kingston, N.Y., and John
Edward, born 20 Sep 1983 in Rochester, Minn.

Susan earned a BA degree with a double major in math and business
from Rice University. She is a Fellow in the Society of Actuaries
and is employed as an employee benefits consultant for Towers
Perrin in Houston, Tex.

1151632 Beverly Ann Tenley

Beverly was born 23 Nov 1933 in Rochester, Minn. On 25 Jun 1960 she
married Robert Lee Nesbit who was born 3 Apr 1934 in St. Charles,
Minn.   Their children are Steven Robert, born 13 May 1961 in
Minneapolis, and Susan Marie, born 29 Apr 1963 in Owatonna, Minn.

Steven married Bonnie Jean Ballstadt in Owatonna, Minn. Bonnie was
born 26 Apr 1962 in Medford, Minn.   Their three children are
Allissa Jean, born 23 Jan 1983 in Austin, Minn.; Katy Lynn, born 9
Oct 1986 in Rochester, Minn.; and Alex Robert, born 11 Jul 1989 in
Minneapolis.

Susan married 10 Jun 1989, in Owatonna, Minn., Scott Allan Wiuff.
Secondly, she married Mark Anthony Maloney on 10 Jun 1989 in
Owatonna, Minn. Mark was born 11 Sep 1961 in Austin, Minn. Susan
and Mark have a son, Kyle Joseph who was born 6 Jun 1990 in
Owatonna, and Sarah Elizabeth who was born 8 Nov 1995.

1151633 Beatrice Evon Tenley

Beatrice was born 23 Jun 1938 in Rochester, Minn. She was married
on 5 Aug 1961, in Rochester, to Jerry Demaray who was born 11 Sep
1935 in Mankato, Minn. Their children are Lynn Ann, born 28 Apr
1963 in Mankato, Jeffrey Joseph, born 13 Nov 1966 in Rochester, and
Kristin Sedate, born 13 May 1968 in Rochester.

Lynn was married 4 Nov 1989 in Rochester to Robert Warren
Splittstoesser who was born 17 Jan 1965 in Rochester. They have
Mitchell Demaray who was born 1 May 1996. Jeffrey married Susan
Ann Hoehn on 8 Mar 1997 in Rochester. Their child is Briana Evon
who was born 27 Jul 1997 in Rochester. Kristin married Alan Sasse
on 20 Jul 1996 in Rochester.

1151651 Mary Kathryn Tenley

Mary was born 25 Mar 1946 in Rochester, Minn. She was married in
Rochester on 1 Mar 1963 to Randolph Louis Stevens who was born 26

Aug 1944 in Rochester.   Their children are Lisa Ann, born 2 Oct 1963 in Rochester, and Robert Louis, born 11 May 1971 in Rochester.

Lisa married 22 Aug 1984 Michael Franken in Rochester; they have since divorced.   She is pursuing a doctorate at the University of Minnesota.   Robert married Dawn Melmer on 15 Aug 1998.   Their daughter, Cortney Deanna, was born 8 Oct 1995.

1151652 Cary Robert Tenley

Cary was born 9 Dec 1951 in Rochester, Minn.   He married in Rochester on 23 Jul 1975 Cindy Mae Fenske who was born 28 Nov 1953 in Rochester.   They had Joseph Robert, born 9 Apr 1979, and Jenna Mae, born 23 Jun 1985, both in Rochester.

1151653 Joel Lynn Tenley

Joel was born 14 May 1957 in Rochester.   He married Gail Harty in 1982.   Later they divorced without having any children. Joel is not remarried and works as a plumbing supply salesman.

1151661 James McConnell Tenley

James was born 6 Aug 1942 in Portland, Ind.   He was with Dayton-Hudson Department Store in Minneapolis before his death on 14 Oct 1999.   On 12 Jan 1963 he married Susan Francis Sullivan in Rochester, Minn.   Susan was born 26 Aug 1943 in Maywood, Ill.   They had James Richard, born 30 Jul 1964 in Rochester, and Jennifer Marta, born 27 Jul 1974 in Anoka, Minn.

1151711 Wayne Edward Boag

Wayne was born 13 Jan 1936 in Oregon City, Ore., and died of cancer 30 Apr 1988 in Duarte, Calif.   He was married in Calif. on 29 Nov 1958 to Mary Margaret Hobbs, born 21 Aug 1938 in Oak Park, Ill. Wayne was an electrical engineer.   They have five children: Cheryl Ann, born 20 Nov 1960 in Corvallis, Ore.; William Edward, born 26 Aug 1962 in Costa Mesa, Calif.; Debra Ann, born 8 Aug 1965 in Costa Mesa; Wayne Edward, Jr., born 25 Feb 1967 in Costa Mesa and died there 19 Jan 1969; and Robert Allen, born 3 Feb 1970 in Costa Mesa.

Cheryl Ann married William Lee Cates on 6 Dec 1986 in Costa Mesa. Their children are Alyssa Marie, born 9 Feb 1990; Brandon Virgil, born 11 Jun 1991 and Garrett Wayne, born 8 Jun 1995.   William Edward married Tamara on 10 Aug 1985 and divorced in 1987.   They had Michael Wayne who was born 27 Dec 1989.   Secondly, he married Vickie LaFaye.   William is a software engineer.   Debra Ann was married on 16 Jun 1990 to James Crozier.   They had Jeffrey Thomas 1 Apr 1991 and Christi Lee 5 Nov 1993, both born in Calif.

1151712 Cecil Clarence Huntley

Cecil was born 3 Dec 1954 in Lebanon, Ore. He suffered from MS and died 10 Apr 1980 in a nursing home in Albany, Ore.

1151721 Karen Lorraine Harper

Karen was born 8 Nov 1943 in Monahans, Tex. On 14 Feb 1964 she married Donald D. Oppel. Their child is Jennifer Marie, born 22 Aug 1968 in Riverside, Calif. Donald was born 24 Apr 1940 and died 26 Aug 1997 in Boise, Ida., where he is buried.

1151722 Shirley Ann Harper

Shirley was born 18 Aug 1945 in Kermit, Tex. She married Larry E. McQuire on 20 Nov 1965, and they divorced after they had Jeremy and Heather. Shirley married secondly Paul Osborne. Heather married Jason Hampton.

1151731 Martha Belle Harper

Martha was born 25 Aug 1943 in San Francisco. She married Dennis Charles Miller on 8 Aug 1964. They had Carrie, Dennis Guy, and Tammara. Martha divorced Dennis and she married David Jones.

1151732 Carolyn Rae Harper

Carolyn Rae was born 10 Aug 1949 in Lakeview, Ore. Her first marriage on 14 Mar 1970 in Davenport, Ia., was to Russell Lee Carpenter who was born 8 Sep 1941. They had Elizabeth who was born 26 Sep 1970 in Portland and Christina who was born 8 Apr 1976 in Portland. Carolyn secondly married Delane Guild on 24 Dec 1989.

Elizabeth "Beth" married Joseph Patrick Miller on 15 Jul 1989. Joseph was born 28 May 1969. They had Christopher who was born 26 Aug 1991 in Manhattan, Kan., and Corinna who was born 24 May 1993 in Manhattan, Kan.

1151741 Mark William Harper

Mark was born 28 Jan 1947 in Portland, Ore. His children are Troy, born in 1966; Julie Ann, born in 1967; and John, born in 1971.

1151742 Roy Allen Harper

Roy was born 25 May 1949 in Grants Pass, Ore.; died 27 May 1949.

1151743 Jerry Dean Harper

Jerry was born 6 Dec 1953 in Corvallis, Ore. He graduated from Rex

Putnam High School in 1972, then enlisted in the U.S. Navy. Later, Jerry was attached to the U.S. Army National Guard. He attended Life Bible College and Clackamas Community College before entering the work force. He started as an assistant manager at KFC, and for the last nine years he has been a transit bus driver. He married Loraina Jane Hunter who was born 8 May 1954 at Mare Island, Calif. They had Jerry Dean, Jr., born 6 May 1977 in Harbor City, Calif., and Shawn Nathaniel, born 27 Jun 1986 in Clackamas, Ore.

Jerry Jr. married Stacey Batch and they had Lillie Ann and Stuart Thomas.

1151761 Marvin Earl Harper, Jr.

Marvin was born 1 May 1954 in Salem, Ore.

1151762 Marvel Elaine Harper

Marvel was born 23 Jun 1955 in Salem, Ore. On 15 May 1976 she married David Michael Garrison in Oregon City, Ore. David was born 5 Jan 1955 in Oregon City, Ore. Their children are Michael who was born 26 Apr 1979 in Pendleton, Ore., and Michelle who was born 15 Dec 1981 in Oregon City.

Michael married Megan Cole in Oregon City on 16 Jan 1999.

1154121 Laura May Barron

Laura was born 24 Aug 1956 in St. Paul, Minn. She married 6 Nov 1976 Lynn Mitchell Blue in Granite Falls, Minn. Lynn was born 19 Dec 1951 in St. Paul, Minn. Laura graduated from high school in 1974. She then attended Alexandria Technical College where she earned a degree in interior design. Laura now owns and operates a gift shop and floral business in Granite Falls, Minn. Lynn is a Dakota native American and is Finance Officer for Firefly Creek Casino. Their children are Charissa Lynn, born 23 Apr 1980 in Landstuhl, Germany, and Marcus Paul, born 3 Aug 1984 in Shakopee, Minn.

Charissa graduated with honors from Granite Falls High School in May 1998 and is attending Mankato State University.

1154122 Linda Ray Barron

Linda was born 27 Feb 1958 in St. Paul, Minn. She graduated from Sartell High School. She holds a BS in Nursing from Mankato State. Linda works in cardiac care at St. Mary's Hospital in Rochester, Minn., an affiliate of the Mayo Clinic. On 13 Aug 1983 Linda married Jon Magnus Alness in St. Cloud, Minn. Jon is co-owner of

Zumbro Valley Forestry, a business which manages landowner's forested land, oversees timber sales and spring planting of seedlings. They have three children: Alyssa Mae, born 11 Apr 1988; Paul Magnus, born 5 Jun 1990; and Elizabeth Carol, born 5 Dec 1992, all born in Rochester, Minn.

1154123 Paul Reid Barron

Paul was born 30 Dec 1960 in St. Paul. Paul was a graduate of Sartell High School. He was killed in a motorcycle accident near his home on 27 Jul 1980.

1154124 Mary Elizabeth Barron

Mary was born 10 Feb 1962 in St. Paul. She graduated from Sartell High School. She is a language arts teacher at Apollo High School in St. Cloud and received her master's degree in 1998. She married 18 May 1985 Roys Francis Traut in Sartell, Minn. Roys was born 5 Oct 1961 in St. Cloud. They operate a dairy farm located fifteen miles north of St. Cloud. Their children are Matthew Barron, born 23 Jul 1987, and Rory Firmin, born 17 Sep 1991, both in St. Cloud.

1154211 Julie Lynn Huber

Julie was born 26 Jul 1957 in Olney, Ill. She earned a BA degree in social work in 1979 from Bethany College, Lindsburg, Kan. She married Gary F. Lucas on 26 Jul 1980. They had Ben Andrew born 25 Aug 1962 in Liberal, Kan., and Alex Daniel born 2 May 1986 in Liberal. Secondly, she married William E. Ward on 8 Jun 1991. The family was living in Shrewsbury, Mass., in 1999.

1154212 Clay Randall Huber

Clay was born 4 Apr 1961 in El Dorado, Kan. He holds a BS degree in biology from Bethany College, and is now living unmarried in Boulder, Colo.

1154221 Janice Lynn Thomson

Janice was born 28 Nov 1959 at Shaw AF Base, S.C., and spent her youth in South Carolina, Japan, Taiwan, Ohio, and Texas. She is a 1982 graduate of Texas Lutheran College in Sequin, Tex., with a BA in psychology and social work. She worked in that field in Dallas before becoming disabled.

1154222 Lori Christine Thomson

Lori was born 13 Nov 1962 at Misawa AF Base, Japan. She lived abroad in her youth before graduating in 1985 from Duke University in Durham, N.C., with a BA in Chinese history. She then earned a MA in Asian journalism at the University of Illinois, Champaign. She is employed by Juneau Empire, Juneau, Alaska, where she lives.

1154223 Cheryl Lee Thomson   See "Late Additions", p. 381.

1155121 Eric Bates Oppen

Eric was born 22 May 1961 in Iowa Falls, Ia. He graduated from Iowa Falls High School in 1979, then advanced his education at St. Olaf College where he earned a degree in East Asian Studies in Jan 1983. He was a National Merit Scholarship semifinalist, and can speak German and Chinese. Eric is a self-employed landlord and freelance writer. Eric, who lives in Iowa Falls, is not married.

1155122 John David Oppen

John was born 23 Feb 1964 in Iowa Falls, and graduated from high school in 1982. The compiler would attest that John made a wise decision by attending Iowa State University where he graduated with a BS degree in mechanical engineering in 1987. He is working for Boeing Aircraft in Long Beach, Calif. John is not married.

1155431 Mark Spence Levi

Mark was born 5 Oct 1961 in Winchester, Va. He attended Clarke County High School in Berryville, Va., through his junior year and went on to college. He earned a BA in philosophy and a master's in business administration. He will attend law school at the University of California in San Francisco, starting in the fall of 1999. Mark served in the U.S. Army, part of the time in Germany. He was working for GSA in San Francisco in 1999, and resided in Albany, Calif.

1155432 Keith Winterton Levi

Keith was born 22 Jan 1963 in Winchester, Va. In 1982 he graduated from James Wood High School in Winchester. He holds a BA and a Master of Teaching from Virginia Commonwealth University. He married Mary Ellis on 31 Jul 1999, and they reside in Louisa, Va.

1155433 Susan Virginia Levi

Susan was born 16 Feb 1965 in Winchester, Va. She graduated from Randolph Macon Academy in Front Royal, Va., in 1983. She then attended the University of New Mexico where she earned a BA in psychology in 1994. Today, she is working as a medical transcriptionist at the Rehabilitation and Occupational Clinic in Albuquerque, N.M.

1155521 Patrick Eugene Klein

Patrick was born 12 Jun 1943. In 1964 he married Norma Jean Trumbauer in Jesup, Ia. Norma was born 15 Dec 1942. Their children are Christopher Keith, born 21 May 1965 in Ames, Ia.; Michell Marie, born 1 Apr 1966; Pamela Jean, born 23 Mar 1967 in Ames; Jennifer Elaine, born 23 Jan 1969 in Waterloo; and Jay Patrick, born 14 Feb 1977 in Shakopee, Minn. Patrick is a vice-president of a construction company and was manager for the construction of Mall of America. Norma is a RN. They make their home near Parker, Colo.

Christopher married Ana Oviedo Cruz who was born 25 Jul 1965. They have three children: Arrianna, born 26 Sep 1989 in Minn.; Nicolas, born 9 Dec 1994; and Thomas, born 9 Apr 1997 in Houston, Tex., where the family was living in 1999.

Michell married Scott Jirik who was born 15 Jan 1966. Scott is in construction and Michell is in charge of a daycare school. Their four children are David, born 28 Jun 1984; Kimberly, born 3 Feb 1987; Jacob, born 31 Jul 1990; and Sarah, born 16 Dec 1995, all born in Minn. They live in Jordan, Minn.

Pamela married Timothy Powers who was born 5 Nov 1965. They had Shane, born 26 Feb 1992; Caitlyn, born 25 Dec 1993; and Kevin, born 12 Apr 1995. Pamela and David are graduates of the United States Air Force Military Academy. David was a pilot for United Airlines in 1999. They live in Camden, Del.

Jennifer is not married, and Jay is serving in the U.S. Navy.

1155522 Rita Ann Klein

Rita was born 4 Jan 1947 in Waterloo, Ia. On 2 Aug 1969, in Gilbertville, Ia., she married George Amling who was born 16 Sep 1944. They had Stacy, born 10 Aug 1976, and Sarah, born 3 Sep 1979, both born in Cedar Falls. Rita teaches business and has computer classes in high school. George is a CPA and farms on the side. They live near Dike, Ia.

Stacy majored in Spanish at the University of Northern Iowa (UNI) in 1998. In 1999 she was pursuing a master's degree at East Lansing, Mich. Sarah attended school in Dike.

1155523 Elaine Marie Klein

Elaine was born 4 Apr 1948 in Waterloo, Ia. She married John Catalano in Gilbertville on 20 Dec 1969. John was born in Brockton, Mass., on 6 Dec 1946, and today is a diesel mechanic. They had

278   The Descendants of Hugh Thomson

Brian, born 24 Sep 1971 in Attleboro, Mass., and Cory James, born 11 Feb 1977 in San Pedro, Calif.

Brian graduated from Cal Poly, Pomona, Calif. In 1999, he was a senior accountant for Toshiba. Cory is a senior at Cal State in Long Beach, where he majored in business and English, and was expected to graduate in 2000.

1155524 Keith Joseph Klein

Keith was born 4 Jun 1949 in Waterloo, Ia. In Gilbertville, he married Nancy Suiter in 1970, and later they divorced. They had Sheri Jo, born 8 Dec 1970, and Steven Patrick, born 12 Sep 1974. Secondly, Keith married Connie Lee in Tempe, Ariz. Keith worked for a glass machining company in Tempe, Ariz., then moved to Boise, Ida., in 1999, where he works as a machinist.

Sheri married Gabe Horcasitas in Las Vegas in 1996 and live in Phoenix, Ariz.

Steven married Crystal in Nov 1996 in Phoenix and they live in Chandler, Ariz. They had Zachary who was born in Jan 1999 in Ariz.

1155525 David John Klein

David was born 11 Nov 1950 in Waterloo, Ia. He served in the U.S. Air Force after graduating from the USAF Academy. He retired as a Lt. Col., and is now with an airline in Colorado Springs. He married Sandra Pyle on 23 Feb 1974 in Phoenix. Sandra was born 7 Aug 1951. Their children are Karin L., born 28 Nov 1975 in Selma, Ala; Kelly M., born 24 Nov 1976 in Charleston, S.C.; and David J., born 5 Aug 1978 in Charleston, S.C. Karin is a graduate of the USAF Academy on 27 May 1998, and Kelly graduated from Colorado State in Dec 1998. David graduated from the USAF Academy in 2000.

1155526 Doris Margaret Klein

Doris was born 18 Jun 1953 in Waterloo, Ia. She married William McAleer on 21 Oct 1978 in Gilbertville. William was born 21 May 1952. Doris is a registered nurse in Omaha while Bill is employed as a telephone installer and trouble shooter. They had Ryan Patrick, born 12 Oct 1979, and Justin Peter, born 20 Nov 1980, both born in Davenport, Ia.

1155527 Larry James Klein

Larry was born 7 Oct 1955 in Waterloo, Ia. He married Catherine (Cathy) Bown on 10 Jun 1983. Cathy was born 7 Mar 1956. She had Matthew by a previous marriage, born in Sep 1978 who was adopted by

Larry. They also adopted Margaret who was born 11 May 1989 and Emily V. who was born 5 Apr 1991, both in Korea. Larry is a machinist at John Deere in Waterloo where Cathy also works.

1155528 Annette Lorene Klein

Annette was born 25 May 1960 in Waterloo. She married Dean Zuck in Nov 1979 in Gilbertville. Dean was born in Jan 1957. They had Rebecca (Becky) Ann, born in May 1980, and Brett Marshall, born in Sep 1983. Annette is a music teacher at Center Point, and Dean is a dairy farmer who recently gave up a coaching job.

1155529 Angela Mary Klein

Angela was born 23 Dec 1962 in Waterloo. She married Paul Hauser 18 Jun 1988 in Gilbertville. Paul was born 2 Jul 1962. They had Kristine, born in May 1963; Philip, born in Aug 1995; Zachary, born 10 Apr 1997, and Mollie Margaret born 1 Sep 1999, all born in Des Moines, Ia. Angie is a RN, and Paul is a mechanical engineer in West Des Moines.

1155541 Elizabeth Catherine Russell

Elizabeth was born in Germany on 15 Apr 1953. She graduated from Kalani High School in Honolulu. She married Stanley Walker on 31 Jul 1971; they are now divorced. They had Anita Elizabeth who was born 23 Feb 1973. Elizabeth works for Siemans Corp. as a quality control manager.

1155542 John David Russell

John was born 25 May 1954 in Germany. He is a graduate of Kalani High School in Honolulu. John is self employed as a business consultant in Walnut Creek, Calif., and is not married.

1157111 Ronald L. Johnson

Ronald was born 18 Feb 1956 in San Diego Co., Calif. He has a MA in computer science and works in that occupation. He is not married.

1157112 Terri Lynn Johnson

Terri was born 31 Aug 1958 in San Diego Co., Calif. She married John Ireton on 28 Jul 1984 and they live in El Cajon, Calif. Terri is an interior decorator while John is in the cable pulling business. Their children are Jennifer who was born 30 Jun 1989, Tom who was born 10 Aug 1992 and Daniel who was born 17 May 1996.

1157511 Richard Arlan Young

Richard was born 31 Jan 1947 in Sandwich, Ill. He graduated from Earlville High School in 1965, then attended Waubonsie Community College for two years where he studied art. He has done murals for homeowners and was commissioned to do wood carving for a church on the historical register.

1157512 Patricia Louise Young

Patricia was born 1 Jun 1948 in Sandwich, Ill. She graduated from Earlville High School in 1966, then became a x-ray technician. Currently she is in nuclear medicine at Copley Hospital in Aurora, Ill. She is married to a Mr. Beilman and their children are Ryan E. who was born in 1977, twins Raegan Michelle and Lauren Kendall born in 1980, and William Andrew who was born in 1999. Patricia also is a grandmother.

1157513 Jonathan Russell Young

Jonathan was born 29 Mar 1961 in Mendota Ill. He is a graduate of Yorkville High School, and has an associate degree in business from Waubonsie Community College. Presently he is assistant manager at Timeless Hobbies in Wheaton, Ill.

1157711 Paula Ann Thomson

Paula was born 28 May 1967 in Princeton, Ill. In 1985 she graduated from Princeton High School, then went on to Illinois State University where she earned a degree in political science in Dec 1988. She is working as a legal assistant. She married Kenneth R. Lough II on 28 Sep 1991 in Princeton and they are living in Ohio, Ill.

1157712 James Patrick Thomson

James was born 23 Jul 1968 in Princeton, Ill. He married Ann Silleker on 14 Apr 1995 at Virginia Beach, Va. Their children are Trevor James who was born 20 Dec 1993 and Lauren Elizabeth who was born 23 Oct 1995. James, who is self-employed, owns WEINK in Richmond, Va.

1157713 Michael Shawn Thomson

Michael was born 13 Apr 1971 in Princeton, Ill. He graduated from Princeton High School in 1989, then attended Western Illinois University where he earned a BA in 1994 and a MS in political science in 1995. He is assistant political director for the Illinois Assembly Speaker of the House. He married Rachael Longman in Oct 1996 in Princeton and they are living in Springfield, Ill.

1157721 Linda Jean Olin

Linda was born 2 Jul 1960 in Princeton, Ill. She married Brian
Shofner and they had Nicole Renee on 9 May 1985 in Princeton, Ill.
Secondly, Linda married Steve Pierce and they had Renee Jeanette on
20 Oct 1992 and Alex LeRoy on 7 May 1995.

1157722 Vicky Renee Olin

Vicky was born 21 Feb 1967 in Princeton, Ill. She married Tim Cass
and they had Allison Marie on 28 Sep 1986. Secondly, Vicky married
Richard Townsend and they had Dalton Morse on 11 Jul 1993.

1157811 Kori Elaine Burkett

Kori was born 19 Feb 1960 in Mount Clemens, Mich. She married Mr.
Rapier and their children are Gloria Jane, born 19 Apr 1984; Randel
Vaughn, born 5 Dec 1988; and Jesse Clayton, born 2 Jan 1991.

1157812 Kristyn Anne Burkett

Kristyn was born 9 Oct 1964 in Mount Clemens, Mich. Kris married
Mr. Kuhn, and they had Michael Allen who was born 2 Aug 1992.

1157821 Karen Sue Platkowski

Karen was born 12 Feb 1970 in Sterling Heights, Mich. She married
Paul Miller on 11 Dec 1999.

115(10)121 Kenneth John Duff

Kenneth (Ken) was born 31 Jan 1940 in Winterset, Ia. His parents
divorced when he was five years old. Before he completed high
school, he enlisted in the U.S. Air Force, and served from 1957 to
1961. While in the service he completed requirements for a G.E.D.
On 20 Nov 1959 he married Carolyn June Deatherage in Chandler, Az.
Carolyn was born 18 May 1942 in McIntosh, N.M. For the past thirty
years, Ken has been in the business of harvesting carrots in the
lower half of Calif. He has his own fabricating shop where he
constructs much of the equipment for his operation. They had four
daughters: Karen Frances born 24 Jan 1961 in Casa Grande, Ariz.;
Sharon Lynn born 9 Aug 1963 in Ventura, Calif.; Cheryl Linnette
born 30 Nov 1969 in Oxnard, Calif.; and Barbara Mae born 25 Jul
1973 in Bakersfield, Calif. Ken and Carolyn were living in
Bakersfield in 1999.

Karen married Bill Simms and they had John, born 3 Jun 1991. Karen and Bill are divorced.

Sharon married Irvin Glenn, and later divorced. They had Kenneth Jordon born 18 Feb 1994.

Cheryl married Christopher Scott Calley and they had Allison Brooke who was born 24 Jun 1999.

115(10)122 Harriett Jo Duff

Harriett was born 7 Mar 1945 in Winterset, Ia. She graduated from Southeast High School in Lincoln, Neb., in 1963. On 20 Mar 1965 she married Timothy Harry Hergenrader who was born 28 Jan 1945 in Lincoln, Neb. Tim graduated from Hastings College in 1967. They have two children, Kim Frances who was born 7 Dec 1966 in Lincoln, and Chris John who was born 15 Oct 1969 in Lincoln.

Kim graduated from Homer High School, Homer, Neb., in 1985, and from Western Iowa Tech Community College in Sioux City in 1987. She married Kevin Michael Schwartz on 11 Jun 1988 in Sioux City. Kevin was born 15 May 1965 in San Francisco, Calif., and graduated from East High School in Sioux City. They had Haley Renee on 30 Nov 1988 and Shelby Leigh on 15 Feb 1996, both born in Sioux City. Chris graduated from Homer High School in 1988, attended Iowa State University Veterinary College in Ames, where he graduated with a degree as a doctor of veterinary medicine in 1996. On 11 Jun 1993 he married Jill Marie Henry in Jewell, Ia. Jill, born 21 Nov 1969 in Ames, is a graduate of South Hamilton High School and the ISU Veterinary College in 1994. They have a child, Emily Jo who was born 27 Dec 1998 in Sioux Falls, S.D.

115(10)131 Michael Andre Spence

Michael was born in Winterset, Ia., on 12 Jan 1945. Immediately after graduating from Clarion High School in 1963, he went to work for the telephone company with his father, and worked for them until his retirement in 1998. He married Fayann Loux on 8 Jun 1963 at The Little Brown Church in Nashua, Ia. Their children are Timothy John who was born 8 Oct 1963, Kim Lee who was born 15 Dec 1964, and Kenneth Dean who was born 8 Nov 1966, all born in Clarion, Ia. Fayann is a housewife and they make their home in Webster City, Ia.

Tim lives in Mass., and is not married. Kim married Ronald Schumaker on 23 Jun 1984 in Webster City. She is a farmer's wife and they live in Jewell. They had Ross Alan who was born 18 Mar 1987 and Alex James who was born 13 Oct 1992, both born in Ames. Ken married Michele Anderson on 30 Jul 1994 in Story City, Ia.

Their son, Ryan Dean, was born 25 Sep 1997 in Des Moines.

115(10)132 Marilyn Louise Spence

Marilyn was born 10 Jun 1946 in Des Moines. She graduated from
high school in Estherville, Ia., then attended Estherville Junior
College before graduating from Mankato State. She earned a MS from
Georgia State University and and a six-year degree from the
University of Ga., in 1996. She is a school teacher in
Cartersville, Ga. She married William Devine on 17 Sep 1966 in
Estherville. Bill is a district manager for Armor-Swift-Eckrich,
a division of Con-Ag, where he is a promoter with supermarkets.
Marilyn has an old trunk believed to have been brought over by her
Spence ancestor from Scotland. Their child is Jennifer Jo who was
born 21 Mar 1972 in Omaha. The family is living in Cartersville,
Ga.

115(10)133 Anne Marie Spence

Anne was born in Clarion, Ia., on 23 Feb 1958. She graduated from
Estherville High School in 1976. She married Joel Benson on 23 sep
1978. They had Amanda Jo, born 23 May 1978, and Nicole, born 10
May 1981. On 14 Feb 1991 in Waterloo, she married Masudur Rahman
who is from Bangladesh. They have Faith Kay who was born 1 Jul
1994 in Waterloo. Anne works for UNI in dormitory maintenance.
Masudur is a computer expert and works for Iowa Beef in Waterloo.
They live in Cedar Falls.

115(11)311 Neal Joshua Thomson

Joshua was born 26 Mar 1966 in Germany. He was living in Munich,
Germany in 1999.

115(11)312 Jennifer Rachel Thomson

Jennifer was born 23 Jun 1970 and was living in New York City in
1999.

115(11)321 Joel Cain

Joel was employed as a chef in New Jersey, and now lives in
Columbus, Ohio. He is married to Lisa.

115(11)421 Lorene Kay Lapham

Lorene was born 10 Jan 1966. On 9 Jul 1994 she and Brian Rumbaugh
were married. Their children are Devyn who was born 5 Jan 1996 and
Peyton who was born 1 Jul 1998.

115(11)422 John Joseph Lapham

John was born 1 May 1967. He married Tina Sjong 3 Feb 1990. Tina was born 30 Dec 1967. They had Megan Olivia 3 Jun 1994, Elizabeth Berit 14 Jun 1997, and Karl Jan Kaspar 19 Jan 2001.

115(11)423 Kathy Lapham

Kathy was born 5 Nov 1972.

115(11)431 Rebecca Aileen Goold

Rebecca was born 15 Dec 1970. On 15 Jun 1991 she married Paul Tindall who was born 21 Jan 1971. They had Alden William James on 16 Nov 1999.

115(11)432 Leah Rae Goold

Leah was born 21 Dec 1973. She married Jeff Johnson on 17 Dec 1994. Jeff was born 21 May 1971.

115(11)433 William Michael Goold

William was born 7 Aug 1977. He married Corinna Gregg on 15 Apr 1998. Corinna was born 12 Aug 1978. They had William Levi in 2001. They live in Bremerton, Wash.

115(11)434 Joshua David Goold

Joshua was born 31 May 1979.
115(11)435 Rachel Joy Goold

Rachel was born 5 Jan 1983.

115(11)441 Ian Eugene Young

Ian was born 1 Oct 1973. He was living in Tempe, Az., in 2001.

115(11)511 Nathaniel Douglas Brown

Nathan was born 19 Oct 1978 in San Diego Co., Calif. He graduated from Columbia River High School in Vancouver, Wash., in 1997. In 2001 he was attending Point Loma Nazarene University.

115(11)512 Lyndsey Elizabeth Brown

Lyndsey was born 8 Jul 1981 in San Diego Co., Calif. She graduated from high school in 1999 and in 2001 was attending Trinity Western University in British Columbia.

115(11)521 Callie Jean Peterson

Callie was born 2 Aug 1972 in Everett, Wash. She is a graduate of Tumwater High School and Washington State University.

115(11)522 Jennifer Lee Peterson

Jennie was born 11 Dec 1974 in Arlington, Wash. She is a graduate of Tumwater High School and Western Washington University. She married Marcus Singer on 1 May 1999 in Lacey, Wash.

115(11)541 Shawn Thomson

Shawn was born 4 Aug 1969. Single, he works for a golf course in Portland, Ore. Shawn attended college for two years.

115(11)542 Kara Thomson

Kara was born 19 Jan 1971. She was engaged to marry Gary McGuire 31 Oct 1998. Kara attended college for two years and has a desire to become an entertainer. Gary is lead guitarist on the Sammy Kershaw band.

115(12)111 Nicholas Robert Thomson

Nicholas, who was adopted, was born 18 Mar 1970. He has two children, Emily and Nathan.

115(12)211 Schuyler Eugene Corson

Schuyler was born 23 Feb 1967. He married Kelly Sheak and they later divorced. They had two sons, Andrew Eli born 10 Aug 1986 and Zachary Benjamin born in Dec 1987. The boys live with their mother in Manhattan, Kan.

115(12)212 Andrew Craig Corson

Andrew was born 20 Nov 1962. He is a 1991 graduate of the University of Northern Iowa, is not married, and is living in Minneapolis, Minn.

115(12)231 Sandra Leigh Wolvington

Sandra was born 12 Apr 1972. She graduated from Chantilly, Va., High School in 1990, then she graduated from the University of Illinois in 1994. She married Gene Sheih on 19 Aug 1995, and they live in Maple Grove, Minn.

115(12)232 Matthew Allan Wolvington

Matthew was born 7 Sep 1974. He is a graduate of Chintilly High
School class of 1993. He graduated from the University of Eastern
Tenn. in 1997. He is not married and was a car wash manager in
Murfreesboro, Tenn. He is now a flight instructor in Nashville,
Tenn.

1161111 Betty Jane Dooley

Jane was born 23 Dec 1920 in Topeka, Kan. She attended the
University of Arizona, Tucson, and graduated in 1942 with a BA
degree in business. She married Raymond William Duffy on 17 Jul
1943. They had Raymond Terrance (Terry) on 10 Oct 1945. Raymond
William Duffy was killed while in the military in May 1947. She
secondly married George Eugene Kunde in Milwaukee, Wisc., on 27 Nov
1948. They had Gerald Alan on 27 Mar 1950 and Susan Gail on 28 Nov
1960. George died in Feb 1981.

Terry married Arda McIntyre in Dallas in 1979. They lived in
Nashville, Tenn., and divorced in 1987.

Gerald Alan "Jerry" Duffy died 31 Jul 1999.

Susan married Thomas Norstrem on 12 Oct 1991. They had Christopher
George on 28 Dec 1991. Tom and Sue divorced in Nov 1999.

1161112 James Beck Dooley

James was born 8 Dec 1922 in Topeka, Kan., and died 8 Mar 1980 in
LaJolla, Calif. James served in the U.S. Navy. He married Hazel
who survived him. They had no children.

1161121 Dot Elizabeth Taylor

Dot was born 21 Jul 1931 in Topeka, Kan. She graduated from Balboa
High School in the Panama Canal Zone in 1949. She attended the
University of Kansas and finished at Washburn University in 1972
with a degree in English and journalism. Dot worked for the Kansas
State Library then the Kansas State Historical Society as a public
information writer until her retirement in 1993. Dot is not
married. She enjoys reading, the company of her dog, and spends a
great deal of time as compiler of a newsletter for her church.

1161131 J. Warren Rosacker

J. Warren was born 17 Feb 1917 in Stafford, Kan. He married Marty
Meyer. They had no children. He was an attorney, and they live in
Portland, Ore.

1161132 Joseph Jackson Rosacker

Known as Joe, he was born 23 Jan 1919 in Stafford, Kan. On 8 Mar 1942 in Oswego, Kan., he married Anita McCullough who was born 1 Oct 1920 in Dennison, Tex. They had Cynthia Lucile on 20 Mar 1944 in Oswego, William in 1948 who survived a few weeks, John on 30 Sep 1951 in Ottawa, Kan., Mary Beth on 30 Jul 1953 and James W. on 30 Sep 1954 in Ia. Jackson died 11 Sep 1996 in Iola, Kan.

Cynthia married Warren Glimpse and they live in Alexandria, Va.

John graduated from Iola High School in 1969 and attended Pittsburgh State where he received a BSEd in 1973, a MA in history in 1974, and a JD from the University of Washburn in 1980. He is an attorney for Kansas Department of Transportation. John married Debra Kay Martin on 11 Apr 1987 in Topeka. Their children are Rebecca Ann who was born 24 Apr 1990, Jennifer Lynn who was born 18 Nov 1991 and twins Hillary Lucille and Nicole Elizabeth who were born 26 Oct 1993.

1161133 Mary Elizabeth Rosacker

Mary was born 4 Mar 1921 in Stafford, Kan. She married Maurice D. (Bud) Edens. Maurice is deceased. They had no children.

1161134 William Keith Rosacker

Bill was born 18 Oct 1923 in Stafford, Kan. He married Joyce Davis. Joyce is deceased. No children.

1161141 Jay Allen Dooley

Jay was born 25 Oct 1931 in Topeka, Kan. He attended Kansas State University and was inducted into the U.S. Army prior to graduating. He died while serving in Germany on 1 Dec 1954, and was buried in Memorial Park Cem.

1161142 Margaret Anne Dooley

Anne was born 23 Jan 1933 in Topeka, Kan. In 1958 Anne graduated from Washburn University with a BA in education. She earned a MA in library from the University of Oregon in 1968. She has taught air force-dependent children in France, Japan, and The Philippines. On 3 Sep 1970 she married Richard E. Martindale in the Lackland AFB chapel in San Antonio, Tex. Dick was born near Providence, R.I., on 10 Jun 1929. He was a graduate of the University of Texas Medical Branch, Galveston, Tex., and completed his residency in anesthesiology in 1969. He retired from the air force in 1975 as a Lt. Col. They were living in Washington state.

1161143 Stephen Peterson Dooley

Stephen was born 25 Jan 1941 in Topeka, Kan. He attended Washburn University but did not graduate. He married Sharon K. Hurd on 14 Sep 1979 in Miami, Okla. Stephen owns a heating and refrigeration business. Sharon is manager of an optical shop. They had no children together, but Sharon had three sons from a previous marriage.

1161151 Thomas Andrew McDonald

Thomas was born 10 Nov 1927 in Norton, Kan. He attended elementary schools in Alexandria, Va., including George Washington High School. He married Julia Cook in 1956, who had Martha and Jennifer by a previous marriage. Thomas attended several institutes of higher learning while taking time to serve in the U.S. Marine Corps from 1945-46. He was a professor at St. John's College in Annapolis, Md., from 1963 to 1991. Thomas and Julia were living in Maryland in 1999.

1161152 Keith Dooley McDonald

Keith was born 15 Jul 1930 in Norton, Kan., but grew up in Virginia. He attended the University of Southern Calif. for a year on a athletic (track) scholarship, and completed his education by earning a B.S. degree in electrical engineering at the University of Virginia about 1953. He married Sarah Anne Miles on 21 Jun 1954 in Martinsburg, W. Va. Their children were Mary Anne, born 18 Aug 1955; Andrew Miles, born 22 Feb 1958; Patricia Jane, born 16 Mar 1959; and John Keith, born 5 Dec 1963. Sarah died 21 Jun 1964. Keith secondly married Carolyn Boynton on 25 Jun 1980 in Alexandria, Va., where they live.

Mary Anne attended J.E.B Stewart High School in Falls Church, Va., and graduated in 1973. She earned a B.A. degree in American studies in 1978, an M.A. degree in folk lore at the University of North Carolina at Chapel Hill, and her PhD in public health in Dec 1999. Mary Anne was a folklorist from 1985 to 1991. She married Dana Loomis on 14 Jul 1984 at Chapel Hill, but kept her maiden name. Dana has a PhD in epidemiology and is a professor in the School of Public Health at Chapel Hill. Their children are Paul Webb Loomis who was born 18 Jul 1988 and Martin McDonald Loomis who was born 11 Feb 1991, both at Chapel Hill. They live in Durham, N.C.

1161153 James Kenneth McDonald

Ken was born 30 Dec 1931 in Norton, Kan. He married Chandley McCann. They are divorced after having two daughters. He holds a

Ph.D. and is employed as a historian. Ken was living in Arlington, Va., in 1999.

1161221 Karen Lynn Zendzian

Karen was born 14 Jul 1938 in Chicago, Ill. She graduated from Shorewood High School in Shorewood, Wisc., in 1956, then attended Northwestern University where she majored in English and speech. After three years at Northwestern, she married Girroy (Gus) Eugene Mansur. Gus was born 31 May 1936 in Milwaukee, Wisc., and died 28 Jul 1994 in Scottsdale, Az. He was a graduate of York High School in Elmhurst, Ill., in 1955, and briefly attended Northwestern University. He entered the U.S. Army and was an officer for two and a half years. He left the service and resumed his education at Northwestern and earned a BS in marketing and finance. After graduation, he worked in New York City, then in 1985, he moved the family to Phoenix, Ariz. There, he successfully assumed management of an electronics firm that had been floundering. Their children were Marsha Ann, Robin Elizabeth, Regan E., Deirdre Gillian, and David Stuart. Karen went back to Arizona State University after a 26-year hiatus and received dual degrees in history and political science. She worked in N.J. as a real estate broker, and now owns her own business in Ariz.

Marcia Ann was born 14 May 1960 in Lawton, Okla. She graduated from Marlboro High School in Marlboro, N.J., and went on to the University of South Carolina in Columbia. In 1982 she graduated with dual degrees in political science and philosophy. She married Jeffrey Wentworth in Columbia 10 Jan 1987. Marcia has been coaching girls and boys track and cross country teams since 1991. She had been a world-class runner for many years and worked for Nike. Jeff manages the sport's complex at Disney World in Orlando, Fla.

Robin was born 7 Sep 1961 in Evanston, Ill. She graduated from Marlboro High School in 1979, and went on to the University of South Carolina. She married Stanley Robertson in Jul 1985 in N.J. Stan is a principle in a construction firm building custom homes. They have a son, Shaun, born 17 Sep 1989, and twin girls, Ashley and Brooke, born 22 May 1992. The Robertson family lived in Scottsdale, Ariz., in 2001.

Regan was born in Baltimore, Md., 17 Jul 1967. She graduated from Red Bank Catholic High School in Red Bank, N.J., and was died 29 Nov 1985 from wounds received in a car accident while a freshman at Arizona State.

Diedre was born 24 Mar 1970 in Rochester, N.Y. She graduated in 1988 from Chapparrel High School in Scottsdale, Ariz., in 1988.

Deirdre then attended Arizona State University and earned a BA degree in philosophy in 1991. In Jan 2001 she started culinary school at Scottsdale Community College. She has worked as an insurance agent and hopes to soon be a chef. She married Tony Stirpe on 27 Sep 1997, and they were living in Chandler, Ariz., in 2001.

David was born 23 Jul 1976 in Red Bank, N.J. He graduated from Chapparrel High School in Scottsdale, Ariz., in 1994, and from ASU where he received dual degrees in political science and history in 1999. He married Erika Engstrom of Shelburn, Vt., on 4 Jul 2000 in Las Vegas, Nev. They were living in Santa Barbara, Calif., in 2001, where Erika was working towards a Ph.D. in geology. David was planning to attend law school after Erika gets her degree.

1161231 Lynne Beck

Lynne was born 21 Nov 1942 in Concordia, Kan. She graduated from the University of Miami in 1964 and became a teacher. She married Jon V. Gable 30 Dec 1064 in Miami. Jon was born 23 Jun 1938 and is a building contractor. Their son is James V. who was born 13 Oct 1969, and is a tile contractor in Tallahassee. He is married to Sarah, a RN, and they have a daughter, Shannon, born 20 Jul 1997. Lynne is looking forward to retiring in 2002.

1161232 Barbara Lee Beck

Barbara was born 19 May 1946. She married George Adams and they live in Tulsa, Okla. Barbara is a 1968 graduate of Kansas State University in Manhattan, Kan., with a degree in elementary education. They have two children, Todd Exavier, born 18 Aug 1970 in St. Louis, and Curt Matthew, born 7 May 1973 in Tulsa.

1161321 Larry Alan Beck

Larry was born 20 Apr 1942 in Indianapolis, Ind. He graduated from Greenfield, Ia., High School in 1960, then attended Iowa State University, then Drake University where he graduated with a BA in 1969. He continued his advanced education by attending graduate school at the University of Northern Texas and earned a MBE in 1971 and a MS in vocational counseling in 1984. He has taught in Dallas and in Plano for a total of 28 years and now is teaching part time at Richland Community College near Dallas, Tex. He married Mary Jo Ruckman in 1970. Mary Jo is a retired elementary school teacher. They have a son, Brian Alan, who was born 2 May 1972 in Dallas.

1161322 Jane Frances Beck

Jane was born 25 Mar 1944 in Indianapolis, Ind. She spent her

youth growing up on a farm near Greenfield, Ia.   She married Ralph
Beaulin and later they divorced.   Their children were Alison, born
about 1971, now of Denton, Tex.; and Gregory; and Andrew, both born
about 1972, of Anchorage, Alaska.   Jane kept her maiden name and in
1999 she moved from Anchorage to Sanger, Tex.   She is teaching in
Louisville, Tex.

1161323 Thomas James Beck

Thomas was born 24 Nov 1948 in Creston, Ia.   He is a graduate of
Greenfield High School, class of 1967.   Tom attended Texas A&M
University, and the University of Texas at Austin where he earned
a BBA in 1972. His career has been in sales, and he now owns Beck
Filter Sales.   On 3 Sep 1993 Tom married Patricia Wallace in San
Antonio, Tex.   Patrice has a degree in accounting and design and
is employed as an accountant.   Their son is Samuel Cronin who was
born 24 Feb 1994.   They live in San Antonio.

1161324 Daniel Joseph Beck

Daniel was born 12 Sep 1955 in Greenfield, Ia.   In 1973, he
graduated from Greenfield Community High School.   He received a BS
degree from Iowa State University in 1977, and a MS degree at the
University of Missouri-Rolla in 1986.   Currently, he is product
development manager of FOSECO, Inc., in the Steel Mill Division, in
Cleveland, Ohio.   He is not married.

1162311 Ruth Pauline Beymer

Pauline married Virgil Norris and they had Linda.   They divorced
later.   Pauline was living in Lincoln, Neb., in 1999.

1162312 Beth Maxine Beymer

Beth was born 5 Sep 1921 in Diagonal, Ia.   On 15 Aug 1940 in
Albany, Mo., she married Velmer DeFrain Stephens who was born 13
Dec 1919 in Diagonal and died there on 26 Sep 1969 of a heart
attack.   Their fifteen children are Judith Ann, Barbara Mae, David
Richard, Donald Lee, Joan Kay, James Edward, Jack Alan, Jerry
Wayne, Susan Jean, Kathryn Joyce, John Edwin, Stephen Jay, Kenneth
Paul, Sheryl Diane and Betty Jane.

(1) Judith was born 23 Dec 1940 in Diagonal.   On 13 Sep 1959 she
married John Oliver Cason who was born 29 Jan 1941 in Star City,
Ark. They had Joy Diane, Joel Paul, and Jeffrey John. Joy was born
13 Sep 1960 at Mt. Ayr, Ia.   Joy married Wayne Franklin Davis on 13
Jun 1981 in Creston, Ia.   Their children are Benjamin John, born 15
Mar 1984, and Anne Louise, born 24 Sep 1985, both born in Creston.
Joel was born 12 Dec 1961 at St. Ignace, Mich.   On 20 Apr 1985, he

married Brenda Teal; they divorced in 1987. Secondly, Joel married Sandra Carol Copeland on 29 Apr 1988 in Macon, Ga. Sandra was born 17 Jan 1965 at McRae, Ga. Joel and Sandra had John Tyler, born 22 Jun 1989, and Storm Conner, born 26 Jul 1994, both in Macon, Ga. Jeffrey was born 27 Dec 1963 in Sault Ste. Marie, Mich. On 29 May 1993 he married Leanne Marie Robinson in Cedarville, Mich. Leanne was born 18 Dec 1966 at St. Ignace, Mich.

(2) Barbara was born 8 Dec 1941 in Diagonal, Ia. On 31 Jul 1960, she married Cecil Leroy Hinshaw in Diagonal. Cecil was born 22 Apr 1941 at Lenox, Ia. Their children are Deborah Rene, who was born 2 Dec 1960 in Des Moines, and Jennifer Ann, born 25 Nov 1974 at Englewood, Colo. Deborah married Doran Scott Adams on 16 Apr 1984 at Estes Park, Colo. They divorced in 1987. Their children are Justin David who was born 11 Mar 1982 at Englewood, Colo., and Ashley Beth who was born 21 Apr 1985 at Denver, Colo. Secondly, Deborah married Brian Charles Moritz at Lake Tahoe, Nev. Brian was born 26 Mar 1959 at Rockford, Ill. Debby and Brian had Allen Brian who was born 31 May 1995 at Rockford, Ill., and Emily Mae who was born 9 Jan 1999 at Rockford. Jennifer married Robert Richard Meinke on 29 Nov 1998 at Rockford, Ill. Robert was born 25 Jul 1972 in Belvidere, Ill.

(3) David was born 2 Dec 1942 in Diagonal, Ia. On 15 Aug 1965, he married Nancy Ellen Blunck in Ringgold, Co., Ia. They had Pamela Kay and Jill Marie. Pamela was born 23 Mar 1966 at Mt. Ayr, Ia. Jill was born 29 May 1968 at Mt. Ayr, and married Michael Zeller on 15 Jul 1989 in Des Moines, Ia. They were divorced in 1990. Secondly, Jill married Tony Crumley on 15 Aug 1990 in Des Moines. Jill and Tony had David William on 8 Oct 1990 in Des Moines, Emily Margaret on 5 Jul 1992 in Columbus, Ohio, Caleb Anthony on 21 Dec 1994 in Columbus, and Rachel Kaylee on 30 Jan 1996 in Columbus.

(4) Donald was born 11 Dec 1943 in Creston, Ia. He married Julia Anne Haley on 19 Dec 1966 in Mt. Ayr, Ia. Julia was born 12 Feb 1948 in Creston, Ia. Their children are Amy Lynn, Tracy Renee and Margi Ann. Amy was born 10 Aug 1967 in Mt. Ayr, Ia. She married John Andrew Ford on 8 Aug 1987 in Maloy, Ia. John was born 29 Oct 1967. They are the parents of twins, Christopher John and Andrew John, born 25 Aug 1984 in Keokuk, Ia., who were adopted by John and Amy on 29 Jul 1991. Tracy was born 4 Nov 1969 in Mt. Ayr, Ia. She and Scott Eric Giles were married on 4 Sep 1993 in Mt. Ayr. Scott was born 18 Mar 1964 in Maryville, Mo. They are the parents of Caitlin Renee who was born 7 Sep 1994 and Connor Eric who was born 27 Mar 1997, both in Des Moines. Margi was born 8 Sep 1974 in Mt. Ayr, and married Joseph Shane Boord on 27 May 1995 in Diagonal, Ia. Joseph was born 2 Jun 1972 in Leon, Ia.

(5) Joan was born 29 Apr 1945 in Creston, Ia. On 5 Mar 1966 she

and Gerald Lee Bond were married in Diagonal, Ia. Gerald was born 21 Aug 1946 in Hastings, Neb. Their children are Brent Lee and Eric Wade. Brent was born 9 Nov 1967 in Lincoln, Neb. He married Wanda Jean Wurdeman on 27 Nov 1992 in St. Edward, Neb. Wanda was born 14 Feb 1969 in Albion, Neb. Their children are Grant Lee who was born 7 Apr 1993 in Lincoln, Neb., Bailey Mae who was born 21 Nov 1994 in Lincoln, and Gage Stephen who was born 3 Jul 1996 in Austin, Tex. Eric was born 19 Oct 1971 in Albion, Neb., and married Heidi Elizabeth Gibson on 14 Feb 1999 in Diller, Neb. Heidi was born 22 Nov 1972. They had Hunter Cole who was born 15 Mar 1998 in Lincoln, Neb.

(6) James was born 5 Nov 1946 in Creston, Ia. On 14 Aug 1968, he married Rose Elaine Ahu in Las Vegas, Nev. Rose was born 23 Jan 1948. They were divorced in 1969. Secondly, James married Sally Saville on 17 May 1971 in Cedarville, Mich. Sally was born 23 May 1950 in Redding, Ia. They had Ryan James who was born 23 Aug 1975 in Council Bluffs, Ia., Scott Patrick who was born 18 May 1978 in Des Moines, and Kevin Paul who was born 27 Dec 1980 in Des Moines.

(7) Jack was born 9 Nov 1947 in Creston, Ia. On 10 Apr 1982, he married Janice Danielson in Diagonal, Ia. Janice was born 11 Sep 1960. Jack and Janice had Matthew Duane who was born 17 Aug 1977 in Creston, Ia., and Sean Caleb who was born 8 Feb 1983 in Des Moines. Jack and Janice divorced in 1988.

(8) Jerry was born 12 Jun 1949 in Creston, Ia. On 4 May 1968, he married Barbara Elaine Jezek in Tingley, Ia. Barbara was born 18 Jan 1951 in Diagonal, Ia. They are the parents of Lesa Jo and Terri Lynne. Lesa was born 26 Aug 1968 in Mt. Ayr and married Roger Dolecheck on 31 Aug 1991 in Diagonal, Ia. They had twins, Kirsten Lynne and Kyle Wayne who were born 5 Sep 1997 in Des Moines. Terri was born 2 Aug 1970 in Mt. Ayr, and married Matthew Todd Higgins on 2 Sep 1995 in Diagonal, Ia. Matthew was born 11 Oct 1970 in Creston. Their child is Alyssa Nicole who was born 28 Sep 1997 in Des Moines.

(9) Susan was born 28 Jul 1950 in Creston. She married John W. Swenson on 26 Dec 1970 in Maryville, Mo., and divorced in 1987. They had Tami Sue, Rebecca Beth, and Andrea Lynn. Tami was born 14 Aug 1971 in Maryville, Mo. Rebecca was born 18 Nov 1976 in Iowa City, Ia. Andrea was born 2 Mar 1979 in Iowa City, and married Marc Allen Morris on 26 Sep 1998 in Littleton, Colo. Marc was born 24 Nov 1976 in Aurora, Colo. They have a son, Kerouac Dakota (Jack) who was born 7 Aug 1997 in Littleton. Secondly, Susan married Duane Edward Keesen on 2 Jan 1993 in Littleton, Colo. Duane was born 21 Jan 1944 in Denver.

(10) Kathryn was born 26 Nov 1951 in Mt. Ayr, Ia. On 23 Apr 1952,

she married Jon Goodale in Diagonal, Ia. Jon was born 23 Apr 1952 in Mt. Ayr. Their children are Cindy Jo, Billi Jean, Mike Adam and Kelli Ann. Cindy was born 27 Jul 1976 in Creston, Ia., and married Darin Ray Goins on 12 Jun 1999 in Diagonal, Ia. Darin was born 30 Dec 1975 in Creston, Ia. Billi was born 30 Mar 1978, Mile was born 8 May 1980, and Kelli was born 10 Apr 1982, all born in Creston.

(11) John was born 14 Apr 1953 in Mt. Ayr, Ia. On 10 Jun 1978 he married Karleen Ann Cronbaugh in Lenox, Ia. Karleen was born 15 Dec 1954 in Marengo, Ia. They are the parents of Adam John who was born 10 May 1981, Abby Lynn who was born 27 Feb 1984 and Alex John who was born 23 Jul 1985, all born in Creston.

(12) Stephen was born 14 Jul 1954 in Mt. Ayr. Ia. On 26 Dec 1986 he married Eydie Lou Deal in Jefferson, Ia. Eydie was born 25 feb 1945 in Jefferson, Ia.

(13) Kenneth was born 19 Oct 1955 in Mt. Ayr. On 25 May 1975 he married Brenda Kay Wurster in Clearfield, Ia. Brenda was born 11 Feb 1957 in Creston, Ia. They had Joshua Joe on 27 Jun 1979, Jacob Paul on 27 Sep 1981 and Joni Kay on 31 May 1985, all born in Creston.

(14) Sheryl was born 24 Aug 1957 in Mt. Ayr. She and Jim Brown, born 16 Nov 1954 in Omaha, were married 29 Jul 1978 in Osceola, Ia. They had Jeremiah Ely on 18 Oct 1979 in Ottumwa, Ia., and Sarah Jane on 13 Jul 1983 in Denver, Colo. Sheryl and Jim divorced in 1995. Secondly, Sheryl married Wesley Keith Benedict on 15 Feb 1997 in Truro, Ia.

(15) Betty was born 17 Nov 1958 in Mt. Ayr. On 18 Jun 1977 she was married to William Walter Robinson in Diagonal, Ia. Bill was born 13 Sep 1954. They had Amanda Ann on 24 May 1986 in Creston, Ia. Betty and Bill divorced in 1995. Secondly, Betty married Timothy Joe Stalker on 11 Jul 1998 in Creston. He was born 12 Apr 1951 in Creston.

1162313 Ronald Arthur Beymer

Ronald married Mildred. Their children are Anne, Ronald, Ricky, and Nancy. Anne married James Norris and had Lori Angela.

1162321 Robert Byron Greene

Robert was born 12 Mar 1921 in Diagonal, Ia. On 11 Aug 1944 he married Bernice Lucille Lytle in Akron, Ohio. Their children are Linda Louise, born 3 Sep 1950 in Havre de Grace, Md., and Stephen Robert, born 11 Aug 1954 in Baltimore, Md. In 1999 Bob was living in Bel Air, Md.

In 1988 Linda was living at the naval air station in Tokyo, Japan.
Stephen married Johanna Mary Knapschaefer on 16 Apr 1983 in
Washington, D.C. Johanna was born 15 Mar 1956 in Philadelphia, Pa.
They had twins, Alicia Dale and Monica Robyn born 25 Jun 1983 in
Washington, D.C., and Philip Edward born 5 May 1986 in Silver
Spring, Md.

1162322 Shirley Louise Greene

Shirley was born 16 Apr 1923 in Diagonal, Ia. She married Donald
Richard Phoenix on 20 Jan 1941 in Princeton, Mo. Donald was born
11 Feb 1920 in Dallas, Ia., and died 12 May 1989, probably in
Fairfield Bay, Ark. Their children are Phyllis Ann, born 15 Aug
1941; Sharon Louise, born 29 Jun 1943; John Richard, born 22 Mar
1947; and Robert David, born 4 Apr 1961.

Phyllis is a school teacher in the Des Moines area, and is not
married. Sharon Louise married James Pickett on 26 Nov 1966. John
married Diana. Robert is not married.

1162323 Phyllis Marie Greene

Phyllis Marie was born in 1927 in Gravity, Ia. She married Raymond
Weikum 13 Jul 1948 in Des Moines, Ia. Ray was born 30 Aug 1926 in
Hazelton, Neb. Their children are Roberta Kay born 18 Sep 1949 in
Riverdale, N.D., Dessa Ray born 11 Jan 1951 in Walla Walla, Wash.,
and Marlin Bryce born 7 Jun 1953. Roberta married David Linn Evans
on 1 Sep 1968 in Harvey, N.D.

1162324 Alberta Jeannette Greene

Alberta was born 30 Jul 1929 in Diagonal, Ia. She married Alfred
Lawrence Brown 4 Mar 1962. Alfred was born 10 Dec 1931 in
Stoneham, Mass. They had Lawrence Edwin born 19 Nov 1963 and
Kendall Erwin born 20 Feb 1965, both born in Watsonville, Calif.

Lawrence married Susan Gail George on 6 May 1985 at Keene, Tex.
Susan was born 12 Mar 1963 in Nacogdoches, Tex. Their children are
Alexandra Gwyneth born 15 Jul 1990 in Chicago, Ill., and Elwin
Miles born 4 Dec 1991 in Seneca, S.C.

1162341 Byron Dale Jessup

Byron was born 10 Mar 1935 in Farson, Ia. He married Beverly May
Wall on 17 Aug 1968 in St. Paul, Minn. Beverly was born 12 Mar
1938. Byron graduated in 1953 from Central High School in Omaha,
Neb., then went on to college. He earned a BA degree at Wheaton
College in Illinois in 1957. He served as a 2nd Lt. in the U.S.
Army. He was a high school English teacher. Beverly graduated from

Wilson High School in St. Paul, and attended Mounds Midway Nursing School. Later, she worked as a teacher's aide. They had David Eric on 29 Apr 1975 in Burlingame, Calif., and Darin Dwight on 11 Oct 1978 in Burlingame.

David earned a BA at Rice University in Texas, and was pursuing a MA at the University of Alaska. Darin was attending the University of Minnesota in 2000.

1162342 Dwight Wiley Jessup

Dwight was born 23 Dec 1937 in Iowa Falls, Ia. On 6 Jun 1959 in St. Paul, Minn., he married Karin Marie Carlson who was born 4 May 1938. Dwight graduated in 1956 from Jefferson High School in Denver, Colo., then in 1960 he earned a BA at Bethel College in St. Paul. In 1978 he obtained a Ph.D. in history at the University of Minnesota. He is dean and v-p at Taylor University in Upland, Ind. Karin attended Johnson High School in St. Paul, then Bethel College where she earned a BA in 1960. She received a special education certificate from the University of Minnesota in 1975. Their children are Randall David who was born 1 Jan 1961, Elisa Marie who was born 24 Apr 1963, and Colleen Michelle who was born 12 Apr 1967, all born in St. Paul.

Randall married Janet Lynn Turnquist on 27 Aug 1983 in St. Paul, Minn. Janet was born 6 Jan 1960. Randall graduated from Kellogg High School in St. Paul in 1979, then earned a BA from Bethel College in St. Paul, a BS in engineering at the University of Minnesota and a MBA at UM. He is working as a chemical engineer at Eco Lab in Minnesota. Janet holds a MA in journalism from the University of Minnesota and has been an editor for technical journals, in addition to being a housewife. Their children are Marc David who was born 4 May 1988, Micah Daniel who was born 30 Jul 1990, and Elise Corrine who was born 8 Sep 1994, all born in St. Paul.

Elisa is a graduate of Kellogg High School in St. Paul, and earned a BA at Taylor University in Upland, Ind., 1985. She married Jay Riley Case on 22 Jun 1985 in St. Paul. Jay, born 26 Sep 1961, earned a BA at Taylor University in 1985, then a Ph.D. in history at Notre Dame University in 1999. He is now a history professor at Malone College in Canton, Ohio. Their children are Karin Ruth who was born 23 Oct 1987, Brenna Nicole who was born 4 Dec 1898, and Kelsey Marie who was born 20 Jan 1991, all born in Kenya, Africa.

Colleen is a graduate of Kellogg High School and Bethel College where she earned a BA in 1989. In 1999 she received a MA in education at the University of Minnesota, and is now a teacher and a housewife. On 27 May 1989 she and Douglas Brian Inwards were

married in St. Paul. Douglas was born 3 Apr 1967. He is a
graduate of the University of Minnesota with a MA in social work.
Their children are Emily Grace, born 15 Jun 1996, and Megan Taylor,
born 9 Jul 1998, both born in St. Paul.

1162431 Mary Belle Doty

Mary Belle was born 8 May 1946 in El Dorado, Kan. She graduated
from Wichita State University with a degree in music education. On
1 Jun 1968 she married Joe David Leach who was from Groesbeck, Tex.
Mary Belle is a teacher in music education-fine arts head in
Houston, Tex. She is active in her church where she plays for
services and coordinates children's choirs. She is another of
several relatives who has visited Scotland and Dhuloch Farm, which
she did in 1975. They have a daughter, Meredith Doty, who was born
12 Apr 1981 and graduated from high school in 1999.

1162511 Richard Charles Amick

Richard was born 2 Mar 1933. He was married on 10 Sep 1955 in
Minneapolis, Minn., to Jacqueline Lehman. They had Mark Charles,
Kurt William, and Karla Ann. They live in Webster, Wisc.

1162512 Marjorie Ellen Amick

Marjorie was born 21 May 1936 in Sioux City, Ia. She married J.
Kent Jerome on 10 Nov 1956 in Des Moines, Ia. Kent was born 1 Nov
1936. Marjorie is a 1954 graduate of West Des Moines High School.
She attended Stevens College in Columbia, Mo., for two years. Kent
is secretary-treasure of Iowa Telephone Association, and will
retire at the end of 1999. Their children are Jeffrey Kent, born
in Jun 1957; Joni Kay, born in Oct 1959; Pamela Sue, born in 1964;
and Bradley Dane, born in 1966.

1162513 Martha Ann Amick

Martha was born 31 Mar 1941. She married Robert Glenn Lindsey and
they had David and Brian. They make their home in Evergreen, Colo.

1162521 Verlee Fay Jones

Verlee was born 13 Jun 1931 in Davenport, Ia. She attended
Hanawalt Elementary School, Callanan Junior High, and graduated
from Roosevelt High in 1949. Verlee finished her education by
earning a BBA from Westminster College in Pa., in 1953. She married
20 Jun 1953, in Des Moines, James Sanky Clinefelter who was born 14
Apr 1930 in New Castle, Pa. James graduated from New Castle, Pa.,
High School, then obtained a BA degree from Westminster College. He
graduated with a Master's in Divinity in 1955 from Pittsburgh Xenia

Theological Seminary in Pittsburgh. He furthered his education at
Iowa State University in Ames with a master's in education. Their
children are Candace (Candy) Lee, born 29 Aug 1955 in Pittsburgh;
twins Steven Frank and David Alvin, born 23 Dec 1957 in Miami,
Fla., and John Garroway, born 1 May 1964 in Miami. They were of
Sun City Center, Fla.

Candace attended McNab Elementary in Pompano Beach, Fla., then Ames
High School where she graduated in 1973, Mankato State Unversity
where she earned a BS in 1977, and the University of St. Thomas in
Minneapolis with a MBA in 1995. She married Ronald L. Bownan on 18
Mar 1978 in Ames, Ia. Ron was born 2 Apr 1952. He graduated from
Ames High School in 1971 and from Mankato State University with a
BA in 1976. They have Jennifer Estella, born 21 Dec 1984 in
Minneapolis, and Alison Faye, born 15 Apr 1986 in Barrington, Ill.

Steven attended McNab Elementary in Pompano Beach, Fla., Central
Jr. High in Ames, Ames High School from which he graduated in 1976,
the University of Northern Iowa, and San Diego State University. He
married Patricia Ellen Bode on 16 Apr 1988 in Pella, Ia. Patricia
graduated from the University of Iowa in dental hygiene in 1983.
They have two children, Steven Daniel, born 10 May 1990 in Las
Vegas, Nev., and Rachel Elizabeth, born 25 Apr 1993 in Las Vegas.

David graduated from Ames High School in Ames in 1976. John
graduated in 1982.

1162522 Susan Marie Jones

Susan was born 4 Sep 1932. She married 18 Nov 1956 Thomas Daubert
in New Castle, Pa. Thomas was born 6 Oct 1932. They reside in
Miami, Fla. Their children are Timothy Bruce who was born 15 Oct
15, 1957; Deborah Marie who was born 24 Apr 1960; and Katherine Sue
who was born 7 May 1961.

Tim married Cathy Shimko on 4 Mar 1995. Cathy was born 6 Jan 1961.
Deborah married Frederick Schirmann on 4 Oct 1980; they were
divorced in Apr 1989. They had Jonathan Charles on 6 Dec 1981, and
twins Brian Thomas and Christopher Todd on 24 May 1983.

Katherine has a son, Anthony Edward Daubert, born 10 Jan 1982.

1162523 Nancy Anne Jones

Nancy was born 2 Jan 1939 in Des Moines. She graduated from TR
High School and attended Iowa State University for two years. She
married Robert Edwin Fisher on 29 May 1959 in Des Moines. Nancy
became a homemaker; Robert was born 30 Jun 1937 in Akron, Ohio,
and graduated from Iowa State University with a degree in

Engineering. At Northern Illinois University, Robert earned a MBA.
He was a Captain in the U.S. Army. They had James Scott who was
born 1 Oct 1960 in Des Moines and Sharon (Sherri) Lynn on 23 Oct
1962 in Ft. Leonard Wood, Mo.

J. Scott is a graduate of Iowa State University and from Oklahoma
with an MBA. He was a Captain in the U.S. Army. He married
Theresa Lynn Brunkow on 30 Dec 1983. From a previous marriage,
Theresa had Jeremy Alan Sime who was born 9 Dec 1981 in Ames, Ia.
J. Scott and Theresa had James Scott Fisher, Jr., born 30 Apr 1986
in Salinas, Calif., and Alexander Todd Fisher, born 15 Apr 1992 in
Ft. Sill, Okla.

Sharon is a graduate of the University of Illinois.

1162524 Thomas Alvin Jones

Thomas was born 7 Oct 1943 in Des Moines. Tom attended grade
school in Des Moines, and graduated from Benson High School in
Omaha, Neb. He entered Iowa State University where he graduated
with a BS degree in Industrial Engineering. He furthered his
education at the University of Iowa, earning an MBA. He served in
the U.S. Army as a lieutenant from 1969 to 1971. Tom is now
employed as an information and technology management consultant.
After living in Calif., Tex. and S.C., they are back in Tex. Tom
is very active in his church community, enjoys playing golf,
teaching and fishing. He married Sharon Marie Sorensen in Ames,
Ia., on 26 Aug 1967. They had Mark Thomas on 2 Feb 1971 and Karen
Renae on 22 Sep 1972; both were born in Berkeley, Calif.

Mark married Wendy Gaskamp on 7 Oct 1996.

Karen married Shannon Papas on 6 Jun 1998. Shannon was born 7 Dec
1968.

1162531 Laurie Jayne Amick

Laurie was born 5 Jun 1948 in Duluth, Minn. She was a 1966
graduate of International Falls High School, then attended Drake
University in Des Moines for two years before working for an
insurance company. She attended a vocational school in Ankeny,
Ia., and found work in a printing plant where she worked until
1980, then she moved to Minneapolis. Laurie then worked for
another printing firm until 1990 and has taken early retirement due
to back surgery. In 1969 she married William Cutler and later they
were divorced. Their child is Jonas Philip. Laurie has not
remarried and is living in Minneapolis.

Jonas was born 10 Nov 1969 in Des Moines, Iowa. He attended

Minnehaha Academy in Minneapolis, then elisted in the U.S. Marine Corps in the fall of 1989. After receiving an honorable discharge he entered the University of Minnesota and graduated in 1998 with a degree in political science. He is working for the VA at Fort Snelling, Minn.

1162532 Birt Clyde Amick

Birt was born 24 Jun 1950 in Duluth, Minn. He graduated from International Falls High School in 1968, then attended vocational school in Hibbing, Minn. He earned an associate of arts degree at Rainy River Community College in International Falls while working full time for Boise Cascade Paper Co. In 1973, he went to Juneau, Alaska, where he worked for a plumbing firm. Birt attained Alaskan residency and moved to Fairbanks where he obtained work on the Alaska Pipeline as a pipefitter. He also worked for the city of Fairbanks for two years before entering into semi-retirement. He is not married and lives in the home he purchased in Fox, Alaska.

1162533 Jabez Hill Amick

Jabez was born 19 Sep 1951 in Duluth. He is a 1969 graduate of International Falls High School. He worked for Boise Cascade Paper Company and graduated from Northwest Electronics School in Minneapolis, then finished his advanced education at the University of Minnesota where he graduated in 1996 with a degree in accounting. He is a C.P.A. in Minneapolis.

1162611 Jeanette Lavonne Larsen

(From the family history prepared by Jeanette Larsen). Jeanette was born 25 Dec 1924 in Shelby County, Ia. She graduated from high school in Atlantic, Ia., in 1942, and then taught rural school for a year. On 28 May 1944 she married Earl Anderson in Atlantic. Earl was born 22 Apr 1923, and attended Iowa State College in Ames before he entered the U.S. Army during World War II. Earl served in the Philippines, Korea, and the U.S. He retired as Regional Director of Railroads, U.S. Department of Transportation. Jeanette attended Indian Valley Colleges in Marin County, Calif., and in 1979 she received an associate degree as a medical assistant. Jeanette is a member of the D.A.R. and is active in genealogy research. Their children are Carol Jeanette, Dwight Earl, and Bruce Kevin. Jeanette and Earl make their home in West Linn, Ore.

Carol was born 17 Mar 1947 in Sioux City, Ia. "Jeanie" graduated from high school in Lake Oswego, Ore., in 1965 and from Oregon State University in 1970. She married Dennis White on 14 Feb 1970 in Portland, Ore. Dennis is a funeral director and operates Mount Scott Funeral Home in Portland. Their children are Edward Earl, born 16 Dec 1972, and Andrea Jeanette, born 14 Jun 1974. Dwight was born 15 Nov 1948 in Elmhurst, Ill. He graduated from high school in Lake Oswego, Ore., and from Willamette University in Salem, Ore., in 1970. He served in the U. S. Army from 1970 to 1973. Later he worked for the Department of Defense doing computer programming. This work has taken him to Alice Springs, Australia, where he spent two years. While he was stationed there, Earl, Jeanette, Bernice, and Annabelle visited him. Dwight married Frances Stribling on 16 Feb 1985 in Warrenton, Va. Frances was born 30 Nov 1948 and she had Karey and Richard from a previous marriage (to Harley Brooks) which Dwight adopted. They spent three years in England before making Markham, Va., their home where Dwight works. Frances has used book stores in Centerville and in Manassas. Their children are Richard Stone, born 25 Sep 1975; Karey McKay, born 26 Feb 1977; Carolanne McKay, born 22 Aug 1985; and Clayton Hubert, born 18 Mar 1987.

Bruce was born 27 Jan 1954 in Geneva, Ill. He graduated from high school in Lake Oswego, Ore., in 1972. He then enlisted in the U.S. Army Air Force for five years during which he spent time in Thailand. On 8 Apr 1977 he married Martha Amelia Sheppard Anderson at Holloman Air Force Base, N.M. Amelia was born 11 Nov 1950 in Austin, Tex. She had been previously married to Lief Eric Anderson and their three children were adopted by Bruce. The children are Eric, born 5 Jun 1973 in Pasadena, Tex.; Martha Jean, born 5 Jun 1973 in Lakenheath, England; Brian Jack, born 2 Oct 1975 in N.M.; and Jennifer Marie, born 13 Jul 1979 in Portland, Ore. Bruce and Amelia were living in Oregon City. Bruce attended Portland State University and was employed by the U.S. Bank of Oregon as Vice-President of Equipment Control.

1162612 Theodore Larsen Jr.

Theodore was born 24 Aug 1926 near Kirkman, Ia. He graduated from Atlantic High School, then helped his father on the farm. On 25 Feb 1947 he married Lois Lavon Deskins in Wessington Springs, S.D. Ted drove a truck for Walnut Grove Products while Lavon worked in the company office in Atlantic, Ia. They had Thelma Ann, Gail Theodore, Glen Edward, Peggy Bernice, Lois Denise, Sandra Kay, and William (Bill) Allen.

Thelma was born 18 Sep 1947 in Atlantic. She graduated from Atlantic High School and then from Iowa State University in Ames. On 25 May 1969 she married Clint Ruby in Atlantic. They were divorced in 1984. Thelma worked for an accounting firm in Red Oak, Ia. The children from this marriage were Lisa Renee, born 29 Jun 1972, and Kimberly Lynn, born 22 Sep 1974.

Gail was born 21 Apr 1949 in Atlantic, Ia., and graduated from high school there. He completed a technical training course at Iowa Western Community in farm mechanics. Gail married Donna Sams on 4 Apr 1970 in Avoca, Ia. Donna had a beauty shop in her home in Emerson, Ia. Their children were Christina Renee, born 10 Oct 1970, and Trisha Marie, born 31 May 1976.

Glen was born 28 Oct 1951 in Atlantic, Ia. He served in the U.S. Navy during the Vietnam War as a gunner's mate. After eight years in the Navy, Glen became Lieutenant on the Atlantic Police Force and was working towards a degree in law enforcement. He married on 8 Jul 1972 Gloria Batolonas in Olongapo, Zambles, The Philippines. Their children are Thomas, born 12 Jun 1974 at Subic Bay, The Philippines, and Christopher Svend, born 2 Jul 1976 at Great Lakes Naval Hospital.

Peggy was born 19 Aug 1954 in Atlantic. After high school she took business courses at Iowa Western Community College. She worked as a florist in Loveland, Colo. She married on 1 Sep 1973 Jeffrey Hetrick; they divorced in 1978. Secondly, Peggy married on 13 May 1984 Terry Cooper in Atlantic. Peggy and Jeff had Cherese Michelle Hetrick, born 29 Jan 1975, and Corey Michael Hetrick, born 26 Nov 1978.

Lois was born 12 Aug 1956 in Atlantic. She graduated from Atlantic High School, then married Gregory Patrick Newberg on 10 Aug 1975. Pat has worked in the insurance business since graduating from Northwest Missouri State College. Pat has worked for Mutual of Omaha. Their home is in Oakland, Ia. Their children are Jason Scott, born 21 May 1978; Brett Tyler, born 2 Dec 1980 in Atlantic; and Zachary Lee, born 12 May 1986 in Council Bluffs.

Sandra was born 9 Dec 1957 in Atlantic. She is a graduate of Atlantic High School and of Northern Iowa Teachers College in Cedar Falls, Ia. She coached soft ball and other sports for three years. A back injury ended her career as a coach, and she then worked for an insurance company in Omaha.

William (Bill) was born 22 Jul 1959 in Atlantic. He completed courses in auto mechanics at Iowa Western Community College and was employed at Henningsen Construction Co. in Atlantic.

1162613 Nellie Faye Larsen

Nellie was born 26 Mar 1936 in Atlantic. She graduated from Atlantic High School, and from Dana College in Blair, Neb., in 1958. She met Raymond Hagberg in college, and they were later married 3 Jun 1956 in Atlantic. Ray was born 5 Nov 1930, and was a graduate of Spencer High School. He served in the U.S. Army and was stationed in Japan. He completed his advanced education at

Dana College, then obtained a master's degree from the University of Minnesota. He was ordained in Tanzania, East Africa in 1973. Nellie and Ray were called as missionaries for the Lutheran Church to Tanzania in 1958. Their children are Lynnae Caroline, Rochelle Jean, and Vaughan Thomas.

Lynnae was born 12 Jan 1959 in Arusha, Tanzania, East Africa. She graduated from high school in East Africa, then she returned to the U.S. to attend Augustana Lutheran at Sioux Falls, S.D., where she graduated in 1981 with a BS degree in nursing. She was a Public Health Nurse in Minneapolis, and worked toward a master's degree in public health. Lynnae married Donald Winnes on 3 Oct 1992 in Minneapolis.

Rochelle was born 20 May 1961 in Arusha, Tanzania, East Africa. After high school in Africa, she attended Augustana College where she graduated in 1983. She married Paul Funk 14 Jun 1986 in Minneapolis. After a year in Germany training for the mission field, they returned to Minneapolis where Paul worked on his Ph.D. in science. Their children are Lynnae Marie, born 23 Jun 1988 and Zachary Raymond, born 28 Sep 1990.

Vaughan was born 27 Jun 1963 in Arusha, Tanzania, East Africa. After high school in Africa, He attended South Dakota State University and received a degree in electrical engineering in 1985. He met Aleda Decker in college and they were married 20 Jul 1985 in Huron, S.D. Aleda also received a degree in electrical engineering. They lived in Saipan where they were employed by the Far East Broadcasting Co. They had Rachel Renae, born 22 Jun 1990, and Luke Hagberg, born 4 Dec 1991.

1162621 George Lewis Saville

George was born 30 Sep 1926 at Redding, Ia. He married Dorothy May Jeanes at the Little Brown Church in the Vale, Nashua, Ia. George received his college degree from Northwest Missouri State Teachers College in Maryville, Mo. He taught at Breckenridge, Mo., and Diagonal, Ia., then devoted full time to being a farmer. Dorothy was a teacher's aid and taught kindergarten in Diagonal. She then worked in the office of the Mount Ayr Community Hospital. They had Sally Jean, Dennis Franklin, Martha Joyce, Neil Lewis, Timothy Leland, and Linda Louise.

Sally was born 23 May 1950 in Redding, Ia. She married James (Jim) Edward Stephens on 17 May 1971 in Cedarville, Mich. Jim was born 5 Nov 1946 in Diagonal. (See James Stephens at 1162312). Both have degrees from Northwest Missouri State University. Sally worked for Meredith Book Publishing Co. in Des Moines. Jim was a farm manager for Farmers National Company in

Omaha, Neb. Their children are Ryan James, born 23 Aug 1975; Scott Patrick, born 18 May 1978; and Kevin Paul, born 27 Dec 1980.

Dennis was born 27 Nov 1951 in Redding. He married on 29 Nov 1986 Timi Sue Price who was born 25 Mar 1959 in Bowling Green, Ohio. Dennis received a BS degree and a MS degree in wildlife management and recreation at the University of Wyoming. Timi worked for the Forest Service. Dennis works for the Bureau of Land Management and lived in Milner, Colo. They had Amy Lynn, born 14 Sep 1990.

Martha was born 15 Feb 1954 in Redding, Ia. She married 6 Aug 1977 Mike Swanson in Redding, Ia. Mike was born 6 Jun 1954. He has worked as a salesman. Martha earned a degree in Home Economics at NMSU, Maryville, Mo.   She taught for three years, and did bookkeeping in Mount Ayr. They lived in Council Bluffs and had David Michael, born 16 Jul 1982 in Leon, and Bethany Jo, born 5 Nov 1985 in Leon.

Neil was born 15 Oct 1955 in Redding. He received a certificate in farm mechanics from Southwestern Community College. He worked for McMurray Construction in Wyoming.

Timothy was born 9 Feb 1958 in Redding. On 4 Jun 1989 he married Lesa Reynolds near Delphos, Ia. He has worked as a construction worker. Lesa had children from previous marriages(?): Joe Garritt and Ashley Reynolds.

Linda was born 31 Aug 1959 in Mount Ayr. She married 24 Jun 1984 Gary Dean Hosfield in Redding, Ia. Gary was born 18 May 1954. Linda received a degree in Respiratory Therapy at Iowa Methodist Medical Center in Des Moines. Gary farms near Mount Ayr where they live. They had Jennifer Rose, born 29 Mar 1988 in Des Moines.

1162622 Eva Saville

Eva was born 19 Dec 1928 in Redding. On 18 Nov 1945 she married Richard Ariel Knapp who was born 7 Sep 1925. Eva taught in a rural school in Missouri and attended summer school at NMSC, Maryville, Mo. They were divorced in 1984. Their children were Cheryl Winifred, born 6 Dec 1946; Richard Lee, born 25 Apr 1951; Margaret Elaine, born 2 Jun 1953; Charles Roy, born 28 Mar 1957; Mark Andrew, born 30 Sep 1959; and Benjamin Joseph, born 11 Jul 1967.

Cheryl married in Jul 1966, on Paris Island, Va., to Ralph Kobbe. Ralph served in the U.S. Army, then sold feed in Grant City, Mo. Their children were Kristeena Thursa, born 2 Mar 1967 in Germany, and Kenneth Ivan, born 15 mar 1969 in Mount Ayr, Ia. Later they were divorced. Cheryl works for an insurance company in Boston, Mass. Secondly, Cheryl married Jerry South on 25 Aug 1990 in

Billerica, Mass.

Kristeena graduated from Worth County High School in 1986 and went to college at Maryville, Mo., for a year. She then worked in a rest home.

Kenneth graduated from Worth County High School in 1987 and worked for his father in a feed store in Grant City, Mo. He married in Feb 1987 Kathy Thompson, and they had Kendall Ivan , born 22 Aug 1987, and Katelyn Kobbe, born 6 Feb 1990.

Richard married Verlene Denney in Dec 1969 in Redding, Ia. They divorced in 1979. Secondly, Rick married Shirley Campbell on 10 Sep 1982. Rick and Verlene had Richael Lee (Shelly) born 11 Jun 1970 in Redding, and Anthony (Andy) Knapp, born 23 Jan 1975. Shelly married Gordon Craven on 9 Dec 1989 at Mount Ayr, Ia. They had Cody Clinton, born 15 May 1990.

Margaret married, 2 Jun 1974 in Redding, Joe Shields who was born 2 May 1953. Both obtained degrees from Iowa State University. Joe was a research assistant of agricultural services with Land-O-Lakes, Inc. in Webster City, Ia. They lived in Fort Dodge, Ia. Their children are Elizabeth Marie, born 30 Jul 1984, and John Michael, born 16 Apr 1987.

Charles married Elena Santiago on 14 Jul 1990 in Phoenix, Ariz. Chuck graduated from NMSU with a degree in accounting. He worked for Code Electrical Contractors in Tempe, Ariz.

Mark received a degree in music from the University of Northern Iowa, Cedar Falls. He worked toward a master's degree in Boston, and worked at a computer learning center.

Benjamin married on 16 Jun 1990 Melanie Ruth Trullinger in Mount Ayr, Ia. Melanie attended NMSU in Kirksville, Mo. Ben was a student at the University of Iowa.

1162623 Pearle Saville

Pearl was born 4 Jul 1941 in Redding, Ia. She married on 26 Jun 1960, to Jimmie Lee James. Pearl received her degree from NMSC in Maryville, Mo. She taught kindergarten and third grade in South Harrison School District. Jim is a barber in Bethany, Mo. Their children are Terry Lee, born 14 Oct 1961; Jerry Jay, born 29 May 1964; and Michael Ray, born 20 Oct 1974.

Terry was killed in a car accident on 24 Jul 1971 on Hwy 36 near Clarksdale, Mo.

Jerry attended Iowa State University in Ames. He married 1 Jun 1986 Penny Sue Colins who was born 17 Jul 1963. Jerry managed a filling station and Penny worked at McDonald's in Ames.

1162631 Jacob Saville

Jacob was born 4 Feb 1937 in Callender, Ia. He married Brenda Kaye Lawrence on 3 Feb 1963 in Gardner, Kans. Jacob received his elementary education in Redding, and graduated from high school in Mount Ayr. He received a BS degree from the University of Iowa in 1959, where he was a ROTC student. He entered the service in 1960 and spent a year in Korea. Later he received his MS degree and worked toward a PhD in science. He was a major in the army and was serving as a helicopter pilot at the time of his death. He was killed in a car accident on 13 May 1972 near Des Moines. He is buried in Rose Hill Cemetery in Mount Ayr, Ia. Their children were Janet Leann, born 5 Oct 1963, and Derric J., born 2 Oct 1964. Janet was born in Colorado Springs, Colo., and was killed along with her father in the car accident. Derric was born in Fort Madison, Ia. He graduated from the University of Iowa, and married Jeannene Irene Abbott on 12 Mar 1987 in Iowa City.

1162632 Anna Mary Saville

Anna Mary was born 23 Apr 1938 in Fort Dodge, Ia. She attended school in Maloy, Redding, and graduated from Mount Ayr High School in 1956. She received a BS then a MS degree from Northwest Missouri State College. On 23 Aug 1957 she married Jerry Ridenour who was born 13 Dec 1937 in Red Oak, Ia. They divorced in 1974. She taught school in Kansas City. Their child was Jeffrey who was born 20 Dec 1958 in Maryville, Mo. Jeff attended college in Maryville, then married Patricia Riddle in Mar 1989 in Lawrence, Kan. Jeff worked for Woolworths while Patty worked in a nursing home in St. Joseph where they lived. Their child was Allysa who was born 14 Oct 1989 in Lawrence, Kan.

1162633 Paula Saville

Paula was born 15 Nov 1939 in Fort Dodge, Ia. She received her education in Redding and graduated from high school in 1958. She attended Northern Iowa College for two years and then taught school in Iowa. She married 27 Nov 1964 in Colfax, Ia., James Dimit who was born 25 Dec 1931 in Grinnell. Jim received a BS degree from Grinnell College and a MS degree from Drake University. He taught at Northeast Missouri State University in Kirksville, Mo. Paula attended NMSU after she and Jim moved there. She obtained a BS degree in education and in art. She taught in Kirksville Public School and continued her art work with Bird's Art Gallery. They had Dana Ellen who was born 14 Sep 1965 in Newton, Ia. Dana graduated from NMSU in 1987 and worked in Albuquerque, N.M. She married Steven McMurty on 19 May 1990. Both worked for State Farm Insurance Co.

1162634 James Saville

James was born 18 Oct 1946 in Creston, Ia. He graduated from Mount Ayr High School in 1965, then entered the University of Iowa before he graduated an honor student from Northwest Missouri State University in 1969. He taught government and social studies at Mount Ayr High School. He also served as a coach of several sports. He married Marilyn Davis on 19 aug 1967 in Mount Ayr. Marilyn, born 18 Mar 1947, graduated from Mount Ayr HS in 1965 and from Northwest Missouri University in 1969 as an honor student. She then taught in elementary schools. Their child was Douglas who was born 28 Dec 1967. Douglas graduated from college and worked for Metropolitan Insurance in Des Moines.

1162635 Ellen Saville

Ellen was born 9 Jan 1948 in Creston, Ia. She graduated from Mount Ayr HS in 1966, then attended junior college in Clarinda, Ia., for a year before graduating from ISU in Ames in 1970. Ellen married Craig Elliott on 10 Jun 1967 in Mount Ayr. Craig graduated from ISU with a degree in wild animal science in 1970. Craig served in the military, then was county agent in Taylor County. He was manager of Elliott Farms Corp. They had Angela Marie, born 26 Oct 1970, and Christopher Craig, born 30 Dec 1974, both born in Mount Ayr.

1162651 Thomas Keith Saville

Keith was born 16 Oct 1935 in Delphos, Ia. He married Muriel Hill in 1955. She was born in 1936 in Stockton, Calif. Tom graduated from Fresno University in fresno, Calif., and later he and Muriel received grants to complete their doctorates at the University of Texas. Tom did complete his doctorate and then taught at Texas A & M for three years. Then he taught in the physcholgy department at Metropolitan College in Denver, Colo. They divorced in 1971. Secondly, Tom married Gloria Schneider in Aug 1971. Gloria had four children from a previous marriage. Tom and Gloria divorced. Together they had Terri Lynn, born 11 Jul 1956, and Thomas Keith, Jr., born 25 Feb 1958.

Terri Lynn was born at St. Devans, Mass. She received her degree in computer programming and worked in Virginia. She married Stu Jarmon in 1982 in Fresno, Calif. Later they were living in San Francisco.

Thomas was born in Fresno, Calif. He attended Fresno University and majored in communications at the same time working at local stations doing advertising, news, etc. He married Shannon Cagle who was born 12 Nov 1984. Shannon died 12 Jul 1985. She had a daughter, Desiree, whom Tom Jr. has custody of and was to legally adopt her. They lived in Fresno.

1162652 Paul Roger Saville

Paul was born 23 Aug 1937 at Delphos, Ia. He graduated from the University of California, Berkeley in 1961 with a degree in engineering. His first employment was with Varian Association. He later transferred to the Los Angeles area, where he started his own computer business. His home and business were in Costa Mesa. Roger married Jan Luna and they were divorced without children. Secondly, he married Shari Pierre on 1 Sep 1978. Shari had two children, Mark, born in Jul 1959, and Dianne. Roger adopted Tianne who was born 25 Feb 1964.

1162661 Shirley Saville

Shirley was born 12 Oct 1939 in Atlantic, Ia. She graduated from Atlantic High School, then attended secretarial school for a year, and worked for three years before she stayed home with her children. She resumed her secretary career later. She married Gerald Anthony Barmettler on 6 Jun 1959 in Atlantic. They divorced in Feb 1984. Secondly, Shirley married John Rettig on 3 Sep 1984. John is a distributor for Booth Fisheries. Shirley and Gerald had Lori Lee, born 24 May 1960; Brian Anthony, born 16 Jun 1961; Timothy John, born 22 Aug 1962; Lisa Ann, born 3 Mar 1965; and Scott Joseph, born 17 Oct 1969.

Lori Lee was born in Omaha. She worked for Mutual Of Omaha as an auditor. She married Robert Johnson on 9 Feb 1979. Robert worked as a mechanic in Omaha. They had Robin Lee, born 11 Jan 1982, and Jennifer Lynn, born 30 Jun 1984.

Brian was born in Omaha. He worked in a factory and was not married as of 1984.

Timothy was born in Omaha. He worked for Mutual of Omaha Insurance Co. He married Diane Duncan on 26 Aug 1983, and they had Michele Elizabeth, born 21 Feb 1984.

Lisa was born in Omaha. She married Kregg Holdorf on 25 May 1984. Their child is Jami Rae who was born 7 May 1987 in Norfolk, Va.

1162662 Larry Saville
Larry was born 19 Feb 1942 in Atlantic, Ia. Larry graduated from

NMSU in Maryville, Mo.   He taught business administration courses and real estate courses at Des Moines Community College. On 1 Sep 1963 he married Janice Elaine Smith who was born 23 Oct 1942 in Truro, Ia. They were divorced in 1975. Secondly, Larry married Karen Downey. Karen worked for Continental of Iowa as a food marketer. Larry and Jan had Tami Lynn, born 25 Dec 1967 in Pomona, Calif.; Todd Michel, born 21 Oct 1970 in Des Moines; and Kristina Kay, born 22 Mar 1974 in Des Moines.

1162663 Lloyd Saville

Lloyd was born 24 Oct 1944 in Atlantic, Ia.   He married Joan Jasperson on 21 Dec 1963 in Des Moines. Joan died of cancer on 2 Sep 1970 in Des Moines. They had Kevin Joseph, born 23 Jul 1964 in Mason City, Ia., and Melissa Ann, born 11 Mar 1969 in Des Moines. Secondly, Lloyd married Paulette Clapham on 26 Jun 1971 in Princeton, Mo.   She was born 21 Jan 1949.   Lloyd is a computer programmer and has his own business in Des Moines.   Lloyd and Paulette had Chad Aaron, born 4 Jun 1972, and Cory Nathan, born 12 Jun 1977, both born in Des Moines.

1162664 Kenneth Saville

Kenneth was born 23 Mar 1945 in Atlantic, Ia. He was married 7 Sep 1976 to Karen Sue Cohrs who was born 28 Feb 1947 in Atlantic. Kenneth graduated with an associates degree in business and accounting from AIB in Des Moines. He was recently a commercial real estate agent in Wichita, Kan. They had Bradley Ryan, born 2 Mar 1971 in Des Moines, and Andrew Brent, born 15 Sep 1977 in Wichita.

1162681 Robert Alan Bristol

Robert was born 7 Oct 1942 in Lawton, Okla. Alan married Margaret Kattenbach on 10 Oct 1970 in St. Louis, Mo. Margaret was born in 1943. Alan graduated from ISU and worked for McDonnel-Douglas.

1162682 John Edward Bristol

John was born 28 Jun 1946 in Des Moines.   He married Petronilla (Pat) Roybal on 16 Sep 1972. John worked for the U.S. Forestry Department and lived in Albuquerque, N.M. They had Phillip, born 25 Jun 1976, and Valarie Anne, born 28 Nov 1978.

1162691 Rachael Susanne Martin

Rachael was born 1 Apr 1946. in Eldora, Ia. She married Michael Moyna on 5 Aug 1967 in Eldora. They divorced in 1977. Susanne has a master's degree and has taught in Waterloo schools. Their children are Patrick David, born 27 Dec 1968; and Brian Thomas, born 23 Jul 1972. Secondly, Susanne married Ron Brainard on 13 Sep 1980 in Waterloo, Ia. Ron owns and operates Radio Communications in Waterloo. Their children are Christina, born 26 Jul 1981, and Debbie Marie, born 22 May 1983.

1162692 Rebecca Faye Martin

Rebecca was born 19 Jul 1947 in Eldora, Ia. On 8 Jul 1972 she married Tom Kubistal. Becky has a BS degree and was an executive secretary before her marriage. Tom was a supervisor for American Can Co. Their children are Brandon John, born 24 Apr 1975; Lesley Marie, born 2 Sep 1977; and Kathleen Joy, born 2 Jun 1982.

1162693 David Warren Martin

David was born 22 Apr 1949 in Eldora, Ia. He married on 21 Oct 1972 Denise Jacobs in Hubbard, Ia. David served in Vietnam with the U.S. army and now owns and operates a farm near Hubbard. Denise worked for a bank in Radcliffe. They had Jennifer Renae, born 22 Jan 1973, and Jason David, born 31 Dec 1974.

1162694 Marilyn Marie Martin

Marilyn was born 17 Mar 1952 in Atlantic, Ia. On 6 Jun 1985 she married Mark Reynolds who was born 10 Oct 1955. Marilyn is a school teacher, while Mark is an account director for Quorum Financial in Calif. They had Alicia Saville, born 25 May 1986; Allison Merril born in Aug 1989; and Anna Marie, born 14 Feb 1991.

1162811 Curtis Vern Mekemson

Curtis was born 3 Mar 1943 in Ashland, Ore. He graduated from Eldorado High School in Placerville, Calif., in 1961, then earned a BA degree in internal relations and political science in 1964 from the University of California, Berkeley. He has worn many hats which initially involved working for the Peace Corps, and more recently, public relations. He married Peggy Dallen on 28 Nov 1992 in Sacramento. Peggy was born 5 Jul 1950, and is a graduate of the University of Tennessee with a BA degree in education and a MA in school administration and special education. She is assistant principal in the Dry Creek School District. Peggy has two children from a previous marriage, Tony Lumpkin and Natasha Lumpkin. They live in Carmichael, Calif.

1162821 Robert Keith Johnstone

Robert was born 16 Sep 1939 in Des Moines, Ia. He is a graduate of Franklin High School in Vallejo, Calif. He enlisted in the U.S.

Air Force and served four years. Robert then worked for United Air Lines, and for a two-year period had an aquarium store. He is not married.

1162822 James LaMont Johnstone

James was born 8 Feb 1942 in Winterset, Ia. He attended barber school and has been a barber all of his working career. He married Pamela Hansen. They had Diana, and Jennifer born 4 Sep 1970.

1162823 Eleanor Elaine Johnstone

Known as Elaine, she was born 25 Aug 1943 in Newton, Ia. Her first marriage was to Gene Rinard, and they had Michael Eugene who was born 9 Nov 1966 in Sacramento, Calif. Lastly, Elaine married "Tex" Taylor, and in 1999 they were living in Sacramento.

1162831 Roberta Joyce Mekemson

Joyce married Arthur Madland who was born 13 Aug 1922 and had lived in Spokane, Wash. He served in the U.S. Navy aboard destroyers during World War II. Later, he was a carpenter and was involved in real estate. He died 23 Jul 1998 in a nursing home in McMinnville, Ore., and was buried at sea off the coast of Depot Bay.

1162841 Carol Anne Schilling

Carol was born 26 Oct 1941, probably in San Francisco. She attended Roseburg High School, then married Clarence (Clancy) Winningham. Their children are Arthur Jay, William John, Michael, and Andrew. They make their home in Nevada.

1162842 Patricia Belle Schilling

Patricia was born 11 Jan 1946 in Ashland, Ore. In 1964 she graduated from Grants Pass High School, then she attended Oregon State and the University of Oregon where she majored in home economics and fine arts. She married Clifton (Cliff) Lewis on the 9th and 10th of Nov 1967 in Germany. Cliff was born 29 Nov 1946. They had Debra Michelle in 1982. Patricia is a homemaker while Cliff is director for the Oregon State Fair. They were living in Salem, Ore., in 1999.

1162843 Doris Gail Schilling

Doris was born 23 Jul 1947 in Ashland, Ore. In 1966 she graduated from Grants Pass High School, then attended Oregon State where she graduated with a degree in dietetics. She now works for Roseburg School District. She first married Al Szymanski and they later

were divorced. They had a son, Mark. Secondly, she married Neil
Koozer and they reside in Roseburg, Ore.

1162844 Andrew Merritt Schilling

Andrew was born 18 Oct 1951. He obtained a high school GED then
became involved in restaurant work. His first marriage was to Gail
Arp and they had a son, Jeff. Secondly, he married Sherri and they
had Tyler Burton. Andrew was killed in a motorcycle accident in
Mar 1982.

1162845 Bruce Harvey Schilling

Bruce was born 30 Mar 1954. He graduated from Roseburg High School
in 1972 and now is working as a cook. He is not married.

1162851 Laura Mekemson

Laura was born 19 Oct 1946. Her first marriage was to John Their
and they had Michael and John. She is now unmarried and has taken
back her maiden name.

1162852 Jeanette Mekemson

Jeanette was born 5 Oct 1947. Her children are Earl and Chadwick
Teats. She is now divorced and living in Kennewick, Wash.

1162853 Douglas Voight Mekemson

Douglas was born 24 Aug 1954 in Roseburg, Ore. He is a 1972
graduate of Newport High School. He was a fisherman in the Pacific
Ocean until 1990, then became a truck driver. He married, first,
Christi Unger and they had Tyson Voight who was born 9 Jun 1975 in
Corvallis, Ore. Secondly, Douglas married Virginia Carroll who was
born 16 Nov 1960 at Andrews AFB, Md. They had Brandy Amber born 10
Jun 1984 in Wrangell, Alaska. Douglas lives in Southbeach, Ore.

1162854 Howard Allen Mekemson

Howard was born 14 Dec 1956 in Newport, Ore. He married Pearl
Rife. Howard works at a waste water treatment plant in Sheridan.

1162861 Susan Jeanne Grisham

Susan was born 16 Jul 1947 in Ashland, Ore. She attended Southern
Oregon College for two years, then finished at the University of
Nevada at Las Vegas. She earned a master's degree in psychology at
the University of Washington in Seattle. She is a practicing
psychologist in Seattle.

1162862 Deborah Lee Grisham

Deborah was born 8 Apr 1949 in Ashland, Ore. She graduated from
high school, then married John Lacey. They had John L., who was
born 8 Mar 1971; Gregory Robert, who was born 2 Apr 1972; and David
Nathan, who was born 20 Jun 1977, all born in Las Vegas, Nev.
Later, Deborah and John divorced. Deborah works in Las Vegas where
she manages an apartment complex.

1162863 Craig David Grisham

David was born 23 Jul 1951 in Anchorage, Alaska. He is a graduate
of the University of Alaska in Anchorage where he majored in art.
He presently is a computer draftsman working in Coeur d'Alene, Ida.
He married Elizabeth Wade on 4 Nov 1978 in Atlanta, Ga. They had
Elizabeth Rose 13 Jul 1980 and Annalee Rose 6 Jan 1983.

Elizabeth is a high school graduate and was attending college while
working at the front desk in a hotel in 1999.

1162864 Jonathan Reid Grisham

Jonathan was born 3 Jul 1955 in Fairbanks, Alaska. He earned a GED
in Anchorage in 1973. In 1999, he was working as a cab driver in
Anchorage. He married Jenny Epply on 9 Sep 1985 in Anchorage. They
had Elijah born on 9 May 1979; Justin Cody born on 22 Jan 1988, and
Ashley, born 28 Apr 1990, all born in Anchorage.

1162911 Berneta Ray Hulshizer

Berneta Ray married Paul A. Baird. They had Leann, born 25 Jul
1953; Karen, born 8 Aug 1955; Jean Marie, born 6 Dec 1958; and
Jeffrey, born 19 Sep 1961. They lived in Pampa, Tex.

1162912 Dorris Ann Hulshizer

Dorris Ann married Dr. John Ashley who was an opthalmologist. Their
children are Mitchell, born 9 Jun 1960, Michael, born 24 Mar 1965,
and Michelle, born 28 Jun 1967. See page 381, "Late Additions."

1162921 Bonnie Delores Hubby

Bonnie was born 6 Feb 1931 in O'Neill, Neb. She earned a Ph.D. in
education at California State University, San Francisco, in 1978.
She married Dr. Dale Bass, a radiologist; they are divorced. Their
children are Jefferson Dale, born 26 Nov 1957, and Jane DeAnn, born
22 Jul 1960. Bonnie is vice-president of research in her family's
firm, and divides her time between Cripple Creek and San Francisco.

Jeff is married and has a child.

Jane married Ken Page and they had Sara and another child.

1162922 Bruce Marts Hubby

Bruce 4 Mar 1933 in O'Neill, Neb. He graduated from high school in
1951 at Wayne, Neb., then attended Neb. State Teachers College
where he graduated in 1960. He spent 1955-1959 serving in the U.S.
Air Force. On 28 Aug 1953 he married Janet Daurine Butcher in
Hillsboro, Neb. Bruce is chairman of the board of his management
consulting firm which has 95 offices in 13 countries. Janet
operates a gift store in Cripple Creek, Colo. They had Tanya Rae
and Brent Weston.

Tanya was born 22 Jul 1959. She married James Farmer and they had
Logan who was born 8 Nov 1988, and Kal who was born 27 Mar 1991.

Brent was born 14 Oct 1964. He married Lesli Wilbanks. Their
child is Turner.

1162931 Paul Wilburn Berg

Paul was born 26 Sep 1934 in Norfolk, Neb., and later changed his
legal name to Pat O'Day while in the radio business. His first
marriage was to Joni Danielson and they had Jerry Paul, born 4 Feb
1957 in Astoria, Ore., Garry Paul, born 13 Feb 1958 in Yakima,
Wash., and Jeffrey Lee, born 21 Aug 1960 in Seattle. Secondly, on
21 Feb 1981 in Tacoma, he married Stephanie Johnson who was born 23
Jul 1954, and is an attorney. They adopted Kelsey who was born 30
Sep 1990 in Las Vegas, Nev.

1162932 David John Berg

David was born 20 Jun 1939 in Havelock, Neb., a suburb of Lincoln.
In Seattle, Wash., he married Marvella Irene Cain on 30 Dec 1961.
Marvella was born 24 May 1943 in Seattle. Their children are
Shelley Ann who was born 18 Aug 1962 in Seattle, Paul Daniel who
was born 19 Nov 1965 in Seattle, Lisa Marie who was born 26 Mar
1968 in Edmonds, Wash., and Brian David who was born 29 Jan 1975 in
Eugene, Ore.

Shelley married Glade M. Hanson on 13 Mar 1982. They have Tyler
Malcolm who was born 23 Aug 1985 and Stacey Ann who was born 13 Mar
1989. Glade is a faux painter, one who does decorative painting of
walls and some fabrics, and he also is involved in construction,
and Shelley is a homemaker.

Paul (Dan) married Teresa Little on 5 Aug 1989. They had Zechariah
(Zack) Daniel who was born 3 Nov 1991 and Katherine Caroline who
was born 14 Jul 1993.   Paul is a school athletic director and
Teresa is an elementary school teacher.

Lisa married Christopher Jay Egger on 21 Apr 1990. Their children
are Madison Marie born 29 Oct 1992; Christopher Cameron (Cam) born
5 Mar 1994; Dalton David born 22 Jun 1997; Brady James born 31 May
1999. Lisa is a homemaker and Chris is in construction and owns a
Go-Cart race track.

Brian works in construction and is not married.

1162933 Daniel Joe Berg

Daniel was born 26 Aug 1943 in Tacoma, Wash.   Daniel attended
Fresno City College, and is currently a telephone technician. He
married Edna Huey and they had John Randall, born 18 May 1965 in
Seattle, Julie Lynn, born 8 Sep 1966 in Spokane, Joni May, born 20
Feb 1968 in Seattle, and Karin Annette, born 23 Apr 1970 in Great
Falls, Mont. On 27 Dec 1996 in Bellingham, Wash., he was married
to Nina Haataja who was born 24 Apr 1954.

Julie married Keith Murphy on 2 Apr 1997 and they have Michael John
Berg who was born 16 Nov 1992.

Joni married Robert Wagner in Coeur D'Alene, Ida., on 17 Nov 1984.
Robert was born 11 May 1966. Their children are Karin Lynne who
was born 22 May 1985 and Ryan Wayne who was born on his
grandfather's birthday, 26 Aug 1996.

1162941 Roger Ellis Wiley

Roger was born in 1934, and died when three days old.

1162942 Max Allan Wiley

Max was born 26 Mar 1935 in Diagonal, Ia., and died of a brain
tumor in Munich, Germany on 14 Jan 1966. He had been a missionary.
He married Nancy Newell. They had Michael Kent 18 Mar 1959, Robyn
Kay 14 Jun 1960 and Steven 7 Apr 1965. See p. 382 "Late Additions."

1162943 Mark Wiley

Mark was born 26 Sep 1942 and was adopted. He graduated from high
school at Bisbee, Ariz. in 1960.   In 1964 he earned a master's
degree in music at Arizona State University.   Later, he was a
corporate jet pilot for Howard Hughes. He married Marcia Weller and
they had Michelle Ann 20 Jun 1962. Secondly, Mark married Lois

Williams. They had Sarah Noel 25 Dec 1974 and Esther Elizabeth 27 Oct 1978. Sarah married Joe Baker.

1162944 Ann Jeanette Wiley

Ann was born 31 Jan 1946 in Omaha, Neb. Lately, she was living in Albuequerque, N.M. She is a writer and has had novels published, including *Angel In Disguise,* published in 1993.

1162951 Theodore Marts

Theodore (Ted) was born 29 Nov 1940 in Minn. He served in the U.S. Army. He married Janet Barb and they had Christopher Patrick, born 25 Nov 1961, Roland Lee (Marty), born 16 Jun 1963, and Tana Marie. Ted was an electrician.

1162952 Thomas Marts

Thomas was born 4 Nov 1942 in Atkinson, Neb. He graduated from Colorado State University and has been a banker for 36 years. He married Coral Anne Eisentraut on 18 Jun 1963 in Colorado Springs. They had Steven Thomas, born 22 Mar 1964, Douglas Dwight, born 5 May 1966, and Todd Lorne, born 17 Jul 1968.

1162961 Shirley Rae Mord

Shirley was born 16 Jan 1945 in San Diego, Calif. She earned a GED and attended secretarial school. She married John Clinesmith on 16 Aug 1962 and divorced in 1971. They had Kathryn Ranae who was born 27 Oct 1962, Larry Allen who was born 31 Dec 1963 and Diana Rae who was born 24 May 1967, all born in Ogallala, Neb. Next, Shirley was married to Terry Allen. Thirdly, Shirley married Larry Williams on 25 Jul 1978, and they were divorced in 1983. Shirley was of Scottsbluff, Neb., in 2001. Kathryn and Larry are both married, and have children.

1162962 Rahe Sterling Mord

Rahe was born 3 Nov 1946 in Tilden, Neb. He graduated from high school in Ogallala, Neb., in 1964, and enlisted in the U.S. Marine Corps where he served from 1968 through 1971, which included six months in Vietnam. He spent two years attending an electrical technical school. He married Linda Stevens on 31 Dec 1978 in Laurel, Neb., and they divorced in 1990. Rahe has worked in the restaurant business and as a farm hand, and lately he has been part owner/manager of a Mens' Transitional Housing facility in Duluth, Minn.

1162963 Judith Kaye Mord

Judy was born 12 Jul 1949 in Osmond, Neb. She graduated from Ogallala High School. On 27 Jun 1970, she married Richard Carlson and they had Scott Richard on 22 Aug 1972, Debra Kaye on 15 Mar 1976 and Sharon Christine on 13 Dec 1979. Judy was living in Laurel, Neb., in 2001, and worked for Market America.

Scott and Sharon are married and have children.

1162964 Betty Ann Mord

Betty was born 19 Jul 1950 in Osmond, Neb. She is a graduate of Ogallala High School, and on 17 May 1969 she married David P. Nelson. Their three children are Matthew James who was born 2 Feb 1972, Paul David who was stillborn 18 Apr 1974, Sara Jo who was born 6 Oct 1976 and Adam John who was born 29 Apr 1979. They farm near Ogallala, Neb.

Matthew (Matt) is married and has a child. Sara Jo has been married and divorced, and has a child. Adam is married.

1162(10)11 Elizabeth Ann Brenneman

Elizabeth was born 16 Aug 1939 in Pawnee City, Neb. She attended Crete High School through the 11th grade. She married Marvin Vance Zamperini on 21 Jun 1957. Marvin was born 21 Aug 1935 and died 7 Jun 1999; he was buried in Oakland Cemetery in Distant, Pa. Marvin had worked 17 years at Pullman-Standard erecting railroad cars. Elizabeth worked at Shera-Bran shirt factory until it closed. They had Jonathan Vance, born 6 Feb 1958, Brenda Lee, born 11 May 1960 and William Edward, born 2 Jun 1962, all born in Kittanning, Pa. Marvin died in Jun 1999 in Seminole, Pa.

Jonathan married Debra Bishop in 1981 in Distant, Pa. Their children are Jonathan Christopher who was born 22 Aug 1982 in Clarion, Pa., and Desiree who was born 13 Aug 1992 in Duboise, Pa.

Brenda married Glenn Shick in 1981 in Oak Ridge, Pa. They had Brandon Scott on 27 Oct 1982 and Brent Michael on 17 Nov 1984, both born in Brookville, Pa.

William married Janice Sloan about 1985 in New Bethlehem, Pa. Their three children are Kylie Christine who was born in July 1986, Chase Taylor who was born 31 Aug 1988, and Logan Tyler who was born 20 Dec 1989, all born in Kittanning, Pa.

1162(10)12 Robert Duane Brenneman

Robert was born 4 Oct 1942 in Pawnee, Neb. He is a 1960 graduate
of Crete, Neb., High School. He started attending Doane College in
Crete, Neb., then enlisted in the U.S. Navy where he served from
1961 through 1965. He returned to college and graduated with a BS
degree in economics. He then worked in the commercial insurance
industry in Boston, Des Moines and Denver before arriving in
Albuquerque, N.M. Robert married Marian Castrol who was from Neb.
Their children are John Martin who was born 27 Apr 1970 in Quincy,
Mass., and Jennifer Marie who was born 7 Dec 1973 in Des Moines.

Jennifer married Tim Nault, and they had Mickinley who was born 30
Aug 1994 and Joleh who was born 19 Dec 1995.

1162(10)13 Kenneth Brenneman

Kenneth was born 8 Aug 1945 in Lincoln, Neb. He attended the
University of Nebraska at Lincoln for three years where he majored
in electrical engineering. He became a self-employed electrician
and owns his own company. He also has been a cattleman. He was
married on 8 Jun 1968 to Mary Olson of Crete, Neb. They had Amy
Annette who was born 24 Jul 1970. Kenneth was living in rural
Springview, Neb., as of 2001. Amy married Berry Frerichs and they
have a son, Brennon Carl, and a daughter, Amber Annette.

1162(10)21 John Robert Mekemson

John was born 27 May 1944. See "Late Additions," page 382.

1162(10)22 David Graham Mekemson

David was born 23 Mar 1946. He served in the U.S. Army and spent
time in Korea. He graduated from the University of Illinois, and
is lately v-p of Continental Bank. In 1964 he married Adrienne
(Irene) Moher. See "Late Additions," page 382.

1162(10)23 Ann Sheldon Mekemson

Shelle was born 29 Aug 1948. See "Late Additions," page 382.

1162(10)24 Wendy Jane Mekemson

Wendy was born 30 May 1954. See "Late Additions," page 382.

1162(10)25 Leslie Elizabeth Mekemson

Leslie was born 1 Oct 1957 in Libertyville, Ill. See "Late
Additions,", page 382.

R, Bottom Row: Brad Jerome, John Clinefelter, Pam Jerome, Beth White, David Lindsey, Brian Lindsey, Betty kemson, Jennifer Brenneman, Michall Taylor, Deana Slone, Jennifer Johnstone, Amy Brenneman, John enneman, Jonas Cutler, Karla Amick. Second Row: Elnor Doty, Marie Hubby, Eleanor Johnstone, Mima kemson, Edna Swenson, Blanche Amick, Mildred Hulshizer, Bernice Larson, Jackie Amick. Third Row: Dorothy kemson, Rita Swenson, Wilma Berg, Esther Lucky, Janet White, Annabell Bristol, Barbara Amick, Louri onan, Betty Saville, Nancy Fisher, Dorothy Saville, Pauline Brenneman, Verlee Clinefelter, Martha ndsey, Marjorie Jerome, Joni Jerome. Fourth Row: George Saville, Beecher Lucky, Kenneth Amick, Bob istol, Leland Saville, Stuart Mekemson, Mary Brenneman, Marian Brenneman, Howard Amick, Betty Greene, Bob eene, Bill Mekemson, Keith Saville, George Hubby, Bob Brenneman, Fred Swenson, John Brenneman. Back Row: m Clinefelter, David Clinefelter, Charles Noonan, Bill Mekemson, Paul Mekemson, Ken Brenneman, Steve inefelter, Dick Amick, Jim Johnstone, Kent Jerome, Jeff Jerome, Joe Mekemson

Mekemson Family Reunion, Des Moines, IA, 1978

1162(10)31 Mary Janine Mekemson

Mary was born 22 Feb 1953 in Estherville, Ia. She graduated from high school in Humboldt, Ia., and earned a Ph.D. in English Literature at the University of Wisconsin. Mary married Robert Baker on 26 May 1983. They both are teaching at UW. Their child is Elizabeth Mekemson who was born in 1991.

1162(10)32 William Brown Mekemson

The seventh generation by this name, he was born 26 Nov 1954 in Estherville, Ia. He is a graduate of Humboldt High School. He then attended Iowa State University where he earned a BS degree in biology. He now works in Ames at Main Stream Living, where he is project coordinator. WBM married Mary Frances Wilson on 26 Jul 1980. Their children are Amy Claire who was born 23 Mar 1982, William Brown (Will) who was born 4 Apr 1985, and Michelle Gayle who was born 12 Dec 1986.

1162(10)33 Paul Randall Mekemson

Paul was born 7 May 1957 in Havelock, Ia. He is a graduate of Humboldt High School. Later he attended South Dakota Business College for a year, then Emmettsburg Junior College where he received a two-year degree in hotel management. Today he is a chef in Dakota City, Ia., and is not married.

1162(10)34 Joseph Gilbert Mekemson

Joseph was born 1 Aug 1961 in Pocahontas, Ia., and graduated from Humboldt High School. He received a BS degree in mathematics and computer science from the University of Northern Iowa. Joseph is unmarried and lives in Des Moines where he is a consultant in the computer field.

1162(11)11 William Howard Swenson, Jr.

William was born 30 May 1957 in Chicago, Ill. He attended Evergreen State College, Olympia, Wash., and earned a degree in film making. After graduation he worked a few years in Hollywood as an editor. Pursuing his love of nature, he achieved a Ph.D. in biological sciences at Binghamton University, New York, in 2001. He married Linda Fader in 1989. She also earned a Ph.D at Binghamton in 2001 with a major in English.

1162(11)12 Esther Estelle Swenson

Esther was born 13 Jan 1960 in Chicago. She attended Evergreen State College and became a child-care specialist in Langley, Wash.

She married David Iles in 1980.   David is multi-talented, and designed and built his own house in Freeland, South Whitby Island, Wash. Their child is Elijah Oliver who was born 17 Sep 1994 in Seattle, Wash.

1162(11)31 Carol Jean Swenson

Carol was born 5 Sep 1956 in Somerville, N.J.   She adopted Katherine Jialin, who was born 15 Sep 1995, and Ann, who was born in Oct 1998 in China.

1162(11)32 Todd Jack Swenson

Todd was born 14 Dec 1958 in Somerville, N.J. He went to Nagoya, Japan, to teach English, and while he was there he married Chika Tanaka who was born there on 22 Jun 1960.   The marriage took place in Nagoya on 22 Nov 1985.   Later, he moved back to the states and is living at Mohegan Lake, N.Y., and is running a private school where he teaches English to primarily Japanese immigrants and business people who need a refresher course. Their children are Kei Tanaka, born 7 Dec 1987, and Wayne Tanaka, born 25 Oct 1991, both born in Nagoya, Japan.

1162(11)33 Stephen Jack Swenson

Stephen was born 25 Jan 1965 in Plainfield, N.J.   On 7 May 1988 in Cumberland, R.I., he married Sandra Mary Jaroska who was born 1 May 1964 in Providence, R.I.

1162(11)34 Ted Swenson

Ted was born 30 Jun 1970. He married Lori Baker on 11 Sep 1994.

1162(11)41 Elizabeth Florence White

Elizabeth (Beth) was born 25 Oct 1963 in Granville, N.Y.   Beth graduated from Shippensburg High School in Pa., and went on to Ohio state University.   She graduated in 1985 with a degree in agricultural engineering, then went to the Medical School at Ohio State and graduated in 1989.   In 1993 she completed a residency in anesthesiology, and she is now in practice at St. Alphonsus Hospital in Boise, Ida.   On 30 Sep 1995 in Payette Lake, Ida., she married Douglas Ray Varie who was born 1 Nov 1963 in Boise. Douglas is the prosecuting attorney for Gem County, Ida.   They had Ian Dennis on 17 Mar 1998 and Kristen Tara on 6 Sep 1999, both born in Boise.

1163111 Lucile Mildred Crisp

Lucile was born 17 Nov 1918 in Dell Rapids, S.D.   She married Howard Wilson Daugaard on 3 Sep 1940 in Sioux Falls, S.D.   Howard was born 28 Jul 1918 in Dell Rapids, and served with the military during World War II.   Their children were John Robert, born 20 Apr 1942; Peggy Jane, born 8 Jul 1947; Nancy Lu, born 16 Apr 1949; and Paul Richard, born 14 May 1950, all born in Sioux Falls, S.D.

John married Cheryl A. Erfman on 21 Jul 1972.

Peggy married John R. Rines on 19 Sep 1969.   Peggy died 23 May 1978.

Nancy married Wilbur P. Harrington, Jr., on 1 May 1971.

1163112 Ralph Glenn Crisp

Ralph was born 14 Jul 1920 in Dell Rapids, S.D.   He married Lorna Lee Hansen on 15 Apr 1956 in Manning Co., Ia.   Lorna was born 10 Jan 1930 in Manilla, Crawford Co., Ia.   Ralph saw service in the military during World War II.   They had Lisa Ann, born 25 Feb 1958 in Omaha, Neb.

1163113 Betty Ann Crisp

Betty was born 29 Jul 1922 in Dell Rapids.   She and Andrew Ray Burkhart were married 4 Dec 1943 in Sioux Falls, S.D. Andrew was born 16 Feb 1920 in Dell Rapids. Their children were Robert John, born 7 Feb 1945 in Dell Rapids, S.D., and died the same day; Thomas Jay, born 5 Jul 1947 in Sioux Falls; and William Ray, born 2 Jun 1949 in Sioux Falls.

Thomas married Jeanette Williams on 29 Dec 1968.

1163114 Robert Hugh Crisp

Robert was born 28 Mar 1925 in Dell Rapids, S.D.   He married Byrne Mercedes Haak on 7 Jun 1947 in Sioux Falls, S.D.   Byrne was born 3 Nov 1924 in Sioux Falls. Their children were Marsha Kay, born 26 Jul 1948 in Garretson, S.D.; Loren Mark, born 25 Oct 1950 in Dell Rapids; twins Kenneth Byron and Kevin Robert, born 4 Sep 1951; and Candice Jean, born 10 Jun 1953 in Dell Rapids.   Robert and Byrne live in Dell Rapids.

Marsha married Franklin J. Hansen on 13 Jan 1969.   About 1975 they were divorced. Franklin was born 15 Apr 1947 and was killed while hunting in Alaska in Aug 1986.   Marsha lives in Sandy, Utah. Their child was Shannon Marie who was born 12 Aug 1969.   On 10 Apr 1999, at the U.S. Naval Academy Chapel in Annapolis, Md., Shannon married Jason Gray Adkinson who, in 1999, was a captain in the U.S. Marine Corps and a Marine Cobra helicopter pilot. Jason graduated from Woodbridge, S.D., High School, then attended the U.S. Naval Academy where he graduated and was appointed a second lieutenant in 1990. He was attending the USNA in 1999 while pursuing a post-graduate degree. Shannon earned a master's degree in physical therapy at Chapman College in Calif., and was working in that field near Annapolis where they reside.

Loren married Judy Koch in 1990 and they live in Sebring, Fla. Judy has two children from a previous marriage: Crystal and Stephanie.

Ken married Debby Stonebach and they have two children, Tiffany and Tom. They live near Sherman, S.D.

Kevin married Paula Schwebach on 12 Oct 1974, and later they divorced. They had Jennifer, Robbie and Michael. Kevin lives near Dell Rapids, S.D.

Candice married Bradley Grossenburg on 17 Aug 1974. They have two girls, Nicole and Anne.

1163115 Reginald Keith Crisp

Reginald was born 9 Mar 1929 in Dell Rapids. He married Villetta Jean Clark on 30 Jul 1963 at Madison, S.D. Villetta was born 7 Mar 1938 in Pocahontas, Ia. Reginald served in the military during World War II. They live in Dell Rapids.

1163116 Max Thomson Crisp

Max Thomson was born 31 Jan 1931 in Dell Rapids. He married Dianne Lenore Moe on 26 Jun 1956 in Baltic, S.D. Dianne was born 9 Mar 1936 in Sioux Falls, S.D. They had David Lynn, born 11 Apr 1957; Gregory Scott, born 8 May 1959; Mark Jud, born 24 Nov 1961; and Mary Dianne, born 30 Oct 1966, all born in Dell Rapids. Max and Dianne live in Dell Rapids.

1163117 Harriet Ruth Crisp

Harriet was born 7 Jun 1932 in Dell Rapids. She and Arnold Smith Brown were married 7 Jun 1953 in Sioux Falls. Arnold was born 30 Mar 1927 in Havre, Mont. Arnold was a minister and a university professor. They had Craig Michael, born 22 Jul 1957 in San Francisco, and Rita Kay, born 24 Jul 1959 in San Francisco. They lived in Flagstaff, Ariz.

1163121 James Oliver Yule

James was born 29 Nov 1927 in Indianapolis, Ind. He married
Elizabeth Hudson on 14 Jan 1956 in Chambersburg, Pa., and later
were divorced. Secondly, James married Meeri Italvoto Makela on 5
May 1963 in Stockholm, Sweden. Meeri was born 20 Jul 1931 in
Helsinki, Sweden. James was a veteran of World War II. Meeri was
a translator. They had Jay Lynne, born 7 Mar 1964 in Rochester,
N.Y.; and Geoffrey James, born 25 Dec 1965 in Plainview, N.Y. Meeri
had a child by a previous marriage, Martina Katrinka Mokela, born
11 Sep 1951 in Helsinki.

1163122 Roger Thomson Yule

Roger was born 10 May 1931 in Indianapolis, Ind. He married Ann M.
Marcoullier on 28 Dec 1957 in Overbrook Hills, Pa. Ann was born 28
May 1936 in Westfield, Mass. Roger was a U.S. Marine and served in
Korea. They had Joanne Marie, born 25 Jul 1961; Robert Burns II,
born 10 Oct 1962; and Michael David, born 30 Dec 1964, all born in
Los Angeles Co., Calif.

1163123 Roberta Ruth Yule

Roberta was born 28 Jan 1934 in Indianapolis, Ind. She married
Karl Gillmeister on 18 May 1957 in Overbrook Hills, Pa., and later
were divorced. She secondly married Norman Owen on 4 Oct 1969 at
Fort Myer, Va. Norman was born 23 Jan 1944 in Los Angeles, Calif.,
and served with the U.S. Army from 1967-1969. They had Jennifer
Joy, born 23 mar 1970, and Robert Henry, born 9 Nov 1976, both born
in Ann Arbor, Mich.

1163211 David Hugh Thomson

David was born 10 Dec 1956 in Eureka, Mont. He graduated from
Flathead High School, Kalispell, Mont., in 1975, attended Canadian
Bible School in Regina, Sask., and graduated from Chapman School of
Seamanship in Stewart, Fla., in 1987. He later was a general
contractor. He married Janet Lee Pezzaniti 3 Sep 1994 in Joliet,
Mont. Janet has published two cook books with a third in progress.
They were living in Joliet in 2001.

1163212 Pamela Adele Thomson

Pamela was born 7 Jul 1959 in Helena, Mont. She graduated from
high school at Kalispell, Mont., in 1977. Then she attended
college for a year at Toccoa Falls College in Ga. In Nov 1979 Pam
married William S. Maxwell; they divorced in Feb 1984. They had
Karen Rebecca who was born 6 Mar 1981 in Stephens Co., Ga., and
Holly Joanna who was born 15 Apr 1983 in Clarkesville, Ga.   Pam

went back to college in 1989 and graduated from Meredith College in Raleigh, N.C., with a BA degree in art in 1993. She has been teaching art for three years at Pretty Eagle Catholic School, which is a mission school on the Crow Indian Reservation. She is studying towards a masters degree in education at Montana State University in Billings while residing in Hardin, Mont.

Karen graduated from high school in 1999 and plans to attend Crown College in Minnesota. Holly will be a junior in Hardin High School in 1999.

1163221 Janet Jean Thomson

Janet was born 4 Feb 1941 in Estherville, Ia. She married Darryl S. Henrickson. They had Brian Wayne, born 13 Dec 1960 in Key West, Fla. and Patricia Eileen, born 8 Jan 1963 in Norfolk, Va. Secondly, Janet married Randall T. Baker on 10 Apr 1971 in Homestead, Fla. They had Randall Thomas, born 16 Oct 1974 in Miami, Fla., and Scott Allen, born 11 Jun 1976 in Miami.

1163222 Dorothy Marlene Thomson

Dorothy was born 18 Feb 1943 in Estherville, Ia. She married Robert Anthony Worthington on 1 Feb 1964 in Iowa City, Ia. Robert was born 15 Jan 1938 in Pittsburgh, Pa. Their children were Kevin Anthony, born 6 Feb 1965 in Iowa City; Adrienne Tracy, born 4 Oct 1967 in Pittsburgh; and Deborah Lynn, born 22 Jun 1970 in Bloomington, Minn.

1163223 Ruth Marie Thomson

Ruth was born 12 Nov 1944 in Estherville, Ia. She married James Duane Peterson in Dec 1970 in Estherville, Ia. James was born 1 Nov 1931 in Harris, Ia. They had Douglas Alan, born 13 Oct 1971 in Estherville. Ruth also had Tony Carl, born 17 May 1968, fathered by Terry Carl Blackert.

1163224 Mary Kay Thomson

Mary was born 2 Apr 1950 in Estherville, Ia. She married Larry Merlyn Wee on 24 Nov 1968 in Superior, Ia. Larry was born 17 Jun 1946 in Estherville, Ia. They had Kenneth James, born 8 May 1971 in Ames, Ia.; Heather Michelle, born 21 Oct 1973 in Waterloo; and Tiffani Jo, born 15 Sep 1979 in Grand Forks, N.D. Mary and Larry divorced; later Mary married Donald Allen and they reside in Marietta, Ga.

1163231 Clark Walter Roby
Clark was born 16 Jan 1944 in Des Moines, Ia. He married Janis Ann

Hyberger on 5 Jun 1971 in Cedar Rapids, Ia. Janis was born 8 Jul 1947 in Elma, Ia. Their child was James Brian, born 1 Jul 1976 in Cedar Rapids.

1163232 Carol Ann Roby

Carol was born 17 Mar 1946 in Cedar Rapids, Ia. She graduated from George Washington High School in 1964, then married David Wayne Solum on 1 Oct 1966 in Cedar Rapids. David is an electrician. Their children are Eric Russell, born 18 Oct 1969 in Cresco, Ia.; Berit Ann, born 3 May 1971 in Cresco; and Kristy Lee, born 23 Sep 1974. Berit Ann married Neal Monroe and they had Collin Wayne 29 Oct 1998.

1163241 Jackie Gwenn Thomson

Jackie was born 26 Aug 1948 in Des Moines, Ia. She was a music teacher in Des Moines.

1163242 Christine Sue Thomson

Christine was born 23 Jun 1951 in Des Moines. She married John M. Short on 24 Nov 1972. John was born 7 Aug 1951 in Cherokee, Ia. They had Timothy Martin, born 4 Mar 1975 in Des Moines.

1163251 Sharon Lee Wilson

Sharon was born 9 Oct 1938 in Winterset, Ia. She married Henry Walter Cheney on 1 Jul 1962 in Springfield, Mo. Henry was born 27 Jun 1940 in McDowell, Wyo. They had Jeffrey Linn, born 17 Jul 1964 in Branson, Mo.

1163252 Donald Dennis Wilson

Dennis was born 14 Jul 1943 in Winterset, Ia., and died 12 Feb 1975. He never married.

1163511 Richard Andrew Reierson

Richard was born 18 Jul 1942 in Biloxi, Miss. He married Eloise Oviatt on 17 Oct 1964 in Cleveland. Their children are Andrew John, born 21 May 1965; Carolyn Jean, born 29 Oct 1966; Kathryn Louise, born 1 Oct 1973; and Jonathan David, born 1 Apr 1975, all born in Cleveland.

1163512 Michael Eric Reierson

Michael was born 19 Jul 1944 in Gulfport, Miss. He married Susan Kathleen Harrison on 16 Jul 1966 in Springfield, Va. Susan was born 16 Aug 1947 in Huntington, Calif. They had Eric Michael, born 21 May 1972 in Ann Arbor, Mich. Secondly, Michael married Cynthia L. Fiola on 13 Nov 1976 in Zion, Ill.

1163513 Patricia Jean Reierson

Patricia was born 29 Aug 1946 in Madison, Wisc. She married Charles (Doc) Ellis on 30 May 1969 in Beloit, Wisc. Doc was born 9 Jan 1947 in Yazoo City, Miss. They had Adrienne Makeita, born 25 Dec 1970, and Karri Margaret, born 1 Jan 1975, both born in Rockford, Ill.

1163521 Robert Elliot Morgan

Robert was born 16 Apr 1941 in Clay Center, Kan. He graduated from Cornell University with a degree in hotel and restaurant management. Today he owns his own business making sails for yachts in Italy. He married Kathleen Holttum on 24 Nov 1963 in New York City. They are divorced. He secondly married Marisa Bassi in 1983. Their children are Bianca Cleia who was born 17 Apr 1986 and Robin Alexander who was born 8 Jan 1991, both in Rappalo, Italy. The family lives in Italy.

1163522 James Shorter Morgan

James was born 9 May 1943 in Clinton, Ok. He is a graduate of Monmouth College. After college, he enlisted in the U.S. Army and in 1965 graduated from Officer's Candidate School as a Second Lieutenant, then saw service in South Vietnam. He was awarded the Silver Star for heroism, and also was awarded a Purple Heart for wounds suffered in battle in 1966. He married Margaret Pearce on 2 Aug 1969 in Elmhurst, Ill. They had Bryan Augustus who was born about 1974, now a West Point graduate of 1995, and Alison Pierce who was born about 1976.

1163523 William Arthur Morgan

William (Bill) was born 8 Jul 1944 in Oklahoma City, Okla. He enlisted in the U.S. Army in 1951. After his military service, he worked for Commonwealth-Edison, Bolling Brook Division in Chicago as head of operations, and retired at age 55. He married Mary Kathleen Lamberty on 13 Feb 1971 in Villa Park, Ill. They had Kelly Marie, born 27 Feb 1972 in Oklahoma City, Okla., and Benjamin Edward born 27 Jul 1974.

Kelly earned a MS degree in psychiatry from Michigan State and now works for St. Luke's Presbyterian Hospital in Chicago.

Ben recently started working for Commonwealth-Edison as a meter reader. He earlier served out an enlistment in the U.S. Navy.

1163524 Thomas Bard Morgan

Thomas was born 24 Dec 1948 in Oklahoma City, Okla. He suffered from juvenile diabetes and died 30 Jan 1983. His remains were cremated.

1163531 John Carroll Hinman

Jack was born 25 Apr 1945 in Chicago, Ill. He is a graduate of Harvard with a degree in sociology. He obtained his masters degree at Austin, Tex. Later, he graduated from Georgetown Law school in 1991 and worked as a lawyer for Medicare. His first marriage was to Sylvia Ann Lenderking on 12 Jan 1966 in Alexandria, Va. They were divorced in May 1971. They had Richard Carroll, born 23 Oct 1966 in Washington, D.C. John has remarried.

Richard is a West Point graduate, class of 1988. He served in Panama with distinction, then at the Savannah Army Air Base as a Ranger. In 1999 he was a Captain teaching desert warfare at Ft. Irwin, Calif.

1163532 Andrea Jean Hinman

Andrea was born 29 Apr 1948 in Washington, D.C. She graduated from Monmouth College in 1970. She married John Rocco Elia on 4 Sep 1971 in Alexandria, Va. John is also a Monmouth graduate and is now vice-president of Day International, Inc., in Ashville, N.C. They had Nancy Ann who was born 8 Oct 1974, Joseph Rocco who was born 16 Oct 1978 and Laura Kathryn who was born 18 Jul 1985.

Nancy married Michael Shepard in Oct 1997. Michael is a graduate of the United States Naval Academy in Annapolis and is a Lt. stationed at Jacksonville, Fla.

1163533 Donald Lee Hinman

Donald was born 18 Jun 19. Frances has used book stos a graduate of Colorado College in Colorado Springs in 1974. He is a professor of economics at the University of Wisconsin at Superior. He is involved in economic development, an occupation that requires him to travel frequently. Donald married Susan Allen.

1163534 Keith Russell Hinman

Keith was born 25 Mar 1953 in Washington, D.C. Keith graduated from the University of California, Santa Cruz, with a major in history. He earned his master's degree at Berkeley. He worked for the EPA, and is now a consultant on environmental issues for a firm in Calif. He married Fritzie Reisner who earned a Ph.D. in economics. They live in Seattle with their three children: Miriam who was born about 1986, Rachel born about 1989, and Joshua who was born 6 Feb 1998.

1163535 Nancy Caroline Hinman

Nancy was born 27 Oct 1954 in Washington, D.C., and died of leukemia on 12 Sep 1955.

1163611 Sheila Ruth Holmes

Sheila was born 26 Mar 1949 in Des Moines, Ia. She died 14 Aug 1958.

1163612 Loren Errol Holmes

Loren was born 31 Mar 1950 in Mora, Minn. She died 9 Dec 1963.

1163613 Alice Carolyn Holmes

Alice was born 29 Apr 1951 in Mora, Minn. She was a graduate of the College of St. Teresa of Winona, Minn., in 1973. She served as a nurse in the U.S. Army from 1973 to 1985. She then served as a nurse in the U.S. Air Force from 1986 to 1994 and retired as a major. Alice holds a master's degree from the University of Texas in Austin, in 1983. Now she is a nurse practitioner in pediatrics. She married Leon Meyer on 25 Jul 1984. He is a retired Air Force M/Sgt and now is a real estate agent. Their children are Amanda Leigh, born 9 Oct 1985 in Germany, and Ashley Noel, born 3 Jan 1989 in Lancaster, Calif.

1163614 Michael Ray Holmes

Michael was born 23 Aug 1954 in St. Paul, Minn. He graduated from high school in 1972, then from the University of Minnesota in 1979. He served in the U.S. Army from 1973 to 1976. Today, he is a computer analyst. Michael married Laurie Jo Bluhm on 9 Sep 1978. She was a hair dresser, then became a school-bus driver. They had Brian Michael, born 20 Aug 1983 in Minneapolis and Katherine Elizabeth, born 13 Jun 1986 in Minneapolis.

1163615 Glen Harold Holmes

Glen was born 23 Nov 1955 in St. Paul, Minn. In 1974 he graduated from high school, then served in the U.S. Army from 1974 to 1978. Today he is employed as a millwright. He married Cheri Johnson on 7 Aug 1993. Cheri works for the state of Minnesota Environmental Dept. They have Heather Lynn, born 28 May 1988 in Minneapolis.

1163616 David Brian Holmes

David was born 26 May 1959 in St. Paul, Minn. He is a 1977 high school graduate. He served in the U.S. Army from 1977 to 1980, and now is a building inspector. He married Carolyn Audrey Downer on 27 Nov 1987 in Los Angeles, Calif. Their children are Christopher Loren, born 29 Aug 1988, Cameron Mitchell, born 6 Dec 1990, and Clayton Joshua, born 17 Oct 1997, all born in Big Bear Lake, Calif.

1163617 Susan Lori Holmes

Susan was born 1 Oct 1960 in St. Paul. In 1979 she graduated from high school and in 1983 graduated from the College of St. Teresa in Winona, Minn., with a nursing degree. She served as a nurse in the U.S. Army from 1983 to 1986. Since 1988 she has served as a nurse with the U.S. Air Force. Susan earned a master's degree in nursing from the University of Arizona in 1999. She married Jeff Charles Irons on 21 April 1984 in San Antonio, Tex. Jeff is an independent craftsman. Their children are Jonathan Taylor, born 7 Feb 1987 in San Antonio; Garrett Michael, born 24 Mar 1991 in Ogden, Utah; and Candace Paige, born 8 Oct 1992 in Ogden.

1163618 Sharon Elizabeth Holmes

Sharon was born 19 Nov 1964 in St. Paul, Minn. She graduated from high school in 1983 and spent two years in college in Anoka, Minn. She now operates a day care facility. She married Christopher Richard Johnson on 15 Jul 1995 in Anoka. He is a sound and lighting specialist for live theater. They had Lauren Ashley, born 17 Nov 1997 and Amber Rose, born 15 Feb 1999, both in Anoka.

1163619 Tamara Iris Holmes

Tamara was born 10 May 1967 in St. Paul. She graduated from high school in 1985 and now works as a manager of a convenience store. She married Mark Guy on 25 Jul 1992 in Anoka, Minn. He works in the manufacture of ammunition. Brandon David was born 1 Mar 1996.

1163621 Robin Lynn Thomson

Robin was born 27 Aug 1960 in St. Paul, Minn. She earned a BS degree in engineering at Texas A & I University, and received a MBA at East Texas State University. She is an aerospace engineer at the Corpus Christi (Tex.) Army Depot. She married Bradley Bonham on 7 May 1988 in Corpus Christi. Brad holds a BA in art and is a management analyst at the Depot. Their children are Jeffrey Taylor who was born 26 Nov 1990 and Leslie Michelle who was born 10 Aug 1998.

1163622 Randall Ray Thomson

Randy was born 3 Jul 1964 in Scandia, Minn. He married Stacy Bartlett in Apr 1990 in Los Fresnos, Tex. Randy is a border patrol officer near Las Cruces, N.M., while Stacy is a school teacher and homemaker. Their children are Anthony Paul who was born 18 Dec 1990 and Tamra Rose who was born 12 Dec 1993 in Tex.

1163623 Holly Lynn Thomson

An identical twin, Holly was born 3 May 1970 in Bowie, Md. She married Jesse Trevino 15 Mar 1990 in San Benito, Tex. Jesse was born 30 Apr 1969 in San Benito. Holly and Jesse served in the U.S. Army, Holly for eight years, which included time in Germany. They had Haley Lynn who was born 23 Apr 1997 in Regensburg, Germany, and Kady Michelle who was born 5 Dec 2000 in Silver Spring, Md. Holly and her sister are importers of Polish pottery. The family resides in Bowie, Md.

1163624 Jennifer Ruth Thomson

Jenny was born 3 May 1970, a twin, in Bowie, Md. She and her twin sister graduated from Los Fresnos, Tex., High School in 1989. Jenny then went to Texas A&M where she received a BS in animal science in 1995. She married James Puckett II in Jacksonville, Fla., on 6 Apr 1996. James was born 25 Jul 1968. He earned a MS from the University of Michigan, then served ten years in the U.S. Navy as a pilot, and now works in contract with the government. They had Morgan Leigh who was born 4 Jul 1999 in Bethesda, Md. They live in Bowie, Md.

1163631 Jacelyn Kay Thomson

Jacelyn was born 7 Apr 1967 in Sandstone, Minn. She is a graduate of College of St. Benedict in St. Cloud, Minn., and now is a corrections officer there.

1163632 Hugh Ryan Thomson

Hugh, "Skip", was born 30 Jun 1970 in Sandstone, Minn. On 10 Oct 1994 he married Gretchen Julene Cherwika who was from Cannon Falls,

Minn.   In addition to farming, Skip is an insurance saleman. Gretchen is an analyst in the medical field in hospitals in Duluth.

1163633 Gary Gene Thomson

Gary was born 25 Jan 1972 in Sandstone, Minn.   He attended an engineering college for a year and also the University of Duluth for a year. He is a driver for UPS.   He lives in Sandstone.

1164121 Roberta Mae Black

Roberta was born 8 Oct 1918 in Madison Co., Ia.   She married Lloyd Jones on 30 Nov 1940.   They did not have any children.   Lloyd was born 23 Jan 1902 and died 4 Mar 1983.

1164122 Iola Maxine Black

Iola was born 16 Nov 1920 in Madison Co., Ia.   She married Merlin Russell Lovely on 18 Aug 1940 in Grant City, Mo.   Merlin was born 15 Jan 1916.   They are living in Greenfield, Ia.   Iola has provided the compiler with a great deal of assistance.   Their children are (1)Marilyn Maxine, born 8 Oct 1942 in Greenfield, Ia., and (2)Susan Virginia, born 4 Sep 1944 in Greenfield.

(1)Marilyn married Rolan David Jensen on 8 Oct 1960 in Greenfield, Ia.   Rolan was born 20 Dec 1940 at Fontanelle, Ia.   They had Pheona Lynn, born prematurely and died 12 May 1961; Melinda Johne, born 15 Jul 1962; Melea Janelle, born 1 Dec 1964; and Blake David, born 27 Aug 1968, all born in Greenfield.

Melinda married Brian Joseph Drees in Greenfield on 6 Aug 1983. Brian was born 5 Mar 1961.   Their children are Nathen Andrew, born 16 Sep 1988 in Kansas City, Mo.; Adam Michael, born 26 Nov 1991 in Grinell, Ia.; and Emily Jo, born 10 Jan 1993 in Grinnell.

Melea married Timothy Dean Goins in Greenfield on 5 Jun 1988. Timothy was born 27 May 1963.   Their children are Breanna Nicole, born 22 Apr 1991, and Garrett Tyler, born 4 Apr 1995 and Abigayle Anne who was born 16 Jul 1999.

Blake married Connie Quinlan in Mason City, Ia., on 26 Sep 1992. Connie was born 14 Aug 1971 near Mason City.   They had Tate Avery, born 23 Mar 1993, and Shea Adeline, born 6 Mar 1998.

(2)Susan married Charles Lee Henry on 19 Mar 1966 in Greenfield, Ia.   Charles was born 9 Aug 1941 at Dubuque, Ia.   They had Bradley Warren, born 7 Nov 1969 in Houston, Tex., and Jennifer Janay, born 28 Jan 1973 in Silsbee, Tex.

Jennifer married Matthew MacGregor (Mac) Rice on 20 Apr 1996 at Columbia, Mo. Mac was born 25 Nov 1968.

1164123 Earl Chase Black

Earl was born 14 Apr 1924 in Madison Co., Ia., and died 6 Jan 1925.

1164124 Eva Rachel Black

Eva was born 30 Mar 1927 in Madison Co., Ia., and died 26 Jul 1996 in Des Moines, Ia. She married Robert Larry Strong and they had four children: Larry Robert, born 15 Jul 1941; Donna Mae, born 8 Nov 1942; Richard Dean, born 12 Mar 1944; and Charles Michael, born 13 Oct 1945. All were born in Greenfield, Ia. Later, Eva and Robert were divorced. Secondly, Eva married Glen Donald Foster at Albia, Ia. Glen was born 4 Apr 1914 at Albia, and died 26 Oct 1990 in Johnston, Ia.

Larry married Linda Hines who was born 21 May 1945. They had Gayle Ann, born 30 Aug 1964; Michele Rae, born 12 Dec 1965; Timothy Alan, born 3 Jun 1967, and Jeffrey Michael born 31 Jul 1968. Gayle married Jeffry Mark Farrell and they had Connor Mark 21 Aug 1995 and Andrew Michael 31 Jan 1997. Michele married Jerry McHargue and they later divorced. They had BrandiLyn JoAnn 17 Dec 1988 and Jeremy Alan 6 Jan 1990. Timothy married Angela Diane Wheeler. They had Alyssa Ann on 15 Oct 1996. Jeffrey married Susan Kay Marshall. They had Kristen Ann 9 Jun 1993 and Matthew Robert 1 May 1995.

Donna was married on 11 Aug 1961 to William Riley who was born 18 Feb 1936. They adopted Kathleen Kay, born 4 Oct 1966; Michael John, born 1 Mar 1969 and died 29 May 1969; and Karen Ann, born 28 Mar 1971.

Richard is married, living in Humble, Tex., and has two children.

Charles married Kathryn Joyce Cook 14 Mar 1965. She was born 1 May 1946. They had Brian Emmett, born 5 Sep 1968, and William Michael, born 10 Jun 1970. They are living in Brighton, Colo.

1164131 Charles Edmund Chase

Charles lived only six months.

1164132 Verl Andrew Chase Jr.

Verl was born 10 Sep 1936 in Dexter, Ia. He graduated from Earlham High School in 1954, then went on to Drake University where he

majored in accounting and earned a BS degree in 1961. Verl then
enlisted in the U.S. Air Force and retired 1 Nov 1983 with the rank
of major.   During his military career, he earned a MS in industrial
management at the University of North Dakota in 1973. He married
Shizuko Miyagi on 9 Jan 1966 at Koza, Okinawa. They adopted Richard
Kangen after his birth on 16 Jun 1971.   In 2001, Verl was self-
employed as a business owner and landlord.

1164133 John Edmund Chase

John was born 22 Jun 1935 in Dexter, Ia. He graduated from Earlham
Consolidated High School in 1953, then attended a commercial
college in Omaha and graduated in 1955.   He then went to work for
Ford Motor Co., Tractor Division for 17 years, during which he took
night classes at Drake University for six years. John was in the
Army Reserves for six months. He married in 1955 Ruby Golightly and
later they divorced; they had one child, David John. David is
married to Mary and they had Dustin, Dillon and Jaydin Leigh.

1164134 Marilyn Ann Chase

Marilyn was born 10 Jun 1941 in Dexter, Ia., and graduated from
Earlham H-S in 1959. She married David James Tobey. Their children
are Michael James, born 3 Sep 1965; Steven Andrew, born 11 Jul
1967; and Duane Franklin who was born 18 Nov 1968; all born in Des
Moines. Michael had Andrew Michael Tobey on 25 May 2001 and Duane
had Jacob Matthew Tobey on 9 Oct 2000. Marilyn and David live in
Des Moines.

1165111 Richard Lewis Edwards

Richard was born 27 Nov 1934 in Spokane. He married Terrill Gail
Mudgett on 17 Jan 1953 in Coeur d'Alene, Ida., and they lived in
Wilbur, Wash.   Terrill was born 31 Dec 1935 in Spokane. Their
children are William Reid, Michael Lewis, Yvonne Darlene, and John
Edward Tracy.

William was born 10 Jun 1953 in Spokane, Wash. He married Cindy
Lou Coppersmith on 10 Oct 1979 in Almira, Wash. Cindy was born 8
Mar 1957 in Coeur d'Alene. William farms while Cindy works in
retail sales. Their children are Danielle Elizabeth who was born
17 Sep 1986, Andrea Lynn who was born 3 Apr 1989 and Kelsey Marie
who was born 25 Aug 1992, all born in Spokane.

Michael was born 19 Sep 1954 in Spokane. He married Sandra Louise
Setterlund on 4 May 1974 in Yakima, Wash. Michael is a farmer in
Hartline. Their children are Christopher Michael who was born 18
May 1978 and Karin Ann who was born 29 Jul 1980, both born in
Spokane.

Yvonne was born 23 Jan 1956 in Spokane, and married Raymond Carl White on 10 Jun 1978 in Wilbur, Wash. Yvonne is a secretary and Raymond a truck driver, after having served in the U.S. Navy. They had Brooke Lindsey who was born 14 Jul 1980 and Ashley Rae who was born 13 Oct 1984, both born in Spokane.

John was born 12 Mar 1960 in Spokane; married Danette Dee Krause on 25 Apr 1981 in Wilbur. He is a farmer in Hartline. They had Tyler Richard Alan who was born 29 Dec 1985 and Brylee Renee who was born 1 May 1988, both in Spokane.

1165131 Frederick Allison Graham

Fred was born 8 Sep 1930 in Chicago, Ill. He graduated from John R. Rogers High School in Spokane, Wash., in Jan 1948. His education was continued at Illinois Institute of Technology (IIT) for two years, then he enlisted in the U.S. Marine Corps and served from 1950 to 1954, then finished up at IIT by earning a degree in electrical engineering in Jan 1957. His first employment was with Automatic Electric in Chicago, then with GTEI, which took him to foreign countries, and he spent 23 years living outside the U.S. His career has basically involved applications and sales of telephonic media. For the last eleven years he has worked for DCM Industries.

In San Gol Qi, Ecuador, he married Lilia Maripza Troncoso on 5 May 1962. Lilia has worked as a bilingual translator for the hospital in San Mateo, Calif. Their children are Frederick Kurt who was born in Nov 1964 in Trinidad, and Franklin Fabian who was born in Jan 1966 in Philadelphia, Pa. Frederick is a technical writer.

1165132 Frances Mildred Graham

Frances was born 26 Aug 1933 in Spokane, and was a graduate of North Central High School in Spokane. She married Michael Delaplain, and later they divorced. Their son is Michael Jr., who lives in Temecula, Calif., and is married to Brenda. Frances died 14 Nov 1998 in Calif.

1165141 Diane Graham

Diane married H. Carlton Smith, and they live in South Colby, Wash.

1165142 Jacqueline Graham

Jacqueline was born 9 Aug 1932. She was married to Robert D. Stoyer and died 21 Oct 1978 in Bakerstown, Pa. She was a member of The Eastern Star.

1165161 Lawrence Eugene Phillipy

Larry was born 27 Mar 1937 in Spokane, Wash. He married Evelyn
Irene "Lynn" Taylor on 6 Jul 1957 in Spokane. He once worked as a
lineman for Pacific Northwest Bell Telephone which became U.S. West
Communications.   Lynn worked at Colbert Grade School in food
service. They have been involved in church activities in their
spare time. They had Mark Alan, Brent and Daren.

Mark is a CAD/CAM senior engineer at Boeing Aerospace. He married
Monica Kyle. Their children are Stacia, Shane, Melanie, Shaunae,
Kalie, Ryan, and Kiara.

Brent married Nikki Peterson. Their children are Bo and Cruz.
Daren graduated from high school in 1992 and worked at a variety of
jobs while saving his earnings for a college education. He left
Spokane in May 1993 for a two-year church mission which took him to
the San Jose, Calif., area. Later, he attended Rick's College in
Idaho on a partial scholarship. He maintains high scholastic marks
and participates on the wrestling team.

1165162 David Allison Phillipy

David was born 26 Dec 1939 in Spokane. He graduated from West
Valley High School in 1958, then went on to Whitworth College where
he graduated in 1962.   He graduated in 1965 from McCormick
Theological Seminary in Chicago and was ordained into the gospel
ministry by the Spokane Presbytery. His first appointment was to
serve as chaplain-intern at Anna State Hospital in Anna, Ill.,
while he trained in preparation for a correctional ministry. He
became a chaplain at the Tennessee Prison for Women in Nashville,
Tenn. He married Joyce Eilene Benner of Merced, Calif., on 27 Jan
1962 in Spokane and they divorced in 1987. They had Gregory and
Joel. Secondly, David married Carol Von Stein on 30 Dec 1989 in
Nashville, Tenn.

Gregory was born in 1974. After he graduated from high school he
enlisted in the U.S. Navy which involved spending time in Scotland.
In 1992, he earned a master's degree in fine arts. His sculptures
won recognition in Nashville's juried art shows, and some of them
were sold. He married Amy Strobel in July 1991. Amy, too, holds
a master's degree in fine arts. They live in Sante Fe, N.M., where
Greg works in a bronze molding factory; he continues to make
artistic metal sculptures.

1165163 Keith Leroy Phillipy

Keith was born in Spokane, Wash., on 14 Oct 1947. He graduated from
West Valley High School in 1966, then enlisted in the U.S. Navy and

served four years on nuclear submarines. After he left the navy, he went to work for Pacific Northwest Bell, later USWest Communications, and has been a cable splicer and central office equipment installer since 1973. On 18 Sep 1976 Keith married Nancy Eileen Smith who was born 14 Nov 1949 in Spokane. Nancy graduated from Shadle Park High School in 1968, then obtained her advanced education at Idaho State University where she graduated in 1972; since then she has been a dental hygienist. They have a son, Matthew Scott, born 12 Feb 1978, a daughter, Meagan Leigh, born 16 Mar 1981, and a son, Todd Andrew, born 26 Feb 1985. They live in Spokane, Wash.

1165171 William Leonard Graham

Leonard was born 10 Nov 1946 in Rotan, Tex. On 26 Dec 1979 he married Karen Sue Southern in Mineral Wells, Tex. Karen was born 8 Apr 1956 in Mineral Wells. William is a BNA sales rep. Their children are Eilene Crystal who was born 6 May 1981 in Fort Worth; Curtis William who was born 6 Jun 1983 in Fort Worth; and Elizabeth Dawn who was born 4 Mar 1989 in Lubbock.

1165172 Janice Fern Graham

Janice was born 11 Jun 1954 in Lubbock, Tex. On 3 Aug 1972 she married John Henry Smith III in Mineral Wells. John was born 16 Jan 1954 in Cheyenne, Wyo. Their children are Robert Henry III who was born 12 Aug 1979 in Bedford, Tex; Ryan Graham who was born 30 Jan 1982 in Hurst; Cara Diann who was born 29 Nov 1984 in Bedford; and Caitlin Elizabeth who was born 22 Nov 1986 in Bedford.

1165211 Philip Edward Graham Jr.

Philip was born 7 Jul 1937 and died 9 Jul 1937 in Los Angeles Co., Calif. He is buried with his parents.

1165212 Mary Margaret Graham

Mary was born 23 Apr 1943 in Long Beach, Calif. She is a 1960 graduate of Long Beach Polytecnical High School. She graduated from California State University at Long Beach in 1964 with a BA degree in elementary education, then earned a MA there in 1972. She has been primarily teaching music for 37 years as of 2001. On 24 Feb 1968 she married Donald C. Gabriel who was born 5 May 1935. Don holds a MS in education from Chapman University in Orange, Calif., and recently was a real estate agent. Their children are Marc David and Jason Andrew. Mary and Don live in San Antonio, Tex.

Marc was born 26 Feb 1973 in Long Beach and has earned BA and MA degrees in architecture from the University of Nevada at Las Vegas. He was working in Boston, Mass., as of 2001.

Jason was born 14 Oct 1974 in Long Beach. He has a BS in civil engineering from California State University at Fullerton. He works for the city of Santa Anna, Calif.

1165213 Patricia Louise Dobyns

Patricia was born 4 Apr 1933 and lived with the Graham family. She married Edward Arthur Hinz Jr. and they live in Rancho Palos Verdes, Calif. They have two sons.

1165221 Judith Lynne Graham

Judy was born 24 Mar 1941 in Oakland, Calif. She graduated from Pioneer High School in San Jose, then attended the University of California-Berkeley, where she majored in art history and earned a BA degree in 1962. Lately, she has developed her own business as a household organizer. She married in 1962, Carl Frederick Dukatz, and they had Eric, who was born 5 May 1963 in Berkeley. Secondly, Judy married Mark D. Baker, and they had Adam Gordon Samuel who was born 12 Apr 1969 in Oakland. They live in Garberville, Calif.

1165222 Darleen Joan Graham

Darleen was born 15 Jun 1945 in San Jose, Calif. After graduating from Pioneer high School in San Jose, she earned a degree in education at the University of California-San Jose. She is a teacher in Denver, Colo. She married Edward Sherman Exum, and they had Amber Laura, born in 1974, and Damon Edward, born in 1976. Darleen and Edward divorced, whereupon she changed her name back to Graham. She lives in Denver.

1165223 Thais June Graham

Thais was born 14 Oct 1950 in San Jose, Calif. She is a graduate of Jackson High School in Jackson, Wyo. At the Utah State University she majored in art and graduated magna cum laude with a BFA degree. For a while she was an artist, and is a sculptor in bronze. She also is involved in property management in Jackson, Wyo.

1165231 Thomas Edward Graham

Thomas was born 11 Jan 1950 in Long Beach, Calif. He received a BA in political science from the University of Calif., L.A., in 1972, and became a writing editor. Tom is also a politics and music buff. In 2001, he was living in Tustin, Calif.

1165232 Christine Diane Graham

Christine was born 9 Mar 1952 in Lexington Park, Md. She earned a
BA in history in 1974 at the University of Calif., Santa Barbara.
In 1976, she graduated from the University of San Diego in the
lawyer assistant program. She worked as a paralegal at law firms
in San Diego, Denver and Colorado Springs, Colo. She married Ronald
G. Crowder 19 Jun 1980 in Colo. Ron is commander of Colorado Army
National Guard. Their children are Kelley Jeanne, born 26 Dec
1981, and Robert Graham, born 12 Oct 1986, both born in Colorado
Springs.

1165233 Robert David Graham

Robert was born 1 Jun 1954 in Corona, Calif. He received a BA from
San Diego University in 1977 with majors in telecommunications and
film journalism. He moved to Colorado in 1978 where he played
guitar and banjo in a local band. Bob worked as a writer and
producer of news and special events and was the host of
documentaries. He was an announcer at KKTV in Colorado Springs. In
1988 he became owner, producer, director and writer of Graham
Productions that produced special videos for corporate clients. Bob
is an avid golfer. He married Dawn Elizabeth Spearman 9 Apr 1983
in Colorado Springs. Dawn was born 17 Dec 1958 in Big Springs, Tex.
She is a talented arts and crafts artist. They have a daughter,
Holly Christine, born 8 Dec 1993 in Colorado Springs where they
were residing in 2001.

1165311 Robert Layman Graham

Robert was born 11 Aug 1918 in Kanawha, a small town in north-
central Iowa, the same town where the compiler spent many of his
childhood years. Robert was married on 12 Aug 1944 to Marilyn
Lugsch in Little Rock, Ark. Marilyn was born 11 Mar 1920 in
Glenwood, Ia. Their children, all born in Omaha, were Kathleen,
born 3 Mar 1953; Arlene, born 21 Apr 1955, and Robert Jr., born 23
Apr 1957.

1165321 Margaret Karen Graham

Margaret was born 18 Dec 1938 near Creston, Ia. She married 7 Jun
1959 James Wilbur Tussey in Orient, Ia. He was born 5 Jan 1937 in
Shannon City, Ia. Their children were Jeffrey James, born 24 Sep
1961 in Des Moines, and Stephen Earl born 28 Mar 1964 in Des
Moines.

Jeffrey married 20 Jun 1981 Peni Jo Huddleson in Greenfield, Ia. They had Jill and Nick.

Stephen married 23 Jul 1985 Teresa Jo Kingery in Greenfield, Ia. Their child is Thad.

1165331 Raymond Earl Light

Raymond was born 14te agent in Wichita, Kan. He married in Kansas City, Mo., Elaine Taylor on 22 May 1955. Ray died 7 Nov 1996 in Phoenix, Ariz. A Elaine Light who was born 10 Dec 1924 died 6 Dec 1993 in Port Angeles, Wash.

1165341 Carol Lee Ross

Carol was born in Winterset, Ia., on 18 May 1936. Carol married Richard Edward Nahas in Des Moines on 2 Jun 1963. Richard was born 12 Aug 1934. Their children were Richard Edward, Jr., born 29 Apr 1964 in Des Moines; Lisa Michelle, born 28 Jun 1968, died 17 Jan 1977; and John Minion, born 15 Jan 1970.

Richard married Linda Leanne Moore on 8 May 1993. Linda was born 4 Aug 1962. They had Logan John, born 27 Aug 1994, and Alec David, born 3 Sep 1996, both born in Des Moines.

1165342 Donald Frank Ross

Donald was born 17 Feb 1938 in Winterset. He married Annabelle Cameron 21 Jul 1957 in Macksburg, Ia. She was born in Winterset on 19 Dec 1936. Their children were Kimberly Ann, born 10 Feb 1960; Pamela Jean, born 14 May 1962; and Susanna Kay, born 25 Jul 1965, all born in Des Moines.

Kimberly married Kurt Vincent Katch on 6 Jun 1981. Kurt was born 14 Mar 1959. They had Ashley Anne, born 21 Oct 1985, and Lauren Leigh, born 26 Apr 1988, both born in Des Moines.

Susanna married Kenneth Howard Hinds on 30 Jul 1983. Kenneth was born 7 May 1964. Their children are Benjamin Lee, born 11 Feb 1986, and Nicole Marie, born 25 Jul 1989, both in Des Moines.

1165343 John Edward Ross

John was born 12 May 1942 in Mount Pleasant, Ia. He married Mary Ellen Anderson in Los Angeles.

1165351 Margaret Jean Graham
Margaret was born 2 Jan 1928 in Macksburg, Ia. She married William Joseph Keyburn in Compton, Calif. William was born 17 Mar 1927 in

Norwalk, Conn. Their children are Robert George, born 3 Sep 1954 in Lynwood, Calif.; Kathy Ann, born 5 Mar 1957 in Lynwood; Terri Lee, born 1 Apr 1959 in Lynwood; and Thomas Edward, born 28 Dec 1960 in Harbor City, Calif.

1165352 Betty Mae Graham

Betty was born 13 Apr 1929 in Council Bluffs, Ia. She married John Herod Barr in Hollydale, Calif. They had Sharon Lee 3 Sep 1954 and Marianne E. 28 Dec 1957, both born in L.A. Co., Calif.

1165353 Harold Edward Graham

Harold was born 27 May 1934 in Greenfield, Ia. He married Eileen Esther McDonald in Whittier, Calif. Eileen was born 23 May 1935 in Canton, Ohio.

1165361 Kenneth Lee Graham

Kenneth was born 12 Feb 1949 in Creston, Ia. He married 20 Jul 1969 Rosalie Ann Freeman in Lenox, Ia. Rosalie was born 22 Nov 1950 in Creston, Ia. Their children are David Lee, born 3 Jul 1971 in Oceanport, N.J; Lori Ann, born 3 Sep 1973 in Creston, Ia; and Jennifer Lynn, born 3 Sep 1975 in Creston. Lori has been married and divorced; she has a child, Ashlie McKinney, born 5 Sep 1992.

1165362 William Robert Graham

William was born 1 Jan 1952 in Greenfield, Ia. He married Alma Leighton 22 Dec 1991.

1165363 Mary Louise Graham

Mary was born 16 Oct 1958 in Creston, Ia. She married Robert Weinstein 10 Jun 1989 in Pa. They have Alexandria Clea, born 3 Feb 1995 in New York.

1165421 Robert Lyle Haworth

Robert was born 18 Nov 1922 in Spokane, Wash., and died 11 Feb 1999 in Eugene, Ore. On 19 Jan 1944 he married Elizabeth Ann (Betty Ann) Woesner in Moscow, Idaho. Both were graduates of the University of Idaho. Later, robert earned a master's degree there. He was in the Battle of the Bulge during WW II when he was blown out of a foxhole. Robert became a realtor and an insurance broker in Springfield, Ore. Their children are Robert Larry, born 8 Aug 1970; James Dennis, born 19 Oct 1950; Gary Williams and Samuel Ray, twins born 10 Aug 1953.

Robert married 8 Aug 1970 Marguerite Ann DeReamer who was born 6 Mar 1951.   Robert graduated from the University of California. They have Graham Whitney, born 22 Aug 1972.

James married 29 Dec 1971 Priscilla Ann Pebley who was born 8 Jan 1949.   James graduated from the University of Oregon.   Their children are Benjamin, born 7 May 1974, and Lindsay, born 16 Aug 1978.

Gary married 31 Aug 1976 Penny Sue Lewellen who was born 22 May 1951. Gary graduated from the Univ. of Oregon.   They have Christopher Sean, born 11 Jul 1978; Aaron, born in 1980; Gavin, born in 1983; and Holly, born in Jul 1984.

Samuel is a graduate of the University of Oregon.

1165422 Donald Raymond Haworth

Donald was born 21 Aug 1926 in Spokane, Wash.   On 3 Jun 1950 he married Jewel Virginia Smith.   They both graduated from Washington State University.   Donald served in the U.S. Navy during World War II, and later was employed by Sperry-Rand as a manager.   He became vice president of University Computers in Dallas, Tex.   This was followed by a career as president and member of the executive committee of Greyhound Corporation, and finally was president of Atlantic Bell, International.   Their children are Linda Katherine, born 24 Feb 1952 in Spokane; Constance Lynn, born 7 Jul 1954; and Julie Ann, born 10 Dec 1957.

Linda married David Nichols in Dallas in 1984.   They have Blaine Haworth, born in Sep 1985.

Constance married 8 Oct 1972 Charles Wesley Hilliard IV.   Their children are Jennifer Lynn, Kimberly Ann, Michelle Leigh, and Charles Wesley Jr.

1165423 Gerald Samuel Haworth

Gerald was born 21 Oct 1928 in Spokane, Wash.   He died of complications following a tonsillectomy in Spokane on 19 Jan 1936.

1165431 Ruth Evelyn Wimmer

Ruth was born in Seattle 6 Mar 1927.   She married Richard Alexander Leggett on 15 Oct 1949 in West Hartford, Conn.   Ruth graduated from Middlebury College with a degree in mathematics, and Richard graduated from Trinity University in Hartford.   Richard went on to become vice-president and actuary of The Travelers Insurance Company.   Their children are Elizabeth Roberts, born 1 Apr 1953;

John Graham, born 21 Sep 1954; Jane Allison, born 12 Sep 1956; Anne Sarah, born 9 Jun 1959; and Martha Starr, born 18 Apr 1962, all born in Hartford.   In 1999, Ruth and Richard were living in West Hartford, Conn.

Elizabeth graduated from Denison College in Ohio with a bachelor's degree in social science.   She was employed at Washington State University in Student Services; she is working on a master's degree at Azusa Pacific College. She married Corbett West in 1979.   Their children are Matthew Alexander, born 1 Jan 1984; Gillian Christine, born 1 Aug 1985; and Martha Lynn, born 12 May 1987.

John graduated with a bachelor's degree in music from Connecticut College. He was in computer sales and programing before joining a computer import-export company.   He married Eileen Sullivan on 16 Oct 1994.   Their children are Alicia Isabel who was born 12 Nov 1995 and Alan Sullivan who was born 4 Nov 1997.

Jane graduated from Middlebury College with a degree in environmental economics and earned a master's degree in urban development from Harvard. She was employed by the EPA and later was stationed in Paris, France.   Jane has Elise Samiha Emil who was born 23 Jun 1994 and Katherine Annette Emil who was born 30 Nov 1995.

Anne graduated *magna cum laude* from Middlebury College with a degree in environmental economics.   She later earned a master's degree in botany at the University of Washington.   Anne married Daniel Billman in 1991 and is employed at HDR Engineering Inc., Anchorage, Alaska.

Martha graduated from Dartmouth with a BA, then was on the staff of an Alaskan senator.   She earned a master's degree in Yale School of Management and Yale Divinity School.   She married John Edward Kennard in 1993. Their children are John Leggett who was born 27 Nov 1994, Maeve Wimmer who was born 16 Jul 1996 and Elizabeth Powers who was born 2 Oct 1999.

1165432 Gordon Lyle Wimmer

Gordon was born 9 Jun 1929 in Seattle.   On 1 Feb 1958 he married Grace Elizabeth Moloy in Loudenville, N.Y.   Gordon graduated with a degree in engineering from Princeton and worked for Westinghouse for fifteen years.   Their children are John Gordon, born 19 Jun 1959; James Lyle, born 14 Oct 1960; and Margaret Mary, born 26 Apr 1963.

John graduated in accounting from Clarkson University in New York, and was employed by Specialty Steel and Metals Manufacturing Co.

James graduated from Niagara College in New York with a degree in accounting, and became a CPA.

Margaret graduated in economics from Colby College in Maine, and attended the London School of Economics. She earned a master's degree at the school of management at Duke University, and is now with a consulting firm in Washington, D.C.

1165511 Samuel Howard Sloan

Howard was born 7 Sep 1944 in Richmond, Va. He attended, but did not graduate from, the University of California at Berkley. He was married to Anda and they had Peter Julius, born 27 Oct 1979 in N.Y.C.; and Mary Rachel, born 18 Oct 1980 in N.Y.C. He divorced Anda in 1981 and married several more times, including Honzagol in Pakistan and they had a daughter, Shamema who was born 16 Oct 1981 in N.Y.C. They divorced in 1982. Shemema was recently of Madison Heights, Va.

1165512 Creighton Wesley Sloan

Creighton was born 27 Jun 1946 in Richmond, Va. He received a AA degree from Louisburg College in N.C., in 1966; a BA from the State University of New York at Buffalo in 1970; and a MBA from the University of North Carolina in 1984. He is employed by the Westinghouse Savannah River Company. Creighton married Gloria Jean Smith on 6 Aug 1972. Gloria was born 5 Jun 1950 in Bellmore, N.Y. She holds a BS from the State University of Buffalo, New York in 1972, and a MS degree from the University of Iowa in 1975. She is employed by the Aiken County Public Schools. They had Cassel Wesley, born 4 Oct 1982 in Durham, N.C., and Armanda Marjorie, born 2 Oct 1985 in Charlotte, N.C.

1165521 Edward Graham Jacobson

Edward was born 31 Dec 1944 in El Paso, Tex. He graduated in 1963 from Cedar Falls High School, and served in the U.S. Coast Guard from 1965 through 1969 on boats that were involved in military actions in the South China Sea. Later he studied for a degree in electrical engineering at the University of Iowa and received a BSEE in 1974. He worked for General Electric Corp. for twelve years which took him to several foreign countries. Since then he has been employed at Los Alamos, N.M., where he is involved in nuclear activities. Ed married Adelaide G. Behan on 20 Apr 1987 in Lumberton, N.C. She was born 10 Nov 1950, and is a graduate of St Bonaventure University with a BBA degree, and of Wake Forest where she earned a jurist doctorate in 1976. Adelaide was once District Court Judge in N.C. Their child is Austin G. who was born 8 Dec 1990 in Los Alamos.

1165531 Carol Elizabeth Jacobson

Carol was born 5 Feb 1951 in Washington, D.C. She married Thomas E. Fenstermacher and the family lives in Silver Spring, Md.

1165532 Karen Jeanette Jacobson

Karen was born in Washington, D.C. on 1 Dec 1954. She married Brian Holmes on 1 Aug 1987 in Silver Spring, Md. She is a graduate of the University of Maryland with a BA in government. She then completed work on two master's degrees, one in hospital administration, the other a MBA which she received in 1989, both from George Washington University. Karen initially worked in the health care field, but more recently she has been a supervisor at U.S. Customs Service.

1165551 Robert Dale Jacobson

Robert was born 21 Apr 1942 in Enid, Okla. He is a graduate of the University of Iowa Law School. He married 14 Jun 1974 Connie Jean Richards in Indianola, Ia. He is a lawyer living in Lumberton, N.C.

1165552 Richard Wesley Jacobson

Richard was born 3 Jul 1944 San Antonio, Tex. In Huntsville, Ala., he married Gail Rodene Borovicki. They had Deborah, born 3 Mar 1970 in Germany, and Julie Elizabeth, born 16 Jul 1971 in Germany. Deborah is married to Mark Grammitico and they have one child. Julie is married to Jason Chamberlain.

1165553 William Allison Jacobson

William was born 19 Apr 1948 in Japan. He lived in Honolulu when he worked for a navy contractor. He is unmarried, and currently living in Lake Port, Calif.

1165554 Philip Alden Jacobson

Philip was born 1 Aug 1950 at Fort Belvoir, Va. He is married to Laura, and they live in Calif.

1165611 Joan Myrtle Bishop

Joan (Jo-an) was born 19 Jun 1930. She married Elmer Hammerschmidt on 9 Jul 1949 in Park Ridge, Ill. Their children are Robert Stephan, born 12 Sep 1952 in Waukegan; Alan Dale, born 2 Jun 1954 in Cherry Point, N.C.; and Lynn Marie, born 16 Apr 1960 in Chicago.

Elmer was in the U.S. Marine Corps and retired as a SSGT after 12 years of service. They live in Park Ridge, Ill.

1165612 Barbara Jean Bishop

Barbara was born 24 Oct 1932 in Chicago, Ill. She married John Markey on 7 May 1954 in Las Vegas and live in Oceanside, Calif. They had Pamela Jean who born 4 Aug 1954 in Camp Lejeune, N.C.; Patricia Ann who was born 1 Jan 1956 in Oceanside; and Teresa Kathleen who was born 10 Oct 1963 in Oceanside.

1165621 John Allison Bishop

John was born 22 Dec 1934 in Milwaukee, Wisc. He graduated from Rufus high school in Milwaukee in 1954, then served in the U.S. Coast guard from 1954 to 1958. He was with the police department for five years then with the sheriff's department for 28 years before retiring. He enjoys traveling, works part-time in a store, and enjoys doing the home cooking. On 25 Jun 1955 he married Shirley Ruth White who was born 2 Oct 1935 in Milwaukee. Their children are Mark Sherwin who was born 24 Mar 1956, Glen Allen who was born 11 Nov 1957, Lori Lynn who was born 16 May 1962, William John who was born 26 May 1965, and Susan Ann who was born 6 Dec 1967. John and Shirley live in West Allis, Wisc.

Mark married JoAnn Salamone and they have Lianna Salamone born 14 Oct 1985.

Glen married Mary Cerwin and they had Jessica Rose who was born 7 Jan 1982. Glen and Mary are now divorced.

Lori married Anthony Fischer. Their children are Jacquelyn Ann born 16 Dec 1982, Gregory Anthony born 7 Jan 1984, and Lance Andrew born 27 Aug 1985. Secondly, Lori married Steven William Eisch and they have a son, Joseph William who was born 26 Sep 1992.

William married Kim Rebro; no children.

Susan married "Scott" Lafleur. They had Zachary Scott who was born 30 Oct 1990. Secondly, Susan married Doneo Berndsen and they had Colton John born 25 Jun 1999.

1165622 Mary Jane Bishop

Mary was born 4 Nov 1938 in Milwaukee. She married James Steinbach on 28 Mar 1959 in West Bend, Wisc. They had Debra Mary who was born 28 Nov 1960 and died 19 Nov 1968, Jeff Lee who was born 2 Jun 1964, Jay Lee who was born 15 Feb 1966, and Jayson Lee who was born 17 Jan 1974, all born in Milwaukee, Wisc.

Jeff married Michelle Hoekstra on 2 Nov 1984 in Fond du Lac, Wisc. Their children are Heather Nicole born 8 Oct 1985, Justin Lee born 19 Jan 1989 and Matilin Johanna born 26 Feb 1998, all born in Waupun, Wisc. Jeff is a graduate of the University of Wisconsin, and is a project manager in the manufacture of portable room partitions for a company in Madison, Wisc.,

1165623 Thomas Wayne Bishop

Thomas was born 6 May 1943 in Milwaukee. In Milwaukee on 18 Aug 1962 he married Kathleen Murphy who was born there 18 Jan 1942. Their four children are Todd Thomas who was born 10 Dec 1963 in Milwaukee, Hollie Ann who was born 1 Mar 1965 in Milwaukee, Dennis Wayne who was born 3 Dec 1967 in West Alice and Brian Wayne who was born 1 Jul 1970.

Todd married Yvonne Kaprelina and they have a son, Maxwell Thomas, born 8 Dec 1991.

Hollie married Ray Szymanowski. They have Shane Ryan born 29 Aug 1986 and Erika Nicole born 5 Nov 1989.

Dennis married Caroline Giacomin on 1 May 1999.

Brian married Jennifer Jacobson on 15 Jun 1990 in Racine, Wisc; and they later divorced. They had twins, Nicole Marie and Dannielle Marie, born on 29 Aug 1990, and Michael Edward, born on 27 Jun 1994.

1165624 Kenneth Claude Bishop

Kenneth was born 30 Jun 1949; he is unmarried and has a son, Kenneth Claude, born 22 Dec 1981. Kenneth served with the U.S. Navy until he was granted a hardship discharge following the death of his father. He now is employed in the production of blue prints.

1165631 Claudette Jane Augustine

Claudette was born 28 Aug 1936 in Osceola, Ia., and died the same day.

1165632 Jim O. Augustine

Jim, who was adopted, was born 1 Jan 1947. He was in the U.S. Marine Corps and was severely wounded during the Vietnam War for which he was awarded Purple Hearts. He may be living in Wisc.

1165633 Jack G. Augustine

Jack was born 2 Jan 1948 and was adopted. He has proven to be a
hard man to locate.

1165641 Richard Alan Morris

Dick was born 4 Apr 1941 in Berwyn, Ill. He graduated from
Creston, Iowa, High School in 1959, then served in the U.S. Navy
aboard submarines. Making use of the GI bill, he attended Iowa
State University where he earned a BS degree in metallurgical
engineering in 1971. He immediately went to work for a naval
research lab in Annapolis, Md., where he worked from 1971 through
1994 when he retired to Buhl, Ida. He worked at the same facility
as the compiler, unaware of their relationship. He married Judy
Bauerle on 11 Aug 1962 in Idaho Falls, Ida. Judy was born 22 Apr
1944 and had worked as a restaurant manager. Their children are
Michael David who was born 6 Jun 1964 in Portsmouth, Va., and Lisa
Ann who was born 12 Nov 1965 in Great Lakes, Ill.

Michael married Kate Lynn Casteel 8 Jun 2001. Lisa married Morris
Richard Davis, and later they divorced. They had a son, Michael
Edward, born 25 Jan 1992 in Norfolk, Va.

1165642 Peter Jon Morris

Peter (Pete) was born 23 Oct 1942 in Berwyn, Ill. He graduated
from Creston High School in 1961, then enlisted in 1962 in the U.S.
Navy and served until 1966. He was married to Jill Herstein who
was previously married. Later they divorced. They had Marty Lee
born 22 Mar 1977 in Des Moines and Shayne Michael born 14 Dec 1979
in Des Moines. He works for the postal service in Des Moines and is
a resident of Indianola, Ia.

1165711 Jerry Keithley Butler III

Jerry was born 19 Oct 1943 in San Diego, Calif. He married 8 Feb
1968 Mary Carolyn Soileau in Marshall, Tex. Mary was born 17 Dec
1946 in Ville Platte, La. They had Geri Kaye who was born 9 Nov
1969 in Ann Arbor, Mich. Jerry and Mary later divorced. Secondly,
Jerry married 7 Jan 1980 Deborah Ellen Patterson who was born in
Tampa, Fla., 9 Apr 1940. Jerry graduated from Louisiana Tech, then
served with the U.S. Air Force. Deborah was a professor of
Humanities at Edison College in Fort Meyers, Fla. Jerry worked for
a newspaper in Fort Meyers.

Geri married Scott Christopher Savoie 1 Aug 1987 in Washington,
La., Scott was born 18 Dec 1967. Scott was a member of the U.S.
Air Force. They had Christopher Ashton and David Scott.

1165712 Robert Graham Butler

Robert was born 28 May 1945 in San Diego. He married Melissa Dianne Idom 19 Feb 1966 at Vivian, La. Robert graduated from Louisiana Tech and became a salesman. They had Robin Melissa, born 21 Oct 1966 in Shreveport, La., and Amanda Susan, born 22 Nov 1970 in Ruston, La.

1165713 Ellen Ruth Butler

Ellen was born 19 Aug 1949 in Cherry Point, N.C. On 11 Apr 1969 she married Larry Elbert Page who was born 3 Sep 1938. Later they were divorced. Their children were Matthew Corey, born 5 Sep 1972 in Shreveport, and Jeremy Foster, born 18 Jun 1979 in Shreveport.

1165714 Lawrence Walter Butler

Lawrence was born 30 Sep 1952 at Barksdale Air Force Base, La. His first marriage was to Jane Boyd on 27 Oct 1970 in Louisville, Ky. They were divorced in 1972. Secondly, Lawrence married Barbara Ella Moore on 19 Oct 1974 in Shreveport, La. Their children are Shawn Michael, born 27 Jul 1974, and Dawn Nicole, born 6 Jan 1977.

1167111 Frank Raymond Eyerly

Frank was born 16 Aug 1945 in Los Angeles Co., Calif., and died 27 Jun 1998 in Lynnwood, Wash. He married Susan E. Rhodes, and they had Frank William who was born 27 Aug 1965 in Los Angeles Co., Calif. Frank and Susan were divorced in 1981. Frank secondly married Rosalie. They had no children. Frank was once a resident of Friday Harbor, Wash. There may have been a genealogy of the Eyerly family published about 1979.

1167112 Jenna Eyerly

Jenna is a resident of Hawaii and is not married.

1167121 Joan Lorraine Billiter

Joan was born 12 Mar 1949 in Los Angeles Co., Calif.

1167141 Millicent Jean Mills

Millicent was born 17 Feb 1954 in Pasadena, Calif. She married Mark Smit, and they had Jessica who was born in 1991, and Eric who was born in Oct 1995.

1167142 Patricia Ann Mills

Patricia was born 5 Apr 1956 in Pasadena, Calif. She is married to Roberto Lopez. They had Rebeca and Heidi Christina. Rebeca married Steven Polac.

1167211 Ruth Ilene Sandusky

Ruth was born 24 Dec 1932 in Earlham, Ia. She married Donald Sayre on 24 Aug 1957 in Madison Co. Donald was born 24 Dec 1930 and died 8 Aug 1970. Their children were Paula Ann, born 8 Aug 1958, and John Arron, born 10 Jan 1965. Secondly, Ruth married Clinton Butler on 28 Nov 1970. They have one child, Robin Lee, born 8 Apr 1973. Paula Ann married Bell Schierlman on 25 Mar 1983.

1167212 Evelyn Lenora Sandusky

Evelyn was born 6 Sep 1934 in Earlham, Ia. She married Felix Cordero on 16 Nov 1953 in Montgomery, Alabama. Felix was born about 1932 and served in the U.S. Air Force for 23 years and left the service as a master sargeant. Their children are Richard Felix, born 3 Sep 1954 and Tina (or Lena ?) Lynn, born 28 Oct 1959, both in Winterset, Ia. Evelyn and Felix are divorced; she was living in San Antonio in 1999.

Richard married JoAnn Lnu on 6 May 1976 in Victorville, Calif. They divorced without children.

1167213 Mary Isabelle Sandusky

Mary was born 11 Jul 1937 in Earlham, Ia. She married Glen Cottle on 6 May 1960 in Madison Co. Glen was born about 1935 in Ia. They had Patricia Ann who was born 29 May 1961 in Madison Co., Ia. Patricia Ann married John Hyall on 20 Nov 1986 in Madison Co., Ia.

1167221 Lenamae Louise Gieber

Lee was born 18 Apr 1941 in Glenwood, Ia. She attended elementary schools in Glenwood and graduated from Omaha Central High School in 1959. She studied at Rhema Bible School during the 1979-1980 term, and from 1986-87 at the School of the Local Church in Tulsa, Okla., and for a while was an ordained minister. Today she teaches Bible classes at a non-denominational church in Lincoln, Neb. She married Leland Brokaw who is probably a distant cousin of other Brokaws mentioned herein. Their children were Kim Marie who was born 17 Oct 1961 in Omaha and Cheryl Lee who was born 17 Nov 1964 in Turlock, Calif. Lee and Leland were divorced and Lee married Warren "Andy" P. Brayton on 13 Feb 1970 in Papillion, Neb. Andy

was born 26 Jun 1943 in Los Angeles. They had a stillborn child,
Andrew John, in Jan 1971. Andy is a self-employed craftsman. Lee
and Warren live in Milford, Neb.

Kim married Ron Engel on 21 Apr 1979 in Milford, Neb. Ron was born
9 May 1959. They have no children.

Cheryl married Warren Brayton Jr. on 11 Jan 1992. Warren was born
19 Aug 1963. Their children were Kaitlyn Dawn who was born 13 Nov
1992 and died 23 Nov 1992, and Breanna Dawn who was born 22 Jun
1994.

1167222 Connie Jo Gieber

Connie Jo was born 28 Aug 1943 in Glenwood, Ia., and died in Omaha
of encephalitis on 25 Jul 1946.

1167223 John Edward Gieber

John was born 10 Nov 1948 in Omaha. He suffered a back injury when
he fell out of a hay mow as a youth. He was once a mechanic for a
trucking firm and is now self-employed. He is not married and
lives in Omaha.

1167231 Nancy Mae McCorkle

Nancy was borin May 1987. Secondly, Patricia married Ronald
Phillips in June 1989 in Omaha. Ron is a architect technician for
the Army Corps of Engineers. Pat works as a legal aid in Omaha.

1167242 Terri Joanne Rold

Terri was born 23 Nov 1957 in Omaha. She attended high school then
studied at nursing school in Omaha and is a LPN. Terri has a son,
Nathaniel Lee Rold, who was born 27 Oct 1982 in Omaha.

1167311 Joanne Elizabeth Wright

Joanne was born 5 Dec 1946 in Denver, Colo. She was a 1965
graduate of Arvada West High School. Joanne is now a finance
manager in an engineering consulting office she owns. She married
Robert E. Sammons on 6 Sep 1967 in Arvada, Colo. Robert was born
13 Sep 1944 and died 30 Mar 1970. She married Larry Gambrell 3 Sep
1976 in Conifer, Colo. Larry was born 26 Mar 1938 and died 1 Feb
1999. Larry was an electrical engineering graduate of Colorado
State University. There were no children. Joanne lives close to
Yellowstone National Park in summer months and near Tucson in the
winter.

1167321 Warren Lee Duff

Warren was born 8 May 1940 in Denver, Colo. He graduated from
Central High School in Pueblo, and attended junior college briefly.
He then enlisted in the U.S. Air Force and was honorably discharged
after serving his full enlistment period. He then was manager of
a beauty supply warehouse. He was married to Gertrude; there were
no children. Warren died 2 May 1995 in Denver and his body was
cremated. Gertrude was born 25 Jan 1926 and died 13 Jul 1991 in
Denver.

1167322 Carole Leanne Duff

Carole was born 19 Sep 1942 in Denver, Colo. She graduated from
Central High School in Pueblo in 1960, and studied business at
Western State in Gunnison for a year. She married David Wesley
Roberts on 19 Jun 1960. They had Loretta Jeanette who was born 24
Aug 1961 in Canon City, Colo. Later, Carole married James Oliver
Horton Jr. on 24 Dec 1980. Carole worked as a advertising traffic
manager for a television station for eight years, then as a payroll
specialist, and is now an administration assistant at Rocky
Mountain Steel Mills. James was born 23 Nov 1934 and died 9 Apr
1998 in Pueblo.

Loretta married Steve Sanchez, then Wayne Canida on 21 Apr 1999.
They live in Pueblo, Colo.

1167331 Shirley Barnes

Shirley was born about 1931.

1167421 Carol Lenora Morse

Carol was born 4 Sep 1961 in Great Falls, Mont. She graduated from
Moore High School in 1979, then attended Montana State College
where she earned a BS degree in nursing. She worked as a nurse in
the Billings area, then married Robert Atchison on 26 Oct 1985 in
Lewistown. Their children are Shelby Lynn who was born 13 Dec 1996
in Billings and Robert Colby who was born 20 Sep 1998 in Billings.
They live in Roundup, Mont.

1167422 Paul Nicholas Morse

Paul was born 21 Nov 1965 in Missoula, Mont. He is a 1984 graduate
of Moore High School. He attended Northern College for two years
and became a diesel mechanic.   He married Rita and they had Ashley

Jean who was born 3 Sep 1987 in Great Falls. Secondly, he married
Cindy Chapel and they divorced without children.

1167423 Julie Ann Morse

Julie was born 13 Apr 1970 in Billings, Mont. After graduation
from Moore High School in 1988, she attended a business college in
Spokane for a year, then studied to become a beautician. She
worked in Bozeman, Mont. Julie married Jon Bengel on 27 Dec 1991
in Coeur d'Alene, Id. Their child is Raegann Michell who was born
20 Nov 1995 in Lewistown, Mont.

1167431 Gregg Edward Morse

Gregg was born 13 Apr 1954 in Great Falls, Mont. He married Paula
Louise Kinsby on 15 May 1976 in Great Falls. She was born about
1956 in Mont. They had Jeffrey Gregg, born 31 Aug 1979, and Dustin
Christopher, born 5 Jul 1982, both in Great Falls.

1167432 Karen Ione Morse

Karen was born 5 Feb 1956 in Great Falls. She married Jim Durnford
and they had Ian James on 20 May 1994 and Nolan Morse on 8 Jan
1997. Karen once worked as a bank inspector for the Federal
Reserve, and is now a homemaker. Jim is a mechanical engineer
involved with marine construction. They make their home in Kent,
Wash.

1167433 Eric Lindsay Morse

Eric was born 29 Apr 1958 in Great Falls, Mont. He is a rancher
near Denton, Mont., where he feeds several cows and grows barley
and other grains. Eric is not married.

1167434 Mark Harry Morse

Mark was born 27 Dec 1959 in Great Falls, Mont. He married Terri
Fraser on 19 Oct 1996, and they live in Renton, Wash.

1167435 Dale Frederick Morse

Dale was born 27 Aug 1961 in Great Falls, Mont. He married
Bridgette Ann Cassidy on 23 Jan 1987 in Great Falls. They have two
daughters, Patricia Norine born 18 Dec 1992 and Ann Marie born 5
May 1995. They live in White Hall, Mont.

1167436 Carla Jean Morse
Carla was born 24 Apr 1963 in Great Falls, Mont. She married Terry
Lee Hoyer on 31 Aug 1985 in Great Falls. Terry was born about 1961

in Mont. They have a girl and a boy, Ariana ?? and Gaylon, and live in Vancouver, Wash.

1167451 Michael Patrick Morse

Michael was born 17 Mar 1952. He married Julie Lnu about 1977. Their children were Eric Andrew on 3 Apr 1978 and Amy born about 1981.

1167452 Rebecca Marie Morse

Rebecca was born 25 May 1953. She married Joseph (Joe) L. Hicks and they had Brandie Elsie and Dustin. In 2001 they were planning on moving away from Menomonie, Wisc., for a warmer climate.

1167453 Patricia Ann Morse

Patricia was born 26 May 1957. She married Michael Kane. Their children are Laura Elaine born 21 Jan 1989, Mary Patricia born 21 Dec 1992 and Scott Edward born 16 Mar 1994.

1167454 Thomas John Morse

Thomas was born 9 Apr 1959.

1167455 Juanita Elaine Morse

Juanita was born 25 Jun 1963. She married Steven Barton on 12 Sep 1985. They have Tara and Annie.

1167456 Joan Ellen Morse

Joan was born 26 Feb 1965. On 21 Dec 1991, she married Suneel Arora.

1167511 Shirley Lee Light

Shirley was born 8 Aug 1930 in Kansas City, Mo. She grew to adulthood in Columbus, Kan., and graduated from Cherokee County Community High School. She gave birth to Daniel Lee Light who was born 13 Dec 1946 in San Francisco. He was adopted in 1950 by Paul and Bernice Fee. Shirley married Russel Randall in Oakland, Calif., where he was stationed while serving with the U.S. Navy. They later settled in Tulsa, Okla., where Shirley was a housewife while Russel worked for a magazine distribution company. While there, they had Russel, Jr., and Sharon. They next lived in Afton, Okla., where William was born. They were divorced while living in Afton. Secondly, Shirley married Edwin Heitkemper in 1954 and they lived in Ariz. for several years. They divorced in 1965 and Shirley returned to Columbus, Kan., where she makes her home with her husband, Gerald Greenlee, whom she married in 1966. Shirley has had varying occupations in her lifetime, and now in retirement, she and Gerald serve as part-time drivers for Social Services.

Russel Rolland Randall, Jr. was born 9 Mar 1948 in Tulsa, Okla. In 1997 he was living in West Richland, Wash. Russ graduated from high school in Columbus, Kan., in 1966, then he attended Kansas State Teachers College at Emporia, Kan., where he received a BA degree. Next he attended Kansas State University in Manhattan, Kan., and earned a PhD. in physics in 1974. He accepted employment with Dresser Atlas Corp. of Houston, Tex., where he was a nuclear physicist and helped design and construct deep-oil well instruments for detecting and determining porosity of rock. After 1991 he continued in the same line of work for Baker Hughes. In 1994 he took a position as nuclear physicist with the Department of Energy, Hartford Site, Richland, Wash. Now he has his own consulting firm. Russ married Bonnie Jean Carpenter on 30 May 1970 in Wichita, Kan. Bonnie was born 24 Mar 1948 in Wichita. They divorced in 1987 in Katy, Tex. Their children are Brent Eldon, born 23 Apr 1976, and Regina Kay, born 1 Feb 1979, both born in Houston, Tex.

Sharon Lee Randall was born 22 Dec 1949 in Tulsa, Okla. She married Wolfgang Eugene Poth in Nov 1968, and divorced in 1970. Secondly, she married Mark Alan Poloschan on 13 Jul 1972 in Yuma, Az., and they divorced in 1981. Mark was born 14 May 1949 in Canton, Ohio. In Massillon, Ohio, their two children were born: Kimberly Michelle, born 13 Dec 1974, and Tiffany Lee, born 3 Dec 1976. Sharon earned a cosmetology degree from Ft. Scott Community College in 1990, and was then a cosmetic consultant for Christian Dior at Famous Barr in Joplin, Mo.

Kimberly graduated from high school in Columbus, Kan., in 1993. She was a member of the math team that year when they won first place in the Missouri Southern Math League. She majored in marketing and finance at Pittsburg State University and was due to graduate in 1998. She married Drew Jason Richards on 3 Aug 1996 in Columbus, Kan. Drew was born 31 Dec 1974 in Columbus. He graduated from high school in 1993 and from Pittsburgh State University in 1998. Drew works at his father's printing plant in Columbus.

Tiffany Lee attended Columbus Unified High School and graduated from McKinley High in Canton, Ohio, in 1995. She married David Andrew Lamp on 26 Jul 1997 in Canton where David was born 25 Oct 1998. He was a graduate of Capital University in 1995 where he was a star soccer player. David and Tiffany were living in Columbus, Kan., where he is manager of a rental car agency.

William was born 2 Dec 1950 in Afton, Okla. He died 2 Aug 1979 in Belton, Mo., and was buried in Belton Cemetery. William was the natural child of Shirley and Russell R. Randall, and was adopted by Delmer and Florena Scott in 1953. He graduated from high school at Belton and from Kansas City Business College. William suffered a fatal heart attack while playing baseball. He had been aware that he had a heart defect known as aorta stenosis which contributed to his death. William married Pamela Jane Robertson on 25 Feb 1972 in Belton, Mo. Their child was Jennifer Louise Scott, born 14 Aug 1972 in Belton. Jennifer has three children: Jaci Lynn, born in 1992; Devin Joseph, born in 1994; and Dakoda, born in Jan 1996; their last name is unknown.

1167512 Jack Scott Light

[Contributed by Jack Light] Jack was born 1 Jan 1932 in Skidmore, Kan., in the rural home of his grandparents, Elmer and Bertha Scott. After graduating from Columbus High School, he joined the U.S. Air Force on 10 Oct 1950. He entered aircraft mechanic training as a private at Wichita Falls, Tex. He was awarded a promotion to corporal for graduating at the top of his class. Next, Jack served at National Airport in Washington, D.C., in the Military Transport Service until 1955 when he rose to Staff Sargeant. While there he met Reta Francine Alfano and they were married at her home in Dewey Rose, Ga., on 6 Apr 1952.

In 1955 Jack applied for Officer Candidate School (OCS) as one out of over 9,000 applicants service wide and became a member of the class of 56C; he took his OCS training at Lackland Air Force Base and graduated as a Second Lieutenant. Next he completed pilot training at Orlando Air Force Base and advanced training in B-52s at Vance Air Force Base in 1957, and graduated with honors at the top of his class with the presentation of the Silver Bowl Outstanding Pilot Award. He took advanced training in the C-118 (DC-6) at West Palm Beach, Fla., and was assigned to the 30th Squadron, McGuire AFB, N.J., in 1958. He flew world-wide routes for eight years and upgraded into the Boeing C-135 (707) jet in 1965.

Through the military education program he earned a BS degree in 1964 from the University of Omaha. In 1966 he was transferred to Charleston AFB where he was Captain, Operations Officer, at the Command Post, and pilot of the Lockheed C-141 Starlifter. He served briefly as Operation Officer in Japan before being transferred to the MATS Command Post in the Phillipines and was promoted to Major. As Pilot and Aircraft Commander he flew for the C-118 Air Evac Squadron in Vietnam one week out of each month for three years where he logged several hundred hours of combat time and was awarded two Air Medals. After twenty years of military

service and after logging over 10,000 flying hours, Major Light
retired from the Air Force on 1 Nov 1970.

Jack entered graduate school at the University of Nebraska in 1971
and graduated with a MS in economics in 1973.   Jack accepted a
position as Economist in the Research Department of the Federal
Reserve Bank of Chicago.   Jack continued his higher education by
attending Northwestern University and received his MM degree in
finance and banking.   He also graduated from the Graduate School of
Bank Management at the University of Michigan.   He worked as an
Economist, Operations Officer, and Assistant Vice President before
he left the Federal Reserve in 1985.   Jack and Reta moved to
Atlanta where Jack worked at the First National Bank of Atlanta in
Monroe, Ga.

In 2001, Jack and Reta left their retirement home in Ponte Verda
Beach, Fla., and relocated to the cooler environment of Buena
Vista, Colo.   Jack enjoys playing golf, doing yard work, reading,
and traveling while conducting genealogy research.   Jack has been
a prolific writer of family genealogies, including considerable
material on a branch of the Samuel Melvin Thomson family.

Reta was born 14 Jun 1933 in Mt. Airy, N.C.   She attended
elementary school in Elberton, Ga.   She graduated from Bowman, Ga.,
then removed to Washington, D.C.   Their three children are Francine
Kay, Edward Scott, and Brad Chandler.   Later Reta worked as a
cosmetic model in Chicago for a few years.

Francine Kay Light was born 24 Jan 1953 in Ft. Belvoir, Va.   She
received her elementary education in Bordertown, N.J., started high
school in the Phillipines, and graduated in Omaha, Neb.   She
attended the University of Nebraska for two years before she
married Jarrett Louis Knoll on 18 Aug 1973 in Omaha.   She worked
for an insurance company and an optometrist.   Jarrett was born 10
Apr 1952 in Spokane, Wash.   He was a self-employed computer
consultant before his untimely death due to colon cancer on 21 May
2001 at his home in Overland Park, Kan. He had been active in the
Boy Scouts of America organization.   Their children are Jason
Jarrett Knoll, born 12 Apr 1978 in Omaha; and Sean Michael Knoll,
born 15 Mar 1984 in Kansas City, Mo.   Jason was active in scouting
and earned the coveted Eagle Scout award in 1994.   He graduated
from high school in 1996 and attended Johnson County Community
College in Overland Park, Kan.   Sean is active in scouting,
participates in soccer, and is a student of the violin which he
plays in the school orchestra.

Edward Scott Light was born 13 Dec 1955 in Ft. Belvoir, Va.   In
1998 he was a resident of Littleton, Colo.   Scott grew up in the
atmosphere of military bases where his father was assigned.   He

attended grammar school at Summerville, S.C., and then at the Clark AFB in the Phillipines. He was a Boy Scout and enjoyed playing football. Scott graduated from high school in Deerfield, Ill., then attended Kearney State College in Neb., from 1973-75. Scott is an accomplished down-hill skier. He has worked for Sears for 18 years in the Colorado area and is now a Facilities Manager for eight stores. Scott married Terri Eilene (Matya) Thiesfeld on 19 Sep 1998 in Roxborough Park, Littleton, Colo. Terri was born 6 Nov 1953 in Karney, Neb. She graduated with a degree in nursing in 1997. Terri has a daughter, Heather Christine Matya, born 12 Sep 1980 in Wheatridge, Colo. She is to be adopted by Scott.

Brad Chandler Light was born 20 Feb 1963 in Princeton, N.J. He attended school in the Phillipines; in Omaha, Neb.; and Deerfield, Ill., before completing high school at Culver Military Academy in Ind. He graduated from Southern Illinois University in 1988 where he majored in drama and theater. Brad has appeared in many TV commercials. He is a customer rep for a health food wholesaler in Chicago while continuing his acting career.

1167513 Edson Leonard Light

Edson was born 11 Jul 1938 in Woolridge, Mo. Leonard started school in Eagle Pass, Tex., where his father was a barber. He also attended school in Texarcana, Tex., and graduated from Park Hill High School in Riverside, Mo. He then worked at several occupations and was last employed by Lubarb Chemical Co. He married Marcella Mary Allen on 29 Oct 1957 in Riverside; they divorced about 1980. She was born 19 Oct 1941 in Salem, Mo. They had Allen Leonard, Paula Jean, and Daryell Wayne. Secondly, he married Evelyn Mary Engerman on 9 Jun 1981 in Independence, Mo. Evelyn was born 10 Mar 1938 in Miami, Okla. They were living in Independence, Mo., in 1997.

Allen Leonard Light was born 11 May 1961 in Kansas City, Mo., and was living in Lees Summit, Mo., in 1997.

Paula Jean Light was born 19 May 1962 in Kansas City, Mo. Her first marriage was to George Short about 1977 in Kansas City, Mo. They had Jason Short, born about 1978, and Christina Short, born about 1981. She married, secondly, Duke _____ about 1994; they were living in Lees Summit in 1997.

Daryell Wayne Light was born 29 May 1964 in Kansas City, Mo. He was living in Lees Summit, Mo., in 1997.

1167514 Paul Albert Light

Paul was born 3 Feb 1943 in Eagle Pass, Tex. He attended Brenner

Ridge Elementary School and graduated from Park Hill High School in Riverside, Mo. He attended night school and received a degree from Rockhurst College in 1974, and worked his way into the company data processing department. In 1997, Paul was living in Kansas City, Mo., where he was a data processing manager for Seaboard Corp. He married Cathleen Yoder on 30 Nov 1979 in Overland Park, Kan. They divorced in 1996. Their children are Paul Anderson, born 30 Dec 1980 in Overland Park, and Caroline Audrey, born 7 Nov 1988 in Overland Park.

1167531 Georga Anne Light

Georga was born 1 Sep 1950 in Kansas City, Mo. She married Bruce Lynn Turpin 25 Apr 1970 in Ft. Jackson, S.C. Bruce was born 16 May 1948 in Bethany, Mo. They had Pride Travis, born 5 Dec 1970 in Kansas City, Kan., and Sage Beatrice, born 15 Jan 1974 in Kansas City, Kan. They lived many years in Anchorage, Alaska, and about 1992 they were located in Las Vegas, Nev.

Pride married Diana Kathleen Tysar on 12 Nov 1994 in Platte, Mo. Diana was born 14 Oct 1974. In 1999 they were living in Parkville, Mo. They had Miranda Lynn on 21 Feb 1995 in Kansas City, Kan., and Chance Patrick on 30 Apr 1997 in Joplin, Mo.

Sage married Sean Lee Neeson on 26 Aug 1997. In 1999, she was living in Trimble, Mo. Sean was born 28 Dec 1965 in Macon, Mo., and died 16 Aug 1997. They had Alec George on 8 May 1995 in Kansas City, Kan.

1167541 William Claude Redd

William (Bill) was born 1 Dec 1935 in Kansas City, Mo. He completed his elementary and high school education in Kansas City, Mo. He attended the University of Missouri and graduated with a degree in business administration. Bill worked for the Exxon Corp. in Milwaukee, Wisc. He retired from Citgo Petroleum in 1998 after 33 years of service. He married Joan Marion Goehrig on 30 Aug 1958 in Milwaukee. Joan was born 27 Aug 1938 in Milwaukee. Their children were Christopher Earl, born 21 May 1962 in Milwaukee, and Sara Anne, born 22 Nov 1966 in Milwaukee.

Christopher received his elementary education in Milwaukee and Tulsa, Okla. He then attended Oklahoma State University where he graduated with a degree in advertising and public relations. In 1999, he was working for Allstate Insurance Co., in Omaha. Christopher was married to Sally Lynn Schlinker on 17 Jan 1992 in Chicago, Ill. Sally was born 13 Jun 1964 in San Mateo, Calif. She graduated from the University of Illinois with a degree in accounting. She worked in Chicago where she met Chris. Their children are Michael Christopher who was born 23 Oct 1992 and Courtney Lynn who was born 6 Jun 1994, both born in Tulsa, Okla.

Sara graduated from high school in Tulsa, Okla., and then attended Stephans College where she graduated with a degree in communications and public relations. She married John Joseph Carney on 20 Sep 1991 in Myrtle Beach, S.C. John was born 10 Apr 1960 in Cumberland, Md. He graduated from Frostburg University in Maryland with a BA degree. He currently is head golf pro and general manager of Brick Landing Plantation in Ocean Isle Beach, N.C. In 1999, Sara was a homemaker and expecting her second child. They had Allison Kate on 12 May 1993 in Wilmington, N.C.

1167551 Connie Ruth Parker

Connie was born in 1939 in Kansas City, Mo. She died there in 1955.

1167552 Earl C. Parker

Earl was born 4 Aug 1938 in Kansas City, Mo. He married Ruth Ann Wenta about 1963. They had Katie who was born about 1964. About 1975 he married Marilyn Lnu, and they had Sydney and Lindsey. Lastly, he married Yvonne Lnu about 1997, possibly in Vacaville, Calif., where he was living. He was in the newspaper business for a time.

1167621 Ricky Lee Landes

Ricky was born 5 May 1948 in Bethany, Mo. He married Judy Ann Alldredge on 18 Jan 1970 in Stansberry, Mo. Judy was born 18 Nov 1948. They had Amy Nicole who was born 2 Mar 1979 and Kristen Erin who was born 31 Aug 1982, both born in St. Joseph, Mo. Amy died 15 Jan 1980 in Stansberry and was buried there in High Ridge Cem.

1167622 Deborah June Landes

Deborah was born 5 Mar 1955 in Bethany, Mo. She was married to Charles "Quentin" Combs on 14 Dec 1973 in St. Joseph, Mo. Quentin was born 18 Aug 1947. They had Melissa Dawn on 6 Jun 1975 and Jonathan Dahl on 27 Apr 1979 in St. Joseph, Mo.

1167631 Brenda Rea Landes

Brenda was born 2 Jan 1949 in Bethany, Mo. She married Richard Lewis Ebersold on 21 Jun 1969 in Harrison Co., Mo. Richard was born 5 Jun 1949 in Union Star, Mo. They had Craig Lewis, born 22

Dec 1973 in Smithville and Natashia Renae on 2 Jan 1976 in St. Joseph, Mo.

1167632 Alan Lynn Landes

Alan was born 23 Nov 1949 in Bethany, Mo. He married Gracie Sharon Merkling on 6 Jun 1970 in Bethany, Mo. Gracie was born 31 Dec 1951 in Harrison Co., Mo. Their children were Amanda Renee, born 7 Nov 1974; Nathan Alan, born 11 Jan 1978; and Anna Marie, born 21 Feb 1979, all born in St. Joseph, Mo.

1167633 Tony Ray Landes

Tony was born 8 Jul 1951 in Bethany, Mo. He married Patsy Gail Crabtree on 1 Apr 1977 in Harrison Co., Mo. Their child is Amber Michelle, born 4 Oct 1977 in Harrison Co., Mo. Secondly, Tony married Karla Knudtson Michels on 8 May 1982 in Harrison Co. Their child is Christina Lynn, born 17 Jan 1984 in San Diego, Calif. Tony and Karla are divorced in 1987. He was married to Rita Green King on 9 Jan 1989 in Bethany, Mo. She died 30 Jan 1994 in Bethany and was buried in White Oak Cem. Tony married Bonnie Jean Bogner on 27 Jul 1996 in Rosedale, Mo. Bonnie was born 19 Apr 1955 in San Diego, Calif.

Amber married Grover Cleveland Hoyle on 20 Apr 1996 in Mitchelville, Mo. Grover was born 22 Jul 1973 in Cameron, Mo. They had Jacob Wesley on 6 Nov 1995 in St. Joseph, Mo.

1167641 David Eugene Landes

David was born 9 Jan 1959 in Bethany, Mo. He married Lori Roseanne Welling on 11 Jun 1994 in Ridgeway, Mo. Lori was born 19 Sep 1963 in Omaha. They manage the family farm north of Bethany.

1167642 Gloria June Landes

Gloria was born 24 Nov 1960 in Bethany, Mo. Gloria works at the school in Ridgeway. Gloria married George Douglas Craig on 6 Jul 1991 in Bethany. George was born 30 Sep 1960 in Bethany. They had George Matthew who was born 24 Jul 1996 in Maryville, Mo.

1167711 Toni Ann McCorkle

Toni was born 17 Mar 1948 in Seattle, Wash. In 1998, she was living in Melbourne, Australia. She married Noel Howard Barlow on 19 Dec 1970 in Aberdeen, Wash. Noel was born 7 Feb 1948 in Klamath Falls, Ore. They left the U.S. in 1976 to live in Australia. Noel is a teacher in high school, while Toni is in the elementary school system. They have no children.

1167712 Terry Lee McCorkle

Terry was born 13 Aug 1956 in Kenmore, Wash. In 1998 he was living in Lake Stevens, Wash.   He married Taleatha "Terri" Andrews on 6 Aug 1983 in Bothell, Wash. They had Toni Lee on 15 Oct 1984 at home in Bothell.

1167721 Nancy Carol McDonald

Nancy was born 26 Jul 1945 in Smith Center, Kan. She married James (Jim) St. Aubyn on 12 Jun 1966 in Smith Center, Kan. Jim was born 5 Sep 1944 in Lyons, Kan. In 1998 Nancy was living in Austin, Tex.

1167722 Kenneth Ray McDonald

Kenneth was born 8 May 1948 in Smith Center, Kan. He married Cynthia Rose Efaw on 8 Feb 1975 in Arlington, Va. Cynthia was born 8 Aug 1947 in Davenport, Ia. In 1998 he was living in Greenbelt, Md.

1167723 Jean Loree McDonald

Jean was born 17 Apr 1949 in Smith Center, Kan. In 1988 she was living in Northglen, Colo.

1167724 Larry Allen McDonald

Larry was born 9 Feb 1958 in Smith Center, Kan. He married Sherry Lynn Baumfalk on 23 Nov 1985 in Smith Co., Kan. Sherry was born 27 Jul 1957. He was living in Colby, Kan., in 1998.

1167725 Cathy Arlene McDonald

Cathy was born 26 Jul 1959 in Smith Center, Kan. She married Benjamin Fulton Johnson on 23 Nov 1985 in Smith Center. Benjamin was born 13 Jan 1954. They had Maegan Carol who was born 22 Apr 1988 and Conor Benjamin on 6 Jun 1991, both born in Brighton, Colo. Cathy was living in Henderson, Colo., in 1998.

1167726 Gary Steven McDonald

Gary was born 13 Aug 1961 in Smith Center, Kan. He married Terry Lynn Roenne on 16 Dec 1989 in Smith Center, Kan. Terry was born 27 Jan 1960 in Osborne, Kan. They had Chelsea Lynn who was born 22 Oct 1990 and Jonathan Chase who was born 8 Mar 1992, both in Beloit, Wisc.

1167731 Donna Beth McCorkle
Donna was born 20 Dec 1947 in Thurston Co., Wash. She married

Larry Curtis Anderson 20 Jan 1967 in Puyallup, Wash. They had Michael Curtis on 14 Feb 1968 in Tacoma, Wash. Secondly, she married Barton Oscar Russell on 16 Mar 1973 in LaJunta, Colo. Barton was born 30 May 1945 in Muscatine, Ia. They had Bridget Katherine, born 13 Jul 1975 in Tacoma, Wash.

Michael married Michie L. Meyers on 24 Jul 1993 in Tacoma, Wash. Michie was born 15 Feb 1966. They had Curtis Michael on 22 Feb 1996 in Tacoma.

1167732 Ronald Allen McCorkle

Ronald was born 25 May 1952 in Thurston Co., Wash. He married Rebecca Marie Brackman on 28 Jun 1975 in Puyallap, Wash. Rebecca was born 17 Jul 1951 in Puyallup. Their children are Joshua David, born 16 May 1978, and Zachariah Peter, born 23 Feb 1982, both born in Puyallup.

1167741 Sharon Kay McCorkle

Sharon was born 21 Jul 1948 in Shawnee, Kan. She married Charles Robert Clelland on 17 Feb 1966 in Sebetha, Neb. They divorced in 1968. They had a son, Mark Alan, born 7 May 1966 in Omaha. Secondly, Sharon married Richard Joseph Dombkowski on 23 Nov 1968 in Omaha. Joseph was born 14 Jun 1947 in Worcester, Mass. They had Jennifer Sue, born 22 Aug 1969 in Omaha. In 1998 Jennifer was living in Topeka, Kan.

1167742 Dennis Scott McCorkle

Dennis was born 26 Sep 1950 in Smith Center, Kan. He married Bonita Ann Ellington on 11 Apr 1981 in Topeka, Kan. Bonita was born 12 Jun 1961 in Hiawatha, Kan. They had Palmer Scott Franklin who was born 29 Sep 1981 in Sabetha, Kan., Amoretta Denise who was born 2 Jun 1984 in Sabetha and Silas McKinley who was born 30 Oct 1991 in Wichita, Kan.

1167743 Jeffrey Harold McCorkle

Jeffrey was born 5 Feb 1962 in Sabetha, Kan. He married Tammy Lynn Leonard on 18 Aug 1984 in Dubois, Neb. Tammy was born 1 Jan 1964 in Omaha. They had Ashley Lynn on 21 Dec 1987 and Alanna Dawn on 27 Mar 1993, both born in Sabetha.

1167744 Norma Jean McCorkle

Jeannie was born 18 Nov 1968 in Sabetha, Kan. She married Wayne W. Rosalis on 2 Sep 1995 in Sabetha. Wayne was born 13 Jul 1969.

1167751 Janet Marie Trent

Janet was born 24 Nov 1946 in Sabetha, Kan. She married John Lester Atkinson 6 Jun 1965 in Smith Co., Kan. John was born 15 Feb 1946, and he died 15 Jun 1990 in Phillipsburg, Kan. They had Jill Joann who was born 22 Feb 1971. Secondly, she married Ronald Louis Horinek on 22 Oct 1994 in Phillipsburg. He was born 27 Apr 1941. They make their home in Scott City, Kan.

Jill married Ronald Dean Boeve Jr. on 19 Oct 1991 in Phillipsburg, Kan. Ronald was born 5 Jan 1969 in Norton, Kan. They had Jordyn Marie on 27 Jul 1993 and Allyson Kae on 26 Jun 1996, both in Phillipsburg.

1167752 Richard Dean Trent

Richard was born 31 Aug 1948 in Smith Co., Kan. He married Dixie Trent who was born 18 Sep 1948 in Smith Co. Later they divorced. Secondly, he married Cindy Pool. They had Brandon who was born 11 Dec 1973 in Phillipsburg.

1167753 Marcia Jane Trent

Marcia was born 22 Mar 1954 in Osborne, Kan. She married Roy James Brown who was born 8 Dec 1952. Their children are Marci who was born 8 Dec 1977 and Trenton James who was born 20 Mar 1982 in Las Cruicus, N.M.

Marci was married to Ernie Cameron Nevarez on 20 Dec 1997 in Las Cruicus, N.M. Ernie was born 10 Jul 1976 in Las Cruicus. They had Ernie Cameron on 19 Jun 1998 in Las Cruicus.

1167754 Sheri Lou Trent

Sheri was born 9 Jun 1959 in Phillipsburg, Kan. She married Jesse Erwin Vance on 26 Jun 1982 in Boulder, Colo. Jesse was born 5 Mar 1956. Their children are Aaron Micah who was born 14 Dec 1982 and Ryan Dale who was born 15 Apr 1985, both in Aurora, Colo.

1167761 Robert Alden McCorkle Jr.

Robert was born 29 Oct 1960 in Denver, Colo. He graduated from Douglas High School in 1978. He works as a maintenance foreman at Martin-Marietta. On 28 May 1982 he married Sharon Kathleen Shrader in Denver. Sharon was born in Denver on 29 May 1962. They had Lindsay Renee who was born 17 Jul 1983 and Tyler John who was born 8 Nov 1986, both in Denver.

1167762 Elizabeth Ellen McCorkle

Elizabeth was born 28 Dec 1962 in Denver, Colo. She attended Rangley College for a year, then worked for Martin-Marietta as a computer specialist, and lately was a manager at U.S. West in Denver. Elizabeth is not married.

1167771 Peggy Sue McCorkle

Peggy was born 29 Dec 1965 in Denver, Colo. She married James Kent "Kenny" Landers on 1 Dec 1989 in Ovid, N.Y. James was born 26 Oct 1967 in Quanah, Tex. They had Jamie Lynn who was born 6 Apr 1990 and Kellie Ann who was born 11 Apr 1992, both born in Amarillo, Tex.

1167811 Linda Jane Lary

Linda was born 1 Mar 1951 in Longview, Wash. In Mar 1970 she married C. Phillip Smith who was born about 1950. Their child is Michelle Lynn who was born 13 Sep 1970. Michelle married Mr. Linse about 1990. Their child is Robert James Lary Linse who was born 27 Jan 1993.

1167812 Charles Halsey Lary

Charles was born 25 Dec 1952 in Longview, Wash. He married Babette Higgins on 26 Aug 1973 in Eugene, Ore. They had Laurel Diane who was born 20 May 1975, Lisa Nicole who was born 6 Sep 1977, and Benjamin Joel who was born 1 Feb 1985.

1167813 Randall Edward Lary

Randall was born 24 Apr 1954 in Longview, Wash. On 20 Dec 1980 he married Stacey L. Burke in Lebanon, Ore. Their children are Amber Rose who was born 2 Oct 1984, Erin Alexandra who was born 23 Apr 1987, and Cassandra Janette who was born 28 Feb 1989.

1167814 Susan Ann Lary

Susan was born 26 Jun 1957 in Longview, Wash.

1167815 Robert McLain Lary

Robert was born 29 Dec 1958 in Longview, Wash.

1167831 Mathew Lary Peters

Mathew was born 20 Feb 1956 in Hood River, Ore. He married Mary Elisabeth Moore in Nov 1979. They had Alise Christine who was born

10 Aug 1981 and Brian Mathew who was born 15 Jan 1984.   Secondly, he married Peggy Packer on 22 Oct 1994 in Hood River.

1167832 Danise Lea Peters

Danise was born 3 Sep 1958 in Hood River, Ore.   She married Larry M. Tice on 30 Jul 1983 in Hood River.   They were living in Molalla, Ore., in 1997.   Their son is Paul Byron who was born 8 Oct 1986.

1167833 Timothy Henry Peters

Timothy was born 26 Jan 1961 in Hood River, Ore.   He married Kristen L. Kliensmith on 27 Jun 1987 in Hood River.   Their children are John Ellis who was born 27 Sep 1988, Katelyn Diane who was born 29 Jun 1990, and David Henry who was born 19 Feb 1993.

1167834 Julann Carol Peters

Julann was born 8 Feb 1963 in Hood River, Ore.   On 29 Jun 1985 she married Robert E. D'Aboy.   Their children are Peter Robert who was born 12 Oct 1987, Joseph Evan who was born 26 Oct 1988, and Thomas John who was born 19 Sep 1991.

1171111 Thomas Marvin Salsman

Thomas was born 2 Feb 1950 in Fort Collins, Colo.   He married Ileene Brimkamp and they had a son, Jonathan Michael who was born 5 Jun 1978 in Calif.   After his divorce, Thomas lived in Cypress, Calif., where he works in quality control for an electronics company.

1171112 Larry Eugene Salsman

Larry was born 3 Jan 1952 in Oakland, Calif.   He was married, then divorced, and was living in Arvada, Colo.   There were no children. Currently, Larry is a bus driver for the city of Denver.

1171113 Kathline Salsman

Kathline was born 9 Mar 1954 in Antioch, Calif.   At one time she operated a pet grooming shop.   She is married to Dennis Elsey and they live in Hooper, Neb.   Their children are Anna Patience who was born 16 Jul 1989 in Denver, and Joseph Ryan who was born 29 May 1997 in Denver.

1171114 Teresa Gail Salsman

Teresa was born 15 Jan 1957 in Denver.   On 17 Sep 1983, in Jackson, Miss., she married Bruce Reeves Bowman, but Teresa kept her maiden name. She graduated from the University of Iowa with a degree in political science in 1984, and later attended Mississippi College where she studied accounting. She was employed as a CPA while in Mississippi. Their children are Robin Victoria who was born 8 Aug 1992 in Pearl, Miss., and John Augustus who was born 31 Dec 1996 in Baton Rouge, La. They live in Baton Rouge, La.

1171115 James Robert Salsman

Jim was born 5 Jun 1959 in Denver. He married Susan Sandquist on 2 Dec 1978 in Des Moines, Ia. They had Christopher James who was born 7 Jul 1979 and Tiffany Sue who was born 12 Sep 1980 in Des Moines. Jim was manager of a grocery store until recently, and was planning to become a plumber. Their home is in Saint Mary's, Ia.

1171211 Stephen Wayne Baker

Steve was born 10 Nov 1949 in Arkansas City, Kan. He married Catherine Ann Hammett on 4 Jan 1974 in Roswell, N.M. Catherine was born 1 Dec 1950. Steve graduated from Roswell High School in 1967, then served in the U.S. Army from 1969-1972. He resumed his education and graduated from the University of New Mexico in Dec 1975 with a degree in business. He worked in retail lumber for 17 years, then became an independent contractor in Eagle Nest, N.M. Their children were Jacob Christopher, born 15 May 1979 in Deming, N.M., and Jessica Cherise, born 30 Jul 1982 in Silver City, N.M. Steve and Catherine live in Eagle Nest, N.M.

Jacob graduated from high school in Cimarron, N.M. in 1997 and was attending New Mexico State University in 2000, majoring in mechanical engineering.

1171212 James Raymond Baker

Jim was born 28 Sep 1951 in Roswell, N.M. On 10 Apr 1976 he married Patrice Ann (Orange) Boehm in La. Jim is a graduate of Roswell High School class of 1969, and of the University of New Mexico class of 1976. He is now working for a geophysical company in Denver, Colo. Their children are Bradley Warren, born 18 Aug 1979, and Kenneth James, born 30 Mar 1981, both born in Houston. Bradley graduated in 1998 from high school in Littleton, Colo. Ken graduated from high school in 1999 and is a student at Colorado State University.

1171213 Allen David Baker

Allen was born 25 Oct 1955 in Roswell. On 14 May 1983 he married Mary Elizabeth Yarbough. Allen was a graduate of Roswell High School with the class of 1973, then enlisted in the U.S. Army where

he served until 1976.   Returning home, he attended National
University in San Diego and earned a B.S. degree in 1987, and a
master's degree in 1989.   He works for Hewlett-Packard as a
computer software engineer in Boise, Ida.   Their children are
Steven Roscoe, born in El Cajon, Calif., in Oct 1985; Lisa Renae,
born in El Cajon in Sep 1986; Caitlin Marie, born in Boise in Sep
1989; and Matthew Ryan, born 27 Mar 1991 in Boise.   Allen and
family live in Garden Valley, Ida.

1171214 Doris Jeananne Baker

Doris was born 6 Aug 1958 in Roswell, N.M.   She graduated from
Roswell High School in 1976.   On 20 May 1978 she married Owen K.
Black in Roswell, N.M.   Owen was born 5 Dec 1953.   They had Krista
Danielle, born 16 Sep 1984 in Tarcana, Calif.; David Owen, born 28
Aug 1986 in Tarcana; and Elizabeth Jean, born 10 Jan 1989 in Van
Nuys, Calif.   Owen is manager of a Walgreen's store. Doris later
attended Eastern New Mexico University and earned a degree in
education in 1995.   She is now teaching in an elementary school in
Roswell, N.M., where they make their home.

1171311 Peggy Ann Weir

Peggy was born 27 Apr 1951 in Burlington, Ia.   She married Stephen
Williams and later they were divorced.   There were no children from
the marriage.   Peggy lived in Tucson in 1992, and in Macomb, Ill.
in 1998.

1171312 William Ray Weir Jr.

William was born 25 Jun 1952 in Burlington.   He married 13 Dec
1975, in Burlington, Theresa Ann Stoll who was born 4 Oct 1954.
They had Neil Alexander, born 24 Oct 1976, and Martha Marie, born
9 Apr 1980.   William died of cancer 6 Aug 1996.   Burial was in
North Henderson Cem.

1171313 John Milton Weir

John was born 28 Jun 1955 in Burlington.   He attended Burlington
Community College briefly.   He owns a radio station in Burlington,
call letters KBUR-AM and KGRS-FM.   He is not married.   The compiler
remembers listening as a child to "The Shadow" on KBUR when he
lived in Burlington from 1944 to 1945.

1171341 Lawrence Mark Anderson

Mark was born 22 Oct 1963 in Burlington.   Mark graduated from
Western Illinois University in 1986.   On 5 Mar 1988 he married Lori
Scott.   Lori is a graduate of Truman University in Kirksville, Mo.

They had Blair, born 7 Aug 1990, and Lydia Brooke, born 29 Mar 1995 in Des Moines.

1171342 Susan Marie Anderson

Susan was born 5 Nov 1959 in Elgin, Ill. She was a 1977 graduate of Union High School in Biggsville, Ill. In 1981 she graduated from Truman University with a BS degree. She teaches 8th grade at Union Elementary School in Biggsville. She married Steven M. Higgins on 14 Aug 1982. Steve graduated from Western Illinois University and works for Monson TV in Monmouth, Ill. Their children are Stephanie Kay, born 2 Jan 1984 in Kirkwood, Mo.; Joshua, born 23 Jul 1985 in Kirksville; and Gretchen, born 11 Jan 1994 in Washington, Mo.

1171343 Laura Kay Anderson

Laura was born 23 May 1961 in Burlington. She graduated from Union High School in 1979. She received a BS degree in 1983 from the University of Missouri in Columbia, and a MA in 1987. On 17 Jun 1989 she married Jeffery Dale Zimmer who was born 9 Jan 1961. Laura is a fifth grade teacher in Troy, Mo., while Jeffery is employed by Farmers Insurance Co. They live in Warrenton, Mo. Their children are Jacob Dale, born 18 May 1991; Jeremiah Daniel, born 11 Jan 1993; and Josiah Dylan, born 16 May 1996 at Lake St. Louis, Mo.

1172111 Marilyn Jeanne Gibb

Marilyn was born 8 Dec 1929 in Monmouth, Ill. On 25 Nov 1946 she married William Edgar Fowler in the Little Brown Church at Nashua, Ia. William was born 14 Sep 1921. Their two children are Denise Lynn, born 31 May 1949; and William Darcy, born 2 Oct 1954. Marilyn and William divorced and neither has remarried. Mariyln has an oblong mirror that is about thirty inches tall and mounted on a stand that has been passed down from her Scottish ancestor, Ann (Milwain) Thomson. She also has a photograph of Ann that is inscribed on the back "niece of John Paul Jones." Who wrote the inscription is not known, but, as mentioned earlier, the compiler has been unable to prove such a relationship.

Denise was married on 25 Nov 1967 to Jerry Eugene Easley who was born 11 Feb 1947. They had Jennifer Lynn, born 13 Nov 1969 and Jason Paul, born 9 Jul 1973, both born in Des Moines, Ia. Jennifer graduated from North Dakota State School of Science in 1990, then enlisted in the U.S. Army. She was a Korean linquist, was involved in cryptology and intelligence, and was discharged in 1994. She also studied at Logan Chiropractic College in St. Louis. There she met and married Su ryong Lee in 1996. Jennifer graduated from Logan with a DC degree in 1998. They divorced in 2000. Jennifer was serving with her reserve unit in Bosnia and was expected to return to the U.S. in 2001. Jason attended North Dakota State School of Science, and worked as a radio announcer. Later, he was a drummer with a traveling band, and was booked as entertainment on cruise ships. He married Bonnie Ann Quam 5 Mar 1996. Bonnie is a 1995 graduate of the University of North Dakota. Lately, Jason was employed at Telex communications and residing in Plymouth, Minn.

William married 3 Aug 1974 Mary Katherine Powell who was born 26 May 1956. They had Katherine JoAnne born 10 Aug 1978.

1172112 Dennis Lee Gibb

Dennis was born 28 Jul 1931 in Henderson Co., Ill. He graduated from high school in 1949 then enlisted in the U.S. Marine Corps, and served in Korea. He is a graduate of Western Illinois University with a degree in education. Dennis taught at Hawthorne High School for about twenty years. Later he worked at the Orange County Court House in Orange, Calif. On 30 May 1959 in Calif., he married Ruth Ann Bowman who was born 27 Oct 1933. They had Michael Douglas, born 28 Feb 1960, Daniel Aaron, born 13 Oct 1962, and William Todd, born 29 May 1970, all born in Calif.

1172121 Linda Lee Gibb

Linda was born 30 Aug 1945. She married on 26 May 1963 at Biggsville, Ill., Wendell Doole. They later divorced. Secondly, Linda married on 17 Sep 1966 at Burlington, Ia., Steven N. Blair who was born 1 Feb 1942 in Henderson Co., Ill. Steven was a factory worker and a member of Biggsville United Methodist Church. He died of cancer 23 Nov 1985 in Burlington, Ia., and was buried in Biggsville Cemetery. They had six children: Darrin Lee, born 27 Jul 1966; Sharon Lee, stillborn 3 Jun 1967; Gale Ann, born 15 Jul 1968; James Bradley, born 16 Dec 1970; Brenda Renee, born 16 Jun 1972; and Kimberly Jean, born 27 Aug 1974.

1172122 Dana Lynn Gibb

Dana was born 30 Apr 1964. In 1982 she graduated from Union High School in Biggsville, Ill.

1172211 Donn F. Price

Donn was born 9 Aug 1927 in Monmouth, Ill. He died at home in Biggsville of a heart attack on 2 Jul 1994. He married Barbara Jean James 16 Feb 1952 in Burlington, Ia. Barbara was born 1 Jul 1930 in Gladstone, Ill. Donn graduated from high school in Chapin, Ill., and attended Monmouth College. He was a Navy veteran and was a plumber and electrician in Henderson Co., Ill. Barbara is a secretary at Union High School in Biggsville. They had two children-Bradley Wayne, born 29 Aug 1952 in Burlington; and Rebecca Sue, born 23 Jun 1954 in Burlington.

Bradley married on 10 Oct 1975 in Decatur, Ill., Mary Christine Reedy who was born 18 Dec 1954. They were divorced in 1979. Brad was a teacher at that time, and they had no children. Secondly, Brad married Carol Jane Ziegele on 5 Oct 1979 at Mackinac Island in Mich. Carol was born 17 Feb 1949 in Waukegan, Ill. She had a child from a previous marriage, Paige Marie Ziegele, born 14 Jun 1974. Brad received his doctorate of Chiropracty in Jun 1994 and is now in the practice in Reddington Beach, Fla. They have a child, Brandon Wayne Ziegele Price, born 14 Apr 1981 in Peoria, Ill.

Rebecca married on 6 Jan 1995 Nathan E. Hoagland in Chillicothe, Ill., where they make their home.

1172212 Robert Leon Price (I)

Robert was born 3 Oct 1928 in Keokuk Co., Ia. He died of a heart attack on 31 Dec 1993 in Monmouth Hospital. He married on 24 Jun 1951 Donna Lee Carothers at Biggsville United Methodist Church. Donna was born 24 Jun 1933 in Biggsville Twp., Henderson Co., Ill. Bob had a career in the U.S. Army. He was buried in Biggsville Cemetery. Their children were Paul Leslie, born 6 Aug 1952 at Fort Lee, Va.; Robert Leon, born 8 Nov 1954 at the U.S. Army Hospital in Calambrone Commune Di Pisa, Italy; and Mary Lou, who was born 25 Apr 1962, died at birth, and was buried in Biggsville Cem.

Paul married on 26 Feb 1977 Judy Lynn Sloan at Austin, Tex. Judy was born 20 Dec 1951 at Omaha, Neb. They have three children: Abra Sloan, stillborn 31 Aug 1982 in Austin, Tex.; Dana Leigh, born 30 Jun 1983 in Austin; and Eric Carothers, date not provided.

Robert Leon Price (II) married 21 Jun 1980 Mary Rita Zachman in Burnsville, Minn. Mary was born 22 Apr 1952 at Owatonna, Minn. They have two children: twins Jacob Zachman and Aaron Zachman, born 6 May 1982 in Minneapolis, Minn.

1172213 Ellen Jane Price

Ellen was born 11 Mar 1933 at Fort Madison, Ia. She married Harry Philip Lehning 26 Jun 1954 in Burlington, Ia. Harry was born 14 Mar 1933 in Chicago, Ill. Jane was a school teacher and Harry a coach. Their three children are Kathleen Anne, born 27 Nov 1956 at Heidelberg State Baden, Germany; Ellen Jo, born 16 Apr 1959 in Kewanee, Ill.; and Michael Philip, born 12 Jul 1961 in Kewanee.

Kathleen married 6 Oct 1978 Brian Paul Lorenzi at Ladd, Ill. Brian was born 30 Jul 1957 at Spring Valley, Ill. Kathleen works as a computer programmer in a bank , and is living in Farnsworth, Ill.

Ellen Jo is living in Miller Place, N.Y.

Michael married Tracy on 12 Jul 1961 in Kewanee, Ill., and they have two children: Nicole Christine, born 23 Dec 1994, and Marcus Philip, born 29 May 1996. The family lives in Bourbonnais, Ill.

1172231 Stephen Wendell Graham Jr.

Steven was born 5 Dec 1932 in Burlington, Ia. He married Mary Elizabeth Martin 17 Oct 1954 in Burlington. Mary was born 11 May 1933 in Burlington. Stephen was a Lt. in the U.S. Air Force, and was a farmer. Mary was a school teacher. Their children were Johanna, born 24 Sep 1955 in Ga.; Jeanne, born 15 Jan 1957 in Va.; Julie, born 3 Nov 1959; Jennifer, born 27 Jan 1962; and Jamiee, born 9 Jun 1965 in Burlington, Ia.

Johanna married 12 Jun 1976 Lloyd Wayne Little at Biggsville, Ill. Lloyd was born 13 May 1948 in LaHarpe, Ill. They had Curtiss Wayne, born 1 May 1980 in Princeton, Ill.; and Stephen Joel, born 25 Mar 1982 in Macomb, Ill.

Jeanne married 26 Apr 1975 William E. Seitz in Burlington, Ia. He was born 19 Nov 1957. Bill is a farmer and Jeanne a teacher. Their four children are Michael Lawrence, born 28 Aug 1975 in Monmouth, Ill.; twins Sarah Ann and Stephanie Ellen, born 15 Jan 1978 in Monmouth; and Mathew William, born 21 Feb 1981 in Monmouth.

Julie married 18 Aug 1989 Scott Johnson in Burlington. They live in Deerfield, Ill.

Jennifer married 26 Jan 1985 John C. Ripp in Biggsville, Ill. They were divorced in 1991. Secondly, Jennifer married Rex Houston.

Jamiee married 4 Sep 1988 Gary Carter, Jr. in Divernon, Ill. Jamiee graduated from Western Illinois University in 1987 and works at Franklin Life Insurance as a systems analyst. Gary is a computer operator in the same company. Their children are Jacob Aaron, born 29 Dec 1989 in Springfield, Ill., and Olivia Graham, born 2 May 1994 in Springfield. They are living in Devernon.

1172232 Mary Ellen Graham

Mary was stillborn 18 Jun 1939 and was buried in Biggsville Cem.

1172233 Jon Kendall Graham

Jon was born 21 Jun 1941 in Burlington. He married 4 Mar 1962
Sharon Kay Galley in Peoria, Ill. Sharon was born 28 Sep 1943 in
Peoria. They have a daughter, Lorella Layne, born 14 Apr 1966 in
Burlington. Lorella married 8 Oct 1988 William Patrick McLaughlin
in Monmouth, Ill. Both are graduates of Western Illinois
University. She is a special ed teacher, and he is a sales
representative for the Neff Co. Their children are Karly Elise,
born 17 Jan 1993 in Peoria, and Hannah Jadeyn, born 8 Apr 1996.
They reside in Edwardsville, Ill.

1172234 Owen Gibb Graham

Owen was stillborn 21 May 1943 and was buried in Biggsville Cem.

1172241 Barbara Jean Milligan

Barbara was born 23 Dec 1930 in Gladstone Twp., Henderson Co., Ill.
On 3 Mar 1951, at Nashua, Ia., she married Daryl "Ozz" Eugene
Baylor who was born 10 Aug 1929 in Independence, Ia. Barb worked
as a bookkeeper off and on until 1988. Daryl was a member of the
U.S. Army from 1951 to 1954 and served in Korea for seventeen
months. In 1954 they moved to a farm at Mt. Union, Ia., where they
lived for eight years. They then bought a farm located west of Mt.
Pleasant, Ia. where they moved to in Jan 1963. Daryl worked for
U.S. Gypsum Co. in Sperry, Ia., and continued to do farm work on
the side. Their children are Kenneth Scott, born 14 Aug 1954 in
Burlington, Ia.; Kyle Wayne, born 29 Oct 1956 in Burlington;
Jeffrey Karl, born 9 Dec 1958 in Burlington; and Karen Ann, born 9
Aug 1962.

Kenneth married on 1 Mar 1972 at Kahoka, Mo., Donna Law who was
born 3 Aug 1955. He joined the U.S. Marine Corps 15 Mar 1972 and
spent a tour in Vietnam. He left the Corps in 1976. Kenneth and
Donna divorced in 1984. They had two children: (1)Janey Lynn, born
13 Aug 1972 in San Bernardino, Calif., she had Tanner Brenton
Holder-Baylor, born 23 Dec 1996; (2)Amy Miranda, born 10 Dec 1975
and died at birth in Mt. Pleasant, Ia. Secondly, Kenneth married
on 23 Apr 1988 Lori Ann Watson in Mt. Pleasant. Kenneth, known as
Scott, is co-owner of a tool and die shop.

Kyle was born 29 Oct 1956 in Burlington, Ia. He married on 27 Jul
1975 Vicky Lee Waterman who was born 19 Jan 1957 in Fort Madison,
Ia. Kyle is manager of an auto parts store in Mt. Pleasant. Their
three children are Janelle Elizabeth, born 29 Dec 1979; Theodore
Michael; and Brian Eugene, born 8 Jun 1988, all born in Mt.
Pleasant.

Jeffrey married 29 Jul 1978 Susan Kay Gustafson who was born 29 Aug 1961. Their child was Brianne Ann born 1 Apr 1979 in Mt. Pleasant. They were divorced in 1983. Jeffrey secondly married 28 Jun 1986 Carol Margaret Westra who was born 11 Aug 1964. They had Katelyn Marie born 16 Nov 1990.

Karen married 30 May 1987 Michael Joseph Fritz who was born 7 Sep 1962 in Burlington, Ia. Karen is a teacher and Mike is in the U.S. Navy. Their children are Zachary Lewis, born 1 Jul 1989; Zane Michael, born 13 Feb 1991; and Zeth William, born 17 Dec 1993, all born in Mt. Pleasant, Ia.

1172242 Jimmy Lee Milligan

Jimmy was born 20 Apr 1933 in Biggsville, Ill. He married Ella Marie Simmons on 19 Dec 1953 in Tacoma, Wash. Ella was born 24 Aug 1933 at Oquawka, Ill. Jimmy graduated from Biggsville High School in 1951. In 1953 he entered the U.S. Army, and took basic training at Camp Gordon in Augusta, Ga. He completed his service in the states and was discharged in 1955. Then he took a position with Caterpillar in Peoria, Ill., and eventually became a design engineer before he retired in 1990. Ella worked most of the time at Bordens. They had two children: Denise Marie, born 30 Aug 1957 at Pekin, Ill., and David Lee, born 28 Jul 1966 at Pekin.

Denise married 2 Jun 1979 at Pekin, Larry James Koetter who was born 10 Aug 1956 at Peoria, Ill. Denise graduated from Methodist Medical Center as a nurse in 1975. She works in the MICU at Methodist Medical Center in Peoria. Larry works as an electrician at Caterpillar. Their two children are Jenny Marie, born 9 Mar 1983 at Peoria, and Matthew James, born 8 Nov 1987 at Peoria.

David married Kelly Greenwald on 16 Aug 1990 at Pekin. Kelly was born 15 Feb 1966 at Sheboygan, Wisc. David graduated from Pekin High School in 1984, and he is now manager of the Aldi Store in Galesburg, Ill. Kelly works at J.C. Penny. They have three children: Jacob Lee, born 7 Feb 1991; Nicholas Brandon, born 27 Aug 1993; and Ian Lucas, born 8 Apr 1995, all born in Galesburg.

1172243 Gerald Earl Milligan

Jerry was born 28 May 1938 at Monmouth, Ill. He married Jeanette Parrish on 15 Feb 1959 at Monmouth. They divorced in 1961. Secondly, Jerry married Sharon Wood in 1967, and they divorced in 1969. Jerry's third marriage was to Carol Hill on 15 Mar 1974 in Fallbrook, Calif. Carol's three children by a previous marriage were adopted by Jerry-- Simmie, born 22 Aug 1966; Roxanne, born 9 Nov 1967; and Laura, born 20 Dec 1969. Jerry and Carol had a child together, Christina, born 10 May 1975 in Calif.

Jerry graduated from Biggsville High School, then enlisted in the U.S. Army which took him to Europe for most of his service. Jerry is a licensed plumber and surveyor in Calif. They now make their home in Sun Valley, Ore.

1172251 Doris Joan Stotts

Doris was born 21 Oct 1933 in Biggsville, Ill. She married William Carl Combs on 13 May 1948 at Bowling Green, Ky. They had a child before they divorced, Carl "Bill" William Combs-Stotts, born 28 Sep 1950 in Bowling Green. Secondly, Doris married Raymond Hummer who was born 13 Oct 1934 in Clarence, Mo. They adopted Violet J., born 14 Feb 1961 in Moline, Ill.

Bill married Marietta Wilson who was born 21 Feb 1950. They had Paul William, born 6 dec 1970 in Bowling Green, and James Raymond, born 17 Apr 1974. Secondly, Bill married Wendy. They live in Moline, Ill.

Violet married John Leuck and they live in East Moline, Ill.

1172252 Ronald Keith Stotts

Ronald was born 6 Sep 1935 in Biggsville, Ill. He married Ruth Neighbors on 10 Jul 1954 at Bowling Green, Ky. Ruth was born 16 Apr 1936 in Warren Co., Ky. Ronald is in electric sales and Ruth is in newspaper advertising. They had Creg Alan, born 24 Sep 1956 in Bowling Green; and Debra Inez, born 18 Sep 1959 in Bowling Green.

Creg married Janet Fuller and were later divorced. They had Jamie born 25 Feb 1985. Secondly, Creg married Jeannie McAllister on 19 Aug 1989 in Santa Clause, Ind. Jeannie was born 13 May 1960 at Dothan, Ala. Creg is in sales and Jeannie is a travel consultant. They live in Antioch, Tenn.

Debra married Quinten Marquette who was born 5 Feb 1948 in Covington, Ky. Debra is a housewife while Quinten is a lawyer; they reside in Bowling Green. They had two children, Lindsay, born 20 Feb 1983 and Jared, born 27 Apr 1984.

1172253 Myrna Bernita Stotts

Myrna was born 27 Nov 1937 in Galesburg, Ill. She married 3 Nov 1955 Carl Adamson in Milan, Ill. Carl was born 20 Jul 1935. Their two children are Gary, born 20 Dec 1957 in Des Moines, and Michael, born 20 Aug 1967 in Moline. Myrna and Carl live in New Windsor, Ill. Gary is married to Karen and living in Alpha, Ill. Michael married Kelly and they live in Viola, Ill.

1172254 Evelyn Jean Stotts

Evelyn was born 27 Aug 1939 in Galesburg, Ill. She married Ronald Partlow 1 Nov 1959 at Milan, Ill. He is a baker. They had Patrick Dean, born 20 Jul 1961 in Moline; Timothy, born 27 Jul 1968 in Moline; and Keleen Luanne, born 22 Oct 1971 in Moline. Evelyn and Ronald divorced in 1980. Secondly, Evelyn married 15 May 1981 Matthew French Johnson in Crockett, Tex. Matthew was born 26 Jan 1937 in Armstrong. Mo. Matthew is a rancher in Crockett, Tex.

Patrick married 21 Sep 1985 Brenda Lee Holmes in Aledo, Ill. Brenda was born 2 Dec 1962 in Moline. Patrick manages a wholesale lumber store. Their children are Bailey Jean, born 19 Mar 1988 in Aledo, Ill.; Logan Luanne, born 18 Sep 1991 in Aledo, and McKayla Patrice, born 29 Nov 1996 in Moline.

Timothy married Shawna Marie Gonzale in Oct 1991 in New Windsor, Ill. He is a dock loader. They have Alicia Suzanne, born 13 Feb 1986, and Shalleen DeVaunn, born 3 Aug 1987.

Kathleen is a chiropractic assistant.

1172261 Terry Edward Leinbach

Terry was born 24 Oct 1941 in Burlington, Ia., and died 6 Aug 1993 of cancer at Burlington Medical Center. Burial was in Stronghurst Cemetery. He married on 16 Nov 1963 Judith McGinnis in Stronghurst, Ill. Judith was born 12 Jan 1944 in Dallas City, Ill. They had two children: Timothy Edward, born 1 Sep 1964 in Carthage, Ill.; and Laurie Leann, born 3 Dec 1968 in Burlington. Judith lives in Dallas City.

Timothy married Linda Lynn Patterson on 9 Jun 1984 in Dallas City, Ill. Linda was born 5 May 1964 at LaHarpe, Ill. Timothy is in the heating and air conditioning business. They have two children: Megan Lynn, born 16 Oct 1988; and Trevor Edward, born 11 Oct 1990, both born in Mercy Hospital in Davenport, Ia.

Laurie married 9 Oct 1993 Bradley Lane Despot in Fort Madison, Ia. Laurie graduated from high school in Dallas City in 1987 and attended the University of Iowa and the University of Illinois at Chicago. They had Dylan Lane, born 26 Jan 1992 in Chicago; and Landon, born about 1997. Laurie and Bradley live in Forest Park, Ill.

1172262 Guy Lynn Leinbach

Guy was born 20 Oct 1950 in Burlington, Ia. He married Mrs. Linda Lee Mitchell-Schroeder on 20 Feb 1976 in Quincy, Ill. She had a son by a previous marriage, Scott Edward Schroeder, born 16 Apr 1969 in Maryville, Mo., and Lynn adopted him. They also had Chad Lynn, born 10 Feb 1977 in Burlington. Lynn is superintendent of Gunther Construction Co., while they make their home in Stronghurst.

Scott first married Kristi. Secondly he married 25 Oct 1997 Angela K. Elmore in Burlington, Ia. Scott graduated from Southern High School and Western Illinois University. They are living in Burlington.

1172271 Charles Francis Tinkham

Charles was born 28 Nov 1943 at Monmouth Hospital, Warren Co., Ill. He died 29 Aug 1979 in a truck-train accident. He was buried in Marshalltown, Ia. He married 4 May 1968 Connie Lively in Cedar Rapids. Their two children are Austin Keith, born 11 Feb 1971 in Clinton, Ia.; and Andrea Renee, born 26 Jan 1975 in Newton, Ia. Connie lives in Marion, Ia. Austin has a child, Kelsey.

1172272 Michael Bradley Tinkham

Michael was born 4 Jun 1945 in the Burlington Hospital. He married Carol Lynne Peters on 18 Jun 1966 in Maxwell, Ia. Carol was born 13 Jun 1947. They had two children: Julie, born 2 Aug 1967, and Steven Russell, born 29 Apr 1972. Julie married 18 Jun 1988 Douglas Calhoun who was born 26 May____. They had Cody who was born 30 Jun 1993.

1172311 Leonard Edwin Brokaw

Leonard was born 5 May 1946 in Dubuque, Ia. He married Shirley Rae Jensen on 15 Jun 1974 in Pierre, S.D. Their children are Michelle Lynn, Brian Allan, and Aaron Eiler. In 1992 they were living in Montgomery, Ill.

1172312 Louise Anne Brokaw

Louise was born 13 Sep 1947 in Dubuque, Ia. In 1992 she was living in Reinbeck, Ia. The Rev. Louise Brokaw was installed as pastor of the United Church of Woodhull, Ill., on Sunday, 26 Jun 1994.

1172321 Karen Sue Brokaw

Karen was born 13 Jan 1942 in Aledo, Ill. Karen married John V. Weaver on 8 Jun 1963 in Aledo, Ill. John was born 28 Apr 1939. Their children are Brian Jon, born 26 Sep 1966 in Moline, Ill., and Bradley Reed, born 4 Feb 1970 in Red Wing, Minn. Brian married Amy Marie Ekum on 26 Apr 1992 in Viroqua, Wisc. Their son, Ethan Jon, was born 9 Jan 1998 in Winona, Minn.

1172322 James Kurtis Brokaw

James was born 3 Jan 1945 in (Davenport, Ia?).   James married
Dereth Melyn Higgins on 24 Jul 1971 in Aledo, Ill.   Dereth died 11
May 1982 and was buried in Peniel Cemetery in Joy, Ill.   They had
Travis James who was born 24 Jan 1977 in Aledo, Ill.   Secondly,
James married Caryn Thirtyacre on 4 Dec 1992 in Aledo, Ill. Caryn's
children from a previous marriage are Justin, Brandon, Ryan, and
Amy. Jim is police chief in Aledo, and Caryn is a Mercer County
Sherriff Department dispatcher.   Jim lived in rural Joy in 1989.

1172323 Philip Weir Brokaw

Philip was born 25 Jan 1948 in Davenport, Ia.   He died 15 Dec 1969
in Turkey while serving in the military.   He was buried in Aledo
Cem., Aledo, Ill.

1172324 Dennis Craig Brokaw

Dennis was born 10 Sep 1949 in Rock Island, Ill. He married Bonnie
Beth Norris on 25 Jun 1972 in Alexis, Ill.   Their children are Chad
Andrew, born 8 Feb 1977 in Galesburg, Ill., and Andrea Dana, born
30 Apr 1980 in Galesburg.   Dennis lived in Peoria as of 1989.

1172325 Michael Jon Brokaw

Mike was born 8 Feb 1956 in Aledo, Ill.   Mike married Laura Lea
Sutherland on 9 Aug 1980 in Aledo, Ill.   Their children are Aaron
Sutherland, born 19 Jun 1983 in Iowa City; Ashley Rae, born 31 Jan
1987 in Muscatine, Ia.; and Amber Leigh, born 26 Feb 1989 in
Muscatine. Mike lived in rural Aledo in 1989.

1172331 Shirley Marie Service

Shirley was born 24 Nov 1941 in Moline, Ill.   She married Joseph
Matthew Culbert, Jr., on 30 Nov 196_ in Sasaebo, Japan.   They had
Carrie Michele, born 4 May 1976 in Frankfort, Germany.   Carrie
married Kevin Brandon Jackson on 18 May 1996 in Guntersville, Ala.

1172332 John Dean Service

Dean was born 21 Jan 1945 in Moline, Ill.   He married Karen Sue
Conn on 6 Apr 1968 in Moline, Ill.   They had Allison Ann, born 18
Mar 1973 in Moline, and Scott Andrew, born 11 Jun 1976 in Moline.

Allison married Michael Ward McCutcheon on 20 Jul 1996 in Moline,
Ill.

1172333 Robert Kent Service

Known as Kent, he was born 19 Jun 1949 in Moline, Ill. Kent
married Lynn Diane Johnston on 9 Oct 1976 in West Union, Ia. They
had Stephanie Lizabeth, born 14 Jan 1981, and Katelyn Nicole, born
15 Apr 1988, both born in Davenport. The family was living in
Bettendorf, Ia., in 2000.

1172341 Paul Scott Brokaw

Paul was born 9 Mar 1957 in Bradenton, Fla. He married Cynthia
Jean McAllister on 11 Jul 1981 in Bradenton, Fla. They have Scott
Thomas, born 17 Jul 1983 in Sarasota, Fla,; and Adam Michael, born
14 Aug 1985 in Sarasota. Paul was living in Atlanta as of 1996.

1172342 Elizabeth Ann Brokaw

Ann was born 13 Aug 1968 in Bradenton, Fla. She was living in
Santa Monica, Calif., in 1996.

1172351 Sharon Ruth Brokaw

Sharon was born 22 Jan 1952 in Aledo, Ill. She graduated from
Winola High School in 1970, and from Illinois State at Normal in
1974 with a degree in home economics. She has been a teacher since
graduation. Sharon married Dennis Mark Warner on 12 Jun 1977 in
Aledo, Ill. They had Justin Mark, born 19 Feb 1980 in Freeport,
Ill.; Andrew Todd, born 17 May 1982 in Freeport; and Robert
William, born 25 Jan 1984 in Freeport. Sharon and Dennis were
divorced in Jun 1986. Secondly, Sharon married Bill Zigmont on 30
Dec 1990 in Elizabeth, Ill., and they had Nathan Lee who was born
3 Aug 1993.

1172352 Debra Dee Brokaw

Debra was born 14 Feb 1953 in Aledo, Ill. She graduated from
Winola High School in 1971 and attended Blackhawk Junior College
for a year. She married Jeffrey Lee Brandon on 19 Jun 1982 in
Viola, Ill. They had Brett Kyle, born 24 Mar 1984 in Kansas City,
Kan.; and Bart Michael, born 8 Jul 1986 in Kansas City, Kan. They
live in Bucyrus, Kan.

1172353 Robert Mark Brokaw

Robert was born 13 Sep 1958 Aledo, Ill. He is a 1976 graduate of
Winola High School. He graduated from the University of Illinois
in 1980 and from Yale in 1986 with a MA degree. He is an off-
Broadway director in New York City. Robert is not married.

1172354 Bradley Kyle Brokaw

Bradley was born 26 Sep 1961 in Aledo, Ill. In 1979 he graduated
from Winola High School. He attended Illinois State University
where he studied agriculture. Bradley married Susan Dawn Deeds on
18 Jul 1987 in Joy, Ill. Their children are Brooke Erin, born 18
Jun 1990 in Rock Island, Ill.; and Sydney Elyse, born 30 Nov 1995
in Moline, Ill. They live in Aledo, Ill.

1172355 Christina Marie Brokaw

Christina was born 19 Dec 1968 in Aledo, Ill. She is a graduate of
Winola High School with the class of 1987. She attended the
University of Illinois before graduating in 1991 from Marycrest
College in Davenport, Ia. There she received a BS degree in
nursing. In 1996 she was awarded an MS degree from the University
of Illinois. She married Brett Lee Nelson on 8 Jun 1991 in Viola,
Ill. They had Jenna Elizabeth, born 15 Jul 1998 in Davenport, Ia.
They live in Andalusia, Ill.

1172361 John Andrew Brokaw

John was born 24 Dec 1952 in Aledo, Ill. He graduated from Orion
High School in 1971. John married Denise Lynn Jackson on 28 Jun
1975 in Orion, Ill. Their children are Calla Marie, born 24 May
1977 in Silvis, Ill.; Jason Andrew, born 11 Nov 1980 in Silvis; and
Sara Amanda, born 25 Apr 1986 in Rock Island, Ill. John worked for
International Harvester. They were living in Lynn Center, Ill.

LATE ADDITIONS

The following information arrived after the main text was finalized.

Page 164. <u>William Herman Swenson.</u> Bill died 8 Jul 2001 after a long struggle with lymphoma. He died in Maryville, Tenn., and was buried there in Grandview Cem.

Page 244. <u>Jerry Lee Snyder.</u> Brent Allen married 3 Sep 1983 Michelle Marie Yeck who was born 27 Dec 1964. They had Ryan Allen 30 Jun 1992 and Christopher Lee 28 Oct 1996. Susan Irene married 4 Jul 1996 Jonathan Wade Miller who was born 11 Jun 1973. They divorced in 2001. They had twins, Danielle Lee and Jordan Lee on 25 Mar 1998.

Page 244. <u>Keith Eugene Snyder.</u> Their children were Mariah Kae, born 17 May 1977; Cissandra Kei, born 13 Jan 1979 and Jamaica Kie, born 17 Oct 1980. Mariah Kay married 10 Jun 2000 Eric Keirn. She is a graduate of IBC in Fort Wayne, Ind., with a certificate in computer programming. Cissandra (Cizzy) had worked for Colwell Industries. Jami is a machine operator at Colwell.

Page 262. <u>Donna Jean Thomson.</u> Donna married Raymond Nelson Galvin in Jan 1969. They founded 'Skill Craft Enterprises' in Huntington Beach and employ 35 people. They have also developed and manage several industrial properties in the city. They are founding members of the Huntington Beach Art Center, the HB Youth Shelter for abused and neglected children, and the Bolsa Chica Wetlands Land Trust. Their children are Stacey Lynn and Michael Thomson.

Stacey was born 11 Aug 1969 in Covina, Calif., and graduated from Fountain Valley HS in 1987. She earned a BS degree in social ecology at the University of California—Irvine, and holds a master's degree in psychology from Chapman University, Orange. Stacey is a licensed marriage and family therapist working in Orange County.

Michael Thomson Galvin was born 21 Feb 1988 in Newport Beach and in 2001 was attending the Pegasus School in Huntington Beach. His interests include computer tecnology and sports.

Page 276. <u>Cheryl Lee Thomson.</u> Cheryl was born 29 Jan 1966 in Euclid, Ohio. She spent some time in Asia with her family, then attended Sam Houston State University in Huntsville where she

382

earned a BA in photo journalism in 1987. She works in that field in Houston while residing in Tyler, Tex.

Page 313. <u>Dorris Ann Hulshizer.</u> Doris gave the compiler a set of letters written in 1981-1982 by her close relatives, as part of a "round robin." She also sent a copy of the text of a talk she delivered at a reunion in 1995. She recalled that her grandpa Marts spent much of his time in his library reading the Bible and preparing sermons. Her mother attended a Christian college to become a teacher. Later in life she attained a master's degree. Dorris grew up in Long Pine, Neb. She also lived in Arnold and in Ogallala. After high school, she worked her way through college.

After marrying Jack Ashley, they lived in Omaha where he attended medical school and Dorris taught, and opened a culinary arts school. In 1985 she started a lecture series. For many years she had a TV cooking series and attended the Culinary Arts Institute in Hyde Park for food styling. More recently she became involved in selling real estate, then became a leader in marketing the company.

In 1995 Dorris and Jack hosted the Nebraskaland Governors Art Show. She was honored for her contributions to the arts.

Page 315. <u>Mark Allan Wiley.</u> Mike married Lisa Rich and they had Sean, born 13 Nov 1985, and Chris, born 19 May 1988. Steve married Julie Wright and they had Ian Maxwell on 23 Jul 1997.

Page 318. <u>John Robert Mewkemson.</u> Jack served in the U.S Air Force and was stationed in Germany and England. In England, he married Tonia Godfrey. Their children are Greer born 1 Dec 1970 in England, and Gavin John born 24 Jul 1973. Greer is a graduate of the Univ. of Mich., and married Mike Dietrich. Gavin graduated *magna cum laude* from UM and is a horticulturist.

Page 318. <u>David Graham Mekemson.</u> The children of David and Adrienne are Lisa Christine, born 21 Feb 1969, and Jamee Marie, born 27 Nov 1971. Lisa married Glen Doering and they had Jason Eric on 13 May 1997 and Ian Stuart on 24 Feb 2000. Jamee married Brian Brown and they had Brandon Clifford on 24 aug 1998 and Cameron David on 19 Jun 2001.

Secondly, David married Irene Petruniak on 17 Mar 1978 in Libertyville, Ill. They had Lindsay born 22 Apr 1979 and Kyle David born 30 Jun 1982.

Page 318. <u>Ann Sheldon Mekemson.</u> Shelle married Andrew Thomas Pentes on 15 Mar 1969. She attended scretarial college and is a graphic design artist. Their children are Geoffrey born 23 Oct

1969 and Christopher born 4 Feb 1973. Geoffrey married Kim and they had Christopher James 13 Oct 1995 and Ryan David 27 Aug 1997.

Page 318. Wendy Jane Mekemson. Wendy married Calvin Detrich Thomas on 9 Jun 1979 in Washington, Ill. Their children are Bethany Elizabeth, born 7 Apr 1982; Christian Marie, born 7 Dec 1983; and Katherine Alexis, born 21 Dec 1989, all born in Waukegan, Ill.

Page 318. Leslie Elizabeth Mekemson. Leslie married Dale Alan Spencer on 19 Aug 1978 in Libertyville, Ill. Dale was born 9 Jul 1958 in Mundeleen, Ill. They had Ryan Matthew on 21 Oct 1979 in Lake Forest, Ill., and Jessica Diane on 27 Aug 1983 in Libertyville, Ill. Ryan married Kelly Barrett and they had Paige Alexis on 19 Jan 1999.

APPENDIX

Poem composed by John Thomson

To my family on my 90th Birthday:

"My days are almost numbered
For my years are four score ten,
I long have passed the average mark
Allowed to most of men.

I have no right to fear grim death
Though he is terror's king
For Jesus met and conquered him
And took away his sting

I have no right to mourn and fret
For leaving friends so kind
I have as good friends gone before
As those I leave behind.
There is father, mother, sister
Two wives and children three
Have all gone on before me there
Some day to welcome me.

I shall be there to meet you too
In that celestial Throng
With Holy joy to welcome you
As you come one by one.

We'll be in that assembly
Around King Jesus' feet
In Holy joy to worship him
And kiss his pierced feet.

And when he comes to judge the world
We shall be near his heart,
The voice that raised up Lazarus
Will raise our mortal part.

With soul and body joined again
Before this glorious throne
The work of His own Spirit
Will seal us for His own.

When we're ascending with Him
With joyfulness we'll sing:
O grave where is thy victory,
O death where is thy sting?

And in his heavenly mansions, He
Will set us by His side
With angels for our waiting maids
And we his loving bride."

INDEX OF BIOGRAPHIES
(Through seven generations)

INDEX OF SPOUSES

(Through seven generations)

Made in the USA
San Bernardino, CA
02 April 2017